SCHOOLS FOR YOUTH

Daniel Tanner

*The University of Wisconsin—
Milwaukee*

SCHOOLS for YOUTH

CHANGE and CHALLENGE in SECONDARY EDUCATION

THE MACMILLAN COMPANY, NEW YORK
COLLIER–MACMILLAN LIMITED, LONDON

To LILLIAN and LAUREL

Fourth Printing, 1967

Library of Congress catalog card number: 65–11600

The Macmillan Company, New York

Collier–Macmillan Canada, Ltd., Toronto, Ontario

Printed in the United States of America

*Credits for photographs appearing on title page (from left to right): first three,
courtesy Vories Fisher; fourth, courtesy Northwestern University; fifth, courtesy
Herb Comess.*

PREFACE

SECONDARY EDUCATION is no longer a privilege. It is a right and an expectation. During the twentieth century, the secondary school has opened its doors to all youth. The universalization of secondary education and the evolvement of the comprehensive high school are recent phenomena—subjected to both praise and criticism at home and abroad. While we can look back on these accomplishments with great pride, we must also face up to the fact that even today many young people are not well served by the schools. How our schools can better serve the youth of our nation is the theme of this book.

This book is addressed to those who are planning to teach in the secondary school. Experienced teachers also will find this book useful in their work. While it is intended to represent a comprehensive overview of the principles and practices of secondary education, this volume seeks to probe the forces underlying the problems, conflicts, and directions of American education.

A modern democracy expects its schools to cultivate the attributes of individual enlightenment and group responsibility. At the same time it demands that our schools prepare youth adequately for a place in the changing world of work and for the pursuit of higher learning. Though these goals are formidable, there is no turning back. Yet, these goals cannot be realized unless adolescents have avenues for success in school and society.

In recent years we have witnessed a growing concern for such problems as reducing school drop-outs and youth unemployment, providing for the academically talented, eliminating educational inequities based

v

on racial and socio-economic-geographic factors, modernizing the curriculum, harnessing new educational resources, organizing and administering the schools more effectively, improving teacher preparation, and professionalizing the work of the teacher. At times, when confronted with Soviet scientific and technological achievement, some critics have been quick to blame the schools for our alleged scientific, military, industrial, and governmental weaknesses. At other times, when we appear to be clearly ahead of the Soviets, such successes, unlike the failures, are not attributed to our schools. There are instances where, as a result of the critics, educators have reacted by exerting increased pressures on our most promising students while giving decreased attention to the least promising. But, fortunately, there are enough wise men among our educators who see the need to challenge and encourage our academically talented youth while helping all youth to find the fullest possible measure of success in school and society.

The author has attempted to focus on these and other problems and issues in order that the reader may gain an understanding of the vital and dynamic forces at work. Each chapter is accompanied by several "Problems for Study and Discussion" that are intended to stimulate the student to probe into sources outside the textbook. The reference lists and footnotes should be useful guides for further investigation and study. It is the hope of the author that, through this book, the reader will find direction and assistance for a successful career as a teacher in the junior or senior high school.

I wish to express my appreciation to many of my colleagues for their interest and encouragement during the preparation of this manuscript: Professors Dan H. Cooper of the University of Michigan, Edgar Dale of The Ohio State University, Gail M. Inlow of Northwestern University, Henry Clay Lindgren of San Francisco State College, Robert C. McKean and Bob L. Taylor of the University of Colorado, and A. M. Rempel and F. J. Woerdehoff of Purdue University.

And, finally, I am grateful to both my mother and my wife for their faith and patience.

Daniel Tanner

CONTENTS

1

Perspectives and Prospects in Secondary Education

My father, who was a blacksmith in the railway shop in Galesburg, couldn't sign his name. He had to use an "X" and maybe we ought to have an organization formed of Americans whose parents couldn't sign their own names. It might tell a lot about this country.
—*Carl Sandburg*

CHAPTER 1

The Development of American Secondary Education.

THE FIRST SETTLERS of America conceived of education primarily as a means of spiritual salvation. The Puritans in New England soon established an educational program patterned after the English system—private tutoring at home and Latin grammar schools for boys who would be entering college for training as ministers.

Although most of the early settlers came to America for religious freedom as well as economic opportunity, they quickly adopted the European practice of a direct tie between the state and a single established church. In Massachusetts, for example, a law of 1631 required membership in an authorized church and ownership of property as the two conditions for voting. And everyone was required, by a law of 1638, to attend the established church on Sundays and to contribute in taxes to its support. Laws were enacted between 1644 and 1659 that decreed banishment for Baptists and Jesuits, and death for practicing Quakers. The single established religion was practiced in the colonies of Massachusetts, Connecticut, New Hampshire, Maryland, Virginia, and the Carolinas. Thus, while the early settlers came to these shores seeking religious freedom, their adherence to a single established church prohibited those of other religious sects from worshipping freely.

EDUCATION IN COLONIAL AMERICA

Massachusetts Law of 1642

The failure to support education voluntarily led to the enactment of the Massachusetts Law of 1642 that required that all children be taught "to read and understand the principles of religion and the capital laws

3

of the country" and trained "in learning and labor . . . profitable to the Commonwealth."[1] Although this law did not order the establishment and support of schools, it nevertheless required that all children be taught to read. This piece of legislation is recognized as the first of its kind in the English-speaking world.[2] The Massachusetts Law of 1642 marked the beginning of compulsory education in the New World. The purpose of this law, however, was not to foster individual enlightenment, but to help man to become a better servant of God and the state.

Massachusetts Law of 1647

Puritan church leaders soon recognized the inadequacy of leaving education to individual families. As a result, the Massachusetts Law of 1647 was enacted requiring every town of 50 householders to appoint a person to teach reading and writing and to pay the wages of the teacher, and every town of 100 householders to establish a grammar school to instruct youth for entrance to the university. This legislation provided for a fine of £5 for failure to comply. The Law of 1647 marked the right of the state to require communities to employ teachers and to establish schools—a law without precedent in the English-speaking world.

The Puritan-Calvinist leaders were directly instrumental in securing the enactment of these laws by the Colony. The main purpose in requiring the teaching of reading was to promote a knowledge of the Scriptures. This purpose is clearly revealed in the preamble of the Law of 1647.

> It being one chief project of the old deluder, Satan, to keep men from the knowledge of the Scriptures, as in former times by keeping them in an unknown tongue, so in these latter times by persuading from the use of tongues, that so at least the true sense and meaning of the original might be clouded by false glosses of saint seeming deceivers, that learning may not be buried in the grave of our fathers in the church and commonwealth, the Lord assisting our endeavors. . . .[3]

The "Olde Deluder Satan Law" of 1647, like the Law of 1642, was a means of promoting the creed of the Puritan sect. Although these laws can be said to represent the recognition of the need for universal education, it should be realized that their purpose was to build adherence to the established religion rather than to promote personal enlightenment. Cubberley cites these laws as significant in that they also represent the right of the state to require the support of education through the levying of a general tax and the right of the state to hold the parent

---

1 See Ellwood P. Cubberley, *Public Education in the United States,* Revised (Boston: Houghton Mifflin Company, 1947), p. 17.

2 *Ibid.*

3 Colony of Massachusetts, *Records of the Governor and Company of the Massachusetts Bay in New England,* II (Boston: William White, 1853), p. 203.

responsible for supporting such education.[4] Nevertheless, the state and church were one, and these laws were designed to promote adherence to the church and commonwealth. But although this legislation was not motivated by democratic aims, it does represent the principle of promoting the education of the young, whether rich or poor, for the benefit of society. Other New England colonies soon followed Massachusetts in enacting similar laws.

Separation of Church and State

The monopoly of church and state by the Puritan Calvinists in New England was broken under the leadership of Roger Williams in Rhode Island. The Rhode Island charter of 1663 guaranteed religious freedom to its people. In Pennsylvania, William Penn led the way to freedom of worship. Pennsylvania's Great Law of 1682 held that the state could not require conformity to any religious establishment. The separation of Delaware from Pennsylvania in 1702 found Delaware adhering to the Pennsylvania practice of religious freedom and separation between church and state.

The heterogeneity of the religious populations of New York and New Jersey prevented the monopoly of church and state that was prevalent in Massachusetts, Connecticut, and New Hampshire. However, in their early constitutions, Delaware, Pennsylvania, and New Jersey required religious oaths and religious qualifications for holders of office.

The settlers of the southern colonies were followers of the English National Church in contrast to the dissenters who established New England. Consequently, there were no significant early efforts in the South to separate church and state.

With the close of the seventeenth century, the domination of the church began to weaken and civil forms of government took the place of the religious forms. Cubberley cites the Salem witchcraft persecutions of 1691–1692 as a factor in weakening the domination of the people by the ministry in New England.[5] Gradually, with the realities of the developing frontier, the growth of commerce, and the more scientifically based conceptions of human nature, the obsession with personal salvation gave way to the desire to deal effectively with the conditions of life.

Educational Beginnings in the Southern Colonies

The early settlers of the southern colonies followed the English practice of leaving education to the home through private tutors and pay-schools. Youngsters of the less privileged classes might resort to pauper schools and apprenticeships. The formation of plantation settlements and the

---

[4] Cubberley, *op. cit.*, p. 19.   [5] *Ibid.*, p. 59.

employment of criminals and paupers brought over from England as indentured white servants quickly established a class structure in the South. The wealthy provided their youngsters with tutors, private schools, and advanced education in England. Following the English custom, compulsory apprenticeship training was provided for poor children.

During the early colonial period in the South, education was regarded by some leaders as a dangerous force. In reply to an inquiry concerning the provisions for the education of children in Virginia, Governor Berkeley declared,

> The same course that is taken in England . . . every man according to his ability in instructing his children. . . . But, I thank God there are no free schools nor printing, and I hope we shall not have them these hundred years, for learning has brought disobedience and heresy and sects into the world, and printing has divulged them and libels against the best government. God keep us from both.[6]

The early settlers of the southern colonies were here for economic gain rather than to escape religious persecution. While the New England settlers were dissenters from the Church of England, the settlers of the southern colonies were adherents of this church. The indentured white servants and Negro slaves in the South supplied no motive on the part of the leaders to provide for common schools. In New England, however, the motive of establishing a new order gave early impetus to compulsory education and common schooling. The so-called compulsory education laws in the South during this period pertained only to the dependent poor and not to the general population.

Apprenticeship Training

Apprenticeship training of the poor, as practiced in England, became established throughout colonial America. Forced or compulsory apprenticeship of orphans or children of the poor was common. Although it was generally the practice for a written agreement to be made and approved by the court, such arrangements tended to favor the master.[7] While the master was required by law to provide for the instruction of apprentices in reading and writing, he was often mainly concerned with economic exploitation of the apprenticeship agreement.

In the southern colonies the apprenticeship system constituted the main form of compulsory education, since children of the well-to-do received private tutoring and attended private schools. In New England, on the other hand, laws were enacted, following the pattern of the Massachusetts Law of 1647, requiring the establishment and support of common

---

[6] John S. Brubacher, *A History of the Problems of Education* (New York: McGraw-Hill Company, Inc., 1947), p. 547.

[7] Cubberley, *op. cit.,* p. 34.

schools. But even in the northern colonies compulsory apprenticing of orphans and children of the poor was practiced under court approval. Voluntary apprenticeships were also arranged through the court for boys and girls of average means.

The Latin Grammar School

While orphans and the children of the poor were largely bound to the apprenticeship system, youngsters of the upper classes in New England attended the Latin grammar school. This type of school, brought over from England, was designed to instruct in Latin—the language of religion. A limited amount of instruction in Greek was provided for its classical significance. Although some teaching of English was included in the curriculum, this left much to be desired, since the main emphasis was given to Latin.

Before entering the Latin grammar school, the youngster went to a "dame" school, run by a woman in her own home, where the basic skills of reading and writing were crudely taught. The dame schools were privately established and were not required by law. The dame schools included both boys and girls, but the Latin grammar schools were open only to boys. The Latin grammar schools, which admitted boys at the age of seven or eight, also prepared some of the students for entrance at the age of fifteen to Harvard College (founded in 1636), where they would receive training for the ministry. Discipline was severe in the schools and colleges of the day. Cubberley describes the practice of disciplining students at Harvard by whipping.

> Thomas Sargent, a Harvard student, convicted in 1674 of speaking blasphemous words, was publicly whipped in the library before all the scholars. The punishment was inflicted under the supervision of the president who preceded the chastisement with prayer.[8]

Twenty-eight Latin grammar schools were established in Massachusetts before 1700. But by the middle of the eighteenth century it was becoming increasingly clear that the Latin grammar schools were failing to meet the growing practical and commercial needs of the times and, as a result, these institutions began to decline in favor of the academies.

The Rise of the Academy

The emergence of great literature in the modern languages, the decline of the old religious orthodoxy, and the need to deal effectively with the mother tongue in commerce left Latin with little relevancy to the realities of the new world. New social and political concepts were also emerging. In 1732, the Grammar School of the City of New York was established. Unlike the Latin grammar school, where instruction was offered prin-

---

[8] *Ibid.*, p. 57.

cipally in Latin, this English grammar school gave heavy emphasis to English and such practical subjects as mathematics, geography, navigation, and bookkeeping. The English grammar schools developed in the cities of the middle colonies, were privately operated, and were attended by those seeking a practical education. Although the English grammar school did not spread beyond the few cities of the middle colonies, this institution served as a forerunner of the academy.

THE ACADEMY. In 1749 Benjamin Franklin published a comprehensive plan for education, *Proposals Relating to the Education of Youth in Pennsylvania*. According to Franklin, a new type of school was needed to meet the practical requirements of the day. The Latin grammar school was clearly not in tune with the times, while the English grammar school varied greatly in the nature of its sponsorship and had failed to expand on a sufficiently broad scale. Franklin proposed an academy with a curriculum giving key emphasis to the English language (literature, composition, and speaking) and such practical studies as mathematics, accounting, geography, political science, modern history, modern foreign languages, agriculture, natural science, and physical education. Franklin viewed his proposed school as a place where youth would be treated with affection and would be assisted in vocational placement. The school would be attractive and well equipped with learning resources.

In 1751 Franklin established the first academy in Philadelphia. Although academies grew rapidly in number and led to the virtual elimination of the Latin grammar school before the close of the eighteenth century, Franklin expressed his deep disappointment at the tendency of many academies to continue to emphasize the teaching of Latin and the classical subjects while neglecting English and other utilitarian studies.

Nevertheless, the academy movement must be regarded as "one of the basic revolutions in the conception of a proper secondary education for American youth."[9] Between 1830 and 1850 the academies reached a peak of some 6,000 in the various states east of the Missouri River. Most academies were private, nondenominational institutions with tuition fees. Despite the inclination of many of the early academies to stress the traditional subjects, considerable curriculum diversity soon developed and such useful subjects as English, mathematics, geography, and science received considerable emphasis in preparing students for commerce and the professions. The academies also provided teachers for the lower schools.

While the old Latin grammar school was limited only to boys, acade-

---

[9] R. Freeman Butts and Lawrence A. Cremin, *A History of Education in American Culture* (New York: Holt, Rinehart and Winston, Inc., 1953), p. 81.

mies for girls were common early in the nineteenth century. In addition to providing a modern secondary curriculum for youth, the academies marked the establishment of secondary education for girls.

With the rise of the public high school during the latter half of the nineteenth century, the academy movement began a sharp decline. The academy had served as a means of developing widespread recognition for the need of popular education.

THE EARLY NATIONAL GOVERNMENT AND EDUCATION

The opening of the War of Independence found most colonies with a state-established religion. Only Rhode Island, Pennsylvania, and Maryland were committed to religious freedom. The Constitution, however, through the First Amendment enacted in 1791, guaranteed freedom of religion and provided that "Congress shall make no law respecting an establishment of religion, or prohibiting the free exercise thereof." The principle of freedom and equality for all mankind had been asserted clearly in the Declaration of Independence in 1776.

> We hold these truths to be self-evident: that all men are created equal; that they are endowed by their Creator with certain inalienable rights; that among these are life, liberty, and the pursuit of happiness; that to secure these rights, governments are instituted among men, deriving their just powers from the consent of the governed.

The principle of separation of church and state and the principle of freedom and equality of all mankind, so early established in our history, were to have profound implications for such problems of the 1960's as federal aid to education and equality of educational opportunity.

The Constitution and Education

The nonsectarian principle that eventually was to govern the development of our public school system is based on the Constitutional provisions guaranteeing religious freedom and forbidding Congress to establish a state religion. While the Constitution made no specific mention of education, its expressed provision that Congress shall "promote the general welfare" has formed the basis for federal support of education to this day.

The Tenth Amendment to the Constitution, ratified in 1791, declared that "powers not delegated to the United States by the Constitution, nor prohibited by it to the States, are reserved to the States respectively, or to the people." Thus, on the basis of the Tenth Amendment, education in the United States has developed as a state function. Unlike the single educational system, characteristic of the European nations, our educational program became organized through many systems. Nevertheless, the interest and role of the Federal Government in supporting education were recognized very early. Education in the United States evolved as a state function, with the general operation of the schools delegated to the local communities and their boards of education. At the same time, the Federal Government came to serve an important supporting role through various grants-in-aid.

Origins of Federal Support of Education

The great territory between the Alleghenies and the Mississippi was designated by the new Federal Government as the domain for future states. In the Ordinance of 1787, which provided for the government of the Northwest Territory, Congress gave clear evidence of its commitment to the promotion of education.

> Religion, morality, and knowledge being necessary to good government and the happiness of mankind, schools and the means of education shall forever be encouraged.[10]

Under the Land Ordinance of 1785 the sixteenth section of every township was reserved "for the maintenance of public schools within said township." Each Congressional township being divided into 36 sections one mile square, the grants for schools amounted to many millions of acres. Through the sale of public lands, Congress also made monetary grants to the states for the support of education during the first half of the nineteenth century.

During the early period of our national government such men as Jefferson and Washington called for an enlightened citizenry through the general diffusion of knowledge. In his opening message to Congress in 1790, Washington stated:

> There is nothing which can better deserve your patronage than the promotion of science and literature. Knowledge is in every country the surest basis of public happiness. In one in which the measure of government receives their impressions so immediately from the sense of the community as in ours, it is proportionally essential.[11]

In 1796 Washington declared in his Farewell address:

> Promote then, as an object of primary importance, institutions for the general diffusion of knowledge. In proportion as the structure of a government gives force to public opinion, it is essential that public opinion should be enlightened.[12]

Jefferson's belief in the importance of providing legislation for the education of the common people is exemplified in a letter written in 1786.

---

[10] *Ibid.*, p. 245.
[11] Ellwood P. Cubberley, *Public Education in the United States,* Revised (Boston: Houghton Mifflin Company, 1947), p. 89.
[12] *Ibid.*

Preach, my dear Sir, a crusade against ignorance; establish and improve the law for educating the common people. Let our Countrymen know that the people alone can protect us against these evils, and that the tax which will be paid for this purpose is not more than the thousandth part of what will be paid to kings, priests and nobles who will rise up among us if we leave the people in ignorance.[13]

In 1779 Jefferson sought the establishment of a complete system of education in Virginia with free elementary schools, secondary schools, and a state college. Although Jefferson failed to secure legislation in Virginia for the establishment of a comprehensive educational system, he was later successful in founding the University of Virginia (1819). Jefferson's writings clearly indicate his conviction that the key to an enlightened citizenry rests with education. In 1816 he wrote:

If a nation expects to be ignorant and free in a state of civilization it expects what never was and never will be. . . . There is no safe deposit for the functions of government, but with the people themselves; nor can they be safe with them without information.[14]

THE ESTABLISHMENT OF FREE SCHOOLS

By 1820 thirteen of the twenty-three states forming the Union had made some specific mention of education in their constitutions. The states of the middle colonies continued for some time to regard education as a responsibility of the church and of private agencies. The southern states, along with Rhode Island, also regarded education as a private matter.

Education and Suffrage

Only four states had enacted universal manhood suffrage by 1815. Property holdings were necessary qualifications for voting in most of the states, but as the new frontier states to the west were formed, complete male suffrage was established. By the middle of the nineteenth century most of the eastern states rescinded their property qualifications for voting and granted full male suffrage.

The election of Andrew Jackson as President in 1828 was symptomatic of the rejection of the old aristocratic traditions. Jackson, unlike his predecessors who represented the propertied class, was a man of the frontier—a man of the people. The general population was developing a new awareness of its rightful role in civil affairs.

Full manhood suffrage demanded that education be a function of the state rather than a private matter. Heretofore voting in most of the states

---

[13] Gordon C. Lee (ed.), *Crusade Against Ignorance: Thomas Jefferson and Education* (New York: Columbia University Press, 1961), p. 100.
[14] Cubberley, *op. cit.*, p. 89.

was the privilege of those who could meet property and/or religious qualifications, and such persons could well afford to provide for the education of their own children through private means. But now that voting had become the right of all male citizens, it seemed necessary that all men be educated. And it was clear that only the state would be capable of providing an educational program on such a mass scale.

The preamble to the first Illinois school law (1825) stated:

> To enjoy our rights and liberties, we must understand them; their security and protection ought to be the first object of a free people; and it is a well established fact that no nation has ever continued long in the enjoyment of civil and political freedom, which was not both virtuous and enlightened.[15]

Governor De Witt Clinton of New York declared in his message to the legislature in 1827 that "The great bulwark of republican government is the cultivation of education; for the right of suffrage cannot be exercised in a salutary manner without intelligence."[16] Daniel Webster, in an address at Madison, Indiana (1837), advocated universal education, saying: "Education, to accomplish the ends of good government, should be universally diffused. Open the doors of the schoolhouses to all the children in the land . . . On the diffusion of education among the people rests the preservation and perpetuation of our free institutions."[17]

Education and Labor

As laboring groups began to organize, they expressed a new awareness of the importance of education. At a workingmen's meeting in Philadelphia in 1829, it was argued that

> No system of education, which a freeman can accept, has yet been established for the poor; whilst thousands of dollars of the public money has been appropriated for building colleges and academies for the rich.[18]

It was a common practice in some of the eastern states to provide public funds for the support of private tuition academies and colleges. This was deplored by many of the workingmen's groups who sought the use of public funds for a universal system of education.

Education and Taxation

The rise of the labor movement in the cities of New York, Philadelphia, Baltimore, and Boston during the period from 1825 to the Civil War found labor leaders agitating for free public education of children. By the middle of the nineteenth century almost all of the northern states

---

[15] *Ibid.*, p. 154. [16] *Ibid.*, p. 155.
[17] *Ibid.*, p. 156. [18] *Ibid.*, p. 173.

had come to recognize the need for free, publicly supported, nonsectarian schools. By 1839 North Carolina had established an elementary school system supported by public taxes.

But there were those who resisted the idea of being taxed to support schools for the education of other people's children. Some persisted in regarding general education of the masses as a danger to established society. The states of New Jersey, Pennsylvania, Delaware, Maryland, Virginia, and Georgia held on to the pauper school idea inherited from English rule. This idea was based on the rationale that state funds were to be used only for the children of parents who could not afford to provide for education under private auspices. Pennsylvania passed a free school law in 1834, and ordered free schools in all districts in 1848. New Jersey abandoned the pauper school with the adoption of its new state constitution in 1844. Shortly after the Civil War, the southern states joined in eliminating the pauper school idea.

As some of the states began to systematize their means of supporting the common schools through special appropriations and direct taxation, communities were required to provide similar school funds through local taxation. In 1827, for example, Massachusetts required all towns to support schools with local taxes, thereby implementing the principles of the Massachusetts Law of 1647. The matching of state funds with local taxes was required in New York in 1812, in Delaware in 1829, and in New Jersey in 1846. Other conditions for state aid were made later, such as minimum length of the school term, size of attendance, repair of school buildings, and provision of supplies.

Thus the state established its function in providing for an educational system and compelled local communities to support education through taxation. Nevertheless, the schools were not yet entirely free. In many of the states, rate bills were in effect that levied charges on parents of school children. This practice, inherited from England, was abolished in all the states by 1871.

Educational Leadership at the State Level

In 1784 New York established the Board of Regents of the University of the State of New York. The purpose of this body was to endow and control secondary and higher education. New York State was first to establish a state school officer in 1812. However, this post was abolished in 1821 and was not reestablished until 1854 when the office of Superintendent of Public Instruction was created. A similar position was established by Maryland in 1826, Michigan in 1836, Kentucky in 1838, Vermont in 1845, Louisiana in 1847, Illinois in 1854, and Pennsylvania in 1857. The function of this office was to apportion state aid to the various school districts, to collect data on attendance and finance, to serve the legislature in matters of school needs, and to encourage the establishment of local schools.

Massachusetts established a state board of education in 1837. Appointed by the governor, the members of the board selected Horace Mann (1796–1859), then president of the state senate, to serve as the chief state school officer under the title of Secretary to the Massachusetts State Board of Education. Mann accepted the post at great financial sacrifice. Although the work of the board and its secretary was limited to gathering data and making recommendations to the governor and legislature, Mann exercised great educational leadership, not only in Massachusetts, but throughout the northern states. His Annual Reports were evaluative documents that awakened great public interest in education. He advocated and achieved measurably greater support for schools through taxation. He established the first institutions for teacher education in America, promoted progressive teaching methods, and established libraries in schools. He fought for free, universal education that would include high school. Through his successful battle for a nonsectarian educational system, the schools of Massachusetts became instruments for a democratic society, rather than for religious goals. He survived many bitter attacks from religious leaders who accused the nonsectarian schools of being godless. Mann saw the need for universal education and nonsectarian schools in a society that was pluralistic in its population and democratic in its ideals.

Another important educational leader of the time was Henry Barnard (1811–1900) who, in 1839, paved the way for the first state school office in Connecticut and served as its chief officer. Barnard promoted more adequate taxation for the support of the schools and sought improved means of teacher education. But Barnard's office was abolished in 1842 by a governor who viewed such work as a "useless expense" and who regarded the higher public schools as a "dangerous innovation."[19] Called to Rhode Island in 1843, Barnard made the first state school survey and later became the Commissioner of Public Schools for that state. He returned to Connecticut in 1851 to head the state normal school. Barnard is credited with playing a leading role in establishing a state school system in Connecticut and Rhode Island. He served as the first United States Commissioner of Education from 1867 to 1870. Barnard viewed the high school as the means of preparing all youth for all stations in life.

The District System

By the middle of the nineteenth century, the district system was well entrenched as the unit of school organization. Since the newly formed

---

[19] Ellwood P. Cubberley, *Public Education in the United States,* Revised (Boston: Houghton Mifflin Company, 1947), pp. 227–228.

state boards of education were weak and lacked legislative support, the local districts frequently abused their powers, hired poorly qualified teachers, and failed to provide adequate taxation for school support. Gradually, under the leadership of Mann, Barnard, and other chief state school officers, education began to operate as a state function under state supervision.

Secularization of the Schools

Many of the cities and states continued to grant aid to church schools during much of the nineteenth century. This practice was inherited from colonial times when the major goal of education was spiritual salvation and when the government recognized the role of the church in education. The great increase in immigration of Catholics between 1820 and 1840 raised the question of whether public funds should be used for parochial and private schools.

The efforts of Horace Mann in establishing nonsectarian schools in Massachusetts finally succeeded in that state in 1855 with the adoption of a constitutional amendment prohibiting the division of funds between public and sectarian or private schools. Similar constitutional amendments had been passed in New Jersey in 1844, Michigan in 1850, and Ohio and Indiana in 1851. Through the last half of the nineteenth century, most of the other states adopted this constitutional prohibition either by amendment or in the framing of their constitution upon admission to the Union. Wisconsin, for example, adopted this in its constitution when admitted in 1848.

In New York City, where many of the different religious groups were vying for public funds for their respective parochial schools, the legislature in 1842 directed the establishment of a public school system under a City Board of Education and declared that public funds were not to be used for sectarian purposes.

Cubberley describes the importance of this question at the national level during President Grant's administration.

> In 1875 President Grant, in his message to Congress, urged the submission of an amendment to the Federal Constitution making it the duty of the States to support free public schools, free from religious teaching, and forbidding the diversion of school funds to church or sectarian purposes. In a later message he renewed the recommendation, but Congress took no action because it considered such action unnecessary.[20]

Although the question of dividing school funds was largely settled during the last quarter of the nineteenth century, the agitation for federal aid for parochial schools continues to this day. And the matter of religious

---

[20] *Ibid.*, p. 240.

prayer and bible-reading in the public schools was not finally settled until the Supreme Court decision of June 17, 1963 prohibiting the requirement of such activity by any state or locality.

PUBLIC SUPPORT OF SECONDARY AND HIGHER EDUCATION

By 1850 the various states were providing for a public program of elementary education. However, secondary school studies were offered primarily in the tuition academies. With the development of a publicly supported, tuition-free elementary school system, it was soon argued that the educational program be extended upward to include secondary-level studies. A number of the western and southern states had already established state universities but had not yet provided for a system of public secondary education. The time was ripe for the development of the American high school, which, unlike the academy, would be free to all students.

The First High Schools

In 1821 a high school for boys was founded in Boston. This was the first high school in the United States. Five years later a high school for girls was also established in Boston, but this institution closed in 1828 because, ironically, it could not meet the tremendous enrollment pressures.

The first high school was known as the English high school because of its emphasis on English and not the languages of antiquity. Other subjects included science, mathematics, history, and logic. The purpose of this high school was not preparation for the university, but preparation for a more useful and satisfying role in a developing commercial and industrial society. Similar high schools were established in Portland, Maine in 1821, Worcester, Massachusetts in 1824, and New York City in 1825.

At this time there was no clear trend indicating that the high schools would eventually supplant the academies. Legislation providing tax support for these schools was strictly on an individual community level and the legality of such taxation was yet to be tested in the courts. In 1825 there were some 5,000 academies in operation and they were still growing in number.

THE MASSACHUSETTS LAW OF 1827. The legislature of Massachusetts passed a law in 1827 requiring every town with a population of 500 families or more to support a high school. This law even went so far as to specify the subjects to be taught (United States history, mathematics, bookkeeping, and surveying). Additional subjects were required in the schools of communities with a population of over 4,000.

This legislation set an important precedent for laws in other states. Moreover, it represented an attempt to provide a program of secondary education uniquely adapted to our nation. But the growth in the number of high schools was slow. Before the middle of the nineteenth century only 55 high schools had been established, while 6,000 academies were in operation. The Civil War period postponed the growth of the high schools and, in each of the various states, the high school was not yet regarded as part of the state common school system.

The Land-Grant Colleges

In 1862 Congress passed the Morrill Act, signed by President Lincoln, providing for the establishment of colleges of agriculture and the mechanic arts in each of the various states. More than 11 million acres of public land were appropriated to the states for the endowment of these institutions, which came to be known as the Land-Grant Colleges and Universities. A number of the states that had already established state colleges or universities chose to identify the existing institutions for land-grant support, while the other states founded their first state college or university as a result of the Morrill Act. The author of this legislation, Senator Justin P. Morrill of Vermont, was not a college graduate. Morrill recognized the limitations of the classically oriented colleges of the day and their failure to meet the educational needs of the nation.

It is interesting to note that George Washington viewed the Federal Government as having a legitimate role in supporting public higher education. Washington envisaged the establishment of a National University in the nation's capital. Washington actually willed a considerable sum to the national government for the new university, which never came into being. Nevertheless, 63 years after Washington's will was made, the national government, through the Morrill Act, provided the basis for the development of a system of great state universities.

The Morrill Act of 1862 marked the recognition of higher education as an instrument for national development rather than an institution of gentlemanly privilege. The Federal Government, at a time of national crisis (Civil War), had opened the way to the development of a system of public higher education that would help build the agricultural and industrial strength of the young nation. The Morrill Act stipulated that other scientific and classical studies were not to be excluded. Its general purpose was "to promote the liberal and practical education of the industrial classes." Today, more than 600,000 full-time students, or one fifth of our nation's total enrollment, are attending land-grant colleges and universities. As of 1964, the majority of living American Nobel Prize laureates earned one or more degrees at a land-grant institution.

In historical perspective, it is important to note that although the Morrill Act of 1862 clearly established the basis of national and state support of public higher education, the high school at that time was yet to be recognized as integral to the common educational system. The private tuition academy was still the dominant institution for secondary-level studies.

The Civil War and Education

Educational progress was far more rapid in the northern states than in the South. Because of the agricultural economy and the institution of slavery, the need for formal education provided through tax funds was not widely recognized in the South. During the 1850's, however, a rising interest in education began to become evident, particularly in some of the larger southern cities. State universities had been established in many of the southern states prior to the Civil War; but while the northern states were clearly committed to the establishment of state systems of free, tax-supported, nonsectarian common schools, the southern states were not yet ready for such a move.

The Civil War (1861–65) checked the development of education in the North and virtually halted it in the South. The postwar reconstruction period found the South falling even farther behind the rest of the nation in its educational development; yet the importance of education to the building of the new South was recognized by many southern leaders. In 1866 Robert E. Lee expressed the need for the education of youth in the postwar period thus:

> So greatly have those interests (educational) been disturbed at the South, and so much does its future condition depend upon the rising generation, that I consider the proper education of its youth one of the most important objects now to be obtained, and one from which the greatest benefits may be expected. Nothing will compensate us for the depression of the standard of our moral and intellectual culture, and each State should take the most energetic measures to revive the schools and colleges, and, if possible, to increase the facilities for instruction and to elevate the standard of learning.[21]

The devastation of the South and the appalling poverty of its people left the region with no taxable resources for the support of education. With the gradual reconstruction of the South and the adoption of new state constitutions after 1875, new school legislation was passed. But educational progress remained slow. In the North, despite the establish-

---

21 Ellwood P. Cubberley, *Public Education in the United States,* Revised (Boston: Houghton Mifflin Company, 1947), p. 432.

ment of public high schools in many of the cities prior to the Civil War, there was considerable opposition to these publicly supported schools during the post-Civil War period. It was argued that it was illegal to levy taxes for the establishment and maintenance of high schools that would benefit only a small portion of the population.

The United States Bureau of Education

In 1867 Congress established the United States Bureau of Education. Until that time there was no agency responsible for the collection and dissemination of information pertaining to the status and directions of education in the United States. The Bureau came into being largely through the efforts of Henry Barnard, then Secretary of the Rhode Island Board of Education. Barnard was appointed chief officer of the Bureau, thus becoming the first United States Commissioner of Education.

The duties of the Bureau of Education were not limited merely to the gathering of data and its dissemination, but provided also "to otherwise promote the cause of education." Over the years this office has come under different federal departments. In recent times it has operated as the Office of Education under the United States Department of Health, Education, and Welfare.

The Kalamazoo Decision

In 1872 the city of Kalamazoo, Michigan, voted to support a high school and employ a superintendent of schools through the assessment of additional taxes. This was promptly challenged in the courts. The Michigan Supreme Court ruled that such taxation was clearly legal in that there was "conclusively a general state policy, beginning in 1817 and continuing until after the adoption of the present state constitution, in the direction of free schools in which education . . . might be brought within the reach of all the children of the state. . . ."[22] The court ruled that tax monies could be used for education at any grade of instruction provided the "voters consent in regular form to bear the expense and raise the taxes for the purpose."[23]

This decision had a bearing on similar cases in other states, and consequently led to legal recognition of the high school as part of the state common school system. The high schools had now entered a period of establishment, and by 1890 the trend was clear: the high school was replacing the tuition academy. By 1900 there were some 6,000 high schools, while the number of academies had declined to approximately 1,200. It was now evident that a public secondary-school system, contigu-

---

[22] *Ibid.*, p. 263.   [23] *Ibid.*

ous with the common schools, had emerged. The threat of a dual system of private schools for those who could afford them and public schools for the poor was dying. Although the high schools were attended by only a small proportion of our youth in 1900, the inclusion of both terminal and college preparatory students under one roof was testimony to our rejection of the dual system of secondary education prevalent in Europe.

THE EDUCATION AND STATUS OF TEACHERS

The development of a system of free schools raised new demands for the education of teachers. As late as the middle of the nineteenth century, teachers were selected on a haphazard basis, the chief criterion being the ability to maintain discipline. The better teachers in the elementary schools were graduates of the academies and the newly established high schools. Salaries were meager and the quality of instruction left much to be desired. Teaching methods tended to be confined to drilling and having the student memorize bits of knowledge, rather than reasoning.

The first school for training teachers in this country was established in 1823 by Samuel R. Hall at Concord, Vermont. Although the level of instruction was not above that provided by the academy, some work in teaching methods and observation was provided. Hall developed a series of lectures into the first professional teaching book in English, *Lectures on Schoolkeeping* (1829).

In 1827 New York provided state aid to the academies for promoting the preparation of teachers. Governor Clinton of New York advocated, in 1827, the establishment of county teacher-training schools.

The Normal School

The first state-supported institution for the training of teachers was established in 1839 at Lexington, Massachusetts. Horace Mann, Secretary of the Massachusetts Board of Education, was largely responsible for its establishment. Two additional normal schools were established in Massachusetts by 1840. In 1844 the State Normal School was founded at Albany, New York. Although subject to considerable debate and criticism, other state normal schools followed in Connecticut and Michigan (1849), Rhode Island (1854), New Jersey (1855), Illinois (1857), Pennsylvania (1859), and Minnesota (1860). The first city normal school was established in St. Louis in 1857. By 1885 the number of public teacher-training schools exceeded 100. And by 1910 there were 200 such schools in operation throughout the United States.

The idea of special institutions for the training of teachers for the common schools was taken from practices in Germany and France, and the name normal was adopted from the French. The American normal school, like its European predecessor, developed as an extension of the common school, and not as a function of the university. The normal school programs ranged from one to four years in length, but even the four-year normal school represented the equivalent of two years beyond the four-year high school.

While many of the secondary school teachers were coming from the colleges and universities, the role of these institutions in teacher education was unclear. Many of the normal schools soon developed programs for the preparation of high-school teachers. But this function required the raising of standards, and during the early part of the twentieth century most of these institutions grew into state teachers colleges with increasing curricular emphasis on the arts and sciences. After World War II the state teachers colleges evolved into multi-purpose state colleges and universities. During the 1960's, the void that once separated the training of teachers from other branches of higher education had virtually disappeared.

Teacher Training in Colleges and Universities

New York University provided a modest teacher-training program as early as 1832, but this was short-lived. Brown University established an education department in 1850, but discontinued it following the founding of a state normal school in 1854. In the East, the colleges and universities showed little interest in the training of teachers for the lowly common schools and, consequently, such work was left to the normal schools.

In the north-central and western states, however, teacher-training programs were started at many of the state universities and colleges, such as Indiana University (1852), University of Iowa (1855), University of Wisconsin (1856), University of Missouri (1868), University of Kansas (1876), University of Michigan (1879), and the State Agricultural and Mechanical College of Kentucky (1881). The growth and development of the high school gave impetus to the role of the university in teacher training, although state normal schools also shared this function.

The growing recognition of the importance of teacher education as a university function was exemplified by the appearance of a *Harper's Weekly* editorial on July 26, 1879, entitled "Teaching How To Teach." This editorial praised the University of Michigan for establishing a professorship in education and stressed the importance of teacher education for our nation in these words: "In a society like ours, whose security depends upon educated intelligence, there is no more important function and service than that of teaching the teachers."

Before the turn of the century, teacher training was established at such universities as Johns Hopkins (1884), Cornell (1886), Stanford and Chicago (1891), California (1892), Illinois and Minnesota (1893), Ohio and Texas (1896), Columbia and Northwestern (1898). But the support for teacher education at the university level remained meager for some time. Gradually, however, the growing magnitude of public secondary education, coupled with the emergence of psychology and child-study as key behavioral sciences, led to the full establishment of teacher education as a university function.

Status of the Teacher

During the nineteenth century teaching became a predominantly female occupation. Even at the turn of the century, wages were ridiculously low and teaching was often regarded as a transitional occupation. Teacher tenure and retirement benefits were virtually nonexistent. The social life of teachers was severely restricted, particularly in rural areas. At a meeting of the American Institute of Instruction in 1864 a Connecticut lawyer commented:

> So long as teachers show, by their conduct, that they have no profession, from an apparent conscious of demerit, just so long will other professions, at great disadvantage, employ teachers as passive tools, and every man become the teacher's censor.[24]

Many school districts of the day were concerned with economy rather than qualifications in the hiring of teachers. State and local teacher organizations began to appear during the latter half of the nineenth century. Although the National Education Association, originally established as the National Teachers Association in 1857, attracted limited membership and effected little influence with local and state educational authorities, the organization served as a vehicle for new educational ideas during the 1880's and 1890's.

During this period, some of the progressive ideas from Europe were appearing in literature and in actual practice at the elementary level. The ideas of Pestalozzi had spread to England and the United States and increasing attention was being given to sensory experience, rather than to rote verbalization.

It should be mentioned that, while the training and status of teachers left much to be desired, similar conditions were prevalent in other professions. In medicine, for example, medical school standards varied greatly and many such institutions were profit-seeking. Few medical schools were engaged in anything resembling research, and students were trained primarily by practitioners of mediocre accomplishment.

---

[24] R. Freeman Butts and Lawrence A. Cremin, *A History of Education in American Culture* (New York: Holt, Rinehart and Winston, Inc., 1953), p. 233.

Beginnings of Education as a Behavioral Science

The work of Darwin (*Origin of Species*, 1859) led to a biological conception of the human mind and the learning process. William James' *Principles of Psychology* (1890) advocated that psychology be developed as a natural science. The work of Freud in Vienna shocked those who regarded the study of the human mind as the proper and exclusive realm of philosophy and religion. There was growing awareness in Europe and America of the conception of mental behavior as subject to biological and environmental forces.

By the turn of the century the study of psychology was being related to instructional methods and the behavior of the learner. G. Stanley Hall, President of Clark University from 1888 to 1919, pioneered the child-study movement with his investigations of the behavior of children.

The doctrine of mental discipline was soon to be challenged and discredited through the application of scientific inquiry to education. The conception of curriculum and method, particularly at the elementary level, acquired new significance as a result of these investigations. A variety of journals on education were appearing, marking the beginnings of education as a field for scientific study. At the close of the nineteenth century it was not uncommon for a college or university in a north-central or western state to have a lectureship, professorship, department, or school of education or pedagogy. But these beginnings were modest and often were subject to criticism by other sectors of the college or university.

SOCIETAL NEEDS AND THE SCHOOL

Broadening the High School Curriculum

During the last quarter of the nineteenth century, manual training was introduced in a number of high schools. John D. Runkle, first president of the Massachusetts Institute of Technology, and Calvin W. Woodward, Dean of the Polytechnic School at Washington University in St. Louis, influenced the establishment of manual training in the high schools. The first specialized manual training high school was established in St. Louis in 1880, with instruction in shopwork and mechanical drawing as well as in the general high school subjects. Publicly supported manual training high schools were started in Baltimore in 1884 and Philadelphia in 1885. Homemaking courses for high school girls were provided in Toledo in 1886. Indianapolis developed a comprehensive homemaking curriculum for girls in its manual training high school established in 1889.

The subject of drawing was required in the schools of larger cities and towns in Massachusetts beginning in 1870. Laboratory instruction in the sciences also began to be included in secondary school and college curricula at this time. Prior to 1870 most science instruction in school and college was strictly from books. The rise of the land-grant colleges gave great impetus to instruction in the laboratory and applied sciences. Gradually the old classical training was yielding to demands for an educational program more realistic for a society entering an age of science and technology. The study of human nature and learning was also emerging and, as a result, the old classical education and the doctrine of mental discipline began to yield to modern studies. Physical training in calisthenics and gymnastics appeared after 1875.

The Negro

Slavery had been abolished with the passage of the Thirteenth Amendment (1865). Through the Fourteenth Amendment (1868), states were enjoined from denying citizens equal protection of the laws and from abridging civil rights. The Fifteenth Amendment (1870) prohibited states from denying or limiting the voting rights of citizens on the basis of "race, color, or previous condition of servitude." The Civil Rights Act of 1875 guaranteed that all persons have open to them the public facilities of services, entertainment, and transportation.

But following the withdrawal of federal troops from the South in 1875, various Jim Crow laws were enacted in the southern states. Negroes were denied the right to vote through the invention of a variety of literacy tests subject to arbitrary interpretation. During the last two decades of the nineteenth century approximately 2,000 lynchings of Negroes occurred in the South. Separate schools for Negro youngsters were established in the southern states along with separate provisions for transportation and other social services.

Even in certain northern areas separate schools were maintained for Negroes. In 1849 a decision of the Massachusetts Supreme Court held that the provision for separate schools for Negro children in Boston was not in violation of their equal rights to education. Boston abolished these separate schools in 1855. A United States Supreme Court decision in 1896 (Plessey vs. Ferguson) upheld the right of the state to require segregation in public transportation. In this decision, Justice Harlan wrote a famous dissenting opinion predicting its eventual reversal. The separate but equal doctrine was now commonly applied to segregated school facilities in the South. At the turn of the century, however, the per capita expenditure for education of Negro children in the South was only $2.71 in contrast to $4.92 for white children.[25]

---

25 Virgil A. Clift, Archibald W. Anderson, and H. Gordon Hullfish (eds.), *Negro Education in America*, Sixteenth Yearbook of the John Dewey Society (New York: Harper and Row, Publishers, Inc., 1962), p. 44.

It was not until the United States Supreme Court decision of May 17, 1954 (unanimous) that the separate but equal doctrine was destroyed with the historic declaration that "separate educational facilities are inherently unequal."

The Work of National Committees

The National Education Association in 1891 appointed a Committee of Ten on Secondary School Studies. Chaired by President Charles W. Eliot of Harvard, this committee examined the program of studies of the secondary school and, through its report in 1893, helped bring about greater uniformity in the high school curriculum. The Committee of Ten was dominated by college professors who tended to view the work of the high school as preparation for college. No attempt was made to study the nature of the learner or the relationship of the curriculum to societal forces.

The Committee on College Entrance Requirements, also appointed by the N.E.A. in 1895, reinforced the conception of secondary education as preparation for college. Although the public high school was not originally designed as a college preparatory institution, the leaders in higher education exerted great influence in making this the dominant function of the high school.

During the last two decades of the nineteenth century, high school and college accreditation agencies were formed to provide regional standardization of curricula and facilities. The New England Association of Colleges and Secondary Schools dates back to 1885. The North Central Association of Colleges and Secondary Schools was established in 1894. The Southern Association of Colleges and Secondary Schools was organized in 1895.

The Growing Diversity of Population

During the first two decades of the nineteenth century the annual rate of immigration was merely a few thousand, coming largely from Protestant northern European origins (England, Scotland, Ireland, and Germany). While the number of these immigrants totalled slightly more than 8,000 in 1820, it mounted to over 50,000 in 1825. The annual immigration rate continued to mushroom, reaching more than 200,000 in 1847 and 427,000 in 1854. The national origins of these immigrants represented a wider diversity than ever before. The potato famine of 1846–1848 brought a million and a quarter Irish immigrants to our shores between 1845 and 1855. Most of these Irish immigrants were Catholics and soon Catholic parochial schools made their appearance.

During the last two decades of the nineteenth century and during the early part of the twentieth century, the national origins of immigrants shifted from the north and west of Europe to the south and east. Many of these immigrants were poorly educated and lacking in financial resources. The great task of creating unity out of diversity was upon us, and much of this job of Americanization was given to the schools. Evening schools increased markedly in the larger cities during the last quarter of the nineteenth century. While the task of assimilation and Americanization of the children and youth fell upon the schools, the labor unions and political bosses assumed a significant leadership role with adult immigrants. Although the movement toward women's suffrage was evident during the last half of the nineteenth century, it was not attained nationally until the Constitutional Amendment of 1919.

High School Enrollment

By 1890 the high school was commonly organized as a four-year institution following the eight-year elementary school. During the 1889–1890 school year, only 6.7 per cent of the 14- to 17-year-old age group was enrolled in school. By 1900 the percentage of the 14- to 17-year-old age group enrolled in school had risen to 11.4.

At the turn of the century many areas of the nation were still without high schools, and only relatively few sections had begun to develop a tradition of high school attendance. The curriculum of the high school was geared more toward preparation for college than to the practical needs of youth.

As we entered the twentieth century the public high school was a rather exclusive institution serving only one out of every ten youths. Universal secondary education was to be attained during the twentieth century through the development of a comprehensive curriculum, the extension of compulsory education laws to older children and youth, and the enactment of effective child labor legislation.

SUMMARY

In coming to this continent the early settlers brought with them many of the traditions and customs of the Old World. Although they came here seeking religious freedom, it was not long before they instituted the European tradition of a direct tie between the government and a single established church. As in the Old World, the aim of education was spiritual salvation rather than individual enlightenment. While the early laws on education in the Massachusetts Colony were intended to ensure adherence to the established religion, their enactment served to establish the right of government to require the support of education through taxation and to hold the parent responsible for supporting such education.

The growing religious and cultural diversity in some of the colonies

THE DEVELOPMENT OF AMERICAN SECONDARY EDUCATION

prevented the development of a singular church-state monopoly. By the end of the seventeenth century, civil forms of government began to take the place of the religious forms. The settlers, concerned with the realities of the frontier, sought to improve the conditions of life.

While children of the poor and orphans were bound to the apprenticeship system transplanted from England, youngsters from the upper classes attended the Latin grammar school, also brought over from England. Instruction in the Latin grammar school emphasized Latin, the language of religion. Failing to meet the practical needs of the day, the Latin grammar school began to yield to the academy during the second-half of the eighteenth century.

Originally conceived by Benjamin Franklin, the academy represented a revolution in secondary education. The curriculum included English and modern foreign languages, as well as other practical studies. Where the Latin grammar school was limited to boys, certain academies for girls were established. But the academies were private tuition schools, and many of them maintained the tradition of teaching Latin and the classical subjects.

The First Amendment to the Constitution guaranteed religious freedom and established the principle of separation of church and state. Although the Constitution made no direct mention of education, the Preamble expressed the goal to "promote the general welfare." Washington, Jefferson, and other founding fathers avowed their belief in education for the common people as essential to a free society. Yet, while the role of the Federal Government in supporting education was recognized very early in the history of our nation, education in the United States evolved as a state function.

Although publicly supported tuition-free elementary schools were well established in the various states by the middle of the nineteenth century, the private academy was still the dominant form of secondary schooling. The academy, while originally designed to meet the practical needs of a nation emerging in commerce, nevertheless was limited to those who could afford the tuition. Moreover, the curricula of many academies remained tradition-bound. The growing demand for a free public secondary school system, contiguous with the common public schools, led to the decline of the academy during the second-half of the nineteenth century.

At the close of the nineteenth century it was clear that a dual system of private schools for the privileged and public schools for the poor was a dying threat. While the public high school was attended by only a small fraction of our nation's youth, the principle of public taxation for the maintenance of secondary education was firmly established.

The great waves of immigrants around the turn of the century, from diverse national and cultural origins, were to leave the imposing task of Americanization with the schools. No other nation was to face such a challenge.

Before we turn to educational developments of the twentieth century, we shall examine in Chapter 2 the aims of education in historic perspective.

PROBLEMS FOR STUDY AND DISCUSSION

1. It is said that the church and state were one in the New England Colonies. What bearing did this have on the early educational legislation in the Massachusetts Colony?

2. Why was severe corporal punishment common in the schools of the colonial period?

3. What forces brought about the adoption of the principle of separation of church and state and the development of secularized public schools? Is the separation of church and state an issue in contemporary education? Why or why not?

4. What forces led to the transition from the Latin grammar school to the academy, and from the academy to the high school?

5. What are the historical bases for the role of the Federal Government in supporting education? Why is there considerable controversy even today regarding the role of the Federal Government in education?

6. What are the historical bases for regarding public education as a state function?

7. How do you account for the early opposition to supporting high schools through taxation? Has such opposition been felt in your own community in recent years?

8. Why didn't we develop a dual system of secondary education patterned after the European approach?

9. How do you explain the development of national and state support of higher education before the high school came to be recognized as integral to the public educational system?

10. Why didn't teacher education have its beginnings in the college and university in our society?

11. Why was it that only one out of every ten youths between 14 and 17 years of age was enrolled in high school as recently as 1900? What percentage of our nation's youth fail to graduate from high school today? Does your local high school maintain dropout statistics?

12. How do you explain the reversal of the United States Supreme Court over the years in decisions relating to the separate but equal doctrine?

13. Do many of our large city schools serve an Americanization function today? Why or why not?

SELECTED REFERENCES

Brubacher, John S. *A History of the Problems of Education.* New York: McGraw-Hill Company, Inc., 1947.

Butts, R. Freeman. *A Cultural History of Western Education.* 2nd Ed. New York: McGraw-Hill Company, Inc., 1955.

——— and Lawrence A. Cremin. *A History of Education in American Culture.* New York: Holt, Rinehart & Winston, Inc., 1953.

Clift, Virgil A., Archibald W. Anderson, and H. Gordon Hullfish (eds.) *Negro Education in America,* Sixteenth Yearbook of the John Dewey Society. New York: Harper and Row, Publishers, Inc., 1962.

Cubberley, Ellwood P. *Public Education in the United States.* Boston: Houghton Mifflin Company, 1947.

Drake, William C. *The American School in Transition.* Englewood Cliffs, N.J.: Prentice-Hall, Inc., 1955.

Edwards, Newton and Herman G. Richey. *The School in the American Social Order.* 2nd Ed. Boston: Houghton Mifflin Company, 1963.

Fellman, David, *The Supreme Court and Education.* New York: Columbia University Press, 1960.

Good, Harry G. *A History of American Education.* 2nd Ed. New York: The Macmillan Company, 1962.

Knight, Edgar W. *Fifty Years of American Education.* New York: The Ronald Press Company, 1952.

Meyers, E. D. *Education in the Perspective of History.* New York: Harper and Row, Publishers, Inc., 1960.

Smiley, Marjorie and John S. Diekhoff. *Prologue to Teaching.* New York: Oxford University Press, 1959.

Thayer, V. T. *The Role of the School in American Society.* New York: Dodd, Mead & Company, 1960.

Kneller, George F. (ed.) *Foundations of Education.* New York: John Wiley and Sons, Inc., 1963.

CHAPTER 2

The Aims
of Education

M OST PEOPLE are aware that education in the United States today is beset by many differences of opinion about the nature of the aims and means to be pursued. But many of us are not aware that this great controversy is as old as civilization itself. In the words of Aristotle,

> As things are . . . mankind are by no means agreed about the things to be taught, whether we look to virtue or the best life. . . . The existing practice is perplexing; no one knowing on what principle we should proceed—should the useful in life, or should virtue, or should the higher knowledge be the aim of our training; all these opinions have been entertained. Again about the means there is no agreement; for differing persons, starting with different ideas about the nature of virtue, naturally disagree about the practice of it.[1]

Historically, educational aims have been divided according to conservative and progressive elements. Ancient Chinese culture embraced an educational program geared to the preservation of a static social order. Eventually, the educational program of ancient China fell far behind the economic and technological advances of the nation, so education, being divorced from life, became an end in itself.

In the Greek city-state of Athens, education for the freeman was directed toward the well-rounded person, with a well-proportioned balance of intellectual, aesthetic, moral, and physical traits. The Athenians were concerned with progressive educational elements as well as conservative ones. They were concerned not only with the preservation of

---

[1] *The Works of Aristotle, Politica,* Book VIII, Ch. 2, translated into English by Benjamin Jowett, Vol. X (Oxford: The Clarendon Press, 1921), p. 1338.

the order of things, but with the improvement of the individual and society. Education for the freeman was aimed at the cultivation of the intellect, since man's mind or intelligence distinguished him from the beasts. The education of the freeman was liberal (from the Latin *liber*, meaning free); the slave, on the other hand, was saddled with the menial labor of the society. While the Athenians recognized physical fitness as an essential educational aim, they were concerned about the danger of over-emphasis on athleticism, which was becoming evident in the Olympics. Aristotle (384–322 B.C.) was critical of the Spartans' obsession with physical education for military purposes and neglect of intellectualized activity.

Plato (427–347 B.C.), in *The Republic,* described an "ideal" state composed of three classes of citizens—the artisans, the warriors, and the philosophers or guardians. The education of the philosophers or guardians would be of the highest and noblest in quality, since they would be the true leaders of the society.

The early Romans, like the Athenians, were concerned with education for effective citizenship on the part of the freeman, but the Romans placed even greater emphasis on the practical needs for citizenship.

EDUCATION FOR SALVATION

While the Greeks and Romans were concerned with education for citizenship or secular life, the Judeo-Christian purpose was education for salvation and life in the hereafter. Education as preparation for the after-world obviously neglected the practical needs of the day. This ideal of education for salvation was dominant through the Middle Ages. The Renaissance brought man to a revival of the Greco-Roman concept of liberal education, combined with the Judeo-Christian concept of salvation. The impact of the Protestant Reformation against the repressive rule of the church, the revival of commerce, the development of printing, and the rise of the universities led to a reemphasis on learning. The printing press was in operation in the leading cities of Europe by 1475. In 1517 Martin Luther began his great dispute against the authority of the traditional Christian Church.

Emerging from the Renaissance of the fourteenth, fifteenth, and six-teenth centuries was a view of man known as classical humanism. This view held that since man was distinguished above the beasts by his intellect, man's education should be concerned with pursuits of a non-materialistic nature. Classical and spiritual studies, therefore, were far nobler for man's purposes than practical studies. A liberal education was founded upon religious and classical foundations. This concept of classical humanism was embraced by many of the intellectual leaders of the American Colonies. The American Colonies were formed by settlers in search of religious and political freedom, most of whom embraced some form of Protestantism. In Chapter 1 we discussed how education in the early colonies was designed for salvation. Children were taught to read in Latin so that they would develop a knowledge of the scriptures.

EDUCATION FOR INDIVIDUAL DEVELOPMENT

Francis Bacon (1561–1626) in England and Johann Amos Comenius (1592–1670) in Moravia began the quest to make educational aims more realistic, in line with the practical needs of life through the study of science and other realistic subjects. In France, Jean Jacques Rousseau (1712–1778) argued for a more natural education of the child. Education for self-development began to be emphasized in place of education for salvation.

But some continued to conceive of education as a means of mental discipline, and classical subjects were retained for the purpose of "sharpening the mental faculties." Although the doctrine of mental discipline was not demolished until the rise of experimental psychology in the twentieth century, new demands were being made for more practical educational aims in harmony with the demands of life.

The noted Englishman, John Locke (1632–1704), emphasized the importance of education for moral character in his work, *Some Thoughts Concerning Education*. Locke did not make any mention of religious education in his writings on the cultivation of moral values and, consequently, is regarded as a forerunner to the rise of secularism. Locke emphasized the importance of using reason in character development. The eighteenth century, often called the Age of Reason, was characterized by a spirit of reflection, brought on by the new age of science.

Jean Jacques Rousseau created a tremendous controversy with the appearance of his iconoclastic book in 1762, *Emile*, the story of a boy's education by a new and radical plan. Rousseau described the education of Emile as natural and free of the coercion and punishment that characterized the schools of the day. Rousseau attacked the rigidity and abuses of ecclesiastical education. He rejected the doctrine of original sin and held that everything in nature was inherently good, not evil. He conceived of education as concerned ideally with life in the present and natural world rather than with life in the hereafter. Although Rousseau's natural program of education bordered on the laissez-faire and contained many exaggerations, *Emile* is regarded as one of the great works of the eighteenth century, and it exerted an important influence on the thinking about education.

The eighteenth century saw a breakdown of the old religious interests. The New England colonists deplored the church's role in the witchcraft persecutions at Salem (1691–1692) and elsewhere, and began to concentrate on the practical demands of frontier existence. Town governments changed from religious to civil forms. New frontier settlements were developing rapidly and commerce was growing. Individualism was rising in Europe and America, and the schools began to change in character.

Pestalozzi (1746–1827) in Switzerland and Froebel (1782–1852) in Germany, deeply influenced by Rousseau, were experimenting with educational approaches in harmony with the individual interests and capacities of the child. The dignity and worth of the individual and the function of education as a means of social correction was beginning to come into recognition. In the words of Pestalozzi,

> . . . the ultimate end of education is not perfection in the accomplishment of the school, but fitness for life; not the acquirement of habits of blind obedience and of prescribed diligence, but a preparation for independent action.[2]

The work of Pestalozzi and Rousseau reflected a new conception of the nature of man that was rooted in the Age of Enlightment. These men attacked the doctrine of original sin and argued that man is made good or evil by his environment. Education, therefore, was part of this environment and, consequently, education should play an important role in the shaping of the individual. The child was not a sinful being to be controlled and molded through harsh discipline and punishment. The child, with a potentiality for goodness, should be surrounded by a school environment epitomizing this goodness. The child should be treated with dignity and kindness, not coercion and punishment, if he is to become a good person.

Johann Friedrich Herbart (1776–1841), a professor of philosophy in Germany, worked out a theory and method of instruction that later caught the attention of educators in Europe and America. Influenced by Pestalozzi, Herbart emphasized the importance of interest in learning and condemned the emphasis on the endless memorization of isolated facts that was so characteristic of the schools of the day. Herbart placed emphasis on the moral aims of teaching and on improved techniques of instruction. Herbart differed with Rousseau's conception of free and natural education and introduced a formal approach to teaching method. He emphasized the importance of reorganizing the content of instruction to fulfill definite purposes in accordance with the development of the learner.

---

[2] L. F. Anderson, *Pestalozzi* (New York: McGraw-Hill Company, Inc., 1931), p. 166.

In Europe and America, education for individual development gathered impetus with the rejection of the concept of education for salvation or for social privilege. The Declaration of Independence stated that "all men are created equal, that they are endowed by their Creator with certain unalienable Rights. . . . That to secure these rights, Governments are instituted among Men, deriving their powers from the consent of the governed." Jefferson and Washington advocated the promotion of education for general enlightenment. The leaders of the new nation recognized the importance of education for the enhancement of democracy.

A society of heterogeneous religious interests developed rapidly in America. The Bill of Rights, in the First Amendment, protected religious freedom for all by prohibiting Congress from making any law respecting an establishment of religion. This amendment ensured against a privileged position for any religious group.

In the early nineteenth century, a controversy was raging in New York and Massachusetts over the exclusion of religion from the curriculum of the public schools. In 1842 New York decided to eliminate any use of public funds to support private church schools. Moreover, religion was excluded from the curriculum of the public schools because of the controversy about the nature of such instruction and the principle of church-state separation.

Horace Mann (1796–1859), as Secretary of the Massachusetts State Board of Education, steadfastly held that the public schools should be nonsectarian. Although Mann was vigorously attacked for promoting godless schools, the battle for secularization of public education gathered impetus in Massachusetts and elsewhere during the second half of the nineteenth century. The principle of separation of church and state was applied to the public schools in order to protect the pluralistic nature of our society. Secularism was needed to prevent the domination of any majority religious group over minority groups. Laws were passed to eliminate any use of public funds for private and church schools and to protect the public schools from disintegrating forces.

EDUCATION FOR MENTAL DISCIPLINE

As the demand for more practical studies grew, certain educators sought a justification for continuing with a perennial curriculum steeped predominantly in the antiquity of Latin and Greek classical studies. The forces of tradition, prestige, and inertia helped retain these classical studies, but they were constantly being eroded by the practical needs of a rapidly expanding industrial society. Earlier in this chapter we discussed some of the tenets of classical humanism that developed in

Europe through the sixteenth and seventeenth centuries and exerted an important influence on education in America from the colonial period through the eighteenth and early nineteenth centuries.

In the nineteenth century the position of the humanistic and classical tradition was seriously challenged by the scientific and practical developments in society. The classical humanists viewed educational aims as a revival of the ancient Greek and Roman ideals of liberal education combined with the Christian purpose of moral salvation; they held that scientific studies, in their practicality, were materialistic. And since the humanists felt that man should be concerned with spiritual and intellectual pursuits of a nonmaterialistic nature, there was no room for science or other practical studies in the curriculum. It was further argued that classical studies were of a higher order than practical studies since the former led to the cultivation of the intellect. True education should be concerned with disciplining the mental faculties, and the classical tradition, it was argued, is the key to intellectual facility.

But the demand for the useful and practical was overwhelming. Benjamin Franklin, in his founding of the academy in Philadelphia in 1751, conceived of a school system geared to the practical and vocational needs of the new nation. He advocated the study of modern languages, especially English, in preference to classical languages. Franklin included in his curriculum of the academy the study of mathematics, social studies (geography, government, history), natural science (including agriculture), and other useful subjects. Although many of the academies failed to follow Franklin's ideas and tenaciously held to the teaching of Latin and other classical studies, the rapid development of the public school system and the decline of the tuition academies at the close of the nineteenth century led to many needed changes in the curriculum.

Throughout most of the nineteenth century, the doctrine of mental discipline received support from the faculty psychologists, who held that certain traditional subjects were valuable for strengthening the mental faculties. Scholarly knowledge, they argued, was rigorous and would result in the sharpening of the intellect. Useful studies designed for living in the modern world were not regarded as capable of sharpening and strengthening the intellect. The mind was conceived as an entity separate and distinct from the body. This conception of man was in harmony with the views of the religionists, who opposed materialism and environmentalism. But the developing revolution in the social, economic, and political conceptions of man led to the downfall of this view of education. The continued development of experimental psychology (behavioral, Gestalt, etc.) led to the general dissolution of faculty psychology.

Although the battle for a more practical curriculum was won decisively through the great scientific and technological revolution of the twentieth century, the controversy over the essential or fundamental studies and the frills continues to this day.

EDUCATION FOR COMPLETE LIVING

The accelerated pace of scientific and industrial development around the middle of the nineteenth century led some thinkers to challenge the classical curriculum and the persistent emphasis on mental discipline. It was argued that the study of science was vital to intelligent living. Teaching methods of incessant drill and repetition were coming under attack.

Herbert Spencer (1820–1903), one of England's greatest scholars, published an essay in 1859 titled "What Knowledge is of Most Worth?" Spencer argued that the purpose of education was "to prepare for complete living." He advocated that science have an important place in the curriculum because it is so useful in life. Spencer stressed the importance of formulating the educational program in accordance with the leading activities and needs of life, and he identified these needs in the following order of importance:

1. Those ministering directly to self-preservation.
2. Those which secure for one the necessities of life.
3. Those which help in the rearing and disciplining of offspring.
4. Those involved in maintaining one's political and social relations.
5. Those which fill up the leisure part of life and gratify taste and feelings.[3]

Spencer's essays on education elicited great interest in the aims and means of education in both England and the United States, and eventually resulted in a new recognition of science as an important area of the curriculum. Moreover, Spencer's writings showed the need for reshaping the purposes and practices of education in harmony with the realities of our daily lives. Essentially, Spencer was advocating a curriculum based upon human needs of health and safety, vocation, family, citizenship, and leisure. Spencer helped us focus on the need for educational reform advocated by many thinkers.

EDUCATION FOR DEMOCRACY AND SOCIAL PROGRESS

In Europe during the latter part of the eighteenth century, men like Rousseau in France and Pestalozzi in Switzerland were exercising influence toward a new recognition of the dignity and worth of the individual.

---

[3] Herbert Spencer, *Essays on Education* (New York: E. P. Dutton & Company, 1911). p. 7.

After the Revolutionary War many leaders of the new nation, including Jefferson and Washington, endorsed education as the means of strengthening and perpetuating liberty and domocracy. But, essentially, the men who had framed the Constitution were from the aristocratic class. In the new nation, qualifications for voting were based upon property holdings and religious faith. The nineteenth century in America, however, was a period characterized by an awakening of educational consciousness. In 1828 Andrew Jackson was elected President. Jackson, as a man of the people, symbolized the spirit of the American frontier. Full manhood suffrage in the states developed rapidly during this period. As the workingmen began to organize, they demanded free education for their children. In 1852 Massachusetts adopted a law for compulsory education at public expense. The pauper school system, inherited from the class system of England, was vigorously attacked and abolished in the middle Atlantic and southern states. The western states had no tolerance for the undemocratic idea of a pauper-school system.

The work of Horace Mann in Massachusetts during the middle part of the nineteenth century pointed to democratic and national goals of education, rather than religious ends. By 1850, elementary school education was available to the masses, but now the demand for public high schools was growing. Before the close of the nineteenth century, the free public high school had become accepted as part of the common school system of the state, and the private tuition academies were rapidly declining.

New Forces for National Progress

During the first two decades of the twentieth century, American educators became increasingly concerned with the need for changes in the character of secondary education. World War I demonstrated the need for technologically trained and physically fit citizenry. Although at the turn of the century only one out of every 10 youngsters of secondary school age actually was enrolled in school, new pressures and demands were being made for making secondary education accessible to a much larger proportion of our youth. By 1920 one out of every five youngsters of secondary-school age was enrolled in school. The trend toward universal secondary education was clearly indicated, and new developments and perspectives in science and technology, coupled with economic and political reforms, pointed to the need for changes in the aims and content of secondary education in our society. The critical period of World War I led to the passage in 1917 of the Smith-Hughes Act of Congress, signed by President Wilson, providing for federal support for vocational education in our secondary schools. The United States emerged from World War I as a world power facing great social problems of the new industrial age. The goals of the schools were coming closer to the practical needs of the nation.

The Modern School Proposal

In 1917, Abraham Flexner of the General Education Board, famous for his Carnegie Foundation studies of medical education, published a paper entitled "A Modern School." Flexner rejected the traditional curriculum of the secondary school and proposed a program geared to the contemporary physical and social world and emphasizing activities in four basic areas.

1. *Science*—This to be the central feature of the school.
2. *Industry*—The occupations and trades of the industrial world.
3. *Civics*—History, civic institutions, and the organization of society and government.
4. *Aesthetics*—Literature, languages, music, and art.[4]

The Cardinal Principles of Seconday Education

Out of this great ferment for modernizing the curriculum and extending secondary education to all youth, the National Education Association designated a committee in 1913 know as the Commission on the Reorganization of Secondary Education. In 1918 the Commission issued an important document called *Cardinal Principles of Secondary Education*. This report pointed to the importance of education for complete living in a democratic society and identified the following seven principles or aims of secondary education:

1. Sound health knowledge and habits.
2. Command of the fundamental processes (reading, writing, arithmetical computation, and oral and written expression).
3. Worthy home membership.
4. Education for a vocation.
5. Education for good citizenship.
6. Worthy use of leisure.
7. Ethical character.[5]

These seven *Cardinal Principles of Secondary Education* were widely discussed and followed. It became clear that they were equally applicable to the elementary and collegiate levels. Some educators recognized in these principles a basic philosophy and purpose of education applicable to all levels of education—with differing programs in accordance with the age group concerned. The Cardinal Principles clearly pointed to the

---

4 Publications of the General Education Board, *Occasional Papers*, No. 3, New York, 1917.
5 Commission of the Reorganization of Secondary Education, *Cardinal Principles of Secondary Education* (Washington, D.C.: U.S. Office of Education, Bulletin 35, 1918).

comprehensive role of the secondary school in its aims of educating for complete living in a democracy. Most of the commissions and individuals who attempted to formulate educational objectives in subsequent years have based their work on the proposals of Herbert Spencer in 1859 and the Cardinal Principles of 1918.

Progressive Education

The work of John Dewey (1859–1952) during the early decades of the twentieth century exerted a profound influence on American education.[6] Although Dewey did not attempt to offer a specific listing of educational objectives, he viewed education as the means of building a democratic way of life. He attacked mental discipline and indoctrination and viewed the educational process as critical thinking and problem-solving through the method of intelligence or the scientific method. Dewey recognized the importance of studying the psychology of learning and both the nature of the individual and his social context. If, according to Dewey, we are to develop enlightened citizens for a democracy, then the heart of the educational process must consist of critical thinking and problem-solving. And since social progress is implicit in democracy, therefore the educational process must be progressive, not static.

No other educator has exerted a greater influence on the shaping of American education than John Dewey. Although his philosophy was greatly distorted by both his followers and his critics, he lived to see many of his ideas gain acceptance in the schools.

Other Objectives for Comprehensive Education

In 1918 Alexander Inglis of Harvard University, a member of the N.E.A. Commission on the Reorganization of Secondary Education, proposed these three fundamental aims of secondary education:

1. The Socio-Civic Aim: the preparation of the individual as a prospective citizen and cooperating member of society.
2. The Economic-Vocational Aim: the preparation of the individual as a prospective worker and producer.
3. The Individualistic-Avocational Aim: the preparation of the individual for life as a free and independent personality and the wise utilization of leisure.[7]

In 1924, Franklin Bobbitt of the University of Chicago, as a result of his curriculum work for the Los Angeles schools, identified these ten major activity areas of education:

---

[6] See John Dewey, *Democracy and Education* (New York: The Macmillan Company, 1916).

[7] Alexander J. Inglis, *Principles of Secondary Education* (Boston: Houghton Mifflin Company, 1918), pp. 367–368.

1. Language activities; social intercommunication.
2. Health activities.
3. Citizenship activities.
4. General social activities.
5. Spare-time activities, amusements, recreations.
6. Keeping one's self mentally fit.
7. Religious activities.
8. Parental activities.
9. Unspecialized or nonvocational practical activities.
10. The labors of one's calling.[8]

Bobbitt's objectives were designed for general education at all levels. In accordance with these objectives, he proposed the following basic studies for all secondary school students:

1. English.
2. Literature.
3. Social Studies.
4. Science.
5. Mathematics.
6. Physical Education.
7. Practical Arts.
8. Music.
9. Arts.[9]

Bobbitt also proposed electives in advanced subjects from the above areas, including foreign languages, vocational education, and others. Although Bobbitt recognized "religious attitudes and activities" as part of his educational objectives, he did not include these in the school curriculum, apparently in recognition of these functions as the role of the home and church.

Education for a New Social Order

During the early 1930's, when our nation was beset by serious economic and social dislocations, some educators looked to the schools as institutions for reconstructing the social order.

> If progressive education is to be genuinely progressive, it must . . . face squarely and courageously every social issue, come to grips with life in all its stark reality, establish an organic relation with the community, develop a realistic and comprehensive theory of welfare, fashion a compelling and challenging vision of human destiny, and become less frightened than it is today at the bogies of imposition and indoctrination.[10]

---

[8] Franklin Bobbitt, *How to Make a Curriculum* (Boston: Houghton Mifflin Company, 1924), pp. 8–9.

[9] *Ibid.*, pp. 68–75.

[10] George S. Counts, *Dare the Schools Build a New Social Order?* (New York: The John Day Company, 1932), pp. 9–10.

These critics argued that the progressives must look to the educational ideal of improving and reconstructing the social order, rather than be concerned with child-centered and individualistic aims. Yet, although our society looks to the schools as institutions for societal improvements, the schools remain instruments of society, and as such are expected to preserve and strengthen the best elements of the social order. With the advent of many social and economic reforms at the national level during the late 1930's, reconstructionism declined in its influence.

Continued Emphasis on Education for Democracy and Social Progress

The Educational Policies Commission of the National Education Association formulated a comprehensive list of goals for American education in a report published in 1938, and summarized them as follows:

1. *The Objectives of Self-Realization.* Inquiring mind, speech, reading, writing, number, health, recreation, esthetics, character.
2. *The Objectives of Human Relationship.* Respect for humanity, friendships, cooperation, courtesy, home membership.
3. *The Objectives of Economic Efficiency.* Occupation, consumer economics.
4. *The Objectives of Civic Responsibility.* Social justice, social understanding and activity, critical judgment, tolerance, conservation, citizenship, democracy.[11]

THE PROBLEMS OF YOUTH AND THE NATION. The great depression of the 1930's led to a new focus on social and economic directions. The American Youth Commission, appointed in 1935 by the American Council on Education to study the problems of out-of-school youth, recommended a program of education designed to meet the following needs of youth:

1. Citizenship.
2. Home and family.
3. Vocational life.
4. Leisure time.
5. Physical health.
6. Mental health.
7. Continued learning.[12]

THE IMPERATIVE NEEDS OF YOUTH. As we were emerging from World War II, in a position of world leadership, the Educational Policies Commission of the N.E.A. prepared a volume entitled *Education for ALL American Youth,* published in 1944. Secondary education was recognized as necessary for all the children of all the people, and although it was

[11] Educational Policies Commission, *The Purposes of Education in American Democracy* (Washington, D.C.: National Education Association, 1938), pp. 50, 72, 92, 108.
[12] See American Youth Commission, *Youth and the Future* (Washington, D.C.: American Council on Education, 1942).

agreed that diversified programs should be provided, it was emphasized that all youth should attend a comprehensive high school together. Moreover, it was emphasized that every citizen should have the opportunity to secure an education to the fullest extent of his capacities. The work of the American Youth Commission during the latter part of the depression years had caused educators to focus on the needs of youth as well as the needs of the nation. In 1944, the Educational Policies Commission, in *Education for ALL American Youth*, identified the "Ten Imperative Needs of Youth" as follows:

1. All youth need to develop salable skills and those understandings and attitudes that make the worker an intelligent and productive participant in economic life. To this end, most youth need supervised work experience as well as education in the skills and knowledges of their occupations.

2. All youth need to develop and maintain good health and physical fitness.

3. All youth need to understand the rights and duties of a citizen of a democratic society, and to be diligent and competent in the performance of their obligations as members of the community and citizens of the state and nation, and of the world.

4. All youth need to understand the significance of the family for the individual and society, and the conditions conducive to successful family life.

5. All youth need to know how to purchase and use goods and services intelligently, understanding both the value received by the consumer and the economic consequence of their acts.

6. All youth need to understand the methods of science, the influence of science on human life, and the main scientific facts concerning the nature of the world and man.

7. All youth need opportunities to develop their capacities to appreciate beauty in literature, art, music and nature.

8. All youth need to be able to use their leisure time well and to budget it wisely, balancing activities that yield satisfaction to the individual with those that are socially useful.

9. All youth need to develop respect for other persons, to grow in their insight into ethical values and principles and to be able to live and work cooperatively with others.

10. All youth need to grow in their ability to think rationally, to express their thoughts clearly, and to read and listen with understanding.[13]

REPORT OF THE HARVARD COMMITTEE.   In 1943 Dr. James B. Conant, President of Harvard University, appointed a committee composed of faculty members from the Arts and Sciences and Education at Harvard

---

[13] Educational Policies Commission, *Education for All American Youth* (Washington, D.C.: National Education Association, 1944), pp. 225–226. (Later revised as *Education for All American Youth: A Further Look*, 1952, p. 216.)

"And you America,
  Cast you the real reckoning for your present?
  The lights and shadows of your future, good or evil?
  To girlhood, boyhood look, the teacher and the school."
                            —WALT WHITMAN

for the purpose of exploring "the objectives of a general education in a free society." The work of the committee was completed in 1945 as the "Report of the Harvard Committee" under the title, *General Education in a Free Society*. In selecting the term general education in place of liberal education, Conant emphasized the democratic ideal of universal education over the traditional concept of liberal education for the privileged few. This famous report focused on the goals and means of general education at both school and college levels. Although this report did not attempt to identify a concise list of aims or goals of education, nevertheless certain guiding principles and aims were explored. Several statements gleaned from various sections of the report are concerned with educational ends and means.

> . . . the aim of education should be to prepare an individual to become an expert both in some particular vocation or art and in the general art of the free man and the citizen. Thus the two kinds of education once given separately to different social classes must be given together to all alike.[14]

In describing the abilities that should be derived from general education, the report emphasized critical thinking.

> These abilities, in our opinion, are: to think effectively, to communicate thought, to make relevant judgments, to discriminate among values.[15]

The report also stressed the importance of gearing education to the whole person. According to the report, the fruition of the four preceding abilities lies in personal integration.

> Education must look to the whole man. It has been wisely said that education aims at the good man, the good citizen, and the useful man. . . . Personal integration is not a fifth characteristic in addition to the other four and coordinate with them; it is their proper fruition.[16]

In defining what is meant by the whole man, the Harvard report cautioned against two dangers:

> First there is the danger of identifying intelligence with the qualities of the so-called intellectual type—with bookishness and skill in the manipulation of concepts. We have tried to guard against this mistake by stressing the traits of relevant judgment and discrimination of values in effective thinking. Second, we must remember that intelligence, even when taken in its widest sense, does not exhaust the total potentialities of human nature. Man is not a contemplative being alone. Why is it, then, that education is conceived as primarily an intellectual enterprise

---

14 Reprinted by permission of the publisher from *General Education in a Free Society*, Report of the Harvard Committee. Cambridge, Mass.: Harvard University Press, Copyright, 1945, by the President and Fellows of Harvard College. P. 54.
15 *Ibid.*, pp. 64–65.   16 *Ibid.*, p. 74.

when, in fact, human nature is so complex? For instance, man has his emotions and his drives and his will; why should education center on the training of the intellect? . . . the fruit of education is intelligence in action . . .

. . . when either thought or action is stressed as an exclusive end, when the teachers look only to scholarly ability and the students (and perhaps the public too) only in proficiency in activities and to "personality" (whatever they may mean), then indeed wholeness is lost.[17]

The Harvard report went on to state that although we can agree on common aims of education, we cannot expect to find an absolute system of implementing these aims.

. . . though common aims must bind together the whole educational system, there exists no one body of knowledge, no single system of instruction equally valid for every part of it. . . .[18] General education must accordingly be conceived less as a specific set of books to be read or courses to be given, than as a concern for certain goals of knowledge and outlook and an insistence that these goals be sought after by many means . . .[19]

Recognizing the comprehensive nature of general education, the Harvard report cited the value of the industrial arts in developing "the capacity to create by hand from a concept in the mind."[20] The report also stressed the importance of providing for special interests and vocational preparation in the curriculum of the secondary school, emphasizing that these special-interest and vocational areas emanate from general education.[21] The report pointed to the role of the school in fostering good physical and mental health,[22] and cited the importance of extracurricular activities in the education of the whole person.[23]

Recognizing the polyglot nature of our societal makeup with regard to religious beliefs, the Harvard Committee cautioned against any inclusion of religious instruction in the curriculum.

We are not at all unmindful of the importance of religious belief in the completely good life. But, given the American scene with its varieties of faith and even of unfaith, we did not feel justified in proposing religious instruction as a part of the curriculum.[24]

In emphasizing the importance of universal education to a free society, the Harvard report also cautioned against neglecting the less gifted youth.

The *Report of the Harvard Committee* exerted considerable influence on educators at both the secondary and collegiate levels, urging educators to reconcile the differences between the traditional and experimental values in education by combining and integrating the best elements of

---

[17] *Ibid.*, p. 75.
[19] *Ibid.*, p. 80.
[21] *Ibid.*, p. 102.
[23] *Ibid.*, p. 172.

[18] *Ibid.*, p. 79.
[20] *Ibid.*, p. 175.
[22] *Ibid.*, p. 168.
[24] *Ibid.*, p. 76.

each system.[25] But despite this plea for reconciliation, the American educational system at mid-twentieth century entered the post-World War II era with sharp divisions about the proper ends and means.

LIFE ADJUSTMENT. At a conference on vocational education, convened by the United States Office of Education in 1945, a declaration was made, later known as the Prosser Resolution (after the name of the author), in which it was stated that the high schools were serving 20 per cent of the youth for college entrance and another 20 per cent for skilled occupations, while neglecting to meet the life-adjustment needs of the remaining 60 per cent of our youth.[26] Many critics of American public education immediately seized upon the term life adjustment and used it to ridicule the current program of education in our schools. This is discussed further in Chapter 3.

DEVELOPMENTAL TASKS. Studies of adolescent needs, given considerable emphasis during the 1930's, received renewed attention at mid-century. Havighurst examined these needs in the light of the tasks necessary for individual development in relation to the demands of our culture. He identified the following developmental tasks of life during the period of adolescence:

1. Achieving new and more mature relations with agemates of both sexes.
2. Achieving a masculine or feminine role.
3. Accepting one's physique and using the body effectively.
4. Achieving emotional independence of parents and other adults.
5. Achieving assurance of economic independence.
6. Selecting and preparing for an occupation.
7. Preparing for marriage and family life.
8. Developing intellectual skills and concepts.
9. Desiring and achieving socially responsible behavior.
10. Acquiring a set of values and an ethical system as a guide to behavior.[27]

The role of the school in relation to other societal institutions and forces in helping adolescents to meet these tasks remains a subject of considerable controversy. Yet, regardless of one's position in defining the role of the school, there is growing recognition that psychobiological and social problems cannot be separated from the function of the school.

THE WHITE HOUSE CONFERENCE. In November of 1955, under the auspices of President Eisenhower, some 1800 lay citizens and professional educators participated in a White House Conference on educational

---

[25] *Ibid.*, p. 51.
[26] U.S. Office of Education, *Life Adjustment Education for Every Youth* (Washington, D.C.: Government Printing Office, Bulletin 22, 1951), p. 16.
[27] See Robert J. Havighurst, *Developmental Tasks and Education* (New York: Longmans, Green and Co., 1948), pp. 111–147.

problems. Among other questions, the topic of "What Should Our Schools Accomplish?" led to the following list of aims or purposes in the report of the Conference:

1. The fundamental skills of communication—reading, writing, spelling, as well as other elements of effective oral and written expression; the arithmetical and mathematical skills, including problem-solving.
2. Appreciation of our democratic heritage.
3. Civic rights and responsibilities and knowledge of American institutions.
4. Respect and appreciation for human values and for the beliefs of others.
5. Ability to think and evaluate constructively and creatively.
6. Effective work habits and self-discipline.
7. Social competency as a contributing member of family and community.
8. Ethical behavior based on a sense of moral and spiritual values.
9. Intellectual curiosity and eagerness for lifelong learning.
10. Esthetic appreciation and self-expression in the arts.
11. Physical and mental health.
12. Wise use of time, including constructive leisure pursuits.
13. Understanding of the physical world and man's relation to it as represented through basic knowledge of the sciences.
14. An awareness of our relationships with the world community.[28]

THE PURSUIT OF EXCELLENCE.   With the dramatic launching of Sputnik I on October 4, 1957, American public education faced a new wave of criticism. Some critics charged that the schools were neglecting the

---

[28] The Committee for the White House Conference on Education, *A Report to the President* (Washington, D.C.: Government Printing Office, 1956).

"How could youths better learn to live
than by at once trying the experiment of living?"
　　　　　—HENRY DAVID THOREAU

Photo by Vories Fisher

gifted child. Others argued for reformulation of the objectives and procedures in our educational program. In 1958 the Rockefeller Brothers Fund began releasing a series of reports in connection with its Special Studies Projects. These reports were designed to examine the major problems of our nation over the coming 10 to 15 years. One such report, released in 1958, was entitled *The Pursuit of Excellence: Education and the Future of America.* However, this report stressed that the need for excellence is not merely manifested by the present state of competition with the Soviets, but by man's incessant need to improve his lot.

The Rockefeller report on education was prepared by a panel composed predominantly of college administrators, professors, officers of the Carnegie Foundation and the Fund for the Advancement of Education (Ford Foundation), and two journalists who specialized in educational affairs. Reviewing the nature of our free society and the development of universal public education, the Rockefeller report stressed the need for both quality and quantity in the educational system of a democracy.

> From time to time one still hears arguments over *quantity* versus *quality* education. Behind such arguments is the assumption that a society can choose to educate a few people exceedingly well *or* to educate a great number of people somewhat less well, but that it cannot do both. But a modern society such as ours cannot choose to do one *or* the other. It has no choice but to do both. Our kind of society calls for maximum development of individual potentialities *at all levels.*[29]

The Rockefeller report supported the comprehensive high school and rejected the dual pattern of secondary education, prevalent in Europe, as unpalatable to our society.[30]

One of the important aspects of this report was the recognition of the serious financial problems in American education. The report recommended that we must at least double our expenditures for education within the next decade in order to meet the immense social and technological challenges of the mid-twentieth century.

THE CONANT REPORT. Under the auspices of the Carnegie Corporation, Dr. James B. Conant, former President of Harvard University and former United States Ambassador to the Federal Republic of Germany, began a study of the American high school early in 1957. The study was completed late in 1958 and released early in 1959 under the title, *The American High School Today.*[31] This report was addressed to members

---

[29] Rockefeller Brothers Fund, *The Pursuit of Excellence: Education and the Future of America, Panel Report V of the Special Studies Project* (New York: Doubleday and Company, 1958), p. 22.

[30] *Ibid.*, p. 31.

[31] James Bryant Conant, *The American High School Today* (New York: McGraw-Hill Company, Inc., 1959).

of school boards, school administrators, and interested citizens throughout the nation. The Conant report supported the important principle of universal education as vital to our democracy, and provided evidence to support the comprehensive high school as an institution capable of meeting the demands for high quality education.

John W. Gardner, President of the Carnegie Corporation, describes the comprehensive high school in the Foreword of the Conant report:

> It is called comprehensive because it offers, under one administration and under one roof (or series of roofs), secondary education for almost all the high school age children of one town or neighborhood. . . . It is responsible, in sum, for providing good and appropriate education, both academic and vocational, for all young people within a democratic environment which the American people believe serves the principles they cherish.[32]

In one phase of his study, Conant compared the quality of instruction in mathematics and science of outstanding specialized academic schools and outstanding comprehensive schools. Using standardized achievement tests, he found that the achievement level of students in the comprehensive schools was approximately equal to that attained in the specialized academic schools, thereby supporting his thesis that quality in education is attainable under the comprehensive high school program.

Unlike many contemporary critics of American secondary education, Conant supported the diversified role of the school in preparing youth for the vocations, as well as providing them with a strong foundation in general education. He recommended improved counseling programs, ability grouping without undue tracking or separation of students, special programs for the academically talented, remedial programs for slow learners, and schools of sufficient size to offer a rich and diversified program of studies. Conant's support of the comprehensive high school rests in its enabling young people to work together democratically, without neglecting their special talents and interests.

> I think it safe to say that the comprehensive high school is characteristic of our society and further that it has come into being because of our economic history and our devotion to the ideals of equality of opportunity and equality of status. . . .
> I trust I have provided at least a clue to my belief in the significance of a unique American educational institution and the importance of supporting and improving thousands of examples of this institution throughout the United States.[33]

RESTATEMENT BY THE EDUCATIONAL POLICIES COMMISSION. In 1961 the N.E.A.'s Educational Policies Commission, while reaffirming its earlier

---

[32] *Ibid.*, Foreword, pp. IX–X.   [33] *Ibid.*, pp. 8–9.

Courtesy Perkins & Will; photo by Joseph W. Molitor

"There is no longer any single highway of learning."
—WOODROW WILSON

statements on educational goals and needs, identified the central purpose of American education as "freedom of the mind" through cultivation of the "rational powers."[34] The report emphasized that the ability to think is vital to all other educational purposes, and that a free society cannot exist without freedom of the mind. The role of the school, according to the report, is to provide conditions under which the inquiring and creative spirit can flourish.

The report cited the need for acquainting students with strategies of inquiry, the need for concerted research on this style of thinking, and the need for teachers and scholars in the disciplines to work together in developing curriculum content and processes which foster the inquiring mind. This statement by the Educational Policies Commission was prophetic of the vast curriculum reforms which began to take root in our schools during 1963 and 1964.

---

[34] See Educational Policies Commission, *The Central Purposes of American Education* (Washington, D.C.: National Education Association, 1961).

Perspectives: Past, Present, and Future

As we look back on the history of American education, we see how the early schools in the colonies were instruments of religion, the aim of education being personal salvation in the hereafter. Practical education was left to the family and to crude forms of apprenticeship training. But with the development of our civilization, the schools changed from instruments of religion to instruments of the state, and consequently acquired vastly different ends and means. In our society of today the school has, in its service to the general welfare, acquired many functions that were once left to the family.

> The school has always been the most important means of transferring the wealth of tradition from one generation to the next. This applies in an even higher degree than in former times for, through modern development of economic life, the family as bearer of tradition and education has been weakened. The continuance and health of human society is therefore in a still higher degree dependent on the school than formerly.[35]

In reexamining the many formulations of aims, goals, objectives, or purposes of education, we see considerable repetition. But we also see considerable evolvement: from education for spiritual salvation to education for the good life; from education for mental discipline and indoctrination to education for individual enlightenment and freedom; from education for the privileged few to education for all the people. Moreover, we see in these aims the tremendously complex and comprehensive role our schools are expected to fulfill in our society. Is it possible for our schools to handle this enormous task? Or should priorities and delineations be established?

The public schools in our polyglot society are the one means of reaching all of the children of all of the people, and consequently our schools have been charged with the enormous task of being all things to all people.

Perhaps the great debate over the ends and means of education will never reach a permanent resolution, because the conditions of society and human existence are dynamic and evolving, not static and inert. Therefore, constant assessment and reassessment of our ends and means of education will always be necessary. Albert Einstein warned us that knowledge is not absolute and immutable, but resembles the statute of Ozymandias.

> . . . with the affairs of active human beings it is different. Here knowledge of truth alone does not suffice; on the contrary this knowl-

---

[35] Albert Einstein, *Out of My Later Years* (New York: Philosophical Library, 1950), p. 32.

edge must continually be renewed by ceaseless effort, if it is not to be lost. It resembles a statue of marble which stands in the desert and is continuously threatened with burial by the shifting sand. The hands of service must ever be at work, in order that the marble continue lastingly to shine in the sun. To these serving hands mine also shall belong.[36]

In his classic work, *The Aims of Education*, Alfred North Whitehead stressed the importance of keeping education fresh and dynamic.

> For successful education there must always be a certain freshness in the knowledge dealt with . . . knowledge does not keep any better than fish.[37]

Emphasizing the rapidly accelerating pace of changing conditions in modern civilization, Whitehead called for an educational program geared to the recognition of change.

> Our sociological theories, our political philosophy . . . and our doctrines of education are derived from an unbroken tradition of thinkers and of practical examples, from the age of Plato . . . to the end of the last century. The whole of this tradition is warped by the vicious assumption that each generation will substantially live amid the conditions governing the lives of its fathers and will transmit those conditions to mold with equal force the lives of its children. We are living in the first period of human history for which this assumption is false.[38]

A democratic society must be dynamic, perpetually seeking progress. And if our aim is to enhance democracy, then we must see to it that both the goals and means of education are consistent with the ideal of democracy. In a democratic society, education must be accessible to all who can profit from it. No one should be denied an education on economic or social grounds. In a democracy, freedom of inquiry is essential. Indoctrination does not develop an enlightened citizenry. If we expect people to deal with problems and controversies with intelligence and wisdom, then the schools must not shy away from problems and controversies. And the school must always seek improvement, just as society seeks improvement. No society can remain static. And as long as our society lives, its citizens must continue to reexamine and reassess the ends and means of education.

CONFLICTING PHILOSOPHIES OF EDUCATION

We opened this chapter with a quotation from Aristotle: "mankind are by no means agreed about the things to be taught . . . Again about

---

[36] *Ibid.*, pp. 31–32.
[37] Alfred North Whitehead, *The Aims of Education and Other Essays* (London: Williams and Norgate, Ltd., 1932), p. v.
[38] Alfred North Whitehead, *Adventures of Ideas* (New York: The Macmillan Company, 1933), p. 117.

the means there is no agreement." In the second half of the twentieth century, the great controversy is concerned with the ends and means of education. As long as human society is dynamic this controversy will never reach final settlement. Yet it is of utmost importance for educators to understand these conflicts and to formulate a rationale through an open-minded exploration of the differing positions. For if we are without convictions, without belief in what we are doing, our educational enterprise will reflect only chaos and decay.

An educational philosophy should not be a party line, but a coherent operational system that links means and ends harmoniously and enables us to act intelligently when confronted with unforeseen problems.

American education is divided by two conflicting philosophic positions, *traditionalism* and *progressivism*. Within each position there are, of course, differing orientations. These conflicts are rooted in man's concept of himself and are reflected not only in education but in man's various social patterns and aspirations. The remainder of this chapter presents an analysis of these conflicting positions and the major variants and cleavages in educational ends and means.

Traditionalism

CHRISTIAN TRADITIONALISM. This philosophical position holds that the supreme goal of education is salvation. Although the roots of Christian traditionalism can be traced back many centuries, this philosophy remains an important force in education today. The Roman Catholic Church and certain other religious groups have established their own elementary and secondary schools because the secular school is not concerned with spiritual dogma and salvation. Moreover, each group feels that it, and it alone, is the possessor of divine truth; consequently, no other form of spiritual and moral education can be satisfactory.

> A school from which religion is excluded is contrary to the fundamental principles of education. Such school in time is bound to be irreligious. The only school that is a fit school for Catholic students is a school controlled by the Church, in which religion is the foundation and crown of the youth's entire training, not only in the elementary grades, but in the high school and college as well.[39]

The secular school, which has been considered so vital to a polyglot society such as ours, is alien to the Catholic point of view. As a result the Catholics have established a vast school system for their own children and youth. Catholic education is aimed at correcting the evils of original sin through supernatural revelation.

---

[39] Francis M. Crowley, "The Catholic Approach to Religion in Education," from Ernest O. Melby and Morton Pruner (eds.), *Freedom and Public Education* (New York: Praeger, 1953), p. 65.

SCHOLASTICISM.   Scholasticism is the term commonly given to the educational philosophy of the Roman Catholic Church, since it is derived from the church schoolmen of the Middle Ages. St. Thomas Aquinas (1225–1274) was the chief author of this educational philosophy.

Since this educational philosophy stems from the divinely instituted church, its educational means are authoritarian. The church is the unimpeachable authority in theocentric matters and the school is expected to educate for salvation. Of course, Christian traditionalism is concerned not only with the supernatural world of salvation but with the natural world as well. For, after all, salvation is dependent upon the kind of life one has led in the natural world. Because of its primary goal of education for salvation, however, the curriculum gives considerable emphasis to religious indoctrination. And since it is a traditional philosophy, great importance is also given to the study of Latin, ecclesiastical history, and the liberal arts. Over the centuries, literary education has been held in high esteem in interpreting St. Thomas Aquinas' views on the importance of words or symbols, rather than objects, in causing knowledge.[40] Literary sources, particularly classical works, have been given great emphasis in Catholic secondary and higher education. The underlying assumption for giving stress to classical literary sources appears to be that such works have great intellectual fiber and that the intellect, not the physical aspects of man, is closest to the spiritual domain. In recognizing the low proportional representation of Catholics among our eminent scientists, the Catholic schools, in recent years, have been attempting to give increased emphasis to modern scientific subjects. Citizenship, recreation, and vocational needs are also important for developing the whole man, "soul united to body in unity of nature."[41]

Despite the well-roundedness of the curriculum, we must keep in mind that the theocentric goal of salvation is essential and foremost in this educational philosophy. Secondly, the church is the infallible source of divine revelation. The learner is not to be allowed to choose among alternatives where such divine truth is concerned. Consequently, the method of this educational philosophy is authoritarian—at least where religious instruction is concerned.

Obviously, the public schools of our polyglot society are committed to secularism. Religion, then, is left to the home and church and parochial school.

CLASSICAL TRADITIONALISM.   While the classical tradition has no theocentric orientation, it shares many of its elements with the Christian

---

[40] See John S. Brubacher, *A History of the Problems of Education* (New York: McGraw-Hill Company, Inc., 1947), p. 108.

[41] Crowley, *op. cit.*, p. 65.

tradition. Not only do they both share a long history, but they both regard man's best literary works of the past as a vital facet of the curriculum.

The classical tradition is rooted in the concept of liberal education derived from ancient Greece. This type of education, as advocated by Plato and Aristotle, was regarded as proper for the free man who could devote himself to leisure and matters of citizenship. On the other hand, the slave was concerned with practical and material duties. Therefore, education for the free man was conceived as a general and well-rounded program of intellectual, spiritual, and physical development. Classical traditionalism or humanism received great impetus during the Renaissance when man sought to free himself from the rule of the church. The goal of this educational philosophy is the perfection of man through his best intellectual and aesthetic (or humanistic) endeavors. Classical traditionalism or humanism, then, focuses on the humanities as the means of developing the best in man's nature. This educational philosophy is often referred to as classical humanism because of the high esteem it holds for classical literature, which represents man's highest achievement. Contemporary classicists believe that man's great literary works of the past are the exemplars of intellectual excellence. The curriculum, therefore, should center around these great works which, presumably, are valid for any period of human existence. History, classical languages, and philosophy also occupy an important position in the curriculum. The social sciences, other than history, are too contemporaneous for many humanists.

The classical traditionalists or humanists believe that true education is concerned solely with the cultivation of the intellect, since man's distinction from the lower animals lies in his intellect. The liberal studies are regarded as the most appropriate education for the development of the mind. The practical or vocational studies, being concerned with man's physical and economic needs, are regarded as training rather than education. A liberal education is essential for the free man. Vocational training is too narrow, specialized, and mundane to be fitting for the true education of man. Although it is conceded that the practical and vocational programs are important in modern society, such training, it is held, should be provided through on-the-job experience or in special technical institutes, rather than be allowed to distract from the legitimate educational role of the school or college.

This educational philosophy is sometimes referred to as perennialism because of its quest for true, everlasting principles governing human existence.

> . . . the perennialist is not so much interested in emphasizing the social heritage as he is in the existence of eternal, absolute principles of

truth, goodness, and beauty outside space and time—which are in a profound sense everlasting, and therefore perennial.[42]

The curriculum that is concerned with the practical or contemporaneous is to be frowned upon, for such a program of education is temporary. The classical humanist believes that the curriculum should not be subject to change. Instead, it should be concerned with the great works of the past that are valid for any time or place.

> One purpose of education is to draw out the elements of our common human nature. These elements are the same in any time or place. The notion of educating a man to live in a particular time or place, to adjust him to any particular environment, is therefore foreign to a true conception of education.
> Education implies teaching. Teaching implies knowledge. Knowledge is truth. The truth is everywhere the same. Hence education should be everywhere the same.[43]

Classical traditionalism holds that since man is elevated above the beast by virtue of his intellect, education should be concerned, therefore, solely with intellectual pursuit or development of the mind. This obsession with cultivation of the intellect leads some classical traditionalists to the position of actually disparaging physical education.

> The best test of where *not* to send your children is a school's requirements for physical education. If they are extensive, you should take your child somewhere else at once.[44]

Because of its pervading concern with the development of man's rational powers, this educational philosophy is also called rationalism. Chief contemporary exponents are Robert M. Hutchins, Stringfellow Barr, Mark Van Doren, and Mortimer Adler.

The classical traditionalists or rationalists advocate a curriculum well grounded in the three R's—with highest emphasis on the language skills, leading to effective study of classical literature.

> The ideal education is not an *ad hoc* education, not an education directed to immediate needs; it is not a specialized education, or a preprofessional education; it is not a utilitarian education. It is an education calculated to develop the mind.
> . . . I have old-fashioned prejudices in favor of the three R's and the liberal arts, in favor of trying to understand the greatest works that the

---

[42] Theodore Brameld, *Education for the Emerging Age* (New York: Harper and Row, Publishers, Inc., 1961), p. 24.

[43] Robert M. Hutchins, *The Higher Learning in America* (New Haven, Conn.: Yale University Press, 1936), p. 67.

[44] Robert M. Hutchins, *On Education* (Santa Barbara, Calif.: Center for the Study of Democratic Institutions, The Fund for the Republic, Inc., 1963), p. 18.

human race has produced. I believe that these are the permanent necessities, the intellectual tools that are needed to understand the ideas and
the ideals of our world.[45]

Although many classical traditionalists acknowledge the importance
of the sciences in the curriculum, such studies are often approached in
terms of man's past experiences.

The classical humanist conceives of mind as a receptacle into which
the timeless facts and principles can be poured. Learners of relatively
modest intellectual means should receive the same educational nutrients
as their more highly endowed colleagues, albeit in smaller quantities
and at a slower pace.

ESSENTIALISM. Another traditionalist philosophy is essentialism. This
position first gained significant momentum during the late 1930's as a
reaction against progressivism. Chief proponent of this position during the
late 1930's was William C. Bagley. Essentialism continued to have a
powerful following during the 1950's and 1960's through such spokesmen
as Professor Arthur Bestor and Admiral Hyman G. Rickover. This position holds that the school curriculum should be geared to the essentials
or fundamentals. Essentialists deplore the dilution of the school curriculum with so-called frill subjects and vocationalism. However, unlike the
Christian and classical traditionalists whose philosophies are rooted in
the past, essentialists are concerned more with the contemporary scene.

The essentialist position has great appeal for those who favor reduced
expenditures for education. A curriculum limited to the fundamentals
is not nearly so expensive as one that requires special facilities and
equipment for such subjects as art, music, homemaking, and vocational
trades and industries.

According to the essentialist, the school curriculum should be limited
to such fundamental subjects as English (reading and writing), mathematics, sciences, history, and geography. Some essentialists, notably Admiral Rickover, have contended that we would do well to emulate certain
aspects of Soviet and European education.[46] However, Rickover and
others are accused of ignoring the democratic ideals of our society and
its schools.[47] And they seem to ignore the rather heavy vocational emphasis in certain phases of Soviet secondary education.

Like the classical traditionalists, the essentialists tend to regard the
student's mind as a vessel into which the facts and principles of the
essential subjects are received and retained. All learners, regardless of
abilities and interests, are to be given the same intellectual brew, although

---

[45] *Ibid.*, pp. 1–2.
[46] See Hyman G. Rickover, *Education and Freedom* (New York: E. P. Dutton &
    Co., Inc., 1959), Ch. 9 and Appendix 3.
[47] Brameld, *op. cit.*, p. 24.

the quantity and rate of the potion should be adjusted to the capacity of the learner. The process of education, in the eyes of the essentialist, is to facilitate the means whereby the learner absorbs the knowledge of the essential subjects to the limit of his capacity.

> The educational process for all children must be one of absorbing knowledge to the limit of their capacity. Recreation, manual or clerical training, etiquette, and similar know-how subjects have little effect on the mind itself, and it is with the mind that the school must solely concern itself. The poorer a child's natural endowments the more he needs to have his mind trained.[48]

As seen in the above quotation, Admiral Rickover, like the classical traditionalists, embraces the long discredited doctrine of mental discipline. The educational process, in the eyes of the essentialists, should place great emphasis on the mastery of the skills and facts that form the subject matter of the essential subjects. A curriculum that takes into account student interests or debatable problems and issues from the contemporary scene is both trivial and time-wasting. The curriculum is regarded as a logical body of essential subject matter that must not be diluted or dissipated through psychological teaching methods or non-essential subjects. Emotional or social factors in the teaching-learning process are either ignored or disparaged by most essentialists. The learner simply must be made to work hard at his studies. However, Rickover's views on the proper environment for his own work seem to run counter to his proposals for the secondary school classroom. Where the high school student should be compelled to rigid discipline and training, Rickover sees his own task force as operating at greatest efficiency when interest, motivation, and freedom are highly valued.

> When I set up my reactor group twelve years ago, I put all my energy into finding the right people and wasted no time creating an "ideal" organization. In fact we still have no formal organization. We have excellent people . . . strongly motivated because of their intense interest in the work. Such people cannot be fitted into the usual hierarchic organization. . . . They must be given freedom to work out their own problems and to assume responsibility for what they do. They need an environment that allows them to be venturesome and does not stifle their initiative with routines . . .[49]

Ironically, the working milieu Rickover advocates for himself and his own men is remarkably similar to the type of atmosphere fostered in our most progressive schools.

Bestor, Rickover, and other leading essentialists have advocated absolute educational standards in our high schools through a program of national examinations. The standard for the high school diploma should

---

[48] Rickover, *op. cit.*, p. 133.   [49] Rickover, *op. cit.*, pp. 18–19.

be uniformly established throughout the nation as representing a specified level of attainment in the essential subjects.[50] In advocating such standards of uniformity or quality control, the essentialists often ignore the fact that even at the college level the bachelor's degree represents a broad spectrum of curricula and a wide range of academic achievement.

Eclecticism

Some educators choose to borrow elements from various philosophies, rather than commit themselves to a singular system or outlook. They believe that each educational philosophy, however divergent or conflicting with other philosophies, carries some value. The eclectic, then, attempts to select the elements that best fit his needs. Because certain elements embraced by one eclectic may differ sharply from the views of another, eclecticism is not a philosophy per se. Instead it is a synthetic formulation of beliefs compounded from several points of view.

The eclectic believes that neither traditionalism nor progressivism embodies the complete and ultimate answer to our educational needs. The Harvard report, *General Education in a Free Society,* represents one of the most significant works of eclecticism in American education. Its eclectic spirit is represented in the statement, ". . . though common aims must bind together the whole educational system, there exists no one body of knowledge, no single system of instruction equally valid for every part of it."[51]

Many teachers appear to function intuitively and without a systematic rationale or commitment to a singular educational philosophy. But this does not mean that they are eclectics. The eclectic consciously derives his views from various philosophic sources. While the eclectic may feel that the greatest strength and validity lies in borrowing the best elements from the various positions, the innate inconsistency of eclecticism must also be regarded as a serious weakness.

Progressivism

The development of progressivism can be traced to two important forces. On the one hand was the growing need for educating people who would be capable of dealing effectively with the pervading problems of modern life. And on the other hand, the scientific study of human behavior resulted in the rejection of traditional educational doctrines. The ideal of universal education, which emerged in twentieth century America, led to an expanding secondary school curriculum to meet the

---

[50] See Arthur Bestor, "What Went Wrong with U.S. Schools," *U.S. News & World Report,* Vol. XLIV, January 24, 1958, pp. 72–73.

[51] Report of the Harvard Committee, *General Education in a Free Society* (Cambridge, Mass.: Harvard University Press, 1945), p. 79.

needs of all the children of all the people. Although progressivism is a twentieth-century phenomenon, its origins can be traced to empiricism, naturalism, and pragmatism.

SENSE REALISM AND EMPIRICISM. The limitations of the verbalistic rituals of seventeenth century humanistic education were recognized by Johann Amos Comenius (1592–1670), a Moravian educator and clergyman. Comenius advocated education that combined verbalization with sense experience. He authored the first illustrated textbook, *Orbis Pictus*.

John Locke (1632–1704), the English philosopher-educator, viewed knowledge as deriving from sense experience. He rejected Plato's proposition that man is born with innate ideas and even challenged the church doctrine of original sin. Sense experience, rather than supernatural revelation, was Locke's key to education.

NATURALISM. Sir Francis Bacon (1561–1626), English philosopher and statesman, advocated the inductive method of experimental science. He recognized the complete inadequacy of the preconceptions man had accepted about his own nature and that of the universe. Bacon recommended a scientific approach to understanding the world of nature. Comenius expressed the view that education should be in harmony with nature.

Jean Jacques Rousseau (1712–1778), the French iconoclast, went even further in linking the educational process with nature. His book *Emile*, published in 1762, described the ideal education of a child. Rousseau rejected the church doctrine of original sin and held that "God makes all things good; man meddles with them and they become evil."[52] In this sense, Rousseau romanticized the goodness of the child. While his educational scheme often bordered on the laissez faire, he placed great stress on cognitive learning and capitalizing on the natural bent of children to seek to understand.

> Teach your scholar to observe the phenomena of nature; you will soon rouse his curiosity, but if you would have it grow, do not be in too great a hurry to satisfy this curiosity. Put the problems before him and let him solve them himself. Let him know nothing because you have told him, but because he has learnt it for himself. Let him not be taught science, let him discover it. If ever you substitute authority for reason he will cease to reason; he will be a mere plaything of other people's thoughts.[53]

Because of his romanticized view of the nature of the child and the extreme freedom he advocated in rearing and educating the child, Rousseau is regarded as a romantic naturalist. Today, many of the extreme

---

[52] Jean Jacques Rousseau, *Emile*, translated by Barbara Foxley, (London: J. M. Dent & Sons Ltd., 1911), p. 5.

[53] *Ibid.*, p. 131.

progressivist views that stem from Rousseau are erroneously attributed to John Dewey.

Johann Heinrich Pestalozzi (1746–1827), a Swiss educator, attempted to put Rousseau's theories into practice by providing a home and school on his farm for fifty abandoned children. He believed that these poverty-stricken children could be regenerated through proper environment and education. He wrote of this experience, "For years I have lived in the midst of fifty little beggars, sharing in my poverty my bread with them, living like a beggar myself in order to teach beggars to live like men."[54]

PRAGMATISM. The accelerating developments in science during the latter half of the nineteenth and early part of the twentieth century brought about radical changes in man's conception of knowledge. In accepting scientific explanations for phenomena, it was necessary for many to reject views of long-standing tradition. The appearance of Darwin's *Origin of Species* in 1859 is a notable example of the forces that shook the foundations of man's preconceived notions of himself. In the United States, Charles Peirce (1839–1914), a mathematician, and William James (1842–1910), a psychologist, developed the philosophy of pragmatism. Rejecting the dogmas and a priori truths of the traditionalists, the pragmatists held that there are no absolute truths or eternal values. Pragmatism was regarded as a method or process of testing and verifying ideas through application. Thus, truth is not absolute, but rather that which, through scientific investigation, proves itself in relation to experience or action. In a sense, the relativistic concept of truth held by the pragmatists finds its exemplar in the theory of relativity advanced in the field of physics by Einstein in 1905.

In his views on psychology, James applied Darwin's biological approach in conceiving of mind as an evolutionary development in bringing the human species toward successful adaptation to environment. Obviously, such views were in direct conflict with the traditionalists, whose fundamental postulates were based on a priori truths and who conceived of mind as a timeless faculty and not a product of natural evolution.

According to the pragmatists, no concept or experience should be immune from investigation and no phenomenon is above natural explanation.

EXPERIMENTALISM. This educational philosophy emerged in the United States during the twentieth century. Although it derives as a synthesis of the progressive philosophies previously discussed, experimentalism exerted a new and profound influence on American education and drew serious attention from many European countries. The great

---

[54] Quoted from Ellwood P. Cubberley, *Public Education in the United States,* Revised (Boston: Houghton Mifflin Company, 1947), p. 345.

orchestrator of experimentalism was John Dewey (1859–1952). When Dewey's work, *Democracy and Education,* appeared in 1916, Walter Lippman described it in the *New Republic* as "the mature wisdom of the finest and most powerful intellect devoted to the future of American civilization."[55]

Dewey viewed education as a means of improving human life. He regarded education as life, rather than a synthetic representation of life or a preparation for life. To Dewey, progress is the keynote of a democratic society. And if our societal ends are democratic, then our means, too, must be democratic. In this respect, Dewey advocated that the means of education must be contiguous with our democratic goals. According to Dewey, a society could not attain democratic ends via totalitarian means. And authoritarian schools are antithetical to democracy.

Born in the year in which Darwin's *Origin of Species* appeared (1859), Dewey viewed education as a force that must be in harmony with man's biological nature. He conceived of education as an evolving and progressive process. To Dewey, education has no point of ultimate fulfillment, but is a process of growth. Obviously, a progressive society requires a progressive education.

The singular societal ideal expounded by Dewey is that of democracy. And democracy requires open-mindedness, freedom from absolutes, and free interaction of ideas. While Dewey is frequently targeted as the founder of life-adjustment education, he actually deplored adjustment and saw education as a means of societal improvement.

> For purposes of simplification we have spoken . . . somewhat as if the education of the immature which fills them with the spirit of the social group to which they belong, were a sort of catching up of the child with the aptitudes and resources of the adult group. In static societies, societies which make the maintenance of established custom their measure of value, this conception applies in the main. But not in progressive communities. They endeavor to shape the experiences of the young so that instead of reproducing current habits, better habits shall be formed, and thus the future adult society be an improvement on their own. . . . But we are doubtless far from realizing the potential efficacy of education as a constructive agency of improving society, from realizing that it represents not only a development of children and youth but also of the future society of which they will be the constituents.[56]

Dewey believed that the means of education and societal improvement are to be found in the "method of intelligence." Here the learner

---

[55] As quoted in Lawrence A. Cremin, *The Transformation of the School* (New York: Alfred A. Knopf, 1961), p. 120.

[56] John Dewey, *Democracy and Education,* (New York: The Macmillan Company, 1916), p. 92.

"The pupils have got to be made to feel
   that they are studying something,
   and are not merely executing intellectual minuets."
                              —ALFRED NORTH WHITEHEAD

encounters problems, formulates hypotheses, applies possible solutions, and reaches conclusions through observation, experimentation, and verification.[57] Dewey rejected the traditional notion of knowledge as an end in itself or as a means of mental discipline. He regarded knowledge as a means of further inquiry and problem-solving. He viewed learning as a process of incessant inquiry and discovery.

> The accumulation and acquisition of information for purposes of reproduction in recitation and examination is made too much of. "Knowledge," in the sense of information, means the working capital, the indispensable resources, of further inquiry; of finding out, or learning, more things. Frequently it is treated as an end in itself, and then the goal becomes to heap it up and display it when called for. This static, cold-storage ideal of knowledge is inimical to educative development. It not only lets occasions for thinking go unused, but it swamps thinking.[58]

Dewey abhorred the separation between theory and practice, between information and doing in education. He rejected the idea that doing something is of a lower intellectual order than knowing something. Experimental science, he observed, has demonstrated that "there is no such thing as genuine knowledge and fruitful understanding except as the offspring of doing."[59] Instead of studying the past for its own sake, it should be viewed in relevancy to the living world. Student needs, interests, and individual variations must be taken into account if effective learning is to ensue. Education, according to Dewey, should lead to improved changes in behavior for the individual and, contiguously, to improvements in society. Experimentation should be the keynote to educational content and method. Independent thinking, not conformity, is education's highest contribution to a better environment and a democratic society. In Dewey's words, "a progressive society counts individual variations as precious since it finds in them the means of its own growth."[60]

Dewey's experimentalism was, and still is, grossly misunderstood and maligned. Distorted interpretations of his educational philosophy were not only forthcoming from his enemies, but from his disciples. Dewey, himself, criticized the progressive extremists and their laissez faire classrooms by arguing that freedom and individuality are not given at birth, but are to be continuously achieved.[61] Some of Dewey's followers developed progressive dogmas and absolutes that were inimical to his experimentalist views. Dewey soundly criticized these followers by cau-

---

[57] *Ibid.*, p. 192.   [58] *Ibid.*, p. 186.
[59] *Ibid.*, p. 321.   [60] *Ibid.*, p. 357.
[61] See Cremin, *The Transformation of the School* (New York: Alfred A. Knopf, 1961), pp. 234–235.

tioning: ". . . any movement that thinks and acts in terms of an 'ism becomes so involved in reaction against other 'isms that it is unwittingly controlled by them."[62]

Cremin observes that the progressive education movement, like many successful reform movements, became a victim of its own success.[63] But the curriculum trends of the 1960's, with the renewed emphasis on inquiry and discovery in the teaching-learning process, indicate that Dewey's experimentalism has had a lasting and renewing influence on American education. While the adherents of the traditional educational philosophies, particularly the essentialists, continue to exert significant influence on our schools, Dewey's experimentalism appears to be irreversible. For experimentalism has awakened our schools to the forces of change that ebb and flow in the society and world around us.

RECONSTRUCTIONISM. The depression of the 1930's caused some progressivists to look for an educational philosophy that would be dedicated to the building of a better society. To these educators, who were appalled by the stagnating effects of the Great Depression, experimentalism was too neutral and individualistic. They saw in the schools the instrument for creating a new social order. The chief exponent of reconstructionism was George S. Counts, Professor at Columbia University's Teachers College.[64] The leading contemporary reconstructionist is Theodore Brameld of Boston University. Brameld sets forth his views on reconstructionism thus:

> The world of the future should be a world which the common man rules not merely in theory but in fact. It should be a world in which the technological potentialities already clearly discernible are released for the creation of health, abundance, security for the great masses of every color, every creed, every nationality . . . Reconstructionism is thus a philosophy of magnetic foresight—a philosophy of ends attainable through the development of powerful means possessed latently by the people.[65]
>
> Education sufficiently dedicated to this purpose no longer remains, to be sure, on the fence of intellectual "impartiality." But it is an education which . . . through the schools of America and of all other democracies, could at last demonstrate its capacity to play no longer a minor but a major role in the rebuilding of civilization.[66]

---

[62] John Dewey, *Experience and Education* (New York: The Macmillan Company, 1938), p. vii.

[63] Cremin, *op. cit.*, p. 340.

[64] George S. Counts, *Dare the Schools Build a New Social Order?* (New York: The John Day Company, 1932).

[65] Theodore Brameld, *Education for the Emerging Age* (New York: Harper and Row, Publishers, Inc., 1961), p. 25.

[66] *Ibid.*, p. 27.

Reconstructionism has never developed into a significant educational movement. Perhaps it had its greatest day during the depression period. Its call for fixed social goals and the role of the schools in achieving these utopian ends seems to neglect the realities governing the educational system of any society. For schools are instruments of society, and as such can only reflect the best, and worst, of society. While the schools can help a society to rebuild, only society can give the schools the calling of reconstruction.

National and global problems of poverty, disease, oppression, missile races, and running hot and cold wars all serve to point to the need for societal and international reconstruction. While in the United States we are concerned with agricultural surpluses, it is recognized that "more than half the world's three billion people live in perpetual hunger."[67] But the force of reconstructionism in our schools cannot develop apart from other societal institutions and forces. Nevertheless, a changing, improving nation requires schools that not only mirror the society, but play a constructive role in the betterment of society.

SUMMARY

From the time of Aristotle man has disagreed about the aims and means of education. Historically, the aims of education have been divided into conservative and progressive polarities. For the early colonists in America the aim of education was spiritual salvation. Traditionally, education was also regarded as the special province of the privileged class in society. As man became more concerned with the practical needs of life and the worth of the individual, he came to regard education as the means for optimum individual development and more complete living.

Men such as Washington and Jefferson viewed education as a force for enlightening the people, building a democracy, and ensuring social progress. Yet, the universalization of secondary education in our nation did not become a reality until we were well into the twentieth century. Two World Wars and the Great Depression gave us cause to reaffirm our faith in free public education as the instrument of democracy and social progress. In a polyglot society this was no mean task.

The movement of progressive education was the embodiment of the new spirit to enhance democracy and social progress through the schools. The branch of progressivism known as experimentalism sought to apply the new and growing knowledge of human behavior to sounder

---

[67] "Hunger Round the World—10,000 Die Every Day," *Newsweek*, June 17, 1963, p. 43.

educational practices. The great orchestrator of experimentalism was
John Dewey. Dewey saw education as relevant to the living world, as
a means of improving human life. He conceived of the method of
intelligence as the force for building an enlightened citizenry and a
vigorous democracy. Knowledge was not something to be put into cold
storage; according to Dewey, knowledge was the means of continued
inquiry and learning.

As experimentalism became subject to a variety of misinterpretations
and distortions through the progressive movement, some of the traditionalists began to be heard. Among the traditionalists were the perennialists, who saw the proper content of education embodied in the great
classical literature. According to the perennialists, such great works were
timeless and, hence, valid for man in any era. To the perennialists,
education should be concerned solely with the cultivation of the intellect.
And what could be more apropos to this aim than man's greatest literary
works?

A more influential traditionalist philosophy during the twentieth
century is essentialism. While the essentialists, like the traditionalists,
deplored the growing diversity of the secondary-school curriculum, the
essentialists wanted the curriculum limited to the fundamental subjects.
They viewed these fundamental subjects as the means of disciplining
the mind. Both perennialism and essentialism embraced the doctrine of
mental discipline, even though this doctrine came to be refuted as a
result of studies in the psychology of learning. But essentialism was very
appealing. It offered a simple and inexpensive formula for the educational excesses of the day: return to the fundamentals. Because the
essentialists recognize the modern studies in science and mathematics
as belonging to the fundamentals, it can be said that the essentialists are
somewhat more concerned with the contemporary scene than are the
perennialists. Yet the essentialists do deplore contemporaneity in the curriculum. They value the study of history, while deprecating the study
of current events, sociology, or vocational education in the high school.

Today, our schools are intended to serve all youth. During the second-
half of the twentieth century, the ends and means of education continue
to be debated.

In a free society, ends and means of education will always be a matter
of debate. In recent years, our secondary schools have continued to offer
a diversified curriculum to meet the needs of youth and society. While
the call to progressive education lies in the past, recent efforts in improving curriculum and instruction in the secondary school are emphasizing
the Deweyan tenets of inquiry and discovery. Increased attention is
being given to strategies of teaching attuned to newer findings in the
psychology of learning.

During the 1960's a growing influence was being felt in using education to mobilize our human resources so as to better serve national needs. Whether this trend will lead to the erosion of the ideal of education as a means of individual enlightenment is yet to be determined.

PROBLEMS FOR STUDY AND DISCUSSION

1. How do you account for the persistence of some contemporary educators in embracing the doctrine of mental discipline?

2. Why does essentialism continue to hold great appeal among many of the intelligensia?

3. Do you agree with Bestor and Rickover that the schools should not attempt to deal with social problems and vocationalism? Why or why not?

4. Conant states that the comprehensive high school is characteristic of our society. Do you agree? Why or why not?

5. Experimentalism is said to be a uniquely American educational philosophy. How do you account for this?

6. How do perennialism and essentialism differ? Which of these two philosophies is more powerful in American education today? Why?

7. It is held that Dewey's views were misinterpreted and distorted, not only by his enemies, but by his followers. How do you account for this?

8. What impact has experimentalism had on higher education?

9. In your opinion, what should be the aims of American public education today?

10. How would you state your philosophy of education?

SELECTED REFERENCES

Alberty, Harold and Elsie J. Alberty. *Reorganizing the High School Curriculum*. 3rd Ed. New York: The Macmillan Company, 1962, Ch. 2.

Bayles, Ernest E. *Democratic Educational Theory*. New York: Harper and Row, Publishers, Inc., 1960.

Bestor, Arthur. *The Restoration of Learning*. New York: Alfred A. Knopf, Inc., 1955.

Brameld, Theodore. *Education for the Emerging Age*. New York: Harper and Row, Publishers, Inc., 1961.

————. *Ends and Means in Education.* New York: Harper and Row, Publishers, Inc., 1950.

Brubacher, John S. *A History of the Problems of Education.* New York: McGraw-Hill Company, Inc., 1947.

Butts, R. Freeman and Laurence A. Cremin. *A History of Education in American Culture.* New York: Holt, Rinehart and Winston, Inc., 1953.

Commission on the Reorganization of Secondary Education. *Cardinal Principles of Secondary Education.* Washington, D.C.: U.S. Office of Education, Bulletin 35, 1918.

Committee for the White House Conference on Education. *A Report to the President.* Washington, D.C.: Government Printing Office, 1956.

Conant, James B. *The American High School Today,* New York: McGraw-Hill Company, Inc., 1959.

Counts, George S. *Dare the Schools Build a New Social Order?* New York: The John Day Company, Inc., 1932.

Cremin, Lawrence A. *The Transformation of the School.* New York: Alfred A. Knopf, Inc., 1961.

Cubberley, Ellwood P. *Public Education in the United States.* Boston: Houghton Mifflin Company, 1947.

Dewey, John. *Democracy and Education.* New York: The Macmillan Company, 1916.

————. *Experience and Education.* New York: The Macmillan Company, 1938.

Educational Policies Commission. *Education for All American Youth: A Further Look.* Washington, D.C.: National Education Association, 1952.

Hook, Sidney. *Education for Modern Man.* New York: Alfred A. Knopf, Inc., 1963.

Hullfish, H. Gordon and Philip G. Smith. *Reflective Thinking: The Method of Education.* New York: Dodd, Mead & Company, 1961.

Hutchins, Robert M. *On Education* (pamphlet). Santa Barbara, California: Center for the Study of Democratic Institutions, The Fund for the Republic, Inc., 1963.

Lee, Gordon C. *Education in Modern America.* New York: Holt, Rinehart and Winston, Inc., 1957. Chs. 5, 6, 7.

Report of the Harvard Committee. *General Education in a Free Society.* Cambridge, Massachusetts: Harvard University Press, 1945.

Rickover, Hyman G. *Education and Freedom.* New York: E. P. Dutton & Co., Inc., 1959.

Rugg, Harold. *Foundations for American Education.* Yonkers-on-Hudson, New York: World Book Company, 1947.

Smith, B. Othanel, William O. Stanley and J. Harlan Shores. *Fundamentals of Curriculum Development* (Revised). Yonkers-on-Hudson, New York: World Book Company, 1957. Chs. 21, 22, 23.

Taba, Hilda. *Curriculum Development.* New York: Harcourt, Brace & World, Inc., 1962. Ch. 2.

U.S. Office of Education. *Life Adjustment Education for Every Youth.* Washington, D.C.: Government Printing Office, 1951.

Whitehead, Alfred North. *The Aims of Education and Other Essays.* London: Williams & Norgate Ltd., 1932.

Woodring, Paul. *A Fourth of a Nation.* New York: McGraw-Hill Company, Inc., 1957.

II

Education for Democracy

. . . no instrumentality less universal in its power and authority than government can secure popular education . . . without popular education, moreover, no government which rests on popular action can long endure. . . .

—*Woodrow Wilson*

CHAPTER *3*

The Twentieth
Century Revolution

THE UNIVERSALIZATION OF SECONDARY EDUCATION is a phenomenon of the twentieth century. The opening of secondary schools to all American youth was accompanied by the development of diversified curricula and the evolution of the comprehensive high school. During the first half of the twentieth century, the humanitarian ideals of progressive education were instrumental in bringing public education in closer harmony with our societal precepts of democracy. But the twentieth century has wrought not only great change but also great conflict in the ends and means of education. The climax of this conflict is often symbolized by the Soviet Sputnik, but the seeds of clashing ideas on education were planted long before the modern era of economic, scientific, military, and ideological competition with the Soviets. In this chapter we shall examine the revolutionary transformation of secondary education in our society and the bases for some contemporary problems.

SECONDARY EDUCATION FOR ALL YOUTH

The Enrollment Revolution

As recently as 1920, only one third of the 14- to 17-year-old age group was enrolled in the secondary school. By 1930, half of the age group was enrolled. This increased to almost three fourths of the age group by 1940. During the 1963–64 academic year, nine out of ten youths of high school age were enrolled.

Many people erroneously attribute this amazing explosion in secondary school enrollment to the increase in our nation's population of 14- to 17-year-olds. But between 1890 and 1962 the number of the 14- to 17-

73

"One generation of the world today represents
a greater volume of intellectual life
than any five centuries ever did before."
—EDWARD BELLAMY

Table 3–1
Enrollment In Grades 9–12
Compared With Population 14–17 Years of Age
1889–90 to 1969–70

School Year	Secondary School Enrollment	Number in 14–17 Age Group	Per Cent of Age Group Enrolled
1889–90	359,949	5,354,653	6.7
1899–1900	699,403	6,152,231	11.4
1909–10	1,115,398	7,220,298	15.4
1919–20	2,500,176	7,735,841	32.3
1929–30	4,804,255	9,341,221	51.4
1939–40	7,123,009	9,720,419	73.3
1949–50	6,453,009	8,404,768	76.8
1959–60	9,590,000	10,985,000	87.3
1961–62	10,800,000	12,004,000	90.0
1969–70*	14,873,000†	15,451,000†	96.2†

* Includes Alaska and Hawaii.
† Projections.
SOURCE: Office of Education, U.S. Department of Health, Education, and Welfare.

year-olds slightly more than doubled in size, while high school enrollment multiplied thirtyfold! Thus it can be seen in Table 3–1 that the dramatic growth in enrollment was caused not by the population increase of adolescents, but by opening the high school to all American youth.

A veritable revolution in education has taken place in our century. What was once an exclusive institution with relatively limited goals has been transformed into a universal institution with comprehensive functions. But the transformation has not been smooth. Today, more than one third of our high school students fail to graduate. Of these dropouts, 70 per cent have the intellectual potential of completing a high school education, and from 6 to 13 per cent are capable of college work. The quality of secondary schooling varies greatly with the ability of the community and state to finance education. Socioeconomic factors play an important role in determining the quality of the educational enterprise. The ideal of equality of educational opportunity is not to reduce education to a common denominator, but rather to raise it to the highest possible level so that the schools will provide the opportunity for all youth to reach their fullest potential.

Enrollment in Nonpublic High Schools

At the turn of the century, 18 per cent of the secondary school enrollment was in nonpublic schools. This declined to 6 per cent in 1940. Today approximately 11 per cent of all secondary school students are in nonpublic schools. Church-related schools handle 88 per cent of the nonpublic enrollment in grades 9 through 12. And 80 per cent of all students in nonpublic schools are enrolled in Roman Catholic institutions.[1] Enrollment trends in nonpublic and public schools for the period 1889 to 1960 are shown in Figure 3–1.

The percentage of secondary school students enrolled in nonpublic schools varies sharply by region. Regions with the highest percentages are New England with 17.3, the Middle Eastern states with 11.9, the Great Lakes with 11.0, and the Plains States with 9.4. In contrast we find percentages of 6.3 in the Far West, 4.1 in the Southwest, and only 3.8 in the Southeast and Rocky Mountains.[2]

Most of the nonpublic high schools are limited to college preparatory programs, with only 16.6 per cent comprehensive (having three or more curriculum choices).[3]

Because religious indoctrination is the basic purpose of the parochial schools, efforts to secure public funds for these schools have been defeated on the grounds that such support would violate the principle of separation of church and state. Neither are public funds provided for the nonsectarian private schools inasmuch as such schools are intended to serve a private, not a public function. On the other hand, certain federal funds have been made available to private as well as public institutions of higher education. Even church-related colleges may receive research grants and funds for the construction of instructional facilities from the Federal Government. The legality of providing public funds for private institutions of higher education is yet to be tested. The issue of public support for nonpublic schools is discussed in Chapter 4.

Compulsory School Attendance and Child Labor

Early in the twentieth century child labor continued to be a problem of national concern. Congress appropriated funds in 1907 to investigate child labor. In 1910 some 18 per cent of the children between 10 and 15 years of age were gainfully employed.[4] The need to protect children from exploitation received increasing recognition between 1910 and 1930, and as a result child labor declined significantly. By 1918 all states had enacted compulsory school attendance laws, though the provisions and enforcement of such legislation varied widely from state to state. Even at midcentury there was considerable variation in these laws and the degree of their enforcement, but what was once a serious social

---

[1] Diane B. Gertler, "Statistics of Nonpublic Schools," *School Life*, Vol. 46, No. 1, October, 1963, p. 35.
[2] *Ibid.*, pp. 35–36.   [3] *Ibid.*, p. 32.
[4] Newton Edwards and Herman G. Richey, *The School in the American Social Order*, 2nd Ed. (Boston: Houghton Mifflin Company, 1963), p. 489.

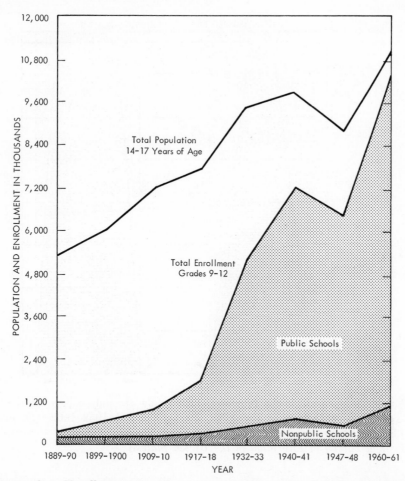

FIGURE 3–1. Enrollment in grades 9–12 of public and nonpublic secondary schools and population 14–17 years of age, for selected years, 1890–1961. [SOURCE: Office of Education, "Statistics of Nonpublic Secondary Schools 1960–1961" (Washington, D.C.: U.S. Department of Health, Education, and Welfare, 1963), p. 12.]

problem was now almost eliminated through the growing humanitarian motive and the provisions for universal education.

Today the problem of helping youth, especially those who have dropped out of high school, to become gainfully employed is a national concern. The unemployment rate among high school dropouts is estimated at over 20 per cent nationally and reaches considerably higher proportions in the slum areas of our major cities.[5]

---

[5] National Education Association, Report of the Project on Instruction, *Schools for the Sixties* (New York: McGraw-Hill Company, Inc., 1963), p. 36.

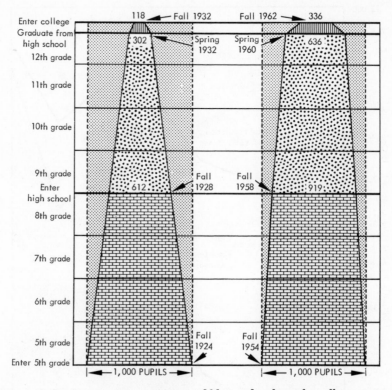

FIGURE 3–2. Approximate retention, fifth grade through college entrance: 48 States and District of Columbia, 1924–1932 and 1952–1962. [SOURCE: U.S. Department of Health, Education, and Welfare, Office of Education, *Biennial Survey of Education in the United States*.]

Retention and Dropouts

Table 3–2 presents comparisons over the years between the number of high school graduates and the total population of 17-year-olds. In 1900 only 6.4 per cent of the 17-year-olds were graduating from high school. This increased to 29 per cent by 1930, 50.8 per cent by 1940, and 64.2 per cent by 1960. We have already observed that, despite this remarkable progress, approximately one third of the 17-year-olds are dropouts. The current dropout rate must be regarded as exceedingly high when one considers that 70 per cent of the dropouts have the intellectual capacity for high school graduation. Lack of motivation, curricular restrictions, ineffective counseling, socio-economic handicaps, and geographic inequities are some of the major factors contributing to this problem.

In Figure 3–2 we see the holding power of our educational ladder comparing the periods 1924 to 1932, and 1954 to 1962. For every thousand pupils enrolled in the fifth grade in 1924, 612 entered high school in 1928, 302 graduated from high school in 1932 and only 118 of these graduates entered college. In comparison, for every thousand who enrolled in the fifth grade in 1954, 919 entered high school in 1958, 636 graduated from high school in 1962 and 336 of these graduates entered college. The increase in the proportion of students graduating from high school from 1932 to 1962 amounted to more than 110 per cent. The proportion of those entering college in 1962 represented an increase of almost 185 per cent over 1933. While compulsory attendance laws served to bring about the dramatic growth in the proportion of youth entering high school, the broadening of the curriculum and the changing educational aspirations of our society have resulted in the great increase in the proportion of those graduating from high school and entering college.

Table 3–2

Number of High School Graduates Compared with Population
17 Years of Age: United States, 1869–70 to 1961–62

School Year	Population 17 Years of Age†	High School Graduates°			Number Graduated Per 100 Persons 17 Years of Age
		Total	Boys	Girls	
1869–70..........	815,000	16,000	7,064	8,936	2.0
1879–80..........	946,026	23,634	10,605	13,029	2.5
1889–90..........	1,259,177	43,731	18,549	25,182	3.5
1899–1900........	1,489,146	94,883	38,075	56,808	6.4
1909–10..........	1,786,240	156,429	63,676	92,753	8.8
1919–20..........	1,855,173	311,266	123,684	187,582	16.8
1929–30..........	2,295,822	666,904	300,376	366,528	29.0
1939–40..........	2,403,074	1,221,475	578,718	642,757	50.8
1949–50..........	2,034,450	1,199,700	570,700	629,000	59.0
1951–52..........	2,040,800	1,196,500	569,200	627,300	58.6
1953–54..........	2,128,600	1,276,100	612,500	663,600	60.0
1955–56..........	2,270,000	1,414,800	679,500	735,300	62.3
1957–58..........	2,324,000	1,505,900	725,500	780,400	64.8
1959–60..........	2,862,000	1,838,000	886,000	952,000	64.2
1961–62‡........	2,762,000	1,930,000	940,000	990,000	69.9

° Includes graduates from public and nonpublic schools.
† U.S. Bureau of the Census.
‡ Preliminary data for 50 States and the District of Columbia.
NOTE: Unless otherwise indicated, data are for 48 States and the District of Columbia.
SOURCE: U.S. Department of Health, Education, and Welfare, Office of Education, *Biennial Survey of Education in the United States.*

The holding power of the high school varies significantly among states and regions. For the nation as a whole, 72.7 per cent of the ninth-graders in 1959–60 graduated from high school four years later (1963). But while 87.5 per cent of the California ninth-graders remained to graduate, only 56.8 per cent of the Georgia youngsters completed high school. Some of the states, other than California, having a retention level of over 80 per cent are Minnesota, Nebraska, Kansas, Washington, South Dakota, Illinois, North Dakota, and Wisconsin. In contrast, states with a holding power below 60 per cent are Georgia, Kentucky, Alabama, New Mexico, and North Carolina.[6]

These geographic differences suggest significant educational and cultural inequities which have an important bearing on the holding power of the high school. Similar relationships are borne out in the illiteracy data for the states and regions.

Illiteracy

Through compulsory education and child labor legislation, the increasing holding power of the schools has led to a marked decrease in illiteracy. The illiteracy rate in 1900 was 11.3 per cent. By 1930 the rate had declined to 4.8 per cent. In 1960 illiterates comprised 2.4 per cent of the total population.

Despite this remarkable progress, however, much work remains to be done. These figures represent those who are "unable to read and write a simple message either in English or in any other language."[7] The population of functional illiterates (those without basic functional language facility or those having completed less than five years of schooling) is much higher. In 1960 there were three million illiterates and more than eight million functional illiterates in the United States.[8]

Illiteracy is also a regional problem reflecting the vast contrasts in the economic, social, and cultural endowment of our people. For example, the illiteracy rate for Iowa is only 0.7 per cent in contrast to 6.3 per cent for Louisiana.[9] Other states with rates of illiteracy below the one per cent mark are Idaho, Oregon, Kansas, Nebraska, South Dakota, Utah, and Washington. The states having an illiteracy rate above four per cent are Louisiana, South Carolina, Mississippi, Georgia, Alabama, and Texas.[10]

---

[6] Office of Education, *School Life* (Washington, D.C.: U.S. Department of Health, Education, and Welfare, May, 1963), p. 33.

[7] Bureau of the Census, "Estimates of Illiteracy by States," *Current Population Reports*, Series P–23, No. 8 (Washington, D.C.: Government Printing Office, February 12, 1963).

[8] *Ibid.*, p. 2.   [9] *Ibid.*, p. 2.

[10] *Ibid.*, p. 2.

The task that remains is not merely the elimination of illiteracy, but the development of functional literacy. Regional disparities and the vast inequalities of educational opportunity must be eradicated.

CURRICULUM CHANGE AND SCHOOL REORGANIZATION

At the turn of the century many educators regarded the high school as serving primarily a college preparatory function. The work of the early committees of the National Education Association, such as the Committee of Ten on Secondary School Studies (1893) and the Committee on College Entrance Requirements (1899), served to fix the idea of the secondary school as a college preparatory institution. The establishment of the various regional standardizing associations, such as the North Central Association of Colleges and Secondary Schools (1894), reinforced the college preparatory role of the high school.

In an attempt to standardize the bookkeeping of high school studies for the convenience of calculating college entrance requirements, the Carnegie Foundation in 1909 proposed the standard unit of credit. This was approved almost immediately by the College Entrance Examination Board and came to be known as the Carnegie Unit. The Carnegie Unit continues to this day as the standard quantitative measure of high school studies. Each unit represents the equivalent of five class periods per week over a full academic year in a major subject. This convenient formula has served in too many instances to inhibit curriculum experimentation. It fails to recognize the capability of some students to accelerate their education by being allowed to progress at their own pace.

Notwithstanding the dominance of the college preparatory function of the high school early in the twentieth century, new modifying forces were becoming evident. The accelerating increase in knowledge, the great technological demands on nations, and the growing diversity of the enlarging secondary-school population forced new demands on the high school. The need for reassessing and reconstructing the secondary school curriculum gained added impetus through the scientific conceptions of human behavior and learning. The social demands of democracy gave renewed recognition to the ideal of educational opportunity, and this in turn necessitated a more liberal and comprehensive view of the role of the secondary school.

Need for Diversified Curricula

An influential proponent of electives and diversified curricula in the secondary school and college was Charles W. Eliot, President of Harvard from 1869 to 1909. In a paper presented to the National Education Association in 1892, Eliot advocated a more flexible and diversified program of studies in the secondary schools to meet the needs of a heterogeneous enrollment.

> Now if the only school that the youth has attended has had a narrow, uniform program, containing a limited number of subjects, without options among them, this important object in secondary education may not have been attained for the individual. A good secondary school must have a program of studies larger and wider than any single pupil can follow, else its range of subjects will be too small to permit the sure fulfillment of this all-important function of a good secondary school— the thorough exploration of all its pupils' capacities. . . .
>
> Anyone who has had much experience in schools or colleges must have learned that as the course of education goes on, and new subjects are set before a class or group of pupils, the bright and dull children not infrequently change places—those that were accounted bright become apparently dull, and those that were accounted dull become, perhaps, leaders. The reason is that the dull children have finally been brought to a subject in which they excel; while the bright ones, who have been exercising a faculty which they possess in large measure, have been brought to a new field to which their powers are not adapted. Flexible and diversified school programs will give all the children their most favorable chance; stiff and uniform programs will not. No machine, like an army, a ship, or a factory, can be a democratic institution; for it demands from the many implicit obedience, and the subordination of the individual energy to the movements of the mass. So far as a school is a machine of uniform product, it must fail, on that account, to serve as it might in the real interests of democratic society.[11]

In 1916 Eliot condemned the useless artificiality of the secondary school curriculum and declared that "the best part of all human knowledge has come by exact and studied observation made through the senses."[12] Although Eliot later came under attack for promoting the elective system in secondary schools and colleges, the liberalization of the curriculum was an inevitable development in a society committed to the ideal of meeting the educational needs of a diverse population.

Abraham Flexner, famous for his monumental Carnegie Foundation report on medical education (1910), presented a paper in 1916 that called for modernizing the curriculum of the secondary school by giving attention to the study of science, industry, civics, and aesthetics.[13] Although the proponents of a more modernized secondary-school curriculum were bitterly attacked by the classicists and essentialists, the handwriting was on the wall. The schools could no longer be divorced from the world of scientific, industrial, and social reality.

---

[11] Proceedings of the National Education Association, 1892, pp. 617–625.

[12] Charles W. Eliot, "Changes Needed in American Secondary Education" (New York: General Education Board, Occasional Papers, no. 2, 1916).

[13] Abraham Flexner, "A Modern School" (New York: General Education Board, Occasional Papers, no. 3, 1916).

During the first quarter of the twentieth century, an increasing proportion of secondary schools departed from the single academic curriculum by allowing students elective options in addition to certain required constants. Other schools introduced multiple curricula such as academic, commercial, industrial, agricultural, homemaking, general, and fine arts.

"Often enough an idea that seems utterly obscure to one generation seems quite obvious to the next generation."

—FRED HOYLE

Courtesy the Ford Foundation; photo by William R. Simmons

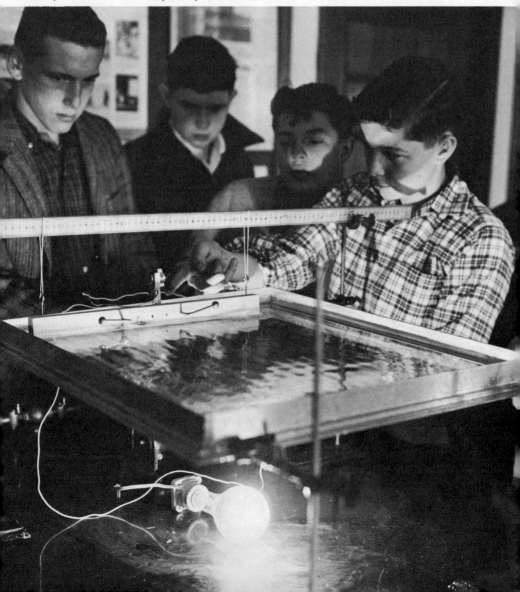

National Needs and Vocational Education

Although some agricultural high schools and trade schools were established before the turn of the century, the general need for vocational education in the United States came to be fully recognized during World War I. Some European nations such as Germany, Austria, Switzerland, France, and Denmark had already developed extensive programs of vocational education for youth of secondary-school age. In this country, the land-grant colleges and universities were making significant contributions to the agricultural and industrial needs of the nation. But it was becoming increasingly apparent that a concerted effort for vocational education of less than college grade was needed.

In 1913 Congress provided for a Presidential Commission to look into the need for national support of vocational education. The Commission, in its report in 1914, revealed that less than one per cent of those engaged in agriculture and manufacturing were adequately trained for these pursuits. The Commission also criticized the narrow academic training of the high schools of the day and pointed to the need of most youth to learn how to earn a good living.

On February 23, 1917, the Smith-Hughes Bill was signed by President Wilson. The nation's needs in agriculture and industry during a wartime emergency influenced the passage of this legislation. This law provided for federal support to the states for vocational education of less than college grade in agriculture, trades, industries, and home economics. Youngsters enrolled in these programs were required to be over 14 years of age. Within five months of the enactment of this legislation, every state had indicated acceptance of the program. Under provisions of the Smith-Hughes Act, matching federal and state funds were allocated to public high schools through the various State Boards for Vocational Education. Participating school districts matched state funds in this cooperative program. Federal funds were allocated to each state according to a formula based on the proportion of the state's rural and urban population to the nation's total rural and urban populations. Subsequent related federal legislation was enacted in 1929, 1935, 1937, and 1946 to provide additional support for vocational education of less than college grade.

By 1931 more than one million students were enrolled in federally supported programs. Enrollment reached two million in 1939, three million in 1949, and four million in 1962. However, despite this notable growth in enrollment, along with the increased holding power of our high schools, the sizable army of dropouts and unemployed youth constitute a most serious problem for contemporary society. Many programs of vocational education are lacking in adequate on-the-job training for successful transition to the world of work. For many of our youth, particularly those in the lower socioeconomic strata, the high school seems to be out of touch with the realities of the working world. And, all too often, the working world tends to ignore the vocational needs of youth.

Aims of Secondary Education are Broadened

The function of the public high school in meeting broad educational needs received increasing recognition. The Commission on the Reorganization of Secondary Education, established in 1913 by the N.E.A., released a widely publicized report in 1918 entitled *Cardinal Principles of Secondary Education.* This report is most famous for its identification of seven objectives of the secondary-school curriculum, encompassing such areas as health, command of the fundamental processes, worthy home membership, education for a vocation, effective citizenship, worthy use of leisure, and ethical character.[14]

As discussed in Chapter 2, subsequent statements by similar groups of educators during the first-half of the twentieth century reaffirmed the need for broadening the aims of the high school. During the 1950's and 1960's, the expanded aims and diversified curriculum of the high school became the subject of heightened attack by the essentialists.

The Comprehensive High School

With the establishment of cooperative federal-state programs for vocational education in 1917, a number of educators were advocating separate specialized vocational schools after the European pattern. But the prevailing sentiment on the part of most educators and parents was against a two-track system with a terminal-technical education for one group and an academic-college preparatory program for the other group.

The opposition to such segregated schooling led to the evolution of a high school aimed at providing (1) a good general education for all citizens of a democratic society, (2) the specialized programs necessary for vocational proficiency for youngsters preparing for the world of work, (3) the specialized program of academic preparation for college, and (4) exploratory courses to meet the individual interests of all students. This multipurpose institution came to be known as the comprehensive high school. It is cited by Conant as characteristic of our society, which is so devoted to the ideals of equality of educational opportunity.[15]

---

[14] U.S. Bureau of Education, *Cardinal Principles of Secondary Education,* Bulletin 35 (Washington, D.C.: Government Printing Office, 1918).

[15] James Bryant Conant, *The American High School Today* (New York: McGraw-Hill Company, Inc., 1959), pp. 7–8.

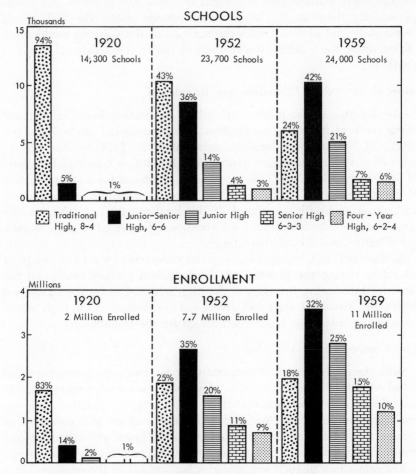

FIGURE 3–3. Types of organization of public secondary schools. [SOURCE: Office of Education, U.S. Department of Health, Education, and Welfare.]

The Junior High School

By 1900 the most widespread form of vertical school organization was an eight-year elementary school followed by a four-year high school. But the 8–4 plan of school organization was questioned by such educators as President Eliot of Harvard, President Harper of Chicago, and Professor John Dewey. These men felt that the 8–4 plan should be reorganized to permit a shortening of the elementary school and enrichment in the program of studies at both the elementary and secondary levels. The eight-year elementary school, with its heavy emphasis on drill in the fundamental processes, was regarded as too long in years and too restrictive in its curricular experiences. Of related concern at the time were questions of promotion, acceleration, remedial work, enrichment, grouping, flexible grading, and holding power.

The first attempts at regrouping grades seven, eight, and nine to form a new school (the junior high) were made at Berkeley, California and Columbus, Ohio in 1909, and in Los Angeles in 1910. The new 6–3–3 type of vertical organization developed rapidly in place of the 8–4 plan, particularly in the cities. In 1920 the traditional four-year high school enrolled 94 per cent of the students. This was reduced to 43 per cent in 1952, and 24 per cent in 1959.

In the smaller population areas, the 6–6 plan has developed, providing for a combined junior-senior high school under one principal. But the 6–3–3 plan has been gaining increasing national popularity, particularly in the larger population centers. Some school districts have followed a 6–2–4 plan, providing for a two-year junior high school while retaining the four-year senior high. In certain sections where the junior colleges are under the administrative control of the public school district, the 6–4–4 plan has emerged, incorporating grades 13 and 14 with the senior high school while providing for a four-year intermediate unit. The city of Pasadena was one of the pioneers in developing this pattern. However, a more popular arrangement provides for a separate junior college facility through a 6–3–3–2 plan under the administration of the public school district. Figure 3–3 shows the changes in patterns of organizing the secondary schools.

The growth of the junior high school during the past half-century has been phenomenal. One of the chief factors in the remarkable development of the junior high school was the economic problem faced by school districts with expanding enrollments at both the elementary and secondary levels. Instead of constructing new elementary and high-school buildings under the 8–4 plan, a given school district could choose the alternative of constructing an intermediate or junior-high-school unit by reorganizing, for example, under the 6–3–3 plan. In this way, enrollment pressure would be reduced in both the elementary school and the high school. Such reorganization proved to be highly feasible and economical for many school districts.

But, in addition to these factors, the junior high school offers numerous educational advantages. It is credited with providing for an increase in the proportion of male teachers serving grades seven and eight. Many junior high schools also boast special facilities, including laboratories and libraries, which are not commonly available in the elementary school. The junior high school also claims the advantage of concentrating on the needs of early adolescents, thereby providing for a better transi-

Courtesy U.S. Office of Education

The one-room school, which once dominated the rural scene, is almost extinct as a result of school consolidation and district reorganization.

Courtesy Perkins & Will; photo by Bill Engdahl, Hedrich-Blessing

tion to high-school studies. The improved holding power of the schools is also attributed to the junior high school by some observers.[16]

Nevertheless, although the vertical reorganization of school systems can help facilitate certain desirable educational outcomes, the key elements in the success of the school are the quality of the faculty, administration, curriculum, learning resources, and the commitment of the home and community to the educational enterprise.

School Consolidation and District Reorganization

With the development of improved roads and automotive transportation, the movement to consolidate schools within districts and to reorganize or combine districts began to take shape. Through such consolidation and reorganization, larger school units with improved physical facilities and a wider variety of curricular offerings became possible. The elimination of the unnecessary multiplicity of small school units resulted in greater economic and administrative efficiency.

In many areas, however, community rivalries and local school loyalties resulted in bitter resistance to consolidation and redistricting. As an increasing number of states offered financial assistance for school construction and pupil transportation, local resistance to larger units of educational organization began to dissipate. Such states as California and New York were particularly successful in the reorganization movement. In many of the southeastern states, school districts have been coterminous with the county, and therefore there was no need to enlarge the administrative units.

In 1930 there were almost 150,000 one-teacher schools. By 1962 the number of such schools was reduced to less than 15,000. In 1932 more than 127,000 school districts were in operation throughout the United States, as compared with some 36,000 by 1962. California, the largest state in population, operates far fewer districts than such states as Nebraska, Kansas, Minnesota, and others of considerably smaller population! In his report on the American high school, published in 1959, Conant observed that of the 21,000 high schools in the United States, 17,000 had graduating classes of less than 100 students.[17] He noted that if the enrollment per high school throughout the nation were to match California's ratio, there would be just over 5,000 high schools in the United States, instead of 21,000.[18] While Conant did not recommend such a

---

[16] Newton Edwards and Herman G. Richey, *The School in the American Social Order*, 2nd Ed. (Boston: Houghton Mifflin Company, 1963), p. 641.

[17] See American Association of School Administrators and Department of Rural Education, *School District Reorganization, Journey That Must Not End* (Washington, D.C.: National Education Association, 1962).

[18] Conant, *The American High School Today* (New York: McGraw-Hill Company, Inc., 1959), p. 81.

reduction per se, he did advocate that the graduating class contain at least 100 students if a comprehensive type of curriculum is to be provided at reasonable cost.[19]

The process of school consolidation and district reorganization has been taking place without relinquishing the principle of local control as symbolized by the district board of education.

SURVEYING, EVALUATING, AND ACCREDITING

The phenomenal growth in secondary school enrollment during the first three decades of the twentieth century, coupled with the great economic and social crises of the depression, led many educators and national leaders to recognize the need for curriculum diversification. Even before the depression it was becoming increasingly apparent that enrollment growth and curriculum change necessitated a comprehensive nationwide study of the status and trends of secondary education. Moreover, the need for reappraising the standards of the secondary school was drawing renewed attention. It was clear that a changing society necessitated a dynamic educational program, but such evolving conditions made the question of how to determine the quality of a secondary school all the more complicated.

The National Survey of Secondary Education

In response to a resolution in 1929 by the North Central Association of Colleges and Secondary Schools, the United States Office of Education undertook a comprehensive study, the National Survey of Secondary Education. The results of this study revealed important data concerning the status and trends of secondary education throughout the United States. Although the survey was more of a fact-finding project than an attempt to prescribe and institute specific changes in the schools, a number of the findings led to some important recommendations. Diversified curricula and vocational education were regarded as means of meeting the needs of all youth in a democratic society. Other findings pointed to the need of schools to provide for individual differences through special remedial, enrichment, and accelerated programs. Also cited were the importance of the library as a central feature of a school, the need for cultural offerings such as art and music, pupil guidance, more functional instruction in the modern foreign languages, teacher participation in curriculum revisions, and curriculum experimentation.[20]

---

[19] *Ibid.*, p. 77.

[20] Leonard V. Koos et al., *National Survey of Secondary Education: Summary*, Bulletin No. 17 (Washington, D.C.: U.S. Office of Education, 1932).

Secondary School Standards

The several voluntary regional accrediting associations, established around the turn of the century, were concerned for many years with evaluating high schools along quantitative lines. Aware of these limitations, the six regional associations (New England, North Central, Middle States, Southern, Northwest, and Western) embarked on an attempt in 1932 to develop evaluative criteria along qualitative lines. Through a national committee, new criteria were formed and tested along such dimensions as the school's philosophy, student population, curriculum, community, faculty, facilities, and other educational factors.

As a result of these efforts, principles were established that recognized the need for schools, within broadly defined limits, to vary their programs according to the particular needs of their own communities and student bodies. Four volumes on evaluative criteria and procedures were prepared.[21] Local school staffs were required to complete a comprehensive self-appraisal of the educational program, followed by an evaluation conducted by a visiting committee of educators from other schools and colleges. The local school then received a report concerning its strengths and areas for improvement in connection with its accreditation status.

The approach of the Cooperative Study was to place key emphasis on continuous growth and improvement, rather than on the meeting of minimum quantitative standards. Self-appraisal, outside expert judgment, objective evidence, and practices in comparable schools with successful programs were identified as important aspects of accreditation. This program, with some variations, continues to this day.

YOUTH, EDUCATION, AND THE DEPRESSION

The great economic depression that began in 1929 compounded the problems of high-school dropouts and youth unemployment. The decade of the thirties was an era of federal programs, including those designed for youth-training and employment, and efforts to study the problems of youth. The National Survey of Secondary Education, conducted in 1929 by the United States Office of Education, had provided some yardsticks in assessing the status and directions of our secondary schools. But the Great Depression caused our national leaders and educators to study and take action on (1) high-school dropouts, (2) youth unemployment, and (3) the problems of youth. Under the New Deal, the Federal Government enacted such emergency programs during the 1930's as the Civilian Conservation Corps, the National Youth Administration, and

---

[21] See Cooperative Study of Secondary School Standards, *Evaluative Criteria*, Washington, D.C., 1960.

the Works Progress Administration. These federal programs came under criticism for operating independently of state and local educational machinery and for lumping education with economic relief programs. But these emergency programs were terminated when World War II ended the national unemployment problem.

The depression period and the New Deal legislation brought about a new focus on the problems of youth both in and out of school. And educators began to give serious attention to the role of the school in the social order.

The Civilian Conservation Corps

In 1933 the Federal Government established the Civilian Conservation Corps. The C.C.C. was designed to provide socially useful employment for out-of-school youth through work projects on soil conservation and reforestation. Lacking any prior experience with such programs and faced with the emergency conditions of the day, the C.C.C. made no provisions initially for the education of its youthful workers. The Department of Labor inducted the youth, the Department of War constructed and managed the work camps, while the Departments of Agriculture and Interior took charge of the projects. It soon became obvious, however, that the educational needs of the C.C.C. youth could not be ignored. Within a few months of the establishment of the C.C.C., the United States Office of Education was designated as the agency for establishing an educational program. The six major objectives of this program were

> to develop powers of self-expression, self-attainment, and self-culture; to develop pride and satisfaction in cooperative endeavor; to develop an understanding of prevailing social and economic conditions, to the end that each man might cooperate intelligently in improving these conditions; to preserve and strengthen good habits of health and mental development; to assist each man, by vocational counseling and training, to meet his employment problems when he leaves camp; and to develop an appreciation of nature and of country life.[22]

Educational advisers and an instructional staff were provided for the camps to establish voluntary programs. Over 90 per cent of the C.C.C. members were enrolled in the educational program by 1939.[23] Despite the limitations on the educational program imposed by the War Department, over 100,000 illiterates learned how to read and write, more than 25,000 attained eighth-grade certificates, and some 5,000 qualified for high school diplomas.[24]

---

[22] Lawrence A. Cremin, *The Transformation of the School* (New York: Alfred A. Knopf, 1961), p. 320.

[23] *Ibid.*, p. 321.

[24] Hollis P. Allen, *The Federal Government and Education* (New York: McGraw-Hill Company, Inc., 1950), p. 94.

Although these notable educational achievements were realized through the C.C.C., the War Department insisted that the organization's prime function be work rather than education. World War II put an end to the C.C.C., but the concern and responsibility for unemployed youth on the part of the Federal Government and educators was clearly demonstrated.

The National Youth Administration

Established in 1935, this federal agency was designed to help needy students remain in school and college by providing part-time employment. This program included students between the ages of 16 and 24. Vocational training was also conducted for jobless youth through the National Youth Administration. Federal funds were granted to schools and colleges that employed needy students in part-time clerical, custodial, and library work. Other federal funds were earmarked for the development of vocational training under the N.Y.A. Although the N.Y.A. was not as ambitious or far-reaching a program as the C.C.C., more than 580,000 youths were participating during the peak year of 1937. With our entry into World War II, the N.Y.A. was discontinued along with other federal emergency relief programs.

The Works Progress Administration

Another important New Deal program of the depression period was the Works Progress Administration. In addition to providing employment through a vast program of public works projects, the W.P.A. served as the administrative agency for the N.Y.A. The W.P.A. also constructed thousands of public schools and college buildings, sponsored nursery schools, and operated an adult educational program that served to teach more than a million illiterates to read and write.

The American Youth Commission

One of the non-governmental agencies that embarked on some important studies during the 1930's concerning the problems of youth was the American Youth Commission, an agency established by the American Council on Education. In investigating 13,500 youth in Maryland, the Commission, noting the high proportion of school dropouts, concluded that "all along the line the schools, as they are now set up, are adapted to neither the needs nor the interests of large numbers of our young people."[25] The Commission reported that a significant proportion of youth had left school because of the inability of their families to support them

---

25 Howard M. Bell, *Youth Tell Their Story* (Washington, D.C.: American Council on Education, 1938), p. 67.

in school.[26] Among other studies and reports calling for curricular reform, the American Youth Commission advocated that schools accept the responsibility for educating youth for a full and successful life.

> These objectives must include the effective preparation of young people for life in all its aspects—for work, for health, for use of leisure time, for home membership, and above all for the obligations of citizenship in a democracy.[27]

The Commission pointed to the need of the high schools to provide a realistic program for the large army of youth who would not be going on to college, including provisions for work experience under competent school supervision. Although the work of the Commission dates back to the Great Depression, its focus on school dropouts and youth unemployment has great relevance for the schools of the 1960's.

The Regents' Inquiry of New York

During the 1930's, an exhaustive study was made of public education in New York State. Sponsored by the state education department, the Regents of the State of New York, the study was published in ten volumes. With regard to secondary education and the needs of youth, the Regents' Inquiry pointed to the failure of the schools to develop readiness for continued learning and job responsibilities not only for the dropouts, but also in the case of those who complete their high-school education. Also criticized was the failure of schools to create enthusiasm for learning, the domination of the academic subjects, and the tendency to regard vocational curricula as suitable only for scholastic misfits. The Inquiry went on to deplore the failure of many teachers to seek to know their students and the wide gap between the curriculum of the school and the needs of youth.[28]

Education and the Great Depression

The Great Depression caused our nation to reassess the role of the school in society. Many adolescents found themselves in the dilemma of being a burden to their families while remaining in school and of being unable to find employment upon leaving school. Educators became increasingly aware of the need to study the problems of youth and to provide the means whereby youth might be better able to come to grips with these problems. A number of people looked to the educational system as one of the prime movers for building a better society.

---

[26] *Ibid.*, p. 67.

[27] The General Report of the American Youth Commission, *Youth and the Future* (Washington, D.C.: American Council on Education, 1942), p. 116.

[28] Ruth E. Eckert and Thomas O. Marshall, *When Youth Leave School: Report of the Regents' Inquiry* (New York: McGraw-Hill Company, Inc.), 1938.

The measures undertaken by the Federal Government to provide for youth employment and education were clearly of an emergency and temporary character. Despite the serious weaknesses of such federal action, including the tendency to bypass many of the existing educational channels, it nevertheless represented the recognized responsibility of our national government in meeting the employment, welfare, and educational needs of our youth.

Although World War II put an end to these concerns of the depression, the postwar period brought to the fore the problem of educating and retraining the vast number of ex-servicemen. The growing competition with the Soviets in science and technology during the 1950's and 1960's brought the schools into the focus of renewed study and criticism. Youth unemployment, a critical problem of the 1930's, was again recognized as a serious societal problem of the 1960's. The age of automation and science had eliminated many of the unskilled jobs while creating new needs for highly skilled technicians and scientists.

PROGRESSIVE EDUCATION

The twentieth century witnessed the application of scientific inquiry to the process of education. Findings in educational psychology challenged and refuted the doctrine of mental discipline and caused educators to reassess their objectives, methods, and the content of the curriculum. Traditional schooling came under attack for lacking the spirit of true education. The tremendous social and industrial changes placed new demands on the schools. The wall between the school and life began to feel the seismic shocks of a new philosophy of education. The new philosophy of progressivism demanded an experimental approach to education and the rejection of synthetic learning. The new goal for our schools was to develop the capacity of the learner in the direction of how to think, not what to think. The new cry was for schools to prepare for and lead to a better life.

John Dewey and Progressive Education

The foremost figure in American educational philosophy was John Dewey (1859–1952). Dewey served as professor of philosophy and education at the University of Chicago from 1894 to 1904 and at Teachers College from 1904 until his retirement. As discussed in Chapter 2, Dewey criticized the formalistic and static quality of the traditional curriculum as representing "the cultural product of societies that assumed the future would be much like the past."[29] He noted the irony in the use of such a

---

[29] John Dewey, *Experience and Education* (New York: The Macmillan Company, 1938), p. 5.

dead curriculum as "education food in a society where change is the rule, not the exception."[30]

Dewey viewed education as inquiry, not indoctrination. He saw schools as democratic institutions consistent with the broader societal ideals of democracy. If they were directly concerned with life, the schools would help us to find the means to a better way of life. Instead of cultivating blind obedience and passivity, the schools, according to Dewey, should energize individual inquiry and social responsibility. Dewey deplored the cataloguing of knowledge and the teaching of subject matter as information rather than inquiry.[31]

Although Dewey's experimentalist philosophy was repellent to any isms, his genius, coupled with the tenor of the times, resulted in an adamant discipleship. The depression of the 1930's gave cause for the reappraisal of the role of education in American life. During this period progressive education gained significant influence in teacher education and in school practices, particularly at the elementary level. Consistent with the findings in educational psychology and harmonious with the principles of democracy, progressive education was a natural and needed development.

The Eight-Year Study

The Progressive Education Association, founded in 1919 with Charles W. Eliot of Harvard as the organization's first honorary president, supported a number of projects designed to bring about important reforms in American education. Perhaps the most influential of the several committees of the Progressive Education Association was the Commission on the Relation of School and College. Established in 1930, this Commission directed its efforts at freeing the secondary schools for experimentation. Then as now, it was felt that the prevailing college-entrance requirements restricted the secondary schools from experimenting with the curriculum and attempting needed reconstruction.

Soon after its establishment, the Commission on the Relation of School and College reported on the failure of the high school to deal adequately with fostering effective citizenship, challenging gifted youth, and motivating all students to their fullest potential. The Commission invited thirty leading secondary schools to develop experimental programs within the framework of its declared purpose.

> We are trying to develop students who regard education as an enduring quest for meanings rather than credit accumulation; who desire to

---

[30] *Ibid.*, p. 5.
[31] John Dewey, *Democracy and Education* (New York: The Macmillan Company, 1916), p. 220.

investigate, to follow the leadings of a subject, to explore new fields of thought; knowing how to budget time, to read well, to use sources of knowledge effectively and who are experienced in fulfilling obligations which come with membership in the school or college community.[32]

Through the cooperation of more than 300 colleges and universities throughout the nation, the thirty secondary schools were free to ignore the usual college entrance requirements. The cooperating colleges and universities had agreed to waive their entrance requirements for recommended graduates of the thirty schools. Thus these schools were free to develop a wide range of curriculum innovation and reconstruction.

The study covered the period from 1932 to 1940 and included 1,475 graduates who had entered college. These graduates of the thirty experimental schools were paired with graduates of other secondary schools according to similarity in socioeconomic background, aptitude, interests, age, race, and other factors. In following up the 1,475 matched pairs in college, the evaluation team reported that the graduates of the thirty experimental schools performed as follows:

1. earned a slightly higher total grade average;
2. earned higher grade averages in all subject fields except foreign language;
3. received slightly more academic honors each year;
4. were more often judged to possess a high degree of intellectual curiosity and drive;
5. were more often judged to be precise, systematic, and objective in their thinking;
6. were more often judged to have developed clear or well-formulated ideas concerning the meaning of education;
7. more often demonstrated a high degree of resourcefulness in meeting new situations;
8. had about the same problems of adjustment as the comparison group, but approached their solution with greater effectiveness;
9. participated somewhat more frequently in student groups;
10. earned a higher percentage of nonacademic honors (i.e. officerships, athletic awards, etc.);
11. had a somewhat better orientation toward the choice of a vocation;
12. demonstrated a more active concern for what was going on in the world.[33]

The study also revealed that the graduates of the more experimental of the thirty schools attained even higher levels of performance in the above areas. Although the Eight-Year Study provided for the careful matching of the two student populations, such factors as teacher competency and educational expenditures for the experimental and control

---

[32] Wilford M. Aikin, *The Story of the Eight-Year Study* (New York: McGraw-Hill Company, Inc., 1942), p. 144.
[33] *Ibid.*, pp. 111–112.

schools were not matched. Nevertheless, it was clearly demonstrated that success in college was not predicated on the completion of the traditional units of college preparatory subjects. Herbert E. Hawkes, Dean of Columbia College, put it this way:

> The results of this Study seem to indicate that the pattern . . . which concentrates on a preparation for a fixed set of entrance requirements is not the only satisfactory means of fitting a boy or girl for making the most out of college experience. It looks as if the stimulus and the initiative which the less conventional approach to secondary school education affords sends on to college better human materials than we have obtained in the past.[34]

While interest in experimentation was encouraged by the results of the Eight-Year Study, most high schools persisted in following rather traditional college preparatory programs. The Michigan Secondary School-College Agreement represented a significant move, however, toward freeing the schools to experiment with new patterns of college preparation. Under this agreement, students from selected accredited high schools were admitted to college upon recommendation from the school with the proviso that they represent the more able members of their graduation class. The experience of this agreement indicates that the traditional units of college preparatory work can be disregarded in favor of the school recommendation.[35]

However, the increasing number of students seeking entrance to college during the 1960's, along with the tendency for critics to see virtue only in rigid patterns of college preparation, indicates a trend toward greater uniformity in the high-school curriculum. The relationship between secondary and higher education needs more attention today than ever before.

Progressive Education Under Attack

Whitehead observed that "in the history of education, the most striking phenomenon is that schools of learning, which at one epoch are alive with a ferment of genius, in a succeeding generation exhibit merely pedantry and routine."[36] Although Whitehead was actually calling for the elimination of inert matter in education, rather than predicting the fate of any particular movement, his words were remarkably prophetic. At the time of Whitehead's writing, the progressive movement in educa-

---

[34] *Ibid.*, p. 150.

[35] Leon S. Waskin, "The Michigan Secondary School-College Agreement," *Bulletin of the National Association of Secondary School Principals*, No. 159, 33:51, January, 1949.

[36] Alfred North Whitehead, *The Aims of Education* (New York: The Macmillan Company, 1929), p. 2.

tion had not reached full momentum. The period of the 1930's and early forties saw considerable innovation and experimentation in our schools. However, many disciples of Dewey misinterpreted his message and developed progressive doctrines of their own.

With our entry into World War II, the tendency toward curriculum retrenchment caused progressive education to lose a great deal of its vigor. The Cold War period saw Dewey and the progressivists being blamed for "soft pedagogy" and, of all things, for the failure of our scientific, military, and industrial establishments to match the Soviet space feats! The cry for a return to the fundamentals and essentials began to split many eardrums. Dewey himself had forewarned in 1938 that "every movement in the direction of a new order of ideas and of activities directed by them calls out, sooner or later, a return to what appear to be simpler and more fundamental ideas and practices of the past. . . ."[37]

Although Dewey's experimentalist philosophy never attained widespread practice in our schools, it has, nevertheless, exerted a profound and permanent influence. Ironically, the curriculum reforms of the 1960's have incorporated many Deweyan principles in the content and process of learning. New emphasis is being given to inquiry and discovery. The trend is to regard a discipline not as a body of inert information, but rather as a mode of inquiry with a symmetry and structure of its own.[38] Recent developments in employing nonverbal media give promise of adding new dimensions to educative experience.

NATIONAL NEEDS AND THE IMPROVEMENT OF EDUCATIONAL OPPORTUNITY

The great conflict between democracy and fascism in World War II gave impetus to the importance of educating youth for democratic values and for understanding the interdependence of the United States and all other nations of the world. World War II was a period of accelerated education, war production training, and intensive training programs for armed forces personnel; it was not a period of curriculum innovation and experimentation in the secondary school.

From 1940 to 1945 almost 7.5 million persons were enrolled in the federally supported programs of Vocational Education for National Defense and War Production Training. Administered through the existing vocational education structure at state and local levels, these programs provided intensive training for war plant employment. The Rural War

---

[37] John Dewey, *Experience and Education* (New York: The Macmillan Company, 1939), Foreword.
[38] See Jerome S. Bruner, *The Process of Education* (Cambridge, Mass.: Harvard University Press, 1960).

Production Training Program was established in 1940 for the education and training of out-of-school youth between the ages of 17 and 24 inclusively. The goal was to train rural youth for war industries, although agricultural production came to be included later.

In addition to attending intensive technical training programs for armed forces personnel, thousands of GI's voluntarily enrolled in correspondence courses for high school and college credit under the United States Armed Forces Institute (USAFI).

During the course of World War II a number of leading educators began to formulate guidelines and policies for the postwar period. Such groups as the Harvard Committee on the Objectives of General Education in a Free Society and the N.E.A.'s Educational Policies Commission made notable efforts in this direction.

Report of the Harvard Committee

Immediately following World War II, the subject of general education received increasing attention. As discussed in Chapter 2, the foremost statement on general education in school and college was the Report of the Harvard Committee, *General Education in a Free Society,* published in 1945. This report emphasized the importance of general education in a democratic society of great population diversity. Attention was also given to the relationship of general education to other areas of the curriculum in school and college, and to the ultimate goal of general education to produce responsible human beings and citizens. This report was a remarkable, statesmanlike document and exerted considerable influence in developing awareness of the need for effective programs of general education in high school and college. The Harvard report is reviewed in considerable detail in Chapter 7.

The Educational Policies Commission

This commission was appointed by the N.E.A. in 1935 for the purpose of studying various educational problems and issues with a view toward issuing key policy statements. Perhaps the most important document on secondary education by the commission appeared in 1944 under the title, *Education for ALL American Youth* (revised in 1952). Looking to the postwar period, this volume set forth an ideal program of secondary education using hypothetical community and state settings. Identifying "Ten Imperative Needs of Youth" (see Chapter 2), the book was a comprehensive blueprint for secondary education in a democracy.

This volume described the role of the comprehensive high school in meeting the general education needs of all youth and the vocational needs of terminal students. The blueprint called for an educational program from grades 7 through 14 in schools of sufficient size to offer a highly diversified curriculum. Also cited were provisions for state and federal support of education to insure equalization of opportunity.

In looking to the schools of tomorrow, *Education for ALL American Youth* was a bold projection incorporating many of the tenets and ideals of progressive education.

Life-Adjustment Education

The depression of the 1930's, followed by World War II, left our school districts with outmoded buildings and facilities. The sharply increased birth rate of the postwar years compounded the need for new schools. Tremendous tax increases were needed to meet these new demands. It was during this crucial period of postwar reconstruction that a new wave of criticism was leveled at the public schools. Some critics were primarily interested in keeping taxes at a minimum. Others wanted to see the schools return to the fundamentals or basic subjects. The favorite catchword of the critics was "life adjustment."

The label "life adjustment" has been given to studies and activities that are nonacademic. The notoriety of the term "life adjustment" grew out of misinterpretation and distortion. A number of educational critics have chosen to interpret life adjustment as education for happy adjustment and conformity.

Actually, the so-called life-adjustment movement had its origin in a resolution by Dr. Charles Prosser at a conference in 1945 sponsored by the Vocational Education Division of the United States Office of Education.

> It is the belief of this conference that, with the aid of this report ("Vocational Education in the Years Ahead"), the vocational school of a community will be able better to prepare 20 per cent of the youth of secondary school age for entrance upon desirable skilled occupations; and that the high school will continue to prepare another 20 per cent for entrance to college. We do not believe that the remaining 60 per cent of our youth of secondary school age will receive the life adjustment training they need and to which they are entitled as American citizens—unless and until the administrators of public education with the assistance of the vocational education leaders formulate a similar program for this group.
> We therefore request the U.S. Commissioner of Education and the Assistant Commissioner for Vocational Education to call at some early date a conference or a series of regional conferences between an equal number of representatives of general and of vocational education—to consider this problem and to take such initial steps as may be found advisable for its solution.[39]

---

[39] U.S. Office of Education, *Life Adjustment Education for Every Youth*, Bulletin 1951, No. 22 (Washington, D.C.: Government Printing Office, 1951), pp. 15–16.

The resolution was unanimously adopted and five regional meetings, sponsored by the Office of Education, were conducted during 1946. The consensus of these regional conferences included the following: (1) our secondary schools were not meeting the life-adjustment needs of perhaps a major portion of our youth; (2) functional experiences were needed in the school curriculum in the areas of practical arts, home and family life, health and physical fitness, and civic competence; and (3) most youth need a supervised program of work experience.[40] As a result of these conferences, the Commission on Life Adjustment Education for Youth was established. The task of this Commission was defined as "designed to equip all American youth to live democratically with satisfaction to themselves and profit to society as home members, workers, and citizens."[41] The Commission clearly indicated that life adjustment was not to be misinterpreted as mere "adjustment to existing conditions, but that it emphasizes active and creative achievements . . . , places a high premium upon learning to make wise choices, since the very concept of American democracy demands the appropriate revising of aims and the means of attaining them."[42]

The first commission functioned for three years and was followed in 1951 by a second commission, which culminated its final report in 1954 with this statement:

> One may conclude that an enormous and necessary task undertaken during the 20th century is but half finished. This is the task of providing universal secondary education for all youth that may live in a society which must make full utilization of scientific discovery. The speed with which this assignment is completed depends in part on the resources which the public through public funds, individually or through foundations are willing to devote to the unfinished business of providing education for all American youth.[43]

A third commission was not established. Criticisms of progressive education were rampant and the label of life adjustment was being applied indiscriminately to virtually any proposal or program that was not purely academic. The term "life adjustment" was an easy target for misinterpretation and attack.

The life-adjustment effort was conceived in recognition of the failure of our secondary schools to meet the life needs of a majority of our

---

40 *Ibid.*, p. 17.
41 U.S. Office of Education, *Vitalizing Secondary Education: Report of the First Commission on Life Adjustment Education for Youth* (Washington, D.C.: Government Printing Office, 1951), p. 1.
42 *Ibid.*, pp. 32–33.
43 U.S. Office of Education, *A Look Ahead in Secondary Education: Report of the Second Commission on Life Adjustment Education for Youth* (Washington, D.C.: Government Printing Office, 1954), p. 95.

youth. During the early post-World War II period, approximately one out of every two youths who entered the ninth grade failed to graduate four years later, and only one out of every five youths of college age was enrolled in an institution of higher education.

Failure to complete a high school education or to enroll in college was clearly not caused only by lack of ability. Many youths failed to see a purpose in the curriculum of the high school, and many were lacking in financial support for continued education. The President's Commission on Higher Education, in its report of 1948, argued that virtually 50 per cent of the population is capable of completing fourteen years of formal education, and that almost one third is potentially capable of completing a four-year college program.[44] While the two Commissions on Life Adjustment Education did not recognize such a high potential for mass higher education, their main task was to encourage the development of more realistic educational programs in our secondary schools to meet the needs of all youth.

But the term "life adjustment" was soon to become a convenient label to be used recklessly by many critics of public education. Life adjustment was to be misinterpreted as education for adjustment and conformity to the common denominators of society. The pronouncements of some of the more vocal and influential critics of contemporary public secondary education are discussed in the next chapter.

Educational Benefits for War Veterans

While pensions for war veterans have been provided since 1776, the first efforts for the re-education of former servicemen was the Smith-Sears Law of 1918. This law was limited to the rehabilitation of disabled war veterans and was administered through the Federal Board for Vocational Education, which in turn had been established under the Smith-Hughes Act of 1917.

Similar provisions, but on a far greater scale, were provided for disabled veterans of World War II with the enactment of Public Law 16 in 1943. Hundreds of thousands of disabled veterans enrolled in a wide variety of occupational training programs under the provisions of this act. Benefits were extended to Korean veterans in 1950.

But the most monumental education program ever undertaken for war veterans was Public Law 346, the Servicemen's Readjustment Act, popularly known as the G.I. Bill of Rights. Enacted by the Seventy-eighth Congress on June 22, 1944, this law was intended to provide opportunities

---

[44] President's Commission on Higher Education, *Higher Education for American Democracy*, Vol. I (Washington, D.C.: Government Printing Office, 1947), pp. 38–39.

for veterans of World War II to recapture educational pursuits that had been interrupted because of the War. An amendment in 1945 enabled virtually every honorably discharged veteran with 90 days or more of service to participate in these benefits. As a result, the G.I. Bill of Rights provided opportunities for millions of veterans to continue their education significantly beyond what might have been expected of a comparable nonveteran population group. Approximately eight million veterans, more than half of all who served in World War II, participated in these benefits at a cost to the Federal Government of some $14.5 billions. The number of veterans enrolled in school totalled 3,430,000, while 2,350,000 enrolled in college and 2,390,000 in on-the-job training. These veterans received subsistence, tuition, books, supplies, equipment, and counseling services under provisions of this legislation. Similar benefits were extended in 1952 to veterans of the Korean conflict.

Educational Opportunity Extends Upward

Higher education has been traditionally regarded as the domain of the socially privileged and academically talented. Although the Morrill Act of 1862 was designed to make higher education an instrument of social policy and national need, it was not until after World War II that higher education came within reach of the masses. Prior to World War II, private colleges and universities enrolled more than half of the students. Today, close to two thirds of the nation's college students are attending publicly supported institutions.

While many people like to think of higher education as a means of personal advancement through private means, federal legislation in recent years has been designed to provide aid and support as a matter of national policy to meet national needs.

Revolution in Higher Education

The G.I. Bill of Rights opened the doors of schools and colleges to millions who otherwise would not have continued their education. Prior to World War II, higher education was generally regarded as the province of a very select group of academically talented youth. In actual practice, however, college attendance was predicated at least as much on financial ability as on academic competence. In the years immediately preceding World War II, only some 15 per cent of the 18- to 21-year-old age group was enrolled in degree-credit programs of higher education. By 1961 this percentage had increased remarkably to 37.6 per cent, and in the fall of 1964 it reached an unprecedented 40 per cent.

That such a high proportion of the 18- to 21-year-old age group would be capable of pursuing higher education was simply undreamed of prior to World War II. However, the matter of higher education for the postwar

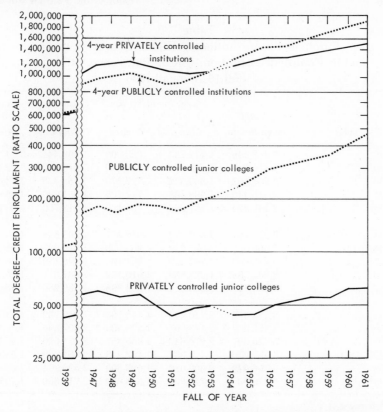

FIGURE 3–4. Trends in degree-credit enrollment for 4-year institutions and junior colleges, by types of institutional control: United States and outlying parts, fall 1939 and fall 1947 through fall 1961. [SOURCE: U.S. Department of Health, Education, and Welfare, Office of Education, Surveys of *Opening (Fall) Enrollment in Higher Education.*]

period was of sufficient national concern that in 1946 President Truman appointed a commission to study and evaluate our current programs in light of future national policies. The President's Commission on Higher Education in American Democracy published its five-volume report in 1947.[45] One of the most controversial aspects of the report was the conclusion that one half of our population has the potential of completing fourteen years of schooling, while one third of our people could complete an advanced liberal or specialized professional education. The Commission proceeded to base its recommendations on this point by calling for a doubling of enrollment in higher education by 1960. Some educators

---

[45] President's Commission on Higher Education, *Higher Education for American Democracy,* Vol. I (Washington, D.C.: Government Printing Office, 1947).

Table 3–3
Enrollment in Institutions of Higher Education, by Sex
and by Control of Institution: United States and Outlying Parts,
Fall 1948 to Fall 1963

Year	Total Enrollment	Enrollment by Sex		Enrollment by Control of Institution	
		Men	Women	Public	Private
1948.............	2,408,249	1,712,283	695,966	1,190,441	1,217,808
1949.............	2,456,841	1,728,672	728,169	1,218,580	1,238,261
1950.............	2,296,592	1,569,322	727,270	1,154,456	1,142,136
1951.............	2,116,440	1,398,735	717,705	1,051,990	1,064,450
1952.............	2,148,284	1,387,094	761,190	1,113,700	1,034,584
1953.............	2,250,701	1,432,474	818,227	1,203,558	1,047,143
1954.............	2,468,596	1,575,227	893,369	1,372,937	1,095,659
1955.............	2,678,623	1,747,429	931,194	1,498,510	1,180,113
1956.............	2,946,985	1,927,863	1,019,122	1,681,671	1,265,314
1957.............	3,068,417	2,003,424	1,064,993	1,780,280	1,288,137
1958.............	3,258,556	2,110,426	1,148,130	1,912,232	1,346,324
1959.............	3,402,297	2,173,797	1,228,500	2,002,868	1,399,429
1960.............	3,610,007	2,270,640	1,339,367	2,135,690	1,474,317
1961.............	3,891,230	2,423,987	1,467,243	2,351,719	1,539,511
1962.............	4,206,672	2,603,072	1,603,600	2,596,904	1,609,768
1963*.............	4,419,000	2,743,000	1,676,000	2,714,000	1,705,000

* Estimated.

NOTE: Prior to 1953, includes only resident degree-credit students; in 1953 and subsequent years, includes resident and extension degree-credit students.

SOURCE: U.S. Department of Health, Education, and Welfare, Office of Education, circulars on *Opening (Fall) Enrollment in Higher Education.*

like President Hutchins of the University of Chicago and President Gannon of Fordham University condemned this as "educational inflation" and concluded that it would lead to a lowering of standards.[46] Nevertheless, the phenomenal growth in higher education during the early 1960's was clear testimony to the fact that a national trend in harmony with the report of the President's Commission had been established. As recently as 1952 the total enrollment in private colleges and universities exceeded that of public institutions. By 1963, however, the public institutions of higher education enrolled almost two-thirds of all students. These data are presented in Figure 3–4 and Tables 3–3 and 3–4.

Other recommendations by the President's Commission included the elimination of racial and religious discrimination in college entrance,

[46] *Time,* July 26, 1948, p. 58.

Table 3–4
Enrollment in Institutions of Higher Education Compared
with Population Aged 18–21: United States,
Fall 1946 to Fall 1963

Year	Population 18–21 Years of Age*	Enrollment	Number Enrolled Per 100 Persons 18–21 Years of Age
1946	9,403,000	2,078,095	22.1
1947	9,276,000	2,338,226	25.2
1948	9,144,000	2,403,396	26.3
1949	8,990,000	2,444,900	27.2
1950	8,945,000	2,281,298	25.5
1951	8,742,000	2,101,962	24.0
1952	8,542,000	2,134,242	25.0
1953	8,441,000	2,231,054	26.4
1954	8,437,000	2,446,693	29.0
1955	8,508,000	2,653,034	31.2
1956	8,701,000	2,918,212	33.5
1957	8,844,000	3,036,938	34.3
1958	8,959,000	3,226,038	36.0
1959	9,182,000	3,364,861	36.6
1960	9,546,000	3,582,726	37.5
1961	10,246,000	3,860,643	37.7
1962	10,745,000	4,174,936	38.9
1963	11,330,000†	4,419,000†	39.0†

* These Bureau of the Census estimates are as of July 1 preceding the opening of the academic year. They include Armed Forces overseas.
† Estimated.

NOTE: Beginning in 1960, data are for 50 States and D.C.; data for earlier years are for 48 States and D.C. Beginning in 1953, enrollment figures include residence and extension degree-credit students; data for earlier years exclude extension students.

SOURCES: U.S. Department of Health, Education, and Welfare, Office of Education, circulars on *Opening (Fall) Enrollment in Higher Education;* and U.S. Department of Commerce, Bureau of the Census, *Current Population Reports,* Series P–25, No. 265.

the rapid expansion of educational facilities, including junior colleges, and a vast program of federal scholarships for needy and talented students.

The Junior College Movement

During the latter half of the nineteenth century, several college presidents, notably Henry P. Tappan of the University of Michigan, William W. Folwell of the University of Minnesota, and Edmund J. James of the

University of Illinois, advanced the idea that some of the early stages of university studies be moved down into the high school. In 1892 President William Rainey Harper of the University of Chicago divided the four-year undergraduate program into two divisions that, by 1896, were officially called Junior College (freshman and sophomore years) and Senior College (junior and senior years). This was the first known use of the term junior college.[47] Harper also encouraged a number of high schools to encompass one or two years of lower-division, college studies. Under Harper's influence, the first public junior college was established in 1902 at Joliet, Illinois.

In 1907 the California legislature authorized high schools to expand their offerings to include postgraduate courses, and in 1917 the legislature enacted a bill authorizing state and county finances for such expansion. In 1921 California provided for the establishment of independent junior college districts. Soon some of the junior colleges in California were offering terminal occupational curricula as well as the equivalent of lower division college studies.

Over the years, a small number of junior or community colleges came to be structured within the 6–4–4 plan of the public school system, providing for one secondary school unit encompassing grades 7 through 10, and another unit including grades 11 through 14. However, the 6–3–3–2 plan, with a separate junior or community college unit under the local public school system, came to be far more popular. A significant number of junior colleges are organized as separate districts independent of the local school district. In some areas the junior colleges are supported and controlled directly by the state. Privately controlled junior colleges comprise some 12 per cent of the total junior college enrollment.

By far the leading state in junior college enrollment is California. Although California also has the most extensive and generously supported four-year state college and university systems, its junior colleges have been enrolling some 73 per cent of all full-time freshmen and sophomores in public higher education.[48] Texas and Florida are other leading states in the junior college movement. Although a majority of the states have enacted legislation relating to public junior colleges, relatively few states have made a concerted effort to establish and support these institutions on a scale sufficient to meet the college enrollment crisis of the 1960's. Nevertheless, their growth in number and size of enrollment over the years is encouraging. From 1951 to 1961, the resident enrollment in public junior colleges more than doubled. Table 3–5 shows the data for

[47] Walter C. Eells, *The Junior College* (Boston: Houghton Mifflin Company, 1931), p. 47.

[48] Leland L. Medsker, *The Junior College: Progress and Prospect* (New York: McGraw-Hill Company, Inc., 1960), p. 211.

Table 3–5
Resident Enrollment in Junior Colleges,* by Type of Control:
United States, 1917–18 to 1963–64

Academic year	All Junior Colleges		Publicly Controlled		Privately Controlled	
	Number	Enrollment	Number	Enrollment	Number	Enrollment
1917–18	46	4,504	14	1,367	32	3,137
1919–20	52	8,102	10	2,940	42	5,162
1921–22	80	12,124	17	4,771	63	7,353
1923–24	132	20,559	39	9,240	93	11,319
1925–26	153	27,095	47	13,859	106	13,236
1927–28	248	44,855	114	28,437	134	16,418
1929–30	277	55,616	129	36,501	148	19,115
1931–32	342	85,063	159	58,887	183	26,176
1933–34	322	78,480	152	55,869	170	22,611
1935–36	415	102,453	187	70,557	228	31,896
1937–38	453	121,510	209	82,041	244	39,469
1939–40	456	149,854	217	107,553	239	42,301
1941–42	461	141,272	231	100,783	230	40,489
1943–44	413	89,208	210	60,884	203	28,324
1945–46	464	156,456	242	109,640	222	46,816
1947–48	472	240,173	242	178,196	230	61,977
1949–50	506	243,839	279	188,794	227	55,045
1951–52	506	231,175	291	184,054	215	47,121
1953–54	518	325,804	293	272,036	225	53,768
Fall, 1955	469	295,553	276	249,928	193	45,625
Fall, 1957	490	349,385	283	297,680	207	51,705
Fall, 1959	509	403,524	310	348,538	199	54,986
Fall, 1963	577	771,637	393	691,678	184	79,959

* Includes 2-year normal schools in 1949–50 and subsequent years.
NOTE: Beginning in 1959–60, includes Alaska and Hawaii.
SOURCES: U.S. Department of Health, Education, and Welfare, Office of Education, *Biennial Survey of Education in the United States;* Circular OE–54025, *Total Enrollment in Institutions of Higher Education, First Term, 1959–60;* Circular OE–54003, *Opening (Fall) Enrollment in Higher Education,* 1963.

resident enrollment in public and private junior colleges from 1917 to 1960.

Students choosing to attend a junior or community college do so for many reasons, such as the opportunity to live at home while attending college, lower fees and tuition charges, inability to gain admission to a four-year college or university, and the opportunity to pursue a terminal-occupational program.

Studies of the performance of junior college students who transfer to four-year colleges and universities are generally favorable. Comparisons between junior college transfers and native students at one of our finest universities, the University of California (Berkeley), reveal that, when both groups were academically eligible for university admission at the time of high school graduation, the transfer students performed about as well as the native students. Even among those transfer students who would not have been eligible for university admission at the time of high school graduation, the record is rather encouraging. Approximately 56 per cent of this ineligible group of transfers made good academic records and almost 90 per cent of the 56 per cent group earned a university degree.[49] This is a remarkable record when one considers that these very same students would have been denied admission to this university on the basis of their high-school records two years previously. Those critics, like Bestor and Rickover, who advocate early and rigid selection practices for college entrance would do well to heed the records of the many late developers.

The Educational Policies Commission and the American Association of School Administrators recently urged that free, universal education be extended two years beyond high school through a vast number of nonselective colleges.[50]

Challenge of the 1960's

Our national commitment to higher education is reflected in comparative data on the percentages of the age group enrolled in the United States and those of other nations. Where Western European nations enroll less than 10 per cent of the age group in colleges and universities, we have reached 40 per cent. The Soviets expect to enroll approximately 20 per cent of the college-age population by 1965, but most of the students will be in part-time studies.[51]

Increases in tuition, fees, and cost of living tend to prevent many of our able students from pursuing and completing college studies. Even our publicly supported colleges and universities have been increasing their tuition and fees. Student loan provisions under the National Defense Education Act of 1958 are restricted to those in science, mathematics, and modern foreign languages. As a free society we like to boast that curriculum choice is up to the individual; yet our Federal Government has placed a premium on certain areas of the curriculum in schools and colleges. The privately supported National Merit Scholarship Program

---

[49] Medsker, op. cit., p. 123.
[50] "Two-Year College for All is Urged," The New York Times, January 2, 1964, pp. 1, 30.
[51] Nicholas DeWitt, Education and Professional Employment in the U.S.S.R. (Washington, D.C.: National Science Foundation, 1961), p. 317.

provides awards for only a very small fraction of our able students. Approximately one half of our college students do not remain to complete their degrees, and most of these students drop out for reasons other than academic. The pursuit of higher learning should be based not on the ability to pay but on the ability and motivation to learn.

With the college-age population today reaching unprecedented levels, the challenge of meeting the educational needs of our young men and women has never been greater.

SUMMARY

The universalization of secondary education is a phenomenon of the twentieth century. The opening of the high school to all youth reflected our growing conviction that educational opportunity is necessary for a free society, and that the schools are the means of perpetuating democracy and social progress.

The twentieth century witnessed child labor legislation, compulsory school attendance, and woman suffrage. Our knowledge of human behavior was greatly accelerated and, coupled with a growing humanitarian conscience, the education of the masses became a realistic goal.

The need to diversify the curriculum of the secondary school was partly influenced by the heterogeneous pupil population, and partly by the great advances in science and technology. The crisis of World War I led to federally supported programs of vocational education in the high schools of our nation. The Great Depression and the high rate of school dropouts and unemployed youth led to a reassessment of the high school curriculum with focus on the problems and needs of youth. The progressive education movement represented the attempt to make education attuned to the needs of our times, rather than the instrument of tradition.

The period following World War II witnessed unprecedented activity by the Federal Government in sponsoring the continued education of ex-servicemen. Leaders in higher education discovered that a far higher proportion of our population than heretofore realized was capable of the successful pursuit of higher learning. Even after the expiration of the G.I. Bill of Rights, the demand for higher education continued to grow at a rate higher than the growth of the college-age population. Shortly after mid-century it was clear that the major responsibility of meeting these needs would rest with the public colleges and universities.

Despite these revolutionary transformations, during the 1960's we are still grappling with problems of youth unemployment, high-school dropouts, and inequities of educational opportunity connected with socioeconomic, geographic, and racial problems. Whereas even the most primitive societies have developed the mechanisms for bringing the adolescent into successful union with the adult world, our own civilization has not solved this basic societal need.

Nevertheless, the twentieth century is a revolutionary period in American education. It is revolutionary because it witnessed the opening of the high schools to all American youth, the expansion of knowledge of human behavior and the psychology of learning, the success of the schools in Americanizing the great populations of immigrants from diverse national and cultural origins, the diversification of the high-school curriculum, the development of the comprehensive high school as a force for improving equality of educational opportunity, the extension of mass education upward to include college and university studies, and the recognized responsibility of the Federal Government in eliminating racial segregation in our schools.

PROBLEMS FOR STUDY AND DISCUSSION

1. What forces led to the universalization of secondary education in our society?

2. Is the current enrollment revolution in higher education a result of forces similar to those that led to the universalization of secondary education? Why or why not?

3. What forces have militated against the realization of equal educational opportunity? What measures do you believe should be taken for our nation to attain equality of educational opportunity?

4. It is said that the American system of education is designed primarily to serve the individual rather than the state. Do you agree or disagree? Why?

5. How do you account for the intensified interest in the problems of youth during the 1930's? Should the problems of today's youth have an influence in shaping the curriculum of the high school? Why or why not?

6. Some critics use the term life adjustment as a label for progressive education. Does this term accurately fit Dewey's concept of progressive education? Why or why not?

7. Although the curriculum of the high school has become increasingly diversified during the twentieth century, some educators hold that by far the greatest diversification of the curriculum has taken place in our colleges. How do you account for such growth in the expansion of offerings in higher

education? Compare the number and types of curricula offered at a large comprehensive high school with that of a junior college and a four-year college.

8. Many college educators maintain that while college enrollment has reached the highest proportion of the age group in our history, academic standards have never been higher. What evidence can you find in support of this position? Against?

9. What arguments are offered in favor of establishing public junior colleges on a wide scale? To what extent, if any, do you believe junior colleges are justified in offering terminal-occupational curricula, as well as preparation for transfer to four-year colleges?

SELECTED REFERENCES

Allen, Hollis P. *The Federal Government and Education.* New York: McGraw-Hill Company, Inc., 1950.

American Association of School Administrators. *School District Reorganization, Journey That Must Not End.* Washington, D.C.: National Educational Association, 1962.

American Youth Commission. *Youth and the Future.* Washington, D.C.: American Council on Education, 1942.

Aikin, Wilford M. *The Story of the Eight-Year Study.* New York: McGraw-Hill Company, Inc., 1942.

Bell, Howard M. *Youth Tell Their Story.* Washington, D.C.: American Council on Education, 1938.

Bruner, Jerome S. *The Process of Education.* Cambridge, Mass.: Harvard University Press, 1960.

Butts, R. Freeman and Lawrence A. Cremin. *A History of Education in American Culture.* New York: Holt, Rinehart and Winston, Inc., 1953.

Conant, James Bryant. *The American High School Today.* New York: McGraw-Hill Company, Inc., 1959.

Cremin, Lawrence A. *The Transformation of the School.* New York: Alfred A. Knopf, Inc., 1961.

Cubberley, Ellwood P. *Public Education in the United States.* Boston: Houghton Mifflin Company, 1947.

DeWitt, Nicholas. *Education and Professional Employment in the U.S.S.R.* Washington, D.C.: National Science Foundation, 1961.

Dewey, John. *Democracy and Education.* New York: The Macmillan Company, 1916.
———. *Experience and Education.* New York: The Macmillan Company, 1938.

Educational Policies Commission. *Education for ALL American Youth—A Further Look.* Washington, D.C.: National Education Association, 1952.

Edwards, Newton and Herman G. Richey. *The School in the American Social Order.* 2nd Ed. Boston: Houghton Mifflin Company, 1963.

Fields, Ralph R. *The Community College Movement.* New York: McGraw-Hill Company, Inc., 1962.

Kneller, George F. (ed.) *Foundations of Education.* New York: John Wiley and Sons, Inc., 1963.

Knight, Edgar W. *Fifty Years of American Education*. New York: The Ronald Press Company, 1952.

Medsker, Leland L. *The Junior College: Progress and Prospect*. New York: McGraw-Hill Company, Inc., 1960.

National Education Association, Report of the Project on Instruction. *Schools for the Sixties*. New York: McGraw-Hill Cmpany, Inc., 1963.

President's Commission on Higher Education. *Higher Education for American Democracy*. Washington, D.C.: Government Printing Office, 1947. 5 Vols.

Thayer, V. T. *The Role of the School in American Society*. New York: Dodd, Mead and Company, 1960.

Whitehead, Alfred North. *The Aims of Education*. New York: The Macmillan Company, 1929.

CHAPTER *4*

Contemporary Conflicts
and Challenges

AT MID-TWENTIETH CENTURY many educational problems and issues were reaching the boiling point. The growing criticism of education during the post-World War II period was shaped by many forces. Cremin attributes this rising criticism to such conditions as the lack of adequate buildings and facilities resulting from the wartime halt in school construction, the population boom, the teacher shortage, the increasing concern with the expansion of communism as a global force, and the critical need for educated manpower.[1]

Some critics were calling for reduced educational expenditures by curtailing the school curriculum to the traditional disciplines. The essentialists attracted considerable notice and support in their attacks on life adjustment and soft pedagogy.

International tensions and ideological disagreements gave birth to McCarthyism and a variety of infringements on academic freedom. Censorship of controversial material in school books and school libraries was not uncommon. And the loyalty oath became a matter of routine for teachers and professors. The Sputnik of 1957 soon led to increased support of education by the Federal Government, particularly in the fields of science, mathematics, and modern foreign languages. There was a growing interest in comparing American education with the school systems of the U.S.S.R. and the Western European nations.

Youth unemployment during the early 1960's received national attention on a scale unparalleled since the depression of the 1930's. High

---

[1] Lawrence A. Cremin, *The Transformation of the School* (New York: Alfred A. Knopf, 1961), p. 338.

115

school enrollments were at an all-time high, yet many youths were dropping out of school only to join the ranks of the unemployed. Automation had created a new prosperity and a new poverty. New vocational education measures were enacted at the federal level to meet these critical demands.

Our nation began to look more and more to the schools and colleges as instruments for serving the national need. With enrollment in higher education surging year by year to unprecedented levels, epoch-making federal legislation was passed for the construction of instructional facilities in our colleges and universities.

A new social awakening was upon us with the growing demand for equal educational and economic opportunity for the Negro. Historic decisions by the United States Supreme Court mandated that we fulfill our democratic legacy by opening the schools to all.

The question of public support for private and church-sponsored schools remained controversial and unsettled despite our traditional principle of separation between church and state. Great inequalities of educational opportunity still persisted according to geographic, economic, and social factors.

Although mid-twentieth century has been a smoldering period of great confusion and conflict, it has also been an era of challenge and action. In this chapter we will review some of these conflicting forces and the measures we have taken for the future.

DEMAND FOR CURRICULUM RETRENCHMENT AND ECONOMY

The 1950's were marked by a great wave of reaction against the expansion and diversification of the high school curriculum that had occurred since the depression. The sharp and sudden rise in the birthrate following World War II produced unrelenting enrollment pressures on our public schools. The critical shortage of school buildings, facilities, and teachers led to marked increases in local property taxes for financing these needs. Many of those seeking to hold the line against tax increases became allied with the critics who were advocating that the schools confine their curriculum to the basic subjects.

Return to the Fundamentals

During the 1950's the rallying cry of essentialists and tax conservatives was "Return to the fundamentals." Tax conservatives sought to reduce school expenditures by curtailing or eliminating the so-called frill subjects along with the expensive equipment and facilities required for diversified curricula.[2] A series of articles in *U.S. News & World Report* and other magazines from 1956 through 1958 advocated greater emphasis on the basic subjects and reduced educational expenditure in our public schools.[3] The schools were even accused of socialism.[4]

Probably the most publicized and influential criticisms of life-adjustment education during the 1950's were leveled by Professor Arthur Bestor of the University of Illinois and Hyman G. Rickover, Vice Admiral of the U.S. Navy. In attacking life adjustment and vocational education, Bestor declared:

> Liberal Education is designed to produce self-reliance. It expects a man or woman to use his general intelligence to solve particular problems. Vocational and "life-adjustment" programs, on the other hand, breed servile dependence. Originality, reason, and common sense are at a discount; maxims, formulas, and rules (the most degraded kinds of book-learning) are at a premium. The nation should view with grave alarm the undermining of that self-reliance upon which our greatness was based. One can search history and biography in vain for evidence that men or women have ever accomplished anything original, creative, or significant by virtue of narrowly conceived vocational training or of educational programs that aimed merely at "life-adjustment." The West was not settled by men and women who had taken courses in "How to be a pioneer." The mechanical ingenuity which is a proverbial characteristic of the American people owes nothing whatever to school-room manipulation of gadgets. I for one do not believe that the American people have lost all common sense and native wit so that now they have to be taught in school to blow their noses and button their pants.[5]

Bestor attracted a following of the intelligentsia, as well as exercising influence on large segments of the general public. Such magazines as *U.S. News & World Report* and *Good Housekeeping* gave Bestor a national platform from which to vent his ire. *Good Housekeeping* went so far as to make Bestor its education editor. In his arguments, Bestor chose to ignore the holding-power problem of a rigidly academic curriculum where dropouts would be cast upon society without salable skills or vocational proficiency. He advocated that vocational studies be eliminated in favor of "a standard academic program."[6]

---

[2] See Roger A. Freeman, *School Needs in the Decade Ahead* (New York: Institute for Social Science Research, 1958).

[3] See *U.S. News & World Report*, "We are Less Educated Than 50 Years Ago" and "A Businessman's View on the Failure of Education," November 30, 1956, pp. 68–82 and 83–86, 89; "Back to the 3 R's?", March 15, 1957, pp. 38–44, 122–124; "Is U. S. Really Too Stingy With its Schools?", July 4, 1958, pp. 68–71.

[4] *U.S. News & World Report*, "A Businessman's View on the Failure of Education," November 30, 1956, p. 86.

[5] Arthur Bestor, *Educational Wastelands* (Urbana, Illinois: The University of Illinois Press, 1953), pp. 63–64.

[6] Arthur Bestor, *The Restoration of Learning* (New York: Alfred A. Knopf, 1955), p. 329.

Educational Efficiency

Cries for reduced educational expenditures were accompanied by demands for increased efficiency in our schools. One writer advocated the assessment of our school system in terms of the production efficiency of the automobile and steel industries.

> . . . the schools, no less than the automobile industry, have an inescapable production problem. Even if we were all agreed on the quality we desired, we would still, presumably, want the schools to turn out students with the greatest possible efficiency—i.e., we would want to optimize the number of students, and we would want to minimize the input of man-hours and capital. In this respect the schools are no different from General Motors. . . . The (steel) industry's productivity has been rising at an average of 3 or 4 per cent a year, and two workers today can produce as much steel as three did in 1947. No comparable economies are visible in the education industry.[7]

The article went on to cite the efforts of the Ford Foundation in supporting technological innovations in the schools for the purpose of improving educational efficiency. An earlier publication by the Ford Foundation presented a blueprint for utilizing television in our schools as a means not only of improving the effectiveness of teaching, but of reducing educational expenditures by solving the shortage of teachers and school buildings.[8] The National Defense Education Act of 1958 provided funds for schools to purchase new educational media including television equipment and teaching machines. The term autoinstructional technology soon gained common usage in educational literature.[9] Many educational researchers and administrators approached the new technology from the angles of increased efficiency and economy rather than how to bring new qualitative dimensions to education.

In attempting to apply industrial standards of efficiency to education, some people seemed to forget that the schools are dealing with human beings and not with automobiles, refrigerators, and washing machines.

SOVIET RIVALRY RAISES FEARS AND CRITICISMS

The growing influence of communism in various sectors of the world during the decade of the 1950's influenced American education in several

---

[7] Daniel Seligman, "The Low Productivity of the Education Industry," *Fortune*, Vol. LVIII, No. 4, October 1958, p. 136.

[8] Alexander J. Stoddard, *Schools for Tomorrow: An Educator's Blueprint* (New York: Ford Foundation, Fund for the Advancement of Education, January 1957).

[9] See Daniel Tanner, *Technological Influences: Automation in the Teaching-Learning Process*, Chapter V, Forty-First Yearbook, The Association for Student Teaching, 1962, pp. 102–117.

ways. Superpatriotic groups scrutinized school textbooks and school libraries for un-American material. Most of our states enacted legislation requiring loyalty oaths as a condition of employment of teachers and professors in publicly supported schools and colleges. Soviet progress in space technology produced a new avalanche of school criticism. As never before, the role of education as an instrument of national purpose became a focal point of debate.

Freedom to Learn

Academic freedom is an abiding principle of any democracy. Freedom of speech and of the press are guaranteed under the First Amendment to the Constitution. Nevertheless, academic freedom is not license to propagandize, but the right and obligation of the teacher and learner to investigate with an open mind all sides of a problem or issue.

Prior to the twentieth century the principle of academic freedom was dealt with mostly in connection with university studies. During the twentieth century, however, the commitment to universal secondary education was accompanied by an increasing concern for developing an enlightened citizenry. Progressive educators were calling for open-minded study of contemporary social problems and issues in our schools through the method of intelligence. But many teachers have avoided controversial questions in the classroom by stressing factual indoctrination in the social studies. It is argued that high school students are not sufficiently mature to come up with the right answers on controversial issues. The tradition of regarding mind as a receptacle or sponge into which appropriate knowledge is to be poured or soaked has also militated against independent thought. Consequently, in many of our schools there has existed a voluntary force for censorship and avoidance of the controversial.

During the 1950's a wave of national insecurity welled up as a result of the growth of communism as a competing world force. The spirit of McCarthyism on the national political scene began to be felt at the state and local levels through the search for subversive material in textbooks and school libraries. The loyalty oath became a contractual condition for the employment of teachers and professors. There were those who saw school censorship and teacher loyalty oaths as essential in protecting our nation from communism, while others warned that such actions served to undermine democracy and "bring to our intellectual and artistic life the same sort of sterility from which the cultural world of our Communist adversaries is already suffering."[10]

---

[10] Address by George F. Kennan, former United States Ambassador to the U.S.S.R. (May 15, 1953), as quoted in V. T. Thayer, *The Role of the School in American Society* (New York: Dodd, Mead & Company, 1960), p. 328.

However, a number of extremist measures eventually came to be challenged and demolished in the courts. The intellectual, who was ridiculed as an impractical egghead during the early 1950's, suddenly became a respected figure—particularly the scientist, who was now to be found in the antechambers of presidents, premiers, and prime ministers. The loyalty oath, once necessary for grants under the National Defense

". . . there is always the temptation in large schools
to omit the endless task of meeting the wants of
each single mind. . . ."

—RALPH WALDO EMERSON

Photo by Vories Fisher

Education Act, was rescinded. Some of the foolish, superpatriotic measures adopted by school boards during the early 1950's came to be dropped voluntarily. For example, the Los Angeles Board of Education in 1957 removed its 1953 ban on the discussion of the United Nations as a controversial subject.

But even today the battle to preserve academic freedom continues. Some of the contemporary measures against controversial material in the schools would assume comic proportions if the implications and possible consequences were not so dangerous. In 1963 the California Superintendent of Public Instruction, upon discovering *The Dictionary of American Slang* in a number of school libraries, suggested that "a little bit of censorship" would be necessary to remove the book from the schools. The resultant tide of controversy put the reference book into the lucrative sales category throughout the state.[11] Also in 1963, the Board of Education of Harlem Township High School in Rockford, Illinois ordered the drama-speech teacher to stop production on the play, "Inherit the Wind," because of its controversial theme (concerning the trial of a biology teacher charged with the teaching of evolution in a Tennessee high school in 1925). In January of 1964 the California State Board of Education rejected a recommendation by Dr. Maxwell Rafferty, State Superintendent of Public Instruction, calling for some editing of the treatment of Darwinian evolution in textbooks.[12]

THE SOVIET SPUTNIK. The launching of the Sputnik by the Russians on October 4, 1957 came as a shock to our nation. However, while our government and the scientific, military, and industrial establishments managed to avoid serious criticism and attack for this Soviet achievement, an avalanche of new criticism fell upon our schools. Bestor and Rickover were among the first to lay the blame on American education. According to Bestor,

> We have wasted an appalling part of the time of our young people on trivialities. The Russians have had sense enough not to do so. That's why the first satellite bears the label "Made in Russia."[13]

Although any honest educator would see considerable room for improvement in American education, one wonders how Professor Bestor managed to blame our schools for the Soviet space lead and not give any credit whatsoever to American education for other notable societal achievements.

---

11 The *New York Times,* July 12, 1963, p. 27.
12 The *New York Times,* January 10, 1964, p. 18.
13 Arthur Bestor, "What Went Wrong With U.S. Schools," *U.S. News & World Report,* January 24, 1958, p. 69.

Ignoring the vocationalism of the Soviet schools, and holding that Russian education is superior to ours, Bestor and Rickover continued to bitterly condemn life-adjustment and vocational education in American schools. In the words of Rickover,

> Apart from the life-adjustment fallacy so prevalent among American educationists, our schools seem unable to concentrate on training young minds because of partiality for so-called "useful" knowledge.[14]

> Unfortunately, we are now harvesting the bitter fruit of an educational philosophy which has set its aims too low. Life-adjustment education merely aspires to adjust the child to life as it is.[15]

> It would be an immeasurable gain if we but stopped at once training *future* teachers of frivolities and concentrated on training teachers of solid subjects . . . .[16]

Rickover further recommended that college-bound students be educated in separate academic programs beginning with grade six or seven.[17] Rickover's concept of education is mind-training, and it is through the academic subjects that, according to Rickover, such mind-training is most apt to be developed.[18]

Another highly influential opponent of vocational education was the late Dr. A. Whitney Griswold, President of Yale University until 1963. President Griswold decried the offering of vocational programs and non-academic subjects in our high schools and colleges. He regarded such offerings contemptuously as "service station courses."[19] However, despite President Griswold's public pronouncements against vocational and service station programs, his own institution, Yale University, continued to offer a Certificate in Transportation for students who successfully completed a graduate-level curriculum at Yale's Bureau of Highway Traffic.

The Comprehensive High School Criticized and Defended

Both Bestor and Rickover severely criticized the American comprehensive high school and held that education in virtually any European nation was superior to ours. In comparing our school system with England's, Bestor observed:

> There is a world of difference between the systems, so far as developing the intellectual resources of the country are concerned. And Sputnik shows that the difference could well be a fatal one to this nation.[20]

---

[14] Hyman G. Rickover, *Education and Freedom* (New York: E. P. Dutton & Co., Inc., 1959), p. 24.
[15] *Ibid.*, p. 180.   [16] *Ibid.*, p. 217.
[17] *Ibid.*, pp. 127–128.   [18] *Ibid.*, p. 133.
[19] "An Interview With A. Whitney Griswold," *The University*, Santa Barbara, California: Center for the Study of Democratic Institutions, November, 1961, 29 pp.
[20] Bestor, *op. cit.*, p. 72.

In his influential report, *The American High School Today* (1959), Dr. James B. Conant focused his attention on the comprehensive high school—"a peculiarly American phenomenon."[21] While Conant offered many recommendations for improving the American high school, he concluded that the comprehensive high school should be maintained.

Nevertheless, Admiral Rickover persisted in advocating the elimination of the comprehensive high school and the establishment of a dual, European type of system of secondary education.

> Education of a kind that only the bright can successfully absorb costs no more—usually less—than bland life-adjustment training. Moreover, the parents of bright children pay school taxes exactly like everybody else. Therefore, failure of the public schools to set up separate secondary education cannot be justified on any sane and fair ground. We are the only advanced nation committed to comprehensive education. The Soviets are *in theory* committed to this concept, but in practice they have devised ways to circumvent it—they are too practical to waste their best minds.
>
> One cannot argue the issue of comprehensive schooling versus separate secondary education on a philosophical basis. But one can argue it on the basis whether the country really has a choice as between efficient education—that is separate schools above the elementary level—and pure "democratic" education which insists on the inefficient, time-wasting comprehensive school. In my opinion, we no longer have that choice. We must opt for efficiency.[22]

Despite Rickover's dogmatic pronouncements, College Board scores and college record comparisons between students from public comprehensive high schools and those from private college-preparatory institutions have tended to favor the former group over the latter.[23] Rickover, on the other hand, has offered no evidence to justify the elimination of the comprehensive high school. The values to be derived from the American comprehensive high school have been described by Conant as follows:

> By organizing our free schools on as comprehensive a basis as possible, we can continue to give our children an understanding of democracy. Religious tolerance, mutual respect between vocational groups, belief in the rights of the individual are among the virtues that the best of our high schools now foster. . . .
>
> What the great "Public Schools" of England accomplished for the future governing class of that nation in the nineteenth century the Ameri-

---

21 James Bryant Conant, *The American High School Today* (New York: McGraw-Hill Company, Inc., 1959), Foreword, p. ix.

22 Hyman G. Rickover, *American Education—A National Failure* (New York: E. P. Dutton & Co., Inc., 1963), p. 89.

23 Herbert L. Brown, Jr., "Are the Public Schools Doing Their Job?", in *The Great Debate* by C. Winfield Scott, Clyde M. Hill and Hobert W. Burns (Englewood Cliffs, N. J.: Prentice-Hall, Inc., 1959), pp. 21–22.

"The teacher is successful at the moment
when his student becomes original."
—MARK VAN DOREN

can high school is now attempting to accomplish for those who govern the United States, namely, all the people. Free schools where the future doctor, lawyer, professor, politician, banker, industrial executive, labor leader, and manual workers have studied and played together from the ages of 15 to 17 are a characteristic of large sections of the United States; they are an American invention. That such schools should be maintained and made even more democratic and comprehensive seems to me to be essential for the future of this republic.[24]

---

[24] James Bryant Conant, *Education and Liberty* (Cambridge, Mass.: Harvard University Press, 1953), p. 86.

RECENT EDUCATIONAL REFORMS IN EUROPE

The heightening of international rivalry between communism and capitalism produced a rash of American school critics who maintained that European and Soviet education are superior to ours. The field of comparative education was raised to a new status as people sought answers to the question: "How does American education compare with education in the U.S.S.R. . . . England . . . France . . . Europe?" Through an Exchange Agreement negotiated by the United States Department of State, an official United States education mission went to the U.S.S.R. in 1958 and, upon returning, described Soviet education as "a kind of grand passion."[25] A second official mission followed in 1959.[26]

While the reports of these two educational missions were objective and balanced, critics like Bestor and Rickover were flatly maintaining that Soviet and European educational systems were superior to ours. A serious and objective study of comparative educational systems leads one to realize, however, that the schools of different cultures and political ideologies cannot be compared on the same basis. A society that professes education for individual enlightenment should be expected to have schools that are somewhat different from a nation that sees the school as an instrument of national purpose only. Likewise, an educational system serving a society with a tradition of aristocracy will be quite different from the schools of a society that holds to the democratic ideal. Consequently, glib comparisons are apt to be misleading and erroneous.

In this section, it is not our intent to go into a detailed study of comparative educational systems. However, a brief review of recent educational reforms in Britain, the U.S.S.R., and some other European nations will illustrate that (1) educational problems are common to all nations, (2) no nation claims to have the best system of education or the final answer, (3) educational change and reform are common to all dynamic societies, and (4) if there is a trend among leading nations, it is toward improving educational opportunity, making education more functional, and regarding education as an important instrument of national goals.

Secondary Education in England

Children enter local primary schools at the age of five and continue until they reach eleven. At this point they go through a rigid selection

---

[25] Office of Education, *Soviet Commitment to Education*, Report of the First Official U.S. Educational Mission to the U.S.S.R. (Washington, D.C.: U.S. Department of Health, Education, and Welfare, 1959), p. 1.

[26] See Office of Education, *Soviet Education Programs* (Washington, D.C.: U.S. Department of Health, Education, and Welfare, 1960).

process known as the 11-plus examination. This examination includes
batteries of intelligence and achievement tests, the results of which
determine which segment of the tripartite secondary school system the
youngster will be eligible to attend. Those making the highest scores
are eligible to attend the local grammar school, which is an academic
or college-preparatory type of secondary school, or they may attend a
technical school. Approximately 20 per cent of the youth thus enter
the grammar school, while some three or four per cent are selected for
the technical school. Some 70 per cent of the youngsters fail to qualify
for the secondary grammar school. This group, with the exception of
those few who can afford to attend independent schools, enter the
modern school—a terminal secondary school they will leave at the
age of fifteen or sixteen. Consequently, the English secondary-school
system consists of the grammar school, the secondary modern school,
and the technical school. These institutions account for some 94 per
cent of the secondary school enrollment. The remaining six per cent
attend independent tuition schools. Dr. Robin Pedley, Director of the
University of Exeter Institute of Education, observes that even the best
British universities have a tradition of contact with particular independent preparatory schools, thereby ensuring special consideration for certain
applicants who do not possess outstanding academic ability.[27] Thus,
parents who can afford the high fees tend to choose the independent
preparatory schools for their youngsters.

Standards in the grammar schools are high. Upon completion of the
grammar school at the age of sixteen or seventeen, a vital examination
called the General Certificate of Education is taken. This examination
is conducted by external boards representing the universities. Only eight
of the original 20, or some 40 per cent of those selected for the grammar
schools manage to attain sufficiently high scores on the GCE to gain
entrance to the colleges and universities. While such high selectivity
may seem impressive, many British educators have been pointing to the
injustices imposed by the system. The findings of a governmental commission in 1959, known as the Crowther Report, pointed to the inac-
curacy of the rigid system of selecting pupils for grammar schools and
modern schools. Pedley describes these implications thus:

> The result of all this immensely honest effort by educational psychol-
> ogists, teachers, and administrators is this: that out of every twenty
> children picked for the grammar school, six or seven turn out to be un-
> suited to that type of education, and they keep out another six or seven
> of the remaining eighty sent to modern schools, who should have been
> admitted. The true picture may be worse, for it is reasonable to suppose

---

[27] Robin Pedley, *The Comprehensive School* (Middlesex, England: Penguin Books
Ltd., 1963), pp. 12–13.

that other modern school children, discouraged by rejection (as they see it), fail to respond there as they might have done had they been allowed to proceed to a grammar school. . . .

The Crowther Report found that twenty-two per cent of Army recruits to national service, and no fewer than twenty-nine per cent of R.A.F. recruits had had the wrong type of schooling. No observer could find such figures less than gravely disturbing. Is there not, he must ask, some satisfactory alternative which could dispense altogether with selection and segregation at eleven-plus?[28]

The Crowther Report also found that two out of five of the most able boys were leaving school by the age of 16.[29] While such critics of American education as Bestor and Rickover were arguing that high selectivity through national examinations and a dual system of secondary education would give our most able students the greatest educational opportunity, the British were reporting that such a system was failing to meet the needs of both talented and average youth. And while Bestor[30] and Rickover[31] were maintaining that we must emulate the educational practices of the British, many British educators were advocating just the opposite. A *New York Times* report describes the presidential address before the 1963 meeting of the British Association for the Advancement of Science.

After comparing educational systems on both sides of the Atlantic, a leading educator has declared British schools unscientific, obsolescent and of value only to a privileged few.

The criticism was made tonight by Sir Eric Ashby, a fellow of the Royal Society and a master of Clare College, Cambridge. . . .

"The Americans have an open door to education," Sir Eric said. "Anyone who has completed a high school course may claim admission to some university. . . ."

Sir Eric deplored British practices on "investment in man."

"By the age of 12," he said, "the door to full-time higher education is all but closed to 80 out of every 100 children. The remaining 20 are selected for specialized, privileged schooling which brings them to the gates of colleges and universities, but only 8 of the 20 get in."

. . . Sir Eric said British selection methods for higher education assumed that "our intellectual resources are limited by genetic factors."

He added: "We have abundant evidence that it is not genetics but inequalities in our society and inadequacies in our educational system which at present limit our investment in man. . . ."[32]

---

28 *Ibid.*, pp. 19–20.　　　　　29 *Ibid.*, p. 108.

30 Bestor, "What Went Wrong With U.S. Schools," *U.S. News & World Report*, January 24, 1958, pp. 72–73.

31 Rickover, *American Education—A National Failure* (New York: E. P. Dutton & Co., Inc., 1963), pp. 287–289.

32 John Hillaby, "British Schools Called Obsolete," *The New York Times*, August 29, 1963, p. 5.

Courtesy British Information Service

There are now more than 150 American-style comprehensive secondary schools in Britain. These views are of the Holland Park Comprehensive School in London, showing the main building and a class in Russian.

Courtesy British Information Service

On July 1, 1963 the London County Council announced its decision to eliminate the 11-plus examinations beginning with the 1964–65 school year. An important factor in bringing about this decision was research that showed "conclusively that a quarter of the children in the country who had failed the 11-plus merited places in grammar (academic secondary) school."[33] And once a youngster is denied admission to the grammar or academic secondary school, he cannot gain entrance to a college or university unless his parents can afford to send him to an independent preparatory school. A number of other districts in England have also chosen to eliminate the 11-plus examination. This leaves the matter of curriculum choice, whether college preparatory or terminal, up to the parents who, in turn, receive consultation and advice from the school authorities.

Another important aspect of educational reform in Britain is the comprehensive secondary school patterned after the American institution. Although the comprehensive schools are still relatively few in number, enrolling only some 11 per cent of the youth, they have been cropping up in different areas of the country. Studies have shown that a much higher proportion of youth continue their education when they are attending comprehensive schools rather than divided schools.[34,35] Moreover, a significantly greater proportion of comprehensive school students are attaining good scores on the GCE examination than under the segregated system.

> . . . whereas a system of separate types of secondary school normally produces around ten per cent of each age-group getting "good" GCE's after five years, comprehensive schools are normally achieving around fourteen per cent. This is a significant improvement. It bears out a simple thesis: that selection at eleven is premature and inaccurate . . . and that if one keeps open the door of full opportunity, many more children will pass through it.[36]

In announcing the elimination of the 11-plus examination, the London Council also indicated its intention to eliminate the dual system of grammar and modern schools in favor of comprehensive secondary schools.[37] An English educator describes the new commitment to the comprehensive secondary school thus:

> The arguments against our divided system of education mount higher day by day. Parents are no longer content to accept the verdict of mental tests at eleven as authoritative. . . .

---

[33] Lawrence Fellows, "London Dropping Test for Schools," The New York Times, July 2, 1963, p. 31.
[34] Edward Blishen (ed.), Education Today: The Existing Opportunities (London: British Broadcasting Corporation, 1963), p. 76.
[35] Pedley, op. cit., p. 107.   [36] Ibid., pp. 96–97.
[37] "To Kill the Terror," Newsweek, July 15, 1963, p. 52.

In examination results, comprehensive schools are already turning the tables on those who raised alarm about the threat to academic standards. Despite the serious handicaps imposed on them, these schools are beginning to suggest that it is the segregated system whose performance may be inferior. . . .

Looking further ahead, it is impossible to put any ceiling to future expansion. The process of education is self-perpetuating, and the whole record of history indicates that increased opportunity begets ever-increasing response.[38]

The tradition of separate schools for boys and girls is being challenged through the coeducational policies of about half of the comprehensive secondary schools. British proponents of the comprehensive secondary school cite the same advantages upon which the American comprehensive high school is based. In addition to keeping the doors open to more advanced education and improving educational holding power, it is claimed that the comprehensive school, by providing for the educational needs of youth from all walks of life, is in greater harmony with the ideals of a democratic society. It is maintained that under a dual, segregated system, students and teachers in the lower echelon school tend to feel inferior, and as a result their performance reflects this attitude. In the comprehensive school, all students and teachers can feel that they are members of a complete educational community.

However, there is no marked trend toward the comprehensive secondary school in Britain. The most significant effort in contemporary school reform is directed at eliminating the traditional 11-plus examination while postponing and broadening the criteria for academic selection. In this connection the government has appropriated unprecedented sums in recent years for the construction of new colleges and universities. Only eight out of every 100 Britons of college age have access to full-time higher education, while almost 40 out of every 100 Americans are enrolled in colleges and universities.[39]

Secondary Education in the U.S.S.R.

In December of 1958, at the urging of Premier Khrushchev, the Supreme Soviet enacted the school reform law. Aimed at developing closer ties between education and productive labor, the school reform law was titled "The Consolidation of Links Between School and Life and the Further Development of the Educational System of the U.S.S.R." The new law regards the main task of Soviet education as follows:

The principal task of the Soviet school should be the preparation of pupils for life, for socially useful work, a further improvement of the

---

[38] Pedley, op. cit., pp. 197–198.
[39] The New York Times, October 24, 1963, p. 1.

standard of general and technical education, the preparation of educated people with a good knowledge of the fundamentals of science, the bringing up of young people with the spirit of deep respect for the principles of socialist society.

The leading principle of education and training in the general secondary school should be a close linking of teaching and work.[40]

This new law puts ever greater emphasis on the utilitarian goals of a society undergoing rapid industrial and technological change. The Minister of Public Education of the Russian Federative Republic describes what is required of the Soviet school and the work-study emphasis in the new curriculum.

In process it must break down the barrier which all previous societies have maintained between mental and manual labor. It must bring the school closer to real life. It must inculcate a profound sense of the social and personal values of productive labor. . . .

The major point in which the new curriculum differs from the old is in its strong and repeated emphasis upon work study tie-up. Work training will have a prominent place in the course of study beginning with the very first grade.[41]

The 1958 school reform law greatly intensifies the work-training and experience programs for all secondary school students, including those who will be going on to higher education. Moreover, under the new program, priority for admission to colleges and universities is given to candidates who have a record of at least two years of successful employment in factories or on farms following completion of secondary school studies.

The basic unit of the Soviet educational structure is a universal eight-year comprehensive school called "general education-labor-polytechnical school." Children enter this school at the age of seven and complete the program at fifteen. They may then enter a three-year comprehensive type of general secondary labor-polytechnical school embracing grades 9 to 11 (ages 15, 16, and 17). Those who begin gainful employment upon completing the eight-year school may continue their education in evening (off-shift) general secondary schools, which include a three-year course of study covering grades 9 to 11. An alternative 11-year complete secondary school is also available in certain areas.

In summary, Soviet school organization provides for an eight-year comprehensive elementary-junior secondary school, followed by a three-year comprehensive secondary labor-polytechnical school or a three-year evening general secondary school, as well as an alternative 11-year

[40] E. I. Monoszon, "The General Secondary School in the U.S.S.R.," Scientific World, London, 4, No. 8, 1959, p. 3.
[41] Yevgeni Afanasenko, "The Soviet School System Reorganized," U.S.S.R. Illustrated Monthly, Vol. 37, No. 10, p. 46.

comprehensive school. Boarding schools along the pattern of the eight-year and eleven-year comprehensive schools are also maintained. Those completing the eight-year or eleven-year programs may enter gainful employment, or they may be eligible for further education in technicums or other specialized schools. University entrance may be gained through competitive examinations after completion of eleven years of schooling plus work experience.

The high degree of comprehensiveness of the Soviet school curriculum is shown in Tables 4–1 and 4–2. Note that Work Training is introduced in the third year (age 9) and that Fundamentals of Industrial Production is taken in the ninth and tenth grades (ages 15 and 16). Theoretical and Practical Vocational Training and Productive Work takes up six hours per week in grade 9 (age 15), twelve hours in grade 10 (age 16), and eighteen hours in grade 11 (age 17). These programs of productive and vocational training and experience are required of all students, including those who will later enter colleges and universities. Heavy emphasis is given to mathematics and science throughout the cur-

Table 4–1
Subjects and Lessons* Per Week
for Grades I through VIII
in an 11-Year Soviet School

Subject	Number of Lessons Per Week in Grades							
	I	II	III	IV	V	VI	VII	VIII
Russian Language	12	12	12	10	6			
						8	6	5
Russian Literature	–	–	–	–	2			
Mathematics	6	6	6	6	6	6	6	6
History, Constitution of the USSR	–	–	–	2	2	2	2	3
Natural History	–	–	–	3	–	–	–	–
Geography	–	–	–	–	2	2	2	2
Biology	–	–	–	–	2	2	3	2
Physics	–	–	–	–	–	2	3	3
Chemistry	–	–	–	–	–	–	2	2
Mechanical Drawing	–	–	–	–	–	–	1	1
Foreign Language	–	–	–	–	4	4	3	3
Drawing	1	1	1	1	1	1	–	–
Music and Singing	1	1	1	1	1	1	–	–
Physical Education	2	2	2	2	2	2	2	3
Manual Training	2	2	2	2	3	2	2	–
Work Training	–	–	2	2	2	–	–	3
Optional Subjects	–	–	–	–	2	–	–	1

*Each lesson is 45 minutes.
SOURCE: *U.S.S.R. Illustrated Monthly*, Vol. 37, No. 10, pp. 50–51.

riculum. All students are required to take the comprehensive program of studies. No ability grouping is practiced in the various grades, and classes are coeducational.

The great stress on modern science and mathematics, modern language, and practical work experience in Soviet schools is indicative of a present- and future-oriented curriculum, rather than one that is tradition bound. Although the proportion of students in the age groups attending secondary school and college in the Soviet Union far exceeds that of the Western European nations, it nevertheless remains below that of the United States.

Upon completion of the eleventh year of schooling, those desiring admission to the university take competitive examinations. However, under the 1958 school reform law, most university applicants are required to have completed a minimum of two years of gainful employment. Evening and correspondence courses are also offered in university level

Table 4–2

Subjects and Lessons* Per Week
for Grades IX through XI
in an 11-Year Soviet School

Subject	Number of Hours Per Week in Grades		
	IX	X	XI
Literature	3	3	3
Mathematics	4	4	4
History	3	4	3
Constitution of the USSR	–	–	1
Economic Geography	3	–	–
Physics	4	3	2
Astronomy	–	1	–
Chemistry	2	3	2
Biology	2	–	–
Mechanical Drawing	2	–	–
Foreign Language	3	3	2
Physical Education	2	2	1
Fundamentals of Industrial Production	2	1	–
Theoretical and Practical Vocational Training and Productive Work	6	12	18
Optional hours for sports, art studies, etc.	3	3	3

* Each lesson is 45 minutes.
SOURCE: U.S.S.R. Illustrated Monthly, Vol. 37, No. 10, pp. 52–53.

studies for those who are employed. Stipends are provided for virtually all full-time university students who maintain good grades.

The Soviet school reform law of 1958 appeared to be a reaction against the growing tendency of education in the U.S.S.R. to become a means of individual advancement at a time of shortage of productive labor.[42] Although the Soviets place great emphasis on maximizing educational opportunity, their educational program is designed clearly to serve the common good, the collectivist state—not the individual. American education, on the other hand, has given considerable emphasis to individual opportunity and development, although in recent years our schools have been increasingly influenced by nationalizing forces. Ironically, the competition with the Soviets has given impetus to these nationalizing influences in American education.

School Reform Elsewhere

We have seen how the United States and the U.S.S.R. embrace the comprehensive system for universal schooling of children and youth. In recent years, England has been experimenting with the comprehensive school as a replacement for the traditional dual or tripartite system of education. Virtually every European country has been undergoing some sort of school reform during the past decade. As people become more educated, they demand even greater educational opportunity for their children. Modern societies, in demanding an enlightened citizenry, turn to the schools for this goal.

Another nation that has been effecting a changeover from the traditional dual system of Europe to the American style of comprehensive school is Sweden. A democratic nation with one of the world's highest standards of living, Sweden began between 1950 and 1960 to experiment with the comprehensive school as a means of breaking down the old class divisions. As a result of generally favorable findings, the Swedish Parliament decided that a shift to the comprehensive school be effected on a voluntary, community basis.

> The major educational trend in Sweden has been a planned and controlled shift from the European-type dual system of schools, representing old class divisions, to the comprehensive, class-less public school, so characteristic of the United States. At the present time—that is, during the autumn semester of 1961—about one-half of the student population of compulsory school age is being taught in the comprehensive mode. . . .[43]

---

42 Nicholas De Witt, *Education and Professional Employment in the U.S.S.R.* (Washington, D.C.: National Science Foundation, 1961), p. 15.

43 Torsten Husén, "A Liberal Democracy Adopts the Comprehensive School System," *Phi Delta Kappan*, XLIII, No. 2, November, 1961, p. 86.

The new Swedish comprehensive school includes children aged seven to sixteen. Youngsters are not differentiated until the ninth grade (age 15), whereupon they follow a college preparatory program, a vocational curriculum, or a terminating general education.[44] The decision regarding the course of study now rests largely with the students and parents rather than with the school authorities. Public opinion studies have revealed that a majority of the Swedish people favor the comprehensive school.[45] Under the old dual system, about one half of the dropouts had I.Q.'s sufficiently high to complete the academic school. It is felt that the comprehensive school will effect a great reduction in this loss of talent.[46]

In France, under the school reform law of 1959, the traditional examination for entrance to the lycée at age 11 has been abolished in favor of a two-year observation cycle for those who have completed the primary school program. Under the old system, only one out of five youngsters succeeded in passing the examination for entrance to the lycée. Studies revealed that, under the old 11-year examination system, "selection has been based much more on social and economic factors than on intellectual merit."[47] Under the new program, all normal students have access to the various courses of study. It is felt that these reforms will improve educational opportunity, enabling a much higher proportion of youth to gain advanced education and serve the scientific and technological needs of a modern nation.[48]

The baccalauréat, a final examination upon completion of secondary schooling, serves as the key to university studies. Despite recent modifications in the baccalauréat to include technical achievement, only a minority succeed in passing this examination. Although there has been a marked increase in the population of college age during the early 1960's, coupled with a growing demand for higher education, the French government has failed to expand college and university facilities to meet these needs. As a result the 1963–64 academic year, marked by student riots, was called a catastrophe, while the 1964–65 academic year was predicted to be a disaster.[49]

During the 1960's, virtually every developed nation in the world has been faced with the sharp rise in the number of youths of high-school and college age, accompanied by an unparalleled demand for opening the doors of secondary and higher education to an increasing proportion

---

[44] *Ibid.*, p. 89.   [45] *Ibid.*, p. 89.
[46] *Ibid.*, p. 91.
[47] Roger Gal, "The Development of Education in France—1945 to 1961," *Phi Delta Kappan*, XLIII, No. 2, November, 1961, p. 61.
[48] *Ibid.*, p. 62.
[49] The *New York Times*, January 16, 1964, p. 79.

of the population. The most massive efforts to meet these expanding
needs have been made in the United States, followed by the U.S.S.R.
In 1964 almost 40 per cent of our nation's 18- to 21-year-olds were
enrolled in colleges and universities, while European nations enrolled
less than 10 per cent of this age group in higher education.[50]

RECENT ASSESSMENTS, INNOVATIONS, AND
NATIONALIZING INFLUENCES IN THE UNITED STATES

The 1950's and early 1960's have witnessed significant attempts in
certain European nations to improve educational opportunity. The comprehensive high school, a product of American education, not only has a
counterpart in the Soviet 8–year and 11–year schools, but is also being
introduced in Sweden and England. The avowed purposes of developing
a program of comprehensive schooling are to improve the holding power
of the schools through increased educational opportunity and to reduce
class barriers. No nation comes close to matching the United States in
the proportion of the age groups attending high school and college.

Unlike the centralized educational systems of European nations, American education is decentralized. Nevertheless, in recent years there seems
to be a trend toward national goals in American education through the
influence of nongovernmental and governmental agencies and new
federal legislation.

Conant's Report on the American High School

As discussed earlier in this chapter, Conant's report on the American
high school, published in 1959, supported the comprehensive high school
and recommended improvements that would not necessitate radical
change.[51]

Conant's recommendations included minimum general education requirements for all, further academic course requirements for the academically talented, improved counseling, increased emphasis on English
composition, diversified programs for marketable skills, the organization
of the high school into larger units of enrollment, and the grouping of
students according to ability levels.

His recommendations on curriculum were concerned mainly with setting quantitative offerings and requirements rather than making qualitative changes. Although very few of his recommendations were formulated
from research data, Conant exerted considerable influence on the schools.

---

[50] The *New York Times*, January 16, 1964, p. 78.
[51] James Bryant Conant, *The American High School Today* (New York: McGraw-
Hill Company, Inc., 1959).

His recommendations and their implications are discussed in some detail in later chapters.

The Private Foundations

From 1951 to 1964, the Ford Foundation's Fund for the Advancement of Education allocated $86.4 million dollars for projects in educational and instructional television. The Fund has also supported a wide variety of educational innovations, including the Advanced Placement Program, which enables high-school students to pursue college level studies, demonstrations with large group instruction and individualized study, the development of more functional and flexible educational facilities for increased efficiency in the utilization of learning resources, and the application of technology to instruction. In the fields of elementary and secondary education, most of the Fund's efforts have been directed toward solving the teacher shortage and reducing educational expenditures through the use of instructional technology and more efficient school management practices.

The Carnegie Corporation, in addition to supporting Conant's study of the American high school, commissioned him to undertake two further studies on American education: an investigation of public education in our major metropolitan areas[52] and a study of teacher education in the United States.[53] Both of these works provoked wide discussion among educators and lay people. The Carnegie Corporation in recent years has also supported projects on programmed learning and autoinstructional technology.

The influence of these two great foundations should not be underestimated. The men governing these agencies are not neutral in their educational views and are not without influence on the national scene. The Carnegie-supported work of Conant, for example, has already exerted considerable influence on the high school curriculum and has stirred up intensive debate and public confusion concerning the education and the competency of our teachers.

The National Defense Education Act of 1958

Less than a year after the Soviets launched the first man-made earth satellite, President Eisenhower signed into law the National Defense Education Act of 1958. The purpose of the act is "to provide substantial assistance in various forms to individuals, and to States and their subdivisions, in order to insure trained manpower of sufficient quality and

---

[52] James Bryant Conant, *Slums and Suburbs* (New York: McGraw-Hill Company, Inc., 1961).

[53] James Bryant Conant, *The Education of American Teachers* (New York: McGraw-Hill Company, Inc., 1963).

quantity to meet the national defense needs of the United States."
Extensions of the act were signed by President Kennedy in 1961 and
President Johnson in 1963.

Provisions of the act cover elementary, secondary, and higher education. During the first five years of the National Defense Education Act,
federal allocations included $181 million for improving instruction in
science, mathematics, and modern foreign languages in public elementary
and secondary schools; over $20 million for new educational media;
$330 million for loans to superior college students who are preparing to
become elementary or secondary school teachers or who are majoring
in science, mathematics, or modern foreign languages; $80 million dollars
for graduate fellowships; almost $43 million for the training of techni-
cians in area vocational programs; and over $5 million to state educa-
tional agencies for the improvement of statistical services. These sums do
not include matching funds by states and local educational agencies
undre certain titles of the act.

The National Defense Education Act is clearly designed to serve the
national need at a time of international emergency. It can be criticized
for favoring certain specific areas of the curriculum, along with the
teachers who work in these areas. Although science, mathematics, and
modern foreign languages are supported under N.D.E.A., and while
vocational education is aided under other federal legislation, the fields
of English language arts and the social studies have received relatively
little support. Surely the communication skills and the social studies are
vital to the perpetuation and improvement of a democratic society.

Many educators feel that what is needed is comprehensive federal
legislation providing general support for public education, rather than
a wide variety of disjointed aid programs, each of which is earmarked
for specific purposes. Otherwise the emergency and defense tenor of our
national legislation on education tends to resemble the strategy of nondemocratic societies in manipulating their human resources.

The National Science Foundation

The National Science Foundation Act of 1950 created in the executive
branch of the Federal Government an agency to improve research and
education in the sciences and mathematics. In addition to supporting
basic scientific research, N.S.F. funds are allocated for improving the
competencies of teachers of science and mathematics through institutes
on university campuses, improving the curriculum in secondary school
science and mathematics, identifying and developing talented high
school and college students, and providing fellowships for graduate
students. During the ten-year period from 1952 to 1962, N.S.F. allocations
for educational programs have increased phenomenally from $1.5 million

to $84.5 million.[54] Federal appropriations to N.S.F. were sharply increased following the orbiting of the Soviet Sputnik and the passage of the National Defense Education Act.

N.S.F. has catalyzed a veritable revolution for curriculum and instruction in science and mathematics through its support of the School Mathematics Study Group (SMSG), the Physical Science Study Committee (PSSC), and the Biological Science Curriculum Study (BSCS). These committees have enlisted the efforts of outstanding scholars and educators in updating the subject-matter content and methods of instruction. Instead of traditional rote learning, the new emphasis is in stimulating students to understand the structure of a discipline and to encounter the subject in a vein similar to that of the scientist. These committees have also employed the media of television and the motion picture for high-school instruction in the sciences. N.S.F. has sponsored special summer programs bringing talented students to university campuses where they may study under accomplished scientists.

N.S.F., like N.D.E.A., is indicative of a rapidly growing trend toward shaping education to fit our national needs. Since the operations of N.S.F. are independent of the United States Office of Education, there is a lack of effective coordination between these two federal agencies as well as among federal, state, and local units.[55]

External Testing Programs

In recent years national testing activities by two nongovernmental agencies, the National Merit Scholarship Program and the College Entrance Examination Board, have exerted considerable influence on the high schools. The National Merit Scholarship Program was established in 1955 through grants from the Ford Foundation, the Carnegie Corporation, and other private sources. This agency provides college scholarships for promising high school students.

Of the 596,241 high school contestants in 1963, only 11,128 were named finalists, and a mere 1,528 survived to become Merit Scholars.[56] This meant that the odds against a contestant being named a Merit Scholar were almost 400:1. Obviously, the number of applicants in proportion to the available awards is so disproportionate that many promising and deserving candidates are denied Merit Scholarships. An average

[54] See Lloyd J. Mendelson, "The National Science Foundation," Chapter 3 in *Nationalizing Influences on Secondary Education* by Roald F. Campbell and Robert A. Bunnell (eds.) (Chicago: Midwest Administration Center, University of Chicago, February 1963), pp. 25–40.

[55] See Campbell and Bunnell, *op. cit.*, pp. 124–128.

[56] National Merit Scholarship Corporation, Annual Report 1963, *The Quest for Intellectual Excellence*, Evanston, Illinois, 1964.

of only one Merit Scholar is named for every ten participating high schools. Despite these discouraging odds, many school administrators feel that refusal to participate would result in severe criticism, particularly in communities where many high-school students are college-bound.[57] There are also indications that schools are unofficially rated, particularly by the press, according to these awards, and that some schools are attempting to coach students for these examinations.[58] Unless the number of awards can be markedly increased in proportion to the number of applicants, the amount of time and effort expended on the National Merit Scholarship Program is subject to serious question. The possibility of federal support for a national scholarship program has been under consideration in recent years, but such a federal program raises the knotty problem of curriculum control.

Another influential nongovernmental agency of external testing is the College Entrance Examination Board. Established at Columbia University in 1901, the CEEB contracts Educational Testing Service to administer the Scholastic Aptitude Test and various achievement tests each year to high school seniors who are applying for admission to one of the more than 400 member colleges and universities. The CEEB also administers the Advanced Placement Program, which enables outstanding high-school students to pursue college level studies and take examinations for advanced placement or credit upon entering college.

New Pressures and Demands

The late 1950's and early 1960's witnessed a huge crescendo of criticisms leveled at our public schools. The realization that the United States was being challenged for global leadership, along with the dramatic performances of the Soviets in space technology, resulted in hysterical accusations directed at our educational system. Our concern with education for individual enlightenment began to be overshadowed by demands that our schools become instruments for meeting the scientific and technological emergencies of our nation. Admiral Rickover's book, *Education and Freedom,* published in 1959, suggested the more appropriate title, "Education for Triumph in World War III."

Even the National Education Association began to give signs of yielding to these forces. Where the N.E.A. literature of the early 1950's pointed to the responsibility of the school to serve the interests and needs of all youth and to foster mental health as well as rational thinking,[59] it did

---

[57] Lorraine La Vigne, "The National Merit Scholarship Program," Chapter 4 in Campbell and Bunnell, *op. cit.,* p. 49.

[58] *Ibid.,* p. 53.

[59] See Educational Policies Commission, *Education for ALL American Youth—A Further Look* (Washington, D.C.: National Education Association, 1952).

not regard the proper role of the school as a form of pressure and demand upon the individual, which is advocated in recent literature.

> It is appropriate in our society to consider education as a demand upon the individual rather than as a privilege or as therapy. Progress and happiness can both be served, it is conceded, when adults get behind the child and push.[60]

In one decade our educational system is under pressure to constrict its role and function, and in another it is forced by society to expand its ends and means. The school cannot divorce itself from society, and therefore every strength and every weakness of society is to be found in the schools. A recent study of a district in Manhattan, conducted by the staff of Cornell University Medical College, found that 80 per cent of the residents exhibited some mental disturbance, and 23.4 per cent of all residents showed "marked, severe, and incapacitating symptoms."[61] Can the schools in such an area choose to ignore mental health, while dealing only with basic education and training in science and technology? Can such schools choose to ignore the problems that youngsters bring with them from their homes and neighborhoods? Can the youngsters shut these problems from their minds the moment they enter the school each day? While the schools cannot, alone, cure the ills of society, neither can they keep themselves in ignorance of these ills.

THE CHURCH, THE STATE, AND THE SCHOOL

In an earlier chapter we stated that separation of church and state is one of the principles of American democracy. This principle derives from the First Amendment to the Constitution: "Congress shall make no law respecting an establishment of religion, or prohibiting the free exercise thereof. . . ." This principle ensures religious freedom as well as protection from singular church domination in a pluralistic society. During the colonial period, most of the colonies prohibited dissent from the established religion. The First Amendment, enacted in 1791, clearly separated religion from the concerns of government.

Educationally, the result of this principle of separation of church and state is the secular public school, which serves all the children of all the people. But the secular school has been subjected to unrelenting pressures that have threatened to erode the principle of separation. These pressures reached a critical point during the 1950's and 1960's and were manifested in the demand for religious instruction in the curriculum of

---

[60] National Education Association, *Schools for the Sixties* (New York: McGraw-Hill Company, Inc., 1963), p. 11.
[61] The *New York Times*, March 30, 1962, p. 1.

the public school, and the demand for the right to secure public funds for the support of nonpublic and church-supported schools.

Secularism and Godlessness

The cry against the godlessness of our public schools was to be heard louder than ever during the late 1940's and throughout the 1950's. One of the most powerful voices venting this accusation was that of the late Canon Bernard Iddings Bell of the Episcopalian Church. Canon Bell accused the public schools, not the homes or the churches, of producing a "nation of religious illiterates."[62] In obvious contradiction, it was Bell who also argued that "one of the chief hindrances to decent education in America today is our overloading of the schools by placing on their shoulders responsibilities which in other times and other countries have as a matter of course been assumed by the home."[63]

Some church groups defended the secularism of the public school in a pluralistic culture and deplored the charge of godlessness that was leveled at public education. For example, the following is taken from an official policy statement adopted in 1957 by the General Assembly of the Presbyterian Church concerning its position on public education:

> Memories of unpleasant experiences of ecclesiastical domination of education in Europe . . . were among the many forces that prompted the body politic to draw the blueprint for a school system compatible with a pluralistic culture. Our public school system is the result. The same constitutional guarantee protecting the church from any tyranny that would stifle freedom of belief and worship was inseparably mixed into the very mortar of this structure and also insured every child and every parent against the imposition of sectarian dogma in the classroom.[64]

The statement went on to caution against unwarranted criticisms of the public schools in matters of religion.

> It is doubtful whether the charge of "godlessness," sometimes hurled at the public school, is understood in its full implication by those who voice dissatisfaction, using this term. . . .
> We object therefore to unwarranted criticism heaped upon the schools without adequate understanding of the position that the schools hold in the structure of society. . . .
> In short, we must never betray the genius of the public schools, nor yet be mesmerized by the fatal assumption that the church can delegate

[62] Bernard Iddings Bell, "Know How vs. Know Why," *Life*, Vol. 29, No. 16, October 16, 1950, p. 97.

[63] Bernard Iddings Bell, *Crisis in Education* (New York: McGraw-Hill Company, Inc., 1949), p. 78.

[64] General Assembly of the Presbyterian Church in the United States of America, *The Church and the Public Schools* (Philadelphia: Board of Christian Education, June 1957), p. 6.

its responsibility to any institution in order to make up for the prevalence of religious illiteracy.[65]

Religious Instruction and Prayer in the Public School

Many statements on the aims of American public education include the promotion of spiritual values.[66] Such statements fail to come to grips with the problem of how spiritual values are to be promoted in the secular schools of a pluralistic society in which church and state are held separate.

Until the historic Supreme Court decisions of 1962 and 1963, prohibiting prayer and bible-reading in the public schools, such religious activity was not only permitted in many schools but was actually required in a number of states. Pennsylvania enacted a law in 1913 requiring bible-reading in all public schools. By 1963 religious exercises and bible-reading were permitted in most of our states, while 13 states required bible-reading by law.[67]

In June of 1962, the United States Supreme Court held that an official school prayer drafted by the New York State Board of Regents constituted an establishment of religion in violation of the First Amendment to the Constitution. This nondenominational prayer had been formulated by the state educational agency and recommended for recital by teachers and students at the start of each school day. The implications of this decision extended beyond New York State in that the promotion of any religious ceremony by a governmental agency for the public schools was regarded as a breach of separation of church and state. The majority opinion by Justice Black included a quotation from James Madison, author of the First Amendment.

> It is proper to take alarm at the first experiment on our liberties. . . . Who does not see that the same authority which can establish Christianity, in exclusion of all other religions, may establish with the same ease any particular sect of Christians, in exclusion of all other sects?[68]

Although students were not compelled to take part in the New York prayer, the court held that "it is no part of the business of government to compose official prayers for any group of American people to recite as part of a religious program carried on by government."[69] At the time of this 1962 Supreme Court decision approximately half of the public school systems in the United States had similar religious ceremonies.[70]

Despite the great importance of this decision, the question of required

---

[65] *Ibid.*, pp. 11–13.
[66] Educational Policies Commission, *op. cit.*, p. 16.
[67] The *New York Times*, June 18, 1963, p. 27.
[68] The *New York Times*, June 26, 1962, p. 16.
[69] *Ibid.*, p. 16. [70] *Ibid.*, p. 1.

bible-reading or recitation of the Lord's Prayer in the public schools was yet to be settled. Almost exactly one year following the New York prayer decision, in June of 1963, the United States Supreme Court ruled that no state or locality may require the reading of bible verses or the Lord's Prayer in the public schools.[71] At the time of this decision 38 states were allowing religious exercises, including bible-reading, in the public schools, while 13 states were requiring bible-reading by law.[72]

The 1963 decision was written by an 8–1 majority, with the sole dissenting vote calling for further hearings rather than challenging the Supreme Court's interpretation of the Constitution. This decision originated in a suit challenging a Pennsylvania state law requiring the reading of "at least 10 verses from the Holy Bible, without comment, at the opening of each public school on each school day," and another case involving a similar ruling by the Baltimore Board of Education. Although the Pennsylvania statute and Baltimore rule permitted students to be excused at their parents' request, the Supreme Court held that such laws and rulings were required of a compulsory school system and thereby had a coercive effect.

It appeared from this ruling that even the voluntary undertaking of such prayers or bible-readings by a teacher would be illegal, inasmuch as such activity would be taking place in a compulsory school system and through an agent of government. Consequently, the 1963 decision of the United States Supreme Court must be regarded as momentous and as having a far-reaching effect in upholding the secular school and in maintaining the strict neutrality of government in matters of religion. This does not mean, however, that studying *about* religion is prohibited or unlawful in the public schools. The Educational Policies Commission of the N.E.A. has held for some time that the public schools can teach objectively *about* religion without promoting a particular sect or creed.[73] However, very few elementary and secondary school teachers are sufficiently versed in the field of comparative religion to teach *about* religion competently and impartially.

RELEASED TIME FOR RELIGIOUS INSTRUCTION. The legality of voluntary released time for religious education, conducted away from public school buildings by the various denominations and without academic credit, was upheld by the United States Supreme Court in 1952 in a 6–3 decision.[74] The minority opinion, however, expressed concern that students not participating in released-time religious instruction were com-

---

71 The *New York Times,* June 18, 1963, p. 1.
72 *Ibid.,* p. 27.
73 Educational Policies Commission, *Moral and Spiritual Values in the Public Schools* (Washington, D.C.: National Education Association, 1951).
74 Zorach vs. Clauson, 343 (U.S.) 306 (1952).

pelled to remain in school; consequently, the public schools were serving "as the instrument for securing attendance at denominational classes."[75] An earlier Supreme Court decision (1948) held 7–1 that religious education in released-time classes could not be conducted on public school property and could not be required or advocated by school authorities.[76]

Today, although 48 of the 50 states have legal provisions for released time for religious instruction, it is estimated that only approximately 30 per cent of our public school systems use released time, and even within these systems many students remain in school rather than take released time for religious instruction.[77] The usual practice of released time is to allow one hour per week near the end of a school day for students who have parental consent to leave the school premises for religious instruction under church auspices. Some Protestant, Jewish, and Unitarian groups have opposed such released time for religious instruction. In his dissenting opinion in the 1952 Supreme Court case, Justice Jackson had this to say about released time:

> If public education were taking so much of the pupils' time as to injure the public or the students' welfare by encroaching upon their religious opportunity, simply shortening everyone's school day would facilitate voluntary and optional attendance at Church classes. But that suggestion is rejected upon the ground that if they are made free many students would not go to the Church. . . .
> . . . schooling is more or less suspended during the "released time" so that nonreligious attendants will not forge ahead of the churchgoing absentees. But it serves as a temporary jail for a pupil who will not go to Church. It takes more subtlety of mind than I possess to deny that this is government constraint in support of religion.[78]

Public Support of Parochial and Private Schools

Approximately one out of every ten youths is attending nonpublic secondary schools, and some 80 per cent of the nonpublic enrollment is in Roman Catholic schools. The Roman Catholic Church has been the leading proponent of the use of public funds for the general support of parochial schools. Catholic leaders have argued that it is unjust for Catholic citizens to be required by law to pay taxes for the support of public schools while, at the same time, they are supporting Catholic parochial schools for the education of their own children.[79] On the other hand, it is argued that the individual is free to choose between

---

[75] Dissenting opinion by Justice Frankfurter, joined by similar opinions by Justices Black and Jackson.

[76] Illinois ex rel. McCallum vs. Board of Education, 333 (U.S.) 203 (1948).

[77] Paul Blanshard, *Religion and the Schools* (Boston: Beacon Press, 1963), p. 176.

[78] Zorach vs. Clauson, 343 (U.S.) 306 (1952).

[79] Msgr. William E. McManus, "The Administration and Financing of Catholic Schools," *Phi Delta Kappan*, Vol. XLV, No. 3, December, 1963, p. 133.

public or private (including parochial) education for his children,[80] but that such choice does not exempt one from taxation nor entitle the private or parochial school to public funds.[81]

A number of church groups, while upholding the right of the individual to choose between public and nonpublic education, have expressed vigorous opposition to the use of public funds for independent and parochial schools. An example of this opposition is the official statement of the General Assembly of the Presbyterian Church.

> There is very real danger that as parochial schools become strong the public school system may be reduced to a second-rate institution. . . .
> It is our conviction that parochial education accentuates differences, causing social cleavage. . . .
> . . . As costs (for education) continue to mount, pressures from parochial-school advocates to obtain tax money will increase through political means . . . by trying to prove that the parochial school is really a part of "community" education. We consider this implication as a prime step in violation of constitutional guarantees against Government support of sectarianism. . . .
> We therefore are unalterably opposed to the support of independent or parochial schools through the use of public funds, since such use virtually favors establishment of religion by government. We know full well that parochial schools, avowedly sectarian, are not amenable to the control of the community from which they seek support. There is a widespread and aggressive movement that asserts that the parochial school is really a part of public education. This contention confuses the public and is contrary to the fact that parochial schools and public schools are erected upon entirely different foundations.[82]

In a 1947 Supreme Court decision, Justice Black's opinion for the majority offered this statement regarding the relationship between the principle of separation of church and state, and the use of taxes for supporting religious activities or institutions:

> No tax in any amount, large or small, can be levied to support any religious activities or institutions, whatever they may be called, or whatever form they may adopt to teach or practice religion. Neither a state nor the Federal Government can, openly or secretly, participate in the affairs of any religious organizations or groups and vice versa. In the words of Jefferson, the clause against establishment of religion by law was intended to erect "a wall of separation between Church and State."[83]

Although the language of the above decision clearly prohibits the use of tax funds for religious activities and institutions, certain sectarian

---

[80] Pierce (Governor of Oregon) vs. Society of Sisters of the Holy Names of Jesus and Mary, 268 (U.S.) 510 (1925).

[81] Everson vs. Board of Education, 330 (U.S.) 1 (1947).

[82] General Assembly of the Presbyterian Church in the United States of America, *The Church and the Public Schools* (Philadelphia: Board of Christian Education, June 1957), pp. 19–20.

[83] Everson vs. Board of Education, 330 (U.S.) 1 (1947).

groups, notably the Roman Catholic Church, continue to demand public funds for the general support of parochial schools. This continuing controversy has served to block a number of federal bills for public education.

INDIRECT AID TO PAROCHIAL AND PRIVATE SCHOOLS. It has been maintained that while the use of tax funds for the direct support of parochial schools is contrary to the constitutional separation of church and state, such public funds can be applied legally to programs designed to benefit the child rather than the parochial school. In other words, under this child-benefit theory, it would be legal to provide public funds for aiding children in parochial and private schools through various services, provided that such programs do not constitute direct aid to these church and private schools.

This doctrine was tested in the United States Supreme Court in 1930 in a case involving a Louisiana law that provided for the free distribution of textbooks by the state to children in public and private schools. The Supreme Court affirmed the child-benefit doctrine on the grounds that the books were distributed for the benefit of the children and the state, and not for the benefit of the private and parochial schools.[84]

If public funds may be used to provide textbooks for students attending private and parochial schools on the grounds of child benefit, what about the legality of other auxiliary services to students in nonpublic schools? In 1947 a case involving the use of public funds for the payment of bus transportation for pupils in Roman Catholic schools in New Jersey was decided by the Supreme Court. In this case the Court held that such transportation payments are legal in that they constitute benefits of public welfare legislation. However, in this very same decision, delivered for the majority by Justice Black, is found the strongest language upholding the principle of church-state separation deriving from the First Amendment.

> The First Amendment has erected a wall between church and state. That wall must be kept high and impregnable. We could not approve the slightest breach. New Jersey has not breached it here.[85]

A dissenting opinion in the New Jersey bus case, written by Justice Jackson, questions the language of the 5–4 majority decision as discordant and fallacious.

> . . . the undertones of the opinion, advocating complete and uncompromising separation of Church from State, seem utterly discordant with its conclusions yielding support to their commingling in educational matters. The case which irresistibly comes to mind as to the most fitting

---

84 Cochran vs. Louisiana State Board of Education, 281 (U.S.) 510 (1930).
85 Everson vs. Board of Education, 330 (U.S.) 1 (1947).

precedent is that of Julia who, according to Byron's reports, "whispering 'I will ne'er consent,'—consented."

. . . It is of no importance in this situation whether the beneficiary of this expenditure of tax-raised funds is primarily the parochial school and incidentally the pupil, or whether the aid is directly bestowed on the pupil with indirect benefits to the school. The state cannot maintain a Church and it can no more tax its citizens to furnish free carriage to those who attend a Church. The prohibition against establishment of religion cannot be circumvented by a subsidy, bonus or reimbursement of expense to individuals for receiving religious instruction and indoctrinaton. . . .

It seems to me that the basic fallacy in the Court's reasoning, which accounts for its failure to apply the principles it avows, is in ignoring the essentially religious test by which beneficiaries are selected.[86]

The opinion of the dissenters in this case observed that the principle of church-state separation established by our forefathers was "set forth in absolute terms, and its strength is its rigidity." This dissenting opinion went on to interpret the intent of the separation principle.

It was intended not only to keep the states' hands out of religion, but to keep religion's hands off the state, and, above all, to keep bitter religious controversy out of public life by denying to every denomination any advantage from getting control of public policy or the public purse.[87]

The dissenting opinion also maintained that the allowance of tax monies for transportation to and from parochial schools did not differ from the use of tax funds for "tuitions, teachers' salaries, buildings, equipment and necessary materials."

Although the 1947 Supreme Court ruling held that the use of public funds for the transportation of students to and from parochial schools is not in violation of the United States Constitution, by 1964 the courts of seven states had ruled that this practice violates their own constitutions and is therefore unlawful.[88] Textbook and other auxiliary grants for pupils attending parochial schools have similarly been regarded by several states as illegal support of sectarian education, thereby holding the child-benefit and child-welfare theories invalid. Nevertheless, at the end of 1963, 16 states were allocating public funds for pupil transportation to and from parochial schools. To many educators and legal authorities the line of demarcation between auxiliary services and direct educational provisions is fuzzy. They fear that the terms child benefit and child welfare may be construed to include the total fabric of parochial education, the result being the ultimate erosion of the principle of separation between church and state.

---

[86] *Ibid.*   [87] *Ibid.*
[88] The seven states are Alaska, Iowa, Missouri, Oklahoma, New Mexico, Washington, and Wisconsin.

PUBLIC SUPPORT OF NONPUBLIC HIGHER EDUCATION. Although the principle of church-state separation, derived from the First Amendment, applies to higher education as well as to elementary and secondary education, church and private colleges have been successful in gaining public funds, particularly in recent years. In its famous report of 1948, the President's Commission on Higher Education held that federal funds for the general support of higher education be granted only to public institutions.

> Federal funds for the general support of current educational activities and for general capital outlay purposes should be appropriated for use only in institutions under public control . . . any diversion by government of public funds to the general support of nonpublicly controlled educational institutions tends to deny the acceptance of the fundamental responsibility and to weaken the program of public education.[89]

Through such programs as the National Science Foundation and the National Defense Education Act, federal funds have been allocated for research at both public and nonpublic institutions of higher education. Also under these programs, loans and scholarships are granted to students attending private and church-related colleges, as well as public institutions of higher education. It is maintained that these loans and scholarships do not violate the principle of church-state separation since they are designed for the benefit of students rather than for the colleges and universities.

But recent federal programs for the construction of college buildings on public and nonpublic campuses clearly appear to benefit the recipient institutions. Since these federal funds for building construction are allocated to church-supported colleges, they appear to constitute a violation of the principle of church-state separation. Since 1959 many private and church-supported colleges have received federal loans for the construction of student housing facilities. The Higher Education Facilities Act, signed into law in December of 1963, provides $835 millions in grants and $360 millions in low-interest loans over a three-year period for the construction of college buildings and facilities. This $1.2 billion measure includes grants and loans to public, private, and church-related colleges and universities. The only limitations on this new federal program are that the funds must be used for instructional facilities in science, mathematics, engineering, and modern foreign languages; no funds are to be used for religious facilities, sports arenas, or auditoriums that would involve admission charges.

Despite these limitations, it is easy to see that recipient church-

---

[89] President's Commission on Higher Education, *Higher Education for American Democracy*, Vol. V, *Financing Higher Education* (New York: Harper & Row, Publishers, Inc., 1948), p. 57.

affiliated colleges would enjoy an improved financial position and would be better able to use their own funds more freely in constructing religious facilities. The legality of church-state commingling at the college level has not been tested in the United States Supreme Court.

TOWARD BETTER EDUCATIONAL OPPORTUNITY

The great challenge of the 1960's is to reduce educational inequalities and to improve educational opportunities. Equality of educational opportunity is a vital principle for a society that holds to the democratic ideal. Good government rests upon an enlightened citizenry. Although the twentieth century has witnessed the universalization of secondary education and the opening of college doors to an unparalleled proportion of young men and women, there remain some serious inequities based on social, economic, geographic, and racial factors.

The equalization and improvement of educational opportunity at all levels of schooling by counteracting geographic, socioeconomic, and racial inequities, is a great national problem. While we in the United States have done more than any other society in keeping open the doors of our schools and colleges, the task remains largely unfinished. In the words of the United States Supreme Court, "In these days it is doubtful that any child may reasonably be expected to succeed in life if he is denied the opportunity of an education."[90]

Geographic and Socioeconomic Influences

Expenditures per pupil in the public schools vary tremendously by geographic area. Our wealthiest states spend from two to three times as much money annually per pupil as our poorest states. During 1963–64 the maximum salary for a teacher with a Master's degree was over $10,000 in New York City and only $5,680 in Birmingham, Alabama.[91] Minimum salary levels reflected similar disparities. Even within the same state there are frequently great differences in per pupil expenditure and teachers' salaries.

At the level of higher education, there is a paradox in that some of our wealthier states, particularly those in the northeast, are failing to expend sufficient funds for public colleges and universities. For example, in 1964 the per capita expenditure for state-supported colleges and universities amounted to only $5.85 in Massachusetts, while California spent $42.72.[92] Although New York ranks with California in wealth and population, New York's per capita expenditure for state institutions of

---

[90] Brown vs. Board of Education, 347 (U.S.) 483 (1954).
[91] National Education Association, "Increases in Scheduled Salaries in Large Districts," *NEA Research Bulletin*, Vol. 41, No. 3, October, 1963, pp. 80–81.
[92] The *New York Times*, January 16, 1964, p. 78.

higher education is among the lowest of the 50 states. Because of the relatively low expenditures for public higher education in the northeastern states, there has been a trend since the end of World War II for high school graduates from New York, New Jersey, Pennsylvania, Connecticut, and Massachusetts to seek entrance to the large state universities of the midwest. This has caused some of the "Big-Ten" universities to devise enrollment quotas for these five northeastern states.[93]

Geographic factors were clearly evident in the results of the Armed Forces Qualification Test during the Korean conflict. Where 16.4 per cent of all selective service registrants failed this test, in one state the rate of failure was only one per cent while in another state it was 56 per cent.[94] Improved state equalization aid and comprehensive federal support for education can reduce these great disparities.

Likewise, social and economic handicaps severely limit the educational potential of a large portion of our population. While our nation is depicted as enjoying the highest standard of living in the world, a recent report tells us that from 40 to 50 million Americans are ill-housed, ill-clad, and ill-nourished.[95] Obviously, youngsters from poverty-stricken families are badly handicapped before they even start school. The school cannot succeed where society has failed. The lower socioeconomic groups are caught in a self-perpetuating cycle of limited realization of potential talents as a result of economic and cultural deprivation. In our large metropolitan areas the problem of equalizing and improving educational opportunity is compounded by the tendency of many teachers to avoid the slum schools and seek positions in the "nice" suburban school districts.

Because of cultural, economic, and educational limitations, the lower socioeconomic groups tend to be underrepresented in colleges and universities in comparison to the higher socioeconomic groups. In comparing aspirations to college attendance among youngsters from high and low socioeconomic strata, we find that such aspirations toward higher education tend to be correlated more with social status than with ability level.

> A majority of sons and daughters of top (social) status expect to go to college even when they are of lowest ability; whereas for children of the bottom (social) status, at no level of ability including the highest do a majority plan college.[96]

[93] The New York Times, January 18, 1964, p. 25.
[94] Benjamin S. Bloom, "The 1955 Normative Study of the Tests of General Educational Development," The School Review, March 1956, p. 122.
[95] Michael Harrington, The Other America (New York: The Macmillan Company, 1963).
[96] Burton C. Clark, Educating the Expert Society (San Francisco: Chandler Publishing Company, 1962), p. 63.

It has been demonstrated in recent years that, when the community and schools make a concerted effort, the educational aspiration level of our lower socioeconomic groups can be raised through intensive programs of guidance, remedial instruction, and cultural enrichment. Special programs with youngsters in the slum areas of New York City have yielded some remarkable gains in aspiration and achievement. In 1956 the Demonstration Guidance Project was launched in a junior high school in Harlem. Of the 1,400 students in the school, only 14 per cent were Caucasian. It was estimated that at least half of the children's families were on welfare assistance and many of these families lived in SRO (Single Room Occupancy) apartments. Half of the entire student body was selected to participate in this program on the basis of showing some glimmer, however slight, of academic potential. The program followed these students through high school and assigned them to smaller classes, remedial instruction, special guidance, and cultural enrichment through visits to museums, college campuses, and attendance at concerts. As a result of the program, reading scores increased from 5.4 in grade 7 (1 year and 4 months below normal) to 9.7 in grade 9 (3 months above normal). In comparison with previous groups, the high-school graduation rate increased by 39 per cent, while the rate of college entrance rose 250 per cent. Although the normal pattern is for verbal I.Q. to decline with age among underprivileged youngsters, the scores for this group rose from a median of 93 in grade 8 to a score of 102 in grade 11. Some of these students have won scholarships to Ivy League colleges.[97]

The success of New York's Demonstration Guidance Program led the City to establish a much broader-scaled program in 1959 known as the Higher Horizons Project. While following the measures for educational and cultural improvement employed in the Guidance Program, Higher Horizons was applied to virtually all youngsters, regardless of ability, in 13 junior high schools and 52 elementary schools serving several of the city's worst slum areas. The Higher Horizons Project has since expanded to include the high schools located in these sections of the community. Preliminary results of Higher Horizons have indicated similarly remarkable gains to those following the Guidance Program.

Higher Horizons has sought to improve the self-esteem of youngsters in order to raise motivation and achievement. Parent workshops are provided and joint school-parent-pupil activities of a cultural nature are sponsored as a form of parent and community education. It has been demonstrated that the raising of self-esteem and the exposure to new educational and cultural vistas can change pipe dreams to aspirations and, eventually, to the realistic pursuit of higher goals. Most slum-reared

---

[97] Office of Education, *Programs for the Educationally Disadvantaged* (Washington, D.C.: U.S. Department of Health, Education, and Welfare, 1963), pp. 45–46.

Photo by Daniel Tanner

"How many students . . . were rendered callous to ideas,
and how many lost the impetus to learn because of
the way in which learning was experienced by them?"
—John Dewey

youngsters, lacking self-esteem, lose themselves to disillusionment and defeatism when the adult world gives them no encouragement or opportunity to pursue realistic goals. In the words of one youngster from the Harlem slums,

> Man, when I was a kid, I used to have dreams that maybe I'd be a scientist and discover all kinds of things. But they were only dreams; when I woke up, there wasn't anything real about them, there couldn't be anything real about them. I've never seen a scientist; I don't understand anything about them; there aren't any scientists or anybody else who has a big job on my block so I haven't got the least idea of what they're like. It's hard to even picture them mentally. These things are so far above us they aren't real. They're like a cloud that looks solid until you grab into it and find it falls apart in your hands.[98]

The St. Louis schools have reported spectacular results in achievement gains among culturally deprived Negro children when teachers are inspired, when cooperation is developed between parents and school, and when teaching by I.Q. is eliminated. This program encompassed 16,000 children in 23 elementary schools located in the city's worst Negro slum area. While these youngsters were far below national achievement norms at the start of the project, they were brought up to the national norms within three years. High-school follow-up revealed that where previously only 7 per cent of these students were classified as above-average achievers, now 20.7 per cent were so classified. And the rate of below-average achievers in high school was reduced from 47.1 per cent to 21.3 per cent.[99]

If children from impoverished homes are to have equal educational opportunity, special efforts for remedial instruction, guidance, and educational enrichment must be made. Otherwise, by being handicapped before they even start school, the learning gap tends to compound itself with each passing school year.

Youth Unemployment

The rate of youth unemployment throughout 1963 averaged close to three times the national rate for all workers. Unemployment among Negro youths is even more severe. In his study of schools in our metropolitan areas, Conant describes some of the conditions in predominantly Negro slums.

> A total of 59 per cent of the male youth between the ages of sixteen and twenty-one were out of school and unemployed. They were roaming the streets. Of the boys who graduated from high school 48 per cent

[98] Richard Hammer, "Report from a Spanish Harlem 'Fortress'," The New York Times Magazine, January 5, 1964, pp. 34, 37.

[99] John A. Hannah (Chairman), United States Commission on Civil Rights, Report 2: Education (Washington, D.C.: Government Printing Office, 1961), pp. 125–127.

were unemployed in contrast to 63 per cent of the boys who had dropped out of school. In short, two thirds of the male dropouts did not have jobs and about half of the high school graduates did not have jobs. In such a situation, the pupil may ask, "Why bother to stay in school when graduation for half the boys opens onto a dead-end street?"[100]

In describing the situation as social dynamite, Conant recommended realistic high school programs of vocational education that led to regular full-time employment upon graduation.[101] Unfortunately, our communities and schools have tended to insulate themselves from these pervading educational needs.

> . . . the community and its schools are organized to a great extent not alone to pass on traditional wisdom and traditional values, but to protect tradition itself. . . . Formal education, while a product of relatively recent times, in many respects has resembled the types of social organizations which we identify with more traditional societies. When vocational education is viewed in this context it becomes increasingly apparent why greater effort has not as yet been forthcoming concerning the preparation of youth for the world of work.[102]

---

[100] James Bryant Conant, *Slums and Suburbs,* (New York: McGraw-Hill Company, Inc., 1961), pp. 33–34.

[101] *Ibid.,* pp. 2, 44.

[102] Wilbur B. Brookover and Sigmund Nostow, "A Sociological Analysis of Vocational Education in the United States," in *Education for a Changing World of Work,* Appendix III, Report of the Panel of Consultants on Vocational Education (Washington, D.C.: Office of Education, U.S. Department of Health, Education, and Welfare, 1963), p. 26.

"Beyond the knowledge of future work,
the student needs an experience in actual work."
    —REPORT OF THE HARVARD COMMITTEE

Courtesy Northwestern University

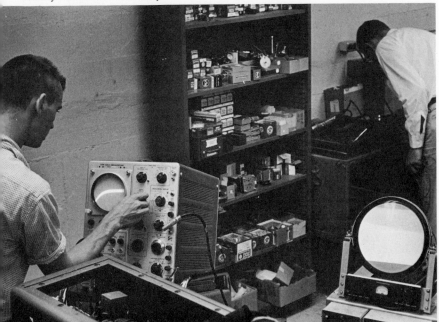

> In actuality, vocational education as it has developed in the United States has become more a reflecting of "appropriate" training for working-class children than a manner of meeting their subsequent vocational needs.[103]

In December of 1963 President Johnson signed two major bills on vocational education. One bill provides federal funds for the construction of vocational schools and financial assistance for youths enrolled in work-study programs. The other bill extends vocational retraining for unemployed youths and adults. These two measures are designed to come to grips with the unemployment problems of the 1960's.

Racial Desegregation

In the light of world opinion, one of the greatest paradoxes and hypocrisies of American life is racial segregation. Until 1954 racial segregation was maintained in the schools of thirteen southern states and in the schools of a number of northern communities on the basis that separate but equal education was perfectly legal. The unanimous decision of the United States Supreme Court on May 17, 1954, delivered by Chief Justice Warren, completely shattered the separate but equal doctrine by declaring that it was in clear violation of the Fourteenth Amendment, which prohibits states from denying to any person equal protection of the laws.

> We conclude that in the field of public education the doctrine of "separate but equal" has no place. Separate educational facilities are inherently unequal. Therefore we hold that the plaintiffs and others similarly situated for whom the actions have been brought are, by reason of the segregation complained of, deprived of the equal protection of the laws guaranteed by the Fourteenth Amendment.[104]

Regarding education as "perhaps the most important function of state and local governments," the Supreme Court pointed to the detrimental social and psychological effects on children who are segregated because of race.

> To separate them from others of similar age and qualifications solely because of their race generates a feeling of inferiority as to their status in the community that may affect their hearts and minds in a way unlikely ever to be undone. . . .[105]

As a result of this decision state legislatures and local school boards were directed to end segregation "with all deliberate speed." Some states and communities have been making notable progress toward compliance with the Supreme Court's ruling, while in other areas, particularly in

---

[103] *Ibid.*, p. 31.
[104] Brown vs. Board of Education, 347 (U.S.) 483 (1954).
[105] *Ibid.*

the deep South, every conceivable tactic for avoiding and delaying the issue has been employed. Although a number of southern states have attempted to avoid desegregation by enacting special statutes and constitutional amendments, the federal courts have consistently held such maneuvers unconstitutional.

An example of the strategy taken to uphold states' rights in the educational domain is the provision of public funds in the form of tuition grants to parents of children attending private schools, along with tax allowances for the maintenance of private schooling. The State of Virginia passed legislation in 1959 giving local authorities the power to suspend compulsory education, to provide tuition grants to parents of children attending private schools, to allow taxpayers to deduct from real and personal property taxes any contributions to private schools, to provide transportation at state expense for children enrolled in private schools, and to make appropriations to public schools on a month-to-month basis—thereby permitting the shutting down of public schools at any time.[106] In June of 1959, Prince Edward County in southern Virginia suspended its public school operations by failing to appropriate funds. A private institution called the Prince Edward School Foundation was established and soon enrolled most of the white students who had previously constituted 48 per cent of Prince Edward's public school population. Beginning in 1960–61 the county gave tuition grants to parents of children in attendance at the private school, allowed tax credits for school contributions, and provided funds to parents for the transportation of their children to and from the private school. Most of the 1,700 Negro youngsters, who had constituted 52 per cent of the total public school enrollment, were left without any provisions for formal education.[107] In May of 1964 a unanimous 9–0 decision of the United States Supreme Court ordered the reopening of the public schools of Prince Edward County. In delivering the opinion of the Court, Justice Black cited the principle of "equal protection of the laws," guaranteed by the Fourteenth Amendment.[108]

The Fourteenth Amendment provides that "No State shall make or enforce any law which shall abridge the privileges or immunities of citizens of the United States . . . nor deny to any person within its jurisdiction the equal protection of the laws."

On July 2, 1964 President Johnson signed into law the Civil Rights Act of 1964. This law authorizes the witholding of funds for federally supported programs in which racial discrimination persists, and gives the Attorney General power to initiate suits or to intervene on behalf

---

[106] Hannah, *op. cit.*, pp. 91–92.
[107] *Ibid.*, p. 91.
[108] The *New York Times,* May 26, 1964, p. 26.

of aggrieved persons on matters of school segregation and discrimination.

The problem of racial segregation is not confined to the schools of the South; it manifests itself in the cities of the North, where Negroes and Puerto Ricans have settled in huge ghettos. The concentration of Negro populations in the slum areas of our large northern cities results in neighborhood schools that are attended almost entirely by Negro children and youth. In New York, Chicago, Philadelphia, and some of our other major northern cities, the nonwhite population of the entire school system approximates 50 per cent. For example, a head count in the Chicago public schools during the fall of 1963 revealed that the nonwhite enrollment was 49.1 per cent.[109] Middle-class white families have abandoned our congested and blighted cities and have moved to the suburbs where home ownership, new schools, and cleaner air compensate for the pressures of commuting. But the out-migration of middle-class white families leaves the cities with a high proportion of nonwhite youngsters from the lower socioeconomic stratum.

Racial segregation in the schools of the South had explicit legal sanction until the United States Supreme Court decision of 1954. Therefore, such segregation by local and state law was termed *de jure*. On the other hand, racial segregation in the schools of the North came about largely because of community housing restrictions and the concentration of lower socioeconomic groups, particularly Negroes, in slum neighborhoods and high-rise slum-clearance projects. Consequently, such segregation in the North, being without explicit legal sanction, is called *de facto* segregation.

In recent years the demand for ending *de facto* segregation in the schools of our northern cities has been receiving increasing attention. In his study of our slum and suburban schools, Conant takes the position that such separation does not necessarily constitute educational inequality.

> In short, if one group of children is separated from another group because of the neighborhood in which they live, the fact of this separation is, of and by itself, no evidence of an inequality in education.[110]

However, Conant's position appears to be at odds with that of the Supreme Court, which declared that "separate educational facilities are inherently unequal." Moreover, if racially segregated schools are harmful to Negro children in the South, why should they not be equally harmful in the North?

Should the school board and school administrator be concerned with the consequences of segregated housing? While it is difficult to imagine

---

[109] *Chicago Daily News,* October 23, 1963.
[110] Conant, *op. cit.,* p. 28.

how school authorities could manage to avoid the educational consequences of segregated housing, Conant takes this position:

> To my mind, the city school superintendent is right who said he was in the education business and should not become involved in attempts to correct the consequences of voluntary segregated housing.[111]

Nonetheless, in studying the case of neighborhood school segregation in New Rochelle, New York, a federal court ruled against the school board and gave it less than three months to submit to the court a plan for desegregation. Since the New Rochelle case involved the school board's deliberate maintenance of a racially segregated school through the gerrymandering of neighborhood boundaries, the question of the legality of *de facto* segregated schools in the North has not been settled. Nevertheless, in the New Rochelle case, the federal court declared that "it is of no moment whether the segregation is labeled by the defendant as *de jure* or *de facto*, as long as the board, by its conduct, is responsible for its maintenance."[112] The court also stated that "the neighborhood school policy certainly is not sacrosanct."[113]

While gerrymandering, or the rezoning of an attendance district to conform to segregated housing patterns, has been employed as a means of concentrating Negro youngsters in certain schools, such rezoning can also be used as a means of desegregating the schools. Likewise, the selection of new school sites can be made by school boards for the purpose of promoting either segregation or integration. If designed for the promotion of segregation, gerrymandering of the attendance zone and the selection of school sites to conform to housing patterns are in violation of the Fourteenth Amendment.

Los Angeles, New York, Philadelphia, and other cities have recently adopted an open-enrollment policy permitting nonwhites to transfer voluntarily from schools that are predominantly nonwhite to those that are mostly white, where sufficient room is available. As we have mentioned, some cities have attempted to rezone and recombine certain neighborhood schools as a means of integration.

While the schools alone cannot correct the ills of society, neither can they ignore them. Voluntary segregated housing is created by socioeconomic forces. This condition in our northern cities is further magnified through high-rise slum-clearance projects that serve to further concentrate the Negro population. The city fathers who plan such projects are compelled by economic considerations to pack the greatest number of people onto the cheapest and smallest parcel of real estate possible. The

---

[111] *Ibid.*, p. 30.
[112] The *New York Times*, January 25, 1961, p. 24.
[113] Taylor vs. Board of Education of New Rochelle, 195 (S.D.N.Y.) 1961.

task of socioeconomic reconstruction in our society is staggering. But it must be done.

The law of the land holds segregation illegal and embraces the democratic ideal of providing all men equal rights and opportunities. One of the most important places to strive toward this ideal is in the schools, where future generations can learn to work together to build a better life for all.

SUMMARY

Criticisms of our public schools were rampant at mid-twentieth century. Tax conservationists were calling for reduced educational expenditures. They were attracted to the essentialist position which advocated curriculum retrenchment. At the same time, the schools were preparing for an unprecedented increase in enrollment as a result of the population boom. Construction of school buildings and facilities, halted during World War II, had now acquired new urgency.

At the same time, world tensions and ideological conflicts gave birth to infringements on academic freedom. A series of dramatic Soviet feats in space during the late 1950's kindled new attacks on American public education. Most of these attacks were led by the essentialists. Strangely, our schools bore the brunt of these attacks while little criticism was leveled at our leadership in government, science, military, and industry. Leading essentialists, ignoring the heavy emphasis on vocationalism in the Soviet schools, advocated that we would do well to emulate certain aspects of Russian and European education. The comprehensive high school, a distinctly American institution, was criticized and defended. While the comprehensive high school survived, new schemes for ability grouping and massive standardized testing programs were adopted by our secondary schools. The new emphasis was on our talented youth.

Federal legislation was passed to support the schools in special areas of the curriculum: mathematics, science, and modern foreign languages. The schools were recognized as instruments for serving the national need. However, legislation for comprehensive federal support of education failed to pass.

During the 1960's, as some of the international crises abated, our interest began to turn to the domestic problems of youth unemployment and racial segregation. Historic decisions by the United States Supreme Court awakened the democratic conscience of the nation by mandating that our schools be open to all children and youth, regardless of race or creed. Other Supreme Court decisions on school prayer and bible reading upheld the secular school and the principle of church-state separation.

While the teacher loyalty oath became commonplace, the principle of academic freedom was eventually reaffirmed. Without freedom to teach, there could be no freedom to learn.

In recent years, increased attention has been given to reducing high-school dropouts and youth unemployment, and improving educational opportunity. The schools were being called upon to better serve the culturally and economically disadvantaged in our society. Whether our schools can meet this task will depend, to no small extent, on whether all institutions of society share this commitment.

PROBLEMS FOR STUDY AND DISCUSSION

1. Sputnik I (1957) triggered a new wave of attacks on American public education. How do you account for the fact that many critics blamed our present-day schools for the space lag while disregarding the responsibility and competency of our scientific, military, and governmental leadership in dealing with this lag?

2. Do you agree or disagree with the following statement by Robert M. Hutchins on the relationship between a nation and its educational system? Why?

> The question most often put to me is: "What is wrong with our educational system?" The answer to this question is "Nothing. . . ."
> The answer to the question asked me may, however, be given in somewhat more general terms. There is never anything wrong with the educational system of a country. What is wrong is the country. The educational system that any country has will be the system that country wants. [Robert M. Hutchins, *Education for Freedom* (Baton Rouge: Louisiana State University Press, 1943), p. 48.]

3. How would you define academic freedom? In view of the following quotation, what limits, if any, would you apply to freedom of teaching and learning in the secondary school? In the college?

> If, in attempting to withstand the onslaughts of communism, we restrain the human mind and deny the Western tradition of freedom of thought, we shall have gone over to the enemy. We shall have abandoned that for which we claim to be fighting, and we shall have lost the support of genuinely freedom-loving peoples everywhere. [Gordon C. Lee, *Education in Modern America* (New York: Holt, Rinehart & Winston, Inc., 1960), pp. 583–84.]

4. Do you agree with Rickover that our nation should adopt a dual, European system of secondary education in place of our comprehensive high schools? Why or why not?

5. How do you explain the heavy emphasis given to socially useful work in the curriculum of Soviet secondary schools—even for academically talented

youths who will be entering the universities? Do you think that a similar program would be desirable for American youth? Why or why not?

6. Do you think our Federal Government is justified in subsidizing such areas of the curriculum as science, mathematics, modern foreign languages, and vocational education, while neglecting the social studies and English language arts? Why or why not?

7. What are the historical and legal bases for secularism in our public schools?

8. If public funds may be used to provide textbooks and transportation for students attending parochial schools, can public funds be used for the general support of church schools? Why or why not? Some of the states have held the child benefit and child welfare theories as invalid. In these states it is illegal to use public funds for providing textbooks and transportation for students in parochial schools. On what grounds are such auxiliary grants denied?

9. While public funds may be granted for the construction of instructional facilities at private and church-affiliated colleges and universities, such public monies are held illegal for the construction of nonpublic elementary and secondary schools. Do you believe that there is justification for this distinction? Why or why not?

10. New York City's Superintendent of Schools, Calvin F. Gross, has been quoted as saying that "we have to do a lot more for some children just to give them the same chance to learn." How do you interpret this statement in terms of the role of the school and the teacher?

11. What is the significance of the following quotation?

> We conclude that in the field of public education the doctrine of "separate but equal" has no place. Separate educational facilities are inherently unequal. [Brown vs. Board of Education, 347 (U.S.) 483 (1954).]

SELECTED REFERENCES

Bell, Bernard Iddings. *Crisis in Education.* New York: McGraw-Hill Company, Inc., 1949.

Bestor, Arthur. *The Restoration of Learning.* New York: Alfred A. Knopf, Inc., 1955.

Blanshard, Paul. *Religion and the Schools.* Boston: Beacon Press, 1963.

Blishen, Edward (ed.) *Education Today: The Existing Opportunities.* London: British Broadcasting Corporation, 1963.

Butts, R. Freeman. *A Cultural History of Western Education,* 2nd ed. New York: McGraw-Hill Company, Inc., 1955, Chs. 15, 16.

———. *The American Tradition in Religion and Education.* Boston: Beacon Press, 1950.

Callahan, Raymond E. *Education and the Cult of Efficiency.* Chicago: The University of Chicago Press, 1962.

Campbell, Roald F. and Robert A. Bunnell (eds.) *Nationalizing Influences on Secondary Education.* Chicago: Midwest Administration Center, The University of Chicago, 1963.

Conant, James Bryant. *Education and Liberty.* Cambridge, Mass.: Harvard University Press, 1953.

———. *Slums and Suburbs.* New York: McGraw-Hill Company, Inc., 1961.

———. *The American High School Today.* New York: McGraw-Hill Company, Inc., 1959.

Cremin, Lawrence A. *The Transformation of the School.* New York: Alfred A. Knopf, Inc., 1961.

De Witt, Nicholas. *Education and Professional Employment in the U.S.S.R.* Washington, D.C.: National Science Foundation, 1961.

Fellman, David (ed.) *The Supreme Court and Education.* New York: Columbia University Press, 1960.

Hannah, John A. (Chairman), United States Commission on Civil Rights. Report 2: *Education.* Washington, D.C.: Government Printing Office, 1961.

King, Edmund J. *Other Schools And Ours.* New York: Holt, Rinehart and Winston, Inc., 1958.

Kneller, George F. (ed.) *Foundations of Education.* New York: John Wiley and Sons, Inc., 1963, Chs. 7, 8, 19.

Lee, Gordon C. *Education in Modern America.* New York: Holt, Rinehart and Winston, Inc., 1957, Chs. 22, 25, 26, 27.

National Education Association. *Schools for the Sixties.* New York: McGraw-Hill Company, Inc., 1963.

Office of Education. *Programs for the Educationally Disadvantaged.* Washington, D.C.: U.S. Department of Health, Education, and Welfare, 1963.

Pedley, Robin. *The Comprehensive School.* Middlesex, England: Penguin Books, Ltd., 1963.

Rickover, Hyman G. *American Education—A National Failure.* New York: E. P. Dutton & Co., Inc., 1963.

———. *Education and Freedom.* New York: E. P. Dutton & Co., Inc., 1959.

Thayer, V. T. *The Role of the School in American Society.* New York: Dodd, Mead & Company, 1960, Chs. 5, 16, 18, 19, 20, 21, 22, 23.

Whyte, William H., Jr. *The Organization Man.* New York: Simon and Schuster, Inc., 1956, Chs. 7 and 8.

CHAPTER 5
Democracy and Education for Enlightenment

B ELIEVING THAT OUR ENDS OR GOALS of secondary education must be contiguous with our means, we find that our methodology must, in turn, be consistent with the cherished ideals of a democratic society.

Thus, we are led to an educational program designed to foster in each individual the optimal power of free and independent thinking. Such a program is dedicated to the dignity and worth of the individual and the realization of man as a social being. Science has shown us that even our most eminent fellowmen have exploited only a minute fraction of their intellectual and motivational potential. The educational system of a democratic society must enable each person to develop and utilize as much of his potential as possible, thereby building an enlightened citizenry and a vigorous democracy.

PROGRESS THROUGH THE METHOD OF INTELLIGENCE

When we analyze our contemporary civilization and view it in historic perspective, we find that the method of intelligence is the taproot of our modern stage of civilization. Moreover, the method of intelligence is the key to the survival and enrichment of our species.

A democratic society stakes its welfare on its faith in this method and the capacity of each member of the society to think critically. We frequently fail to appreciate the newness of this concept. Today's public schools are responsible to all of the children of all of the people, whereas only one out of ten youths were being served in the secondary schools of this nation only a half century ago. Where do we go from here? The answer seems to lie in the educative task of our schools and our total society.

We frequently fail to realize that our abiding faith in the potential of the common man is a revolutionary concept in human experience. Furthermore, we often take for granted that man should and must gauge his thoughts and actions according to the method of intelligence. We can really appreciate how far we have progressed in this light when we realize that only a short while ago in the course of human experience human slavery was common, the right to vote was denied to our women and limited to property owners, the insane were treated as criminals, suspected criminals were tortured into confession and then tortured for their crimes. It was not so very long ago that child labor was common under conditions of appalling exploitation and degradation.

The Schools and the Open Mind

Schools must be places where minds are open to the testing of new ideas. But minds cannot be open without respect for the opinions of others, and without a willingness to share and test these new ideas. Democracy requires open channels of communication, and the school is a place where these channels can be opened and kept open. We tend to close our minds to new ideas when we are insecure or fearful that these ideas will threaten or disrupt the equilibrium of our established notions and biases. But progress is not made in a state of equilibrium or under conditions of restrictive thought. Man's interdependence does not mean conformity. With an open mind we can learn from one another.

> This cannot be an easy life. We shall have a rugged time of it to keep our minds open and to keep them deep, to keep our sense of beauty and our ability to make it, and our ability to see it in places remote and strange and unfamiliar; we shall have a rugged time of it, all of us, in keeping these gardens in our villages, in keeping open the manifold, intricate, casual paths, to keep these flourishing in a great, open, windy world; but this, as I see it, is the condition of man; and in this condition we can help, because we can love one another.[1]

THE PRINCIPLES OF AMERICAN DEMOCRACY

Many opponents of democratic methods in the schools have chosen to confuse democratic principles with laissez-faire conditions. But the principles of democracy are positive, not neutral. What are these principles? How do they apply to school and society?

CULTURAL HETEROGENEITY, INTERDEPENDENCE, AND ASSIMILATION. From two to eight million immigrants have entered our shores each decade since 1840. The great task of assimilating this diversity into the continuity of democracy was thrust upon the schools. No other society

---

[1] J. Robert Oppenheimer, "Prospects in the Arts and Sciences," in *Man's Right to Knowledge* (New York: Columbia University Press, 1955), p. 115.

or school system in the history of mankind has been charged with such a task. Even today, Americanization classes are being conducted in school systems with sizable groups of immigrant children. And, especially today, we are faced with the problems and challenges that call for the assimilation of the Negro and other minority groups in our schools and communities.

Although our nation has pretty well succeeded in the great task of Americanization, we continue to find ourselves plagued by problems of cultural assimilation. In our northern cities, we see youngsters segregated in schools according to the socioeconomic status of the neighborhood. A school located in a slum neighborhood will draw its student body from the low socioeconomic strata, while a school located in a wealthy neighborhood will draw its student body from the upper socioeconomic strata. With the vast development of our mushrooming uppermiddle and upper-class suburbias, we find similar segregating forces at work in our communities and schools.

The principle of cultural interdependence and assimilation in a democracy does not mean the denial of individuality for the sake of conformity. A democratic society is dependent upon diversity for its very existence, and such diversity must become part of the lifeblood of a free society. Nevertheless, cultural assimilation is vital to the attainment of equality of opportunity. And the interdependence of man is essential to the common good.

SOCIAL MOBILITY. One of the important principles of American democracy is social mobility, as contrasted with Old World delineations by social position according to lineage and economic station. We have already pointed to some of the apparent disparities and contradictions in American society, but such stratifications are not inherent in our system. Therefore, our society and its schools must be committed to the principle of providing each citizen with the opportunity of becoming all that he is capable of being. To deny this is to deny one of the abiding principles of democracy.

Through free public education, our nation rests its faith on the potential of human intelligence. And through our system of free public education, each individual has a chance to fulfill his ultimate capacities. In the words of the Declaration of Independence, "We hold these truths to be self-evident, that all men are created equal, that they are endowed by their Creator with certain unalienable rights, that among these are Life, Liberty and the pursuit of Happiness." And it is in this connection that we strive for equality of educational opportunity, equality before the law, and equality of voice in political determination.

It is indeed unfortunate that some individuals have chosen to take issue with this principle so aptly issued in the Declaration, by distorting equality into mediocrity and conformity. In American democracy, equality refers to access or opportunity. Inherent in this principle is the conception of man as an individual, differing from his fellowman in motivations and capacities, and therefore free to excel and reach to his highest aspirations and capabilities. Democracy cherishes individuality, but holds no distinctions regarding individual worth.

A democracy must be dedicated against stratification by cultural and economic determination. And so we find ourselves committed to slum clearance, elimination of poverty, fair employment practices, and so forth.

Social mobility is, of course, closely linked to economic opportunity. And economic opportunity is, to a great extent, dependent upon our next principle—educational accessibility.

EDUCATIONAL ACCESSIBILITY AND EDUCABILITY OF THE PEOPLE. America's vast system of publicly supported and publicly controlled education is financed by general taxation, is free of tuition, and is open to all regardless of social or economic position. So important is the principle of educational accessibility to American democracy that free universal education has been made available through the high school level in virtually every state. Today, almost nine out of every ten youths from 14 to 17 years of age are enrolled in secondary school. In 1900, only one out of ten was enrolled. Educational opportunity has even been extended to include the college level through publicly supported community and state institutions of higher education. Today, almost 40 per cent of the college age group is enrolled in higher education. Higher education in the decade of the 1960's is more readily accessible than secondary education was during the first two decades of the century. Nevertheless, many inequities continue to challenge us. Accessibility to higher education, and even to secondary education, is still dependent upon the ability to meet considerable financial demands. Many promising students are still unable to complete high school or to continue their education beyond high school because of socioeconomic problems. Even today, of our high-school graduates in the top third in ability, some 40 per cent of the boys and more than half of the girls do not go on to college.

The principle of educational accessibility also extends to matters of school integration. The historic decision of the United States Supreme Court on May 17, 1954 shattered the separate but equal doctrine and held racial segregation to be illegal in public education. Desegregation in the schools is one of the great challenges of our time.

The principle of educational accessibility and educability of the people is an expression of faith in the perfectibility of man and in man's capacity for individual and social improvement.

GOVERNMENT BY CONSENT OF THE GOVERNED. In a democracy each man has the right to a voice in his own destiny. Self-government is essential to man's sense of dignity and worth. Democracy abhors special privilege. Each man is treated with equality before the law. There is no tolerance for any doctrine of fixed caste, class, or slave system. The people are the masters of the state, not its instruments.

All decisions in a democracy are derived through common counsel. Decisions are never final and immutable, but are always open to reappraisal and change. These decisions are formulated and acted upon by rational process. Differences of opinion are not only tolerated, but encouraged. Resolution of conflict is by rational and peaceful means.

Although the principle of majority rule is important in a democracy, it is of no greater importance than the principle of minority protection. There is no room for tyranny. The law provides equal protection for all men just as the law, itself, is derived from the people for the purpose of serving them.

MAXIMUM INDIVIDUAL AND ACADEMIC FREEDOM—COMPATIBLE WITH THE GENERAL WELFARE. Freedom of thought and expression is vital to a democratic society and its institutions of education. Although the principle of *academic freedom* has long been recognized as one of the fundamental pillars of our democracy, the midcentury period of loyalty oaths and investigations has driven many to timidity and caution.

The continuity of democracy depends upon intellectual freedom and diversity; yet our society must determine when such freedom is incompatible with the general welfare. This is one of the vital controversies of our time. How can we maintain a free and dynamic society if we are afraid to deal with unpopular ideas and controversial issues? And when do such ideas and issues constitute a present danger to the general welfare?

Although we have rule by the will of the majority, the rights of each individual are respected. And reciprocally, individual freedom cannot exist without responsibility to the group. This is the equilibrium of democracy.

The principle of individual and academic freedom recognizes that human progress is dependent upon human reason. A dynamic society must always be discontent with the *status quo*. It must always be open to new ideas if it is to progress. The quest for knowledge and the experimental attitude are necessary conditions of a free society. In the words of John Dewey, "The only freedom that is of enduring importance is freedom of intelligence."[2] Unless the teacher is free to teach, the learner is not free to learn.

SEPARATION OF CHURCH AND STATE. Secularism is one of the important

---

[2] John Dewey, *Experience and Education* (New York: The Macmillan Company, 1938), p. 61.

principles in insuring religious freedom and in keeping the civil government free of influence and control by any dominating religious sect. This vital principle of separation of church and state was established by the end of the nineteenth century. Nevertheless, it remains an important issue, particularly with regard to the use of public funds for private and parochial schools.

Since religious heterogeneity prevails in the United States, the divorce of church and state insures against a privileged position in civil affairs for any particular religious group. This principle is embodied in the First Amendment to the Federal Constitution.

During colonial America, when each colony represented religious homogeneity, religious minorities could be ignored or discriminated against because there was no divorcement between the civil government and the dominant religious group. Separation of church and state did not originate in hostility toward religion, but in the desire to provide independence and freedom to all sects, as well as to protect the state from dominance by any single group. As a result, religious instruction has been excluded from the curriculum of the public schools.

Today, the principle of separation of church and state is vital to many problems and issues in our society. The decision whether public funds, including federal monies, can be used for educational purposes under private and parochial auspices hinges on this principle.

Hook emphasizes the importance of the school as a democratizing influence, in contrast to the churches, sects, and other institutions that may separate one man from another.

> Its function is to serve as a common institutional ground in which are forged the attitudes of reasonableness, of scientific inquiry, and devotion to shared human values which must underlie all differences within a democratic culture if it is to survive. Where churches and sects and nations divide, and men will always be divided, the schools can unite by becoming the temples and laboratories of a common democratic faith.[3]

Human Equality and Individual Excellence

Many people are confused about the ideals of human equality and individual excellence in a democratic society. They see these ideals as antithetical rather than complementary to each other. But individual excellence would be thwarted without human equality because the latter produces the opportunity for each person to develop his fullest potentials. The Rockefeller Report discusses this complementary relationship between individual excellence and equality of opportunity thus:

---

[3] Sidney Hook, *Education for Modern Man* (New York: Dial Press, 1946), p. 65.

The fundamental view is that in the final matters of human existence all men are equally worthy of our care and concern. Further, we believe that men should be equal in enjoyment of certain familiar legal, civil and political rights. They should, as the phrase goes, be equal before the law.

But men are unequal in their native capacities and their motivations, and therefore in their attainments. In elaborating our national views of equality, the most widely accepted means of dealing with this problem has been to emphasize *equality of opportunity*. The great advantage of the conception of equality of opportunity is that it candidly recognizes differences in endowment and motivation and accepts the certainty of differences in achievement. By allowing free play to these differences, it preserves the freedom to excel which counts for so much in terms of individual aspirations, and has produced so much of mankind's greatness. . . .[4]

In his book, *Excellence*, John W. Gardner, President of the Carnegie Foundation for the Advancement of Teaching, addresses himself to the question, "Can we be equal and excellent too?" Gardner answers this seeming paradox by emphasizing the need for excellence, and opportunity for excellence, in all walks of human society.

We need excellent physicists and excellent mechanics. We need excellent cabinet members and excellent first-grade teachers. The tone and fiber of our society depend upon a pervasive and almost universal striving for good performance.

And we are not going to get that kind of striving, that kind of alert and proud attention to performance, unless we can instruct the whole society in a conception of excellence that leaves room for everybody who is willing to strive—a conception of excellence which means that whoever I am or whatever I am doing, provided that I am engaged in a socially acceptable activity, some kind of excellence is within my reach.[5]

Democracy in Teaching and Learning

We can begin to appreciate the significance of man's progress as a social being when we realize the nature and extent of his capacity for inquiry and improvement. Man's obligations to his fellowman, as a social being, are not antithetical to his rights and obligations for dignity and individuality. The teacher, in a democratic society, occupies a key position in developing in each individual pupil respect for the rights of other individuals, along with an appreciation of the obligations and responsibilities that emerge from being a member of a human community. Each individual needs recognition, approval, and significance. Studies even in nondemocratic, military, industrial, and business groups have shown that

---

[4] Rockefeller Brothers Fund, Inc., *The Pursuit of Excellence: Education and the Future of America* (New York: Doubleday & Company, Inc., 1958), p. 16.

[5] John W. Gardner, *Excellence* (New York: Harper and Row, Publishers, Inc., 1961), pp. 131–132.

the highest performance levels are attained when these factors of approval, recognition, and consideration for the individual are held important by the leadership.

Democratic classroom methods must not be confused with laissez-faire methods. The democratic classroom necessitates the utmost in planning on the part of the teacher. In the democratic classroom, the teacher is a guide, a diagnostician, a leader, and a catalyst. In a democratic society, as in a democratic classroom, the group is striving toward the attainment of certain goals or ideals. In order to reach these goals, rules and regulations are found necessary to facilitate the functioning of the group. It is erroneous to assume that a democratic classroom is characterized by laissez-faire permissiveness. However, in a democratic classroom the pupils are given choice and consideration as well as guidance and direction.

Rules and regulations are necessary in a democratic classroom to help insure that no individual will encroach upon the rights of other members of the group. When the pupils themselves recognize the importance of these rules and see to it that all members of the group abide by these agreements, then we have reached an understanding of these rules. On the other hand, when the rules are established solely and arbitrarily by the teacher, and when no attempt is made toward helping the pupils understand the need for these rules, then the enforcement may have to come from the teacher along threatening and punitive lines.

In a democratic classroom, the teacher enables each pupil to develop a shared responsibility for the success of the total group. In the democratic classroom, pupils are taught how to think, and not what to think. Critical thinking, not indoctrination, is the goal.

DEMOCRATIC PRINCIPLES APPLIED TO EDUCATION. We have emphasized the precept that the means of a society must be contiguous with its goals. Therefore, a society professing to embrace the ideals of democracy must have a democratic educational program. This not only means equality of educational opportunity, but also has an important bearing on the educational environment provided in the school and classroom. Democratic ends cannot be reached through autocratic means. The democratic school and classroom should be concerned with the following goals, which are consistent with principles of a democratic society:

1. Learning to fulfill one's obligations and responsibilities to the total group.
2. Learning to respect the dignity and worth of each individual in the group.
3. Developing the capacity for independent thinking and responsible self-direction.

4. Learning to be open-minded and objective in one's thinking.
5. Providing schools that are open to all regardless of social, economic, racial, religious, or cultural background. The only doctrine acceptable to the school is the doctrine of democracy.

The faculty and administration of the Ohio State University School, in a statement of the School's philosophy and purposes, have identified the following tasks related to democratic values:

Curriculum Experiences Directly Related to Democratic Values
1. Developing social sensitivity.
2. Developing cooperativeness.
3. Developing the ability and zeal to utilize the method of intelligence in solving all problems of human concern.
4. Developing creativeness.
5. Developing skills in democratic living.
6. Interpreting democracy.
7. Developing self-direction.

Curriculum Experiences Implied by Democratic Values
1. Developing communication skills and appreciations.
2. Developing skills in measurement and the use of quantitative symbols.
3. Developing skills in utilizing goods and services.
4. Promoting social adjustments.
5. Promoting health and safety.
6. Developing vocational adjustments and standards.
7. Developing adequate recreational outlets.
8. Developing standards of personal appearance and grooming.[6]

In recent years an increasing number of colleges and universities have given special attention to the function of their general education programs in instilling democratic attitudes, values, and behaviors. The faculty at one state university formulated a list of continua for all of its general education courses. These continua are summarized below because they are applicable not only to higher education, but to secondary education as well.

1. Belief in discussion and majority decision versus acceptance of arbitrary action on the part of the minority.
2. Rejection of all authority versus uncritical acceptance of authority.
3. Active participation in democratic processes versus indifference and nonparticipation.
4. Respect for the general welfare versus unconcern for the rights of society or of elements of society.
5. Respect for and demand for evidence versus uncritical acceptance of unvalidated statements.

---

[6] *The Philosophy and Purposes of the University School* (Columbus, Ohio: The Ohio State University, 1948), pp. 9–10.

6. Concern for, and interest in, all fields versus limitation of interest to a specialized field.
7. Open-mindedness versus uncritical adherence to law and custom.
8. Active concern for others versus self-centeredness or indifference.
9. Definite goals or philosophy versus simple expediency.
10. Acceptance of responsibility for decision and action versus indecision.[7]

DEMOCRACY AND DISCIPLINE. Self-direction and self-discipline are vital to the democratic classroom. The autocratic teacher imposes his rules on the youngsters and expects blind obedience to these rules. The democratic teacher helps the youngsters to understand the rules and why these rules are important.

Many teachers encounter difficulties with class discipline because they are vague and inconsistent in their methods and dealings with youngsters. At times they are tolerant of certain behavior, while at other times they are intolerant of these same actions. Youngsters have a natural zest for testing their teacher's tolerance or expectation level, and if they find that the teacher is inconsistent and vague, they become confused, irritated, and even resentful toward the teacher. The teacher who is autocratic and punitive tends to be feared and resented by the learners. The teacher who is democratic and constructive tends to be respected and admired by the learners. The democratic teacher becomes a worthy model for emulation. The effective teacher knows that certain conditions must prevail if democratic discipline is to be attained.

1. Classroom rules are established cooperatively with the teacher and pupils, and together they develop and utilize methods of self-government and self-direction. All rules are clearly defined, and are established and maintained through reason.
2. All pupils understand that their actions must be consistent with the general welfare.
3. The teacher uses methods and procedures that stimulate and maintain pupil interest and participation.
4. Class activities are designed to be stimulating and challenging to each individual and to the total group.
5. The climate of the classroom is cooperative and constructive. The teacher employs methods of cooperative teacher-pupil planning and evaluation.
6. Evaluation is continuous and consistent with the standards and goals set for each individual. Such goals must be challenging and realistic.

---

[7] Lewis B. Mayhew, "And in Attitudes," in *Evaluation in the Basic College at Michigan State University*, Paul L. Dressel (ed.) (New York: Harper and Row, Publishers, Inc., 1958), pp. 217–218.

7. The teacher recognizes individual differences and provides for differentiated activities in accordance with these differences. Individual problems are dealt with on an individual basis.

8. The dignity and worth of each individual is respected by the teacher and the pupils.

9. The teacher is always consistent and fair in all interpersonal and group relationships.

10. The teacher strives to prevent problems from arising, but if and when they do arise they are handled promptly and constructively.

11. The teacher plans carefully for immediate and long-range goals and activities, but flexibility, not rigidity is the rule.

12. Critical thinking and the use of reason is the rule; arbitrary regulation and blind obedience are avoided.

Albert Einstein stressed the importance of democratic principles in the school and classroom with regard to discipline.

> To me the worst thing seems to be for a school to work with methods of fear, force and artificial authority. Such treatment destroys the sound sentiments, the sincerity and the self-confidence of the pupil. It is no wonder that such schools are the rule in Germany and Russia. I know that the schools in this country are free from this worst evil; this is so in Switzerland and probably in all democratically governed countries. It is comparatively simple to keep the school free from this worst of all evils. Give into the power of the teacher the fewest possible coercive measures, so that the only source of the pupil's respect for the teacher is the human and intellectual qualities of the latter.[8]

COOPERATION AND COMPETITION.   Some educators have chosen to make an issue between activity that is cooperative and activity that is competitive in the teaching-learning process. Research has shown that either of these activities may be desirable or undesirable, depending upon the conditions to which they apply. Experiments in the field of group process have shown that many cooperative situations lead to results that are superior to those of competitive situations. Yet, group processes, when misused, can lead to conformity and restriction of individual effort.[9]

GROUP PROCESSES AND INDIVIDUAL DIFFERENCES. Teachers have a tendency, however, to overemphasize the competitive situation, and as a result many anxieties and feelings of hostility and inadequacy develop in the learner. With reference to the principles of democracy and the democratic classroom, we have emphasized the importance of both

---

[8] Albert Einstein, *Out of My Later Years* (New York: Philosophical Library, 1950), p. 34.

[9] See Solomon E. Asch, "Opinions and Social Pressure," *Scientific American*, November, 1955, pp. 3–7.

individuality and the total group. These should not be antithetical, but mutually supportive. Einstein, in an essay on education, emphasizes the importance of avoiding destructive competitive forces in the school and to develop learning as a pleasurable and constructive force.

> Therefore one should guard against preaching to the young man success in the customary sense as the aim of life. For a successful man is he who receives a great deal from his fellowmen, usually incomparably more than corresponds to his service to them. The value of a man, however, should be seen in what he gives and not in what he is able to receive.
>
> The most important motive for work in the school and in life is the pleasure in work, pleasure in its result and the knowledge of the value of the result to the community. In the awakening and strengthening of these psychological forces in the young man, I see the most important task given by the school. . . .
>
> The awakening of these productive psychological powers is certainly less easy than the practice of force or the awakening of individual ambition but is the more valuable for it. . . . If the school succeeds in working successfully from such points of view, it will be highly honored by the rising generation and the tasks given by the school will be submitted to as a sort of gift. I have known children who preferred schooltime to vacation.[10]

EDUCATION AND THE METHOD OF INTELLIGENCE

Since the method of intelligence is the key to human progress, it would seem reasonable to assume that this method would be common to our schools. Yet, how often do we find our schools imbued with the task of teaching our youth to memorize rather than to think, to regurgitate what the teacher and textbook say rather than to hypothesize and analyze? Unfortunately, many teachers and students find it less perplexing and less frustrating to avoid inquiry in favor of simple memorization-regurgitation. But the process of memorization-regurgitation is indeed a poor excuse for education.

The Need for Inquiry and Cognition

Despite all the newer findings in the science of psychology and their implications for learning, we find that we have a long way to go before these findings are implemented to any great extent. Instead of functioning as a chain of exciting explorations and discoveries, the teaching-learning process is all too frequently limited to impressing the pupil with pre-digested facts, rules, and principles that must be regurgitated upon demand either orally or via the true-false, multiple choice, fill-in, or matching type of examination. In the traditional classroom the pupil is

---

[10] Einstein, *op. cit.*, pp. 34–35.

seldom required to formulate problems, to analyze, to weigh evidence, to explore alternatives, to select pertinent data, and to test assumptions and conclusions for validity in solving significant problems.

We know that the great majority of our population is capable of critical, reflective thinking. Moreover, a democratic society rests its faith on these premises. Unfortunately, far too many of our elementary and secondary schools are geared to traditional principles and methods of teaching. And some of our so-called modern or progressive principles and methods are distorted in their applications when good classroom citizenship means conformity to decision without reason or analysis.

We tend to view the curriculum far too narrowly when we fail to bring students into situations of inequilibrium so that they may be triggered into independent thinking and the discovery of the countless intellectual, esthetic, and emotional satisfactions. We distort modern educational principles when we regard learning as application, regardless of whether or not it is based upon understanding and comprehension. Learning by doing must not imply doing without understanding.

There is no sharp line of demarcation between method and subject matter content in the teaching-learning process. People learn to think when they are given the opportunity and the stimulation to uncover and to discover things. Man has developed understandings, concepts, and new discoveries through the method of intelligence. Through this method, there can be no knowledge without understanding, and no understanding without wisdom.

Many educators have been led to the dangerous misconception that since critical thinking is dependent upon knowledge, therefore such thinking is automatically derived from knowledge, and consequently knowledge should be the prime goal of learning. But knowledge is not an end in itself; it can lead to understanding and creativity only if it is governed by a spirit of inquiry and skepticism. Too frequently our schools turn out students who are able to come up with the correct answers, but who are incapable of formulating provocative questions. Thelen puts it this way:

> It is in the formulation of the problem that individuality is expressed, that creativity is stimulated, and that nuances and subtleties are discovered. It is these aspects of inquiry that give birth to new social movements . . . and that are central in the emergence of insight. Yet it is precisely these aspects of inquiry that schools ignore, for they collapse inquiry to mere problem-solving, and they keep the student busy finding "solutions" to "problems" that are already formulated, externalized, depersonalized, and emotionally fumigated.[11]

---

[11] Herbert A. Thelen, *Education and the Human Quest* (New York: Harper and Row, Publishers, Inc., 1960), p. 26.

While our schools, to a very great extent, have been training students to derive correct answers, we are now living in an age where machines can give answers, but only man can formulate significant questions. Consequently, it would seem that our schools need to place key emphasis on inquiry and cognition. Facts and skills are the tools or means of inquiry and understanding, and not the end result of education. "The difference between an educated man and an uneducated man is the ability to ask fruitful questions."[12] Moreover, the ability of the student to come up with the right answer does not necessarily mean that cognition has taken place. Dewey emphasized the importance of cognition or meaning in learning thus:

> To grasp the meaning of a thing, an event or a situation is to see it in its *relation* to other things: to note how it operates or functions, what consequences follow from it, what causes it, what uses it can be put to . . . since all knowing aims at clothing things and events with meaning it always proceeds by taking the thing inquired into out of its isolation. Search is continued until the thing is discovered to be a relative part in some larger whole.[13]

Each discipline is not merely a body of factual information, but rather a mode of inquiry governed by a symmetry of principles. Consequently, we should think of each discipline as a unified, coherent process of investigation, not as a cancer that grows haphazardly and without meaning. Yet, as a result of their experiences in school, students tend to regard subject matter as a body of facts and skills heaped in an endlessly growing pile. More teachers need to understand the major principles governing their discipline and the inquiry mode that makes continued learning and discovery possible. In the teaching-learning process, we need to relate the information and skills to the framework of principles that form the symmetry of a field or discipline. Bruner refers to this symmetry as the structure of a subject.

Another important force often neglected in the teaching-learning process is that of intuition. Many teachers actually discourage students from using the powers of intuition. They penalize students for guessing. Yet intuition is a vital facet of the inquiry process, enabling the learner, or even the creative scientist, to develop unique perspectives, fresh combinations, or new solutions. Bruner stresses the importance of the intuitive sense in developing an excitement about discovery and building self-confidence:

> Mastery of the fundamental ideas of a field involves not only the grasping of general principles, but also the development of an attitude toward

---

12 *Ibid.*, p. 34.
13 John Dewey, *How We Think* (Boston: D. C. Heath & Company, 1933, pp. 137–138.

learning and inquiry, toward guessing and hunches, toward the possibility of solving problems on one's own. . . . To instill such attitudes
by teaching requires something more than the mere presentation of
fundamental ideas. Just what it takes to bring off such teaching is something on which a great deal of research is needed, but it would seem
that an important ingredient is a sense of excitement about discovery . . .
with a resulting sense of self-confidence in one's abilities.[14]

A democratic society requires citizens who are capable of independent
thinking and group responsibility. These two forces are complementary,
not conflicting. Without independent thinking, the group or society is
vulnerable to manipulation and totalitarianism. Therefore, the schools
have a responsibility to foster reflective thinking. And since we are
students in school for only a certain segment of our lives, our power to
continue learning must be cultivated by the school. "If young people
do not learn to think while in school . . . how are they to keep on
learning?"[15]

The Need for Desirable Attitudes and Emotions

Reflective thinking or the method of intelligence should not be devoid
of attitudinal or emotional responses. The attitudes and emotions are key
elements in intuition. Curiosity and drive for continued learning are also
dependent on our attitudes and emotions. Roe has revealed that the attitudes and feelings of our eminent scientists play a vital role in their
achievements.[16] Bloom cites "interests, attitudes, and values, and the
development of appreciations"[17] as forming one of the three major
domains in his taxonomy of educational objectives.[18] Yet, all too often,
students develop undesirable attitudes toward learning as a result of
their school experiences. Learning can be exciting and rewarding. The
inquiry-discovery process, properly applied, can foster desirable attitudes and feelings toward learning. The interests and feelings of the
learner should not be ignored if his thinking is to be vibrant and constructive.

The mind is never passive; it is a perpetual activity, delicate, receptive,
responsive. . . . You cannot postpone its life until you have sharpened it.

---

[14] Jerome S. Bruner, *The Process of Education* (Cambridge, Mass.: Harvard University Press, 1960), p. 20.
[15] H. Gordon Hullfish and Philip G. Smith, *Reflective Thinking: The Method of
Education* (New York: Dodd, Mead & Company, 1961), p. 3.
[16] Anne Roe, "A Psychologist Examines 64 Eminent Scientists," *Scientific American,*
November, 1952, 187:21–25.
[17] Benjamin S. Bloom (ed.), *Taxonomy of Educational Objectives* (New York: David
McKay Company, Inc., 1956), p. 7.
[18] Bloom refers to this as the "affective domain." The other two domains are the
cognitive and psychomotor, according to Bloom. The cognitive deals with
understanding, while the psychomotor concerns skills like reading and writing.

Whatever interest attaches to your subject-matter must be evoked here and now; whatever powers you are strengthening in the pupil, must be exercised here and now; whatever possibilities of mental life your teaching should impart, must be exhibited here and now. This is the golden rule of education. . . .[19]

The Need for Useful Application

It is not enough for the learner to understand and to have a desirable attitude toward learning. He must be able to apply what he learns in the context of his experience. This does not mean that all learning is to be derived from direct experience, for this is an impossibility. The learner cannot literally relive the period of the American Revolution or the Civil War, but he can relate these periods to the living principles of modern American democracy that affect his own life. This is what Whitehead meant when he declared, "Education is the acquisition of the art of the utilization of knowledge."[20] Useful application also implies bringing about desirable changes in behavior. Whitehead cautioned against our obsession with inert ideas in the educational process.

> . . . above all things we must beware of what I will call "inert ideas"—that is to say, ideas that are merely received into the mind without being utilized, or tested, or thrown into fresh combinations.[21]
>
> Pedants sneer at an education which is useful. But if education is not useful, what is it? Is it a talent to be hidden away in a napkin? Of course, education should be useful, whatever your aim in life.[22]

The Need for an Enlightened Citizenry

Democracy rests its faith on the potential of each citizen to develop and utilize his capacity for independent, reflective thinking through the method of intelligence. Our society looks to the schools for the development of an enlightened citizenry. Enlightenment of the people is a fundamental requisite of democracy. In the words of Jefferson, "Enlighten the people generally, and tyranny and oppressions of body and mind will vanish like evil spirits at the dawn of day."

During the twentieth century, considerable progress has been made in extending education to an increasing proportion of our population. We have discovered that universal education has helped raise the intelligence of our people. Comparisons between inductees of World Wars I and II on the Army Alpha Test reveal a highly significant improvement in test scores. The median score for the World War I group was only 62, as compared with a median of 104 for the World War II group. This

---

[19] Alfred North Whitehead, *The Aims of Education* (New York: The Macmillan Company, 1929), p. 9.
[20] *Ibid.*, p. 6.   [21] *Ibid.*, pp. 1–2.
[22] *Ibid.*, p. 3.

median score of 104 was at the 83rd centile of World War I scores.[23]
The average World War I inductee had an eighth grade education, while
the World War II average had risen to two years of high school. Despite
these gains, studies of World War II inductees showed that less than
one fourth of those who were capable of earning a bachelor's degree
actually reached this goal.[24]

During the 1960's, the task of extending educational opportunity to
all who can profit thereby remains one of our most important goals. The
barriers of socioeconomic status and race need to be eliminated if equality
of educational opportunity is to be attained.

But merely providing an increasing proportion of our population with
more and more formal education is not enough. The quality of education
and the spirit in which it is pursued are all-important. For although we
have discovered a great deal about the principles and conditions of learning and the elements that evoke reflective thinking, we have yet to
transpose these findings to general practice.

> I think our present situation is grave; more, it is immoral. For to act
> ignorantly when knowledge is available, to deny realities that patently
> exist and make a genuine difference is the worst crime of civilized man.[25]
> If one judges by prevailing practices in many high schools today, the
> most plausible assumption about knowledge is that it is a packaged com-
> modity to be given in exchange for the time of the student, and that
> neither it nor the student is much affected by the transaction. The
> package will contain instructions for the use of its contents—like an
> Erector set—and as long as one is content or unimaginative enough to
> build only the adult-anticipated objects, the contents of the package will
> be inadequate. Fortunately these limitations don't matter much because
> the chief educational product is a certificate saying that one has had the
> right courses and bought the same packages as the Jones boy down the
> street.[26]

While this is not a very encouraging picture of secondary education,
there is a growing body of research that points to a new model of the
teaching-learning process. This model is an inquiry-discovery mode based
on the method of intelligence. Through this mode, education should
result in the inquiring person, the enlightened individual—not the person
who is adept merely at collecting so many credit hours of packaged
information.

---

[23] R. D. Tuddenham, "Soldier Intelligence in World Wars I and II," *American Psychologist*, 1948, 3:54–56.

[24] Dael Wolfle, "Intellectual Resources," *Scientific American*, September, 1951, 185:
42–46.

[25] Herbert A. Thelen, *Education and The Human Quest* (New York: Harper and
Row, Publishers, Inc., 1960) p. 26.

[26] *Ibid.*, pp. 29–30.

Some Principles and Conditions of Effective Learning

Research findings in the psychology of learning lead us to several key principles and conditions for effective learning. Effective learning involves cognition, and results in improved behavior and incessant inquiry. These principles are summarized as follows:

1. Learning should be meaningful to the learner.
2. Learning is most meaningful when it is useful to the learner.
3. Learning should consist of key ideas and generalizations, rather than dissociated and inert facts; and such key ideas should be used in formulating many new combinations of principles.
4. Learning should be intrinsically challenging and rewarding.
5. Learning involves inquiry and discovery.
6. Learning requires activity and participation by the learner; the learner must want to learn before learning can take place.
7. Learning involves interaction between the learner and his environment and, consequently, results in behaviorial change.
8. Learning includes the development and modification of attitudes and appreciations, and not merely knowledge of facts and ability to perform skills. Continued learning is dependent upon a wholesome attitude toward exploration and discovery.
9. Learning, in its highest form, leads to creativity.

Dressel identifies four psychological conditions for effective learning:

1. The student is motivated to learn through grasping the purpose of learning and the relationship to his own needs of what is to be learned.
2. There is a relationship between what is to be learned and the previous experience of the student.
3. When the student is an active contributor rather than a passive recipient.
4. When the material learned is shortly used or applied in dealing with other materials or problems.[27]

In far too many instances, these important principles and conditions of learning are ignored and even violated. The following represent some precautions against common pitfalls in the teaching-learning process:

1. The acquisition of information without understanding does not lead to knowledge.
2. No matter how thoroughly a teacher may know his subject matter, no real learning occurs until the ideas, motives, attitudes and behaviors of the learner have been developed, influenced, and modified.

---

[27] Paul L. Dressel, *Evaluation in the Basic College* (New York: Harper and Row, Publishers, Inc., 1958), p. 24.

3. No subject field exists in a vacuum. Each discipline is inter-related with other disciplines, and real education cannot occur unless the learner understands and appreciates the interdependence of knowledge.

4. If certain subject matter is of no significance to the learner in his present state, he will not automatically store it for use at some later date.

5. Information accepted on authority alone is abhorrent to real learning and is dangerous to democracy. Critical thinking can only be developed when the learner experiences the stimulation of analyzing, challenging, and thinking for himself.

6. Learning never really reaches a final stage, but continues throughout life. The truly educated person is one who has attained self-direction for continued learning.

7. The emotions of the learner play an essential role in his intellectual development. Without the right kinds of attitudes and drives, the teaching-learning process will be doomed to failure.

8. Coercion by and conformity to authority prevents independent thinking, open-mindedness, and creativeness.

9. Paper-and-pencil tests frequently fail to assess the full dimensions of learning. Such tests tend to be restricted to knowledge of information and concepts, along with the ability to perform certain skills—while failing to gauge ability to think critically and creatively when confronted with an unforeseen problem.[28]

The effective teacher realizes that learning is actually a power or force within the learner. It is the task of the teacher to help unleash this force. The teacher who constantly dominates the classroom, and thereby prevents students from learning to explore and discover on their own, tends to inhibit the inquiry process. The effective teacher looks to the learner for clues and is able to alter his teaching strategy according to the behavior of the learner. The process of learning is one of growth and development. Through learning one should develop a better understanding of himself and thereby effect improvements in his behavior.

A great deal has been discovered about the learning process, but relatively little of what is known is being applied in actual practice. The process of learning should be stimulating, exciting, and adventuresome. But all too often, the methods employed in the teaching-learning process are dull, routine, and tiresome. This does not mean that learning should lead to self-satisfaction, because the self-satisfied person is indeed a very

28 See Earl C. Kelley, *Education for What is Real* (New York: Harper and Row, Publishers, Inc., 1947), pp. 13–23.

poor learner. Hilgard identifies some generalizations on which learning theorists are in substantial agreement.

1. In deciding who should learn what, the capacities of the learner are very important.
2. A motivated learner acquires what he learns more readily than one who is not motivated.
3. Motivation that is too intense (especially pain, fear, anxiety) may be accompanied by distracting emotional states, so that excessive motivation may be less effective than moderate motivation for learning some kinds of tasks, especially those involving difficult discriminations.
4. Learning under the control of reward is usually preferable to learning under the control of punishment.
5. Learning under intrinsic motivation is preferable to learning under extrinsic motivation.
6. Tolerance for failure is best taught through providing a backlog of success that compensates for experienced failure.
7. Individuals need practice in setting realistic goals for themselves, goals neither so low as to elicit little effort nor so high as to foreordain to failure.
8. The personal history of the individual, for example, his reaction to authority, may hamper or enhance his ability to learn from a given teacher.
9. Active participation by a learner is preferable to passive reception when learning, for example, from a lecture or a motion picture.
10. Meaningful materials and meaningful tasks are learned more readily than nonsense materials and more readily than tasks not understood by the learner.
11. Information about the nature of a good performance, knowledge of his own mistakes, and knowledge of successful results, aid learning.
12. Transfer to new tasks will be better if, in learning, the learner can discover relationships for himself, and if he has experience during learning of applying the principles within a variety of tasks.
13. Spaced or distributed recalls are advantageous in fixing material that is to be long retained.[29]

THE INQUIRY-DISCOVERY PROCESS. Too many teachers gauge the progress of their classes in terms of the number of pages covered in the textbook. Teachers and pupils are rated not by the questions they ask and the knowledge they seek, but by the packaged answers they can give. Dr. Isidor Rabi, Nobel Prize Winner in physics, attributes his interest in science and his questing for discovery to the influence of his parents. Rabi relates how his immigrant family lived on the Lower East Side of New York early in the century, and how his mother tirelessly inquired as he returned from school, "Did you ask any good questions in

---

[29] See Ernest R. Hilgard, *Theories of Learning*, 2nd Ed. (New York: Appleton-Century-Crofts, 1956), pp. 486–487.

school today?"[30] Rabi attributes his interest in science and his drive for discovery to the influence of his parents.

PROBLEM-SOLVING IN CRITICAL THINKING.   The importance of utilizing problem-solving and the scientific method as the keystone in education was emphasized by John Dewey in his famous work, *How We Think*. Dewey rejected the doctrine of mental discipline and conceived of thinking as problem-solving and the application of the scientific method

---

[30] Francis Bello, "Great American Scientists: The Physicists," *Fortune*, LXI, March, 1960, p. 115.

"Now if the students are encouraged to think for themselves, we may call the man a good teacher."
—CONFUCIUS

Photo by Vories Fisher

"There are, oddly, no technical rules for success in science."
—J. BRONOWSKI

Photo by Vories Fisher

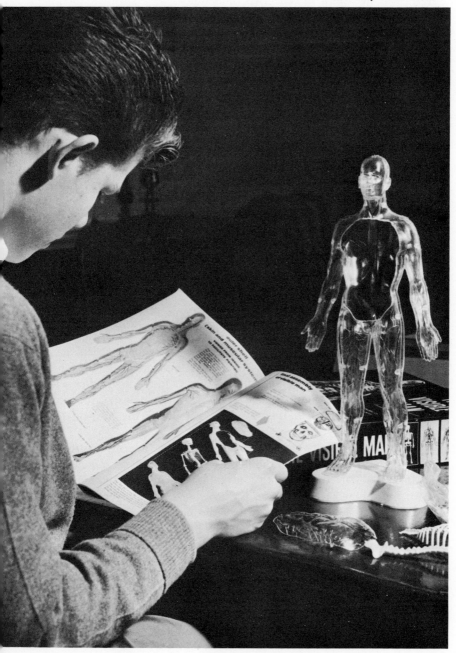

to all types of problems. This revolutionary approach to education was formulated on the basis of the need for an enlightened citizenry in a democratic society. Essentially, Dewey expressed this method of intelligence as five steps in reflective thinking:

1. A felt difficulty.
2. Its location and definition.
3. Suggestion of possible solution.
4. Development by reasoning of the bearings on the suggestion.
5. Further observation and experiment leading to its acceptance or rejection; that is the conclusion of belief or disbelief.[31]

Although these steps in reflective thinking are not necessarily distinct, and although many problems are solved through a great variety of approaches, including sudden insights, intuition, and even accidents, it is generally agreed that most problems of any consequence demand a systematic method of inquiry. This method of inquiry may be approached in a variety of ways.

1. Identifying and formulating the problem.
2. Observing the conditions bearing on the problem.
3. Formulating hypotheses for the solution of the problem.
4. Designing a plan of action for solving the problem.
5. Gathering data pertinent to the problem and pursuing the course of action toward the solution of the problem.
6. Analyzing the data and testing the data.
7. Deriving conclusions, solutions, and applications.

Some people have the erroneous idea that there exists a single, definitive sequence called the scientific method or the method of intelligence. In actuality, there are many pathways in the method of science.[32] But certain elements of critical thinking and analysis are commonly found in what is called the scientific method or the method of intelligence.

The great challenge to American democracy and its institutions of public education rests on whether our society and its schools will develop in students the capacity and habit of critical thinking.

An enlightened citizen, then, is one who is able to recognize when a problem exists; he is able to realize the nature and significance of the problem; he is able to gather and apply information and data relevant to the problem; and he is able to test and derive valid conclusions and solutions to the problem. Dressel and Mayhew list the following problem-solving aspects of critical thinking:

---

[31] John Dewey, *How We Think* (Boston: D. C. Heath & Company, 1933), p. 72.
[32] James B. Conant, *On Understanding Science* (New Haven, Conn.: Yale University Press, 1947).

1. *Ability to Recognize the Existence of a Problem*
   (a) To recognize related conditions in a situation.
   (b) To recognize conflicts and issues in a situation.
   (c) To locate "missing links" in a series of ideas or incidents.
   (d) To recognize problems which have no solution.

2. *Ability to Define the Problem*
   (a) To identify the nature of the problem.
   (b) To understand what is involved and required in the problem.
   (c) To recognize ways in which the problem can be phrased.
   (d) To define difficult and abstract elements of the problem in simple, concrete, and familiar terms.
   (e) To break complex elements of the problem into workable parts.
   (f) To identify the central elements of the problem.
   (g) To place the elements of the problem into an order in which they can be handled.
   (h) To eliminate extraneous elements from the problem.
   (i) To place the problem in its context.

3. *Ability to Select Information Pertinent to the Solution of the Problem*
   (a) To distinguish reliable and unreliable sources of information.
   (b) To recognize bias upon which information is selected and rejected.
   (c) To recognize information relevant to the solution of the problem.
   (d) To select adequate and reliable samples of information.
   (e) To systematize information.
   (f) To select information from personal experience relevant to the solution of the problem.

4. *Ability to Recognize Assumptions Bearing on the Problem*
   (a) To identify unstated assumptions.
   (b) To identify unsupported assumptions.
   (c) To identify irrelevant assumptions.

5. *Ability to Make Relevant Hypotheses*
   (a) To discover clues to the solution of the problem.
   (b) To formulate various hypotheses on the basis of information and assumptions.
   (c) To select the more promising hypotheses for first consideration.
   (d) To check the consistency of the hypotheses with the information and assumptions.
   (e) To make hypotheses concerning unknown and needed information.

6. *Ability to Draw Conclusions Validly from Assumptions, Hypotheses, and Pertinent Information*
   (a) To detect logical relationships among terms and propositions.
   (b) To recognize necessary and sufficient conditions.
   (c) To identify cause and effect relationships.
   (d) To identify and state the conclusion.

7. *Ability to Judge the Validity of the Processes Leading to the Conclusion*
   (a) To distinguish validly drawn conclusions from others chosen, for example, because they are in accord with values, preferences, and biases.

    (b) To distinguish a necessary inference from a probable one.

    (c) To detect formal logical inconsistencies in the argument.

8. *Ability to Evaluate a Conclusion in Terms of Its Application*

    (a) To recognize conditions which would be necessary to verify a conclusion.

    (b) To recognize conditions which would make a conclusion inapplicable.

    (c) To judge the adequacy of a conclusion as a solution of the problem.[33]

In the social sciences, as well as in the natural sciences, Dressel and Mayhew identify the following critical abilities:

1. To identify central issues.
2. To recognize underlying assumptions.
3. To evaluate evidence or authority.
    (a) To recognize stereotypes and clichés.
    (b) To recognize bias and emotional factors.
    (c) To distinguish between verifiable and unverifiable data.
    (d) To distinguish between relevant and nonrelevant.
    (e) To distinguish between essential and incidental.
    (f) To recognize the adequacy of data.
    (g) To determine whether facts support a generalization.
    (h) To check consistency.
4. To draw warranted conclusions.[34]

Watson and Glaser identify the following as major factors in the ability to think critically:

Inference

Ability to discriminate among degrees of truth or falsity or probability of certain inferences drawn from given facts or data.

Recognition of Assumptions

Ability to recognize unstated assumptions in given assertions or propositions.

Deduction

Ability to reason deductively from given premises; to recognize the relation of *implication* between propositions; to determine whether what *seems* an implication or necessary inference between one proposition and another is indeed such.

Interpretation

Ability to weigh evidence and to distinguish between unwarranted generalizations and probable inferences which, though not conclusive or necessary, are warranted beyond a reasonable doubt.

Evaluation of Arguments

Ability to distinguish between arguments which are strong and im-

---

[33] Paul L. Dressel and Lewis B. Mayhew, *General Education Explorations in Evaluation* (Washington, D.C.: American Council on Education, 1954), pp. 177–178.

[34] *Ibid.*, pp. 38–40.

portant to the question at issue and those which are weak and unimportant or irrelevant.[35]

‧These factors in the ability to think critically have important implications for an understanding of human behavior. In our daily lives, we often fall into the traps of making generalizations or reaching conclusions from single or exceptional instances, without taking the trouble to examine and weigh all the evidence. Too often, we apply our personal viewpoints to existing situations, without being consciously aware of our prejudices or preconceived preferences. As George Bernard Shaw pointed out, we use our reason to support our prejudices.

THE OPEN MIND. Man's incessant quest for discovery has demonstrated how knowledge facilitates the acquisition of more knowledge. In other words, each new discovery enhances the possibilities for more new discoveries. These principles of critical thinking have important implications in the teaching-learning process. The goal of education is the open and incessant questing for understanding and improving one's environment. And the drive for exploring and discovering is the essence of education. One critic of contemporary education condemns our obsession with facts and information as ends in themselves.

> Indeed, the whole tendency of the pedagogic tradition is toward following the book. We have tried to remove all uncertainty from subject matter. In doing so, we have repeatedly taken the life out of it. In the name of teaching a corpus, we have taught a corpse, and called it a course. We have taught "the shows of things, instead of the things themselves." We have taught facts and principles in the name of science, prosody in the name of poetry, computation in the name of mathematics, dates and events in the name of history. We have taught rhetoric or grammar in the name of writing. . . . The student is given ready-made formulas for dealing with reality, in a world in which the ability to make new formulas is the crucial need. Rarely, if ever, is he invited to try formulating for himself. . . .
>
> It doesn't have to be this way. Subjects can be brought to life. It is possible to teach in a way that penetrates the shell of the 'given' subject. Although most of us have had little experience with such teaching, we've had at least a little. If your experience is like mine, what is most vivid is not what was done to you or for you, but what you did for yourself.[36]

Unfortunately, too many teachers indoctrinate for these facts and skills, without unleashing the natural drives of curiosity and creativity in the young learner.

INFORMATION OR REFLECTIVE THINKING? The teacher of literature, mathematics, science, social studies, homemaking, industrial arts—what-

---

[35] Goodwin Watson and Edward M. Glaser, *Watson-Glaser Critical Thinking Appraisal Manual* (Yonkers-on-Hudson, New York: World Book Company, 1952).

[36] Arthur W. Foshay, "What is the Message?", *Saturday Review XLIII*, February 13, 1960, pp. 60–61.

Photo by Daniel Tanner

"Solitude has also its lessons."
—EMERSON

ever the specific subject—must be concerned with the problem of helping the learner to think critically and to act effectively in life situations.
Unfortunately, too many courses of study place major emphasis on the
acquisition of subject matter information or narrowly defined skills. The
student of social studies learns, by memorization, the technique of matching dates and events for the temporary expediency of passing a paper
and pencil test. The science student memorizes countless formulas that
are applied only for purposes of passing a written examination. Seldom
is the student tested for evidence of scientific thinking and behavior

as a result of science courses in school. Through a maze of orthodox and mechanical exercises and applications in the science classroom or laboratory, the student meets the necessary course requirements; but he is left without real comprehension of the bases for the complex origins of the concepts behind these exercises and applications.

Many people have the mistaken notion that the basic curriculum in the secondary school is virtually inert—that is, that the basic material never really requires overhauling because it is founded on essential principles of knowledge. We frequently hear people saying, "A good teacher, above all, must know his subject." Yet, whenever one encounters a truly creative person in a given field, we find that he is not concerned with inert knowledge, but with dynamics of inquiry and discovery. Albert Einstein warned educators that they must not become obsessed with knowledge for its own sake.

> Sometimes one sees in the school simply the instrument of transferring a certain maximum quantity of knowledge to the growing generation. But that is not right. Knowledge is dead; the school, however, serves the living.[37]
> The development of general ability for independent thinking and judgment should always be placed foremost, not the acquisition of special knowledge.[38]

In defining the content and process of any curricular area, we tend to make the error of distilling from each subject field the essential atoms of facts and skills without an awareness of the incessant change necessary to the lifestream of any discipline. The various disciplines are not inert and absolute. On the contrary, they are dynamic. Without the incessant questing for solutions to man's problems, we would be at an impasse and, worse yet, we would fall prey to a tragic dogmatism that would make us unable to cope with changing conditions.

The inquiry-discovery process does not minimize the importance of subject matter knowledge; on the contrary, it makes such knowledge all the more significant, meaningful, and vital to the learner. What is the reason underlying the development of curricula that are confined to established knowledge and the acquisition of subject-matter information? Perhaps it is because such subject-matter information is the easiest and safest type of knowledge that can be taught and evaluated by the teacher. Perhaps it is because many of our teachers have failed to develop adequately their own powers of inquiry and discovery.

Students who may be adept at acquiring and regurgitating facts may

---

[37] Albert Einstein, *Out of My Later Years* (New York: Philosophical Library, 1950), p. 32.
[38] *Ibid.*, p. 36.

be incapable of weighing and applying evidence, recognizing inconsistencies, identifying bias, verifying data, discriminating between the relevant and the irrelevant, formulating valid conclusions, and applying these habits of critical thinking to life situations.

If true learning is to take place, we must have more than mere information. Teaching must include the why of things. The importance of true understanding in the teaching-learning process is recognized by the young child who incessantly observes and studies his surroundings, and who tirelessly seeks to know the why of experience. Our schools must not avoid the discomfiture of the problems and issues that derive from the living world. Our schools must develop the inquiring, open-minded individual. Learning how to think is vital to the survival of a democracy. Learning what to think is merely the basis for indoctrination.

To develop the powers of reflective thought and action, students should encounter interpretative situations where they explore different hypotheses, opinions, issues, and alternatives—where they are given the opportunity to find pathways of their own. In too many classrooms, students give rote reports that simply represent a mechanical regurgitation of the authoritative information from the teacher or textbook.

Emulation is an important factor in behavior. The teacher who loves learning is more likely to stimulate students to self-impelled learning than is the teacher who conceives of education as information storage and retrieval. The effective teacher is a guide, catalyst, and behavioral model. He helps the student to learn how to deal effectively with the problems, events, and conditions of life.

The more narrowly sophisticated and inhibited we become as adults, the more shallow and limited we are in terms of our potential for growth in learning and understanding. In a sense, the critical thinker, the person who is searching for solutions to problems and the discovery of new knowledge must, if he is to be successful, retain the refreshing naivete of the young child who is always excited at the marvels that derive from the brink of the unknown. The highest goal of all learning is to instill a lifelong passion for incessant discovery. The process of inquiry is both a worthy end and a worthy means in education, for it leads to the improvement of the human community. Creative intelligence abhors adjustment and conformity to the *status quo*. Instead of adjusting to society, the forces of inquiry lead to the improvement of society. Without inquiry, the human community would be static and arid.

RECENT CURRICULUM REFORMS.   In recent years, particularly as a result of the efforts of the National Science Foundation and the support of the National Defense Education Act, a great wave of reform in course content and methodology in science and mathematics has begun to take hold in our secondary schools. The rationale behind this reform movement is to enable the learner to understand the fields of science and mathematics as systems of inquiry, as processes of unfinished and continuing explorations.

The new curricula are organized so as to penetrate more deeply into the structure of the field or discipline through an understanding of basic principles and generalizations which comprise the bases for contemporary thought. The traditional encyclopedic approach in organizing subject matter and the traditional didactic approach in disseminating information are rejected in favor of strategies in content and process that closely resemble the scientist or mathematician at work. Students learn to hypothesize, to inquire, to generalize, and to test their conclusions in the classroom and laboratory. Treatment is given not only to known material, but to problems for which answers are being sought in the community of scholars. Each field or discipline is treated as a unified process of inquiry with a symmetry and harmony of its own, rather than as a shapeless, disjointed, and additive body of inert facts and skills.

In implementing these reforms, leading scholars in the various disciplines have joined forces with high-school curriculum workers and teachers.

Reforms also have been taking place in the teaching of modern foreign languages, particularly as a result of the support provided by the National Defense Education Act.

The promising results of these efforts at the secondary level have led to similar movements in curriculum reform at the elementary and college levels. The nature and impact of recent curriculum reforms at the secondary level are discussed in greater detail in Chapters 7 and 8.

The English language arts and the social studies, unfortunately, have not been given support for curriculum reform on a scale comparable to that given the sciences, mathematics, and modern foreign languages. We need to recognize these latter two fields as of no less importance to a democratic society than the other areas of the secondary school curriculum.

MOTIVATION, ACHIEVEMENT AND GIFTEDNESS. There is a great deal of truth in Edison's statement that "genius is 99 per cent perspiration and only 1 per cent inspiration." For no matter how high one's intellectual potential may be, his achievement level will not transcend his motivational intensity. Motivation is so vital to the teaching-learning process that students with extremely high I.Q.'s will attain only mediocre grades if they are lacking in drive. And students with average I.Q.'s can, in a number of respects, do superior work if they have the motivation or drive. Most of us use only a very small fraction of our learning potential.

There is danger in looking upon intelligence or giftedness in the narrow perspective of the so-called I.Q. score. We have already stressed the fact that the I.Q. score fails to assess the motivational forces and drives so vital to outstanding achievement. Moreover, the I.Q. test score is not always reliable and valid, since it is affected by physical, psychological, and cultural factors bearing on the learner. But of no less importance is the fact that giftedness acquires a multiplicity of manifestations. Giftedness is not merely limited to the combination of verbal and mathematical facility as evinced by many intelligence tests. The Rockefeller Report on Education makes this point clear.

> *Our conception of excellence must embrace many kinds of achievement at many levels.* There is no single scale or simple set of categories in terms of which to measure excellence. There is excellence in abstract intellectual activity, in art, in music, in managerial activities, in craftsmanship, in human relations, in technical work.
>
> Second, we must not assume that native capacity is the sole ingredient in superior performance. Excellence . . . is a product of ability and motivation and character. And the more one observes high performance in the dust and heat of daily life, the more one is likely to be impressed with the contribution made by the latter two ingredients.
>
> Finally, we must recognize that judgments of differences in talent are not judgments of differences in human worth.
>
> To sum up, it is possible for us to cultivate the ideal of excellence while retaining the moral values of equality.[39]

The Harvard report also stresses the importance of opportunity and motivation in moving individuals toward the multiple dimensions of excellence.

> There are the mechanical who like to work with their hands, and the meditative, often clumsy with their hands but quick at words and ideas. There are the literal, at home in everything exact, and the artistic, who see things intuitively and by symbols. These and similar differences . . . run through all social classes. Yet they are of course fostered or repressed by background and even by the general character of an age. There seems no reason to believe that altogether exceptional artistic talent existed in ancient Greece or Renaissance Italy, or that scientific and executive gifts, to a degree far beyond all others, are inborn in Americans. Opportunity, rather, gives play to some gifts, repressing others, and a chief role of general education is precisely to check the too iron working of current forces, to the end of eliciting the varied powers innate in people, thereby enriching both them and the community.
>
> Finally, there is a vastly important but equally obscure difference in will power and fidelity to purpose. Even the best intellectual gifts come to little without this virtue, and less than the best gifts may go far with it . . . whatever its origin, this quality of will power is something different from intelligence, though in the long run may help it. Hence any

---

[39] Rockefeller Brothers Fund, Inc., *The Pursuit of Excellence: Education and the Future of America* (New York: Doubleday & Company, Inc., 1958), pp. 16–17.

test of intelligence gives very incomplete grounds for judging a person in his changing years, and knowledge thus gained must be augmented by some test of actual accomplishment and by judgment of teachers.[40]

At no time in our history has the problem of identifying and nurturing giftedness and creativeness been so important as it is today. Standardized test scores and academic grades are far from accurate in assessing the qualities or potentials for giftedness and creativeness. An important study reported that the coefficient of correlation between intelligence and academic achievement was only .60 for elementary-school children, .50 for high-school pupils, and .45 for college students.[41] Moreover, many investigators have emphasized that psychological testing is inadequate for predicting success in life.[42]

While the gifted youngster may learn to perform well in whatever is expected of him in the classroom situation, thereby attaining an outstanding academic record, the creative youngster may do poorly in his school work because, through nonconforming means, he seeks unusual and unique channels of learning. History is marked by many cases pointing to the fallibility of tests and teachers in identifying and nurturing the creative youngster. Albert Einstein was regarded as a "slow learner" in school. Thomas Edison's teacher viewed the boy as "dull, if not actually half-witted." Young Darwin was held to be "a difficult child, hard to arouse, slow to learn, seldom eager, a self-centered day-dreamer, timid and stammering."[43]

Roe's study of eminent scientists yielded some interesting findings concerning their backgrounds and attitudes toward their work.[44] The purpose of this study was to determine the elements that go into the making of outstanding men of science. Such factors as background or upbringing, education, intelligence, personality, values, and other attributes were explored. Exhaustive tests, interviews, and analyses of life histories were made in this connection.

In our struggle for survival in the latter half of the twentieth century, the destiny of our society will depend upon our scientific creativity. In this investigation the problem of how an eminent scientist is made was explored. The findings of this study may surprise some people. The factor

[40] Reprinted by permission of the publisher from *General Education in a Free Society*, Report of the Harvard Committee. Cambridge, Mass.: Harvard University Press, Copyright, 1945, by the President and Fellows of Harvard College, pp. 85–86.
[41] Herbert A. Carroll, *Genius in the Making* (New York: McGraw-Hill Company, Inc., 1940).
[42] Charles C. Cole, Jr., *Encouraging Scientific Talent* (New York: College Entrance Examination Board, 1956).
[43] Carroll, *op. cit.*, p. 250.
[44] Anne Roe, "A Psychologist Examines 64 Eminent Scientists," *Scientific American*, November, 1952, 187:21–25.

that triggered most of these scientists into their careers was the sudden realization that new knowledge was discoverable and that everything was not known. When did this realization occur? Unfortunately, it was rarely developed in the elementary or secondary school. These eminent scientists reported, almost invariably, that the first realization that there was a great and exciting frontier of the unknown to be explored and discovered did not come to them until their junior or senior year in college, when they were given an opportunity to do some independent research. The possibility of finding things out for oneself came as a sudden realization and as a unique challenge in the educative experience of these men. A teacher had provided a student with the challenge of independent, critical thinking. Instead of limiting the educative experience to known facts, principles, laws, and events, as evinced through the textbook and the lecture, these students were liberated to find the challenges, rewards, and responsibilities of independent thinking. Conformity was dispelled for creativity. But even at the college level, it was the exceptional situation that provided creative conditions of learning through exploration and discovery. These eminent men of science reported that insufficient opportunity was afforded for creative thinking at all levels of their schooling.

Everyone is familiar with the natural curiosity and exploratory drives of the child. But all too often this curiosity is channeled through the home and schooling into patterns of conformity. Although conformity is required of every member of any society, it should not be attained through the loss of creativity.

In too many instances, our elementary and secondary school programs give youngsters the impression that everything worth knowing is already known, and that acquiring this most consequential and final knowledge is an end in itself. By taking away exploration and discovery from education, we lose the real vitality of learning. Teachers do too much telling and explaining, denying students the joy of exploring and discovering on their own. Quotations from these eminent scientists illustrate the importance of this in setting their life goals.

> I had no course in biology until my senior year in college. . . . It was my first contact with the idea that not everything was known, my first contact with research. In that course I think my final decision was really taken.
>
> One of the professors took a group of us and thought if we wanted to learn about things, the way to do it was to do research. My senior year I carried through some research. That really sent me, that was the thing that trapped me. After that there was no getting out.[45]

---

[45] *Ibid.*, p. 25.

The investigator summarizes the importance of discovery and finding things out for oneself as essential to creativity.

> That research experience is so often decisive is a fact of very considerable importance for educational practice. The discovery of the possibility of finding things out for oneself usually came through experience in school with a teacher who put the students pretty much on their own.[46]

This study also pointed to the importance of motivation to the creative process. The investigator concludes with this statement:

> The one thing that all of these 64 scientists have in common is their driving absorption in their work. They have worked long hours for many years, frequently with no vacations to speak of, because they would rather be doing their work than anything else.[47]

Now, we are not saying that the goal of education is to make creative scientists out of everyone. Even if this were possible, it probably would not be very desirable. The important thing is that we have done little in the way of making education a stimulating experience. We have long neglected the creative process in teaching and learning. In too many of our schools, the curriculum is geared merely to the textbook and workbook. Students are given little opportunity for independent study, critical thinking, and problem-solving. Information is taught as an end in itself. But our future survival will depend upon our creativity and resourcefulness in exploring and discovering from the horizons of the unknown.

Relatively little is known about the creative process. But we do know that the creative person is obsessed with inquiry. Some of the factors generally recognized as characterizing the creative individual are

1. An incessant inquisitiveness and drive for exploration and discovery.
2. A vivid imagination, transcending the orthodox or conventional modes of investigation and analysis.
3. A concept of the ideal that goes beyond existing conditions or limitations. Such existing limitations are regarded as temporary or relative. Moreover, the ideal is not regarded as a final and ultimate state, but a goal for improving existing conditions or solving existing problems.
4. An experimental attitude and an open-minded willingness to try the unlikely and reach for the impossible. Nothing is regarded as immutable, sacred, or immune from investigation.

---

[46] *Ibid.*, p. 25.   [47] *Ibid.*, p. 25.

5. A power of insight or capacity to seize upon unconventional solutions to seemingly insoluble problems.

6. A capacity for synthesizing existing elements into new combinations, relationships, and applications.

Erich Fromm states that one of the prime requisites of the creative attitude is the capacity to be puzzled. He observes, ironically, that this capacity is often stultified through the process of education.

> First of all, it requires the capacity to be puzzled. Children still have the capacity to be puzzled. Their whole effort is one of attempting to orient themselves in a new world, to grasp the ever-new things which they learn to experience. They are puzzled, surprised, capable of wondering, and that is what makes their reaction a creative one. But once they are through the process of education, most people lose the capacity of wondering, of being surprised. They feel they ought to know everything, and hence that it is a sign of ignorance to be surprised at or puzzled by anything.[48]

In his description of the creative process, Bronowski stresses the importance of induction. Rather than deductively selecting data from available facts, the creative scientist induces a theory through imaginative choice transcending the factual information.

> The power which the scientific method has developed has grown from a procedure which the Greeks did not discover: the procedure of induction. . . .
> Francis Bacon in 1620 and Christian Huygens in 1690 set down the intellectual bases of induction. They saw that it is not possible to reach an explanation of what happens in nature by deductive steps. Every explanation goes beyond our experience and thereby becomes a speculation. . . .
> The man who proposes a theory makes a choice—an imaginative choice which outstrips the facts. The creative activity of science lies here, in the process of induction. For induction imagines more than there is ground for and creates relations which at bottom can never be verified. Every induction is a speculation and it guesses at a unity which the facts present but do not strictly imply.
> To put the matter more formally: A scientific theory cannot be constructed from the facts by any procedure which can be laid down in advance, as if for a machine.[49]

> A fact is discovered, a theory is invented.[50]

Other conditions for creativity, according to Fromm, are the ability to concentrate and the ability to accept conflict and tension resulting from polarity.[51] Guilford cites the factors of spontaneous flexibility and

---

[48] Erich Fromm, "The Creative Attitude," in *Creativity and its Cultivation*, Harold H. Anderson (ed.) (New York: Harper and Row, Publishers, Inc., 1959), p. 48.

[49] J. Bronowski, "The Creative Process," in *Science and Society* by Thomas D. Clareson (ed.) (New York: Harper and Row, Publishers, Inc., 1961), p. 50.

[50] *Ibid.*, p. 47.   [51] Fromm, *op. cit.*, pp. 48–54.

adaptive flexibility as important traits of creativity.[52] Traditionalists hold to the idea that one cannot think effectively unless one is first fully impregnated with prior knowledge. But the psychological evidence points to the need to function in an atmosphere free from excessive domination, where a spirit of inquiry, divergence, and freedom are cultivated rather than suppressed.

The social consequences of reflective and creative endeavor are an improved society. Our schools must not only be charged with the task of transmitting the common heritage; they should play a vital role in nurturing individuals who are free to think independently.

The intuitive process, so often discouraged in the classroom, is said to be a key factor in inductive and creative thought.[53] High intelligence, alone, does not guarantee creativity, though it is a vital factor in certain types of creative endeavor. Many investigators believe that while creativity is a rare quality, even among highly intelligent people, it is, nevertheless, within the province of almost all of us.[54]

Thus, we have two views of creativity. One view conceives of creativity as the capacity for original thought, thought that brings about new theories, rather than mere inventions, through the inductive process. Where inventiveness and innovation derive from the interpretation and application of available facts, creativeness involves the induction of unique conceptions into a problem situation. Obviously such creativeness is extremely rare, even among our most highly intelligent population.

The other type of creativity deals with man's capacity to be spontaneous, imaginative, self-confident, and free from artificial fears and coercion, so that he may attack a problem with an open mind and with self-discipline, thereby being capable of reaching constructive solutions. Each person is regarded as a unique and valuable being, and this capacity for uniqueness and individuality contributes to the improvement of the human community. Such a conception holds that, by virtue of this individuality and uniqueness of every man, creativity is within the capacity of the general population, even though only a relatively small proportion of us realize this capacity to any considerable extent. Jane Addams was referring to this kind of creativity when she stated: "The most precious moment in human development is the young creature's assertion that he is unlike any other human being, and has an individual contribution to make to the world. Variation from the established type is at the root of all change, the only possible basis for

---

[52] J. P. Guilford, "Traits of Creativity," in Anderson, op. cit., p. 147.
[53] Jerome S. Bruner, The Process of Education (Cambridge, Mass.: Harvard University Press, 1960), p. 20.
[54] Harold H. Anderson, "Creativity in Perspective," in Anderson, op. cit., p. 249.

Photo by Vories Fisher

"The engagement of the imagination is the only thing
that makes any activity more than mechanical."
—John Dewey

Dr. Melvin Calvin, Nobel Laureate in Chemistry; courtesy Learning Resources Institute

"A gifted man cannot handle bacteria or equations
without taking fire from what he does
and having his emotions engaged."
—J. Bronowski

progress, all that keeps life from growing unprofitably stale and repetitious."[55]

INQUIRY, EMOTIONS, AND NEEDS

Critical Thinking and the Emotions

In emphasizing the importance of critical thinking, problem-solving and the method of intelligence in the teaching-learning process, we do not wish to negate the emotional factors. We have already emphasized the importance of learning as a challenging, rewarding, and joyful ex-

---

[55] Jane Addams, *The Spirit of Youth and the City Streets* (New York: The Macmillan Company), 1909, pp. 8–9.

perience. These are important motivational considerations. Indeed, we cannot separate the intellectual from the emotional. The stimulus that spurs an Einstein in the creative process is both intellectual and emotional. Without the feelings of desire and drive, no amount of critical or creative thinking could take place.

Of course, the critically thinking person must be able to recognize and prevent his biases from influencing his data. He must be able to approach problems open-mindedly. He must be free of superstition and ulterior motive. But this does not mean that he is without emotion. On the contrary, he must have a thirst for exploration and discovery; he must have a drive for continued learning. Without this drive for continued learning, human progress would cease.

Unfortunately, too many teachers make learning so unrewarding, so meaningless, and so punishing that the learner leaves school swearing never to open a book again. The twelfth-grade student of English literature may, through his experience in the course, learn that he finds Shakespeare distasteful. Likewise, the high school student in algebra may develop a distaste for higher mathematics. Obviously, our emotions have such a great influence on our capacity for learning that it would be fruitless to conceive of education as a purely intellectual experience, completely devoid of feelings or attitudes or emotions.

Yet, there are many educators and critics of education who see a divorcement between what is intellectual and what is emotional. This is unfortunate because knowledge does not, of itself, mold feelings or ideals. The study of American history and government does not guarantee that an individual will be more understanding and tolerant in his dealings with minority groups. The study of world literature does not guarantee that an individual will gain a lifelong passion for the great books.

When the educator considers the whole person, he is taking into account the multiple aspects of learning—the intellectual, emotional, and physical—none of which can be separated from the others. The feelings of the learner are so vital to the educative process that they are inseparable from the so-called intellectual pursuits. And, of course, the physical well-being of the learner has a great deal to do with his feelings and drives where education is concerned.

The intellectual and emotional processes belong to what we may call the unity of learning. Corey stressed the importance of viewing learning in its multiple dimensions.

> One of the basic characteristics of learning—and a characteristic that
> is frequently overlooked by persons interested primarily in intellectual
> development—is the "feeling" aspect. We like or dislike, accept or reject,
> feel pleased, or displeased, in greater or lesser degree, with every ex-

perience we have. Whatever is learned about a person, a group of persons, an object, a practice, an institution, or an idea is accompanied by an evaluation of it. Any sharp distinction between intellectual and emotional experience is unrealistic.[56]

Bronowski observes that "a gifted man cannot handle bacteria or equations without taking fire from what he does and having his emotions engaged."[57]

HUMAN NEEDS AND EDUCATION. In addition to our physiological needs of food, clothing, shelter, and sex, humans strive to fulfill other needs that have an important bearing on the educative process. One investigator has identified these other needs as follows:

1. Security and safety.
2. Acceptance—affection, love, affiliation, belonging, companionship, friendship.
3. Approval, recognition, prestige, status.
4. Self-esteem, self-respect, self-satisfaction.
5. Mastery, success, achievement.
6. Independence.[58]

As we analyze these important psychological needs, we come to realize that they are related to the process of maturity. If education is growth, then education is concerned with the development of the mature individual. Maturity is not an ultimate attainment, but a process of approximation. Adults, as well as children, can be found to behave immaturely. Whitehorn identifies four stages of immaturity:

I. *Infantile Level*

At the infantile level one expects from others a limitless amount of service and consideration—without any automatic feeling of reciprocal obligation. . . . The outstanding emotional need at this level is for affection or attention.

II. *Childish Level*

At the childish level, there has developed some sense of responsibility, but it is a delegated responsibility of the kind that is completely erased by a good excuse. The alibi habit is the characteristic expression of this stage. . . . Persons at the childish level of immaturity expect reliability in others, but only formal effort, up to the "excused" level, in themselves. They may expend much more effort in framing acceptable excuses than might be required to get a job done. Praise or blame is the focus of attention. The great emotional need of the childish level is for security, characteristically sought in attachment to

---

[56] Stephen M. Corey, "Psychological Foundations of General Education," National Society for the Study of Education, Fifty-first Yearbook, Part I, *General Education* (Chicago: University of Chicago Press, 1952), pp. 58–59.
[57] Bronowski, "The Creative Process," in Clareson, *op. cit.*, p. 47.
[58] A. H. Maslow, "Preface to Motivation Theory," *Psychosomatic Medicine*, 1943, 5:85–92.

others—older or more powerful persons who may appear reliable and interested.

III. *Early Adolescent Level*

At the early adolescent level, exhibitionism and prestige-seeking are the outstanding manifestations of a strong push to gain personal significance, and to sustain it by repetitive demonstration. The striving for self-sufficiency requires extrafamilial supports, and those are characteristically found in idealistic hero worship and in gangs.

Badges and trophies have high value as demonstrable symbols of prestige. The sense of group responsibility develops at this level, limited in range to the gang or even more limited to one's buddy, but rather fanatical in its intensity. The great emotional need at this stage is for assurance as to personal significance, rather than simply affection or security.

Now personal significance can show off only in a social setting. It can never be wholly individualistic. There is therefore at this level a correlated growth of social sense expressed in personal loyalty or small group loyalty.

IV. *Late Adolescent Level*

The late adolescent level is the stage of -isms—romanticism, idealism, or cynicism, for example. The sense of social responsibility has become more generalized in the form of loyalty to a cause, as well as to a person or group. The tendency to excess is still present as in earlier adolescence, but it is doctrinaire excess rather than physically strenuous excess. The pseudosophisticated "line" of talk, the "wisecrack," and the sophomoric savant are easily recognizable manifestations. Sexual interests are expressed in pairing off and in courtship behavior, but success in that field, or the anticipation of success, has the emotional quality of a conquest rather than of mutual devotion.[59]

It would be folly for us to draw a sharp line of demarcation between intelligence and the emotions in the educative process. The intellectual needs of man cannot be divorced from his emotional needs. Both are complementary forces in the process of growth and maturity. Whitehorn, in summation, identifies three basic emotional needs:

1. The need for affection
2. The need for personal security
3. The need for personal significance[60]

These emotional needs reflect man's interdependent position as a social organism. We strive for belonging while asserting our individuality. The mature individual does not regard freedom and security as antithetical forces. One has to be reasonably secure in order to enjoy freedom, and one has to be free in order to enjoy a sense of security and well-being. The teacher who recognizes these important emotional needs will be in

---

[59] John C. Whitehorn, "The Development of Mature Individuals," *Adult Leadership*, 5, January, 1957, 7:206–208, 222.
[60] *Ibid.*, p. 208.

a better position to work successfully with youngsters and adults. One cannot consider the nature of intelligence without an understanding of the psychological drives and emotional needs that influence human behavior.

Some investigators have identified these human needs in terms of attraction and repulsion, or appetite and aversion. A human need, vital to the educative process but often neglected by teachers, is the need for questing, exploring, and discovery.

1. Human beings tend to behave in ways involving movement away from being bored and finding life dull and monotonous toward adventure, new experience, and zestful activity.
2. Human beings tend to behave in ways involving movement away from failure, thwarting, and disappointment toward success, mastery, and achievement.
3. Human beings tend to behave in ways involving movement away from being ignored or looked down upon toward being looked up to, recognized, approved, admired.
4. Human beings tend to behave in ways involving movement away from being unwanted toward being loved and given intimacy, tenderness, and a sense of belonging.
5. Human beings tend to behave in ways involving movement away from being worried, anxious, fearful toward release, security, and peace of mind.[61]

These needs for exploring, success, recognition, belonging, and so on point to the importance of interpersonal relationships in education. These newer findings about human behavior have come about through work in Gestalt psychology, psychoanalysis, and social psychology. And these findings cannot be ignored by the competent teacher. Once again, we must emphasize that interpersonal relationships in the educative process must provide for a maximum of individual freedom. And, of course, in a democratic society, individual freedom exists in a setting of social responsibility.

Albert Einstein emphasized the role of the school in meeting these important human needs, but cautions us against using the need for recognition as an instrument to fulfill individual ambitions at the expense of social responsibility.

. . . the aiming at recognition and consideration, lies firmly fixed in human nature. With absence of mental stimulus of this kind, human cooperation would be entirely impossible; the desire for the approval of one's fellowman certainly is one of the most important binding powers of society. In this complex of feelings, constructive and destructive forces lie closely together. Desire for approval and recognition is a healthy motive; but the desire to be acknowledged as better, stronger or more

---

[61] G. B. Watson and R. B. Spence, *The ABC of Educational Psychology* (New York: The Macmillan Company), 1930, p. 326.

intelligent than a fellow being or fellow scholar easily leads to an excessively egoistic psychological adjustment, which may become injurious for the individual and for the community. Therefore the school and the teacher must guard against employing the easy method of creating individual ambition, in order to induce the pupils to diligent work.[62]

THE INQUIRING LEARNER OR THE QUIZ KID? Our machines are far more efficient than humans at storing and retrieving information. These machines are not bored by this regurgitative process; but men do become bored with mechanical routine. On the other hand, the inquiry process is challenging and exciting. The climate of our schools can be revitalized through the inquiry process. But the adult world is sometimes afraid to allow youngsters to grapple with real problems such as racial segregation, socioeconomic inequities, world government, conflicting political systems, and so forth. Instead, we are more comfortable when we see the schools develop quiz kids who are most adept at retaining factual information. Is it any wonder, then, that the most exciting aspect of many high schools and colleges is the athletic event?

Instead of information-giving-custodial institutions that are divorced from the realities of life, our schools should be learning laboratories through which the student inquires into real problems. In this way the lust for learning, so common in the young child, will become manifest also in adolescents and adults. Inquiry has long been resisted as a mode for our schools, not only because of our obsession with absolute and invalid doctrines of learning such as mental discipline, but because we are often afraid of allowing many authority-derived rules and processes to be questioned. Then too, it is not an easy task to develop the inquiring individual in a society that expends far more for advertising each year than for public secondary education. Yet, the democratic ideal and the need for societal improvement require that our schools develop the inquiring mind.

SUMMARY

American democracy rests its faith on perhaps six principles that have an important bearing on our educational system: (1) cultural heterogeneity, interdependence, and assimilation; (2) social mobility; (3) educational accessibility and educability of the people; (4) government by consent of the governed; (5) maximum individual and academic freedom, compatible with the general welfare; and (6) separation of church and state.

During the twentieth century, each of these principles has been

---

[62] Albert Einstein, *Out of My Later Years* (New York: Philosophical Library, 1950), p. 34.

tested. Our schools have met the major task, early in the century, of building unity from cultural diversity. Our high schools have opened their doors to all youth. We have rejected the class and caste system which plagues many other societies. We have affirmed our faith in freedom to teach and freedom to learn as essential ingredients of a free society. And we have maintained the secular school as vital to the general welfare of a pluralistic people.

While the principles of American democracy have not been fully realized, they have served as goals for the continued improvement of society. If the schools are to be instruments of democracy, they must function as democratic institutions. A democracy rests its strength upon an enlightened citizenry. Unless students gain experiences in inquiry and independent thinking, they will not acquire these powers automatically when reaching adulthood. The capacity for critical thought and action is enhanced when students are stimulated to discover problems and to find their own solutions.

Studies have revealed that much of what passes for education results in convergent or conforming thinking. Recent reforms in curriculum and instruction in certain areas of the secondary school curriculum represent a reawakening of the responsibility of the school to foster inquiry, cognition, and even divergent styles of thinking. Indoctrination by the school can only lead to the closing of minds. In today's world, it is the opening of minds that will lead to creative solutions to pervading problems.

Through the comprehensive high school we have rejected the notion that the secondary school is the exclusive domain of the academically talented. Yet, we have just begun to recognize that excellence is manifested in many walks of life, and that our schools are responsible for developing a wide spectrum of talents.

PROBLEMS FOR STUDY AND DISCUSSION

1. How do the principles of American democracy apply to practices in American public education?

2. The Rockefeller Report, *The Pursuit of Excellence*, states that the ideals of human equality and individual excellence are not antithetical, but complementary forces in a democracy. How do you see these two ideals or forces as complementary rather than conflicting?

3. Why is intuition an important factor in the inquiry process? Bruner observes that many teachers ignore or even discourage intuitive thinking. How do you account for this?

4. Bruner refers to the structure of a subject as the means whereby we are able to recognize the applicability or inapplicability of an idea to a new situation. Drawing from your own major field, give an example of how an understanding of certain major ideas would enable the learner to deal with new situations or problems.

5. Why are attitudes and emotions so important in the teaching-learning process?

6. It has been said that "the attempt to teach thinking to children who are tied to school desks is like offering a correspondence course in swimming to a Bedouin in the desert of Arabia" (Joseph K. Hart in *Education in The Humane Community*). Do you think this statement is applicable to many of the procedures in our high schools? Why or why not?

7. Describe a situation in which you, as a teacher, would employ the inquiry-discovery mode with your students.

8. Dewey stated that "education is the fundamental method of social progress and reform." Do you agree or disagree with this statement? Why?

9. What connection do you see between the method of intelligence in our schools and the development of an enlightened citizenry?

SELECTED REFERENCES

Anderson, Harold H. (ed.) *Creativity and its Cultivation.* New York: Harper and Row, Publishers, Inc., 1959.

Bayles, Ernest E. *Democratic Educational Theory.* New York: Harper and Row, Publishers, Inc., 1959.

Bloom, Benjamin S. (ed.) *Taxonomy of Educational Objectives.* New York: David McKay Company, Inc., 1956.

Bode, Boyd H. *How We Learn.* Boston: D. C. Heath and Company, 1940.

Brameld, Theodore. *Education for the Emerging Age.* New York: Harper and Row, Publishers, Inc., 1961.

Bruner, Jerome S. *The Process of Education.* Cambridge, Mass.: Harvard University Press, 1960.

Burton, William H., Roland B. Kimball and Richard L. Wing. *Education for Effective Thinking.* New York: Appleton-Century-Crofts, Inc., 1960.

Cantor, Nathaniel. *The Teaching-Learning Process.* New York: Holt, Rinehart and Winston, Inc., 1953.

Dewey, John. *Democracy and Education.* New York: The Macmillan Company, 1916.
———. *How We Think.* Boston: D. C. Heath and Company, 1933.

Farber, Seymour M. and Roger H. L. Wilson (eds.) *Conflict and Creativity.* New York: McGraw-Hill Company, Inc., 1963.

Gardner, John. *Excellence: Can We Be Equal and Excellent Too?* New York: Harper and Row, Publishers, Inc., 1961.

Getzels, Jacob and Philip Jackson. *Creativity and Intelligence.* New York: John Wiley & Sons, Inc., 1962.

Hart, Joseph K. *Education in The Humane Community.* New York: Harper and Row, Publishers, Inc., 1951.

Hilgard, Ernest R. *Theories of Learning.* New York: Appleton-Century-Crofts, Inc., 1956.

Hook, Sidney. *Education for Modern Man.* New York: Alfred A. Knopf, Inc., 1963.

Hullfish, H. Gordon and Philip G. Smith. *Reflective Thinking: The Method of Education.* New York: Dodd, Mead & Company, 1961.

Kelley, Earl C. *Education for What is Real.* New York: Harper and Row, Publishers, Inc., 1947.

Lee, Gordon C. *Education in Modern America.* New York: Holt, Rinehart and Winston, Inc., 1957. Ch. 3.

Murphy, Gardiner. *Human Potentialities.* New York: Basic Books, 1958.

National Society for the Study of Education. *Theories of Learning and Instruction.* 63rd Yearbook, Part I. Chicago: The University of Chicago Press, 1964.

Report of The Harvard Committee. *General Education in a Free Society.* Cambridge, Mass.: Harvard University Press, 1958.

Rockefeller Brothers Fund, Inc. *The Pursuit of Excellence: Education and the Future of America.* Special Studies Report V. New York: Doubleday & Company, 1958.

Taylor, Calvin W. and Frank Barron. *Scientific Creativity: Its Recognition and Develment.* New York: John Wiley & Sons, Inc., 1963.

Thelen, Herbert A. *Education and The Human Quest.* New York: Harper and Row, Publishers, Inc., 1960.

Warner, W. Lloyd, Robert J. Havighurst, and Martin G. Loeb. *Who Shall Be Educated?* New York: Harper and Row, Publishers, Inc., 1944.

Wertheimer, Max. *Productive Thinking* (Revised). New York: Harper and Row, Publishers, Inc., 1959.

Whitehead, Alfred North. *The Aims of Education and Other Essays.* New York: The Macmillan Company, 1929.

III

The Curriculum: Change and Challenge

I am the last person to question the importance of genuine literary education. . . . An exclusively scientific training will bring about a mental twist as surely as an exclusively literary training. The value of the cargo does not compensate for the ship's being out of trim.

—*Thomas Henry Huxley*

CHAPTER 6

The Subject
Curriculum

THE SUBJECT-CENTERED CURRICULUM has long been the dominant approach to organizing the program of studies in the American high school. The 1930's witnessed considerable experimentation with other patterns of curriculum organization. Although these efforts yielded great promise for curriculum improvement, our schools, by and large, have adhered to the subject-centered approach. Nevertheless, the 1960's are marked by new efforts to improve course content and methodology in the secondary school. There have also been some notable modifications of the traditional subject-centered curriculum.

In this chapter we shall examine the advantages and limitations of the subject-centered curriculum. We shall also examine the origin and status of the Carnegie Unit, and discuss its relationship to the subject curriculum and the program of studies of the secondary school. Moreover, the problem of curriculum articulation and improvement will be explored.

WHAT IS CURRICULUM?

The term curriculum is defined in many ways. To some it means the aggregate of courses offered by an educational institution. Others think of curriculum as those courses required of a student enrolled in a school. The terms extracurricular or cocurricular activities are generally confined to school offerings that are not patterned as courses, carry no academic credit, and are conducted on a voluntary basis. Thus, school-sponsored clubs, athletic teams, student organizations, publications, and other similar functions may be classified as extracurricular. However, many educators strongly object to the term extracurricular since it im-

213

plies that it represents the noneducational aspects of the school program. It is common practice for schools to sponsor student clubs in photography, modern languages, science, mathematics, and other areas having real educational value. Consequently, a number of educators prefer the term cocurriculum to designate those school-sponsored activities that are not patterned as formal courses. On the other hand, many educators would offer a still broader definition of the term curriculum. They would regard curriculum as the sum total of experiences that are sponsored by the school. This broad definition makes the terms extracurricular and cocurricular meaningless. The following statement represents this broad concept of curriculum:

> In literate societies instruction in group ways becomes partly a specialized function. An institution—the school charged with the responsibility for teaching certain things—is created. A sequence of potential experiences is set up in the school for the purpose of disciplining children and youth in group ways of thinking and acting. This set of experiences is referred to as the curriculum.[1]

Another broad definition of the term curriculum is offered by Harold Taylor, former president of Sarah Lawrence College, who holds that a curriculum is much more than the subject-matter content for some courses of study.

> The establishment of a strong curriculum with serious intellectual content is not a question of adding more subject-matter in order to give children more to do, or to make the curriculum "harder," so that the mind will be trained. It is a question of holding in one's mind a double image of what the curriculum must be and what it must do, just as the composer writes down what he is composing and hears his own sounds as he writes. A curriculum is a composition in just this sense, and it consists not merely in textbooks and readings, but in questions, experiences, atmosphere, attitudes, remarks, interests. A true curriculum can only be made by one who knows intuitively what his plan of education will be like in action, what kind of response it can evoke in the learner.[2]

Some educational critics, however, would take issue with these broad definitions of curriculum. They would view a curriculum as a specific set of formal courses. Professor Bestor, for example, advocates that the elementary school curriculum be confined essentially to the fundamental subjects, and the curriculum at the secondary level should focus primarily on the recognized academic disciplines. He would recommend an academic curriculum for all students, regardless of ability or interest.

---

[1] B. Othanel Smith, William O. Stanley, and J. Harlan Shores, *Fundamentals of Curriculum Development* (Yonkers-on-Hudson, New York: World Book Company, 1957), p. 3.
[2] Harold Taylor, "The Whole Child: A Fresh Look," *Saturday Review,* December 16, 1961, p. 58.

Photo by Vories Fisher

"One can no more say what music is than one can say
   what life itself is. . . . Like life itself, music
   never ends, for it can always be re-created."
                                    —AARON COPLAND

Such a curriculum, he argues, is best for teaching youngsters how to use their minds.

> In my judgment, the real purpose of a school is to teach youngsters how to use their minds effectively. You have reading, writing and arithmetic as the first steps in this process. Then, in high school you get science, history, English and foreign languages.
>
> Of course, you have other school activities, too. But these ought to be additions to the school program.[3]

While Professor Bestor recognizes the need for some vocational education in high school, he recommends no academic credit for such studies.[4] Thus we see a basic conflict of opinion between those educators who conceive of curriculum as the sum total of experiences provided by the school and those educators who see it as a group of standard courses. In addition, there is the conflict between those educators who advocate a diversified program of studies at the secondary level, and those who confine the curriculum to a narrow group of academic subjects. These issues, obviously, are rooted in differences in educational philosophy.

THE CURRICULUM, THE INDIVIDUAL, AND SOCIETY. We must bear in mind that no matter how good a curriculum may seem to be on paper, the true test is how it affects the ideas and behaviors of the learners. Thus, the competency of the teacher is a vital element of the curriculum. In too many of our schools, the curriculum is thought of as the combined courses of instruction and subjects that students are required to take for graduation. Few attempts are made at developing a functional relationship between and among the various curricular elements. Rarely does a faculty attempt to develop an educational philosophy in harmony with the ideals of our society and the needs of our youth.

In a dynamic society, the curriculum cannot remain static. When we examine the secondary school curriculum in historical perspective, we come to realize that it has undergone continual change—perhaps not so much for purposes of experimentation and articulation, but rather in response to the changing needs and demands of society. In Chapter I we discussed how Benjamin Franklin proposed and implemented a utilitarian program of education at the secondary level, as contrasted with the prevailing classical and religious educational emphasis of the colonial period.

Even during the twentieth century, the curriculum of the American secondary school has undergone some significant changes. But unfortunately, many of these changes have come about by merely adding courses

---

[3] Interview with Professor Arthur Bestor, "We Are Less Educated than 50 Years Ago," *U.S. News & World Report,* November 30, 1956, p. 69.
[4] Arthur Bestor, *The Restoration of Learning* (New York: Alfred A. Knopf, 1955), p. 51.

where they seemed to be needed, while gradually dropping others that seemed outmoded, without giving adequate attention to the effects on the curricular content and structure. The role of the secondary school today is quite different from its predecessor of 1900. The modern mandate is education for all youth. Today, there are many crosscurrents of opinion about what subjects should be taught, how these subjects should be taught, and for what purpose.

THE CARNEGIE UNIT

The traditional role of the high school was preparation for college. Until the rapid development of the junior high school during the 1920's and 1930's, the prevailing pattern was an eight-year elementary school and a four-year high school. In 1909 the Carnegie Foundation for the Advancement of Teaching proposed the standard unit as a measurement for high-school credits. The purpose of this proposal was to overcome the prevailing confusion regarding the application of high-school credits toward college admission. At that time, there was a wide divergence in college admission requirements and in the time-allotment of subject fields in the high schools. The standard unit, as proposed by the Carnegie Foundation, was aimed at overcoming this confusion. The College Entrance Examination Board promptly approved the standard unit proposal, and thus the Carnegie Unit was imposed on the high schools.

The Carnegie Unit represents the standard of measurement of high school credits according to the amount of time spent on a particular subject in the classroom. One Carnegie Unit is gained when a student has successfully completed a minimum of 120 clock hours in a subject during a school year. Using the four-year high school as a basis, the student must attend a daily class session from 40 to 60 minutes in length, over an academic year of from 36 to 40 weeks, in order to earn a unit of credit. The assumption is that 16 such units over the four-year period qualifies a student for high school graduation. This quantitative standard was readily adopted by the high schools since their primary purpose at the time was the preparation of students for college. The colleges quickly accepted this unit of measurement because it helped them overcome the existing confusion in evaluating high-school credits for college admission. Moreover, the Carnegie Foundation exerted considerable influence on the colleges at that time. Even today, the Carnegie Unit is the standard unit of measurement for high-school credits. Yet the high school of today is far different from that of 1909. The modern comprehensive high school is responsible for educating the many who will not go on to college. Indeed, almost two thirds of our high-school youth will not enter college. As a result, the high schools have diversified their offerings to meet the needs of a heterogeneous student population.

Shortcomings of the Carnegie Unit

The Carnegie Unit is a quantitative measurement and ignores qualitative variations in teaching and learning. Students are placed in a convenient lockstep where they attend virtually the same classes each day for the same period of time, regardless of their learning capabilities.

> Those urging the reexamination of the Carnegie Unit as a useful means of measuring pupil progress point out that these time allotments reduce high-school graduation to a question of covering certain bodies of subject-matter regarded as approximately equal to one another, and suggest that each pupil achieve in each a similar degree of mastery. Followed blindly, as it often is, they say that this concept (1) asks few questions about a pupil's ability to master the required bodies of knowledge, (2) pays too little attention to what he already knows, (3) forgets conveniently that some learn the same facts or skills in a fraction of the time required by others, (4) fails to reconcile wide variations in teaching skill and efficiency, and (5) ignores the many other facts about teaching, learning, testing, and marking which do not in fact conform to such a simple, quantitative formula as the Carnegie Unit. At its worst, the Carnegie Unit is accused of being a road-block to the building of modern high-school curricula, to needed reconstruction in the schedules of instruction, to sound evaluation of pupil progress, and to the improvement of high school-college relationships.[5]

Of the 25 trustees of the Carnegie Foundation in 1909, 22 were college presidents. And although the primary interest of the Foundation was in the realm of higher education, the universal acceptance of the Foundation's proposal for a standard unit has exerted a profound influence on the quantitative aspects of the high school curriculum. Surprisingly, there was no criticism of the Carnegie Unit by high-school educators during the years immediately following its adoption.

The widespread use of the Carnegie Unit today is testimony to its administrative convenience and to the failure of educators to come up with a suitable alternative system. The Carnegie Unit does not prevent the high schools from developing certain qualitative measures and improvements in the curriculum, but it does hold the schools to a rigid quantitative standard of measurement. For example, it tends to inhibit the development of accelerated programs that might allow students to secure more units in less time. The limitations of the Carnegie Unit are summarized as follows:

---

[5] Tompkins, Ellsworth and Walter H. Gaumnitz, The Carnegie Unit: Its Origin, Status, and Trends (Washington, D.C.: U.S. Department of Health, Education, and Welfare, Office of Education, 1954, pp. 1–2.

1. It lends prestige to those subjects acceptable to colleges in terms of entrance Units, and discriminates against other subjects excellent in their own right but as yet unacceptable for Unit measure.
2. It considers of equal magnitude *all* subjects for which classes meet an equal number of minutes per semester, provided outside pupil preparation is required. Five periods of English is equal to five periods of mathematics, etc.
3. It tends to make inflexible the daily and weekly time schedules of the school, for the Carnegie Unit nourishes the idea that a class should meet one period a day five times a week.
4. It restricts the development of a more functional curriculum based upon students' abilities, interests, and life-needs, because it has been difficult for the high school to obtain units of credit acceptable to the colleges in certain more functional subjects.
5. It measures quantitatively experiences in different subjects and in different schools and counts them as similar in outcome.
6. It ranks pupils in graduating class despite the fact that few of them ever have exactly the same program of studies and despite the fact that seldom are all the years in school counted in the ranking of the pupil.
7. It measures a high-school education (and diploma) in terms of *time* served and credits earned by the pupil.[6]

Yet, despite all of the limitations and handicaps of the Carnegie Unit, it would be unfair to rest all of the blame on the Unit for our failure to do more in the way of curricular innovation and experimentation. The Carnegie Unit did not create the traditional structure of curriculum organization and the inertia that preserves it. But the Carnegie Unit is particularly adapted to the traditional subject curriculum, which is in widespread practice today.

The Program of Studies

In examining the program of studies in the secondary school, we find that it embraces three comprehensive categories:

1. General education or common learnings
2. Exploratory or special-interest education
3. Specialized education
   (a) Academic or college preparatory
   (b) Vocational

General education or common learnings refer to those studies that are required of all students regardless of their particular avocational or vocational interests. The curriculum in general education is designed to meet the common needs of all citizens of our society.

Exploratory or special-interest education refers to those studies taken as electives. The usual practice is to allow the student to take at least

---

[6] *Ibid.,* p. 19.

one elective course each semester. Such electives may be restricted to certain subject fields, or the student may be free to select his electives from any of the courses offered by the school.

Specialized education represents the area or areas of concentration by the student for either vocational or academic purposes. The high-school student who plans to go on to college will follow a college preparatory program as his area of specialization. Other students may follow a vocational program. For those students not planning to go on to college, but who are uncertain of their vocational interests, a general program with a liberal choice of electives may be followed.

Obviously, the above classification is based upon the purposes for which various studies are pursued, and consequently there are no sharp lines of demarcation between the curricular categories. For example, because everyone in our society needs to communicate effectively, English is a required subject for all students, and consequently is classified as a general education requirement. On the other hand, a student specializing in business education takes typing as a vocational requirement, while another student in the college preparatory program may take the same course as an elective.

The three broad curricular categories of general education, exploratory education, and specialized education are treated in considerable detail in the chapters that follow.

The Comprehensive High School and the Specialized High School

The comprehensive high school has been called "a peculiarly American phenomenon."[7] While the traditional European pattern of secondary education has followed a dual-track system of dividing students according to academic and terminal-vocational categories, the predominant pattern in the United States has been a comprehensive high school designed to meet the educational needs of all youth.[8]

In many of our larger cities, specialized academic and vocational high schools are provided. The merits of the comprehensive high school versus those of the specialized high school are discussed in detail in the next chapter, but it is important to understand that the comprehensive high school, by its very nature, must offer a well-diversified curriculum. One of the key problems presented by a diversified program is that of developing continuity and cohesion in the curriculum, particularly for purposes of general education.

[7] John W. Gardner, in the Foreword of *The American High School Today* by James Bryant Conant (New York: McGraw-Hill Company, Inc., 1959, p. IX.
[8] *Ibid.*, pp. IX–X.

THE SUBJECT CURRICULUM IN OPERATION

Although our high schools vary greatly in the number and variety of specific course offerings, there are sixteen commonly accepted broad subject fields. (Those with asterisks may be offered as vocational programs under federal subsidization.) They are:

Agriculture*	Home Economics*
Art	Industrial Arts
Business Education	Mathematics
Distributive Education*	Music
Driver Education	Physical Education
English	Science
Foreign Languages	Social Studies
Health Education	Trade and Industrial Education*

While the above subject fields may be broken down into hundreds of courses or subjects offered at the high school level, too little attention is given to developing a functional or organic synthesis of these studies. The high-school curriculum is often a conglomeration of courses offered in a fragmented and dissociated manner, leaving many gaps as well as having unnecessary overlapping of curriculum material. Subjects are added and divisions are created without sufficient attention given to curricular relationships.

CURRICULUM TRACKS. A common practice in comprehensive and general high schools is to designate the curriculum according to several fixed areas or tracks, such as college preparatory, vocational, general, etc. An example of such a curriculum is shown in Table 6–1. Under this multiple track system, the student, with the advice of his counselor, chooses his area of specialized education (college preparatory, vocational, general, business, etc.). But regardless of the specific track a student pursues, there are certain courses, notably English, social studies, mathematics, biology, and physical education, that all students may be required to take. Such universal requirements may be classified as the core or general education sequence, or as constants of the curriculum. In addition to this so-called core or general education sequence and the specialized education sequence, certain electives are offered. Students may be free to elect any course offered by the school or they may be required to select electives from certain fields only. For our purposes, we have not indicated any differentiation between free electives and restricted electives in Table 6–1. In any case, such electives may be classified as exploratory or special-interest education.

In some high school programs, students may be required to com-

Table 6-1

Sample Program of Studies in a Large Comprehensive Four-Year High School

Year	College Preparatory	General	Practical Arts	Vocational Education	Business Education	Fine Arts
FRESHMAN* (9th Grade)	English I Social Studies Algebra Physical Educ. Foreign Lang. Elective	English I Social Studies Mathematics Physical Educ. General Science Elective	English I Social Studies Mathematics Physical Educ. Industrial Arts or Homemaking Elective	English I Social Studies Mathematics Physical Educ. Trades & Industs., Vocational Homemaking, or Distrib. Occup. Elective	English I Social Studies Mathematics Physical Educ. General Business Elective	English I Social Studies Mathematics Physical Educ. Art or Music Elective
SOPHOMORE (10th Grade)	English II Biology Physical Educ. Geometry Foreign Lang. Elective	English II Biology Physical Educ. Math or Algebra Elective Elective	English II Biology Physical Educ. Math or Algebra Industrial Arts or Homemaking Elective	English II Biology Physical Educ. Math or Algebra Trades & Industs., Vocational Homemaking, or Distrib. Occup. Elective	English II Biology Physical Educ. Math or Algebra Typing Elective	English II Biology Physical Educ. Math or Algebra Art or Music Elective
JUNIOR (11th Grade)	English III U.S. History Physical Educ. Advanced Alg. Foreign Lang. Elective	English III U.S. History Physical Educ. Elective Elective Elective	English III U.S. History Physical Educ. Industrial Arts or Homemaking Elective Elective	English III U.S. History Physical Educ. Trades & Industs., Vocational Homemaking, or Distrib. Occup. Elective Elective	English III U.S. History Physical Educ. Typing Shorthand or Bookkeeping Elective	English III U.S. History Physical Educ. Art or Music Elective Elective

SENIOR (12th Grade)					
English IV	American Gov't.	American Gov't.	American Gov't.	American Gov't.	American Gov't.
American Gov't.	Physical Educ.	Physical Educ.	Physical Educ.	Physical Educ.	Physical Educ.
Physical Educ.	Elective	Industrial Arts or Homemaking	Trades & Industs., Vocational Homemaking, or Distrib. Occup.	Shorthand or Bookkeeping	Art or Music
Chemistry or Physics	Elective	Elective	Elective	Elective	Elective
Elective	Elective	Elective	Elective	Elective	Elective
Elective	Elective	Elective	Elective	Elective	Elective

* School systems with a three-year junior high school and a three-year senior high school (6–3–3), absorb this into the final year of the junior high school.

plete a major and minor sequence. For example, this may consist of two majors of three years each, and two minors of two years each.

The organization of the curriculum into separate tracks, as shown in Table 6–1, is opposed by a number of educators. They argue that it is entirely unnecessary to track students according to college preparatory, vocational, or other designations. They believe that such tracking not only labels the curricula, but also labels the students. They would prefer dividing the curriculum into two very broad areas: required and elective courses. In this way, the labeling of students would be avoided and there would be less tendency to restrict students to rigid programs. In other words, except for those general education courses required of all students, the selection of courses would be made on an individualized basis. Students would not be compelled to restrict themselves to a fixed track.

Let us examine the curriculum at Abraham Lincoln High School—a large comprehensive high school in San Francisco. The graduation requirements at Abraham Lincoln High School are as follows:

> To graduate from high school, a student must show evidence of trustworthy character and must earn at least 150 semester periods of credit beyond the ninth grade. One subject taken every day for a semester counts 5 semester periods. The following specific requirements must be completed:
>
> 1. Six semesters of English in grades 10–12.
>   (Unless excused by the Principal from the 12th grade work.)
> 2. Two semesters of United States History and two semesters of Senior Civics.
> 3. Two semesters of laboratory science in grades 10–12.
> 4. Eighth grade proficiency in arithmetic.
>   (Test given in grade 11.)
> 5. Driver Education (30 class hours)
> 6. Physical Education or R.O.T.C. each semester.
> 7. Swimming (proficiency test given)
> 8. Field of Interest—Grades 9–12:
>   English—45 Semester periods
>   Social Studies—40 semester periods
>   Other—30 semester periods
> 9. 150 semester periods in grades 10–12 or
>   200 semester periods in grades 9–12.[9]

In Table 6–2 we see that the curriculum at Abraham Lincoln High School is organized according to five tracks or programs of study: academic, business, practical arts (homemaking and industrial arts), fine arts (music and art), and general education. The academic program is obviously designed for college entrance. The curriculum in general edu-

---

[9] *Master Program of Studies*, 1964–1965, Abraham Lincoln High School, San Francisco, California.

cation allows a student to pursue a wide range of electives. Although this is a large comprehensive high school, the vocational program is limited. For example, the curriculum in practical arts does not provide for vocational education in trades and industries or distributive occupations.

Table 6–3 reveals that there are thirteen departments offering no less than 90 subjects in grades 10 through 12 at this high school.

The programs of study in Tables 6–2 and 6–3 illustrate one approach in organizing a subject curriculum in a large comprehensive high school. The advantages and limitations of the subject curriculum are discussed later in this chapter.

The United States Office of Education describes the general purposes of the comprehensive high school and the nature of its curriculum as follows:

> The comprehensive high school curriculum is designed to provide secondary education for pupils who are preparing to enter college, for pupils who are preparing for vocational careers, for future homemakers, and for pupils who have not yet made a choice of careers. Such a curriculum contains certain school subjects which are required of all pupils and as wide a range of elective subjects as the total school enrollment can support.
>
> In general, one-half of the courses taken in the 4 years of secondary schooling are required and one-half are elective. Courses most commonly required of all pupils include 4 years of English, 2 years of social studies, 1 year of science, and 1 year of mathematics. In many schools, courses in health and physical education are taken each year, one-fourth of a unit credit being given for each year's course.
>
> Recently, there have been movements to increase the requirements in mathematics and science from 1 year to 2 years.[10]

Thus we see that the subject approach, with certain *broad-fields* modifications, constitutes the prevailing curriculum structure in our high schools. Options are provided for exploratory electives and specialization according to academic or vocational interests and aptitudes. The curriculum of the comprehensive high school, though structured according to a subject-centered and broad-fields approach, is diversified to meet the needs of a cosmopolitan student population.

Junior High School Studies

The junior high school may be organized as either a two-year or three-year institution. The two-year junior high school embraces grades seven

---

[10] Office of Education, U.S. Department of Health, Education, and Welfare, *Progress of Public Education in the United States 1960–61* (Washington, D.C.: Government Printing Office, 1961), p. 40.

Table 6–2
Abraham Lincoln High School Programs of Study
San Francisco, California

	Ninth Grade	Tenth Grade	Eleventh Grade	Twelfth Grade	Recommendations
ACADEMIC	English 1–2 Social Studies 1–2 Algebra 1–2 Foreign Language 1–2 Counseled Elective P.E.	English 3–4 One of the following: W. Hist., Biol. or Geometry 1–2 Counseled Elective Foreign Language Driver Ed.; Counseled Electives P.E. or R.O.T.C.	English 5–6 U.S. History 1–2 Adv. work in two: Foreign Lang., Math or Science Counseled Elective P.E. or R.O.T.C.	Adv. Comp.; World Lit.; Senior Eng. Lit. Senior Civics Adv. work in two: Foreign Lang., Math or Science Counseled Elective P.E. or R.O.T.C.	Consult current college catalogs for college entrance requirements.
BUSINESS	English 1–2 Social Studies 1–2 Algebra 1–2 or Math 1–2 Typewriting 1–2 Counseled Elective P.E.	English 3–4 One of the following: Biology or App. Science Business Elective Typewriting 3–4 Driver Ed.; Counseled Electives P.E. or R.O.T.C.	English 5–6 U.S. History 1–2 Business Elective Business Elective Counseled Elective P.E. or R.O.T.C.	Bus. Eng.: English Elective Senior Civics Business Elective Business Elective Counseled Elective P.E. or R.O.T.C.	Students are to specialize in one of the following areas: Bookkeeping Clerical Merchandising Secretarial
PRACTICAL ARTS	English 1–2 Social Studies 1–2 Algebra 1–2 or Math 1–2 Homemaking 1–2 Counseled Elective P.E.	English 3–4 One of the following: Science or Counseled Elective Homemaking Elective Counseled Elective Driver Ed.: Counseled Electives	English 5–6 U.S. History 1–2 Homemaking Elective One of the following: Science or Counseled Elective Counseled Elective P.E.	English Elective Senior Civics Homemaking Elective Homemaking Elective Counseled Elective P.E.	Students are to enroll in at least three of the following areas:
Homemaking					Child Development Clothing & Textiles Foods & Nutrition Home Management

Industrial Arts	English 1–2 Social Studies 1–2 Algebra 1–2 or Math 1–2 Mechanical Draw. 1–2 Counseled Elective P.E.	English 3–4 One of the following: Science or Counseled Elective Ind. Arts Elective Counseled Elective Driver Ed.; Counseled Electives P.E. or R.O.T.C.	English 5–6 U.S. History 1–2 One of the following: Science or Counseled Elective Ind. Arts Elective Counseled Elective P.E. or R.O.T.C.	English Elective Senior Civics Mechanical Draw. Adv. Ind. Arts Elective Counseled Elective P.E. or R.O.T.C.	This program of study should include, in addition to shop subjects, Shop Math and two semesters of Mechanical Drawing.
FINE ARTS *Music*	English 1–2 Social Studies 1–2 Algebra 1–2 or Math 1–2 Music Elective Counseled Electives P.E.	English 3–4 One of the following: Biology or App. Science Music Elective Counseled Elective Driver Ed.; Counseled Electives P.E. or R.O.T.C.	English 5–6 U.S. History 1–2 Music Elective Counseled Elective Counseled Elective P.E. or R.O.T.C.	English Elective Senior Civics Music Elective Counseled Elective Counseled Elective P.E. or R.O.T.C.	This program of study should include a semester each of History of Music and Harmony.
Art	English 1–2 Social Studies 1–2 Algebra 1–2 or Math 1–2 Art Elective Counseled Elective P.E.	English 3–4 One of the following: Biology or App. Science Art Elective Counseled Elective Driver Ed.; Art Appr. P.E. or R.O.T.C.	English 5–6 U.S. History 1–2 Art Elective Counseled Elective Counseled Elective P.E. or R.O.T.C.	English Elective Senior Civics Art Elective Counseled Elective Counseled Elective P.E. or R.O.T.C.	This program of study should include two semesters of History of Art.
GENERAL EDUCATION	English 1–2 Social Studies 1–2 Alegbra 1–2 or Math 1–2 Counseled Elective Counseled Elective P.E.	English 3–4 One of the following: Biology or App. Science Field of Interest Counseled Elective Driver Ed.; Counseled Electives P.E. or R.O.T.C.	English 5–6 U.S. History 1–2 Field of Interest Field of Interest Counseled Elective P.E. or R.O.T.C.	English Elective Senior Civics Field of Interest Field of Interest Counseled Elective P.E. or R.O.T.C.	It is possible for a student to take a wide range of electives in this program; but a field of interest must be completed.

SOURCE: *Master Program of Studies*, 1964–1965, Abraham Lincoln High School, San Francisco, California.

Table 6-3
Subjects Offered, Grades 10 through 12,
Abraham Lincoln High School,
San Francisco, California

Department and Subject	Grade Level	"H" Needs Home Prep.
ART		
Art Appreciation	L10–H12	
Design	L10–H12	
Freehand Drawing	L10–H12	
Ceramics 1–4	L10–H12	
Commercial Art 1–4	L11–H12	H
Crafts 1–4	L10–H12	
Illustration 1–4	L11–H12	
Stagecraft 1–6	L10–H12	
History of Art 1–2	L11–H12	H
BUSINESS EDUCATION		
Clerical Records	H10	H
Business Mathematics	L10	H
Consumer Mathematics	L11–H12	H
Bookkeeping 1–4	L11–H12	H
Machine Calculation 1–2	L11–H12	
Office Practice 1–2	L11–H12	
Office Practice 3–4	L12–H12	
Sales 1–2	L11–H12	H
Merchandising	L12–H12	H
Shorthand 1–3	L11–H12	H
Transcription	L11–H12	
Secretarial Training	H12	H
Typewriting 1–4	L10–H12	

Department and Subject	Grade Level	"H" Needs Home Prep.
MATHEMATICS		
General Mathematics Review	L10–H10	H
Algebra 1–2	L10–H10	H
Geometry 1–2	L10–H11	H
Advanced Algebra 1–2	L11–H12	H
Trigonometry	H11–H12	H
Mathematical Analysis	L12–H12	H
Matrix Algebra	L12–H12	H
Probability and Statistics	L12–H12	H
Basic Mathematics	L12	H
Calculus—Advanced Placement Math	L12–H12	H
MUSIC		
Band	L10–H12	
Intermediate Band	L10–H12	
Orchestra	L10–H12	
Boys' Glee, Girls' Glee	L10–H12	
Mixed Chorus	L10–H12	
A Cappella Choir	H10–H12	
History of Music 1–4	L11–H12	H
Harmony	L10–H12	H
Music Appreciation	L10–H12	H

ENGLISH

Course	Grades	
English 3–6	L10–H12	H
Senior English Literature	L12–H12	H
World Literature	L12–H12	H
Senior English Review	L12–H12	H
Advanced Composition	H12	H
Drama 1–2	H10–H12	H
Journalism 1–2	H10–H12	H
Public Speaking 1	H10–H12	H
Public Speaking 2 (Forensics)	L11–H12	H
Yearbook 1–2	L12–H12	H

HOMEMAKING

Course	Grades	
Clothing 1–6	L10–H12	
Clothing Selection	L10–H12	H
Foods 1–2	L10–H12	H
Home Living 1–2	L12–H12	H

INDUSTRIAL ARTS

Course	Grades
Electric-Radio Shop 3–6	L10–H12
Graphic Arts 3–6	L10–H12
Machine Shop 3–6	L10–H12
Mechanical Drawing 1–8	L10–H12
Woodshop 3–6	L10–H12
Shop Math	L10–H12

LANGUAGES

Course	Grades	
Chinese 1–6 (Mandarin)	L10–H12	H
French 1–8	L10–H12	H
German 1–8	L10–H12	H
Italian 1–8	L10–H12	H
Latin 1–8	L10–H12	H
Russian 1–6	L10–H12	H
Spanish 1–8	L10–H12	H

Advanced Placement as needed.
Native speakers placed by dept. head.

SCIENCE

Course	Grades	
Applied Science 1–2	L10–H12	H
Biology 1–2	L11–H12	H
Advanced Biology 1–2	L11–H12	H
Chemistry 1–2	L10–H12	H
Physiology 1–2	L11–H12	H
Physics 1–2	L11–H12	H
Chemistry 3	L12–H12	H
Physical Science 1–2	L11–H12	H

SOCIAL STUDIES

Course	Grades	
World History 1–2	L10–H12	H
U.S. History 1–2	L11–H12	H
Senior Civics 1–2	L12–H12	H
California History	L12–H12	H
Current Geography—Pacific Relations	L12–H12	H
Economics	L12–H12	H
History of Music	L11–H12	H
History of Art	L11–H12	H
Local Government and History	H12	H
Latin American Relations	L12–H12	H
European History (Advanced Placement)	L12–H12	H

PHYSICAL EDUCATION

L10–H12

R.O.T.C.

L10–H12

DRIVER EDUCATION

L10   H

Every student and his parents should look ahead and plan a course of study through the twelfth grade. Counselors can give helpful advice in this. It is reasonable to expect that an educational plan made for three or four years ahead will need to be adjusted to changing circumstances. The school will always help students so that necessary changes can be made from term to term and still insure progress toward an educational goal. There should be no slackening of effort in the senior year.

Table 6–4
Sample Program of Studies in a Three-Year Junior High School

Grade 7	Grade 8	Grade 9
Homeroom	Homeroom	Homeroom
English	English	English
Social Studies	Social Studies	Social Studies
Arithmetic	Mathematics	Mathematics or Algebra
General Science	General Science	
		Physical Education
Physical Education	Physical Education	
		Elective°
Elective°	Elective°	
		Elective°

° Choice of art, music, industrial arts (boys), homemaking (girls), foreign language.

and eight, while the three-year junior high school also includes grade nine.

Although the pattern of studies at the junior high school level is commonly organized along the lines of the subject-centered curriculum, the usual practice is to designate the courses as broad fields or areas, rather than specific subjects. Such broad fields include English, social studies, arithmetic or mathematics, science, and so forth. Table 6–4 presents a sample program of studies in a three-year junior high school, while Table 6–5 illustrates the electives commonly offered in three-year junior high schools.

There has been more of a tendency to experiment with different approaches to curriculum organization at the junior high school level than at the senior high school. For example, a number of junior high schools have combined the English language arts and the social studies with the homeroom, where one teacher is responsible for working with a group of pupils during a block of time that covers at least two periods. This teacher is responsible for general guidance and counseling of these pupils, as well as for the instructional program in the areas indicated. This approach claims certain advantages. The larger block of time reduces the number of different pupils in the teacher's daily load. As a result, the teacher has a better opportunity to know the students as individuals because of the additional time spent together during the school day. And since most of the elementary schools are organized on a self-contained classroom pattern, where a single teacher is responsible

Table 6–5
Electives Commonly Offered in a Large Junior High School

GRADE 7 (choice of one)	GRADE 8 (choice of one)	GRADE 9 (choice of two)
Art	Art	Algebra *
Foreign Language	Dramatics	Art
Homemaking	Foreign Language	Dramatics
Industrial Arts	French	Foreign Language *
Music	German	French
	Spanish	German
	Homemaking	Spanish
	Industrial Arts	General Business
	Graphic Arts	Homemaking
	Metals	Industrial Arts
	Woods	Graphic Arts
	Music	Mechanical Drawing
	Band	Metals
	Orchestra	Woods
	Vocal	Music
		Band
		Orchestra
		Vocal
		Speech
		Typing

* Usually recommended for pupils who plan to take the college preparatory program in senior high school.

for instruction in virtually every area of the curriculum, the transition from the elementary school to the junior high school is less abrupt under this system.

The longer time block may be developed under several variations or options—for example, the teacher may follow a traditional pattern of teaching the English language arts and the social studies as distinctly separate broad-fields courses; on the other hand, the two fields may be related to one another under a correlated approach; or they may lose their traditional identity as separate courses through fusion;[11] finally, they may be resynthesized into a core program based upon student problems and interests selected from the combined curricular areas. The core problem-centered approach represents a sharp departure from the tradi-

[11] An example of such fusion would be the unification of American history, literature, and composition under the central theme, "Our Cultural Heritage." Traditional subject lines are dissolved. While the tendency is to fuse courses that are from the same subject field, the fusion of courses from different subject fields (that is social studies and English language arts) is often referred to as a core approach. The core curriculum may be centered either around broad themes or the problems and interests of students.

tional system of curriculum organization, and is discussed in considerable detail in Chapter 7. Other, less drastic approaches to curriculum synthesis, such as correlation, fusion, and broad fields are described later in the present chapter.

Advantages and Limitations of the Subject Curriculum

WHY IS THE SUBJECT-CENTERED CURRICULUM FAVORED? The subject-centered curriculum is the dominant approach to curriculum organization in our high schools. Alberty lists six major arguments in favor of the subject-centered curriculum:

1. Systematic organization is essential to the effective interpretation of experience.
2. The organization of the subject-centered curriculum is simple and easily understood.
3. The subject-centered curriculum is easily changed.
4. The subject-centered curriculum is easily evaluated.
5. The colleges have generally approved and perpetuated the subject-centered curriculum through admission requirements.
6. The subject-centered curriculum is generally approved by teachers, parents, and students.[12]

Most textbooks at the high school level are geared to this type of curriculum organization. These textbooks arrange the subject matter in a logical and systematic manner that conveniently coincides with the subject-centered curriculum. Under this system, many teachers find it easy to follow the textbook, page by page and chapter by chapter. In other words, the course of instruction is synthesized in the textbook, and this is of great convenience to the teacher. The curriculum is kept up to date by following the simple policy of adopting new textbooks every so often.

Administratively, the subject-centered curriculum is easy to schedule. The usual practice is to allow one class period daily to each subject. Also, the students can follow these subjects in an ordered sequence year by year. For example, the usual practice is to offer general science in the ninth grade, biology in the tenth, chemistry in the eleventh, and physics in the twelfth. Moreover, the subject-centered curriculum is in harmony with the Carnegie Unit and the usual practice of stating the requirements for college entrance in terms of credits or units. And most college curricula are organized on a subject-centered basis.

The high-school student and his parents readily comprehend the subject-centered curriculum pattern and the requirements for graduation. Failure in a given subject can be made up without disturbing the general pattern. Also, new subjects can be added to the curriculum with-

---

[12] Harold B. Alberty and Elsie J. Alberty, *Reorganizing the High-School Curriculum*, 3rd Ed. (New York: The Macmillan Company, 1962), pp. 173–180.

out molesting the existing structure. Most of the so-called changes in the high-school curriculum are a matter of simple accretion.

Teachers at the high-school level tend to regard themselves as subject specialists inasmuch as their own college preparation requires the completion of a major and minor in specific subject fields. Consequently, the nature of their preparation for teaching is designed for the subject-centered curriculum. Beginning high school teachers, therefore, are very familiar with the subject-centered pattern of curriculum organization.

WHAT ARE THE LIMITATIONS AND DISADVANTAGES OF THE SUBJECT-CENTERED CURRICULUM? While the subject-centered curriculum offers a number of significant advantages in the construction and administration of a logically organized curriculum, it has some serious limitations and weaknesses.

The subject-centered curriculum is not consistent with our knowledge concerning the psychology of learning. Under this system, the primary focus is on the logical organization of the subject matter, and the problems and interests of the learners may be ignored or treated as of secondary importance. Students may learn facts and information from the textbook only to pass examinations, but they may retain very little of this type of learning once the examinations have been passed and the course is completed. The motivation for learning is too often geared to the extrinsic reward of receiving a passing grade. And what has been learned may soon be conveniently forgotten simply because it was artificial to the student in the first place. John Dewey emphasized the fallacy and artificiality of such learning.

> Facts are torn away from their original place in experience and rearranged with reference to some general principle. Classification is not a matter of child experience; things do not come to the individual pigeonholed. The vital ties of affection, the connecting bonds of activity, hold together the variety of his personal experiences. The adult mind is so familiar with the notion of logically ordered facts that it does not recognize—it cannot realize—the amount of separating and reformulating which the facts of direct experience have to undergo before they can appear as a "study" or branch of learning. A principle, for the intellect, had to be distinguished and defined; facts have had to be interpreted in relation to this principle, not as they are in themselves. They have to be regathered about a new center which is wholly abstract and ideal. . . . The studies as classified are the product in a word, of the science of the ages, not of the experience of the child.[13]

This should not be interpreted to mean that all learning should be confined to the spontaneous interests of the learner. The story is told of the teacher who, upon greeting the children at the beginning of the

---

[13] John Dewey, *The Child and the Curriculum* (Chicago: The University of Chicago Press, 1902), pp. 10–11.

school day, asked cheerfully: "Now, what do we want to learn about today?" A boy in the back of the room raised his hand for recognition, and in a voice of disappointment and exasperation exclaimed: "Do we *have* to learn what we want to learn again, today?" Unfortunately, some educators have gotten the notion that much of the material of instruction should emanate from the learner. Since the learner's universe of experience is limited, such learning procedures would be of limited value. But good teachers know that the logical material in a subject field must be tied to the experience of the learner if significant educational goals are to be attained. Effective teachers are aware of the importance of student attitudes toward learning. Even if the student achieves a grade of A, indicating the highest mastery of the subject matter, the real educational value is lost if, as a result of this experience, he now finds the subject distasteful. If education is to lead to lifelong learning, then we must find ways to enable the learner to understand and appreciate what learning is, and to partake of its joys. In this way, the subject matter is not minimized, but on the contrary is made even more significant to the learner.

Even within the limits of the subject-centered curriculum, good teachers utilize a wide variety of instructional resources and strive to stimulate student interests. In other words, even within the framework of the subject-centered curriculum, it is possible for the teacher to employ sound psychological techniques and procedures. But too many teachers follow the textbook as the bible of learning and condition students to learn quantities of information and skills, to be parroted back at examination time, without a real understanding of the significance and vitality of learning. Using the subject of mathematics as an example, Jacques Barzun relates the futility of learning without understanding.

> . . . because of the tribal bugbear about "math," the mind stumbles more often over ciphering than over anything else. Is it a bugbear that can be traced to its den and slain? My impression is that its point of origin is the mystery created around numbers from the moment a child encounters them. It is an ever-deepening mystery, for as he grows older the pupil is asked to do more and more complicated things in increasing darkness of mind. The right answer is in the back of the book, but the right principles to explain it never seem to be in the front. At least I do not remember reading informatively about numbers until I hunted down books on the subject for my own pleasure long after school.
>
> Then I have more than an impression—it amounts to a certainty— that algebra is made repellant by the unwillingness or inability of teachers to explain why we suddenly start using a and b, what exponents mean apart from their handling, and how the paradoxical behavior of $+$ and $-$ came into being. There is no sense of history behind the teaching, so the feeling is given that the whole system dropped down ready-made from the skies, to be used only by born jugglers. This is

what paralyzes—with few exceptions—the infant, the adolescent, or the adult who is not a juggler himself.[14]

Many people have the mistaken notion that the basic curriculum in the secondary school is virtually inert—that is, the basic material never really requires overhauling because it is founded upon essential principles of knowledge. Under the subject-centered curriculum, we frequently hear people saying, "A good teacher, above all, must know his subject." Yet, whenever one encounters a truly creative person in a given field, we find that he is not concerned with inert knowledge, but with dynamics of exploration, discovery, and learning.

Through the incessant emphasis on the learning of known facts and skills, many youngsters are conditioned to regard human knowledge as a finite and static system, rather than as an infinite and dynamic system. Psychology tells us that we learn much more effectively through exploration and discovery than through rote tasks. Yet, many teachers under the subject-centered curriculum confine students to the established knowledge that is represented in a textbook, and the students are graded according to their facility in the acquisition of subject-matter information and skills. Students who are adept at acquiring and regurgitating facts may be incapable of identifying problems, weighing and applying evidence, recognizing inconsistencies, recognizing bias, verifying data, discriminating between the relevant and the irrelevant, formulating and testing conclusions, and applying these habits of critical thinking to life situations. In one of his most famous works, the noted British mathematician and philosopher, Alfred North Whitehead, cautioned educators against the teaching of inert ideas.

> In the history of education, the most striking phenomenon is that schools of learning, which at one epoch are alive with a ferment of genius, in a succeeding generation exhibit merely pedantry and routine. The reason is, that they are overladen with inert ideas. Education with inert ideas is not only useless: it is, above all things, harmful. . . . Every intellectual revolution which has ever stirred humanity into greatness has been a passionate protest against inert ideas.[15]

Most beginning high-school teachers will find themselves teaching within a subject-centered curriculum pattern. Fortunately, the limitations of this curriculum pattern can be overcome to a considerable extent by an imaginative and resourceful teacher.

Another limitation of the subject-centered curriculum is that it tends to separate knowledge into unrelated blocks. The curriculum is divided

---

[14] Jacques Barzun, *Teacher in America* (New York: Little, Brown, and Company, 1951), p. 82.

[15] Alfred North Whitehead, *The Aims of Education* (New York: The Macmillan Company, 1929), p. 2.

and subdivided into so many dissociated segments that students fail to grasp the interdependence of human knowledge and experience. For example, students may learn about graphs and equations in the algebra class, but they often fail to connect this with the interpretation of data in the social studies and science classes. Whitehead bitterly criticized the schools for this artificial compartmentalization of knowledge through the subject-centered curriculum.

> The result of teaching small parts of a large number of subjects is the passive reception of disconnected ideas, not illumined with any spark of vitality.[16]
> The solution which I am urging, is to eradicate the fatal disconnection of subjects which kills the vitality of our modern curriculum. There is only one subject-matter for education; and that is Life in all its manifestations. Instead of this single unity, we offer children—Algebra, from which nothing follows; Geometry, from which nothing follows; Science, from which nothing follows; History, from which nothing follows; a Couple of Languages, never mastered; and lastly, most dreary of all, Literature, represented by the plays of Shakespeare, with philological notes and short analyses of plot and character to be in substance committed to memory. Can such a list be said to represent Life, as it is known in the midst of the living of it? The best that can be said of it is, that it is a rapid table of contents which a deity might run over in his mind while he was thinking of creating a world, and had not yet determined how to put it together.[17]

The sharp boundary lines between subjects serve as deterrents to the integration of educational experiences. Relationships among subjects at a given grade level may be ignored. Also, there may be little if any attempt to correlate subjects from one grade level to another. For example, students may fail to see a working relationship between general science and mathematics in the ninth grade; and, furthermore, they may fail to see a relationship between biology in the tenth grade and chemistry in the eleventh grade.[18] Each course is conceived as fitting into a watertight compartment; each course is an entity unto itself. And each teacher may isolate himself in accordance with his own specialized subject area.

A further criticism of the subject-centered curriculum is that it does not require cooperative faculty planning in the determination of educational goals and means. Just as the different subjects are separated, so are the various members of the faculty. Even though a teacher may be a member of a subject department in a large high school, he may find that he alone is responsible for determining the elements that make up the course of

---

[16] *Ibid.*, p. 3.   [17] *Ibid.*, pp. 10–11.
[18] See Ralph W. Tyler, "Curriculum Organization," *The Integration of Educational Experiences*, Fifty-seventh Yearbook of the National Society for the Study of Education, Part III (Chicago: The University of Chicago Press, 1958), p. 107.

instruction in his special subject field—or he may simply choose to follow the textbook as the course of instruction. Few opportunities are provided for working together with other faculty members in various subject specialties for the purpose of correlating and integrating the disparate elements of the curriculum. Consequently, the teacher of mathematics in the ninth or tenth grade may seldom if ever work on improving curricular relationships with the teacher of chemistry or physics in the eleventh or twelfth grade.

While many schools have faculty committees working on various projects relating to the curriculum, such committees rarely have sufficient time or resources to achieve their goals. For example, a faculty committee may develop an impressive list of educational objectives for the school. But while these objectives may be endorsed by the total faculty and administration, rarely is the curriculum tested to determine the extent to which these objectives are being met. Too often, one finds relatively few connections between stated objectives and actual classroom practices. The solution to this problem is not the forming of more faculty committees, but developing faculty recognition of the need for cooperative planning and providing the means for implementing such plans. Critics of the subject curriculum argue that such cooperative action is exceedingly difficult when teachers regard themselves as subject-matter specialists in their individual province or domain.

It is also felt that the subject-centered curriculum is too remote from the life of the students. The adolescent often fails to see any direct or immediate connection between his own life and the study of American history, English literature, algebra, chemistry, and other subjects. Few provisions are made for individual needs and interests. A course in American government may have little or no connection with the development of democratic values in the behavior of adolescents. It does not necessarily help youngsters appreciate the values of cooperation and respect for individuality. Likewise, a course in science may not improve the student's ability to think with objectivity and precision, and to appreciate the vast areas for exploration and discovery. The organization of subject matter into logical systems of knowledge may represent mere verbalism in the eyes of the student, and consequently may have little or no part in effecting significant changes in the student's pattern of behavior.

Many educators would agree that the role of the school (and its curriculum) in society is to bring about an improvement in human behavior for the improvement of society. But the mere learning of verbalized material from various logically organized subject areas is no guarantee that the student's life experience will be changed or improved.

The subject-centered curriculum is cumulative; yet, it can cover only a very small fraction of human knowledge. Since the universe of human experience is not finite, but infinite in nature, man's organization and conceptualization of knowledge must undergo constant reappraisal. As new explorations and discoveries are made, and as man continues to revise his way of living, so the curriculum of the school must change. Consequently, the adding of new knowledge to the curriculum and the revision of old knowledge presents an enigma to curriculum workers under the subject-centered approach.

Whitehead observed that knowledge keeps no better than fish. This perishable nature of knowledge, combined with the incessant expansion of new knowledge, means that students can only be exposed to a minute fraction of subject matter. The many new areas of subject specialization lead to a great proliferation of courses. Even if the student, however gifted he may be, were to spend his entire life in school, he would encounter only a tiny portion of the subject matter that man has accumulated. Because human knowledge is dynamic and evolving, a cumulative approach to the organization and cataloguing of subject matter presents serious difficulties in curriculum development. The tendency to arrange and present knowledge in expository form, while permitting a fairly wide degree of coverage, often leads to learning by repetition and memorization. As a consequence, the student is often left with the erroneous impression that knowledge is static and permanent.

Can Teachers Overcome the Limitations of the Subject-Centered Curriculum?

We have observed that most high school teachers adapt easily to the subject-centered curriculum. Their own college preparation and their experiences in student teaching tend to be based on the subject-centered approach. And it is easy for a beginning teacher to follow the textbook as the course of instruction under this system of curriculum organization. Many teachers are so well accustomed to the subject curriculum that they prefer it to any alternative curriculum design. The subject-centered curriculum is so firmly entrenched that proposals for radical change are vigorously resisted. Moreover, teachers rarely have a voice in curriculum design—partly because they do not show sufficient interest in these matters, and also because such decisions are, for the most part, left to the administrators and their boards of education. But even when teachers are given a voice in curriculum determination, they are prone to stick with the *status quo*. Curriculum experimentation is too upsetting to established habits and comfortable routines. Nevertheless, in recent years, an increasing number of teachers seem to be taking an interest in matters of curriculum determination, and more school administrators seem to be calling on their faculties for advice and assistance.

The question then arises as to whether the teacher, working within the structure of the subject-centered curriculum, can overcome its limitations. While, in the next chapter, we examine various attempts at overcoming the limitations of the subject-centered curriculum by turning to other types of curriculum design, it should be emphasized that the key person, in addition to the learner, in the educational process is the teacher. In other words, no curriculum design, no matter how well conceived, can be successful without competent teachers in the classroom. After all, it is the individual classroom teacher who works face to face with the learner and decides what methods of instruction should be employed. Consequently, it is possible for a competent and imaginative classroom teacher to overcome many of the limitations associated with the subject-centered curriculum. The classroom teacher of a given subject can help youngsters relate this subject to other areas of the curriculum, and provide activities that are based on student interests and needs. Individual and group projects can be developed through cooperative teacher-pupil planning. Activities can be provided to enable youngsters to work together democratically. Problems and issues can be explored in a stimulating way. The creative teacher can instill in youngsters a genuine love of learning.

Teachers can work together, even under the subject-centered curriculum, to bring about improved teaching methods and to develop a better synthesis between and among the various subject areas of the curriculum. But unless the need for such cooperative planning by the faculty is recognized, each teacher under the subject curriculum may tend to isolate himself according to his own area of subject specialization. The subject-centered curriculum too often results in the delineation of learning areas into many unrelated components and the failure to develop effective communication among faculty members. The faculty of a school need to work together in (1) identifying educational objectives, (2) developing a synthesis and continuity of curricular elements, (3) improving the methods of instruction, (4) improving instructional materials and devices, (5) developing the total school program, including guidance and student activities, and (6) assessing learning outcomes. While it is important for each teacher to have professional independence and freedom, he cannot isolate himself from the total school program.

For many years it has been fashionable to say that a good teacher, above all, must know his subject. But "knowing" one's subject has never been adequately defined. Moreover, studies of teacher competence reveal that many complex dimensions go into the making of a good teacher. It should be emphasized that even the outstanding scholars do not claim to know their subject. The scholar's task is to explore and discover in his own field, with the goal of expanding human knowledge and under-standing. Since knowledge is dynamic and evolving, the effective teacher must keep abreast of new developments in his own area of specialization and in related areas. He must also be competent in utilizing techniques and resources to make learning significant in the lives of his students. To do this, the teacher must understand the learning process.

Expansion and Modification of the Subject-Centered Curriculum

There has always been resistance to curriculum change. But changes in society have led to changes in the curricula of our schools. For example, the schools and colleges did not begin to offer laboratory sciences until the great impact of scientific and industrial changes in society were clearly evident during the middle and latter half of the nineteenth century. The teaching of modern foreign languages was largely ignored until the nineteenth century. And only after our nation was in the midst of the great technological crisis of World War I did vocational education receive real impetus.

In his remarkable and humorous fictional work, *The Saber-Tooth Curriculum*, published in 1939, Harold Benjamin ridiculed this resistance to curriculum change and the insistence on holding fast to subjects that are traditionally established, however useless and outmoded they may be. The story takes place in cave man society, where one of the tribesmen becomes concerned with the need to educate the children so that they will learn "to live with full bellies, warm backs, and minds free from fear."[19] In this parody, the thinking tribesman decides to establish a curriculum based on activities that are necessary for survival. Since the cavemen must catch fish with their bare hands, he establishes the subject of "fish-grabbing with the bare hands." And since the tribesmen must protect themselves by driving away the saber-tooth tiger with fire, he adds anothers subject to the curriculum: "saber-tooth-tiger-scaring-with-fire." The children soon find this purposeful curriculum much to their liking, and enjoy it much more than merely playing with colored stones. Gradually, these subjects became accepted as the heart of the educational system, as the really fundamental subjects. But after some years, the rivers become muddied and it is no longer possible to catch fish with bare hands. And to add to their woes, the saber-tooth tiger becomes extinct. Finally some young, thinking tribesmen suggest a new curriculum adapted to the changed conditions of society. They want such subjects as "fishnet-making and using" and "bear-catching and killing." But the conservative members of the tribe object to these new

---

[19] Harold Benjamin, *The Saber-Tooth Curriculum* (New York: McGraw-Hill Company, Inc., 1939), p. 28.

subjects as frills, and point out that the standard cultural subjects of
fish-grabbing and tiger-scaring are the real fundamentals.

> "With all the intricate details of fish-grabbing, . . . and tiger-scaring—
> the standard cultural subjects—the school curriculum is too crowded
> now. We can't add these fads and frills of net-making . . . and—of all
> things—bear-killing. . . . What we need to do is give our young people
> a more thorough grounding in the fundamentals. . . ."
>
> "But damn it," exploded one of the radicals, "how can any person
> with good sense be interested in such useless activities? What is the
> point of trying to catch fish with the bare hands when it just can't be
> done any more. . . . And why in hell should children try to scare tigers
> with fire when the tigers are dead and gone?"
>
> "Don't be foolish," said the wise old men. . . . "We don't teach fish
> grabbing to grab fish; we teach it to develop a generalized agility which
> can never be developed by mere training. . . . We don't teach tiger-
> scaring to scare tigers; we teach it for the purpose of giving that noble
> courage which carries over into all the affairs of life and which can never
> come from so base an activity as bear-killing. . . ."
>
> ". . . If you had any education yourself," they said severely, "you
> would know that the essence of true education is timelessness. It is
> something that endures through changing conditions like a solid rock
> standing squarely and firmly in the middle of a raging torrent. You
> must know that there are some eternal verities, and the saber-tooth
> curriculum is one of them.[20]

While the above parody is outlandishly overdrawn, it nevertheless
parallels the long persistence in teaching Greek and Latin while resisting
modern languages in the secondary-school curriculum. And it parallels
the resistance against the introduction of laboratory sciences during the
middle and latter half of the nineteenth century. *The Saber-Tooth
Curriculum* vividly illustrates how the school curriculum must be dynamic if it is to have meaning in relation to the changing conditions of
society.

Traditionalists have deplored the development of such high-school
programs as vocational education and driver education, and the offering
of electives. Even some of the recent reforms in the content and methodology of teaching the sciences, mathematics, and modern foreign
languages have been resisted by the traditionalists. While the new curriculum reforms are discussed in Chapters 7 and 8, it should be emphasized that the curriculum cannot be static if society is dynamic.

APPROACHES TO CURRICULUM ARTICULATION

However, under the subject-centered curriculum, the temptation is to
keep abreast of new knowledge and the myriad areas of specialization

---

[20] *Ibid.*, pp. 41–44.

by adding more courses to the curriculum. In many of our larger high schools it is only possible for a student to take a sampling of the total course offerings. While the elective system has some real merits, the problem of providing students with a well-balanced curriculum is compounded as the curriculum options are multiplied. Furthermore, the problem of curriculum articulation becomes more acute as the number of courses and areas of specialization are increased. Many separate subject departments are formed. While this departmentalization may lead to desirable faculty planning within a subject field, it generally tends to set off one subject field against another.

Two Dimensions of Curriculum Organizaton

Within the framework of the subject curriculum, there have been many attempts to improve the articulation between and among subjects. When we strive to improve the interrelationships between ninth-grade general science and tenth-grade biology, tenth-grade biology and eleventh-grade chemistry, eleventh-grade chemistry and twelfth-grade physics —we are referring to the *vertical* organization of the curriculum. On the other hand, when we attempt to improve the articulation between seventh-grade English and seventh-grade social studies, or between seventh-grade general science and seventh-grade mathematics, we are concerned with the *horizontal* organization of the curriculum.

An analysis of the vertical organization of a given curriculum may reveal serious gaps and omissions in subject-matter content and activity; or it may reveal a great deal of unnecessary duplication and overlapping. Teachers often find themselves going over the same ground in grammar or mathematics because the students have apparently failed to retain the material they had supposedly learned during the previous academic year. In many cases, such review work is required from year to year because the abstract study of grammar or mathematics, for example, never became truly meaningful to the students. The study of grammar was not connected effectively with the actual writing and reading skills and habits of the students. It was merely studied as a discipline unto itself, and the students were required to rely heavily on drill work and memorized rules. Research shows that many teachers fail to connect the study of grammar with experiences in composition and reading, and as a consequence what is learned one semester is forgotten the next.[21] It is common to hear teachers complain about the need for such repetitive drill and review from one grade level to another. This is obviously a

---

[21] See John J. DeBoer, "Grammar in Language Teaching," *Elementary English*, 1–9, October, 1959; also see Bergen Evans, "Grammar for Today," *The Atlantic*, March, 1960, 205:79–82.

problem of improper instructional methods and content, as well as inadequate vertical articulation of the curriculum.

With regard to the horizontal organization of the curriculum, the common pitfall is the failure to draw relationships between and among subjects at a given grade level. Teachers in the secondary school tend to regard themselves as subject specialists, and learning is compartmentalized into separate subjects. Recognizing the failure of students to relate one subject to another, various attempts have been made to improve the horizontal articulation within the framework of the subject curriculum. These efforts are referred to as curriculum correlation, fusion, and broad-fields: The need for curriculum articulation has come about as a result of the finding that students do not automatically transfer what they learn in one subject to another subject. If such transfer is to occur, it must be carefully planned and worked for. Correlation, fusion, and broad-fields represent attempts at articulation while still preserving the subject curriculum. These approaches, therefore, are not radical or revolutionary. But they are, nevertheless, significant attempts to alter the curriculum structure in order to reduce the large number of boundary lines between subjects. The goal of improved curriculum articulation is to bring about an integrated conception of knowledge in the mind of the student. In this way, it is hoped that the student will be able to relate this synthesis of knowledge to experiences and problems throughout life.

Correlation

This approach to curriculum articulation retains the usual subject divisions. However, it attempts to bring together certain common relationships between or among two or more courses. For example, the teacher of United States history and the teacher of American literature may decide to relate the two subjects. As a result, the students may be assigned to read Thomas Paine's *Common Sense* in the literature class at the same time as they are studying the American Revolutionary Period in the history class. Likewise, the reading of Steinbeck's *Grapes of Wrath* in the literature course might parallel the study of the American Depression of the 1930's in the history course. In a similar vein, a correlated approach might be developed between history and geography, science and mathematics, and so on. The correlation of history and literature, or of science and mathematics, involves an attempt to articulate not only two subjects, but two instructional fields. On the other hand, the correlation of history and geography involves two subjects in the same instructional field.

Correlation may be attempted by a single teacher who instructs in two or more courses and attempts to relate these subjects to one another (for instance, geography and history). Or it may be attempted by two or more teachers with the goal of helping students understand and appreciate the common threads between subjects. Such correlation does not disrupt the existing curriculum or the class schedules. But when it involves two or more teachers, a great deal of cooperative planning is necessary. This may be an inconvenience to teachers who must find additional time for such planning. Unless teachers appreciate the need and value of curriculum correlation, they will simply approach each course in an isolated and compartmentalized way.

Correlation may be provided under a variety of administrative combinations, as follows:

1. The teachers plan the work together, but do not necessarily have the same students. Each teacher, however, uses some material from another teacher's field.
2. The teachers plan their work together and have the same group of students, but not at the same time. Section A may have literature the first period with the English teacher, and history the second period with the history teacher.
3. The teachers have separate classes on a criss-cross schedule that permits combining the groups on occasion. Take two groups, A and B, and two teachers, X and Y. Group A has English with teacher X during the first period, while group B has history with teacher Y at the same time. In the second period, group A has teacher Y in history and group B has teacher X in English. When desired, groups A and B may meet with both teachers, X and Y, for the two periods, possibly for films or a field trip.[22]
4. Two teachers meet with the class for two periods and cooperate not only in the planning but in the teaching. This is obviously an expensive arrangement and not likely to be widely used.[23]
5. One teacher, with competence in both fields, teaches the class for both periods.[24]

Some educators believe that while curriculum correlation is based upon sound principles, it does not go far enough. They argue that although correlation represents an attempt to reduce or eliminate the isolationist and compartmentalized characteristics of the subject-centered curriculum, it nevertheless leaves each subject intact. Correlation does not necessarily require changes in the actual methods of teaching. The subject matter may continue to follow a logical pattern of organization

---

[22] In recent years, such cooperative efforts have been referred to as team-teaching.
[23] This team-teaching arrangement can be economical when classes are combined.
[24] See Edward A. Krug, *The Secondary School Curriculum* (New York: Harper & Row, Publishers, Inc., 1960), pp. 200–201.

—ignoring the interests, needs, and motivations of the learner. But again, the reader is cautioned to remember that an effective teacher, regardless of the curriculum pattern, centers his instructional methods around the learner. Nevertheless, the type of curriculum pattern can have a marked influence on the effectiveness of the teacher and on the quality of learning. In too many instances, correlation is merely approached on a chronological basis. In other words, the course in United States history and the course in American literature are merely made to run parallel chronologically.

Fusion

This is regarded as a more advanced step toward curriculum articulation than correlation. Two or more subjects are merged, thereby replacing those subjects previously offered separately. While fusion may involve the merger of two or more couses from different subject fields, it most commonly occurs within the same field.

Examples of fusion are the merger of botany and zoology into biology, or the combining of ancient, medieval, and modern history into world history. While fusion claims advantages similar to correlation, it differs in the sense that fusion represents the merger of related subjects into a new course, while correlation simply repesents an attempt at relating two or more different subjects with one another. Under correlation, the subjects remain intact. Theoretically, fusion should lead to improved curriculum synthesis, but its success also depends upon the teachers concerned. Obviously, the teacher must be committed to the need for such synthesis, and he must be able to draw functional relationships between and among areas of knowledge that were once taught as separate subjects. If the teacher approaches the fused course as a group of separate components, nothing is gained; the teacher is merely teaching two or more different subjects under the title of a single course.

As in correlation, fusion does not require changes in the actual methods of teaching. The teacher may continue to follow the subject matter in a logical pattern—or he may choose a problem-centered approach. But if true fusion is to be achieved, the subjects once taught separately should be brought together as a functional and organic whole.

Broad-Fields

In an effort to avoid an unmanageable multiplicity of courses, many schools and colleges have developed a broad-fields curriculum. Instead of merely fusing the content of two or more courses, the broad-fields approach is an attempt to synthesize an entire branch of learning into a common unity. Broad-fields courses may appear under a variety of title designations, such as Social Studies, Social Relationships, or American Studies. They may be organized as broad content areas or as unifying themes. Some representative patterns of the broad-fields curriculum are:

1. Language Arts.
2. Social Studies.
3. Science and Mathematics.
4. Health and Physical Education.
5. Fine Arts and Music.[25]

The broad-fields approach is not new. This pattern of curriculum organization was advocated in a 1933 report by the Curriculum Committee of the North Central Association of Colleges and Secondary Schools. This committee suggested four broad-fields to encompass the various subjects in the secondary school curriculum:

1. Health and Physical Fitness.
2. Leisure Time.
3. Vocational Activities.
4. Social Relationships.[26]

The broad-fields approach, however, was supposed to have been attempted in England long before its beginnings in the United States.

> The earliest beginning of the broad-fields curriculum is not found in America but in England, in a course given as a series of lectures by Thomas Huxley to London children at the Royal Institution in 1869 and later published under the title of *Physiography*. The preface indicates Huxley's prophetic views with respect to changes in the conventional subject curriculum. He opposed "an *omnium-gatherum* of scraps of all sorts and undigested and unconnected information." The course was inductively developed and aimed at unity not only by bringing the facts and principles of related fields into juxtaposition but also by choosing the Thames basin and the activities of its people as the unifying factor. This was a happy choice, which anticipated by two generations the regional and community ideas in education.[27]

Huxley's ideas on curriculum reorganization were remarkably advanced, not only from the standpoint of recognizing the need for developing a meaningful unity out of many disparate subjects, but also in his attempt to develop this broad-field from the living conditions of a region. Instead of a logical approach to the subject matter, he attempted a problems approach.

---

[25] Nelson L. Bossing, *Principles of Secondary Education* (Englewood Cliffs, N.J.: Prentice-Hall, Inc., 1955), p. 376.

[26] Lewis W. Webb *et al.*, *High School Curriculum Reorganization* (Ann Arbor, Mich.: North Central Association of Colleges and Secondary Schools, 1933).

[27] B. Othanel Smith, William O. Stanley, and J. Harlan Shores, *Fundamentals of Curriculum Development* (Yonkers-on-Hudson, New York: World Book Company, 1957), p. 256.

The value of a broad-fields pattern of curriculum organization at the college level began to be recognized in the United States early in this century. In his inaugural address as president of Harvard University in 1909, A. Lawrence Lowell advocated the establishment of comprehensive courses to "give to men who do not intend to pursue the subject further a comprehension of its underlying principles or methods of thought.[28]

In the early 1900's, courses in general science and problems of democracy began to appear in the curriculum of some high schools. Today, many elementary and secondary schools categorize their curricula according to such broad-fields as general arts, language arts, general mathematics, general science, social studies, and so on.

In 1914 Amherst College established a broad-fields course called Social and Economic Institutions. The University of Chicago, between 1923 and 1925, is credited with having developed the first complete broad-fields curriculum at the college level with such general education courses as The Nature of the World and of Man, Man in Society, The Meaning and Value of the Arts, and Introduction to Reflective Thinking. Beginning in September of 1946, Harvard College inaugurated an experimental program in general education consisting of such broad-fields courses as Social Sciences, Natural Sciences, and others. This program became permanent in 1949.[29] Yale College has also followed a broad-fields approach in general education. The field of American Studies at Yale encompasses history, art, literature, and social sciences. Selected freshmen at Yale may pursue "interdepartmental studies"—consisting of the "interrelationships of literature and the visual arts, of history and philosophy, of sciences and mathematics."[30]

Today many colleges follow a broad-fields approach in general education. The organization of the general education curriculum into broad-fields does not eliminate the specialized courses at the advanced levels of study. The broad-fields curriculum is widely practiced in general education with the aim of giving the student a comprehensive overview of a field of knowledge. The separate subjects, on the other hand, tend to be organized sequentially so that each course represents a small segment of specialized knowledge. It is ironical that the secondary schools should be accused of watering down the curriculum when they attempt to improve the articulation among certain areas of learning through a broad-fields approach—especially when many of our leading

---

[28] A. Lawrence Lowell, "Inaugural Address, October 6, 1909," *Atlantic Monthly*, Vol. 104, November, 1909, p. 692.

[29] See *Courses in General Education* (Cambridge, Mass.: Harvard University Press, 1961–62.

[30] See Bulletin of Yale University, *University Catalogue Number 1961–1962*, New Haven, Conn., November 1, 1961, p. 123.

colleges are recognizing the need for a more unified and integrated curriculum in general education.

CURRICULUM ARTICULATION AND REVISION

Integrating Elements of the Curriculum

Tyler identifies three elements that are the basis for organizing learning experiences: (1) concepts, (2) skills, and (3) values.[31]

> Three kinds of elements are commonly to be found in current curriculum guides and courses of study which are used as the basis for the organization of learning evperiences. Concepts comprise the most common type. For example, the concept of the interdependence of human beings is a concept which occurs again and again in many courses of study beginning with the kindergarten and running through the senior high school. . . .
>
> A second common type of organizing element is that of skills. A skill like reading serves as an element that is acquired at a very simple level in the early grades and is broadened and deepened as the pupil moves on through the elementary school and the high school. . . .
>
> A third type of element which sometimes appears in curriculum guides and courses of study is that of values. Values include aesthetic qualities, ideals, and objects and activities which learners are expected to develop loyalty to or interest in as a part of the educational program. One value which is found most commonly in social studies courses is that of respect for the dignity and worth of every individual regardless of his race, religion, occupation, nationality, or social class. . . . Values appear to represent the organizing elements related to objectives of attitudes, interests, appreciation, and the like.[32]

If the educational program is successful, these concepts, skills, and values will be reflected in the behavior of the learner. In putting together the subject matter of a given specialty, relatively few faculties have given sufficient thought to the common elements or threads that make up the material, color, and design of a discipline; and often ignored is the interdependence of the various disciplines. The chief factor that distinguishes a discipline from an inert body of facts and information lies in the coherence of content and process or the unity of structure that is sustained at all levels of education—from the elementary school to the graduate school.[33] When we ignore this unity, the subject matter becomes a mere additive process and takes on the properties of a formless cancer, rather than the symmetry and harmony of a growing tree.

---

[31] Ralph W. Tyler, "Curriculum Organization," Chapter VI, *The Integration of Educational Experiences,* Fifty-seventh Yearbook of the National Society for the Study of Education, Part III (Chicago: The University of Chicago Press, 1958), p. 112.

[32] *Ibid.,* pp. 112–114.   [33] *Ibid.,* see pp. 112–114.

ORGANIZATION OF THE COURSE.   Whether we have a traditional subject curriculum or a broad-fields approach, there has been a trend in recent years toward reorganizing the internal structure of each course into somewhat larger blocks. Instead of merely presenting the course as a long series of quite separate lessons, the tendency has been toward organizing the subject matter into fairly broad topics. But many curriculum workers have found the topical approach inadequate because it often fails to reduce the number of discreet elements within the course itself. Consequently, they have turned to a unit approach that organizes the subject matter around key problems or purposes. The unit approach has the twofold advantage of reducing the large number of course topics and boundaries into more related blocks, and of making the subject more appealing psychologically through problems and activities related to the interests and needs of the learner.

CRITICISMS OF THE BROAD-FIELDS APPROACH.   We have already pointed out that the creation of a broad-fields curriculum does not automatically result in subject-matter integration. Such integration can only take place in the mind of the student. In other words, the test of a curriculum is in what the student has learned and how such learning leads to more effective behavior in the life of the student.[34] Education should lead to lifelong learning—an attitude of inquiry and open-mindedness. Perhaps the true test of a curriculum is not so much what the student has learned, but what he seeks to learn, and also how he is able to harness such learning in the improvement of his life and the life of others.

To a considerable extent, the success or failure of a curriculum hinges not so much on its particular type of design or structure as on the kind of teacher in the classroom. If the broad-fields approach is to fulfill its purpose of developing new relationships between and among a multiplicity of disparate subjects, teachers must have a broad range of competencies in their chosen area of instruction and they must be committed to the need for curriculum continuity and articulation. The design or structure of a curriculum can help or hinder the educational process, but the final success or failure of this process is utterly dependent on the teacher in the classroom.

---

[34] Professor Bestor observes that "the test of a school, after all, is how much the students learn." (*The Restoration of Learning*, New York: Alfred A. Knopf, 1955, p. 106). But education is not this simple. For example, a student is motivated to obtain a grade of A in a literature course and, at the end of the semester or academic year, he actually achieves this high grade. This is no guarantee that the student will have developed a passion for reading good literature on his own. He has been motivated to get a high grade and he has fulfilled this goal. But he is not necessarily motivated to read good literature in his normal, out-of-school routine. Indeed, he may have developed a negative attitude toward such literature as a result of his experiences in the academic setting.

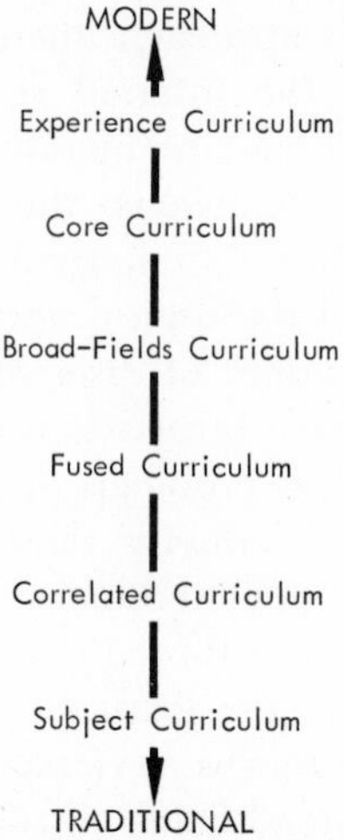

MODERN

↑

Experience Curriculum

|

Core Curriculum

|

Broad-Fields Curriculum

|

Fused Curriculum

|

Correlated Curriculum

|

Subject Curriculum

↓

TRADITIONAL

FIGURE 6–1. Types of curriculum design. [Based upon curriculum classifications as seen by Harold Spears, *The Emerging High-School Curriculum* (New York: American Book Company, 1948), p. 52.]

Some critics of the broad-fields approach argue that it does not go far enough. They would prefer an activity or core curriculum more realistically centered around life problems. The broad-fields approach, they would argue, too often follows a traditional and logical sequence of subject-matter organization without giving sufficient attention to the psychological needs of students. While these critics might concede that the broad-fields is a step in the right direction, they would like to eliminate all of the traditional subject boundaries in general education and develop a curriculum focused on the problems and needs of youth. Such proposals for curriculum reform are treated in detail in Chapter 7.

Representing quite another view are those critics who prefer the traditional subject curriculum. The following statement by an historian criticizes the "worship of contemporaneity" in the curriculum, and decries the "submersion" of the subject of history into the social studies or social sciences:

> In the public schools today the shortsighted worship of contemporaneity is producing its most devasting effects within the area which educationists call "the social studies." This label has itself contributed so greatly to educational confusion and stultification that it ought to be abandoned forthwith. The mature world of scholarship recognizes a number of disciplines that are concerned primarily with the institutions of organized society. Among these are economics, political science, sociology, anthropology, social psychology, and jurisprudence. . . .

History is the one discipline in the traditional secondary-school curriculum which is perennially and consistently concerned with the perspective of time. . . . History cannot perform this essential function if it is submerged in the social sciences and loses its identity. History co-operates with and learns from the other disciplines concerned with man and society, but it has its own tasks, its own techniques, and its own system of values.

A course in history, described and taught as history, cannot possibly neglect the perspective of time or dodge the problems of change and development. A course in "the social studies," on the other hand, can easily narrow its scope to strictly contemporary questions. If its organization is topical, the occasional references it makes to historical "background" may result in so unsystematic and even garbled an understanding of chronology as to destroy historical perspective entirely.[35]

While Professor Bestor is known primarily for his criticisms of the secondary school, his argument against the broad-fields curriculum runs counter to many prevailing practices in the general education programs of some of our most illustrious colleges. In other words, even at the college level the need for curriculum integration is recognized, as evidenced by broad-fields courses at such institutions as Yale College, Harvard College, and the University of Chicago. The attempt at curriculum integration in the social sciences is not to emphasize contemporaneity at the expense of history, but to capitalize on the interdependence of these disciplines. Without such attempts, a great profusion of separate courses develop and it becomes virtually impossible for the high-school student or college freshman to gain an intelligent overview of a field of learning. Moreover, the broad-fields curriculum in general education does not lead to the elimination of the specialized subjects. As the student completes his general education, he is able to pursue the more advanced courses in his chosen areas of specialization.

At advanced levels of scholarship, significant efforts are being made to develop greater unity and coherence among related fields. Interdisciplinary approaches to instruction and research are being taken in the social sciences at Princeton University, for example:

New avenues to a comprehensive view of the social sciences will be opened as the result of a $1,400,000 grant, received last week by Princeton University, for the study of human relations. In sharp contrast to the academic habit of departmental specialization, the Roger Williams Straus Council on Human Relations at Princeton will combine the faculties and principles of history, political science, economics, sociology, anthropology and social psychology to do research on specific problems. . . . the Princeton venture emphasizes the combination of forces to illuminate a problem rather than the general education of the student. It will attempt to increase the values of cooperation by concentrating on

---

[35] Arthur Bestor, *The Restoration of Learning* (New York: Alfred A. Knopf, 1955), pp. 126–129.

one area: the principles of human relations as a tool for resolving human conflicts. Dr. Robert F. Goheen, president of the university, described the need: "The findings of social psychology must be put to work immediately in political science, and sociology must help enlighten economic analysis."[36]

Attempts at curriculum integration are also being made in a number of professional schools, including medicine and dentistry.[37] Some of these programs go far beyond the broad-fields approach in an attempt to develop an integrated curriculum. It seems paradoxical that attempts at curriculum unity are being criticized at the secondary school level, while at the same time there is recognition for such curriculum development in general education and professional education at the university level. Professor Bestor and other critics of secondary education argue that such integration constitutes a hodgepodge or watering down of the curriculum. But if students at the undergraduate college level and advanced professional level are in need of a more unified, cohesive, and interdisciplinary approach to learning, it seems unreasonable to expect the high school student to develop an educational synthesis automatically from the many disparate and departmentalized courses in the subject curriculum. Indeed, it might be argued that the subject curriculum, with its departmentalized organization, results in a hodgepodge of learning as far as the high school student is concerned.

Again, it should be emphasized that the broad-fields approach is not designed to reduce subject matter to its lowest common denominator. Indeed, a poor teacher of history under the traditional subject curriculum may develop nothing but a watered-down hodgepodge of information to be learned by the unfortunate student. Of course, some attempts at curriculum articulation and integration have been misguided and ineffectual. But the failure to provide learning experiences that are stimulating and challenging is not an inherent characteristic of any particular type of curriculum. Rather, such a shortcoming is more of a reflection on the school faculty and administration. The promise of curriculum articulation lies in the increased opportunities for bridging gaps in the educative experience through greater cooperative effort on the part of school faculties. The success or failure of attempts at articulation rests not on the curriculum structure alone, but to a great extent on what is done within the structure. The structure of the curriculum can only help or hinder the efforts for improved articulation.

RETRENCHMENT OR CHANGE? A number of academic specialists in the

---

[36] "Bridge for Social Studies," The New York Times, September 17, 1961, p. E9.
[37] The School of Medicine at Western Reserve University instituted an integrated medical curriculum in 1952. A similar program was developed for the University of Texas School of Dentistry beginning 1961–62.

universities have criticized the curricula of the schools in recent years. Paul Woodring expresses his belief that many such specialists are really not qualified to determine the curriculum for the elementary and secondary school because their own experiences are confined to teaching the relatively high-ability student.

> It has been proposed by critics of the contemporary trends that the curriculum of the elementary and high schools should be made by the academic specialists in the universities because they are presumed to know the most about the world of knowledge. But this is the course which was followed prior to the present century, the course which proved unfeasible with the extension of universal education up through the secondary school. It was because the scholars refused to face the problems of universal education that the classroom teachers, confronted with students of all levels of ability, turned to the new philosophy for a way out of their dilemma. . . .[38]

Professor Bestor is also critical of what he terms the worship of contemporaneity in the curriculum. But the dynamics of knowledge are such that many disciplines, including some of those cited by Professor Bestor, such as sociology and social psychology, are relative newcomers to the academic scene. The avoidance of contemporaneity in the curriculum would have prevented many now recognized academic disciplines from gaining a foothold. For example, the competent scientist and social scientist today needs to be well grounded in statistics. Yet, the science of statistics is really a twentieth-century phenomenon. The science of genetics is also a very young discipline. The point is that within the twentieth century, many new disciplines have been born. The schools cannot keep contemporaneity out of the curriculum. The schools are always being criticized for being too far behind the times, and the needs of society are such that the schools must constantly reappraise and revitalize the curriculum. Obviously, this issue of contemporaneity is rooted in the educational aims that society establishes for its schools. A successful industrialist and outspoken critic of American secondary education puts it this way:

> Our curricula today are largely the result of tradition. They are the carry-over of past generations in which classical education predominated. I think it is time that a fresh look be taken by unprejudiced, imaginative and able educators, persons who can throw off the shackles of blind adherence to tradition. Let these persons look at the world as it is today and ask themselves, "What knowledge, what training, what skills does the youth of today need to prepare him best for the problems he will encounter in his lifetime?"[39]

---

[38] Paul Woodring, *A Fourth of a Nation* (New York: McGraw-Hill Company, Inc., 1957), p. 93.

[39] Arnold O. Beckman, "A Businessman's View on the 'Failure' of Education," *U.S. News & World Report*, XLI, November 30, 1956, 22:89.

The traditionalists and essentialists are advocating that the secondary schools return to a subject-centered curriculum limited to the recognized academic disciplines. The curriculum, as they see it, should be confined to intellectual training:

> The business of the school can no longer be with social adjustment, emotional security, entertainment, or even with character. Such matters, if they are teachable, belong to the home, the church, or the family doctor. The school has the child only one-sixth of his waking hours in any calendar year. Therefore, let it concentrate on the job it alone can do: develop the intellectual equipment of *every* child to its maximum point, and let it never underestimate that point.[40]

In sharp contrast, a professor of philosophy argues that the schools in a free society must be concerned with moral and ethical values, and that the curriculum is not an end but a means to an end.

> Each time I hear someone who knows (or pretends to know) what, in detail, education should consist of, I shudder. For their position usually rests on the assumption that a human can be made into this or that or the other thing. But if humans can be made into this or that or the other thing, then they become mere things and are not human beings. To be human is to be morally responsible, and to be morally responsible is to be free. A rigid doctrine of education negates this freedom.
>
> . . . . I suspect that . . . the traditionalists who want children taught foreign languages and mathematics fail to see that these subjects are merely means for developing moral character. . . . My own specialty is logic, certainly one of the most disinterested of all the disciplines. Logic is certainly an extremely important and valuable course, yet it is a mistake to regard logic, by itself, as anything other than a skill. Learning logic can be an enormous advantage to a person—it can make him more logical in his pursuit of virtue or it can make him more logical in his pursuit of vice. Similarly with the other academic subjects we arts professors are so keen for. They are merely skills, and what one does with them is finally independent of how well he has mastered them. Churchill and Hitler were both masters of the skills of rhetoric. To say that teaching a child mathematics will, by itself, make him a better person is to be guilty of reprehensible naïveté.[41]

The dilemma facing the educator is how moral and ethical values can be developed in school when the reality of society often militates against such values. The construction of family bomb shelters and the devising of protective measures for keeping the neighbors out of these shelters is difficult to reconcile with the ethic "Love thy neighbor." And can the schools counterbalance the materialistic values conditioned by the inces-

---

[40] Statement by Admiral H. G. Rickover, quoted by James D. Koerner, "Admiral Rickover: Gadfly," *Saturday Review*, April 15, 1961, p. 63.
[41] Robert E. Larsen, "Education and Ethics," *Saturday Review*, April 15, 1961, pp. 65–66.

sant waves of television advertising? These questions do not imply that the task of the schools in the areas of morality and ethics is hopeless and should therefore be ignored. But the educator finds that progress in such areas is slow, and the problems are so great that there is a tendency to succumb to the temptation of keying the curriculum to the subject matter, rather than to human behavior. When the home and society fail to inculcate humane values and ideals, we find a variety of educational critics attacking the schools for failing to meet this task. The schools in a free society cannot turn their backs on matters of democracy, morality, and ethics—but they are beset with the dilemma of how to cope with the many contradictions and paradoxes of an imperfect society.

NEW KNOWLEDGE AND CURRICULUM CHANGE. Another problem confronting educators is that of vitalizing the curriculum so that it will keep pace with rapidly accelerating developments in human knowledge. The curriculum, in too many instances, has tended to lag behind societal needs. The traditionalists would like to see our schools turn to a subject curriculum that focuses on the academic disciplines, while the modernists are calling for greater experimentation and flexibility in the curriculum. In recent years, more and more educators have come to the opinion that the method and content of various subject-matter areas need to be changed radically, in line with the revolutionary changes in human knowledge. Despite criticism from the traditionalists, the schools today are under great pressure to bring their curricula up to date. The twentieth-century revolution in science and mathematics is beginning to lead to a curriculum revolution in the schools, a revolution somewhat similar to that advocated by John Dewey early in the century. Consider this modern assessment of mathematics, for example:

> Going modern means mainly two things: pruning out dead wood and introducing some of the new fundamental ideas which within the last century have given more meaning and unity to all the traditional branches of mathematics.
>
> As an example of dead wood one can cite the considerable attention devoted in trigonometry textbooks to solving triangles with logarithms. This was the only method available to surveyors and navigators a century ago; today, technicians punch out the answer in calculating machines. Also in the category of dead wood are some of the classic Euclidean "proofs" of geometry; they are not really proofs at all. Today a mathematician attacks these problems with the calculus and the idea of limits, and arrives at truly rigorous proofs.
>
> Mathematics as now taught in the lower schools and even in college seems to be a collection of separate subjects. Each has its own apparently arbitrary rules taught by rote. But work on the foundations of mathematics in the last century has shown that all branches of mathematics can be reduced to purely abstract terms, with common properties. As

numbers are the elements of algebra, so points and lines are "primitive" elements of geometry, and we can deal with sets of either in the same way—indeed with the same operations. The rules of mathematical logic are universal. These basic ideas and logical processes can be taught even to school children, the modernists believe. In learning them, students will find mathematics more understandable and more meaningful. They will also get at least some aquaintance with modern thinking in mathematics.[42]

Similar reappraisals are being made in the sciences, social studies,[43] modern languages, and other curricular areas. And there is correspondingly growing recognition of the need for effective in-service education of teachers. In an Academic Year Institute for experienced high-school science and mathematics teachers, sponsored by the National Science Foundation, it was found that very few of these teachers had an adequate understanding of the history and philosophy of science. When required to conduct a demonstration teaching assignment, their performances were confined to known facts and principles, ignoring the method of scientific inquiry.

> Evidence that the fellows had not learned to teach students much about the way in which scientific progress is achieved was given by their sample teaching performances. Each of a representative group of fellows gave a half-hour talk on a topic of his own choice designed for a high school classroom. In these short talks the fellows were almost entirely preoccupied with presenting the known facts and principles of science and mathematics. Very seldom was any effort made to convey a sense of the *way* in which scientific thought unfolds—the thinking and research lying behind the material the teacher was presenting. The history leading up to a scientific discovery and the consequences of such a discovery were never discussed.[44]

In another report, the investigator indicates that more active participation by students is necessary if the subject matter (science) is to unfold as a way of thought. The constant telling and explaining by the teacher implies that the subject matter is merely a body of established facts and doctrines, not subject to further inquiry and verification. He hypothesizes that these passive-receptive methods of teaching condition the student *not* to think.

> . . . why do training programs stressing the passive-receptive teaching methods foster the teaching of science as established knowledge while programs stressing active participation foster the teaching of science as

---

[42] E. P. Rosenbaum, "The Teaching of Elementary Mathematics," *Scientific American*, May, 1958, 198:64–65.

[43] See Charles R. Keller, "Needed: Revolution in the Social Studies," *Saturday Review*, September 16, 1961, pp. 60–62.

[44] Howard E. Gruber, "Science Teachers and the Scientific Attitude: An Appraisal of an Academic Year Institute," *Science*, 132:468, August 19, 1960.

a way of thought? Two somewhat different hypotheses suggest themselves. First, it may be that listening to lectures actually suppresses any embryonic tendencies to approach science as a process of intellectual inquiry. The listener, constantly striving to keep up with a highly trained, well-prepared lecturer must discipline himself *not* to think, otherwise he will lose the thread of the lecture and his notes will become a disorganized jumble of his own questions and ideas confused with the instructor's presentation. This might not affect the listener's general intellectual development if a lively discussion followed the lecture, but with students pushing a busy schedule this is rarely the case. Secondly, the process of discussion is itself perhaps a form of thought similar to scientific inquiry. The main function of a lecture is usually the *presentation* of knowledge; the main function of a discussion is the *exploration* of ideas. The social dialogue begun in discussion is continued as an inner dialogue, or thought. In discussions of science, the prospective science teacher has the opportunity to try his own skill at formulating and reformulating the thinking that lies behind the formidable array of established knowledge. Without an abundance of such discussions he may never penetrate the facade of certainty to the arena of doubt in which intellectual inquiry unfolds.[45]

Almost half a century ago, John Dewey called for learning as a process of inquiry, rather than passive absorption and regurgitation of information.

> Excessive reliance upon others for data (whether got from reading or listening) is to be depreciated. Most objectionable of all is the probability that others, the book or the teacher, will supply solutions readymade, instead of giving material that the student has to adapt and apply to the question in hand for himself.
> . . . Pupils who have stored their minds with all kinds of material which they have never put to intellectual uses are sure to be hampered when they try to think.[46]

The passive-receptive role of the student in the traditional curriculum was soundly criticized by Dewey and others early in the twentieth century. Research in the psychology of learning strongly supported Dewey's position. But certain curriculum workers went to extremes in their reaction to traditional education. The activity curriculum at the elementary level placed great emphasis on activity as an end in itself, rather than as a means to an end.[47] Child-centered schools developed, and in many cases a laissez-faire atmosphere prevailed that allowed children a maximum of freedom. Some of these schools that followed an experi-

[45] Howard E. Gruber, *Science as Thought* (Boulder, Colorado: University of Colorado, Behavior Research Laboratory Report No. 16, May, 1961), p. 27.

[46] John Dewey, *Democracy and Education* (New York: The Macmillan Company, 1916), pp. 185–186.

[47] National Society for the Study of Education, *The Activity Movement*, Thirty-third Yearbook, Part II (Chicago: The University of Chicago Press, 1934).

mental pattern remain in existence today, adhering to many of their original tenets.[48] But the trend today is to interconnect learning with vital experience. The problem method or the discovery method are being developed with increasing success in the secondary school, particularly in the areas of science, mathematics, and social studies. Some curriculum theorists, however, contend that such reforms in instructional methods cannot be fully effective unless accompanied by a significant reconstruction of the curriculum design. In other words, they propose a curriculum, particularly in general education, that transcends the usual subject structure and focuses on significant problem areas. Alberty observes that the conflicting concepts of the subject-centered curriculum versus the experience-centered curriculum can be reconciled.

> A curriculum based upon direct, personal experience is much more apt to be meaningful to the student than one based upon the logical organization of subject matter. Such a curriculum, however, must draw heavily upon logically organized subject matter if it is to be effective.
> The subject-centered approach to learning is almost universally practiced in the American high school. It has been assumed that logically organized race experience is a satisfactory basis for organizing learning experience. It has persisted in spite of its psychological shortcomings and its relative ineffectiveness in contributing to democratic purposes . . . A number of significant studies looking toward the improvement of the subject-centered curriculum are in progress. Most of them propose the organization of the subject in terms of central ideas, concepts, or generalizations, rather than facts and information. There is also much emphasis upon the psychological aspects of learning such as problem-solving and discovery of significant ideas, which more readily transfer to novel situations.
> It is possible for experience-centered and subject-centered programs to exist side by side in a school and to supplement and reinforce each other.[49]

There has been a tendency to hold fast to the subject-centered curriculum and to resist attempts to break down the traditional subject-matter boundaries. Proposals for a more experiential curriculum through a core approach in general education at the secondary level have been adopted on a very limited scale. Nevertheless, certain schools and colleges have been successful in their attempts at curriculum reconstruction.

The vocational education curricula in our high schools have been noted for their experience-centered emphasis. Programs of supervised work experience have long been practiced even at the highest levels of professional education, notably internship in medical education. Some col-

---

[48] See A. S. Neill, *Summerhill, A Radical Approach to Child Rearing* (New York: Hart Publishing Company, Inc., 1960).
[49] Harold B. Alberty and Elsie J. Alberty, *Reorganizing the High-School Curriculum*, 3rd Ed. (New York: The Macmillan Company, 1962), pp. 196–197.

leges, Antioch for example, recognize the value of work experience as a liberalizing influence for undergraduate students. The next chapter deals with a number of the major proposals for curriculum reform in general education for our secondary schools.

SUMMARY

Modern educators have come to reject the traditional concept of curriculum as a body of subjects offered or required by an educational institution. Instead, they see the curriculum embodied in the nature of the responses evoked in the learner, as a result of a particular design of school-sponsored experiences. However, no matter how elaborate or promising the design, the true test of a curriculum lies in its influence in bringing about improvements in behavioral strategies.

Despite its serious limitations, the subject-centered approach to organizing the curriculum of the secondary school continues to prevail. It is a convenient way of organizing and administering the program of studies. The subject-centered curriculum also conveniently fits the usual patterns of college entrance requirements. Most textbooks are designed for the subject-centered curriculum, and many teachers find it convenient to rest the responsibility for curriculum design with the author of the textbook.

It has been recognized for some time that the traditional subject-centered curriculum tends to compartmentalize knowledge, so that the transfer of learning from one subject to another is often disappointing, even within the same discipline. With the primary focus on the logical organization of the subject matter, this type of curriculum design has tended to give secondary attention to the psychology of learning. Under the logical organization of the subject matter, there has been the tendency for too many teachers to equate information with knowledge. To them, learning is measured through the power of one's memory to recall information. The degree to which this type of learning brings about new patterns or strategies of behavior is ignored. Knowledge is regarded as static, not dynamic.

Nevertheless, we must bear in mind that changes in the way in which a program of studies is packaged does not necessarily guarantee that the contents of the package will acquire new properties. In recent years, some highly promising approaches have been attempted in reorganizing the content and methodology within the framework of the subject curriculum. In science and mathematics, for example, the new emphasis is more student-centered, with content and process designed to elicit strategies of inquiry and discovery.

Despite these promising changes, the subject curriculum often impedes learning transfer. As the accelerated pace of new knowledge continues, there is the temptation that new courses will be added without revitalizing or even eliminating old courses.

In the final analysis, curriculum experimentation and reconstruction depend less upon any paper plans or lists of objectives, than upon the quality and commitment of the teacher and the entire faculty of a school. Improvement is not possible in the absence of a willingness to experiment.

PROBLEMS FOR STUDY AND DISCUSSION

1. How would you define curriculum? Explain why you have defined it this way.

2. How is one's definition of curriculum related to one's philosophy of education?

3. How did the curriculum of the high school you attended compare with the multiple curriculum in Table 6–1? What courses were you required to take? What electives did you choose? If you had it to do over again, would you elect different courses? Why?

4. Why has there been a greater tendency to experiment with different approaches to curriculum organization at the junior high school level than at the senior high school level?

5. Do you agree or disagree with the following statements by Albert Einstein? Why?

> Sometimes one sees in the school simply the instrument of transferring a certain maximum quantity of knowledge to the growing generation. But that is not right. Knowledge is dead; the school, however, serves the living. . . . [Albert Einstein, *Out of My Later Years* (New York: Philosophical Library, 1950), p. 32.]
> The development of general ability for independent thinking and judgment should always be placed foremost, not the acquisition of special knowledge. [*Ibid.*, p. 36.]

6. What did Alfred North Whitehead mean in the following statement? Do you agree with him? Why?

> The solution which I am urging is to eradicate the fatal disconnection of subjects which kills the vitality of our modern curriculum. There is only one subject-matter for education, and that is Life in all its manifestations. [Alfred North Whitehead, *The Aims of Education* (New York: The Macmillan Company, 1929), p. 10.]

7. In your own field of subject specialization, can you give an example of a concept, a skill, and a value? For each of these three elements, describe an activity you might assign to a high school class.

8. Many illustrious colleges and professional schools have successfully implemented integrated curricula. Why is it, then, that some critics attack such attempts at the secondary school level as a hodgepodge and watering down of the curriculum?

9. Do you agree or disagree with the following statement by Admiral Rickover? Why?

> The business of the school can no longer be with social adjustment, emotional security, . . . or even with character. Such matters, if they are teachable, belong to the home, the church, or the family doctor. [H. G. Rickover, *Saturday Review* (April 15, 1961), p. 63.]

10. How is our conception of learning related to the matter of curriculum design (i.e., the subject curriculum versus broad-fields)?

SELECTED REFERENCES

Alberty, Harold B., and Elsie J. Alberty, *Reorganizing the High-School Curriculum* (3rd Ed.) New York: The Macmillan Company, 1962. Ch. V.

Alexander, William M. and J. Galen Saylor. *Modern Secondary Education.* New York: Holt, Rinehart & Winston, Inc., 1959. Chs. IX and X.

American Council of Learned Societies and the National Council for the Social Studies. *The Social Studies and the Social Sciences.* New York: Harcourt, Brace and World, Inc., 1962.

Benjamin, Harold. *The Saber-Tooth Curriculum.* New York: McGraw-Hill Company, Inc., 1939.

Bent, Rudyard K. and Henry H. Kronenberg. *Principles of Secondary Education.* New York: McGraw-Hill Company, Inc., 1961. Chs. XI and XII.

Bestor, Arthur. *The Restoration of Learning.* New York: Alfred A. Knopf, 1955. Ch. IV.

Dewey, John. *Democracy and Education.* New York: The Macmillan Company, 1916. Ch. XIV.

Douglass, Harl R. (ed.) *The High School Curriculum* (3rd Ed.) New York: The Ronald Press Company, 1964.

Goodlad, John I. *School Curriculum Reform in the United States.* New York: The Fund for the Advancement of Education, March, 1964.

Gwynn, J. Minor. *Curriculum Principles and Social Trends* (3rd Ed.) New York: The Macmillan Company, 1960. Ch. XIII.

Hand, Harold. *Principles of Public Secondary Education.* New York: Harcourt, Brace and World, Inc., 1958. Ch. XI.

Heath, Robert W. (ed.) *New Curricula.* New York: Harper & Row, Publishers, Inc., 1964.

Krug, Edward A. *The Secondary School Curriculum.* New York: Harper & Row, Publishers, Inc., 1960. Chs. VI and VII.

Leese, Joseph, Kenneth Frasure, and Mauritz Johnson, Jr. *The Teacher in Curriculum Making.* New York: Harper & Row, Publishers, Inc., 1961. Chs. VII and X.

Leonard, J. Paul. *Developing the Secondary School Curriculum.* New York: Holt, Rinehart & Winston, Inc., 1956.

National Society for the Study of Education. *The Integration of Educational Experiences.* Fifty-seventh Yearbook, Part III. Chicago: The University of Chicago Press, 1958.

Smith, B. Othanel, William O. Stanley, and J. Harlan Shores. *Fundamentals of Curriculum Development* (Revised). Yonkers-on-Hudson, New York: World Book Company, 1957. Ch. X.

Spears, Harold. *The Emerging High-School Curriculum.* New York: American Book Company, 1948. Chs. I–III.

Taba, Hilda. *Curriculum Development.* New York: Harcourt, Brace & World, Inc., 1962.

Whitehead, Alfred North. *The Aims of Education.* New York: The Macmillan Company, 1929.

Woodring, Paul. *A Fourth of a Nation.* New York: McGraw-Hill Company, Inc., 1957. Ch. IV.

CHAPTER *7*

General Education,
Common Learnings,
and the Core Curriculum

IN ANCIENT GREECE the term liberal education was used to describe the kind of education that was fitting for the freeman, in contrast to the training given to the slave.[1] The liberally educated freeman was to be well rounded in the development of his physical, intellectual, and moral qualities. The freeman took part in the activities of citizenship and had leisure time for educational pursuit, while the slave was expected to carry out the menial labors necessary in society. The word liberal is derived from the Latin word *liber*, meaning free. The curriculum for the freeman consisted of a *trivium* of grammar, logic, and rhetoric—to which was added a *quadrivium* of arithmetic, geometry, music, and astronomy.

GENERAL EDUCATION IN A FREE SOCIETY

Modern democratic societies respect the dignity of labor. The millionaire in our society today is more apt to seek a useful career in government or industry than to pursue a life of leisure. Our society does not regard liberal education as the domain of an elite or privileged class.[2] Since the democratic nations of our modern world hold all citizens to be free, and since each citizen is entitled to an equal voice in voting and other activities of citizenship, the task of universal education for general enlightenment is of vital importance.

---

[1] See John S. Brubacher, *A History of the Problems of Education* (New York: McGraw-Hill Company, Inc., 1947), pp. 474–476.

[2] Despite the ideal of equal educational opportunity embraced by our society, there are many social and economic barriers that prevent many of our youth from obtaining a college education. It is estimated that the total college population is matched by an equally large group of intellectually capable youth who, because of social, economic, or personal problems, are unable to attend college.

In the United States during the twentieth century, we have witnessed a remarkable revolution in making secondary education available to all the children of all the people. But a heterogeneous population in the secondary school has necessitated a diversified curriculum to meet the wide variety of needs and range of capacities of our youth. Nevertheless, a free society, where each citizen enjoys equal rights and exercises an equal power of voting, stakes its strength on an enlightened citizenry. This means that there are some common educational aims all citizens must share—regardless of their special interests or talents. Because of the historic stigma attached to the term liberal education, we have come to use the term general education to describe this core of objectives necessary for all citizens. This does not mean that all persons must be exposed to an identical curriculum in general education. It means that, insofar as possible, our educational system must strive to develop enlightened citizens for a free society.

In the preceding chapter, we reviewed some of the current practices and requirements in general education, subject specialization, and vocational studies at the secondary level. In this chapter we will focus on the major proposals for curriculum improvement in general education in the secondary school since World War II.

Interpretation of General Education

We have already indicated that general education is concerned with the understandings and competencies that all citizens in a democracy must share. It has been defined as "that which prepares the young for the common life of their time and their kind. . . . It is the unifying element of a culture."[3] Programs of general education in school and college may follow widely differing patterns. The traditionalists advocate a program emphasizing the more abstract and verbal type of learning, with key emphasis on man's cultural inheritance. The Great Books program championed by Robert M. Hutchins, former president of the University of Chicago, is an example of this approach. On the other hand, the modernists advocate a program focused to a great extent on current problems and issues for man and society. Emphasis is given to the student's living participation in democratic processes in the school and classroom. Attention is given not only to the so-called intellectual processes, but also to emotional, attitudinal, social, and physical factors.[4] It should be noted that the traditional approach does not completely

---

[3] Earl J. McGrath, et al., Toward General Education (New York: The Macmillan Company, 1948), p. 8.
[4] See T. R. McConnell, "General Education: An Analysis," in General Education, Fifty-first Yearbook, Part I, National Society for the Study of Education (Chicago: The University of Chicago Press, 1952), pp. 4–5.

ignore current problems or issues, but it does place primary focus on cultural inheritance, intellectual processes, and literary sources. Conversely, the modern approach to general education does not ignore completely man's cultural inheritance and literary sources. But the key focus is on contemporary problems and issues, and strong emphasis is given to human personality and behavior. This dichotomy may be summed up thus:

> To some exponents of general education, the purposes are to be attained by transmitting to each new generation of students the tested ideas and values of its cultural inheritance. To others, they are to be realized by making learning the "creative agent of cultural and social progress." To some, the process of general education is the inculcation of some accepted set of values and interpretations of individual and social experience. To the more venturesome, it is the process of encouraging students to discover for themselves the ideas and ideals which seem to hold the greatest promise for human beings and for society.[5]

The modern approach attempts to evolve a program based on what is known about human behavior. The traditional approach, on the other hand, is concerned primarily with man's recognized attainments of the past and how these relate to the current scene. As we study various recommendations for general education later in this chapter, we will see that differences in interpretation lead to different ways and means of organizing the curriculum.

CURRICULUM PRIORITIES. As we examine the major proposals for the improvement of general education at the secondary level, we will see that there are many differences of opinion. Also, in view of the changing forces in society, there is a tendency to provide special support for those curricular areas that seem to meet our most immediate needs. The increasing demands and pressures for educational specialism in an age of accelerating scientific and technological development, coupled with our society's competitiveness with the Soviets, have caused us to give special attention and support to such areas as science and mathematics.[6]

The emergency of World War I led to increasing emphasis on vocational education and physical fitness. The period of World War II was accompanied by attempts to improve the physical fitness programs in our secondary schools. The current space age has resulted in great emphasis on science and mathematics in the curriculum. Our new technology has led to a shrinkage of time and distance so that modern foreign languages have suddenly become an important area of emphasis in the curriculum.

---

[5] *Ibid.*, p. 5.

[6] The National Defense Education Act of 1958 provided federal funds for the improvement of the curriculum and the upgrading of teacher education in the areas of science, mathematics, and modern foreign languages.

Considering the total task of general education in a free society, it would be dangerous for us to create a severe imbalance in the curriculum. If we emphasize science and technology to the neglect of the social studies and the arts of communication, then we may be diminishing our capacity for self-determination and a democratic way of life. Certainly the task of communicating effectively in one's native tongue (English language arts) and the ability to make relevant judgments and to discriminate among values (social studies) are of vital importance to a free society. But the temptation is to meet emergency conditions with emergency programs. Are such priorities soundly conceived? Will they have damaging affects on attempts for a balanced curriculum in general education? In all probability, this emergency program will eventually give way to a more balanced, long-range approach to curriculum improvement.[7]

Since World War II, there have been a number of serious efforts to reformulate our approaches to general education in the secondary school. This chapter is devoted to reviewing the most significant of these efforts.

REPORT OF THE HARVARD COMMITTEE

In January of 1943, Dr. James Bryant Conant, President of Harvard, appointed a faculty group to serve as a University Committee on the Objectives of a General Education in a Free Society. This Committee released its report in 1945 in the form of a book bearing the title, *General Education in a Free Society.*[8] This report was concerned with general education in both school and college, and must be regarded as one of the most significant statements ever made on this question.

In Chapter 2 we examined the Harvard report briefly in terms of its relevancy to the goals or aims of education in our society. In the present chapter, however, we are concerned with the pervading thesis of the report: general education in a modern, democratic society.

The Task of General Education

The Harvard Committee identified four abilities to be developed by general education: to think effectively, to communicate thought, to make relevant judgments, and to discriminate among values.[9] The Harvard Committee defines general education as "education for an informed

---

[7] Under the auspices of the U.S. Office of Education, a program called Project English was initiated in September, 1961 on a very modest scale for the purpose of improving the teaching of English in schools.

[8] Report of the Harvard Committee, *General Education in a Free Society* (Cambridge, Mass.: Harvard University Press, 1945).

[9] *Ibid.*, p. 65.

responsible life in our society" that seeks to fit young persons "for those common spheres which, as citizens and heirs of a joint culture, they will share with others."[10]

The other tasks of education involve the meeting of special-interest and vocational needs of our youth and our society to "help young persons fulfill the unique, particular functions in life which it is in them to fulfill."[11]

With the incessant expansion of human knowledge, the need for more and more specialized education, and the universalization of secondary education, the task of general education becomes increasingly complex. At the same time, it seems to be easier to criticize our educational institutions for failing to meet the changing needs of a changing society.

> The unparalleled growth—one could almost say eruption—of our educational system, taking place as it has while our way of life was itself undergoing still vaster changes, is like a mathematical problem in which new unknowns are being constantly introduced or like a house under construction for which the specifications are forever changing. To have embarked toward the ideal of free secondary education was surely to cut out work enough. But to have done so when life was always raising new demands, when the prospects facing young people were never stable, and when the very goals of education had therefore to be constantly revised, was to undertake more even than was bargained for. The wonder is not that our schools and colleges have in some ways failed; on the contrary, it is that they have succeeded as they have.[12]

Although the Harvard Committee focused its efforts on general education in school and college, it recognized the need for a diversified curriculum in the secondary school to meet the special interests and vocational requirements of a heterogeneous student population. In defining the meaning of general education, the committee emphasized the interdependence of general education and vocational education in a free society where everyone shares a responsibility and voice for self-government.

> It (general education) is used to indicate that part of a student's whole education which looks first of all to his life as a responsible human being and citizen; while the term, special education, indicates that part which looks to the student's competence in some occupation. These two sides of life are not entirely separable, and it would be false to imagine education for the one as quite distinct from education for the other. . . .
>
> Modern democratic society does not regard labor as odious or disgraceful; on the contrary, in this country at least, it regards leisure with suspicion and expects its "gentlemen" to engage in work. Thus we attach no odium to vocational instruction. Moreover, in so far as we surely re-

---

[10] *Ibid.*, p. 4.   [11] *Ibid.*, p. 4.
[12] *Ibid.*, pp. 5–6.

ject the idea of freemen who are free in so far as they have slaves or subjects, we are apt strongly to deprecate the liberal education which went with the structure of the aristocratic ideal. Herein our society runs the risk of committing a serious fallacy. Democracy is the view that not only the few but that all are free, in that everyone governs his own life and shares in the responsibility for the management of the community. This being the case, it follows that all human beings stand in need of an ampler and rounded education. The task of modern democracy is to preserve the ancient ideal of liberal education and to extend it as far as possible to all members of the community. . . . To believe in the equality of human beings is to believe that the good life, and the education which trains the citizen for the good life, are equally the privilege of all.[13]

Recommendations of the Harvard Report

The major recommendations of the Harvard Committee for general education in the secondary school are summarized as follows:[14]

1. At least half of the student's program should be devoted to a core of studies in general education. All students need not pursue exactly the same courses, but their general education should embrace common aims and ideals. Instead of a watered-down program for the less able, however, new and authentic approaches are needed to make these studies meaningful and valuable.

2. The general education program should be distributed throughout the entire four years of high school.

3. The minimum of eight units of general education should consist of three units in English, three in science and mathematics, and two in the social studies.

4. Those planning to attend college should pursue further studies in one or more of the above areas in high school. For those not going to college, added work in general education may be pursued in the areas of art, music, English, American life, and general science.

5. Students not planning to attend college should be able to devote approximately one third of their studies to specialized education, including programs in the vocational and business areas. But even these studies should not be wholly vocational in intent; they should bear a relationship and spirit similar to studies in general education, as does further work in mathematics or languages for those preparing for college.

In summarizing the above recommendations concerning general education and specialized education in the secondary school, the Harvard

---

13 *Ibid.*, pp. 52–53.   14 *Ibid.*, pp. 99–102.

report observes that this scheme "accepts the claims of a common culture, citizenship, and standard of human good, yet also the competing claims of diverse interests, gifts, and hopes. Certainly some such scheme cannot be absent from American education if it is to produce at one and the same time sound people and a sound society."[15]

In addition to the quantitative recommendations embodied in the above five points, the Harvard report calls for the avoidance of mechanical repetition of uncomprehended material, greater cooperation among teachers to dissolve the rigid barriers that prevent the transfer of learning from one subject to another, and increased emphasis on critical thinking.[16]

The secondary school population today is comprised of such a great range of interests, drives, and talents that one wonders how a program of general education can be made meaningful to all. While the Harvard report claims no pat answer to this problem, it observes that this diversity is characteristic of a democratic society where people with different aptitudes and specialties share a common task of responsible citizenship.[17] The Harvard report emphasizes that everyone, regardless of specific abilities or ambitions, should share in the same educational ideals, though different means must be employed to make such education meaningful. Schools might well experiment with a variety of approaches to general education, within a framework of common ideals and purposes.[18]

The report points out that there are many deficiencies in the makeup and use of textbooks in our schools, observing that in too many cases the textbook presents the material to be learned in such predigested fashion that the student is compelled to "memorize the account of a trip which he never took."[19] In other words, the subject matter should be made significant and real to the learner, not trite and artificial.

The Harvard report also states that some of the so-called nonacademic studies, such as the industrial arts, may be valuable, not only for those students who will not be entering college, but also for those who intend to follow scientific and technological pursuits, and also for the general education of all.

> In an earlier section we spoke of the importance of shop training for students who intend to go into scientific or technological work. Such experience is important for the general education of all. Most students who expect to go to college are now offered an almost wholly verbal type of preparatory training, while hand training and the direct manipulation of objects are mainly reserved for the vocational fields. This is a

---

[15] *Ibid.*, p. 102.
[17] *Ibid.*, pp. 93–94.
[19] *Ibid.*, p. 109.

[16] *Ibid.*, see pp. 73–74, 116–117.
[18] *Ibid.*, pp. 96, 99.

serious mistake. The bookish student needs to know how to do things and make things as much as do those students who do not plan to take further intellectual training. The direct contact with materials, the manipulation of simple tools, the capacity to create by hand from a concept in the mind—all these are indispensable aspects of the general education of everyone.[20]

In the area of student activities, the report points out that such activities should not be regarded as something separate from the class-room, but as an extension of it.[21] Educators have recognized that activities and responsibilities in student government, the Science Club, French Club, Debating Society, or Glee Club may be in full harmony with the educational goals of the school. The report observes that it would be desirable if some of the zest for activities were also characteristic of the attitude toward formal studies.

The Harvard report recognizes the need for considering the whole person in the educational program. Emphasis is given to the responsibility of the school to be concerned with the physical and mental well-being of our youth. Recognizing that the home and family may not be up to the task, the report stresses the legitimate role of the school in these areas.[22]

Major Areas of General Education

The Report of the Harvard Committee goes on to describe each of the areas of general education in the secondary school, with recom-mendations for improving the instructional content and methods in English (literature and composition), the arts (music, painting, drawing, and modeling), social studies, science, and mathematics. While space does not permit an elaboration of the observations and recommendations offered in each of the individual areas of general education, a few brief summations may serve to convey some of the highlights.

ENGLISH.[23] The study of literature should continue through the four years of high school, with the focus on the potentialities and norms of living as presented by the best authors. The material should be chal-lenging, but modifications in approach should be made to suit individual differences. Too many texts prematurely digest the material for the student, leading to memorization without understanding. Old and new

---

[20] *Ibid.*, p. 175. A number of comprehensive high schools, such as George Washing-ton High School in San Francisco, require that college preparatory students take a unit in a nonacademic field for purposes of rounding out their education. At the junior high school level, a common practice is to require all boys to take a unit in industrial arts and all girls to complete a unit in homemaking as part of the general education program. Similar requirements may apply for art, music, etc.

[21] *Ibid.*, p. 172.   [22] *Ibid.*, p. 168.

[23] *Ibid.*, see pp. 107–119.

Photo by Daniel Tanner
Words alone cannot express what we see and feel.

works should be proportioned, with the new taking precedence as more immediate and leading to the more remote.

Mechanical repetition of uncomprehended words and phrases should be avoided, and technical literary terminology should be postponed until college. Instruction in English language arts should be the joint task of all teachers. Excessive emphasis on mechanical rules and mere imitation should be avoided.

THE ARTS.[24]   Although formal courses in each of the art subjects may not be required of students, instruction in the arts should be considered a part of general education. Aesthetic sensitivity to music and the fine arts can enhance the happiness of people. Although art may be regarded as the "discernment and communication of beauty," it is really much more than this; art also deals with the discovery and expression of life's values.

Art instruction should include understanding of our heritage from the past, as well as opportunity for the enhancement of present experience and the universal realm of value. Art is not merely self-expression, but also self-transcendence; it is not creativity alone, but also discovery. It is the means through which idea and feeling can be merged with concrete material. Instruction in the arts should not be aimed only at developing skills for leisure activity, but also for the general enrichment of experience. Such instruction should enable the learner to develop aesthetic tastes that will affect his daily living.

THE SOCIAL STUDIES.[25]   Schools can contribute to effective citizenship through both formal courses and student activities (student government, forums, debating societies, discussion groups, and the like). The formal course work in the social studies should deal not only with immediate problems, but also with our heritage. A variety of materials and methods of instruction are necessary for students of different backgrounds and abilities; but everyone shares the problems and responsibilities of citizenship.

Every school should have an over-all plan of instruction in the social studies for continuity throughout the four years of high school. Every student should develop an understanding of the history of modern civilization. Geography should be linked with the study of general history. The study of American history should provide a basis for the study of American life and society and for effective citizenship. Detailed chronological coverage too often dulls the student's interest in the subject and should be avoided. Nor should such studies be limited to the confines of a textbook.

Students should have experience in the gathering and weighing of evidence and the development of skills in critical thinking. The pursuit of facts for their own sake should be avoided. The culmination of work in the social studies should be a course dealing with contemporary society and focusing on topics from the fields of government, economics, and sociology. Greater emphasis should be given to interpretation. Moralizing about proper attitudes is not a desirable approach to education for

---

[24] *Ibid.*, see pp. 127–132.   [25] *Ibid.*, see pp. 132–150.

effective citizenship. Teachers should enjoy academic freedom and the classroom should carry the spirit and practice of inquiry and discussion.

SCIENCE.[26] One of the most important contributions of science instruction to general education is the power of direct observation and precision. For purposes of general education, science instruction should be characterized by broad integrative elements. These include not only comparisons of the various sciences with one another, but comparisons of scientific with other modes of thought, and the relation of science to human history and societal problems. These aspects are given insufficient attention in our schools because they are erroneously regarded as extras. But these broader perspectives can have lasting value.

With the exception of vocational-technological education, virtually all science instruction below the college level should be geared to general education. Even vocational education should carry elements of a general scientific attitude.

Early education in science should be organized in large comprehensive units that transcend conventional subject boundaries and derive their central themes from the student and his environment. Students should have the opportunity to explore for themselves and to solve natural problems through direct observation and experimentation. They should develop a real familiarity with the world of nature beyond the classroom.

The so-called steps in the scientific method should not be rigidly followed, because such a formalistic approach may actually stultify learning; besides, the working scientist uses previous knowledge, intuition, trial and error—as well as the logic of the scientific method.

As the student advances through high school, science instruction can be expanded beyond his immediate environment and experience. Differences in points of view and approaches through the various divisions of science should be emphasized. An understanding of the history of science and the discussion of major concepts and hypotheses should be developed. Such work may constitute a basic background in science to be followed in the ninth or tenth grade by a course in biology. The study of biology should include an objective treatment of personal and community hygiene, nutrition, and sexual reproduction; the work of the great biologists should be studied; individual student projects should parallel the classroom work.

Students not going on to college, and those who plan to enter college but do not intend to pursue science at the higher level, tend to terminate their study of science with the completion of high school biology. These students may well benefit from a general course drawing from the fields of physics, chemistry, geology, and astronomy, with key emphasis on

---

[26] *Ibid.*, see pp. 150–160.

basic concepts and principles.[27] The aims of such a course should also be for general education. Those students who intend to pursue advanced work in science at the college level would also benefit from such an integrated course, followed by a year of high school chemistry or physics or both.

MATHEMATICS.[28] Mathematics plays an indispensable part in the study of many fields where increasing use is being made of graphic data, statistics, algebraic formulas, and so on. Mathematics is important not only in formal education in various subject fields such as science, economics, psychology, and sociology, but also in general living and vocational endeavor.

By the time the student finishes the seventh grade or the middle of the eighth grade, he should have developed reasonable proficiency in the language of arithmetic with some competence in the solution of arithmetical problems and some appreciation of the use of mathematics in the real world in formulating and solving problems. The basic aspects of geometry should also be developed at this time. And finally, for those who will not be able to study advanced high school mathematics, an appreciation for the use of formulas, graphs, simple equations, and basic trigonometry should be developed. These aspects should be mastered by the middle of the ninth grade. Such students should have an opportunity to apply mathematical concepts in other subjects, including mechanical drawing, industrial arts, agriculture, etc. Prospective college students should have some additional study of mathematics, particularly in algebra and demonstrative geometry. Mathematics should not be a ritual of memorized formulas and skills.

Implications of the Harvard Report

The Harvard Committee was composed of twelve of the university's leading educators from the Faculty of Arts and Sciences and the Faculty of Education. The appearance of the Harvard report in 1945 was eloquent testimony to a growing awareness on the part of some college faculty that the secondary school much be much more than a college-preparatory institution. Too many college faculty members regard the high school as an academic institution whose main task is to prepare students for higher academic work in college. Although the Harvard report was also

---

[27] Although such courses are commonly offered at the college level during the freshman or sophomore year, very few high schools provide such an offering. And while courses in general science are commonly found in grades seven, eight, and nine, the Harvard Committee's recommendation calls for an advanced general course in grade eleven or twelve, encompassing a more mature approach than is possible at the junior high level.

[28] *Ibid.*, see pp. 162–167.

concerned with general education in college, major emphasis was given to general education in the secondary school, with particular consideration for the majority of youth who will not pursue higher education. In the words of President Conant at the time the committee was appointed,

> This committee . . . I hope will consider the problem at both the school and college level. For surely the most important aspect of this whole matter is the general education of the great majority of each generation—not the comparatively small minority who attend our four-year colleges. . . .[29]

Another significant aspect of the Harvard report lies in its preference for the term general education over liberal education. Many academic traditionalists deplore the term general education.[30] But the Harvard report embraces the concept of general education as a universal ideal for twentieth-century democracy. The traditional concept of liberal education for the privileged or leisure class is rejected.

The Harvard report probably is the most incisive statement ever made on the nature and purpose of general education. It represents a synthesis of the best that can be derived from tradition with the best that modern experimentalism can offer. It is not a middle-of-the-road position or a bland attempt at reconciling the pervading cleavages and conflicts in educational philosophy.

> Education can therefore be wholly devoted neither to tradition nor to experiment, neither to the belief that the ideal in itself is enough nor the view that means are valuable apart from the ideal. It must uphold at the same time tradition and experiment, the ideal and the means, subserving, like our culture itself, change within commitment.[31]

REPORT OF THE EDUCATIONAL POLICIES COMMISSION: EDUCATION FOR ALL AMERICAN YOUTH

During World War II, another group of educators formulated a plan of secondary education for mid-twentieth century United States. This group was the Educational Policies Commission of the National Education Association. Their comprehensive plan appeared in 1944 under the title, Education For ALL American Youth.

The Educational Policies Commission was established in 1936, during a period when our leading educators began to take a new look at the

---

[29] Ibid., p. viii.

[30] See Arthur Bestor, The Restoration of Learning (New York: Alfred A. Knopf, 1955), pp. 402–403.

[31] Report of the Harvard Committee, General Education in a Free Society (Cambridge, Mass.: Harvard University Press, 1958), p. 51.

problems of youth in a society beset with economic and social maladjustment. But the depression was followed by World War II—a period
during which school construction was at a standstill; many teachers had
left the classroom to serve in the armed forces or to devote themselves
to more lucrative positions in industry; and our in-school youth could
look forward to imminent military service upon graduation from high
school.

The task of the Educational Policies Commission during the war years
was to formulate a plan for public education in the postwar period.[32]
The commission's membership was composed of some of our leading
educators, including Dr. James B. Conant, President of Harvard, who,
during this same period, initiated the work of the Harvard Committee
on The Objectives of a General Education in a Free Society.

In 1952, eight years after *Education for ALL American Youth* was
first published, the commission produced a revised edition carrying the
additional title, *A Further Look*.[33] Dr. Conant was chairman of the commission at this time. The volume was a comprehensive plan or model
for youth education. Using the mythical state of Columbia as the setting,
the report portrayed an idealized educational program for all youth. But
the report was not intended as a Utopian scheme. It attempted to
present a sample of an educational program that might be achieved
during the third quarter of the twentieth century.

This idealized program of youth education was formulated against a
realistic background of educational problems in our society. The report
pointed to the fact that, despite the generally accepted principle of
universal secondary education, approximately half of American youth
do not complete high school; and among this army of dropouts are some
of our most intellectually gifted students. It stressed the need for our
schools to develop comprehensive programs to meet the variety of educational needs and aptitudes of our youth, and urged that our youth
must not be deprived of an education because of social and economic
status. The report called for a comprehensive secondary-school program,
with free public education extending through the junior-college level.
A concerted program of school district reorganization and school consolidation was also recommended.

The commission identified ten "Imperative Needs of Youth," around
which its program of secondary education is based. These needs include
effectiveness in salable skills, health, democratic citizenship, family and

---

[32] The Educational Policies Commission also produced such volumes as *Educational
Services for Young Children* (1945), and *Education for ALL American Children* (1948).

[33] Educational Policies Commission, *Education for ALL American Youth: A Further
Look* (Washington, D.C.: National Education Association, 1952).

societal living, consumer economics, scientific understandings, aesthetics, leisure, and ethical values.[34]

Common Learnings

Although the commission's report was concerned with all aspects of youth education, including provisions for vocational needs, we shall attempt to confine this analysis to the points that deal with general education or common learnings (the latter term being used throughout the report). In formulating its program of common learnings, the commission addressed itself to two questions: "What are the learning experiences which all boys and girls have in common? And how may these be organized so as to be most effective?"[35]

A CORE CURRICULUM. While the proposals of the Harvard Committee were largely within the general framework of the subject and broad-fields curriculum, the Educational Policies Commission advocated a core curriculum in general education. Instead of prescribing a list of separate required courses to cover each of the areas of common study, the commission's plan in general education covered a continuous block of time of two or more hours daily in grades seven through fourteen (two years of junior college are included). The rationale for this block or core approach was to make possible the fullest integration of learning experiences in general education. In this way, conventional subject lines would be dissolved and the interrelationships of human knowledge and activity would be made more vivid. This daily block of time to be devoted to general education was called common learnings, and the aim was to tie such learnings in with the needs of life that all people share in common. The basic course in common learnings would encompass studies and activities in the fields of citizenship, economics, family living, literature, the arts, and English language arts. Some science might be included in this common learnings core, or it might be offered as a separate required course as part of the total general education sequence.[36]

It was felt that since our daily experiences in family life, civic activity, leisure time, and so on, are bound together, the traditional separate subject approach would therefore be insufficient to the task. The common-learnings block or core would permit the study of broad problems that require information and the application of principles from a number of subject-matter areas. This plan would also provide greater flexibility in the use of time for a variety of activities and projects. Another advantage of the proposed plan is that it would permit the teacher of common learnings to have fewer pupils and to spend more time with them,

---

[34] *Ibid.*, p. 216.
[35] Educational Policies Commission, *op. cit.*, p. 223.
[36] *Ibid.*, see p. 228.

In this way, the common-learnings teacher could also serve in a guidance and counseling capacity. Assuming a teaching schedule of six periods, the common-learnings teacher assigned to two blocks of three periods each would have only 60 pupils daily (30 pupils in each group). But under the traditional separate subject approach, a teaching schedule of six periods would mean contact with 180 different pupils daily (30 pupils in each group).

There are, of course, some possible difficulties in the core approach. It requires a teacher who is knowledgeable in the purposes of general education and possesses considerable breadth and depth of understanding in a variety of learning areas. Such teachers are not easy to come by. Consequently, some schools have used a team-teaching approach within the core structure in general education.

Another possible difficulty in the core approach lies in developing the instructional content and process. In the traditional subject curriculum, the content is usually well defined. But in the core approach, there is greater latitude for flexibility and spontaneity when the instructional content and methods are developed around broad problems. Many more alternatives are available to the teacher and learner in the core curriculum, and while this may prove to be challenging and stimulating, it nevertheless requires considerable versatility and ingenuity.

AIMS OF THE COMMON LEARNINGS COURSE. The commission identified six purposes of the course in common learnings:

1. To help all youth grow in knowledge of their community, their nation, and the world of nations; in understanding of the rights and duties of citizens of the American democracy; and in diligent and competent performance of their obligations as members of the community and as citizens of the state and nation.
2. To help all youth grow in knowledge of the operations of the economic system and in understanding of the human relations and problems in economic activities, particularly of the relations between management and employees.
3. To help all youth grow in understanding of personal relations within the family, of the conditions which make for successful family life, and of the importance of the family in society.
4. To help all youth grow in ability to purchase and use goods and services intelligently, with accurate knowledge of values received by the consumer and with understanding of the economic consequences of one's acts.
5. To help all youth grow in appreciation and enjoyment of beauty in literature, art, music, and nature.
6. To help all youth grow in ability to listen and read with understanding and to communicate their thoughts with precision and clarity.[37]

---

[37] *Ibid.*, p. 238.

The area of science is conspicuously absent from the above objectives. While the commission agreed that science should be an integral part of the common learnings course, it decided to offer science instruction separately because of the shortage of qualified science teachers and the difficulty of obtaining the services of common learnings teachers who are also competent in this area.[38] However, the commission did recommend that a general education course in science be taught during the tenth grade in close cooperation with the common-learnings course.[39] While mathematics is universally regarded as a vital part of general education, it is not explicitly mentioned in the six objectives of the common learnings course. Apparently it would be included as needed in the study of economic problems and topics. It would also be included in the exploratory work during grades seven through nine, and in the vocational and college preparatory studies beyond the ninth grade. The area of health and physical fitness, not included in the six objectives for common learnings, is also offered as a separate course because of its specialized nature. This area is required for all students in grades seven through fourteen through the allotment of one period daily.

The commission also identified five aims common for every course, including the common learnings, to help youth develop:

1. In ability to think rationally and in respect for truth arrived at by rational processes.
2. In respect for other persons and ability to work cooperatively with others.
3. In insight into ethical values and principles.
4. In ability to use their time efficiently and to budget it wisely.
5. In ability to plan their own affairs, as individuals and as groups, and to carry out their plans efficiently.[40]

METHODOLOGY OF THE COMMON-LEARNINGS COURSE. The commission called for considerable freedom for the teacher and students in planning and executing the program of common learnings. The faculty would preplan the broad areas of common learnings for each grade level and pupils would be given opportunities to investigate problems.

> Within the broad areas planned for the year, classes can begin their work in any year with the problems and purposes of which students are most keenly aware at the time.[41]

---

[38] A good number of teacher candidates are prepared with a major-minor combination of English language arts and social studies, or vice versa. This combination is particularly fitting for teaching in a common-learnings program. The commission, however, fails to indicate how competent instruction in the arts will be provided, unless, of course, a team-teaching approach is employed for this purpose.

[39] Educational Policies Commission, *op. cit.*, p. 228. This course would be titled "The Scientific View of the World of Man."

[40] *Ibid.*, p. 239.   [41] *Ibid.*, p. 225.

Orderly sequences of learning might be expected in this course, quite as much as in single-subject courses. But there would be various types of sequences, each deliberately chosen by teacher and class because it seemed best suited to the task at hand. Sometimes the class would follow the method of scientific inquiry to conduct an experiment or solve a problem. Sometimes it would trace the relations of cause and effect through the events of history. Sometimes it would follow the logic of organized bodies of knowledge. And sometimes the order of learning would be that appropriate to growth in appreciations. To be able to choose a sequence of learning appropriate to one's aim is again an intellectual achievement.[42]

RELATIONSHIP OF COMMON LEARNINGS TO OTHER AREAS OF THE CURRICULUM. In addition to the core program in common learnings, the commission organized the curriculum into four major areas: personal interests or exploratory studies (grades seven through nine), individual interests or electives (grades ten through fourteen), vocational and college preparatory studies (grades ten through fourteen), and health and physical fitness (grades seven through fourteen).

In Figure 7–1 we see the relationship of the common-learnings core to the other areas of the curriculum in grades 7 through 14, as proposed by the commission. In grades 7 through 9, the pupil devotes half of the school day (three periods) to common learnings, one third (two periods) to personal interests (exploratory work in art, music, science, crafts, and so on), and the remaining one sixth (one period) to health and physical fitness. Upon entering grade 10, the student begins to pursue some vocational studies or college preparatory work. In grades 11 and 12, the common-learnings program is diminished to two periods daily, while the vocational or college-preparatory studies are expanded to two periods. One period daily is devoted to an elective beginning in grade ten.

It can be seen that, in addition to common learnings, this plan provides for specialized studies in vocational and academic subjects, and exploratory and elective courses. We have already mentioned that because the teacher in charge of the common-learnings core spends from two to three periods daily with a given group of pupils, he meets with fewer youngsters each day. On the other hand, the teacher who devotes his entire day to instruction in college-preparatory or elective courses has a greater number of different students. But it should be remembered that the common learnings teacher is also responsible for the guidance of his pupils. Specialized counseling personnel are also available in the school. In a given school, it is possible for a teacher to have only one common-learnings class, devoting the remainder of the day to teaching the specialized or exploratory courses. Obviously, the

---

[42] *Ibid.*, p. 226–227.

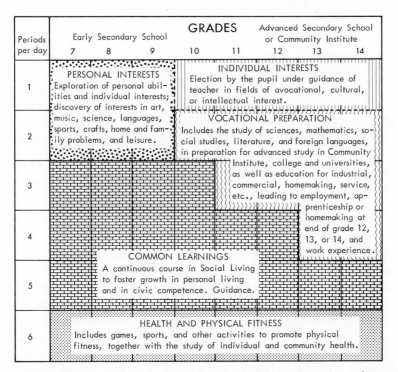

FIGURE 7–1. The curriculum in American City, grades 7 through 14. [SOURCE: Educational Policies Commission, *Planning for American Youth,* Revised (Washington, D.C.: National Educational Association, 1951), p. 48.]

plan shown in Figure 7–1 permits considerable flexibility of curriculum construction.

Areas of Common Learnings. While the common-learnings program in the junior-high grades encompasses a very broad spectrum of studies, it becomes more narrowly defined during the senior high school and junior college years, with major concentration on the social studies. From grade ten through grade fourteen, the areas of study are summarized as follows:[43]

> *Grade 10*
> Orientation to the Senior High School
> The Community at Work
> Civic Competence
> Consumer Economics
> Family Life
> Use of the English Language

---

[43] *Ibid.,* see pp. 240–252.

Grade 11
  Civic Competence
  History of American Civilization
Grade 12
  National and International Problems
  Literature and the Arts
Grades 13 and 14 (community college)
  Community, Regional, National and World Problems

Although the broad areas listed above are predetermined by the faculty, there is considerable teacher-student cooperation in determining the nature and sequence of studies and activities within these areas. Despite the apparently heavy emphasis given to the social studies, the common-learnings classes are continually involved in developing written and oral reports for individual and group analysis. Literature is also studied as an integral part of the social studies.

Implications

Education for ALL American Youth was significant for a number of reasons. It called for leadership by state departments of education in effecting school-district reorganization. It reaffirmed the importance of vocational education in the secondary-school curriculum. It followed the 6-3-3-2 pattern of vertical organization, providing for a junior high school, a senior high school, and finally, a tuition-free community college —all supported through the resources of a unified school district. It supported the comprehensive secondary school where all the youth of all the people can study and work through a diversified curriculum. It raised the period of compulsory education to the age of 18 or graduation from high school. It emphasized the importance of a continuous program of guidance and counseling. And it recognized the need for a core curriculum in general education.

Since we are primarily concerned in this chapter with the general education aspects of the commission's report, we will summarize with a brief reexamination of the "Imperative Needs of Youth" and the common-learnings program.

ARE THE EDUCATIONAL OBJECTIVES TOO BROAD? The educational programs presented in this document were formulated around the so-called Ten Imperative Needs of Youth. It will be recalled that these were identified as effectiveness in salable skills, health and physical fitness, democratic citizenship, family and societal living, consumer economics, scientific understandings, aesthetics, leisure, and ethical values.[44] The Educational Policies Commission obviously viewed the school's role

---

[44] *Ibid.*, p. 216.

as encompassing virtually all aspects of learning that relate to effective living.

While many educators would agree with the comprehensive role of the school in meeting these needs of youth, there are others who would prefer to see the schools limited to instruction in the traditional academic disciplines. They feel that the schools should leave such matters as family living, health, and emotional adjustment to other community agencies. And if these other agencies are not doing their job properly, it is still not the duty of the school to assume such responsibilities. The school, they argue, should be limited to the task of intellectual training. In taking issue with the Educational Policy Commission's broad interpretation of the role of the school, Professor Bestor offers this argument:

> The fact that other social institutions may not be doing their jobs as well as, or in the manner that, one would like is no reason for inducing the school to neglect its own tasks, too, in an ill-considered attempt to remedy the deficiency.
> . . . Much of the cant about education for "home and family living" is a disguised way of saying that the school must take the responsibility for things that the family today is supposedly failing to do. . . . Even if it were true, for example, that parents are not giving adequate sex instruction to their children. . . , does anyone seriously expect an embarrassed schoolteacher to explain the physiology of human reproduction to boys and girls in public, and to use franker and more explicit terms than their parents are willing to employ in private?[45]
> . . . There is one particular need that schools—and only schools—are peculiarly adapted to satisfy. That is the need for intellectual training.[46]

Despite Professor Bestor's pronouncements, however, there are many teachers of basic biological science in our schools and colleges who are providing instruction in the "physiology of human reproduction" with frankness and objectivity, and without embarrassment. Moreover, it is difficult to understand what Professor Bestor means by "intellectual training." Is an understanding of human physiology or nutrition less intellectual than an understanding of supply and demand, the Monroe Doctrine, or gravitation?

Since our public schools comprise one of our society's most effective unifying agencies, at times we may seem to expect much more from the schools than our investments would justify. Nevertheless, the schools are often the most effective agency for many important societal tasks—ranging from Americanization to tuberculosis testing. For some underprivileged youngsters, the school lunch provides the major source of their daily nutritional needs. We have come to realize that youngsters must

---

[45] Arthur Bestor, *The Restoration of Learning* (New York: Alfred A. Knopf, 1955), p. 119.
[46] *Ibid.*, p. 120.

have adequate nutrition and emotional stability if they are to learn effectively. The school cannot be oblivious to such needs if they are not being met in the home. In recent years, even our colleges have been giving increasing attention to such matters as emotional problems and mental health.

> Emotional problems on the campus have become so numerous that the National Institutes of Health recently awarded $237,115 to expand the University of Florida's five-year program in preventative mental hygiene. . . .
> Psychological testing, along with intensive counseling by resident advisers in the dormitories, have produced one striking result: Since the program began there have been no student suicides. . . . Before then, an average of five students committed suicide a year.
> At Florida, the psychiatric clinic is at its busiest just before exams. The same is true on almost every other compus.
> Dr. Graham Blaine, who is one of ten psychiatrists who serve Harvard's 11,500 students, says:
> "The panic (final examinations) started right after Christmas holidays and has built up so that now we're each seeing about ten students daily—even though we've stopped therapy for our regular patients until after finals. Of course, there'll be another fifteen or twenty cases we'll get when exams actually start."
> At other times, each Harvard psychiatrist sees only fifteen patients a week, half of them with problems related to study.[47]

Since the emotional and physical health of the student have a strong bearing on his capacity for learning, the school or college cannot limit its role to so-called intellectual training. This does not mean that the schools alone must provide every type of rehabilitative service. But the schools, by virtue of their daily contact with youngsters, are expected to identify the emotionally disturbed and refer them to agencies for psychiatric treatment. Unfortunately, very few communities are adequately equipped to handle such referrals, and the schools must carry the burden alone. And even in the rare instances where such community agencies are adequate to the task, the schools are expected to play an important role in the rehabilitative process.

The position of the Educational Policies Commission in viewing the school as an agency to help youngsters live effectively is in sharp contrast to those who see the school as a vehicle for intellectual training only. But intellectual training is not divorced from emotional and physical needs of adolescents. Moreover, our schools cannot divorce themselves from the deficiencies of the family or society.

A five-year study by the Mayor's Juvenile Delinquency Evaluation Project in New York City revealed that almost half of the city's 1,000,000

---

[47] *Newsweek*, LIX, No. 4, January 22, 1962, p. 58.

public school students require additional counseling help from their schools.[48] The study showed that from 10 to 20 per cent of the youngsters have "learning difficulties arising from emotional or mental disturbance." The report observed that at least one third or more of the youngsters are from homes that are culturally and economically deprived. The Bureau of Attendance for the New York City schools carried a case load of more than 350,000 during the 1960–61 school year, according to this study.

In recent years, the public schools of New York City have embarked on a program to improve the academic and cultural levels of students from underprivileged homes. This program, called Higher Horizons, involved 65 schools in 1961–62. Higher Horizons has sought to identify potentially able students from socially and economically deprived neighborhoods and assist them through special counseling and social enrichment. Higher Horizons has enabled underprivileged and underachieving youngsters to come in contact with the legitimate theatre, concert hall, art museum, and other cultural experiences for the first time in their lives. A good number of these students, who otherwise would have been school dropouts, have gone on to the successful pursuit of higher education.

These are just a few examples of what can be accomplished when the educative role of the schools is broadly interpreted, as recommended by the Educational Policies Commission.

CORE CURRICULUM IN COMMON LEARNINGS. Another highly significant aspect of *Education for ALL American Youth* is the key emphasis placed on a core curriculum for general education or common learnings. The traditional subject curriculum was rejected, and in its place a core program was developed that would enable teachers and students to study problems that cut across conventional subject-matter lines. Rather than a multiplicity of required courses in general education, the daily block of time devoted to common learnings would permit teachers and students to draw materials and select their learning activities from a variety of subject-matter fields. Greater flexibility in curriculum planning and organization would be possible under the core curriculum in common learnings. The approach to general education embodied in the common-learnings core proposed by the Educational Policies Commission is very much in harmony with the proposals for curriculum integration by many educators.[49]

Considerable emphasis would be given to teacher-student planning and

---

[48] The *New York Times*, September 11, 1961, p. 1.
[49] See The National Society for the Study of Education, *The Integration of Educational Experiences*, Fifty-seventh Yearbook, Part III (Chicago: The University of Chicago Press, 1958).

the role of the core teacher as a guide and counselor. Since the core teacher in grades 7 through 12 would be spending from two to three periods daily with the same group of students, he would have fewer different youngsters with whom to work. Consequently, the core teacher would be in a good position to know his students as individuals and counsel them more effectively. One of the chief problems under the core approach, however, is securing the services of teachers who have the breadth and depth of competencies in the common learnings, and who possess the interest and capacity to serve in a counseling function.

It should be remembered that the proposed plan does not eliminate a more traditional subject curriculum in areas outside the common learnings, such as the college-preparatory, vocational, elective, and exploratory programs.

THE CORE CURRICULUM FOR GENERAL EDUCATION

What is Core?

Some schools apply the term core to that part of the curriculum required of all students, whether it consists of a group of separate subjects, or whether attempts are made to correlate or fuse two or more of these required subjects. According to this interpretation, regardless of the organizational structure, the core is the part of the school curriculum that deals with general education and is required of all students.

On the other hand, some curriculum workers would define core differently. They would argue that it breaks sharply from the subject curriculum in integrating the various areas of study for general education. Like the common learnings proposed in *Education for ALL American Youth,* the true core curriculum rejects the formal organization of separate subjects and attempts to deal with broad problem areas. It strives to avoid the atomistic organization of studies into artificial compartments called subjects. In most cases where the core approach is applied to general education, the school follows a subject curriculum or broad-fields approach for the exploratory electives, vocational courses, and college-preparatory work.

Some definitions of core curriculum are as follows:

> A continuous, carefully planned series of experiences which are based on significant personal and social problems and which involve learnings of common concern to all youth.[50]
> . . . that part of the curriculum which takes as its major job the

---

[50] Hollis L. Caswell *et al., The American High School,* Eighth Yearbook of the John Dewey Society (New York: Harper & Row, Publishers, Inc., 1946), p. 143.

development of personal and social responsibility and competency needed by all youth to serve the needs of a democratic society.[51]

. . . a way of organizing some of the important common learnings in the high school curriculum, using a problem-solving approach as its procedure, having social and personal problems significant to youth as its content, and the development of the behaviors needed in a democratic society as its purpose. This represents a fundamental reorganization of the curriculum of the secondary school, rather than just a combination of the traditional subject matter.[52]

. . . a group of structured problem areas, based upon the common problems, needs, and interests of adolescents, from which are developed teacher-student planned learning units or activities.[53]

From these definitions we can see that the core approach rejects the conception of the general education curriculum as a set of separate required subjects; instead, it is regarded as the learning experiences, personal and social, that all youth in our society should have as a result of the school program. The focal point of the core, according to the above definitions, is on adolescent problems. The major characteristics of the core curriculum are summarized thus:

1. The core approach represents an attempt to organize the general education curriculum in a manner that is consistent with what is known about human behavior and with the psychology of learning. It is formulated around learning experiences designed to bring about desirable changes in behavior. Students are encouraged to seek their own solutions and conclusions, rather than to ingest and regurgitate established subject matter. The core reflects a concern for educational and behavioral outcomes rather than for a specific set of prescribed courses for general education. The focus is not on the subject matter per se, but on the learner—his aspirations and capabilities.

2. The general education function of core derives from an attack on broad problem areas, personal and social, which all the youth of a democratic society share.

3. The attack on broad problem areas is designed to take into account the widely varying aptitudes and interests of students, since considerable latitude is provided for individual and group projects and activities. Therefore, ability grouping by separate classes is not necessary.

4. Through an examination of broad problem areas, the interrelationships of several areas of knowledge are unified and integrated. Conven-

---

[51] J. Paul Leonard, *Developing the Secondary School Curriculum*, New York: Holt, Rinehart, and Winston, Inc., 1953), pp. 396–397.

[52] Vernon E. Anderson, *Principles and Procedures of Curriculum Improvement* (New York: The Ronald Press Company, 1956), p. 9.

[53] Harold Alberty, "A Sound Core Program—What It Is and What It Isn't," *NEA Journal*, Vol. 45, January, 1956, p. 20.

tional subject-matter boundaries are crossed in order to bring all pertinent sources of knowledge to bear on the problem. Instead of compartmentalizing the various areas of knowledge into separate subjects, the core permits an attack on problems through many sources and activities. Material from several logically organized subjects may be brought to bear on a broad problem area.

5. The method of intelligence and critical thinking are the key means of defining problems, gathering evidence, testing hypotheses, reaching solutions and testing conclusions. Students learn to examine all sides of issues without prejudice or bias.

6. The core teacher functions as a guide and counselor in working with the individual and group needs of students.

7. Cooperative curriculum planning by faculty members is necessary in selecting problem areas, determining sequences and methods, and developing resource units. In some schools, a team-teaching approach is used to provide core teachers with specialized assistance when needed.

8. Cooperative teacher-student planning is emphasized, and democratic values are fostered. Students learn to respect the opinions and rights of others.

9. A block of time consisting of two or more class periods is provided for the core. The block-time makes possible extended activities that could not be squeezed into the single period. The multiple period also enables the teacher to work with fewer different pupils each day, thereby having a better opportunity for more individualized instruction.

10. The core approach draws on the community as a laboratory for learning.

11. The core curriculum is required of all students. It represents the common learnings or general education program essential for all citizens of a democratic society, regardless of special aptitudes or vocational interests.

DEVELOPMENT OF THE CORE. The core curriculum began to make inroads during the 1930's and early 1940's. The Lincoln School of Teachers College did much pioneering work by organizing the general education sequence into core areas from grade 7 through 12. Instead of the usual set of required subjects for general education, the faculty established such core areas of study as "Man and his Environment" in the seventh grade, "Living in a Power Age" (culture and environment) in the eighth and ninth grade, "Ancient and Modern Cultures" in the tenth and eleventh grades, and "Living in Contemporary America" (social and economic problems) in the twelfth grade.[54] This revolutionary approach

----

[54] See Lawrence A. Cremin, *The Transformation of the School* (New York: Alfred A. Knopf, 1961), pp. 281–290.

required a tremendous amount of cooperative faculty planning in establishing the problem areas and activities connected with each of the core areas. The traditional textbook and recitation approach was rejected in favor of a problem-solving method that transcended the conventional subject-matter boundaries. The core program developed at the Lincoln School focused on a cultural-history approach to curriculum unification. Such an approach was designed to relate the various areas of man's experience (art, music, literature, government, economics, and so on) through broad cultural-historical themes.

During the 1930's, a number of colleges and universities established laboratory schools under the administration of their schools of education. These laboratory schools were designed to serve as centers for educational experimentation and demonstration. Core programs for general education were developed in many of these schools.

Several schools connected with the Eight-Year Study, launched by the Progressive Education Association in 1932, were noted for their experimentation with the core approach. The Eight-Year Study, involving 30 experimental secondary schools, revealed that "the more experimental the school, the greater degree of success in college."[55]

Some educators have criticized the cultural-history core as being too heavily oriented to the past. It was argued that its chronological emphasis was not suitable to the psychological and social needs of youth in contemporary society. As a result, the adolescent-needs core was developed. The adolescent-needs core was designed to focus on the common problems of youth in "personal-social-civic-economic living."

Since the adolescent-needs core tends to be derived largely from the school studies, some educators have proposed a more comprehensive core of unified studies or common-learnings that would be organized around problems and themes from the several major areas of knowledge. The common learnings program proposed by the Educational Policies Commission is an example of such a core.

A SAMPLE CORE PROGRAM. For some years, the University School at The Ohio State University, established in 1930, has experimented with core approaches based upon adolescent needs, problems, and interests. The curriculum is preplanned by the faculty through the designation of a wide range of problem areas for investigation. These problem areas are based on the maturation levels of adolescents with focus on

1. Personal Living—problems related to growing up.
2. Personal-Social Living—problems related to living with and understanding others.

---

[55] Dean Chamberlin *et al.*, *Did They Succeed in College?* (New York: Harper & Row, Publishers, Inc., 1942, p. 209.

3. Social-Civic-Economic Living—problems related to living in and understanding the immediate and wider community and world.[56]

The faculty of the University School at Ohio State identifies six characteristics of the core classes.

In the secondary program at the University School the core classes
1. Are required of all students.
2. Are scheduled for a longer period of time than are other classes. (Approximately three hours—grades seven, eight, and nine. One and one-half hours—grades ten, eleven, and twelve).
3. Are responsible for a major part of common learnings which are defined as the learning activities that are thought to be basic to the education of all students.
4. Provide learning activities which cut across conventional subject lines.
5. Provide learning activities and experiences which are in harmony with adolescent interests, needs, and concerns.
6. Function in such a way as to care for individual differences in a learning climate conducive to personal and class guidance.[57]

The core curriculum is organized around preplanned problem areas designated according to grade level. Resource units, developed by the faculty, are made available to students studying specific aspects of these problem areas. A wide variety of reading materials are used. Such reading materials are not confined to a specific subject field. Instead, an attempt is made to draw relationships from many areas of knowledge that bear on the problem under study.

Through teacher-pupil planning, problems for study are selected from the list designated by the faculty. The teacher and students cooperatively determine the ways and means of investigating these problems. Heavy emphasis is given to the method of intelligence as each problem is studied and conclusions are reached. Students are given opportunities to select areas of investigation, define objectives, undertake individual and group projects, gather and analyze data, and draw conclusions. The total program is designed to enhance such qualities of the democratic process as open-mindedness, respect for the opinions of others, and faith in the method of intelligence. A list of core problem areas used in recent years at The Ohio State University School follows:

Problem Areas—Grades Seven, Eight, and Nine

1. Understanding my Body
2. Beliefs and Superstitions
3. Hobbies

---

[56] Faculty of the University School, A *Description of Curricular Experiences: The Upper School*, revised (Columbus: The Ohio State University, 1952, Mimeographed), p. 12.
[57] *Ibid.*, p. 10.

4. Managing my Personal Affairs
5. Sports and Recreation
6. Living in University School
7. Living in the Home
8. Living in the Neighborhood
9. Personality and Appearance
10. Earning a Living
11. Housing
12. Natural Resources
13. Community Agencies and Services
        Recreation
        Protection
        Government
        Education
        Welfare
14. Communication
15. Living in Columbus
16. Living in Ohio
17. Living in Another Country or Other Countries

Problem Areas—Grades Ten, Eleven, and Twelve

Tenth Grade
1. Problems of Healthful Living
2. Problems of Living in an Urban Society
3. Problems of the Family as a Basic Social Unit
4. The Development of the American Scene

Eleventh Grade
1. Problems of Living in the Atomic Age
2. The Problems of Establishing Beliefs
3. The Problems of Making a Living (Exploring Vocations)
4. Current World Problems

Twelfth Grade
1. Problems of Producer-Consumer Economics
2. Implications of Scientific Advancement
3. Major Conflicting Ideologies
4. The Bases for Determining Values by which to Live[58]

Although the faculty of The Ohio State University School states that the core classes "are responsible for a major part of common learnings which are defined as the learning activities that are thought to be basic to the education of all students,"[59] an examination of the above list of core problem areas reveals a predominant emphasis on the social studies. If the core curriculum is to embrace the full spectrum of common learnings or general education, then the above list appears to be deficient in problem areas relating to literature, science, mathematics, and the fine arts. On the other hand, if the purpose of the core is to deal with

---

[58] *Ibid.*, pp. 12–13.   [59] *Ibid.*, p. 10.

those personal and social problems the youth of a democracy share, then the above list appears to be adequate. But because of the heavy emphasis on the social studies in the latter approach, some curriculum workers argue that additional learning experiences in such areas as literature, science, mathematics, and the fine arts would be necessary to fill out the common learnings or general education phase of the school curriculum. In other words, the adolescent-problems core is too narrowly confined to the social studies and, consequently, it can be argued that such an approach cannot be expected to represent the full spectrum of general education or common learnings.

TWO RATIONALES FOR THE CORE.   The core curriculum evolved from two different rationales.[60] The first represents an attempt to transform the multiplicity of separate subjects into a unified and coherent nucleus of studies for common learnings or general education. Such a synthesis was designed to bring about an understanding of the interrelations of the various areas of human knowledge and activity. It attempts to embrace the full spectrum of common learnings all citizens must share.

The rationale of the second approach is based on the premise that man's common concern is with the social values, problems, and issues that prevail in modern society. This rationale explains the dominance given to the social studies (social functions and social problems) and adolescent needs in many core programs.

> . . . the core of the curriculum consists in large part of the socio-moral rules comprising the core of the culture. In the society of the United States, these rules are chiefly those that constitute the democratic value-system. The core curriculum, therefore, places considerable emphasis upon the deliberate study of the moral content of the culture—especially as this content bears upon the resolution of social issues that divide the people and thereby prevent effective social action.[61]

The above rationale also explains the emphasis given to democratic processes in the core approach. But if the core is to encompass the full spectrum of general education, and if general education is concerned with the universal cultural as well as social aspects of society, then it can be argued that the core should not be limited to social problems and issues. Thus, an argument for a more comprehensive core approach may be justified. This would involve the study of the cultural and social elements that are universal to our society, including problems, concepts, and activities related to science, fine arts, mathematics, literature, and other areas not derived directly from the social studies.

---

[60] See B. Othanel Smith, William O. Stanley, and J. Harlan Shores, *Fundamentals of Curriculum Development* (Yonkers-on-Hudson, New York: World Book Company, 1957), pp. 311–312.

[61] *Ibid.*, p. 315.

The complexity of such a curriculum synthesis for common learnings can make great demands on the core teacher. In some core programs, a team-teaching approach has been developed whereby the core teacher may call upon teacher specialists for assistance in developing resource units and in conducting special learning activities.

Alberty has formulated 19 problem areas as a proposed core design:

1. Orientation to the School
2. Home and Family Life
3. Community Life
4. Contemporary Cultures
5. Contemporary America Among the Nations
6. Competing Political, Social and Economic Ideologies
7. Personal Value Systems
8. World Religions
9. Communication
10. Resource Development, Conservation, and Use
11. Human Relations
12. Physical and Mental Health
13. Planning (Individuals, Communities, Nations, and World)
14. Science and Technology
15. Vocational Orientation
16. Hobbies and Interests
17. Public Opinion
18. Education
19. War and Peace[62]

Alberty's proposed list of problem areas is also weighted heavily in the social studies, though some latitude is present for integrative work in the language arts (reading, composition, literature) and sciences. This list is designed to meet the common needs of adolescents. Similar lists can be developed cooperatively by a school faculty. The faculty may determine the sequence of these preplanned problem areas from grade to grade.

Alberty observes that this type of core program offers many advantages:

1. Such a program makes possible a direct attack upon the needs of youth and the problems which beset them in our present-day confused culture. . . .
2. Such a program provides an effective means of bridging the gap between education and guidance, between the curriculum and the extra-curriculum, between general and special interest education. . . .
3. It tends to break down the class barriers which so frequently are maintained in the traditional program. The use of broad, comprehensive units of work makes possible provision for individual differences in abilities and in rates of learning, thus obviating the necessity for sectioning or ability grouping. . . .

[62] Harold B. Alberty, *Reorganizing the High School Curriculum*, revised (New York: The Macmillan Company, 1953), pp. 178–180.

4. It facilitates the unification of knowledge. . . .
5. Such a program is consistent with the newer theories of learning and transfer. . . .
6. Such a program encourages the teaching staff to plan and work together. . . .
7. Such a program encourages the use of democratic practices in the classroom. . . . The student has a role in identifying problems, in planning the attacks upon them, and in evaluating the effectiveness of the work. . . .
8. It encourages the use of the community as a laboratory for learning. . . .
9. Such a program makes it possible for teachers to reduce materially the student loads which they are required to carry in a traditional program.[63]

The core approach also gives youngsters the opportunity for responsible self-direction. They have experience in making decisions. In the traditional classroom, students must rely on the teacher for virtually all decision-making in curriculum determination. The core approach is designed to foster qualities of responsibility and maturity. Another advantage of the core curriculum is that it enables the teacher and students to work together each day on a block-time basis. Extended activities and projects can be developed during a multiple period. The keynote of the core is learning how to learn. Provisions are made for individualized learning experiences, rather than keeping all students in a textbook lock-step, chapter by chapter.

CORE CURRICULUM WITHOUT FORMAL STRUCTURE. We have already described a core approach that is structured through problem areas that are predetermined by the faculty. In some schools, these problem areas may be designated specifically by grade level, whereas in other schools the list of problem areas may serve merely as a general guideline.

A few secondary schools have attempted to go a step further in developing a student-centered approach in common learnings.[64] In order to provide the students with a maximum of freedom in selecting problems and activities that fit their needs and interests, the block-time devoted to core is not prestructured. Instead, the teacher and students are free to decide upon and work out an educational program that seems most fitting. Emphasis is given to the values of group process and self-determination. The center of organization for learning is the student, not preselected problem areas or subject matter.

This approach is not laissez faire since it calls for a systematic examination of problems or topics once these are determined by the students and

---

[63] *Ibid.*, pp. 187–189.
[64] See Harold B. Alberty and Elsie J. Alberty, *Reorganizing the High School Curriculum*, 3rd Ed. (New York: The Macmillan Company, 1962), pp. 222–225.

teacher. The method of intelligence is applied to the process of selecting, investigating, and reaching conclusions concerning various problems or topics. Those who prefer a core without formal structure argue that this approach is more likely to deal with the genuine problems and concerns of adolescents. They observe that a structured core with preplanned problem areas and resource units often leads to the rigid formalism characteristic of the subject curriculum.

Obviously, since this type of core is without formal structure, it relies heavily for its success on the versatility and resourcefulness of the students and teacher. Since there are no predetermined problem areas, resource units are not always available to guide the students in their work. While the teacher and students may develop a systematic approach for working on problems or units, once these are determined, no advance attempts are made by the faculty to organize the core around problems dealing with adolescent needs, contemporary issues, cultural epochs, or other concerns. Some teachers in such a core program prefer to require students to base their selections of problems or units according to broad criteria for general education.[65] But because of the lack of prestructured guidelines, relatively few teachers and administrators feel comfortable with this approach.

THE TEACHER.   The success or failure of the core approach hinges on the teacher. As we have emphasized repeatedly, no curriculum plan or system of organization can of itself guarantee satisfactory learning outcomes. Curriculum organization is a means, not an end. Core programs require a considerable amount of cooperative faculty planning. Teachers need to be highly resourceful under such a flexible core plan. They need to have the breadth and depth of competencies and interests to make learning rich and rewarding for students. Since the textbook is not used as the basis for curriculum determination, high-quality resource units must be developed, and the school library and community become a vital part of the learning laboratory.

If the teachers are not committed to the philosophy and purposes of the core curriculum, or if they do not have the background and training for it, the program is likely to be self-defeating. Since most secondary teacher trainees pursue a subject major and minor through specialized courses in a college or university, they are likely to regard themselves as subject specialists, very much along the lines of the college professor. But the organization of knowledge for higher education may not be the best approach for the young adolescent in the junior or senior high school. This poses a real challenge for teacher education.

---

[65] See Roland C. Faunce and Nelson L. Bossing, *Developing the Core Curriculum,* 2nd Ed. (Englewood Cliffs, N.J.: Prentice-Hall, Inc., 1958), pp. 141–145.

Even within the limitations of the subject curriculum, it is possible for the teacher to make use of many techniques and procedures that are indigenous to the core approach. The effective teacher will strive to provide for individual differences, problem-solving, student needs and interests, behavioral goals, and democratic processes. Such a teacher, despite the compartmentalized structure of the subject curriculum, will strive to relate his particular area of subject matter to other fields and vice versa. For example, the effective teacher of science will make use of mathematics as an important tool, will foster the method of inquiry and discovery, and will relate the sciences to personal and social problems. It must be acknowledged, however, that the core approach provides the structure and climate most favorable for curriculum integration in common learnings.

THE CORE CURRICULUM AND THE JUNIOR HIGH SCHOOL.   Core programs of one type or another are most common at the junior-high level, rather than in the senior high school. One reason for this is that the junior high school is a transitional institution whereby children from the self-contained elementary classroom move into a more departmentalized program of instruction as they enter adolescence. Another reason for its greater popularity at the junior-high level is that this institution is not so obsessed with the college preparatory role as is the senior high school. Moreover, at the senior-high-school level, most teachers are disposed to regard themselves as specialists. The junior high school, as a transitional institution, is in a position to adopt the most promising practices from both the elementary school and the senior high school. It should also be remembered that the junior high school is a relatively new phenomenon, and therefore less apt to be bound by tradition. In 1920 there were fewer than 1,000 public junior high schools in the United States. Only ten years later, there were more than 4,000 such schools.[66] Today, it is estimated that approximately three fifths of the twelve-to-fourteen age group are attending junior high schools. Variations of core programs are rather widely followed at the junior-high level in the states of Maryland, Florida, and California. Also, many large city school systems have developed core programs.[67]

Probably the most common core program in the junior high school is where the social studies and English language arts are combined in a block-time of two or more periods daily. A single teacher is responsible for developing an integrated instructional program in these two fields.

---

[66] Ellwood P. Cubberley, *Public Education in the United States* (Boston: Houghton Mifflin Company, 1947), p. 631.
[67] National Society for the Study of Education, *The Integration of Educational Experiences*, Fifty-seventh Yearbook, Part III (Chicago: The University of Chicago Press, 1958), pp. 208–209.

This teacher also serves in a counseling capacity, since the block schedule permits him to spend more time with the youngsters and since he has fewer different pupils with whom to work. In some cases, while the block-time system is followed and a given teacher is responsible for instructing in the social studies and language arts, no attempt is made to integrate these two areas of study. The teacher simply organizes the program of study as two separate subject fields. Obviously, this defeats one of the primary purposes of the core approach: the integration of learning. It is estimated that one out of every three junior high schools employs some type of block-time program.[68]

In some schools, the block-time consists of a genuine core curriculum organized around broad problem areas that are cooperatively preplanned. This approach is designed to bring about optimum curriculum integration since it permits great flexibility in cutting across traditional subject-matter barriers. The faculty members responsible for the core curriculum cooperatively determine which problem areas should be developed at each grade level.

THE CORE AS AN EXPERIENCE-CENTERED CURRICULUM. We have observed that some schools use the term core simply to describe a block-time in which two or more subjects may be taught separately. Obviously, such an approach is not a core curriculum. Faunce and Bossing caution us against this abuse of the term and emphasize that the core is essentially an experience type of curriculum.

> Failure to recognize the fundamental nature of core as a pervasive form of organization of the experience type curriculum has led to some ill-advised practices in schools professing to use core, and to serious danger of a poorly balanced, fragmentary, and inadequate set of learning experiences for pupils.
> Many schools which claim to be using the core idea have in fact nothing but a number of independent groups of pupils and teachers meeting for a two or more hour block of time.[69]

One of the chief failures of the traditional subject curriculum is its preoccupation with the material to be learned, rather than with the task of bringing about desirable change in the behavior of the learner. The learner may derive certain sets of facts, pieces of information, and skills from his courses without undergoing desirable behavioral modifications. The student who has received a passing grade in a class in English literature or music appreciation, for example, may leave school with a strong distaste for these subjects. The core approach is an attempt to

---

[68] Commission on Secondary Curriculum, *The Junior High School We Need* (Washington, D.C.: Association for Supervision and Curriculum Development, National Education Association, 1961), p. 10.

[69] Faunce and Bossing, *op. cit.*, p. 57.

provide the learner with experiences that foster positive attitudinal and behavioral change. This experiential emphasis in curriculum design does not mean that the logical organization of subject matter should be ignored. Intelligence requires the systematic organization of experience. And such organization facilitates the process of relating various systems of knowledge to our lives. But to confine the curriculum to the acquisition of knowledge without relating it to behavioral experience can be deadly indeed. Unfortunately, many instructional programs fail to bridge the gap between knowledge, attitude, and behavior.

> Research indicates that secondary education thus far has exerted relatively little impact upon the values of young people. . . . Adolescence, research shows, is an age of reorganization and redirection, yet, evidently, education has concerned itself very little with these phenomena. Certainly, if any period of growth lends itself to change through education, the period of adolescence, with its emphasis on exploration and discovery, is especially amenable to change.
> . . . Knowing the nature of the early adolescent, the quest for values should become a prime focus of junior high school education. Facts may change, and skills may vanish through disuse, but values, once accepted and acted upon, can grow and strengthen and make a difference—for a lifetime.[70]

THE CONANT REPORT:
THE AMERICAN HIGH SCHOOL TODAY

While some critics of American education have advocated specialized academic and vocational high schools, Conant's study revealed that the comprehensive high school can be more advantageous.[71] Not only are youngsters able to secure a high-quality college preparatory or vocational education in the comprehensive high-school setting, but this type of institution enables all the youth of all the people to work together under one roof. Though the comprehensive high school, by its very nature, offers a highly diversified curriculum, all students, regardless of special interests and needs, can share in a common program of general education and student activities. In this way, the comprehensive high school can be likened to a miniature democratic society in which each citizen has specialized competencies and duties within a common framework of responsible self-government.

Through various achievement tests administered in specialized academic schools and in comprehensive schools, Conant found that students in the latter type of institution performed at least as well as those in the

---

[70] *Ibid.*, pp. 19–20.
[71] See James Bryant Conant, *The American High School Today* (New York: McGraw-Hill Company, Inc., 1959), 140 pp.

academic high schools. Unlike other critics of the American high school, Conant did not seek to set the Russian or any other foreign educational system as the model for us to follow. Instead, he attempted to identify those aspects of the American high school that are best suited to the ideals and aspirations of our nation.[72]

Since the focus of this chapter is on general education, we shall devote this section to the major provisions for such studies embodied in the Conant report.

Recommendations

Conant emphasized that the first objective of the comprehensive high school is to provide a good general education for all students. His key recommendations relating to general education are summarized as follows.[73]

1. Students should not be classified or labeled through separate tracks such as college preparatory, vocational, or commercial. Each student should have an individualized program. Considerable flexibility should exist in programming the student's course of study. The school should avoid rigid divisions or tracks.

2. The general education requirements for graduation for all students should include four years of English; three or four years of social studies, including two years of history (one year of American history), and a senior course in American problems or American government; one year of mathematics in the ninth grade (algebra or general mathematics); and at least one year of science in the ninth or tenth grade (biology or general physical science).

3. The general education program should constitute more than half of the student's total course work.

4. All students should be urged to elect art and music.

5. Since the general education courses are required of all students, irrespective of ability, a passing grade should be given if the student has worked to full capacity. A rigid grading structure for passing and failing should not be maintained in general education. On the other hand, high grading standards should apply in the academic sequences for college preparatory work.

6. Students should be grouped according to ability, subject by subject, following a high, average, and below average gradation. The system of ability grouping should be sufficiently flexible so that a given student, for example, might be in the high section in English but in the middle group in history.

---

[72] *Ibid.*, p. 7. Dr. Conant observes that the comprehensive high school has no counterpart in any other nation.

[73] *Ibid.*, see pp. 46–76.

7. Of the total time devoted to the study of English, approximately half should consist of English composition, with an average of one theme required per week. The themes should be evaluated by the teacher and each teacher should have no more than 100 pupils. A schoolwide composition test should be administered in every grade and, in grades 9 and 11, should be graded by a faculty committee. A special course in English composition should be offered in the twelfth grade for those students whose grade on the eleventh-grade composition test is below their English aptitude score. A developmental reading program should be available to all students on a voluntary basis.

8. There should be at least six periods in the school day in addition to the time required for physical education and driver education. If the day is divided into seven or eight periods, work in the laboratory or in industrial arts should be arranged as double periods. A seven- or eight-period day permits greater flexibility in electing courses and arranging programs.

9. Every student should develop some understanding of science and the scientific approach through a required course in physical science or biology.

10. Homerooms should not be organized according to academic abilities or vocational goals. Students should remain with the same heterogeneous homeroom group throughout their senior high school programs. The homeroom should be a significant social unit, with representatives elected to the student council.

11. The senior course in American problems or American government, required of all students, should be grouped heterogeneously. Emphasis should be given to discussion of current topics and controversial issues. Material on economics should be included. The course should be designed not only to develop understandings in American government and economics, but also mutual respect between and among students of different aptitudes, interests, and backgrounds.

Conant also gave key emphasis to improving the counseling system by recommending one full-time counselor for every 250 to 300 students. Other recommendations were concerned with improving the college preparatory, vocational, and elective offerings. The importance of the large school unit to allow a diversified curriculum received strong emphasis. A minimum-sized graduation class of 100 students was considered necessary to support a diversified curriculum.

Implications

Dr. Conant's report was based on a survey of 103 high schools in 26 states. Extensive testing of academic students in comprehensive high schools with students in specialized academic high schools revealed that the former groups were at least equal in achievement to the latter. These data tended to support Dr. Conant's conviction that the comprehensive high school is capable of providing a high-quality academic program within a setting of diversified curricula and a broad range of student abilities.

Although many critics in recent years have argued for a system of secondary education patterned somewhat after the European system, which separates the academic students through preuniversity schools, Conant pointed to the uniqueness of the American comprehensive high school. Whereas higher education is open to more than a third of the college-age group in the United States, only one fifteenth or one twentieth of the college-age group are enrolled in institutions of higher education in the European countries. The comprehensive high school permits greater fluidity in accommodating the changing aspirations and achievement levels of adolescents. And, according to Conant, the comprehensive high school is consistent with the values and ideals of a democratic society where all citizens, however diverse their occupations and capacities, share in the common task of self-government.

Conant's conclusion that "American secondary education can be made satisfactory without any radical changes in the basic pattern"[74] was testimony to his faith in the comprehensive high school and also indicative of his aversion to radical reforms. Not all of the recommendations in the report were based on objective data or established research, however. Although Conant advocated ability grouping in the high school, he presented no research data to support this recommendation.

The report provided no guidelines or recommendations concerning the area of physical education and athletics. No explanation was offered why this was not included. Physical education is almost universally required of all able-bodied students in our secondary schools. Most schools require students to devote one period daily to classes in physical education. In recent years, physical education has come under increasing criticism for its obsession with team sports and gymnastics and its neglect of more individualized sports and recreational activities, which are more likely to carry over into the life of the young adult.

Conant's recommended program in general education in the senior high school was based on the traditional subject curriculum and the Carnegie Unit. His proposed subject approach to general education can be criticized for failing to deal with the problem of curriculum integration. Perhaps an even more serious criticism was that he formulated most of his recommendations on how much of which subjects students should be required to take, rather than on the need to improve the

---

[74] *Ibid.*, p. 96.

content and process of instruction in the various areas of the curriculum in general education. It should be remembered, however, that the recommendations put forth by Conant were derived by studying existing schools and selecting what appeared to be the most successful practices from the best of these schools. The key emphasis was on the best in current practice, rather than on the most promising experimental approaches or idealizations of what might be done in our high schools.

The Conant report appeared at a time when many rash criticisms were being directed at our schools. The study gave support to diversified curricula and vocational education in a period when many critics were arguing for a curriculum based on the academic essentials. The report also emphasized our need to recognize individual differences and to avoid rigid and absolute standards of grading in the required general education courses. Conant's warning that school boards must distinguish between policy-making and administration came in a period when many well-meaning school boards were busily usurping and undermining the administrative responsibilities of the school superintendent.

This study failed to point to promising experimental practices, and relatively few of the recommendations were derived from experimental evidence. For the times, it represented a moderate approach toward improving the American high school.

THE CONANT MEMORANDUM:
EDUCATION IN THE JUNIOR HIGH SCHOOL YEARS

After completing his study of the senior high school, Dr. James B. Conant turned to the junior high school with a "memorandum to school boards," appearing in 1960, titled *Education in the Junior High School Years*.[75] This study, also supported by a grant from the Carnegie Corporation, was made during the 1959–60 school year and involved 237 schools in 90 school systems in 23 states.

Recommendations

In this study, Dr. Conant did not indicate a preference for any particular type of vertical organization (8–4, 6–6, 6–3–3, 6–2–4, 6–4–2, and so on), but observed that the curriculum is the most important consideration. His recommendations, relating both directly and indirectly to general education, are summarized as follows:[76]

1. The subjects required of all pupils in grades seven and eight should be English, social studies, mathematics, and science. Heavy emphasis

---

[75] James Bryant Conant, *Education in the Junior High School Years* (Princeton, N.J.: Educational Testing Service, 1960), 46 pp.
[76] *Ibid.*, see pp. 16–32.

should be given to reading skills and composition in English, while the social studies should include emphasis on history and geography. Furthermore, instruction in art, music, and physical education should be required of all pupils. All boys should take work in industrial arts and all girls should receive instruction in home economics.

2. Instruction in the basic skills should continue from the elementary school into the junior-high years. With the exception of the mentally retarded, by the end of the ninth grade even the poorest readers should have developed a minimum of sixth-grade reading competency. Special remedial instruction in the basic skills should be provided where needed.

3. The transition between the elementary and the junior-high grades should be as smooth as possible. A block approach, at least in grade 7, should allow one teacher to work with the same group of pupils over two or more periods each day. This teacher would, in most cases, be responsible for instruction in English and social studies. The block-time teacher should be in a position to counsel pupils, inasmuch as he is working day to day with fewer different youngsters and is spending more time with them. This block-time approach is not recommended beyond the eighth grade.

4. The daily schedule should be sufficiently flexible so that students are not put in the position of being unable to elect an important subject because it conflicts with another course. A seven-period day is preferred over a six-period schedule because it permits greater flexibility in programming.

5. Students should be grouped in the academic courses according to three ability levels to meet the range of individual differences. Such grouping should be determined subject by subject.

6. The curriculum in the ninth grade should provide for the continuation of the required work in general education (English, social studies, mathematics, and science). If general science is provided adequately in grades 7 and 8, the ninth grade science may include biology or a special course in physical science with appropriate laboratory facilities. The general education program in the ninth grade should follow the recommendations in *The American High School Today.* Elective sequences in art, music, industrial arts, typing, and various academic subjects including foreign languages should be provided.

7. Student activities in music, dramatics, assemblies, homerooms, clubs, intramural athletics, and student council should be regarded as part of the total school program.

8. Specialized guidance services should be provided with a full-time worker for every 250 to 300 pupils in grades 7 through 9.

9. Homework should be meaningful, and teachers of various subjects should coordinate the homework assignments.

10. The academic courses in grades 7 and 8 should be governed by high standards to insure mastery of basic skills. This applies to the required courses in academic areas. While the implication is that some pupils might be held back, care should be taken to avoid the psychological and social problems with over-age pupils.

11. The school library should be well stocked and should comply with the standards established by the American Library Association. The gymnasium should include locker rooms and showers. Properly equipped facilities should be provided in home economics and industrial arts. Auditorium or assembly space should be sufficient to accommodate at least half the student body, and cafeteria space for at least one third of the school enrollment should be provided. Special art, music, and science rooms are desirable.

12. Articulation should be provided in the various subject fields through coordinated programs that cut across school and grade lines. Competent coordinators of instruction should be employed in every one of the subject fields, rather than only in the special fields of art, music, physical education, and so on.

13. There should be a minimum of 125 pupils in each of the junior-high grade levels in order to support an effective program of specialized instruction.

Implications

Although Dr. Conant did not advocate any particular type of vertical organization of the school system, such as a 6–3–3, 6–6, 8–4, or some other basis, he observed that a unified 6–3–3 or 6–2–4 system may be desirable where there are at least 250 pupils in each of the junior-high grade levels. This would avoid a six-year high school that would be too large, while providing for sufficient enrollment to ensure an adequate program of specialized and diversified instruction at the junior-high level.

The required subjects for general education include those areas recommended in his report on the senior high school, except that instruction in art and music are provided at the junior-high level. In addition, Conant recommended that all girls receive instruction in home economics and all boys take industrial arts in grade seven or eight. The inclusion of art, music, home economics, and industrial arts as part of the required program of general education was particularly significant, since this recommendation came at a time when many critics were advocating that the general education sequence be limited to the so-called academic disciplines.[77] And although many of these critics were also attacking

---

[77] Arthur Bestor, *The Restoration of Learning* (New York: Alfred A. Knopf, 1955), p. 326.

the student activity programs, Dr. Conant chose to recognize the educative worth of such activities by recommending that they be regarded as a legitimate part of the total school program.

The study also indicated the need to provide for a smooth transition from the self-contained elementary classroom to the departmentalized program in the junior high school. In this connection, Dr. Conant recommended a block-time program in grade 7, and possibly grade 8, where one teacher would spend at least two periods daily with the same group of pupils. The block-time teacher might be responsible for instructing in the areas of English and social studies, for example, as well as serving in a counseling capacity with these youngsters. This recommendation was not an endorsement of core teaching, since Conant did not indicate any particular need for integrating the learning material and activities in the block-time program. It was recommended merely as a means of allowing a given teacher to devote more time each day to instruction and counseling with a given group of pupils.

Although he did not advocate the integration of subject matter from different fields through a core curriculum in the block-time program, Conant recommended improved articulation within each subject field by means of coordinated programs that cut across school and grade lines. He recognized that the high level of population mobility in our society contributes to the difficulty of providing a smooth transfer from one school program to another.

Unlike his report on the American high school, where considerable data were gathered to compare the academic achievement of students in comprehensive schools with those in specialized academic schools, Dr. Conant supported his recommendations regarding the junior high schools only on the basis of direct observations and interviews in 237 schools throughout the country.

Many of the recommendations embodied in his report on the American high school were also contained in this study, particularly the ones pertaining to the need for specialized guidance and testing services, homogeneous grouping of students by subject, and provisions for diversified curricula. Ability grouping was recommended as a means of challenging the wide range of abilities in the student body. Again, no objective data were presented to support this recommendation for ability grouping.

Conant observed that his recommendations were "purposely conservative," since they reflect what he believes are the best in established practices. But he also expressed his feeling that, although there are many promising developments for improving instruction at the junior-high level, "these await the test of time."[78]

---

[78] James Bryant Conant, *Education in The Junior High School Years* (Princeton, N.J.: Educational Testing Service, 1960), p. 45.

SOME DEFICIENCIES IN OTHER AREAS OF GENERAL EDUCATION

As we study various proposals for general education in the secondary school, we note that considerable attention is given to the key areas of English, mathematics, social studies, and science. Our purpose here is to review briefly the contributions to general education from other areas and the need for certain improvements.

The Fine Arts

One has only to look at the environment that man has created to realize the terrible absence of aesthetic values in our daily lives. In the building of our cities and suburbs, we have torn down the trees and we have created a geometric uniformity that cannot be easily counteracted. Our tastes in television programming seem to be geared to escapism and violence. The architecture of our newly constructed schools is often indistinguishable from factories and offices. If our lives are to be richer, we must find ways to bring the aesthetic into our material world.

Aesthetic sensitivity can be developed through school experiences in music, drawing, painting, modeling—and a study of our heritage in the arts. Opportunities for creative expression should be provided. The study of music should lead to improved taste. Learning to appreciate a wider range of musical works can lead the adolescent to a lifelong enjoyment of good music. Group singing can also be rewarding.

Many junior high schools require every student to take a semester or two in a general art or music course. But experiences in such classes should be more than developing skills in drawing, singing, or playing an instrument. The cultivation of aesthetic attitudes and tastes should not be neglected. Although there are those who regard the fine arts as fads and frills, we must realize that our lives would be drab indeed without aesthetic values. The application of the arts to the modern world of business, industry, community planning, and home living can bring greater richness and meaning to our lives.

Homemaking and Industrial Arts

A popular requirement in grade seven is a homemaking class for all girls and an industrial arts class for all boys. Since virtually all girls look forward to an eventual career of homemaking, including those who have other occupational aspirations, a course in this area can make significant contributions to general education.

> Home economics consists of those courses, activities, and units of instruction which are designed to meet the home and family life needs of all students and the vocational needs of some students. The program

provides practical learning experiences with a variety of goods, services, and equipment used in home and community. The program is concerned with assisting individuals to develop ability to carry their respective home responsibilities in relation to food, shelter, clothing, child care, health, home care of the sick, and family relationships. In addition to the development of homemaking skills, emphasis is placed on the development of desirable understandings, habits, attitudes, and ideals needed in the home and family life in a democratic society.[79]

The academic traditionalists argue that education for home and family living is the responsibility of the home and not the school.[80] But these critics fail to take into account the number of homes that are deficient. Many youngsters come to school without an adequate breakfast. Their parents may not have a proper understanding and appreciation of the nutritional needs of the adolescent. Parents may have poor taste in home decoration and clothing. They may fail to budget wisely in this era of installment buying and deficit financing. Consumer education has become increasingly important in an age of incessant waves of television advertising. Since programs of adult education cannot be mandatory, the responsibility for meeting such deficiencies rests with the education of our in-school youth.

Unfortunately, some teachers of homemaking follow a textbook approach imitative of the academic studies—with emphasis on the learning of factual information. The study of homemaking should be concerned primarily with the development of desirable attitudes, skills, and behaviors.

The requirement of industrial arts for all boys in grade seven can also serve a general education function by acquainting students with the industrial aspects of our society. It can contribute to a better understanding of various occupations and consumer goods and services. Aesthetic appreciation may be developed through the study of industrial design and architecture. Through the industrial arts, students can be given the opportunity to plan and develop a variety of projects that draw on mathematical skills and concepts.

In recent years, this area also has been deprecated as a frill subject by critics who are oriented toward the so-called academic disciplines. But the Harvard report observes that "direct contact with materials . . . the capacity to create by hand from a concept in the mind . . . are indispensable aspects of the general education of everyone."[81]

Beyond the basic general courses in homemaking and industrial arts,

[79] National Study of Secondary School Evaluation, *Evaluative Criteria* (Washington, D.C.: The Study, 1960), p. 141.
[80] Bestor, *op. cit.*, p. 119.
[81] Report of the Harvard Committee, *General Education in a Free Society* (Cambridge, Mass.: Harvard University Press, 1958), p. 175.

most secondary schools offer electives for exploratory and specialized work.

Health and Physical Education

The early Greek and Roman civilizations gave great importance to physical education. The American secondary school today requires the student to devote as much time to activities in physical education as to the study of English. The Second World War gave tremendous impetus to the need for physical fitness. Studies indicated that approximately one out of every two youths had a physical defect that should have been prevented or corrected earlier in life.[82]

Recent emphasis on science and mathematics in the secondary school curriculum as a result of the Soviet successes in the space race has led to proposals for reducing the amount of time required in physical education. Despite such proposals, however, most students in grades 7 through 12 are required to take a daily period in physical education. In many schools, health and hygiene instruction are integrated in the physical education class.

In some communities, the success of the physical education program is measured by the record of the school's athletic teams in interscholastic competition. But only a minority of students can participate in varsity athletics. The physical education program should foster good physical conditioning, improved health habits, good sportsmanship, and wholesome lifelong recreational activity. Physical education programs have been criticized for excessive emphasis on team sports, which do not have sufficient carry-over into the recreational activities of young adults. Such sports as swimming, golf, and tennis are often neglected because of limited facilities.

In recent years, there has been increasing pressure to make driver education mandatory in the high school. Ordinarily, it is offered as an elective course under the general program of health, safety, and physical education. Actuarial statistics show that persons having completed such a course in high school are safer drivers than those without this special training. Some critics argue that driver training, however important, does not belong in the high school curriculum.

RESISTANCE TO CURRICULUM EXPERIMENTATION

Alfred North Whitehead observed that "there is only one subject-matter for education, and that is Life in all its manifestations."[83] Our

---

82 Office of Education, *Life Adjustment Education for Every Youth,* Bulletin 22 (Washington, D.C.: U.S. Department of Health, Education, and Welfare, 1951), p. 70.

83 Alfred North Whitehead, *The Aims of Education* (New York: The Macmillan Company, 1929), p. 10.

adherence to the traditional subject-centered curriculum can be likened to an attempt to produce a tree by nailing some slabs of wood together. Although experimental programs with various forms of curriculum integration show that the core approach can lead to significant gains in critical thinking and other dimensions of learning,[84] there has been a strong resistance to curriculum experimentation and change. Some of the reasons for this resistance are

1. It is easy to adhere to the traditional. Experimentation with unfamiliar approaches to curriculum organization presents a risk that the learning outcomes may prove to be of no advantage over the traditional subject-centered approach.
2. Requirements for college entrance have long been established according to the subject curriculum and the Carnegie Unit.
3. Most teacher education programs tend to prepare teachers as specialists in a major and minor subject field. And such subject-matter specialization at the college level tends to be organized along specific subject lines.
4. Approaches to curriculum integration necessitate corollary changes in instructional methods, materials, and content. The textbook is no longer the bible of learning. Problem-solving methods require great skill on the part of the teacher. And teachers may not be sufficiently knowledgeable and resourceful to break down the traditional separations of subject matter.
5. Curriculum experimentation requires an experimental philosophy on the part of teachers and administrators who, for the most part, tend to be conservative.
6. Curriculum change necessitates changes in administrative arrangements of the school. Problems of scheduling, assignment of teacher personnel, grouping of students, and organization of learning resources may not be easily solved.
7. The scientific and technological competition with the Soviets has led to many rash criticisms of our schools. In recent years, great pressure has been exerted on our schools to toughen up the curriculum by stressing the fundamentals and by placing increasing emphasis on the sciences, mathematics, and other so-called academic subjects. Under such conditions, great emphasis has been directed at meeting the emergency needs of society, rather than the psychobiological needs of the individual. Curriculum improvements have been concentrated within certain subject divisions—such as science, mathematics, and modern

---

[84] See The National Society for the Study of Education, *The Integration of Educational Experiences,* Fifty-seventh Yearbook, Part III. (Chicago: The University of Chicago Press, 1958), pp. 212–214.

foreign languages—without real regard for integrative problems between and among these subjects.

Integration in General Education in College

While the preceding factors may seem insurmountable, significant efforts, nevertheless, are being made for improved curriculum coherence in general education. In recent years, even the colleges have undertaken experimental programs of notable proportions. For example, Boston University has established a College of General Education encompassing the freshman and sophomore years with a prescribed program of interacting courses, and emphasis on counseling and guidance. The textbook approach was discarded in order to develop interrelationships from various areas of knowledge.[85] Michigan State University established a Basic College for general education in 1944. The Basic College curriculum is comprised of four broad courses prescribed for lower division students (communication skills, natural science, social science, and humanities). Faculty seminars with representatives from each of these broad fields are designed to deal with matters of curriculum integration. Comprehensive examinations are conducted to evaluate the ability of the student to synthesize the material.[86] Sarah Lawrence College has followed a more individualized approach to general education by allowing the student to select courses and areas of study. Considerable emphasis has been given to student self-direction and self-appraisal under the guidance of a faculty adviser. Field experiences have been stressed through such integrative areas of study as Development of a Community.[87] Antioch College is noted for its emphasis on field work throughout its undergraduate curriculum.

These are only a few examples of attempts to integrate the general education curriculum at the college level. Many such programs put notable emphasis on guidance and counseling, student self-direction and self-appraisal, and faculty planning on an inter-divisional basis.

Integrated Programs for Professional Education

Curriculum integration has been found valuable not only for general education, but also for professional education. For example, the School of Medicine at Western Reserve University inaugurated an integrated medical curriculum in September, 1952. The new curriculum eliminates the traditionally separate departmental courses and laboratories. Interdepartmental faculty committees have reorganized the curriculum into broad, functional areas that provide for greater coherence and continuity

---

85 *Ibid.*, see pp. 221–224.   87 *Ibid.*, see pp. 229–235.
86 *Ibid.*, see pp. 224–229.

of learning. The traditional medical curriculum of separate courses was discontinued in favor of the new program for these reasons:

> Fragmentation of the medical school curriculum into specialized, isolated courses has become a serious problem which is already disturbing medical educators. As new knowledge and skills are developed, more specialized groups appear . . . demanding a quota of the students' time for more separate courses. . . .
>
> Any group planning an assault on the medical school curriculum today must also recognize a new interest in medical schools about the whole learning process. There is wide belief that at the medical school level there is little to be gained by presenting a mass of information to a student and requiring him to learn it long enough to pass a written examination. There is ample evidence that the intellectual residue from such an effort is small, and may be overbalanced by an overt hostility the student develops toward the material largely because an indigestible dose is given by eager specialists under conditions in which the student has no intellectual readiness. There seems to be a vast difference between teaching isolated facts on the one hand and on the other creating a situation in which the mature student is eager to learn.[88]

Other weaknesses of the traditional curriculum in medical education at Western Reserve prior to September of 1952 are described thus:

> At this time it was found that the curriculum had grown steadily by accretion and was extremely crowded and specialized. The student often was instructed in a course that was characterized by rigidity and a lock-step schedule which gave him little freedom. Frequently the student was treated as a school boy and given as many as 32 examinations in one year. Departmental barriers were found to be firm, with little or no intercommunication and little hope for change.[89]

The new integrated curriculum at Western Reserve provides for interdepartmental planning and coordination of instruction. Greater attention is given to concepts and principles, rather than to isolated factual information. Multidiscipline laboratories enable the student to interrelate his learning from many areas of the curriculum. Attention is given to fostering attitudes more closely related to the practice of medicine. Some of the advantages cited for the new curriculum are quoted as follows:

> . . . the mass of important medical information has expanded beyond the ability of any faculty to cram it all into a four-year curriculum. There must be some mechanism to decide what will be selected for presentation to medical students. The interdepartmental teaching plan

---

[88] John J. Caughey, Jr., "The Medical School Phase of the Education of a Physician," *American Journal of Mental Deficiency*, July, 1958, 63:44–45.

[89] Thomas Hale Ham, "The Approaches of the Faculty to Medical Education at Western Reserve University," *The Journal of Medical Education*, December, 1959, 34:1163.

permits this selection to be guided by the faculty as a whole rather than by each department separately. . . .

. . . interdepartmental teaching helps the student "think like a physician" from the start of his medical education. . . . We believe it will diminish the tendency some students have to think of separate courses in the preclinical sciences as hurdles they must get over, and leave behind them, on their way to the practice of medicine. . . .

. . . interdepartmental teaching reduces the amount of undesired or unwitting duplication of coverage that may occur when separate departments give their own courses without knowing what other departments are teaching. . . .

. . . interdepartmental teaching is a valuable project for the faculty. It brings together people who might not otherwise have contact and fosters cooperative efforts in other areas than teaching of medical students. . . .

Finally . . . the curriculum becomes more malleable and can be modified in response to needs recognized by the faculty as a whole.[90]

In addition to resynthesizing the curriculum through functional units in place of separate subjects, the medical curriculum at Western Reserve was redesigned to stress comprehensive medical care and an understanding of human behavior. Beginning with the freshman year, the medical student is assigned to a family, which he studies and serves. His responsibility increases as he progresses through the years of his medical education. He also gains experience in working with a health team of psychologists, nurses, social workers, and medical specialists.

In recent years, similar attempts at curriculum integration have been undertaken in a number of professional schools of medicine and dentistry. Curricula in teacher education, law, and engineering also seem to be placing greater emphasis on experiential sequences and interdisciplinary approaches to instruction.

Critics of secondary public education are quick to find fault with attempts at curriculum integration in our schools by attaching labels to these approaches such as watering down, soft pedagogy, and progressive education. But we have seen that the need for curriculum coherence and continuity applies to all levels of education, from the elementary school to the professional school. If curriculum integration is desirable for general education at the undergraduate level, and if it is also desirable at the graduate professional level, one wonders how we can expect the adolescent student in the secondary school to develop his own integrated knowledge from a fragmented subject curriculum. The answer is that the average adolescent under the traditional subject curriculum fails to achieve any real measure of integrated learning.

---

[90] John L. Caughey, Jr., "Medical Education Based on Interdepartmental Cooperation," *The Journal of the American Medical Association*, June 23, 1956, 161:5–7.

RECENT REFORMS IN CURRICULUM AND INSTRUCTION

Traditionally, the expansion of knowledge has been treated as an additive process. In our secondary schools we have attempted to cope with this expansion by covering more material in the time allotted to us. In our colleges and universities we have witnessed a great proliferation of courses and specialties. Yet we have known for some time that no high-school or college student can be expected to learn all there is to know in a given discipline. Even the mature scholar cannot attain complete mastery, since any discipline is an incessant quest for knowing.

In recent times we have begun to turn away from the endless quantitative and descriptive manner of cataloguing subject matter in the elementary and secondary schools. We have become concerned with education as a process of inquiry. We are coming to see each of the various disciplines as an area of ordered inquiry rather than as a formless package of information. The content and process of learning are being treated as a continuum. Problems and areas of inquiry are being developed on an interrelated basis and as an organic part of the total structure of the discipline. And we are witnessing increased efforts toward building curriculum content and process around cognitive styles of learning.

A notable development in the current reforms is that leading scholars are participating in the creation of curricular materials for our elementary and secondary schools. In the past, such scholars have shunned the idea of working at these levels because such efforts lacked prestige and reward. Now these scholars are gaining national recognition and impressive financial support for their efforts.

The chief force behind the programs of course content and improvement in the sciences and mathematics is the National Science Foundation —an agency created in 1950 in the executive branch of the Federal Government. The National Defense Education Act of 1958 has provided funds for the improvement of school instruction in the fields of science, mathematics, and modern foreign languages.

On a more modest scale, the United States Office of Education initiated Project English and Project Social Studies in 1962. Both of these projects involve research, demonstration, and the dissemination of ideas relating to new approaches to curriculum and instruction.

Chapter 8 contains a discussion of the nature of the reforms taking place in the college preparatory subjects of modern foreign languages, physics, and chemistry. The study of biology is so placed in our high school program as to serve a general education function. Therefore, biology is included in the following summary of recent efforts at improving the content and methodology in the various areas of general education.

Curriculum Improvement in Biology

In 1959 the American Institute of Biological Sciences (AIBS) instituted a program at the University of Colorado to improve the high-school biology curriculum. The project was named the Biological Sciences Curriculum Study (BSCS). Because of the great diversity of approaches in studying the life sciences, the project developed three curricular versions: the Yellow version emphasized the genetic and developmental, the Blue stressed the biochemical and physiological, and the Green represented the ecological and evolutionary perspectives. In addition to producing textual works representing these three versions, the group produced teachers' guides and material for laboratory experiments. The AIBS program was tested on a national scale in 15 geographic centers during 1960–1961. The materials were then revised for more extensive testing in the high schools during 1961–1962 and, finally, were made available to the schools in 1963. The rationale of BSCS is similar to those guiding curriculum revision in the other scientific disciplines. The high-school students, rather than relying on the authority of the teacher or the textbook for information, and rather than following the laboratory manual like a cookbook, are engaged in laboratory inquiry where they must test their own hypotheses. Attention is given also to problems that are yet unsolved in the world of biological science. The laboratory studies center around such molar areas as plant growth and development, animal growth and development, interdependence of structure and function, and so forth. Teachers are free to select from a number of these molar areas or blocks to fit their own preferences, preparation, and locality. Some of the findings from the BSCS approach are that students show new enthusiasm for learning, and some who had been considered of below-average ability were now revealing aptitudes heretofore concealed on verbal tests.

In summary, curriculum change in the sciences is designed to provide learning experiences similar to scientific inquiry. None of the new approaches should be regarded as final and definitive, but they do reflect a trend in teaching that is long overdue. Rejected is the traditional approach of didactic exposition by the teacher, explanations by the teacher, or demonstrations by the teacher. Rejected also is the cookbook approach to laboratory work where the student does not formulate questions and where the student merely follows someone else's directions. Instead of attempting to cover a myriad of facts and bits of information, the new materials are designed for interrelatedness so that students gain a real perspective of the discipline. Each of these approaches necessitates effective programs of in-service teacher education. Most difficulties with the new curricula originate with the teachers who are set in their ways, rather than with the students. Curriculum can no longer be regarded as what is covered by the teacher. Curriculum is what is experienced by the learner.

Curriculum Improvement in Mathematics

Since 1952 a group of mathematicians, curriculum specialists, and teachers have been working at the University of Illinois on improving curriculum and instruction in secondary-school mathematics. The group is called the University of Illinois Committee on School Mathematics (UICSM). The key emphasis of the project is to develop a program of instruction that enables students to understand mathematics through student inquiry leading to the discovery of key generalizations. In other words, the student encounters learning experiences that lead him to mathematical principles and rules. Rather than having the teacher or textbook explain the rules and procedures to be initiated by the student, the learner is stimulated to discover or invent the necessary principles and procedures.

Another notable program for improving mathematics instruction in the school is the School Mathematics Study Group (SMSG), now at Stanford University. This project began in 1958 in an effort to revise the entire mathematics program of our schools. Unlike the traditional approaches that rely heavily on rote rather than meaning, SMSG stresses the understanding of the content, process, and structure of mathematics. Through the efforts of mathematicians and mathematics educators, sample textual materials were developed as an integrated sequence for grades 7 through 12 and made available to schools beginning in 1960. In addition to its continuing efforts to revise the existing material, SMSG is developing a variety of new materials for both the elementary and secondary levels.

In addition to the above programs, a number of centers throughout the nation are engaged in revising the school mathematics curriculum. Some of the general trends in curriculum revision and reform are (1) the elimination of relatively unimportant material, (2) the integration of certain important topics, (3) the introduction of newer developments (that is, probability and statistics), (4) the emphasis given to structure and interrelatedness of the discipline, (5) the provision of mathematical ideas at earlier levels, and (6) the concern for cognitive styles of learning rather than imitative and rote manipulation.[91]

While it is not our purpose to make comparisons between the specific aspects of UICSM and SMSG, both programs show promise of improving student (and teacher) attitudes toward the study of mathematics. Both

---

[91] See Allen F. Strehler, "What's New About the New Math?" *Saturday Review,* March 21, 1964, p. 69.

programs seek to develop cognitive styles and intuitive powers in mathematical learning. And both programs represent the dynamic qualities
of the discipline of mathematics. UICSM and SMSG have exerted considerable influence on the new commercial textbooks in mathematics. As
in the case of curriculum reform in the sciences, we are witnessing a
new trend in which the scholars, the curriculum specialists, and the
teachers are working together in improving the content and process of
education.

Curriculum Improvement in the English Language Arts

As we have mentioned, efforts toward improving the content and
process of instruction in the English language arts have not been supported on a scale comparable to the sciences, mathematics, or the
foreign languages. The National Council of Teachers of English, nevertheless, have been influential in stimulating some important reforms in
secondary school English. We have seen attempts since the 1930's at
relating literature and composition to the world of the adolescent. We
have witnessed efforts at correlating, fusing, and integrating English
with the social studies. And we have observed some promising attempts
at incorporating elements of semantics and studying the techniques of
mass media and propaganda in the high-school curriculum.

Nonetheless, there appear to be some wide gaps between current
practices and our research findings on learning in the English language
arts. A great deal of drill work in prescriptive grammar is still provided
without any functional relationship to language usage and development.
Literary selections are often treated in such a way that the adolescent
learns to dislike literature. Youngsters are given insufficient opportunity
to deal with critical ideas in oral and written expression. Literature,
language, and communication too often are treated as separate entities
rather than as functioning parts of an organic discipline. Students are
given insufficient opportunity to compare literary works and develop
their own ideas through writing about the literature they read. In many
classrooms a great deal of time is spent studying for teacher-made tests
that require the recall of factual information rather than interpretation
and reflective thought.

In 1962 the United States Office of Education inaugurated Project
English by establishing a number of curriculum study centers on
university campuses. These centers are engaged in examining current
materials, developing and testing new curricula and methods, and disseminating information concerning revised content and new practices.
An overriding concern is the development of coherent programs of
learning experiences from elementary school through high school. Inductive approaches to the teaching of literature and composition are

also being studied at some of the centers. The centers are applying their findings to the education of future teachers and in-service teachers.

Curriculum Improvement in the Social Studies

Considerable emphasis was given to curriculum reform in the social studies during the 1930's and 1940's. Attempts were made to relate the social studies curriculum at that time to the problems and needs of youth. However, like the English language arts, this curriculum area has not been blessed with the research and development support given to the sciences, mathematics, and modern foreign languages since the late 1950's.

Curriculum work in the social studies encompasses the fields of history, geography, government, economics, sociology, and anthropology. How to develop the interrelatedness of these disciplines without subverting their uniqueness has been a difficult problem. In too many high-school classrooms, there has been a tendency to treat the social studies content in a descriptive and additive manner. The teacher tells and tests, while students are given little opportunity to work with a variety of sources, to examine controversial problems and issues, and to derive generalizations on their own. The textbook is often treated as the only definitive source of information (other than the teacher, of course). Controversial issues relevant to our life and times are frequently neglected in the study of history. Tests deal with *who, what, when,* and *where,* but seldom with *why.* In some instances, students are taught by indoctrination rather than through the objective weighing of evidence.

Since the middle 1950's, the National Council for the Social Studies has been engaged in reviewing the entire social studies curriculum. In 1958 the American Council of Learned Societies took steps to encourage its member groups in the social sciences to make efforts toward improving the high-school curriculum. One joint project of the ACLS and the National Council for the Social Studies involved an analysis of the content objectives of the high-school social studies curriculum.[92] It became clear through this project that the scholars in the disciplines and the school-curriculum workers need to work together on a sustained basis if significant improvements are to be made in the teaching of the social studies.

In late 1962 the United States Office of Education initiated Project Social Studies along lines similar to Project English. The major goal is to improve the curriculum and instruction in the social studies throughout the elementary and secondary levels. Efforts are being made to

---

[92] American Council of Learned Societies and National Council for the Social Studies, *The Social Studies and the Social Sciences* (New York: Harcourt, Brace & World, Inc., 1962).

develop sequential and cumulative programs of studies, employing interdisciplinary approaches where desirable without subverting the key structural elements of the specialties. Obviously, this is a formidable task. Although the level of support for Project Social Studies is modest, it is nevertheless an important venture.

Dr. Harold Taylor finds it ironic that the reforms now taking place stem from the work of John Dewey and his colleagues.[93] Although progressive education is deprecated by many critics, some of the most promising reforms in education today are derived from the progressive ideas that were advanced during the early decades of this century.

The need for experimentation in curriculum design and instructional methodology is now receiving important recognition at all levels of education. Such experimentation is vital to curriculum improvement.

SUMMARY

General education is concerned with the learnings that all citizens of our culture must share. It is not a specific list of courses required of all students in the secondary school. It involves much more than the preservation of our best cultural traditions. General education is generative learning; that is, it enables one to learn continually, even under changing conditions. General education is of particular importance in a society that holds to the ideal of giving each citizen a voice in his own destiny. It should not be regarded as a separate and independent phase of the curriculum, since general education is necessary also for the building of specialized learning.

During the 1930's and 1940's, there were some notable attempts to improve the articulation of the general education curriculum in the secondary school. Efforts were made to focus the common learnings on the problems and needs of youth through more experience-centered approaches. Considerable emphasis was given to fostering democratic values and meeting individual differences.

In more recent years, curriculum workers and teachers have been joined by scholars in the various disciplines in projects to improve course content and methodology. These projects have been supported at the national level and give promise of bringing about the reconstruction of the secondary school curriculum in science and mathematics. However, it is unfortunate that most of the support for curriculum improvement has been concentrated on the fields of science and mathematics. While science and technology are vital to modern society, of

---

[93] See Harold Taylor, "Debate Over the Progressive Idea," The *New York Times Magazine,* November 26, 1961, p. 30.

equal importance to our civilization are the abilities to communicate effectively, to understand and deal constructively with social problems, and to apply aesthetic values toward the building of a harmonious physical environment.

While the national projects are directed at specific subject fields, such as science and mathematics, we must not lose sight of the need to develop greater coherence in the total general education curriculum of the secondary school.

PROBLEMS FOR STUDY AND DISCUSSION

1. Why is general education considered so important for a democratic society?

2. What subjects were you required to take in your high school? How do these requirements compare with the recommendations proposed in the Harvard and Conant reports?

3. Do you favor a core or subject approach to general education? Why?

4. What are the advantages and disadvantages of the core curriculum? The subject curriculum?

5. What areas do you believe should be required for general education in the secondary-school curriculum, and what areas should be offered as electives? Why?

6. Do you agree with Professor Bestor that the schools should be concerned only with intellectual training? Why or why not?

7. Why does there appear to be more curriculum experimentation at the junior-high-school level than at the senior-high-school level?

8. Do you agree or disagree with Conant's recommendations on ability grouping? Why? Does ability grouping eliminate the need for differentiated learning activities within a given course of instruction? Why or why not?

9. Why do many teachers adopt a textbook as the course of instruction for a particular subject? What are the possible hazards of such an approach?

10. Some critics argue that youngsters are not sufficiently mature to have a voice in selecting learning activities. How do you feel about this?

11. How might you as a teacher working in a subject curriculum attempt to overcome the limitations generally attributed to this type of curriculum organization?

12. What is the difference between the *logical* and *psychological* organization of subject matter? Describe a hypothetical teaching-learning situation that illustrates each approach.

SELECTED REFERENCES

Alberty, Harold B. and Elsie J. Alberty. *Reorganizing the High School Curriculum* (3rd Ed.) New York: The Macmillan Company, 1962.

Alcorn, Marvin D. and James M. Linley (eds.) *Issues in Curriculum Development.* New York: Harcourt, Brace & World, Inc., 1959.

Association for Supervision and Curriculum Development. *Balance in the Curriculum.* 1961 Yearbook. Washington, D.C.: The Association, 1961.

Bestor, Arthur. *The Restoration of Learning.* New York: Alfred A. Knopf, Inc., 1955.

Cremin, Lawrence A. *The Transformation of the School.* New York: Alfred A. Knopf, Inc., 1961.

Educational Policies Commission. *Education for ALL American Youth: A Further Look.* Washington, D.C.: National Education Association, 1952.

Faunce, Roland, and Nelson Bossing. *Developing the Core Program,* (2nd Ed.) Englewood Cliffs, N.J.: Prentice-Hall, Inc., 1958.

Hock, Louise E. and Thomas J. Hill. *The General Education Class in the Secondary School.* New York: Holt, Rinehart and Winston, Inc., 1960.

Krug, Edward A. *The Secondary School Curriculum.* New York: Harper & Row, Publishers, Inc., 1960.

Leese, Joseph, Kenneth Frasure, and Mauritz Johnson, Jr. *The Teacher in Curriculum Making.* New York: Harper & Row, Publishers, Inc., 1961.

Leonard, J. Paul. *Developing the Secondary School Curriculum* (revised) New York: Holt, Rinehart & Winston, Inc., 1953.

Lurry, Lucile L. and Elsie J. Alberty. *Developing a High School Core Program.* New York: The Macmillan Company, 1957.

National Society for the Study of Education. *Adapting the Secondary-School Program to the Needs of Youth.* Fifty-second Yearbook, Part I. Chicago: The University of Chicago Press, 1953.

———. *General Education.* Fifty-first Yearbook, Part I. Chicago: The University of Chicago Press, 1952.

———. *Individualizing Instruction.* Sixty-first Yearbook, Part I. Chicago: The University of Chicago Press, 1962.

———. *The Integration of Educational Experiences.* Fifty-seventh Yearbook, Part III. Chicago: The University of Chicago Press, 1958.

Report of the Harvard Committee. *General Education in a Free Society.* Cambridge, Mass.: Harvard University Press, 1958.

Smith, B. Othanel, William O. Stanley, and J. Harlan Shores. *Fundamentals of Curriculum Development.* New York: Harcourt, Brace & World, Inc., 1950.

Taba, Hilda. *Curriculum Development.* New York: Harcourt, Brace & World, Inc., 1962.

Venable, Tom C. *Patterns in Secondary School Curriculum.* New York: Harper &
  Row, Publishers, Inc., 1958.
Whitehead, Alfred North. *The Aims of Education and Other Essays.* New York:
  The Macmillan Company, 1929.
Wright, Grace S. *The Core Program, Unpublished Research 1956–1962.* Washington,
  D.C.: Office of Education, U.S. Department of Health, Education, and Wel-
  fare, 1963.

CHAPTER 8
Before College

A T A TIME WHEN COLLEGE ENROLLMENTS and the demand for higher education are at record levels, we find ourselves in the midst of a great wave of curriculum innovation, revision, and reform in our elementary and secondary schools. At the same time we see new demands and pressures being directed at our youth toward ever higher standards of academic attainment. The great watchword of the 1960's is excellence. Educators everywhere are seeking to identify it, pursue it, capture it, and parcel it out in doses guaranteed to satisfy school critics, parents, and the general public.

But excellence is more than getting the highest grades in the right courses in the best high schools and in the finest colleges. Excellence is manifested in all walks of life where people are given the fullest opportunity to do the best that is in them. Excellence is not possible unless people want to do their best because they love their work and take pride in a sense of personal achievement and social contribution.

In many instances the college-bound high-school student faces a growing condition of supercompetitiveness where the race is for high grades and superior test scores. But under such conditions there is danger that the love of learning will not be cultivated. Fortunately there are countervailing forces at work that foster desirable attitudes of inquiry, rather than negative and conforming attitudes toward learning. Nevertheless, the competitive pressures for college entrance are growing. Many teachers, parents, and students tend to regard high-school education in terms of grades, scores on external aptitude and achievement tests, and admission to the right college. The concern for college admission today is being felt even in the junior high school. One noted authority recommends that potentials for college entrance be assessed in the elementary grades.

As early as the elementary grades the guidance officers ought to begin their program of realistic and frank discussions with parents about the *kind* of college to which their offspring might expect to gain admission.[1]

One is compelled to wonder whether it will soon be recommended that guidance officers begin their frank discussions with parents concerning college plans as soon as their offspring are admitted to nursery school!

In this chapter we shall examine the changing practices in college-preparatory programs and explore the problem of how to improve the opportunities for higher education during a period when the portals of many colleges are becoming more restrictive and selective.

THE CHANGING COLLEGE SCENE

There is great diversity in American higher education. We have junior and community colleges, technical institutes, liberal arts colleges, and multi-purpose universities—capped by graduate and professional schools. Curricular offerings vary widely and so do the standards for admission and retention. We seem to have colleges suitable for virtually anyone of normal to superior intelligence who possesses the interest and drive for postsecondary school studies. No other society has provided for higher education on such a massive scale. Yet, we are just now entering a period of reassessment at a time of dramatic growth. Changes in the college scene will obviously effect changes in the high-school scene. Consequently, let us briefly examine some of these developments and problems in American higher education.

Quality and Quantity

In view of the increases in our college-age population, coupled with the growing demand for higher education, it is estimated that college enrollments between 1960 and 1985 will at least double.[2] As we enter this period of dramatic growth in college and university enrollments, we can also observe that, despite certain inequities in educational opportunity, we have demonstrated that it is possible to provide education of high quality on a massive scale. C. P. Snow, the eminent British scientist and author, addresses American educators with this tribute to higher education in our country:

> You should feel much more pride about the education your colleges provide. I regard it with both envy and admiration.

---

[1] James Bryant Conant, *Slums and Suburbs* (New York: McGraw-Hill Company, Inc., 1961), p. 101.

[2] Sidney J. Tickton, *Letter to a College President* (New York: The Fund for the Advancement of Education, May, 1963), p. 17.

You were the first people in the world to bring education to an enormous slice of an enormous country and to remove it from the privilege of a small elite. . . . Your country . . . did it on a very big scale without any encouragement from the rest of the world and with a great deal of discouragement from superior Englishmen.

You are now reaping the rewards from your system of higher education. The process has, as we all know, sometimes been wasteful, but it has been a generous waste. If we are going to make mistakes about human possibilities, for God's sake let's make them on the generous side. You have done this, and I am certain you are going to be paid time and time again.

I have no doubt whatever that college education over the whole width and breadth of America is one of the real achievements of this world.[3]

SELECTIVE ADMISSIONS. Although there are those who continue to maintain that we cannot have both quality and quantity in higher education, it seems clear that our society has not only begun to demonstrate that it can be done, but that it must be done. Neverthless, the growing enrollment pressures and increasing taxes for the support of public higher education have produced certain mechanisms for more selective admissions. For example, the state of California, long regarded as a pacesetter in public higher education, has limited its state university enrollment to the top ten per cent of high-school graduates. The California state colleges have been selecting the top third, while the junior colleges have admitted all high-school graduates and persons over 18 years of age who show promise of benefiting from this level of study. The California Master Plan for higher education, adopted in 1960, calls for even more selective standards for admission to the state university and state colleges. Despite this high degree of selectivity and track system, California has kept the doors open for successful junior-college students who desire to transfer to the third year of work at a state college or university campus. The records show that such transferees do very well indeed, thereby lending strong support to the validity of maintaining an open-door policy between one type of institution and another.

Some California educators have revealed concern that more rigid standards of college selectivity may be used chiefly as a vehicle for reducing or limiting the tax burden. Concern has also been expressed over the growing tendency of colleges to place the burden of academic success on the student while assuming little if any responsibility for helping the student to succeed in college.[4]

---

[3] C. P. Snow, "Higher Education in America," NEA Journal, 53, April, 1964, 4:11.
[4] See Robert R. Smith, "Prospects for New State College Admission Policies: The Context for Re-Study of State College Admission Policies," Journal of Secondary Education, March, 1961, 3:163–170.

Although in the past it has been the practice of many of our nation's state-supported universities and colleges to admit most high-school graduates, there is a growing trend toward selection from the upper half of the high-school graduating class and requiring the fulfillment of certain high-school subjects.

Increased enrollment pressures obviously are directed at the publicly supported institutions of higher education. Early in this century the private colleges and universities enrolled some 60 per cent of the students. Between 1930 and 1950 the enrollment was evenly divided between public and private institutions. In 1960 almost 60 per cent of the enrollment was in public colleges and universities. It is estimated that by 1985, publicly supported institutions will enroll 80 per cent of the students.[5] California's public system of higher education already accounts for 80 per cent of the total enrollment in that state.

Many of our state universities are now exercising higher standards of academic selectivity than a good portion of our private universities. Indeed there are relatively few private universities that are limiting their freshman class enrollments to the top 8 to 10 per cent of the high-school graduation class, as in the case of the University of California. Because of the much higher tuition required at private institutions, selectivity at the private colleges tends to be determined by financial as well as academic factors. But with the increases in fees and costs of living away from home, even the state-supported institutions are becoming financially selective.

High-school faculties and students are feeling the pressures of increased academic selectivity for college entrance. While some educators may regard this as a desirable trend toward higher academic standards in our high schools and colleges, such pressures are apt to repress curricular experimentation in our secondary schools while also preventing many late bloomers from realizing their potentials. Many of the ex-G.I.'s with poor high school records made excellent college students during the years following World War II. Linus C. Pauling, the only person to win two Nobel Prizes, failed to earn a high-school diploma. Fortunately, he managed to gain entrance to the Oregon Agricultural College in 1918 without graduating from high school.

If, in the years ahead, our colleges become very highly selective, our society may well find itself faced with the problem of a shrinking proportion of people with realized talents and aspirations. A democracy cannot afford such waste and discontent. For instead of fostering excellence, we will be making it more restrictive and exclusive.

---

[5] Tickton, op. cit., p. 17.

CRITERIA FOR COLLEGE ENTRANCE

Standards for admission to college, even among our very best institutions, vary significantly. Most institutions have been revising their admission practices almost annually in accordance with the quantity and quality of applicants. Different admission committees at different institutions will vary in the weight given to the several criteria for college entrance. In this section we shall review briefly the major criteria for college admission.

College-Preparatory Subjects

Historically, colleges and universities have exerted considerable influence over high-school curricula. However, college admissions officers have come to realize that satisfactory completion of a rigidly prescribed college preparatory program does not guarantee success in college. The Eight-Year Study, conducted between 1932 and 1940, revealed that students could succeed in college even though they had been enrolled in experimental high schools with curricula that differed significantly from the traditional college-preparatory programs.[6]

Today, many colleges and universities rely on multiple criteria for admission. In addition to recommending or requiring the completion of a certain minimum number of units in given high-school subjects, candidates are also evaluated through external testing, grades, rank in high-school class, recommendations, interviews, and other criteria. Most colleges tend to recommend certain high-school subjects and units, rather than holding applicants to rigidly prescribed credits. But even in cases where an applicant's high-school record does not meet the college admission requirements, he may qualify for entrance by examination. Admission by examination may be provided for persons over 18 years of age who are not high-school graduates, candidates from nonaccredited high schools, or those who may be lacking certain college-preparatory subjects.

Although some state universities, state colleges, and public junior colleges are open to any graduate of an accredited high school, virtually all institutions of higher education make some specific recommendations regarding high-school subjects and units. The following statements from a variety of colleges and universities illustrate the patterns of high-school subjects and number of units recommended or required for admission:

---

[6] Dean Chamberlin et al., *Did They Succeed in College?* (New York: Harper & Row, Publishers, Inc., 1943).

Interviewing for admission to college.

YALE UNIVERSITY. Yale recommends a secondary school curriculum which includes four years of English; at least two and preferably four years of one foreign language continued through the final year of school; at least three and preferably four years of mathematics; at least one year, and preferably two, of both science and history. . . .

The pattern described above is highly desirable. But the applicant who, because of unusual interests, altered plans, or conflicting advice, has not followed it is not excluded from consideration. Nor must an applicant necessarily complete four years of secondary-school work. Quality of achievement is more important than the accumulation of credits, or the extent to which a given pattern has been followed.[7]

---

[7] Yale University, *University Catalogue Number for the Year 1963–1964*, p. 114.

THE UNIVERSITY OF CHICAGO. The College has no fixed prerequisities of secondary-school study for admission, but it does look much more favorably on the candidate who has taken extensive work in science, mathematics, English and English composition, history, and foreign languages, all of which provide the solid foundation for advanced study. If a student has taken advanced or "accelerated" programs, that is a credit in his favor. . . .[8]

OBERLIN COLLEGE. The minimum unit requirements in specific study fields are 3 units of English, 1 unit of history, 1 unit of laboratory science, and 3 units of mathematics.[9]

MICHIGAN STATE UNIVERSITY. The normal requirement is at least 16 units of high school work. A recommended distribution of units would include: 4 units of English, at least 7 units from mathematics, science, language and social sciences, a minimum of 3 or more units from any of the above or vocational, commercial and industrial subjects or art or music. Remaining units may be from other subjects accepted by the secondary school for graduation.

Several programs require college mathematics courses which are based upon adequate knowledge in college preparatory mathematics.[10]

UNIVERSITY OF CALIFORNIA (Berkeley).
a. History, 1 unit.
b. English, 3 units.
c. Mathematics, 2 units.
d. Laboratory science, 1 unit.
e. Foreign language, 2 units (in one language).
f. Advanced course, 1 or 2 units (in mathematics, foreign language, or science).
g. Electives (to complete a minimum of 15 units).
   At least an average grade of B is required in courses taken in the tenth, eleventh, and twelfth years. . . .[11]

SAN JOSE STATE COLLEGE. For admission to a state college (California), a high school graduate, or other applicant must, as a minimum, meet one of the following:
   (a) Have earned 14 or more semester grades of A or B (70 semester periods or 7 Carnegie units) on a five-point scale in subjects other than physical education, military science, and remedial courses during the last three years in high school, including at least 6 college preparatory subject grades. College preparatory courses include one or more of the following fields:
      1. English
      2. Foreign Languages
      3. Mathematics
      4. Natural Sciences
      5. Social Sciences

[8] The University of Chicago, *College Announcements 1963–64*, p. 29.
[9] Oberlin College, *General Catalogue, 1962–1964*, p. II–2.
[10] Michigan State University, *Michigan State University Catalog 1963–64*, p. 34.
[11] University of California (Berkeley), *General Catalogue, 1963–1964*, pp. 24–25.

 (b) Have earned ten or more semester grades of A or B (50 semester periods or 5 Carnegie units) on a five-point scale in subjects other than physical education, military science, and remedial courses during the last three years in high school. . . .

 An applicant may be admitted to a state college when in the judgment of the appropriate college authorities, he has equivalent preparation to that in (a) or (b) above.[12]

The increasing competitiveness for college admission may well tempt many colleges to prescribe specific subjects and units for entrance; yet, the body of research does not support such requirements as highly valid predictors of success in college. Recognizing the growing competitiveness, however, most high-school counselors today are advising college-bound students to carry predominantly academic programs in line with the recommendations of our leading colleges and spokesmen.

The tendency to hold students to rigidly prescribed courses and units for college entrance neglects the nature of the educative experience itself. In other words, it fails to give adequate attention to the quality of the content and process of learning. For example, Conant prescribes the following minimum high-school program for academically talented students: four years of English, four years of mathematics, four years of one foreign language, three years of science, and three years of social studies.[13] Conant even goes so far as to prescribe at least 15 hours of homework per week for these students.[14] Unfortunately, he gives little attention to the quality of the educative experience and totally ignores the importance of cultivating a love of learning on the part of the academically talented.

High School Grades and Rank in Class

Because high-school grading practices vary widely, most colleges have placed less emphasis on the grade point average, while turning to the student's rank in his high-school class as a key criterion. Rank in class provides college admissions officers with a clearer conception of what an applicant's high-school grades mean. For example, a graduate from one high school using a letter-grading system may have a B average, while a student from a school using a numerical grading system may have an average of 83. On the other hand, two students from different high schools in different cities may have identical averages of 83, but one student ranks tenth in his class of 200 while another ranks eighty-sixth in his class of 195.

---

[12] San Jose State College, *General Catalog 1963–64*, p. 23.
[13] James Bryant Conant, *Slums and Suburbs*, (New York: McGraw-Hill Company, Inc., 1961), p. 89.
[14] James Bryant Conant, *The American High School Today* (New York: McGraw-Hill Company, Inc., 1959).

However, while rank in high-school class is the best single predictor of success in college, it is far from perfect because many students gain seriousness of purpose after high school. Moreover, a student's rank in one high school may differ significantly from what his rank might be in another high school. Although it has been demonstrated that certain corrections can be made for these variables, rank in class remains an imperfect predictor. Getzels reports that such rankings favor the good convergent student over the good divergent or creative student.[15]

Standardized Aptitude and Achievement Tests

In a further effort to improve student selection through prediction of success in college, an increasing number of institutions of higher education have been employing standardized testing. The most popular and influential aptitude examination is the Scholastic Aptitude Test (SAT) of the College Entrance Examination Board. In many high schools, juniors are given a dry run for the SAT through the College Board's Preliminary Scholastic Aptitude Test (PSAT). Also gaining in popularity are the subject-achievment batteries of the College Board.

Although these external testing programs have grown phenomenally, such tests leave much to be desired as valid predictors of success in college. For one thing, they fail to measure a student's drive for learning or how hard he is willing to work at his studies. And they cannot predict changes in motivation as the student matures through late adolescence and into early adulthood.

Rank in high-school class continues to be a more valid predictor of success in college than any battery of standardized aptitude and achievement tests. Nevertheless, an increasing number of high schools and colleges find such testing programs attractive because of their mechanical convenience, the neatly quantitative data they provide, and the pseudo-scientific objectivity of external, standardized testing.

Many educational critics and authorities rely heavily on these tests for identifying the so-called academically talented students. For example, Conant considers a student academically talented if his Scholastic Aptitude Test score is in the upper 15 per cent of the national norms.[16] Yet such test results may be indicative of socio-economic and cultural differences, rather than differences in academic talent. And these test results ignore the factors of motivation and quest for learning that are vital in the lives of people who make important contributions to society. Getzels

---

[15] J. W. Getzels, "Non-IQ Intellectual and Other Factors in College Admission," in *The Coming Crisis in the Selection of Students for College Entrance* (Washington, D.C.: National Education Association and the American Educational Research Association, 1960), p. 28.

[16] Conant, *op. cit.*, p. 59.

offers this warning that such standardized testing programs along with high-school class rankings tend to favor the conforming type of student over the creative type:

> . . . all of these measures are biased in favor of the student with what Guilford calls "convergent intellectual ability" as against the student with "divergent intellectual ability." That is, these indices favor the student who is retentive and docile—the one who tends to seek the single, pre-determined, "correct" answer to an intellectual problem—as against the student who is constructive and creative—the one who tends to seek the multiple, experimental, "novel" answer to an intellectual problem.[17]

Creative students tend to be less interested in grades and not so bent on pleasing the teacher as high-achieving convergent youngsters. Consequently, the creative ones are not as highly esteemed by teachers and tend to receive lower grades than the convergent ones.[18]

The remarkable growth in external testing programs for college admissions is reflected in the data on the number of College Board examinations administered. For example, during 1950–1951, these examinations numbered only 105,000. However, by 1960–1961 almost 2,000,000 College Board examinations were given.[19]

Advanced Placement and Scholarship Testing

Through the Advanced Placement Program, initiated in 1955 by the College Entrance Examination Board, it is possible for superior students to pursue certain advanced courses in high school and gain college credit or advanced college placement by examination. The Advanced Placement Program is growing impressively, because many people believe that it is an effective vehicle for college admissions. During 1963–64 advanced placement and college credit were offered in eleven courses available in certain high schools: American history, biology, chemistry, English composition, European history, French, German, Latin, literature, mathematics (calculus and analytic geometry), and Spanish.

Another mechanism gaining considerable influence in college admissions is the National Merit Scholarship Program. Although this is a rather young program, having begun in 1955, almost all of our larger high schools are now participating in this giant testing operation. Candidates must survive a qualifying test that selects the semifinalists who in turn submit to a second test. While the number of grantees is very small (numbering only 1,528 in 1963), and although the awards are modest (38 per cent of the 1963 awards were under $250), being an award

---

[17] Getzels, op. cit., p. 23.
[18] Ibid., p. 27.
[19] Educational Testing Service, Annual Report 1960–61 (Princeton, N.J., 1961), pp. 56–57.

winner can help one gain admission to a prestige college if he can also meet the financial demands of higher education. In 1963 more than 13,000 semifinalists received Certificates of Merit and over 36,000 students were given Letters of Commendation—designations useful in gaining admission to many colleges.[20]

High-School Recommendations

Many colleges attach notable weight to recommendations from the high-school principal, counselor, or other high-school officials. Such recommendations, however, are used with other criteria in determining admission to college. High-school recommendations encompass both intellective and nonintellective judgments. Among the latter are opinions regarding personality, appearance, participation in extra-class activities, and so on.

Other Criteria for College Admission

Most state-supported institutions of higher education give preference to state residents, while private colleges tend to seek wide geographic representation. Preference is often given to children of alumni in both public and private colleges, though this factor probably is of greater importance to the latter type of institution. Parental occupation and socioeconomic status influence some admission committees more than others. Moreover, socioeconomic factors obviously function as an important screening device. In the higher socioeconomic levels, even students with I.Q.'s below 100 manage to gain admission to college, while bright slum children may not even have the opportunity to finish high school.[21]

Admission to certain departmental or divisional programs at universities frequently entails significant variations in selection standards within the same institution. Coeducational colleges tend to hold girls to higher admission standards than boys, often because of student housing limitations. Sociocultural factors continue to prevent many intelligent girls from pursuing higher education. Although the number of female college students has never been greater, the number enrolled in proportion to the total female population continues to lag behind that for males.

Inasmuch as the opportunity for the pursuit of higher education varies significantly state by state and region by region, geographic residence is a crucial factor for many youths who seek admission to college. A resident of Massachusetts or New York State is apt to encounter considerably less opportunity for gaining entrance to a desired curriculum

---

[20] See National Merit Scholarship Corporation, Annual Report 1963, *The Quest for Intellectual Excellence*, Evanston, Illinois, 1964.

[21] James Bryant Conant, *Slums and Suburbs*, (New York: McGraw-Hill Company, Inc., 1961), p. 115.

in a state college or university than a resident of California or Michigan.

Another important factor in determining admission or rejection is the competition for openings in any particular year. Admission boards must constantly compare applicants against one another. And, finally, even the way in which an applicant handles himself during an interview or the manner in which he fills out his application may have an important bearing on admission.

MANPOWER AND THE HUMAN BEING. As college admissions become more competitive, they tend to become more impersonal and mechanical, with automatic indices and weightings attached to the criteria for selection. We would do well to heed this advice in our haste to regard students as resources of manpower or brainpower for our national needs:

> . . . as the crisis in college admission becomes more severe, we may drift unwittingly from our concept of selecting the college student individually as *Man* into a concept of selecting the college student mechanically as *Manpower*. It is the convergent student who is the most ready source of manpower, the divergent individual the best hope of Man. It is in this sense that I venture a plea here for making provision in our college selection procedures not only for the superior convergent student but for the superior divergent student as well.[22]

ACADEMIC SUBJECTS TAKEN BY HIGH-SCHOOL STUDENTS

Some educational critics have maintained that students of high ability are not taking a sufficient number of academic courses in high school. Recent studies, however, tend to contradict this notion. To begin with, the general education courses required of all students in virtually all of our high schools tend to be concentrated in the academic subjects. A national survey of the courses required of all students, regardless of their ability level or enrollment in college-preparatory or vocational curricula, revealed that the typical graduation requirements are: three to four years of English, two to three years of social studies, one year of mathematics, and one year of science.[23] This means that in order to meet the minimum graduation requirements, all students, regardless of ability level or special interests, must devote approximately half of their high-school studies to academic subjects.

Student Abilities and Courses Taken

The United States Office of Education's national study of courses taken by high-school students revealed that students in the upper

---

[22] Getzels, *op. cit.*, p. 28.
[23] Edith S. Greer, "The Academically Talented," *School Life*, 45, 5:9, March, 1963.

ALL PUPILS — ALL SCHOOLS

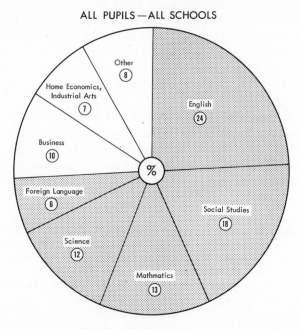

FIGURE 8–1. Proportion of high school pupil programs devoted to certain subject matter areas. [SOURCE: Edith S. Greer and Richard M. Harbeck, *What High School Pupils Study* (Washington, D.C.: Office of Education, U.S. Department of Health, Education, and Welfare, 1962), p. 110.]

quartile in ability were earning 80 per cent of their high-school credits in the five standard academic subject areas. For all ability levels combined, the typical high-school student was devoting 72 per cent of his studies to the five academic fields. And even the pupils in the lower third in ability were earning 66 per cent of their credits in these academic areas.[24] These data are presented in Figures 8–1 and 8–2.

As shown in Figure 8–2, students in the upper quartile of ability were taking 39 per cent of their high-school work in the fields of mathematics, science, and foreign languages. The data in Figure 8–3 show the subjects according to students' class rank. Since class rank tells us about actual achievement, rather than aptitude as measured by standardized tests, it is useful to examine the subject areas pursued as related to rank in class. It is seen in Figure 8–3 that the relationship between class rank and the subject areas taken is very similar to the

---

[24] Edith S. Greer and Richard M. Harbeck, *What High School Pupils Study* (Washington, D.C.: Office of Education, U.S. Department of Health, Education, and Welfare, 1962), p. 117.

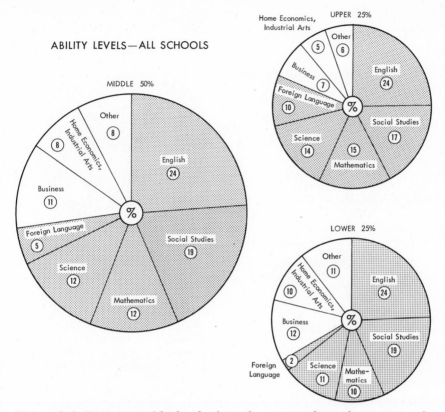

FIGURE 8–2. Proportion of high school pupil programs devoted to certain subject matter areas, by pupil ability level. [SOURCE: Edith S. Greer and Richard M. Harbeck, *What High School Pupils Study* (Washington, D.C.: Office of Education, U.S. Department of Health, Education, and Welfare, 1962), p. 111.]

data for ability levels as shown in Figure 8–2. In other words, students ranking high in achievement, as well as those of high ability, pursue more academic courses than those of middle or lower ranks and ability. But even those youngsters in the lower third in class rank were taking 69 per cent of their programs in the five academic areas. The differences between those in the top third and middle third in class rank do not appear to be significant. While the top group took 77 per cent of their course work in the five academic areas, the middle group devoted 74 per cent of their programs to these fields.

Obviously, the higher-ability students and the higher-achieving students are not seeking the easy credits, as some critics of education would have us believe. Equally significant is the extent to which students of

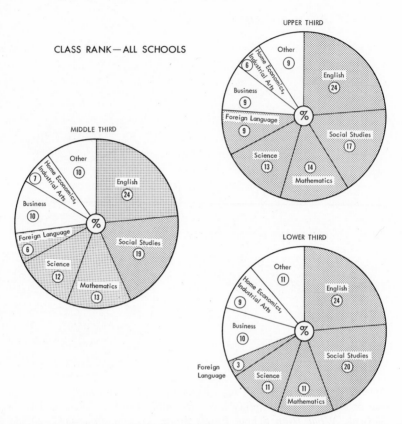

FIGURE 8–3. Proportion of high school pupil programs devoted to certain subject matter areas, by class rank. [SOURCE: Edith S. Greer and Richard M. Harbeck, What High School Pupils Study (Washington, D.C.: Office of Education, U.S. Department of Health, Education, and Welfare, 1962), p. 112.]

average and lower ability are pursuing courses in the five academic areas.

Since 1954 there has been a notable increase in both the total number and proportion of high-school students enrolled in mathematics, science,[25] and modern foreign languages.[26] In the field of foreign languages, the twentieth century has witnessed a dramatic decline in the number and

---

[25] Kenneth E. Brown and Ellsworth S. Obourn, Offerings and Enrollments in Science and Mathematics in Public High Schools (Washington, D.C.: Office of Education, U.S. Department of Health, Education, and Welfare, 1962, p. 28.

[26] Fred M. Hechinger, "Foreign Languages Stage a Comeback," Saturday Review, February 16, 1963, pp. 64–68.

proportion of students studying Latin, while the modern foreign languages have made notable gains during the past decade. As we have already mentioned, the increasing competition for admission to college is causing more of our higher- and average-ability students to pursue a greater proportion of academic courses.

Ability and Achievement

While the pursuit of academic courses may, in itself, be considered desirable, it does not assure us that students are developing better attitudes toward learning or that talented youngsters are being provided with improved opportunities for success in such academic programs. Recent research reveals that, of the students in the top third in academic ability, 40 per cent were actually achieving below this level (28 per cent were achieving at the middle-third ability level, while 12 per cent were achieving at the lower-third level). On the other hand, among the lower third in ability, 42 per cent were achieving above this level (28 per cent were achieving at the middle level and 10 per cent were achieving at the upper-third level).[27] Obviously, interests, motivation, and socio-economic and cultural factors play a vital role in achievement. Yet we often tend to neglect these factors in our efforts to induce students to work harder and pursue more academic courses.

Furthermore, the data that reveal that a significant number of the so-called lower-ability youngsters actually perform at superior and normal levels has an important bearing on grouping practices. Educators should be cautioned against the grouping or pigeonholing of students on the basis of the single criterion of standardized aptitude test scores.

While some investigators have coined the term over-achiever to describe the student of lower ability whose grades are superior or average, the author doubts that there is any such thing as over-achieving. The fact that a student earns superior grades indicates that he is capable of such attainment.

We also need to restudy the developing hierarchy in the way in which the subject fields are regarded. In examining our growing national trend toward emphasizing the academic courses, the question arises as to why students of higher academic ability are often discouraged from taking some electives in art and music. It seems unfortunate that these two areas, so badly neglected in American life, have been regarded as frill subjects in our high schools.

Academic Subjects in the Junior High School

We have observed a growing trend toward emphasizing academic programs and preparation for college as early as the seventh grade. Conant has recommended that prospects for college admission be dis-

---

[27] Edith S. Greer, "The Academically Talented," *School Life*, 45, March, 1963, p. 10.

cussed between school authorities and parents as early as the elementary grades![28] But rather than treat the junior-high-school curriculum as specific preparation for college, it should be designed to enable young adolescents to cultivate desirable attitudes, skills, and behaviors. The junior-high-school curriculum should provide exploratory opportunities as well as a sound program of experiences in general education. Our devices for identifying and preparing youngsters specifically for college are not so perfect as to justify rigid screening at the age of 12 or 13. Such screening may well serve to eliminate rather than assist our most promising youth.

During the junior-high-school years, the heavy concentration given to the academic subjects should be intended for general education upon which exploratory and specialized studies may be developed. Let us examine briefly the current requirements and offerings, particularly in the academic subjects, in the junior high school.

ACADEMIC SUBJECTS REQUIRED OF ALL STUDENTS. Again, as in the case of the senior high school, some critics would have us believe that youngsters are allowed to pursue mostly elective subjects in the junior high school. However, the actual facts show quite another picture. A recent national survey of 1,360 junior high schools, conducted by the United States Office of Education, revealed that the overwhelming practice was for the schools to require every student to take a course in each of four academic areas in grades 7, 8, and 9.[29] The four academic areas are English, mathematics, social studies, and science.

In Table 8–1 we see the percentages of those junior high schools · requiring study in specific subject areas in each grade level. In addition to taking courses in the four academic fields, the survey revealed that almost all students are required to take physical education throughout the three years. A large minority of schools treated science as an elective during the ninth grade. In effect, then, the typical junior-high-school youngster was carrying four academic courses, physical education, and one or two nonacademic courses during each of the three years. In schools where science was not required during the ninth grade, the student was allowed to elect a course in science or choose an additional course from a nonacademic field. Approximately half of the schools required a course in health, industrial arts, homemaking, music, or art during the freshman year.

RECOMMENDATIONS BY CONANT. The academic courses recommended

---

[28] James Bryant Conant, *Slums and Suburbs*, New York: McGraw-Hill Company, Inc., 1961), p. 101.

[29] Grace S. Wright and Edith S. Greer, *The Junior High School* (Washington, D.C.: Office of Education, U.S. Department of Health, Education, and Welfare, 1963).

by Conant at the junior-high-school level are as follows:[30] English, social studies, mathematics, and science for all students in grades seven and eight. Heavy emphasis should be given in English to reading and composition, and the social studies should include emphasis on history and geography. Conant also recommended that the very able students begin algebra in grade 8 and that some, if not all, students begin in grade 7 the study of a modern foreign language (conversational) under a bilingual teacher. According to Conant, if the study of a foreign language is begun in grade 7, provisions should be made for its continuance throughout the junior and senior high school. By beginning algebra in grade 8, Conant sees the very able student pursuing college level mathematics in grade 12. In grade 9 Conant advocates that the able students, in addition to continuing their subjects in general education, pursue an elective sequence in further academic studies. Also recommended for able students is a laboratory course in introductory biology or physical science.[31]

Conant does not ignore the nonacademic studies at the junior-high-school level. For example, he recommends some art and music for all students, and industrial arts for boys and homemaking for girls. Beginning in grade 9 he allows for the beginning of a sequence leading to the development of a marketable skill for those not preparing for college. Nevertheless, the able student is heavily loaded with academic courses during junior high school. Regrettably, Conant fails to treat the matter of cultivating desirable attitudes toward learning during these important formative years. The emphasis of his report is more on courses and credits rather than on stimulating and challenging the able student.

SPECIAL PROGRAMS FOR HIGH ACHIEVERS

During the past decade there has been growing emphasis on improving the education of the more able student through a variety of special programs. We have seen the growing influence of standardized aptitude and achievement testing for college entrance, the competition for National Merit Scholarships, and the efforts of various agencies to improve course content and methods in the academic areas. We have already discussed some of the implications of external testing for college admissions and scholarship awards. Reviewed later in this chapter are some of the recent efforts at improving curriculum and instruction within the various academic fields. Therefore, let us turn now to such provisions for

---

[30] James Bryant Conant, *Education in the Junior High School Years* (Princeton, N.J.: Educational Testing Service, 1960), pp. 16–18.
[31] *Ibid.*, p. 30.

Table 8-1

Percent of Junior High Schools Requiring Study in Specific Subject Areas by Grade, Type, and Size of School

Type and size (enrollment) of school	Language arts (English)	Social studies	Mathematics	Science	Physical education (boys)	Physical education (girls)	Health	Foreign language	Business education	Agriculture	Vocational education	Art	Music (including band and orchestra)	Art or music making	Industrial arts or home making	Other
GRADE 7																
Junior high schools																
Total	99.9	99.7	100.0	82.6	94.7	93.4	57.7	2.9	0.6	0.5	3.1	49.8	50.5	12.1	55.5	3.0
75 to 299	99.6	99.1	100.0	89.6	91.3	88.0	61.0	3.3	.8	.0	1.2	27.0	33.6	11.6	30.3	2.5
300 and above	100.0	100.0	100.0	79.5	96.3	95.5	53.0	2.8	.5	.8	4.0	60.0	58.0	12.3	61.0	3.3
Junior-senior high schools																
Total	100.0	97.7	99.5	92.0	88.4	83.1	57.1	1.0	.3	5.1	3.2	28.5	35.2	11.0	35.3	.5
125 to 499	100.0	97.2	99.4	91.3	87.2	81.4	59.3	.6	.3	6.8	3.1	21.7	30.1	11.2	29.5	.3
500 and above	100.0	99.3	100.0	93.8	91.9	88.6	50.6	2.3	.3	.0	3.6	48.7	50.3	10.8	52.6	.9
GRADE 8																
Junior high schools																
Total	99.9	99.8	100.0	89.0	93.1	91.9	51.9	3.6	2.5	0.1	4.4	32.8	33.9	9.3	54.7	3.3
75 to 299	99.6	99.2	100.0	93.8	89.2	85.9	55.2	3.3	.8	.4	2.1	24.1	28.6	10.8	40.2	2.5
300 and above	100.0	100.0	100.0	86.9	94.8	93.6	50.5	3.7	3.2	.0	5.4	36.7	36.2	8.6	61.1	3.7
Junior-senior high schools																
Total	99.8	98.0	99.7	92.2	89.4	84.5	55.0	1.8	.8	6.4	4.1	26.0	31.2	9.4	39.4	.9
125 to 499	100.0	97.9	99.7	91.9	88.2	82.4	54.7	1.2	.9	8.4	4.3	20.2	26.8	9.8	34.6	.6
500 and above	99.4	98.3	99.7	93.2	92.9	90.3	55.8	3.7	.8	.8	3.7	42.2	43.6	8.2	52.7	1.7

GRADE 9

Junior high schools																
Total	99.8	76.2	91.4	61.2	90.6	88.8	43.5	1.4	1.6	0.2	2.3	9.1	10.5	1.6	18.6	1.4
75 to 299	99.0	83.2	94.7	80.5	84.9	79.6	42.5	.9	.9	.9	1.7	7.1	9.8	1.7	28.2	.9
300 and above	100.0	74.4	90.6	56.2	92.1	91.2	43.8	1.5	1.8	.0	2.4	9.7	10.6	1.5	16.1	1.5
Junior-senior high schools																
Total	99.7	69.9	91.2	83.7	87.1	82.9	39.4	1.5	1.4	7.3	2.0	6.3	8.5	2.8	24.1	.0
125 to 499	100.0	68.7	92.4	85.2	85.2	80.3	37.4	1.2	1.4	9.3	2.3	3.5	6.1	2.6	23.5	.0
500 and above	98.6	73.4	88.0	79.7	92.6	90.3	44.8	2.3	1.1	1.7	1.1	14.0	15.4	3.1	26.0	.0

SOURCE: Grace S. Wright and Edith S. Greer, *The Junior High School* (Washington, D.C.: Office of Education, U.S. Department of Health, Education, and Welfare, 1963).

the more able students as honors classes and special grouping, early entrance to college, advanced placement, and other related practices.

HONORS CLASSES AND ABILITY GROUPING. One of the most influential advocates of ability grouping is Conant. Since the appearance of his reports on the high school in 1959 and the junior high school in 1960, the practice of ability-grouping has become commonplace in our larger secondary schools. Without offering any research evidence, Conant recommended that students be grouped, subject by subject, beginning in grade 7, according to three levels of ability.[32] While most high schools had heretofore provided for the streaming of pupils according to their election of college-preparatory, general, vocational, or commercial programs, the popular trend today is to sort students further according to ability or achievement levels.

The task of grouping for honors or for bringing together the more able students can become highly complicated. To begin with, the available research fails to show any clear-cut evidence of superior achievement as a result of such grouping.[33] It appears that it may not be so important to package students according to ability groups as it is to alter the teaching-learning strategy to meet the needs of the particular group.

> Examination of research reveals that factors other than particular grouping procedures used account for differences when they do occur in tested pupil achievement between children grouped according to ability and those grouped heterogeneously. Some studies seemed to show achievement gains in favor of ability grouping and some in favor of heterogeneous grouping. Still others show little or no statistically significant differences among grouping methods in pupil achievement as measured by standardized tests.[34]

While the practice in most schools is to handle the honors' sections in the usual class style of 30 students per teacher, some schools are experimenting with seminars and independent study for the more able youngsters.

Second, the problem arises as to whether students should be grouped according to aptitude, achievement, interest, or according to a combination of these factors. Third, we need to determine what instruments and procedures to use if we are going to differentiate students. For example, should we use standardized tests, previous academic grades, teacher recommendations, or a combination of these? As discussed earlier in this chapter, studies reveal that 40 per cent of the high-ability youngsters

---

[32] *Ibid.*, p. 26.
[33] Jane Franseth, *Toward Effective Grouping* (Washington, D.C.: Office of Education, U.S. Department of Health, Education, and Welfare, 1962).
[34] *Ibid.*, p. 25.

are not high achievers; and 28 per cent of the low-ability students are achieving at the average level, while 10 per cent are performing at the upper-third level.[35] Standardized aptitude and achievement tests are of imperfect validity and fail to account for important motivating forces. Fourth, many adolescents show marked changes in motivation and resultant achievement. Experiences with ex-servicemen under the G.I. Bill of Rights revealed many with poor high-school records who were able to pursue college-level studies with great success.

It would appear that honors courses for high-school students of outstanding aptitude, achievement, and interest could serve a useful purpose if the nature of ·the learning experiences in these courses is attuned to the needs of such students. Otherwise, the research will continue to show no significant differences in learning outcomes between grouping and nongrouping of these students. In too many instances the honors groups, rather than being stimulated and challenged, are simply primed with more subject matter to be covered under increased competitive pressure. Precautions must also be taken against the tendency of such grouping to reflect socioeconomic and cultural differences, rather than differences in actual talent. Moreover, there is evidence, already mentioned, that such honors grouping may eliminate the divergent or original-thinking student.[36] Administrative implications of high-school grouping practices are discussed further in Chapter 11.

ADVANCED PLACEMENT. As discussed earlier in this chapter, an increasing number of high schools are providing certain college-level courses for selected students. Sponsored by the College Entrance Examination Board since 1955, the Advanced Placement Program enables high-school students to gain college credit and/or advanced placement when entering college. Upon completing one or more advanced courses in high school, the student submits to external examinations sponsored by the College Board. These examinations are prepared by committees of college professors and high-school teachers. Examination results are submitted to the college the student enters and, if satisfactory, the college will give credit or place the student in an advanced course.

While most participating high schools provide standard college-level courses to prepare students for the advanced placement examinations, other means can be used such as tutorial instruction, independent study, or television. The results indicate that advanced placement students perform successfully in college. However, one study of 312 Advanced

---

[35] Edith S. Greer, "The Academically Talented," *School Life,* 45, March, 1963, p. 9.
[36] J. W. Getzels, "Non-IQ Intellectual and Other Factors in College Admission," in .
    The Coming Crisis in the Selection of Students for College Entrance (Washington, D.C.: National Education Association and The American Educational Research Association, 1960).

Placement Program graduates revealed considerable dissatisfaction because of the poor quality of the high-school instruction in such courses, the failure of colleges to make adequate provisions for placement or credit, and the failure of many students to attain adequate scores on the College Board examinations.[37]

EARLY ADMISSION TO COLLEGE. The Advanced Placement Program is largely an outgrowth of experiences with the Program of Early Admission to College, initiated in 1951 by 11 colleges and universities with the support of the Fund for the Advancement of Education.[38] The Fund provided scholarship assistance to 1,350 youngsters who participated in this program. Approximately 42 per cent of these students had completed only 10 years of schooling when admitted to college and almost one third were under 16 years of age. The scholars were selected according to high aptitude and social and emotional maturity. Although matched against older college students of comparable ability, the scholars tended to match or exceed the comparison students in academic performance and achievement tests. The scholars, as a group, also tended to make satisfactory social and emotional adjustments in college, despite their younger ages than the regular college population.

Although some colleges maintain programs for early admission, there appears to be no clear trend toward this type of academic acceleration at the present time. Despite the very favorable results from academic acceleration of carefully selected high-school students, parents are somewhat reluctant to have their youngsters enter college and leave home at the end of the sophomore or junior year of high school.

OTHER SPECIAL PROGRAMS. A number of colleges and universities are offering special noncredit summer programs for promising high-school students. The purposes are to acquaint these youngsters with the university and to provide them with learning enrichment. The National Science Foundation supports summer training programs on various college campuses for outstanding high-school students. N.S.F. also sponsors a visiting scientist program for secondary schools and traveling science libraries. An increasing number of school districts are providing summer courses for the acceleration and enrichment of high-achieving students.

RECENT REFORMS IN CURRICULUM AND INSTRUCTION

In Chapter 7 we discussed some of the recent reforms in curriculum and instruction for certain traditionally recognized areas of general

---

[37] Cyril W. Woolcock, "We're Not Doing Right by the Gifted," *NEA Journal,* 52, November, 1963, 8:31.
[38] See The Fund for the Advancement of Education, *They Went to College Early,* Evaluation Report Number 2 (New York: The Ford Foundation, 1957).

education. In this section we will summarize the principal changes taking place in fields which were not included in Chapter 3 under general education: physics, chemistry, and modern foreign languages.

Of course, the reforms in content and methodology in the various general education subjects relate also to the college preparatory function. And, conversely, some of the so-called college preparatory subjects can serve a general education function.*For example, in the Scandinavian countries, the study of modern foreign languages, particularly English and French, has been geared to serve for general education. Youngsters of normal intelligence, exposed to proper methods, are able to develop functional fluency in a foreign tongue. In our own society, however, the study of foreign languages has been limited primarily to those high school students who are college bound. Recent approaches in introducing foreign languages in our elementary schools, however, demonstrate that children of average intelligence can develop reasonable fluency in a second language. Nevertheless, present trends indicate that, for the most part, the study of foreign languages in our secondary schools will be directed at those students who are preparing for college.

Curriculum Improvement in Modern Foreign Languages

Since the early 1950's the Modern Language Association has been making efforts to improve our approaches to foreign language teaching in the elementary and secondary grades. Prior to 1950 very little foreign language teaching was to be found in the elementary schools. And the study of foreign languages in the high schools was limited largely to college preparatory students. But even after three or four years of studying a foreign language in the high school, most students were unable to speak, read or write with any real degree of fluency. The traditional approach was to study *about* a foreign language rather than *learn* the language. Under the traditional approach the student was required to think constantly in English. It was assumed that one began the learning of a language through grammar and vocabulary drills and memoriter work, even though no child ever learned his native tongue in this way.

However, since the turn of the century the direct method of foreign-language instruction has been practiced in Denmark, enabling youngsters to develop functional fluency in a foreign tongue. Today in Denmark, many youngsters who are not going on to college are able to develop conversational and reading facility in one and even two foreign languages.

Under the leadership of the Modern Language Association of America, and with the support of N.D.E.A. funds, a significant change is taking place in the methods and materials of foreign-language teaching. Students begin by hearing and speaking the language without the necessity of constant translation to English and back again to the foreign tongue. While this approach has been labeled the audio-lingual or aural-oral method, the learning of a language is facilitated through visual experiences. Even the facial expressions and gestures of the conversants are important in conveying meaning and feeling. Moreover, language-learning is facilitated through observing and participating in situations involving conversation. Such situations require many visuals that are integral to the conversational episode. Consequently, we might more accurately use the term audio-visual-lingual method.

The newer approaches utilize formal grammar only when it serves in a functional context. Even the reading and writing is learned quite directly while being related constantly to the hearing and speaking of the language.

Technological aids are being employed to simulate the natural contexts of language learning. The development of the language laboratory, and the use of television, motion pictures, and audio recordings have facilitated language learning. The employment of team teaching enables students to observe and hear conversations in role-playing situations.

Because of our geographic isolation it is not possible for students to make use of a foreign tongue in everyday life. Unless language facility is constantly developing and growing, it tends to melt away. This is a real problem in attempts at learning a foreign language in our country. Another problem is the in-service training of foreign language teachers who have been practicing traditional methods. But considerable progress is being made through N.D.E.A. sponsored language institutes for teachers.

Curriculum Improvement in Science

Since 1956 the Physical Science Study Committee (PSSC) at the Massachusetts Institute of Technology has been developing materials for improving the content and process in high school physics courses. Under an annual budget of some $300,000, this group has completely overhauled the high school curriculum in physics. In addition to new textual material, the PSSC has developed a series of motion pictures, teacher guidebooks, and examinations—all of which are designed for integrated use. The films provide inquiry approaches to experiments conducted by outstanding physicists with equipment that may not be available in the high school. Emphasis is on developing in the student the attitudes and skills characteristic of scientific investigation. Instead of merely following a laboratory manual like a cookbook, the student must think very much like a scientist who is attempting to solve a problem. The curriculum in physics is developed around key concepts that form the structure of modern physics. Emphasis is not on covering more information in physics, but rather in developing the capacity for generative learning. Instead of merely emphasizing encyclopedic knowledge or accumulated facts, the stress is on how to discover knowledge.

Other projects in the improvement of science in the high school share very similar goals and attributes as PSSC. The Chemical Education Material Study (CHEM), initiated in 1960, and now located at the University of California at Berkeley, represents an approach to high-school chemistry based on inquiry through experiments. CHEM has developed a textbook, teachers' guide, equipment for experiments, motion pictures, and other visual materials. Experiments follow an inquiry mode and are designed to precede the reading material in the textbook. The films provide opportunities to study experiments that cannot be undertaken in the regular high-school laboratory. The laboratory experiences in school are designed to stimulate students to hypothesize and discover generalizations for themselves. The textual material deals with concepts that, insofar as possible, can be tested by the student through experimental inquiry. All the examinations are administered on an open-book basis, enabling students to learn how to use reference materials effectively, rather than to rely on rote information or the recall of facts.

Secondary Education and Higher Education

In this chapter we have been concerned with the changing college scene and the changing academic curriculum in the secondary school. In the changing college scene we find some educators and critics of education who prefer to see the college as a more selective institution. But selective measures often have a tendency of becoming restrictive measures. European higher education is now feeling the pangs of this dilemma. Improving educational opportunity rather than restricting it is the great challenge of our times. In 1964 the Educational Policies Commission of the N.E.A. released a report advocating two years of free universal public education beyond the high school.[39] While this recommendation may appear Utopian to many people, it should be remembered that California's public junior colleges are already providing this opportunity.

Increased competitiveness and selection for higher education may tend to cause colleges to become more prescriptive regarding college preparatory work, either explicitly or implicitly, through their admissions practices. In efforts to meet the competition, high schools may tend to play it safe with a conventional and conforming college-preparatory

---

[39] Educational Policies Commission, *Universal Opportunity for Education Beyond the High School* (Washington, D.C.: National Education Association, 1964).

Photo by Herb Comess

". . . the discovery of facts and the creation
of one's own conclusions are the ultimate
joys of learning."

—HAROLD TAYLOR

curriculum, rather than experimenting with different patterns and combinations.

Turning to the changes in course content and process in the academic fields, we see a clear trend at the national level to give priorities to science, mathematics, and modern foreign languages. It is time that we recognize the areas of English language arts, the social studies, and the arts as no less important to our well-being.

On the positive side, there are some beginning efforts to build better balance in the curriculum. And there is a growing tendency on the part of university scholars to turn from criticism and to work constructively with school people on curriculum improvement. Perhaps the most exciting and promising changes now taking place in the academic curriculum lie in the renewed emphasis being given to inquiry and discovery. For true education is not a matter of knowing; it is seeking to know.

SUMMARY

The tremendous growth in college enrollments during the 1960's is the result of (1) the increase in the college-age population, and (2) the unprecedented demand to pursue higher education. The great enrollment pressures have led to higher standards of selectivity being exercized by both public and private colleges and universities.

The growing competitiveness for college admission has resulted in increased reliance on external testing programs and renewed emphasis on prescribed college-preparatory subjects. Rank-in-class also has become an important criterion for college admission.

Through more rigid selection practices there is danger that some of our students with high potential may be denied entrance to college. The divergent thinker, the later bloomer, and the boy or girl from a socially deprived environment may be turned away without being given a chance to meet the challenges and opportunities of a higher education.

Existing research fails to support standardized aptitude and achievement tests as valid predictors of academic performance. Moreover, there is no conclusive evidence that a specific list of course credits or units will produce success in college. Yet these factors are becoming increasingly important as criteria for college admission.

In some states the public junior college is helping more youths to continue their education while living at home. Our national need is to find the ways and means to improve the opportunities for higher education, rather than to seek devices for curtailing enrollments.

In too many high schools there is danger that the college-preparatory curriculum will become primarily a test or hurdle through which students seek high grades for admission to the right college. The curriculum before college should carry the challenges and satisfactions of enlightenment.

PROBLEMS FOR STUDY AND DISCUSSION

1. In referring to the degree to which a society provides opportunities for the higher education of its youth, C. P. Snow makes this appeal: "If we are going to make mistakes about human possibilities, for God's sake let's make them on the generous side." What does Snow mean by this? Do you agree with him? Why or why not?

2. What differences in admission standards exist in your own state on the part of the state university, state colleges, and public junior colleges?

3. Paul Woodring observed: "If Harvard is to be given credit for Kennedy's achievements, Southwest Texas State Teachers College deserves equal credit for the special talents of the new president. It is not likely to get it."[40] Do you agree with Woodring? Why or why not?

4. Construct several hypothetical high-school records and other data for some fictional applicants to your university. Then have individual students in your class rank these high-school applicants in order of preference. How do these rankings differ? What weightings would you assign to various criteria for college admissions?

5. Compare your high-school and college grade point averages. Do the differences appear significant? How do you account for these differences or lack of differences?

6. How do you account for the failure of studies to show any best or preferred curriculum patterns in preparing high-school students for college? Should high schools be encouraged by colleges to experiment with different college-preparatory curricula? Why or why not?

7. Do the data in this chapter support the accusation that higher-ability students in our high schools tend to seek the easy credits? How do you account for the discrepancies often found between ability and achievement?

8. What is meant by structure of a discipline? Why is this deemed so important in curriculum-making and in teaching methods?[41]

---

[40] Paul Woodring, "Can State Colleges Educate for Excellence?", *Saturday Review*, April 18, 1964, p. 55.

[41] See Jerome S. Bruner, *The Process of Education* (Cambridge, Mass.: Harvard University Press, 1960), p. 7.

9. It is frequently argued that the newer curricula require a reduction in the amount of subject matter to be covered. Assuming that this is often the case, what counter-arguments can you offer regarding the advantages of the newer curricula?

SELECTED REFERENCES

Alberty, Harold B. and Elsie J. Alberty. *Reorganizing the High School Curriculum* (3rd Ed.) New York: The Macmillan Company, 1962, Ch. 7.

Alexander, Uhlman S. (ed.) *Supervision for Quality Education in Science.* Washington, D.C.: Office of Education, U.S. Department of Health, Education, and Welfare, 1963.

American Educational Research Association. *Review of Educational Research,* "Higher Education," Vol. 30, No. 4, October, 1960.

Anderson, Kenneth E. (ed.) *Research on the Academically Talented Student.* Washington, D.C.: National Education Association, 1961.

———. *The Coming Crisis in College Admissions.* Washington, D.C.: National Education Association, 1960.

Association for Supervision and Curriculum Development. *Using Current Curriculum Developments.* Washington, D.C.: The Association, 1963.

Bestor, Arthur. *The Restoration of Learning.* New York: Alfred A. Knopf, Inc., 1955.

Black, Hillel. *They Shall Not Pass.* New York: William Morrow & Co., Inc., 1963.

Broudy, Harry S., B. O. Smith and Joe R. Burnett. *Democracy and Excellence in American Secondary Education.* Chicago: Rand McNally & Company, 1964.

Bruner, Jerome S. *The Process of Education.* Cambridge, Mass.: Harvard University Press, 1960.

Campbell, Roald F. and Robert A. Bunnell (eds.) *Nationalizing Influences on Secondary Education.* Chicago: Midwest Administration Center, The University of Chicago, 1963.

Chamberlin, Dean et al. *Did They Succeed in College?* New York: Harper & Row, Publishers, Inc., 1943.

Cole, Charles C., Jr. *Encouraging Scientific Talent.* New York: College Entrance Examination Board, 1956.

College Entrance Examination Board. *The Behavioral Sciences and Education.* Princeton, N.J.: The Board, 1963.

———. *The Changing College Preparatory Curriculum.* Princeton, N.J.: The Board, 1962.

Conant, James Bryant. *Slums and Suburbs.* New York: McGraw-Hill Company, Inc., 1961.

———. *The American High School Today.* New York: McGraw-Hill Company, Inc., 1959.

Educational Policies Commission. *Universal Opportunity for Education Beyond the High School.* Washington, D.C.: National Education Association, 1964.

Fraser, Dorothy M. *Curriculum Studies in Academic Subjects.* Washington, D.C.: National Education Association, 1962.

Fund for the Advancement of Education. *They Went to College Early.* New York: The Ford Foundation, 1957.

Gardner, John W. *Excellence.* New York: Harper & Row, Publishers, Inc., 1961.

Greer, Edith S. and Richard M. Harbeck. *What High School Pupils Study.* Washington, D.C.: Office of Education, U.S. Department of Health, Education, and Welfare, 1962.

Heath, Robert W. (ed.) *New Curricula.* New York: Harper & Row, Publishers, Inc., 1964.

Jacob, Philip E. *Changing Values in College.* New York: Harper & Row, Publishers, Inc., 1957.

Krug, Edward A. *The Secondary School Curriculum.* New York: Harper & Row, Publishers, Inc., 1960, Chs. 6, 7, 9, 10, 11, 12, 13.

McConnell, T. R. *A General Pattern for American Public Higher Education.* New York: McGraw-Hill Company, Inc., 1962.

National Education Association. *Schools for the Sixties.* New York: McGraw-Hill Company, Inc., 1963.

————. *The Scholars Look at the Schools.* Washington, D.C.: The Association, February, 1962.

Rickover, Hyman G. *American Education—A National Failure.* New York: E. P. Dutton & Co., Inc., 1963.

Rockefeller Brothers Fund. *Education and the Pursuit of Excellence.* Garden City, N.Y.: Doubleday & Company, Inc., 1958.

Rosenbloom, Paul C. and Paul C. Hillestad (eds.) *Modern Viewpoints in the Curriculum.* New York: McGraw-Hill Company, Inc., 1964.

Sanford, Nevitt (ed.) *The American College.* New York: John Wiley & Sons, Inc., 1962.

Whitehead, Alfred North. *The Aims of Education and Other Essays.* New York: The Macmillan Company, 1929.

CHAPTER 9

Education for the World of Work

THE HARVARD REPORT, *General Education in a Free Society,* compares general education to "the trunk of a tree from which branches, representing specialism, go off at different heights. . . ."[1] In this chapter, we shall examine the specialism known as vocational education. In a sense, we can say that even general education contributes to vocational proficiency. In other words, there is no sharp line of demarcation between general education and vocational education. While general education may be defined as those curricular experiences designed for all citizens in a democratic society, vocational education is concerned with those curricular experiences necessary for proficiency in a specific vocation. Obviously, general education is the foundation for any vocation.

Every productive member of our society is engaged in a specific vocation, whether a nuclear physicist, a farmer, or a homemaker. Almost every major statement on the goals of secondary education in the twentieth century includes vocational education as an important aim. One of the seven *Cardinal Principles of Secondary Education,* proposed by the NEA Commission on the Reorganization of Secondary Education in 1918, was education for a vocation. In 1944, the Educational Policies Commission of the NEA declared in its report, *Education for ALL American Youth:* "All youth need to develop salable skills and those understandings and attitudes that make the worker an intelligent and productive participant in economic life."[2] The Conant report of 1959 also called for

---

[1] Report of the Harvard Committee, *General Education in a Free Society* (Cambridge, Mass.: Harvard University Press, 1945), p. 102.

[2] Educational Policies Commission, *Education for ALL American Youth* (Washington, D.C.: National Education Association, 1944), p. 216.

353

diversified programs in our comprehensive high schools for the development of marketable skills.[3]

BACKGROUND AND DEVELOPMENT

In the American colonies, orphans and children of the poor were bound out to masters as apprentices. Such apprenticeship was compulsory under provisions of the poor law. Parents of average means, on the other hand, might arrange for a voluntary agreement for apprenticing their youngster in a given trade. The schools of colonial America, as discussed in Chapter 1, were obsessed primarily with education for spiritual salvation, rather than being concerned with the life needs of a frontier settlement.

Benjamin Franklin's academy, which was the dominant form of secondary education in America between 1760 and 1870, included some practical studies in its curriculum. But the academy was a private, tuition school, enrolling only a very small proportion of the youth.

During the first half of the nineteenth century, a number of schools were established here on the pattern of Fellenberg's school in Switzerland, which combined schooling with farming. Such schools were founded in Connecticut (1819), Maine (1821), Massachusetts (1824), Kentucky (1826), New York (1827), Pennsylvania (1829), New Jersey (1830), Virginia (1831), Georgia and Tennessee (1832), and North Carolina (1834). A number of similar schools for industrial training were later established in New York, Massachusetts, and elsewhere. But lacking legislative support, the manual-labor school began to disappear around the middle of the nineteenth century. Some of these schools evolved into such institutions of higher education as Rensselaer Polytechnic Institute, Western Reserve, Oberlin, and Knox.

While vocational education had become well established in such European countries as Switzerland, Germany, Austria, Denmark, and France by the last half of the nineteenth century, a real movement in this area did not get under way in the United States until after World War I. Some privately sponsored trade schools had been established here before the turn of the century, but these did not constitute a concerted public movement.

The Land-Grant Colleges

The Morrill Act of 1862, signed by President Lincoln, provided each state with 30,000 acres of public land for each congressman—the proceeds of which were to be used in establishing colleges of agriculture

---

[3] James Bryant Conant, *The American High School Today* (New York: McGraw-Hill Company, Inc., 1959), p. 81.

and the mechanic arts. This federal act led to the formation of state colleges and universities in many states where, previously, higher education had been left to private interests. In other states, the existing state university was designated as the land-grant institution. Agriculture, engineering, and other applied sciences became recognized as important elements of higher education in our society as a result of this far-reaching legislation.

While the Morrill Act stipulated that other scientific and classical studies not be excluded, the vocational intent of the legislation was clearly stated. Thus, vocational education of college grade was enacted by law long before the existence of a systematic, publicly supported vocational program at the secondary level.

Vocational Education of Less Than College Grade

Although some of the states had established modest programs for vocational education of less than college level before the turn of the century, progress was indeed slow and erratic. In 1913 a Presidential Commission was established to investigate the need for federal aid for vocational education. The commission's findings strongly supported the need for national vocational education by pointing to the fact that less than one per cent of the millions of persons engaged in agriculture, manufacturing, and mechanical pursuits had adequate opportunity for vocational and technical training.

America's need for food, fiber, and technically trained manpower during World War I led finally to the passage of the Smith-Hughes Act of 1917. This legislation provided federal funds to be matched, dollar for dollar, for vocational education of less than college grade for persons over fourteen years of age. In most cases such vocational education programs were administered as an integral part of the existing public schools. Instructional programs in agriculture, home economics, industry, and commerce were now clearly in the domain of the public secondary school.

Additional federal funds for vocational education have been provided through such subsequent legislation as the George-Reed Act of 1929, the George-Ellzey Act of 1935, and the George-Deen Act of 1937. The George-Deen Act provided a substantial increase in funds on a continuing basis for vocational education in agriculture, home economics, trade and industrial education, and distributive education. In 1946, the George-Barden Act provided increased appropriations for programs of vocational education.

During the depression years, vocational classes were provided for unemployed persons over 16 years of age through the Works Progress Administration. The National Youth Administration sponsored vocational classes for youth enrolled in its work-project program. Many of these work projects were operated in public secondary schools and public institutions of higher education.

In 1940 the National Defense Training Program was established to prepare workers for defense industries. Under this program, many schools provided day classes for in-school youth and night classes for training workers for defense industries.

Vocational Education and Rehabilitation of War Veterans

Rehabilitation programs for disabled veterans date back to World War I. Under the Smith-Sears Act of 1918, more than 128,000 disabled veterans completed training courses in a ten-year period from 1918 to 1928. Public Law 16 provided for the vocational rehabilitation of disabled veterans of World War II. Some 639,000 disabled veterans participated in this program between 1943 and 1955.

The Servicemen's Readjustment Act of 1944, commonly known as the G.I. Bill of Rights, provided funds for veterans of World War II to pursue educational opportunities. Although many of the veterans entered college, more than 3.8 million veterans enrolled in education programs below college level. About ten per cent of these entered high school, while the others enrolled in special trade and industrial schools or pursued correspondence courses. A number of proprietary trade schools were established to accommodate these veterans, since the public schools were limited in facilities. Some of the proprietary schools were of dubious value, and soon after the expiration of the G.I. Bill such schools disappeared.

Federal subsistence payments were also made for veterans participating in on-the-farm and on-the-job training. More than 1.5 million veterans enrolled in such training programs.

Under the G.I. Bill over 7.8 million veterans participated in instructional programs at a cost of over 14.5 billion dollars. Similar benefits were extended to veterans of the Korean conflict in 1952.

Recent Federal Legislation

The Area Redevelopment Act (1961) provided federal funds (to 1965) for vocational education for persons in economically distressed areas. The Manpower Development and Training Act (1962) allocated federal funds (to 1965) for training and skill development programs in connection with unemployment problems.

In December of 1963 President Johnson signed a bill extending and broadening the provisions of the 1962 act. The new measure provides for basic education in reading and writing in connection with job training. Under the 1962 act, many unemployed persons were ineligible because of their inability to meet minimum aptitude and sixth-grade literacy requirements. The 1963 act includes these disadvantaged persons.

Also in December of 1963, President Johnson signed a measure allocating federal funds for the construction of vocational schools and providing financial assistance for youth pursuing work-study programs. This bill marked the first time that federal funds were allocated for vocational school construction. Through its financial assistance and work-study provisions, many youths will be encouraged to remain in school. This section of the measure has a precedent in the National Youth Administration of the 1930's.

The 1963 bills on vocational education will more than double the current level of federal appropriations by 1965, and will effect a five-fold increase by 1967.

ENROLLMENTS AND EXPENDITURES IN COOPERATIVE FEDERAL-STATE PROGRAMS

The federal vocational education acts provide funds to stimulate and assist programs that are under public supervision and control, of less than college grade, and for persons over fourteen years of age. The over-all purpose of vocational education under these federal acts is "to fit persons for useful employment."[4] The cooperative federal-state programs of vocational education are designed for both in-school and out-of-school youths, as well as for adults. Encompassed by these programs are the fields of agriculture, distribution, homemaking, and trades and industry. In addition, the programs provide for the training of skilled technicians to meet national defense needs and requirements in other specialized areas, such as practical nurse education.

Enrollment and Expenditures

Today, more than four million students are enrolled in federally reimbursed programs of vocational education of less than college grade. Each state has a board for vocational education empowered to carry out the provisions of these federal vocational education acts. The annual expenditures for such vocational education programs today amount to more than $51.4 million from the Federal Government and over $232 million from state and local sources. Although the annual federal contribution to vocational education of $51.4 million is a significant sum, the cost of one Polaris submarine in 1963, excluding the missiles and warheads, cost the Federal Government over $116,000,000.

---

[4] Office of Education, *Public Vocational Education Programs* (Washington, D.C.: U.S. Department of Health, Education, and Welfare, April, 1960), p. 1.

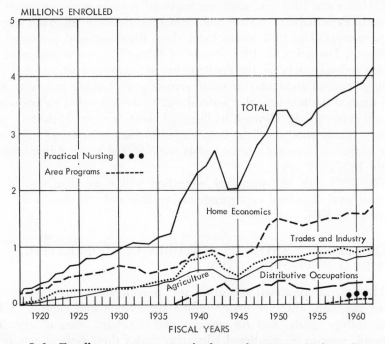

FIGURE 9–1. Enrollment in vocational classes by type of class. [SOURCE: Office of Education, *Digest of Annual Reports of State Boards for Vocational Education* (Washington, D.C.: U.S. Department of Health, Education, and Welfare, 1963), p. 3.]

Figure 9–1 shows the enrollments in various vocational classes from 1917 to 1962. Expenditures of federal, state, and local funds for vocational education are shown in Figure 9–2 and Table 9–1.

Of the more than 4 million enrolled in vocational education of less than college grade in 1962, some 42 per cent were in homemaking, 25 per cent in trades and industries, 20 per cent in agriculture, 8 per cent in distributive occupations, and 1 per cent in practical nursing.

Federal-State-Local Relationships

As required by the federal vocational education acts, each state has designated a state board for vocationl education to cooperate with the United States Office of Education in the development and supervision of vocational education. The chief state school officer in each state usually serves as the executive officer of the board. Each state develops a plan for vocational education, which includes standards for teachers, supervisors, and directors of vocational education. While the plans and

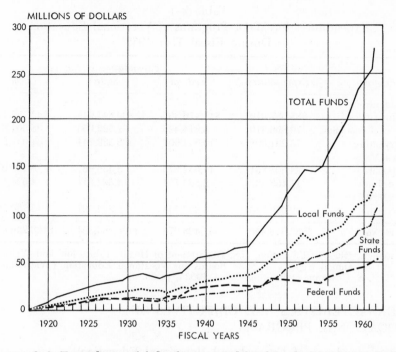

MILLIONS OF DOLLARS

FIGURE 9–2. Expenditure of federal, state, and local funds for vocational education. [SOURCE: Office of Education, *Digest of Annual Reports of State Boards for Vocational Education* (Washington, D.C.: U.S. Department of Health, Education, and Welfare, 1963), p. 4.]

standards vary somewhat from state to state, they must be approved by the Office of Education to qualify for federal support. Federal funds are appropriated to the state and the expenditure of such funds is administered through the state board for vocational education.

Federal appropriations to each state must at least be matched by state and/or local funds for vocational education. Consequently, although every state participates in these federal vocational programs, enrollment and expenditures vary widely from state to state, as shown in Table 9–2. The range in enrollment per 1,000 population varied from 5.0 for New Jersey to 40.2 for Georgia in 1961.

Nationally, state and local expenditures for vocational education far exceed the federal appropriations. Federal funds are used primarily for salaries and travel of teachers, teacher educators, supervisors, and directors of vocational education.

An organization chart showing the federal-state-local relationships for public vocational education is shown in Figure 9–3.

Table 9–1

Expenditures for Major Programs of Vocational Education
During Fiscal Year 1962

| Program | Total Expenditures | Expenditures by Source | | |
		Federal	State	Local
Trades & Industries	$85,087,010	$11,476,867	$30,847,949	$42,762,194
Home Economics	79,898,310	8,874,426	32,522,053	38,501,830
Agriculture	73,291,898	13,644,907	28,589,744	31,057,246
Area Vocational	24,605,851	11,042,875	5,456,967	8,106,010
Distributive	11,405,837	2,564,754	4,302,611	4,538,472
Practical Nursing	9,659,540	3,834,245	2,544,997	3,280,299
TOTAL	$283,948,446	$51,438,074	$104,264,321	$128,246,051

SOURCE: Office of Education, U.S. Department of Health, Education, and Welfare, *Digest* of Annual Reports of State Boards for Vocational Education (Washington, D.C.: U.S. Government Printing Office, 1963), p. 28.

CHARACTERISTICS AND OBJECTIVES OF VOCATIONAL PROGRAMS

Interdependence of General and Vocational Education

Despite the specificity of the federal acts, vocational education should not be conceived as narrow training for skills in various job categories. Neither should it be regarded as an entity completely divorced from the rest of the school curriculum.

> It is more inclusive than training for job skills: It also develops abilities, understandings, attitudes, work habits, and appreciations which contribute to a satisfying and productive life. . . .
> The vocational education program does not take the place of general academic education: It supplements and enhances it for students who want training for a chosen occupation. . . . Vocational education is an important part of a well-balanced school program—not a single subject. It is a part of a well-rounded program of studies aimed at developing competent workers and recognizing that the American worker should also be competent economically, socially, emotionally, physically, intellectually, and in a civic sense.[5]

A good general education program is just as important for the vocational student as for the one who is preparing for college. Both have an equal vote in determining our political leadership and decision-making on vital community questions. Moreover, all vocations and professions

---

[5] Office of Education, *Public Vocational Education Programs* (Washington, D.C.: U.S. Department of Health, Education, and Welfare, April, 1960), pp. 1–2.

Table 9–2

Population, Enrollment, and Expenditures for Vocational Education Under the Smith-Hughes and George-Barden Acts in Selected States for Fiscal Year 1961

State	Population (1960 Census)	Enrollment	Enrollment Per 1,000 Population	Total Expenditures (Federal, State, and Local)
California	15,717,204	438,753	27.9	$18,586,550
Colorado	1,753,947	55,324	30.3	2,202,829
Florida	4,951,560	128,817	26.0	8,771,830
Georgia	3,943,116	158,860	40.2	8,512,764
Illinois	10,081,158	113,376	11.3	10,608,158
Iowa	2,757,537	62,466	22.6	3,829,970
Maryland	3,100,689	25,707	8.3	2,408,271
Massachusetts	5,148,578	67,568	13.1	9,220,411
Minnesota	3,413,864	94,117	27.6	6,573,180
New Jersey	6,066,782	30,151	5.0	4,491,867
New York	16,782,304	187,984	11.2	14,640,903
Pennsylvania	11,319,366	102,967	9.1	10,478,282
Texas	9,579,677	366,434	38.3	19,607,404
Washington	2,853,214	106,309	37.9	5,735,413
West Virginia	1,860,421	31,370	16.8	2,402,198
Wisconsin	3,951,777	102,446	26.0	6,370,555

source: Report of the Panel of Consultants on Vocational Education, *Education for a Changing World of Work* (Washington, D.C.: Office of Education, U.S. Department of Health, Education, and Welfare, 1963), pp. 71–72.

Office of Education, *Digest* of Annual Reports of State Boards for Vocational Education (Washington, D.C.: U.S. Department of Health, Education, and Welfare, 1961), p. 13.

require certain basic understandings and competencies that derive from general education.

Many educators believe that vocational education programs should be provided within the framework of the comprehensive high school. In this way, students enrolled in vocational programs are not segregated from those enrolled in college-preparatory, general, and commercial programs of study. In the comprehensive high school, all students, regardless of special interests or vocational plans, are able to pursue a common general education curriculum and participate in common school activities.

Characteristics of Good Vocational Education Programs

Technological changes are occurring at such an accelerated pace that programs of vocational education must be dynamic and realistic if they

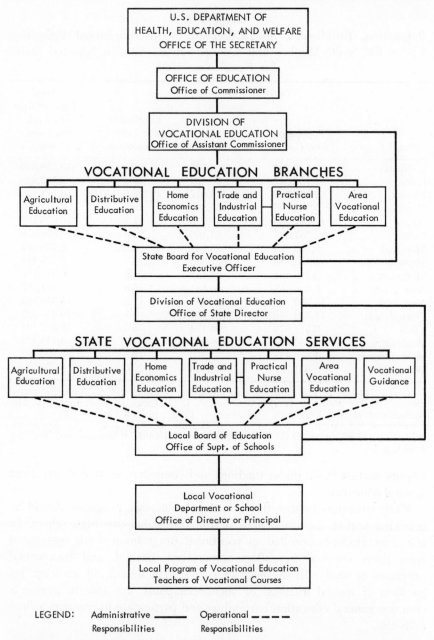

FIGURE 9–3. Organization chart for public reimbursable vocational education. [SOURCE: Office of Education, *Public Vocational Education Programs* (Washington, D.C.: U.S. Department of Health, Education, and Welfare, April, 1960), p. 18.]

are to be successful. Twelve essentials of an effective program of vocational education are

1. The program is directly related to employment opportunities, determined by school officials in cooperation with occupationally concerned and competent individuals and groups.
2. The content of courses is confirmed or changed by periodic analyses of the occupations for which the training is being given.
3. The courses for a specific occupation are set up and maintained with the advice and cooperation of the various occupational groups concerned.
4. The facilities and equipment used in instruction are comparable to those found in the particular occupation.
5. The conditions under which instruction is given duplicate as nearly as possible desirable conditions in the occupation itself and at the same time provide effective learning situations.
6. The length of teaching periods and total hours of instruction are determined by the requirements of the occupation and the needs of the students.
7. Training in a particular occupation is carried to the point of developing marketable skills, abilities, understandings, attitudes, work habits, and appreciations sufficient to enable the trainee to get and hold a job in that occupation.
8. Day and evening classes are scheduled at hours and during seasons convenient to enrollees.
9. Instruction is offered only to persons who need, desire, and can profit from it occupationally.
10. The teachers are competent in the occupation for which they are giving instruction and possess adequate professional qualifications for teaching.
11. Vocational guidance, including effective follow-up of all students who finish or drop out of a course, is an integral and continuing part of the program.
12. Continuous research is an integral part of the program.[6]

PROGRAMS OF VOCATIONAL EDUCATION AND THEIR OBJECTIVES

There are six major federally aided programs of vocational education: agricultural education, distributive education, home economics education, trade and industrial education, practical nurse education, and area vocational education. Vocational education in agriculture is designed to train present and prospective farmers for proficiency in farming. Distributive education applies to occupations concerned with marketing or distributing goods and services, and managing or operating a retail, wholesale, or service business. Vocational homemaking education is concerned with the education of present and prospective homemakers for

---

[6] *Ibid.*, pp. 2–3.

proficiency in the vocation of homemaking. Trade and industrial education deals with the "designing, producing, processing, assembling, maintaining, servicing, or repairing of any manufactured product."[7] This area of vocational education includes the technical occupations such as laboratory technicians, draftsmen, and craftsmen. Practical nurse education applies to the development of proficiency in the performance of nursing duties under the supervision of a licensed physician or registered nurse. The lower age limit is 16 years. Area vocational programs are designed for rapidly developing occupational fields that include highly skilled technicians in engineering and laboratory work. Such programs also provide for the retraining of workers affected by industrial and technological change. Participants in area vocational education programs must be over 16 years of age.

Vocational Education in Agriculture

The efficiency of agricultural production in the United States is at the highest level in our history. But the need for vocational education in agriculture is as great as ever in view of the scientific and technological developments affecting farm production. The farmer who cannot keep abreast of these developments is soon out of business. And although our nation appears to be faced with a problem of agricultural surpluses, the world picture shows a critical and growing need for food and fiber. It is estimated that more than half of the world's population is living in hunger. While the world's population continues to grow, the land area for agricultural purposes has failed to expand. In 1900 the density of world population was approximately 29 persons per square mile of land area. In 1960 it was estimated that there were 46 persons per square mile.

Vocational education in agriculture became part of the curriculum of our rural secondary schools as a result of the Smith-Hughes Act of 1917. Instruction of less than college grade is provided for three groups: (1) day-school students regularly enrolled in high school, (2) out-of-school youth enrolled in young farmer classes, and (3) adult farmers enrolled in evening classes.

Day-school students of vocational agriculture are usually in grades nine through twelve. The classes in vocational agriculture meet about seven clock hours per week. The rest of the time is spent in other high-school studies. Each student in vocational agriculture is required to carry out an approved supervised farming program. The teacher of vocational agriculture supervises this program, which is often conducted on the family farm. Many students of vocational agriculture are able to enter farming on a full-time basis as a result of their expanding super-

---

[7] *Ibid.*, p. 5.

Table 9-3

Characteristics of Vocational Education in Agriculture

Types of Programs	Purposes (All Programs)	For Whom Intended	By Whom Taught	By Whom Instructor Is Employed (All Programs)	How Courses Are Initiated (All Programs)	Advisory Committees (All Programs)
Adult farmer classes—(Meeting at least 10 times per year).	Make a beginning and advance in farming. Produce farm commodities efficiently. Market farm products advantageously. Conserve soil and other natural resources. Manage a farm business. Maintain a favorable environment. Participate in rural leadership activities.	Adult farmers enroll to improve themselves in specific farming occupations.	All types of classes are taught by a qualified teacher who is—farm reared. A graduate of an agricultural college or institution which has been approved by the State Board for Vocational Education to train teachers of vocational agriculture. In special cases instructors other than the above may be employed to teach young farmer and adult farmer classes. They must have had recent and successful experience in the particular jobs or work in which they are to instruct.	The teacher of vocational agriculture is employed by the local school board. Teachers must meet qualification standards outlined in the State Plan for agricultural education.	Courses are initiated by the teacher of agriculture with recommendations from (1) local school officials and (2) local advisory councils or committees, when they exist. Course content is based upon problems in producing and marketing various livestock and crop enterprises and other farm problems of students enrolled in various types of classes. Problems are taught on a seasonal basis. Each student enrolled must conduct a supervised farming program in agriculture for at least six months each year.	A. Composition—Usually composed of from five to nine farmers and business men who represent the agricultural interests in the community. B. Selection—The teacher of vocational agriculture along with the principal and/or superintendent of schools nominate committee members for approval by the board of education. C. Function—To serve in an advisory capacity in planning a program designed to further develop and promote agriculture in the community.
Young farmer classes—(Meet not less than 10 times per year).	Same as above.	Young men who are out of school enroll to develop ability to establish themselves and improve their proficiency in farming.				
Day classes—(Organized in public secondary schools, meeting each school day).	Same as above.	Students who are over 14 years of age and are preparing for farming.				

SOURCE: Office of Education, *Public Vocational Education Programs*, Pamphlet No. 117 (Washington, D.C.: U.S. Department of Health, Education, and Welfare, 1960), p. 11.

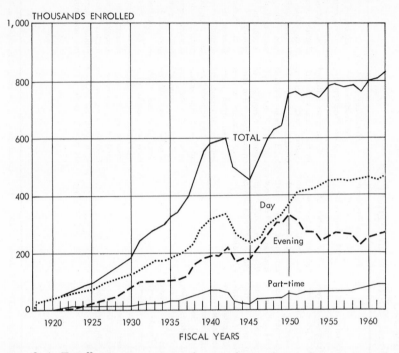

FIGURE 9–4. Enrollment in vocational agriculture classes, by type of class. [SOURCE: Office of Education, *Digest of Annual Reports of State Boards for Vocational Education* (Washington, D.C.: U.S. Department of Health, Education, and Welfare, 1963), p. 7.]

vised farming programs. The teacher of vocational agriculture is employed on a 12-month basis and makes regular visits to the homes of students in order to supervise their farming programs and to consult with parents.

Most day-school students of vocational agriculture hold membership in the Future Farmers of America. The F.F.A. is regarded as an integral part of the vocational agriculture curriculum and F.F.A. activities include community leadership and service projects. Because of the tradition of racial segregation in the schools of the South, the New Farmers of America, or N.F.A., was established to serve Negro youth enrolled in vocational agriculture in segregated schools. As such schools are desegregated, the N.F.A. will become absorbed into the F.F.A.

Young farmer classes for out-of-school youth are required to meet for a minimum of 30 clock hours per year, while adult farmer classes meet for at least twenty clock hours per year. Figure 9–4 shows the growth in enrollment of vocational agriculture classes. In 1962 some 883,000 students were enrolled, of which approximately 474,000 were day students.

Vocational Education for Trades and Industries

The Smith-Hughes Vocational Education Act of 1917 established vocational education in trades and industries for high-school youth and adults. This program is aimed at developing skills and technical proficiency in industrial occupations. Classes in vocational industrial education include (1) youth regularly enrolled in high school, (2) youth in supervised work-experience programs combined with systematic classwork in school, and (3) adults who may be employed and are enrolled in special classes.

Full-time day students may spend one half of the school day in technical classes and shop work, with the remaining half day devoted to other high-school subjects. Out-of-school youth may enroll on a part-time basis. General continuation classes for cooperative diversified occupations are designed to provide supervised work experience for high-school youth in a number of occupations. Such students devote at least 15 hours per week to on-the-job experience, which is supervised by the school and supplemented by related classroom studies. Other part-time classes may be provided for employed adult workers. Like all federally reimbursed programs of vocational education, all enrollees must be at least 14 years of age. Vocational industrial education programs have become increasingly important as technology has increased the demand for skilled workers while bringing about unemployment among the unskilled labor force. In 1962 over 1,000,000 persons were enrolled in vocational classes in trades and industries, of which more than 294,000 were day students. Figure 9–5 shows the enrollment trends in the various classes from 1917 to the present. In recent years, a number of junior colleges and community colleges have been developing programs for training the highly skilled technician.

Vocational Education for Distributive Occupations

With the tremendous rise in industrial production in our nation during the twentieth century, the process of distributing and servicing these products has grown to enormous proportions. Vocational distributive education developed as part of the federally aided program of vocational education during the 1930's. Today some 321,000 are enrolled in distributive education classes. However, almost 90 per cent of this enrollment is comprised of out-of-school youth and adults in evening classes.

Distributive occupations include workers in advertising, wholesaling, retailing, transporting, storing, employing, and so on. It is estimated that at least half of the consumer's dollar goes into the cost of transferring

Table 9-4

Characteristics of Vocational Education in Trades and Industries

Types of Programs	Purpose	For Whom Intended	By Whom Taught	By Whom Instructor Is Employed	How Courses Are Initiated	Advisory Committees (For All Programs)
Trade extension (evening, part-time).	To give instruction and training to supplement the job experience in a craft or occupation in which training is to be provided.	Employed trade and industrial adult workers including supervisors and foremen.	An instructor of ability, skill, experience, and standing in the trade.	Generally by local board of education through cooperation with advisory committees.	By local board of education on: Request from management and/or labor, or Request from advisory committee, or Request from group or individual workers.	A. *Composition*—Equal representation from management and labor in general advisory or craft committees with school representation to serve in a consultative capacity. B. *Selection*—Appointed by the school authority on the basis of recommendations from management and labor. C. *Functions Relating to Programs:* 1. Assist in determining training needs. 2. Recommend competent persons to provide instructions in industrial subjects. 3. Assist in determining course content and length of courses. 4. Inform the respective groups of training services available.
Apprentice instruction (evening or day-time).	To provide technical shop and other related instruction supplementary to the job experience. Subjects to be taught usually determined in cooperation with joint apprenticeship committees.	Persons employed as bona fide apprentices in a trade or industrial occupation.	Skills taught on-the-job by employers; related instruction same as for trade extension.	Generally by local board of education through cooperation with advisory committees.	By local board of education on: Request of joint apprenticeship or craft committee, or Request of management and/or labor union.	
Preemployment training (evening or day-time).	Brief intensive training for entrance into employment in a specific industrial job or retraining the worker for a new position.	Out-of-school youth and/or adults.	An instructor of ability, skill, experience, and standing in the occupation.	Generally by local board of education through cooperation with advisory committees.	By local board of education on: Request from employment service, or Request from employers, or Request from groups of individual workers.	

						(Same for all programs)
Part-time cooperative (day-time).	To provide training in the occupation at which he is employed and at the same time complete a general education. Not considered apprenticeship.	Students in schools who are legally employed and working at least 15 hours per week as learners in an industrial occupation.	Skills taught on-the-job by employers; related technical and general education subjects by instructors.	Instructors of related and general subjects in public schools employed by local board of education usually through cooperation with advisory committee.	By local board of education through: Desires and needs of students for training through part-time employment, and Discovery of opportunities for such employment training through cooperation with employers and advisory committees.	
Preparatory training full-time (day schools).	To prepare for entrance into useful employment in an industrial occupation and provide an opportunity to continue a general education. It is that type of vocational education given in full-time day trade or technical institute classes.	In-school youth who have selected a specific occupation.	Vocational work taught by an instructor of ability, skill, experience, and standing in the trade; general subject taught by instructors regularly qualified for teaching the subjects.	Local board of education employs all instructors. Instructors of vocational subjects in day trade schools usually selected through cooperation with advisory committees.	By local board of education through: Survey of employment opportunities in community, and Desires of students to remain in school full-time and receive initial training in specific trades or industrial occupations in which there is a need, and Cooperation with craft committees in planning facilities and courses.	

SOURCE: Office of Education, *Public Vocational Education Programs* Pamphlet No. 117 (Washington, D.C.: U.S. Department of Health, Education, and Welfare, 1960), pp. 14–15.

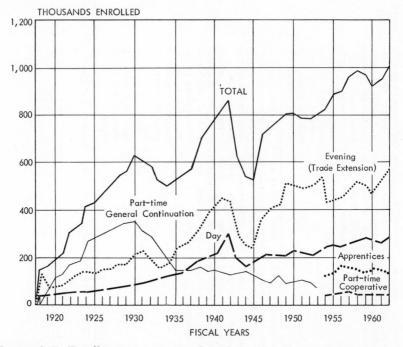

Figure 9–5. Enrollment in vocational trades and industry classes, by type of class. [Source: Office of Education, *Digest of Annual Reports of State Boards for Vocational Education* (Washington, D.C.: U.S. Department of Health, Education, and Welfare, 1963), p. 17.]

goods from the producer to the consumer and providing the necessary services. Approximately one fifth of the employed civilian labor force is engaged in distributive occupations.

Cooperative part-time classes are provided by the secondary school for students who combine their high-school studies with supervised work experience in a distributive occupation. On-the-job experience must equal or exceed the time spent in school studies. Supervision of work experience is provided by the school and the employer. The in-school program includes students in grades 11 and 12 and the first two years of post-high-school work including the junior college.

Adult extension classes are also provided for workers engaged in distribution. Figure 9–6 shows the enrollment trends in vocational distributive education classes. The sharp decline in enrollment between 1950 and 1955 was caused by a temporary decrease in federal funds for this program. The enrollment in vocational distributive education is very small considering the size of the work force in distributive occupations.

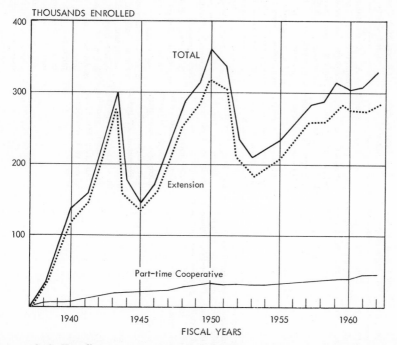

THOUSANDS ENROLLED

TOTAL

Extension

Part-time Cooperative

FISCAL YEARS

FIGURE 9–6. Enrollment in vocational distributive occupations classes, by type of class. [SOURCE: Office of Education, *Digest of Annual Reports of State Boards for Vocational Education* (Washington, D.C.: U.S. Department of Health, Education, and Welfare, 1963), p. 9.]

Vocational Home Economics Education

More than 1.7 million students are enrolled in federally reimbursed programs of vocational education in home economics. Enrollment has expanded rapidly since the passage of the Smith-Hughes Act of 1917. Over one million students were enrolled in regular day classes in 1962, with 663,000 in evening and part-time courses.

Classes are provided for full-time high-school students in grades 9 through 12, and also for out-of-school youth and adults. In-school students generally devote one clock hour or two forty-five-minute periods daily for a full unit of credit over the school year. The rest of the student's schedule is generally devoted to four other high-school subjects in addition to homemaking.

The homemaking curriculum is concerned with foods and nutrition, clothing and textiles, home-planning, and family relationships. Adequate nutrition remains a serious problem for large segments of our population.

Table 9–5

Characteristics of Vocational Education in Distributive Occupations

Types of Programs	Purpose	For Whom Intended	By Whom Taught	By Whom Instructor Is Employed	How Courses Are Initiated	Advisory Committees (Where Such Committees Exist)
Extension classes (day or evening).	To give technical instruction and skill training to supplement job experience of worker.	Adults employed as distributive workers, including managers, department heads, and supervisors.	An instructor who has vocational competence in the occupation taught.	Generally employed by or under direction of local school board.	By local school board on: Request of individual or groups of individuals, or Request of management or employees, or Advice of an advisory committee where such committee exists.	A. *Composition*—Representative from employers and/or employees on general committees. School representatives and representatives of the public, sometimes as committee members, attending the meetings. B. *Selection*—Appointed by the superintendent of schools from lists recommended by the local coordinator of distributive education. C. *Functions Relating to the Program:* 1. Advise on training needs. 2. Advise on various topics relating to instruction such as course content and length of courses. 3. Advise on and often assist in the promotion of the training program or individual classes. 4. Advise on qualifications and activities of teaching personnel.
Cooperative part-time high school courses.	To provide basic and supplementary training in the occupation in which the student is employed, and at the same time, complete his high school education.	Students in secondary schools who are legally employed at least 15 hours per week in a distributive occupation.	Training on the job by a sponsor employed by the establishment and training in school by a qualified distributive instructor and general school teachers.	Instructors in school are employed by public school authorities. On-the-job sponsors paid by the employer.	By local school board on: Survey of training needs in local communities, Requests of individual students who need training through instruction and part-time employment, and Promotion of training for employment by school officials, management, and/or, Advisory committee where such committee exists.	

SOURCE: Office of Education, *Public Vocational Education Programs,* Pamphlet No. 117 (Washington, D. C.: U.S. Department of Health, Education,

Table 9-6

Characteristics of Vocational Education in Home Economics

Types of Programs	Purpose	For Whom Intended	By Whom Taught	By Whom Instructor Is Employed	How Courses Are Initiated	Advisory Committees
Adult education in home economics (homemaking).	To help homemakers improve the quality of their family life through better use of human and material resources.	Any adult man or woman who has responsibility for homemaking and family living.	Home economics teachers certified to teach in the State or skilled workers from some occupations closely related to homemaking.	Local board of education.	By request from adult groups, provision of local school for instruction for adults or upon recommendation of the Advisory Committee.	(Both programs) Many communities have advisory committees made up of representatives of various groups interested in education for home and family living. These committees advise with the homemaking teacher and local school administrators on needed content for homemaking courses for youth and adults and on ways of providing learning experiences.
In-school (day) instruction in home economics (homemaking).	To prepare in-school adolescent students for their part in family living, and for assuming management responsibilities in homemaking. Through these to help enrich their total educational program.	All students in public high schools.	Home economics teachers certified to teach in the State.	Local board of education.	By the local school administrators and boards of education —often at request of pupils, parents, community groups, and advisory committees.	

SOURCE: Office of Education, *Public Vocational Education Programs*, Pamphlet No. 117 (Washington, D. C.: U.S. Department of Health, Education and Welfare, 1960), p. 13.

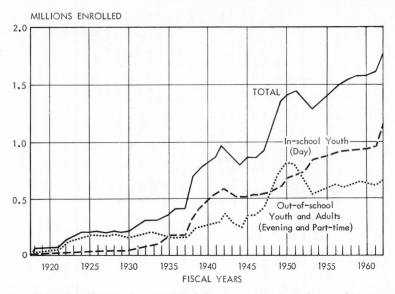

FIGURE 9–7. Enrollment in vocational home economics classes, by type of class. [SOURCE: Office of Education, *Digest of Annual Reports of State Boards for Vocational Education* (Washington, D.C.: U.S. Department of Health, Education, and Walfare, 1963), p. 11.]

Home economics education is also of great importance as a means of consumer education. Since our nation now spends over twelve billion dollars annually in advertising, it has become increasingly necessary for consumers to be able to analyze critically such advertising and to budget their incomes wisely. Problems of human relationship have also led to family difficulties, unhappy marriages, and divorces. With more and more women entering the labor force, leading to the rise of the two-income family, added stress is placed on the job of the homemaker. The enrollment trends in vocational home economics education, from 1917 to 1962, are shown in Figure 9–7.

PRACTICAL NURSE EDUCATION.   Established in 1957 under the George-Barden Act, the average program of preparation amounts to some 1,750 hours of classroom, laboratory, and clinical instruction. Most of the enrollees are high-school graduates. Enrollments in practical nursing and related health programs totalled approximately 49,000 in 1962.

AREA VOCATIONAL EDUCATION.   Designed for the preparation of technicians, area vocational education was established through the National Defense Education Act of 1958. Enrollees include students in the upper levels of the high school, high-school graduates in the thirteenth and fourteenth years of schooling (junior colleges and technical institutes),

Table 9–7

Characteristics of Vocational Education in Practical Nursing

Types of Programs	Purpose	For Whom Intended	By Whom Taught	By Whom Instructor Is Employed	How Courses Are Initiated	Advisory Committee (Where Such Committee Exists)
Preparatory.	To prepare for entrance upon the work of the practical nurse in hospitals, other health agencies and the home.	For persons in or out of school who have reached an age specified by a State's plan for practical nurse training. Lower age limit 16 years of age. In many States 18 years of age. No upper age limit.	A registered professional nurse who has had training for teaching.	By local or State board of education. Supervisor of clinical instruction is sometimes employed by the cooperating hospital or other health agency.	By local or State board of education on request from hospitals, physicians, or other health agencies or on recommendation of an advisory committee.	A. *Composition.*—Representatives of medical profession, hospitals, nurses associations, or other health agencies and the public. B. *Selection*—Appointed by the local or State board of education on basis of recommendations from groups to be represented. C. *Functions.*—Assist in determining training needs; recommend competent persons as teachers or supervisors; assist in determining content and length of course; informing groups and the public of training courses available.
Extension classes.	To give instruction in new techniques to those who are registered practical nurses and to give instruction needed by nonlicensed practical nurses to qualify for licensure.	For persons in or out of school who have reached an age specified by a State's plan for practical nurse training. Lower age limit 16 years of age. In many States 18 years of age. No upper age limit.	A registered professional nurse who has had training for teaching.	By local or State board of education.	By local or State board of education on request from hospitals, physicians, or other health agencies or on recommendation of an advisory committee. Also, on request of a group of practical nurses.	

source: Office of Education, *Public Vocational Education Programs*, Pamphlet No. 117 (Washington, D.C.: U.S. Department of Health, Education, and Welfare, 1960), p. 16.

and adults. Extension courses are also available for workers already engaged in technical work. Technical occupations include such industries as electronics, mechanical, chemical, aeronautical, data-processing, and other fields.

Our nation's demand for technical personnel to assist engineers and scientists far exceeds the available supply. The enrollment in Area Vocational Education programs, after only four years of operation, amounted to almost 150,000 students in 1962. Although these programs are of less than college grade, it is not unusual for graduates to move on to college for engineering studies.

VOCATIONAL BUSINESS EDUCATION. We have already discussed the federally reimbursed programs in distributive education. Legislation in 1963 permits federal funds to be used for vocational business education as well as distributive education. Over the years most high schools have been providing a business education curriculum without federal funds. Commercial education subjects include bookkeeping, stenography, typewriting, office machines, business arithmetic, general business, and other subjects. Some high schools have developed cooperative programs that enable students to gain work experience while attending school. Despite the great enrollments in commercial courses at the high-school level, the demand for skilled typists, stenographers, and business machine operators continues to exceed the existing supply. Many junior colleges are now offering programs in business education.

TECHNICAL EDUCATION. Under provisions of the National Defense Education Act of 1958, federal funds are provided for programs to train highly skilled technicians. These programs are offered in high schools, area vocational and technical schools, junior colleges, technical institutes, and four-year colleges. Such fields as data-processing, computer-programming, electronics, aeronautical and chemical design, and production technology are included. In 1962 enrollment in federally supported programs of technical education reached 149,000. Over 13,000 were enrolled in high-school programs while 40,000 took two-year post-high-school courses. More than $11 million in federal funds were expended on technical education programs in 1962.

VOCATIONAL GUIDANCE AND OCCUPATIONAL INFORMATION. Federal funds have been used for vocational guidance services since 1938, when the United States Commissioner of Education authorized such expenditures through the Smith-Hughes and George-Deen Acts. The George-Barden Act of 1946 provided specifically for vocational guidance services. The National Defense Education Act (Title V) provides considerable federal funds for guidance, counseling, and testing. Such N.D.E.A. funds, however, were not earmarked for vocational guidance per se, but were

Table 9–8

Characteristics of Area Vocational Education

Types of Programs	Purpose	For Whom Intended	By Whom Taught	By Whom Instructor Is Employed	How Courses Are Initiated	Advisory Committee (Where Such Committee Exists)
1	2	3	4	5	6	7
Extension.	To provide training in the direct application of specialized functional aspects of science, mathematics, and advanced technical skills and information needed by highly skilled technicians.	For employed persons over 16 years of age who because of new and changing technologies need additional training as described under "Purpose."	A person who has had experience as an engineer or as a highly skilled technician in a recognized occupation requiring training as described under "Purpose."	By State or local board of education.	By State or local board of education as a result of surveys to determine need for such training or upon request from management and/or labor, advisory committees, or groups wanting training.	A. Composition.— Equal representation of employers and employees in the field, representatives of the public schools and and other interested persons. B. Appointment.— By the school authority. C. Functions: 1. Assist in determining training needs. 2. Recommend instructors. 3. Assist in determining course content and length of course.
Preparatory.	Do.	For persons over 16 years of age who are preparing to enter occupations requiring training as described under "Purpose."	Do.	Do.	Do.	Do.

SOURCE: Office of Education, *Public Vocational Education Programs*, Pamphlet No. 117 (Washington, D.C.: U.S. Department of Health, Education, and Welfare, 1960), p. 17.

aimed at encouraging the more able high-school students to continue their studies and enter college.

During 1962, 18 states made use of federal funds for vocational guidance. The Federal Government contributed $423,000, while the states and communities expended $1.1 million for vocational guidance in 1962.

CURRENT PROBLEMS, ISSUES, NEEDS, AND RECOMMENDATIONS

We have seen how vocational education has come to play a significant role in our secondary schools beginning early in the present century. Enrollment in federally reimbursed programs has grown remarkably from one million in 1930 to two million in 1945 and to more than four million students today. Our rapidly developing technology requires citizens who have technical skills and who are adaptable to changing conditions in industry and agriculture. But despite the growth and success of vocational education in our high schools, many of our youth continue to drop out of school and enter the labor market without adequate preparation for skilled employment. The army of unemployed youth today is comprised largely of those who dropped out of high school and who are lacking in vocational skills.

In recent years, certain critics have argued that the high schools should limit their curricula to the so-called essentials or academic type of courses. Some of these critics seem more concerned with the goal of reducing educational expenditures by eliminating the expensive vocational programs. But it is indeed poor economy to have huge numbers of youth leaving high school each year in search of jobs for which they are unqualified. And nothing can be more devastating to an adolescent than the inability to find productive work and the hopeless feeling of rejection encountered by the unemployed.

Vocational Education Under Attack

During the post-World War II period, vocational education came under sharp attack by critics who embraced the traditional academic subjects as the rightful curriculum for our secondary schools. Ignoring the problems of school dropouts, youth unemployment, and the increasing heterogeneity of an expanding high-school enrollment, the essentialists advocated a return to the traditional academic disciplines. Vocational and other nonacademic subjects were labeled frills and life-adjustment courses.[8] The appeal for a return to the fundamentals attracted a surprisingly large group of members of the intelligentsia who regarded the

---

[8] Arthur Bestor, *Educational Wastelands* (Urbana, Illinois: The University of Illinois Press), 1953, pp. 63–64.

best education as closely resembling the traditional academic program that they themselves had surmounted. Tax conservationists viewed the return to the fundamentals and the elimination of vocational and frill subjects as a sure means to economy.

The Soviet Sputnik of 1957 served to heighten the criticism leveled at our schools. Admiral Hyman G. Rickover, ignoring the Soviet emphasis on vocational education, condemned the vocationalism of our schools and held that our salvation hinged on a return to the solid disciplines.[9]

Criticisms of vocational education, however, were counterbalanced by a growing national awareness of the problems of school dropouts and youth unemployment. One of the persistent societal problems of the 1960's was to prepare youth for the world of work. If anything, existing programs of vocational education in our high schools needed to be up-dated and made more realistic through improved personnel, facilities, equipment, and supervised work experience. Cooperative effort on the part of educators, employers, and unions would be essential to the development of effective programs of vocational education.

Need for Diversified Programs

The universalization of education in our society has led to a recognition of the need for diversified educational programs. The high schools at the turn of the century enrolled only one out of ten youths in the 14- through 17-year-old age group. These schools were concerned primarily with academic studies. They were not expected to serve nine tenths of the adolescent population.

Over the years, the holding power of the American high school has improved steadily. What was once an exclusive educational institution has become, during the course of half a century, a universal institution for adolescent society. Credit for this must be given not only to compulsory education laws, but also to the diversification of the high-school curriculum. Today, some two thirds of those who enter the ninth grade graduate from high school four years later.

Despite the severe criticism heaped upon nonacademic subjects in recent years, many educators not only see vocational education playing an important role in the high-school curriculum, but they would like to see such programs updated and expanded. Each year thousands of youths drop out of high school and enter the labor market without adequate preparation in marketable skills. The United States Labor Department estimates that more than seven million youngsters will drop out of high school during the decade of the 1960's. And most of these dropouts will be ill prepared to enter a labor market that has no need

---

[9] Hyman G. Rickover, *Education and Freedom* (New York: E. P. Dutton & Co., Inc., 1959), p. 180.

for unskilled workers. During the early 1960's, according to Labor Department data, unemployment among teen-agers was almost three times the national average. Teen-agers lacking in marketable skills account for the major portion of this great army of unemployed adolescents. Despite the improved holding power of our high schools, one third of our teen-agers fail to complete a high-school education. James B. Conant warns that by ignoring the problems of high-school dropouts and teen-age unemployment, "we are allowing social dynamite to accumulate in our large cities."[10] The Mayor's Juvenile Delinquency Evaluation Project in New York City reported that nearly half of the city's schoolchildren need additional assistance and guidance from their schools.[11] During the 1962–63 academic year, almost 77,000 youths in New York City alone were out of school and without regular full-time employment.[12] Each year, throughout our nation, almost 1,000,000 students drop out of high school. Studies of dropouts reveal that 70 per cent are of sufficiently high intelligence to complete high school, and from 6 to 13 per cent are capable of college work.[13] Many of these dropouts see no purpose in schools that are bound by traditional academic curricula. Updated programs of vocational guidance and vocational education would help these youngsters remain in school and gain the skills required by society for productive employment.

Youth Unemployment

It is estimated that, during the decade 1960–1970, 26 million youths will be added to the labor force of 58 million.[14] If many of these youths enter the labor market without a high-school education and marketable skills, an already critical problem will be compounded enormously. In June of 1963, the number of jobless in the United States totalled more than four million, or 5.9 per cent of the total labor force. The Secretary of Labor stated that teen-age unemployment "could develop into one of the most explosive social problems in the nation's history."[15]

A recent survey of 3,733 high schools in the states of Alabama, Georgia,

---

10 James Bryant Conant, *Slums and Suburbs* (New York: McGraw-Hill Company, Inc., 1961), p. 2.
11 "City Delinquency Unit Says Half of Students Need Help," The *New York Times*, September 11, 1961, p. 1.
12 "City Youth Plight Shown to Mayor," The *New York Times*, December 8, 1962, p. 15.
13 Fred M. Hechinger, "Uneducated Youth," The *New York Times*, March 18, 1962, p. E7.
14 Summary Report of the Panel of Consultants on Vocational Education, *Education for a Changing World of Work* (Washington, D.C.: Office of Education (OE No. 80020), 1962), p. 1.
15 "Rise in Teen-Age Jobless Pushes U.S. Rate to 5.9%," The *New York Times*, June 7, 1963, p. 1.

Iowa, Nebraska, Ohio, and Pennsylvania, revealed that only five per cent offered distributive education and only nine per cent offered trade and industrial courses.[16] However, it is not only necessary for more of our schools to offer curricula in vocational education, but such programs need to be updated for the modern world of work. Labor unions and management in business and industry must be willing to cooperate in on-the-job experience and occupational placement for vocational students. Business and labor have long neglected the vocational needs of youth.

The growth of technology is rapidly eliminating many unskilled tasks while placing a premium on the highly skilled worker. Our schools are faced with the enormous task of vitalizing the curriculum so that all young people see the value of secondary education and become productive members of society upon completion of their education.

VOCATIONAL EDUCATION AND TECHNOLOGICAL CHANGE. Robert Hutchins, an opponent of vocational education in the secondary school, has argued that technological advances are occurring with such great rapidity that the person trained in a specific marketable skill in high school is apt to find that his skill is obsolete by the time he enters the labor market. But follow-up studies reveal that youth unemployment among those having completed vocational education in high school is only a third of the rate for other high-school graduates.[17] The girl who graduates from high school with skills in typing, stenography, bookkeeping, and business machines is in great demand in the business world. Obviously, the vocational graduate is far better prepared to enter the labor market than the adolescent who drops out of high school because it offers him only an academic or general curriculum.

In agriculture, the need for vocational education continues despite our so-called overproduction. A century ago, approximately 85 per cent of our country's population was engaged in farming. Today only 15 per cent of our population is on the farm. The proportion of farm workers is expected to decline further during the coming years. With the application of science to agricultural production and the mechanization of the farm, American agriculture has been able to keep pace with our improving standard of living and growing population. Many marginal farmers will have to qualify for nonfarm employment as they fail to meet the higher efficiency levels and demands of modern agricultural production. But despite the declining farm population, vocational education in agriculture continues to play an important role. The technical and scientific know-how for efficient agricultural production and marketing have

---

[16] *Ibid.*, p. 11.
[17] Summary Report of the Panel of Consultants on Vocational Education, *op. cit.*, p. 9.

created increased demands for the education of future and practicing farmers. Furthermore, while our society appears to be faced with a problem of agricultural surpluses, the world as a whole is plagued with a critical shortage of food and fiber. We are faced with the immense challenge of improving the production and distribution of agricultural commodities around the globe. Underdeveloped nations are struggling to make the transition from an agricultural to an industrial economy. We have learned that the spectres of hunger and want can lead to revolution and communism.

In an age of scientific and technological acceleration, the demand for balanced and realistic programs of vocational education in our secondary schools becomes ever greater. Such programs must not be allowed to contribute to a stratified social system, but should be geared to enable each youngster to reach his fullest potential. The avenues between the vocational and academic curricula should be sufficiently open to allow a youngster to alter direction in view of his changing potentials and aspirations. This places added emphasis on the need for excellent programs of general education and guidance in our high schools. Many high schools need to update their curricula in vocational education. Some vocational educators are concerned about the tendency for their programs to serve as dumping grounds for youngsters who are unable to meet the academic requirements of the school. But the real problem of universal secondary education is how to develop an educational program that is in tune with the dynamics of our time and that offers each educable youngster the opportunity and stimulation to achieve at his fullest capacity.

SOME RECOMMENDATIONS BY CONANT.   A staunch supporter of diversified programs within the context of the comprehensive high school is James Bryant Conant. He recognizes the importance of vocational goals as a motivational factor at the high-school level.

> To my mind, it is desirable for as many boys and girls as possible in high school to have an ultimate vocational goal. It may well be that many of them will change their minds before the high school course is over or in later years. But, if a student thinks that what he or she is studying in school is likely to have significance in later life, the study in question takes on a new importance. There is less tendency for such "committed" students to waste their time or have a negative attitude toward their schoolwork.[18]

Conant goes on to recommend diversified programs for the development of marketable skills within the structure of the comprehensive high school.

---

[18] James Bryant Conant, *The American High School Today* (New York: McGraw-Hill Company, Inc., 1959), p. 127.

Courtesy the Ford Foundation; photo by William R. Simmons

"I submit that in a heavily urbanized
and industrialized free society
the educational experiences of youth
should fit their subsequent employment."
—JAMES B. CONANT

Programs should be available for girls interested in developing skills in typing, stenography, the use of clerical machines, home economics, or a specialized branch of home economics which through further work in college might lead to the profession of dietitian. Distributive education should be available if the retail shops in the community can be persuaded to provide suitable openings. If the community is rural, vocational agriculture should be included. For boys, depending on the community, trade and industrial programs should be available. . . . In each specialized trade, there should be an advisory committee composed of representatives of management and labor. Federal money is available for these programs.[19]

Some people seem to confuse the standard programs in industrial arts with vocational education. But learning to manipulate a few machines

---

[19] *Ibid.*, pp. 51–52.

in turning out a small trinket or gadget in the wood shop or metal shop is not vocational education. Vocational education is a systematic program designed to develop marketable skills that lead to skilled employment. Although Conant recommends industrial arts as part of the general education requirement during the junior-high-school years, he sees the need for realistic programs of vocational education at the senior-high level. In this sense, he is highly critical of the superficial approach to industrial arts that supposedly acquaints the student with our industrialized society. Conant maintains that such minor manipulations with a variety of crafts does no such thing. He also observes that many of the wealthy suburban communities are failing to provide programs for the development of marketable skills for those students who will not be going on to college. He recommends that such schools develop effective programs in areas like electronics, auto mechanics, and supervised work experience.[20]

RECOMMENDATIONS BY THE EDUCATIONAL POLICIES COMMISSION. In 1944 and 1952, the Educational Policies Commission of the N.E.A. published a blueprint for a comprehensive program of postwar education in a hypothetical rural and urban community.[21] This plan recommended programs of supervised work experience and vocational guidance in the high schools. Programs of terminal vocational education were also recommended at the community college level. Among "ten imperative educational needs of youth" identified in this plan was one concerning vocational education:

> All youth need to develop salable skills and those understandings and attitudes that make the worker an intelligent and productive participant in economic life. To this end, most youth need supervised work experience as well as education in the skills and knowledge of their occupations.[22]

RECOMMENDATIONS BY THE PANEL OF CONSULTANTS ON VOCATIONAL EDUCATION. In 1961, President Kennedy, in his Message to Congress, requested that the Secretary of Health, Education, and Welfare convene an advisory body to review and evaluate the federally supported programs of vocational education. A panel of consultants was promptly appointed and completed its report at the end of 1962. Benjamin Willis, Chicago Superintendent of Schools, served as chairman of this panel.

In reviewing the notable accomplishments of existing programs over the years, the panel also pointed to certain serious deficiencies. For example, it was reported that less than 10 per cent of the nation's high schools were offering trade and industrial training programs. Such

---

20 James Bryant Conant, *Slums and Suburbs* (New York: McGraw-Hill Company, Inc., 1961), pp. 106–108.
21 Educational Policies Commission, *Education for ALL American Youth* (Washington, D.C.: National Education Association, 1944), pp. 264–288.
22 *Ibid.*, p. 216.

programs were providing an annual output of only 160,000 persons, while projected needs indicated openings for one million skilled workers per year.[23] Similar deficiencies were cited in other areas, such as distributive occupations and office occupations. The latter has been included under federally supported programs since 1963.

The failure to meet the vocational needs of rural youth moving to urban centers was also cited. The panel recommended that vocational programs be made available to more high-school students, existing programs be modernized in accordance with present-day needs, and that occupationally oriented programs be developed to lead to actual employment for youth not served adequately by traditional programs. Other recommendations called for improved services in vocational guidance, development of more cooperative school-work programs, and expansion of post-high-school occupational training.

THE SCHOOL SETTING

The Comprehensive High School

The Harvard report showed that vocational education is vital to modern democratic society and should not be administered separately to different social classes.[24] The Report of the Harvard Committee also stressed that we must not conceive of vocational education and general education as completely separate entities. Every person in our society must be concerned with vocational preparation and activity. And every person is faced with the responsibility for effective citizenship.

Conant observed that the comprehensive high school is consistent with the ideals of a democratic society, and appears to have become ". . . as permanent a feature of our society as most of our political institutions."[25] Conant supported his position with data showing that the academic achievement of students enrolled in good comprehensive high schools is at least as high as that of students in specialized academic high schools.[26]

The A.S.C.D. Commission on the Education of Adolescents sees the comprehensive high school as a miniature democratic society.

> If a major task of the public school system of America is to develop the basic values of a free society and mutual respect for the range of persons and groups within our diverse culture, students must have an opportunity to live and work together. The comprehensive secondary school is an essential element in the development of a common view-

---

23 Report of the Panel of Consultants on Vocational Education, op. cit., p. 120.
24 Report of the Harvard Committee, General Education in a Free Society (Cambridge, Mass.: Harvard University Press, 1949), p. 54.
25 James Bryant Conant, The American High School Today (New York: McGraw-Hill Company, Inc., 1959), p. 8.
26 Ibid., pp. 33–36.

point sufficiently strong to hold our nation together. If specialized high schools which divide the population along social and economic lines were substituted for comprehensive high schools, it would further the division that exists among groups and decrease the possibility of maintaining and developing the qualities that unite us as a free people.[27]

The Specialized High School

While the comprehensive high school has proven itself, and while most educators and parents support this institution, some of our large cities have been operating one or more specialized high schools. Such specialized high schools are designed as either academic or vocational institutions. In certain areas, admission to these specialized high schools is selective. The argument for such separate schools is primarily a financial one. In a large city system, it would be very expensive to provide each and every high school with the equipment, facilities, and personnel necessary for a high-quality vocational or technical program. Other advantages cited for the specialized high school are the recognized unity of purpose and function of the school, the simplification of administrative and supervisory functions, and the physical plant can be designed and developed more functionally in accordance with the central purpose of the school.

There are some serious disadvantages of the specialized high school. Students are segregated by interests, aptitude, sex, and socioeconomic level. While such criteria for selection are not deliberate, the fact remains that the student body in such vocational schools tends to represent a lower socioeconomic grouping than that of the academic high school. Moreover, there is a tendency for vocational schools to be designed for boys only or for girls only, whereas most comprehensive high schools are coeducational. Once a student finds himself in a specialized vocational school, it becomes exceedingly difficult for him to muster enough drive to transfer to an academic school, even if his interests and aspirations have changed. On the other hand, it would be much easier to change one's program from vocational to academic, and vice versa, in the comprehensive high school. In many cities, the vocational schools have inferior physical facilities. Moreover, teachers who are charged with instruction in areas of general education and academic subjects tend to have a preference for teaching in the academic or comprehensive high school. As a result, the general education program in the vocational high school tends to suffer. And while the subjects of mathematics and science are exceedingly important in the vocational or technical high schools, many teachers of these subjects prefer to be situated in a more academic setting. Another problem concerns the transportation of stu-

---

[27] Kimball Wiles and Franklin Patterson, *The High Schools We Need* (Washington, D.C.: Association for Supervision and Curriculum Development, NEA, 1959), pp. 5–6.

dents. Since specialized high schools draw students from all parts of a metropolitan center, enrollees are required to commute to such schools.

New York City has what is probably the most specialized system of vocational high schools. Some of these are the Brooklyn High School of Automotive Trades, Central Commercial High School, High School of Fashion Industries, Food Trades High School, Machine and Metal Trades High School, Manhattan High School of Aviation Trades, and the New York School of Printing. While such career high schools may be criticized for segregating students even more severely than the general vocational high schools, it can also be argued that such specialization has some distinct advantages. The facilities, equipment, and teaching staff in these career schools could not otherwise be duplicated in the many general vocational and comprehensive high schools. And it might be argued that such career schools can be more realistically attuned to effective vocational preparation. The City of New York also boasts such specialized high schools for talented youth as the Bronx High School of Science, Brooklyn Technical High School, High School of Music and Arts, High School of Performing Arts, High School of Art and Design, and others. The Bronx High School of Science marked its 25th anniversary during the 1962–63 academic year. Founded in 1938 with an enrollment of 300 boys, the school has grown to 2,800 boys and girls. Each year, of the 4,500 students who apply for admission, approximately 1,000 are selected by competitive examinations. General education is not neglected in these specialized career high schools. Students at the Bronx High School of Science, for example, are required to take four years of English, four years of social science, and three years of a foreign language.

Obviously, only our largest metropolitan centers are able to provide such highly specialized career schools. The enrollment in the public schools of New York City is approximately one million students. Only four United States cities have total populations in excess of the public school enrollment of New York City (Chicago, Los Angeles, Philadelphia, and Detroit). Conant observed that New York City's public school enrollment exceeds the entire school population in each of 39 states.[28]

One can readily appreciate the economic advantages in providing for such specialized career schools rather than attempting to establish effective vocational programs in each of the city's 86 high schools. Of the 86 public high schools in operation in New York City during the 1963–64 academic year, 29 were vocational and three were selective academic schools. The remaining 54 high schools were general and comprehensive in nature. A number of the vocational high schools of New York City are selective and require entrance examinations. These schools are the High School

[28] James Bryant Conant, *Slums and Suburbs*, (New York: McGraw-Hill Company, Inc., 1961), pp. 54–55.

of Art and Design, High School of Fashion Industries, Aviation High School, Brooklyn High School of Automotive Trades, New York School of Printing, and Samuel Gompers Vocational High School.

In many American communities, the so-called comprehensive high school is not, in the strict sense, truly comprehensive. Such schools do not offer programs of vocational education, even though a significant portion of the students will not continue their education beyond high school. These schools might be better termed general high schools. Terminal students may pursue work in industrial arts, but this is not vocational education.

In most of our communities, the general and comprehensive high schools predominate. Our large cities, however, have developed academic and general vocational high schools. New York City stands alone in specialized academic and vocational career schools.

A number of critics of education have advocated that we adopt the traditional European type of dual or unilateral school program (separate academic and vocational-terminal schools). But it should be recognized that our comprehensive high schools have been developed to help fulfill the unique goals of our society. In recent years, some European nations, such as Sweden[29] and England,[30] have been experimenting with the comprehensive type of school for purposes of improving educational opportunity and fostering cultural and social unity.

FURTHER RECOMMENDATIONS, CRITICISMS, AND DEVELOPMENTS

Vocational Education and Occupational Placement

Although federally supported programs for vocational education at the high-school level have been in operation since 1917, the vocational needs of many of our youth remain unmet. Relatively few communities provide adequate vocational programs. More than one third of our youth drop out of high school and some 70 per cent of these dropouts are of normal or above average intelligence. Such youngsters, lacking in vocational skills, are unable to find regular employment. Their rate of unemployment in 1963 constituted three times the national average for all workers. Unemployment leads to delinquency, and delinquency is very costly to society. It has been said that no other nation wastes the resources of its youth as we do in the United States.[31]

---

29 See Torsten Husén, *School Reform in Sweden* (Washington, D.C.: Office of Education, U.S. Department of Health, Education, and Welfare, August 1961), p. 37.
30 See Robin Pedley, *The Comprehensive School* (Middlesex, England: Penguin Books Ltd.), 1963.
31 "Nation Prodded on Jobs for Youth," *The New York Times*, June 16, 1962, p. 20.

In recent years, certain critics of education, failing to acknowledge these problems, have been concerned only with upgrading the academic curricula of our schools. In fact, many of these critics have advocated the elimination of vocational programs.

The problem ahead is to develop programs that enable our youth to see the real values of a high-school education. In this way, the hopes and aspiration levels of our youth can be raised. But we also need realistic programs of occupational placement for youths who terminate their formal education with high school. Conant identified this as a very serious problem and advocated that the high school accept occupational placement as one of its important responsibilities.

> *I submit that in a heavily urbanized and industrialized free society the educational experiences of youth should fit their subsequent employment.* There should be a smooth transition from full-time schooling to a full-time job, whether that transition be after grade 10 or after graduation from high school, college, or university.[32]
>
> . . . The obligations of the school should not end when the student either drops out of school or graduates. . . . To my mind, *guidance officers, especially in the large cities, ought to be given the responsibility for following the post-high school careers of youth from the time they leave school until they are twenty-one years of age.*[33]

Conant observed that such placement responsibilities have long been recognized in our colleges and universities—so why not in our high schools?[34] He acknowledged that, under existing conditions where the high schools fail to assist dropouts and graduates with productive employment, it is exceedingly difficult for youth to gain admission on their own to apprenticeships that require union approval.

> It is far more difficult in many communities to obtain admission to an apprentice program which involves union approval than to get into the most selective medical school in the nation.[35]

Obviously, such problems will not be solved until high schools work together with union officials and employers to seek on-the-job training for youth. Moreover, labor unions and employers must meet their responsibility in helping youth find a place in the world of work.

Conant sees vocational education receiving greatest emphasis in grades 11 and 12, but not taking up more than half of the student's program. Prospective dropouts and slow learners, according to Conant, should be able to begin their vocational studies earlier.

Many vocational educators argue that their programs are too often used as dumping grounds for poor achievers and behavioral problems. They point out that the technical work entailed in effective programs of vocational education requires reasonable intelligence and diligent application.

---

[32] Conant, *op. cit.*, p. 40.
[34] *Ibid.*, p. 40.

[33] *Ibid.*, p. 41.
[35] *Ibid.*, pp. 46–47.

Perhaps additional programs in remedial work and terminal occupational training would serve an important function for slow learners. Behavioral problems obviously need careful professional counseling, but not enough schools are giving adequate attention to such students.

Tracking in the Comprehensive High School

Many general and comprehensive high schools segregate their students according to college-preparatory, general, vocational, and commercial tracks or channels. Although Conant recommended ability grouping, subject by subject, in the general education and so-called academic courses, he warned against compartmentalizing students through a track system. Instead, he regarded these programs of college-preparatory, vocational, and so on, as elective areas. In other words, the student would not be required to commit himself to a specific track, but would elect his coursework each year through consultation with his counselor.[36] Obviously, this flexible arrangement of individualized programs would avoid labeling students and would permit a student to shift his school program according to his changing interests and aptitudes. Such individualized programs are favored over tracking by a number of educators, presumably for the very reason that they advocate the comprehensive over the specialized high school.

However, some critics prefer fixed tracks in the high-school curriculum. The San Francisco Board of Education in 1959 commissioned a group of eight liberal-arts professors, from Stanford University and the University of California at Berkeley, to undertake a study of the curricula of the San Francisco public schools. In its report of 1960, this Curriculum Survey Committee recommended the tracking of students through fixed curricula beginning in the ninth grade.

> We recommend that beginning with the ninth grade separate, fixed curricula—such as academic, commercial, general, and industrial arts (sic)—be established. Students should be held to one of these on the basis partly of achievement, partly of preference and interests, with the possibility of shifting from one curriculum to another according to achievement. Such a system would prevent able students from taking easy courses in order to make high grades with little effort; it would prevent all students from wasting time with dubious or irrelevant electives; and, by reducing programming to a simple routine easily handled by administrative clerks, it would relieve many teachers from counselling and return them to the more important work of teaching.[37]

The above rationale for separate fixed curricula is not shared by many educators. Student programming should not be reduced to a simple cleri-

---

[36] *Ibid.*, pp. 64–65.
[37] *Report of the Curriculum Survey Committee* (San Francisco: Board of Education, San Francisco Unified School District, April 1, 1960), p. 10.

cal chore. This is a time when fruitful counseling can be accomplished. With effective guidance, there would be no excuse for a student to "waste time with dubious or irrelevant electives." If programming is reduced to a simple routine and clerical chore via separate fixed curricula, it would be exceedingly difficult for a student to change his curriculum in view of his changing aspirations and achievement level. Separate fixed curricula may be a convenient way to handle students, but it also labels them unnecessarily and restricts their programs according to rigid tracks.

Continuation Education

Compulsory school attendance laws have extended the age of leaving to sixteen in most states, and up to eighteen in some states. Recognizing the problems of economic hardship and the inability of some youth to adjust to a full-time program of high-school studies, most states have enacted legislation permitting part-time schooling. Such laws were passed in New York in 1910, Wisconsin in 1911, Ohio in 1913, and Pennsylvania in 1915.

In California, for example, where school attendance is compulsory to high-school graduation or to eighteen years of age, a youngster of sixteen or seventeen with parental consent may enroll in part-time schooling. Such youngsters may be unable to participate in full-time schooling because of (1) economic hardship or (2) maladjustment in the regular school program. Part-time or continuation education may be offered through the regular high school during the usual school hours. In such cases, continuation students are enrolled either in the regular classes or in separate classes. Some cities have separate continuation high schools, and others hold special Saturday classes. San Francisco maintains a separate school known as Continuation High School. Advantages of such a separate school are many. Youngsters need not be embarrassed about being unable to attend school on a full-time basis. The faculty and curriculum can be geared more specifically to continuation students, with concerted emphasis given to guidance and vocational placement. San Francisco Continuation High School, for example, offers a special course, Workers' Goals, for students employed full-time. Classes are small to facilitate individualized and small-group instruction.

But separate continuation schools have serious difficulties. Since the student body is comprised of those youths who must work because of economic hardships and those who cannot adjust to a regular high school for reasons of academic or behavioral deficiency, student goals are not very compatible. Moreover, the separate continuation school sometimes tends to carry an undesirable social stigma in the minds of students and the community.

A study of continuation students in California revealed that 50 per cent of the students were of normal or above in mental ability.[38] The record of students completing their high-school education as a result of part-time schooling attests to the importance of providing every possibility for educational continuation. For a large segment of the student body enrolled in part-time schooling, improved programs of vocational education and guidance are sorely needed. With more than a third of our nation's youth dropping out of high school, the task of effective continuation education remains one of our greatest challenges.

Meeting Educational Needs Out of School

Many people in responsible positions seem to be of the opinion that the only key to successful employment and societal adjustment is the attainment of a high-school diploma. Our society often uses the high school as a means of keeping adolescents off the labor market and off the streets, rather than as a means of providing youth with realistic preparation for the world of work. Adolescence is a period of seeking personal worth and responsibility. By denying our teen-agers constructive and responsible contact with the world of work, we should not be surprised to find them channeling their energies into socially undesirable activities.

We have stressed the need to develop realistic programs of vocational education so that the world of learning and the world of work become closely related. Cooperative school-community work experience programs, allowing adolescents to earn money while in school, would go a long way in helping our youth to find constructive and responsible roles in society. But there are, nevertheless, some youths for whom school is artificial and time-wasting. For such youngsters a full-time on-the-job training program may provide learning experiences that are, in the eyes of the youngster, more genuinely attuned to his needs than any formal school-sponsored program. Such full-time work experience, carefully planned and coordinated, could be of great benefit to the individual and society. Evening classes sponsored by the high school could provide opportunity for such youth to continue their education if they should so choose. But this type of program would require significant changes in the policies and attitudes of our government, employers, labor unions, and educators. The potentialities for meeting the educational needs of youth through the world of work must not continue to be ignored.

The Junior College and Technical Institute

The rapidly accelerating technological advancements are requiring technical vocational skills at higher and higher levels. California stands in the forefront in junior college education. Most of these junior colleges

---

[38] E. Evan Shaffer, Jr., *A Study of Continuation Education in California* (Sacramento: California State Department of Education, August 1955), p. 39.

are free of tuition and are administered through the community school district. In addition to the customary academic programs, they commonly offer terminal programs of a vocational nature. New York State has a number of state-supported agricultural and technical institutes that are post-high school and offer preemployment programs of a two-year duration. A number of the community colleges in New York State also offer occupational training programs. As the need for more technicians grows in our society, it appears likely that the role of the junior college will become increasingly important in the area of technical education.

Democracy and Social Mobility

While attempting to meet the important vocational needs of our adolescents, we must guard against the development of a social class and caste system in our schools. Although some sociologists may claim that a semblance of such a system already exists, our society still maintains a fairly high degree of social mobility. The comprehensive high school, with realistic programs of vocational and academic education, is an important instrument in fostering such mobility. Considerable curriculum flexibility is needed, however, to allow students to alter their programs in view of changing interests and aspirations. Adolescence is a period of change—physically, intellectually, and emotionally. And the record shows that there are enough late bloomers to warrant the opening of academic channels, rather than the hardening of these arteries.

Youths who do not go on to higher education should be prepared by the secondary school to enter the world of work. Youths who leave school lacking vocational competencies find that there is no place for them in society.

A 1964 report of the American Council on Education severely criticized the American educational system for being almost totally geared to the objectives of youth who are preparing for college.[39] According to this report, many youths, failing to gain success experiences in the academic-oriented high school, find themselves forced out of school. They become push-outs rather than dropouts. The study not only called for the reconstruction of the high school to meet the work needs of youth, but advocated a drastic change in the narrow academic bias of many junior colleges and four-year colleges.

SUMMARY

Although the federally-supported programs of vocational education at the high-school level date back to 1917, many of our youths are not reached by these programs. Vocational education is more expensive than

---

[39] Grant Venn, *Man, Education and Work* (Washington, D.C.: American Council on Education, 1964).

education that is limited to textbooks and, despite cooperative federal and state support, local school districts need considerable funds to operate effective vocational programs. Moreover, most of our schools have maintained a bias toward the traditional academic subjects, inherited from the time when the primary goal of the high school was preparation for college.

All too often the high schools have been content to allow students to become dropouts without making a concerted effort to determine the causes and to take preventive measures. Lacking vocational preparation, and being deficient in general education skills, the dropout fails to become gainfully employed. Yet, virtually every human being has vocational goals and strives for a sense of worth. When young people are neglected by school and society, there is likely to be trouble.

The Vocational Education Act of 1963 provides federal funds for the training of unemployed youth. The 1963 legislation includes training in areas not covered by previous bills, such as the training of technicians, office workers, and workers in the service industries. Junior colleges are expected to participate in the training programs for technicians.

More schools need to study their dropouts to determine how many youngsters are forced out of school and into the ranks of the unemployed. Industry and labor unions will have to meet their share of the responsibility to help youth make their way in the world of work.

Effective high-school programs in vocational education can be provided within the comprehensive high school. Students enrolled in vocational programs should not be tracked separately from other students. All should participate in the same general education programs at levels suitable to needs and aptitudes. Because adolescence is a period of change, curricula should be sufficiently flexible to allow for changes in motivation and achievement. Part-time evening classes should be provided to enable employed dropouts to earn a high-school diploma.

Every human being needs a sense of significance and a feeling of having something to contribute to the larger society. In modern society we have made many youths unwelcome to the world of work. The hopelessness and despair of unemployed youth is one of the great wastes and tragedies of our time.

PROBLEMS FOR STUDY AND DISCUSSION

1. What caused the Federal Government to establish an interest in the support of vocational education? Is vocational education of any less importance today? Should the Federal Government also support general education?

2. How would you define vocational education? What is the difference between industrial arts and vocational education in trades and industries? What is the difference between trades and industries and area vocational programs?

3. What is the relationship between vocational education and general education?

4. What is the relationship of the federal, state, and local agencies in administering programs of vocational education? Has federal support for vocational education led to federal control of these programs?

5. Industrialization of our society has led to a marked decline in our farm population. Yet, it is said that the need for vocational education in agriculture is as great as ever. How do you account for this?

6. What programs of vocational education, if any, were offered by your high school?

7. How do you account for the severe criticism leveled at vocational education in recent years?

8. Why has unemployment among youth become a growing problem?

9. What are the differences between the comprehensive high school and the general high school?

10. What are the advantages and disadvantages of the specialized high school in comparison with the comprehensive high school?

11. What is the role of the junior college and technical institute in providing for terminal programs of vocational education? How does this role relate to that of the high school?

12. What are the arguments against the tracking of students by curricular programs in the comprehensive high school?

13. Should the high school have a responsibility for job placement and follow-up of dropouts and graduates? Why or why not?

SELECTED REFERENCES

Alberty, Harold B. and Elsie J. Alberty. *Reorganizing the High School Curriculum* (3rd Ed.) New York: The Macmillan Company, 1962, Ch. 7.

Alcorn, Marvin D. and James M. Linley (eds.) *Issues in Curriculum Development.* Yonkers-on-Hudson, New York: World Book Company, 1959.

Benjamin, Harold. *The Saber-Tooth Curriculum*. New York: McGraw-Hill Company, Inc., 1939.

Bent, Rudyard K. and Henry H. Kronenberg. *Principles of Secondary Education*. New York: McGraw-Hill Company, Inc., 1961, Ch. 16.

Bestor, Arthur. *The Restoration of Learning*. New York: Alfred A. Knopf, Inc., 1955.

Byram, Harold M. and Ralph C. Wenrich. *Vocational Education and Practical Arts in the Community School*. New York: The Macmillan Company, 1956.

Conant, James Bryant. *Slums and Suburbs*. New York: McGraw-Hill Company, Inc., 1961.

———. *The American High School Today*. New York: McGraw-Hill Company, Inc., 1959.

Cremin, Lawrence A. *The Transformation of the School*. New York: Alfred A. Knopf, Inc., 1961, Ch. 2.

Educational Policies Commission. *Education for ALL American Youth: A Further Look*. Washington, D. C.: National Education Association, 1952.

Goodman, Paul. *Growing Up Absurd*. New York: Random House, Inc., 1960.

Keller, Franklin J. *The Comprehensive High School*. New York: Harper & Row, Publishers, Inc., 1955.

Krug, Edward A. *The Secondary School Curriculum*. New York: Harper & Row, Publishers, Inc., 1960.

Lichter, Solomon, Elsie Rapien, Frances Seibert, and Morris Sklansky. *The Drop-Outs*. New York: The Free Press of Glencoe and The Macmillan Company, 1962.

National Society for the Study of Education. *Adapting the Secondary-School Program to the Needs of Youth*. Fifty-second Yearbook, Part I. Chicago: The University of Chicago Press, 1953.

Office of Education. *Digest of Annual Reports of State Boards for Vocational Education*. Washington, D.C.: U.S. Department of Health, Education, and Welfare, 1963.

———. *Educational Objectives in Vocational Agriculture*. Washington, D.C.: U.S. Department of Health, Education, and Welfare, 1955.

———. *Public Vocational Education Programs*. Washington, D.C.: U.S. Department of Health, Education, and Welfare, 1960.

Parker, J. Cecil, T. Bentley Edwards, and William H. Stegeman. *Curriculum in America*. New York: Thomas Y. Crowell Company, 1962. Ch. 13.

Report of the Harvard Committee. *General Education in a Free Society*. Cambridge, Massachusetts: Harvard University Press, 1958.

Report of the Panel of Consultants on Vocational Education. *Education for a Changing World of Work*. Washington, D.C.: Office of Education, U.S. Department of Health, Education, and Welfare, 1963.

Rickover, H. G. *Education and Freedom*. New York: E. P. Dutton & Co., Inc., 1959.

Shaffer, E. Evan, Jr. *A Study of Continuation Education in California*. Sacramento: California State Department of Education, August 1955.

Shartle, Carroll L. *Occupational Information: Its Development and Application*. Englewood Cliffs, N.J.: Prentice-Hall, Inc., 1959.

Sutherland, Sidney S. and Orville E. Thompson. *Training Required by Workers in Agricultural Business and Industry*. Sacramento: California State Department of Education, 1957.

Roberts, Roy W. *Vocational and Practical Arts Education*. New York: Harper & Row, Publishers, Inc., 1957.

IV

Educational Resources, Organization, and Services

The larger world can neither be given nor taught in lessons. It is an adventure of the one making the adventure, and teachers and schools should get out of the way—if they cannot learn how to help advance the adventure.

—Joseph K. Hart

IV

Educational Resources,

Organization, and

Services

CHAPTER *10*

Resources for Effective Learning

T HE DEVELOPMENT OF THE MOTION PICTURE and television during the twentieth century has effected a profound change in man's time-life space. He has available to him a window to the world. Yet, our schools have hardly begun to make effective use of these media for bringing new dimensions to the teaching-learning process. It is paradoxical that while almost every home has a television receiver, the typical secondary-school classroom operates as though such an instrument had not yet been invented. Nevertheless, an increasing number of schools and colleges are making serious efforts to use instructional technology to expand and enrich educational experience, or to improve the efficiency of the school program. Some educators see these new media as instruments for bringing about a veritable revolution in curriculum and instruction, while others regard them chiefly as means for reducing educational expenditures in the face of rising enrollments. In this chapter we shall examine some of the developments and proposals for harnessing instructional technology for the secondary school.

READING AND LISTENING

Children learn the spoken language without formal education. To the child, such learning is not drudgery. The preschool child does not study the logical structure of language and memorize the rules and vocabulary definitions. The learning of spoken language occurs in the context of life experience. The child observes situations and derives meaning from what he sees and hears. The learning of language is more than mere imitation and repetition; it requires an understanding of the connections between seeing and hearing, between events and consequences. Although this is one of the most complex forms of learning, the child pursues it eagerly, without strain or boredom, because it is integral to his life experience. Whitehead observed that by holding to rigid antecedents and strict forms for organizing knowledge, dull teachers have "produced in education the dryness of the Sahara."[1]

In formal education we have many practices that stem from traditions rather than from research evidence on the nature of learning. We still insist on a considerable amount of memorization without understanding. Yet, the development of writing and printing eliminated the need for a great deal of sheer memoriter drill. The computer is far more efficient than man in its capacity for information storage and retrieval. And the computer, unlike man, never gets bored with repetitive tasks. But man has the wonderful capacity for intuition, insight, dissent, and play, which lead to novel questions and creative solutions. The schools need to give less attention to rote tasks and more attention to processes which develop the best in human learning and behavior.

Many teachers seem to follow the notion that learning must be made difficult, abstract, and remote from reality if it is to discipline the mind. This ancient dogma has stifled many a learner's enthusiasm for inquiry while it has grossly distorted the real nature of learning.

The Lecture and the Textbook

Before the invention of printing, when books were scarce, professors at the medieval universities read to students from hand-copied books. Students took notes from these readings and committed this material to memory. As books became plentiful through printing, the lecture changed to commentary and interpretation by the teacher. Although the first textbooks appeared around 1600, it was not long before someone saw the need to connect visualization with the verbalized material. In 1657 a textbook containing drawings was published in Nuremberg, Germany by Johann Amos Comenius. This book, titled *Orbis Pictus* (*Visible World*), was designed as a first reader and came to be translated into 14 languages. Comenius also recommended that, wherever possible, the actual objects be shown to students.

Objections to oververbalization in teaching have been raised through the centuries since the time of Comenius. For example, in 1838, Daniel Webster observed,

> We teach too much by manuals, too little by direct intercourse with the pupil's mind; we have too much of words, too little of things. Take any of the common departments, how little do we know of the practical

---

[1] Alfred North Whitehead, *The Aims of Education* (New York: The Macmillan Company, 1929), p. 26.

detail, say geology. It is taught by books. It should be taught by excursions in the field. So of other things.[2]

Today, the textbook, along with talk and chalk, is given a prominent role in education. Although the textbook is primarily a source for verbal communication, many modern textbooks include a rich variety of pertinent visualization through diagrams, charts, graphs, drawings, and photographs. The textbook is economical and provides the teacher and students with an organized approach to subject matter.

In too many classrooms, however, the textbook is treated as the course of study. The teacher merely serves to translate the textbook material, while the students are drilled as though its contents were some sort of catechism. The class follows a page-by-page lockstep of reading assignments and accompanying workbook exercises. Such a situation is not really a criticism of the textbook per se, but of the way in which it is used in the classroom. Through this approach, the selection of textbooks is akin to curriculum-making.

More teachers need to help students utilize a greater variety of printed matter. Learning to use several sources and to interpret conflicting material can be provided through the classroom library and the school library. Greater emphasis on understanding rather than memorizing, on interpreting rather than regurgitating, would help students to gain real meaning from the verbalized material. Working with a rich variety of sources and contexts would enable students to probe more deeply into certain areas of special interest.

Too many textbooks are merely an author's logical approach to the organization of subject matter. The effective teacher will seek to know the students as individuals and will organize the course of instruction on a sound psychological basis. The learning process should be that of inquiring into problems and issues, rather than acquiring factual information for its own sake.

Frequently, when new and complex verbalized material is being treated, the learner is unable to gain cognition unless the verbalizations are accompanied by visualization or direct experience. Otherwise, the learner is apt to attach imitative and synthetic meanings to these verbal symbols. The healthy mind tends to forget that which is without real meaning.

Radio and Recordings

Products of twentieth-century technology, radio and recordings can offer some unique and authentic learning experiences. Radio can provide live and recorded music, and live current events such as political debates,

---

[2] *American Journal of Education*, Vol. 1, 1856, p. 590.

The school can help transform abstractions into reality.

speeches, and interviews. Teachers can make audio tape recordings of important broadcasts. Dramatizations of historic events and plays can be highly effective via radio. Recording companies now offer a rich and growing variety of discs and audio tapes featuring dramatizations by noted actors, poetry readings by famous poets, and concerts by the world's outstanding symphonic groups.

However, even before the advent of television, radio gained only limited use in our schools. One of the reasons for its limited development as an instructional medium in the United States was the fact that radio was immediately exploited as an instrument of private enterprise rather than public service. The lure of the advertising dollar resulted in programming geared to entertain vast audiences. Broadcasters were not required to allocate time for educational programs. Although several hundred radio stations were in operation by 1922, it was not until 1938 that the Federal Communications Commission reserved part of the radio spectrum for noncommercial broadcasting. A number of universities have been operating educational radio stations offering a variety of programs for people of all ages. Some school systems also have been operating their own stations. But despite arrangements for program exchanges, the low operating budgets of educational stations have limited their attractiveness and impact.

The British, on the other hand, have been more successful in utilizing radio for educational purposes. By regarding electronic communications as a natural resource, the British have come to use radio for serving the public interest. Through the noncommercial resources of the British Broadcasting Corporation, high-quality broadcasts are beamed to the schools. Teachers and students are also provided with source books containing maps, pictures, and suggested projects for following-up the broadcasts.

While recordings do not offer the sense of immediacy and realism of live radio, they can be scheduled at the will of the teacher and they can be preheard, evaluated, and edited by the teacher. The magnetic tape recorder enables the teacher to record radio programs and the audio message from television, as well as to make recordings of interviews, guest speakers, and the students themselves.

The language laboratory has gained widespread use in modern foreign-language instruction. Through this electronic system, students are able to listen to phrasings and conversations by experts, as well as to record and play back their own voices for comparison and self-improvement. A central control console permits the teacher to use his own voice, select prerecorded material, and tune in on individual students. The spectacular adoption of the language laboratory in our high schools has been aided considerably through N.D.E.A. funds.

VISUALIZATION AND VERBALIZATION

Many of our thoughts and emotions cannot be verbalized adequately through the written and spoken word. Just as we have developed music that appeals to the auditory sense in a way in which the spoken word would be totally inadequate, so too have we developed visual media that cannot be described adequately through verbalization. Yet we cannot consider visualization entirely separate from verbalization in the teaching-learning process. We have pointed out how the preschool child learns the spoken language by seeing, hearing, and doing. Visualization links the written and spoken word with reality.

Visual Symbols and Audio-Visual Communication

The chalkboard is a traditional device for conveying not only verbal symbols, but certain visual symbols as well. As previously mentioned, the modern textbook contains a wide variety of visual symbols. Below are listed some of the forms of auditory, visual, and audio-visual communication commonly employed in the teaching-learning process:

AUDIO-VISUAL INSTRUMENTS AND MEDIA

AUDITORY
- Phonograph
- Radio
- Audio-tape recording
- Language laboratory

VISUAL
- Diagrams
- Charts
- Graphs
- Sketches
- Maps
- Cartoons
- Drawings
- Paintings
- Photographs
- Slides and filmstrips
- Sculpture
- Models and globes
- Mock-ups
- Artifacts and specimens
- Displays and Exhibits

AUDIO-VISUAL
- Demonstrations
- Dramatizations and role playing
- Sound motion pictures
- Television: live and recorded
- Guest speakers or interviewees
- Field trips
- Experiments
- Direct Experience

Opposition to Audio-Visual Media. We have mentioned how some educators regard the printed word as the epitome of intellectual communication. They see audio-visual resources as either largely unnecessary or as belonging to a rather low echelon of educative endeavor.

> Audio-visual aids (to use the educators' jargon) are subject to the same law of diminishing returns. Pictures have their place in even the most mature forms of learning. But in general the human mind advances from pictures to words and to abstract symbols. Once it has made the advance, many kinds of visual aids become timewasting, round-about, burdensome methods of conveying information that can be got more quickly, accurately, and systematically from the printed page.
>
> Once a pupil has learned to study a discipline systematically and to

"But observation is not enough. We have to understand
the significance of what we see, hear, and touch."
                                        —John Dewey

Photo by Daniel Tanner

think in abstract terms, it is nothing short of an educational crime to thrust him back to the infantile level again. After all, the importance of abstract thought itself has never been in question. The realization that one cannot *begin* at the abstract level does not proceed toward it. And once a child has learned to generalize, good teaching requires that his power to do so be continually exercised and expanded.[3]

While it is of course true that audio-visual media can be misused by employing these resources to convey material that is distracting or geared to a low level of thinking, the same criticism can be attached to the textbook. After all, the real value of the textbook lies not in the covers, which package the material, or on the pages that carry the verbal and visual symbols, but in the content and organization of the message itself —and ultimately in the response evoked by the learner.

Yet, many critics of audio-visual media seem to hold the notion that

[3] Arthur Bestor, *The Restoration of Learning* (New York: Alfred A. Knopf, Inc., 1955), pp. 108–109.

High-school symphony orchestra performs on educational television.

Photo by Barbara M. Marshall; courtesy the Ford Foundation

because these devices deal with sensory experience, they are of poorer intellectual fiber than the printed word. But can it really be said that a painting by Rembrandt, Van Gogh, or Picasso—or a musical composition by Beethoven, Brahms, or Bartok—is of a lower intellectual order than a literary work from the 100 Great Books? And how many chemists and physicists would be willing and able to conduct research without three-dimensional models of molecular constructs and without laboratory apparatus? For example, a great step in unraveling the mystery of life was made through the construction of a huge, three-dimensional, multi-colored molecule of DNA. It was while attempting to arrange in this model the way in which the atoms and molecules of DNA are bonded together that the investigators gained the insights that led to a key breakthrough. In recognition of their work, these investigators, Professor H. C. Crick of England and Professor James D. Watson of the United States, were awarded the 1962 Nobel Prize in medicine.

Audio-visual media can provide us with intellectual and emotional experiences that are unique and beyond the province of verbalized symbols. And these media can attach richer and more authentic meanings to the printed word.

While each of the various forms of visual communication are worthy of extended discussion, we shall limit our treatment in the ensuing sections of this chapter to such broadly encompassing media as the motion picture, television, and the teaching machine. These latter media have been given a prominent role in recent proposals for effecting radical changes in the design and operation of the secondary-school program. Therefore, we shall also examine the implications of the new educational media for changes in the total secondary-school program.

The Motion Picture

Although the origin of the motion picture can be traced back to 1894, the development of sound movies did not come until 1925. The sound motion picture soon came to be recognized in some quarters as a means of revolutionizing education by bringing the world to the classroom. However, although the revolution did not occur in the classroom, it did take place in the entertainment habits of the American people. But instead of bringing the world to the people, it was used to a great extent as a vehicle for fantasy and escape.

Gradually, however, 16 mm educational and instructional films were produced. Film distribution centers were created at many universities and through private agencies. But it was not until during and after World War II that the motion picture gained any real impact for instructional purposes. Between 1940 and 1955 the number of 16 mm sound motion picture projectors in the United States increased from

25,000 to more than half a million.[4] Early research on the effectiveness of the motion picture revealed that it was capable not only of increasing the amount of learning over verbalized approaches, but that it often resulted in improved retention of the material.[5]

EXPANDED USE OF THE INSTRUCTIONAL MOTION PICTURE. During World War II the Armed Forces expended considerable sums for research and development of sound motion pictures. This medium was used with great effectiveness in shortening the time required for training in certain technical operations. The military was also successful in using the motion picture to influence the attitudes of men toward the war effort. Through animation, the photographing of live images, and the use of color, the motion picture proved to be a truly compelling medium. Since World War II, the Armed Forces have continued to use the motion picture for training purposes. Business, industry, and government also came to use this medium on a broad scale.

In the years following World War II, most schools acquired equipment for motion picture usage and many of the larger school districts employed audio-visual coordinators and established film libraries of their own. Yet, the use of the motion picture as a means of systematic instruction was disappointing. Most films were primarily self-contained units or enrichment lessons. And many teachers and school administrators treated the motion picture as a diversionary medium—unconnected with the ongoing curriculum of the school. School budgets for motion pictures were pitifully small and most teachers found it more convenient to hold to the traditional vehicles of talk, chalk, and textbook. Budgets for the production of most instructional motion pictures continued to be low, and much of the work was lacking in creative appeal.

THE PROMISE OF RECENT DEVELOPMENTS. The National Defense Education Act of 1958 has provided funds for research on the effective utilization of the motion picture, television, and other related media of instruction. Schools are also reimbursed up to 50 per cent for the acquisition of equipment used for improving instruction in science, mathematics, and modern foreign languages.

The Physical Science Study Committee (PSSC), established in 1956 at the Massachusetts Institute of Technology through support from the National Science Foundation, has developed materials for improving instructional content and methods in high-school physics. Among these materials is an inquiry-oriented series of motion pictures that provide

---

[4] James W. Brown, Richard B. Lewis, and Fred F. Harcleroad, *A-V Instruction Materials and Methods* (New York: McGraw-Hill Company, Inc., 1959), pp. 158–159.

[5] See Walter A. Wittich and Charles F. Schuller, *Audio-Visual Materials,* (3rd Ed.) (New York: Harper & Row, Publishers, Inc., 1962), pp. 382–384.

experiments and lessons under the directorship of an outstanding authority. Similar work is being carried out by the Biological Sciences Curriculum Study, also with the support of the National Science Foundation.

The motion picture is being used also for systematic instruction in modern foreign languages. Through the support of N.D.E.A., several film series are available that enable the students to learn the language by seeing and hearing how people communicate in realistic situations and authentic locations. Flashback techniques permit repetition without boredom. The motion picture, in this way, brings the world to the classroom. The development of 8 mm sound film makes it practicable to use the motion picture for individual viewing or as part of a multimedia system.

Television

Television has been hailed as "the most powerful medium of communication yet devised by man."[6] The capacity of television to transmit live images, as well as recorded material, makes it man's window to the world. Television, too, is our most eclectic medium of communication. It can transmit recorded material on film or video tape. It can transmit events as they are actually happening. It can deal with a remarkably wide continuum of audio-visual experiences. Television is such a compelling medium that most children and youth spend approximately one sixth of their waking hours with their eyes on the video tube.[7] This means that the average youngster, on a year-round basis, devotes more time to watching television than to attending school. Not only is television a compelling medium for entertainment and fantasy, but it also carries great impact for realism. Studies show that television conveys greater credibility in covering news events than the newspaper.[8]

Yet, television has been described as a vast wasteland by the former chairman of the Federal Communications Commission. From its very beginning in the United States, the dominant emphasis has been on exploiting the medium as a business enterprise rather than as a means of serving the public interest. Network profits are enormous. From 1952 to 1960 the net profits for the three networks increased tenfold.[9] It seems ironic that the continued rise in advertising profits has made commercial television time much too valuable for educational and instructional purposes. In order to compete for the advertising dollar, each of the three

---

[6] Fund for the Advancement of Education, *Teaching by Television* (New York: The Ford Foundation, 1961), p. 2.

[7] Wilbur Schramm (ed.), *The Impact of Educational Television* (Urbana, Illinois: University of Illinois Press, 1960), p. 216.

[8] J. Tebbel, "What Does the Public Believe?", *Saturday Review*, March 10, 1962, pp. 43–44.

[9] The *New York Times*, January 24, 1962.

networks vie for the greatest audiences by offering programs of crime, violence, situational comedy, sports, quiz shows, soap operas, and other forms of pap, fantasy, and escapism.

The great potential of the medium is realized on occasion through high-quality documentaries, dramatizations, concerts, and public affairs telecasting. But the audience ratings and the advertising dollars have been the key determinants of the type of programming offered the public. Upon leaving his post as chairman of the Federal Communications Commission on June 1, 1963, Newton Minow indicated his disappointment at the failure of commercial television to provide sufficient time for programs of educational and cultural value. He deplored the excessive commercialization of the medium and sought federal legislation to empower the FCC to limit television advertising. However, the proposal failed in Congress. Although the National Association of Broadcasters has maintained a voluntary code that limits the proportion of time devoted to commercials, a study by the FCC revealed that 40 per cent of the stations have been violating this code.[10]

But the picture is not all black. Developments in noncommercial television, designed for educational and instructional purposes, are beginning to gain real momentum. We must remember that the first use of television for formal instruction dates back only to 1953. In view of this short history of using the medium for instructional purposes, the accomplishments are significant and the prospects are promising. Let us now examine some of these developments and the prospects for the future.

EDUCATIONAL TELEVISION. Educational television includes any programming that is intended for educational or cultural value. Instructional television carries the more specific definition of applying to programming that is used in formal learning situations—usually carrying academic credit in school or college.

Recognizing the great potential of television for educational and instructional purposes, the FCC reserved a number of channels some years back for the eventual development of noncommercial stations. Such stations operate on a nonprofit basis and are designed to serve educational needs. They may be of the community type, operated by local civic, cultural, and educational groups; or they may be operated by universities, school systems, or state educational TV commissions. The first such station began operations in Houston in 1953. By 1964 some 95 noncommercial stations were in operation. While the increase in the number of noncommercial stations is impressive, many of them have encountered financial problems. Supported by public contributions, edu-

---

[10] The *New York Times*, February 28, 1964, p. 49.

Television can bring the Nobel Laureate to the high-school classroom.
Here we see Nobel Laureate Dr. Linus Pauling (second from right),
Dr. John W. Baxter (center), and assistants examining models for a
TV lesson in chemistry.

cational institutions and agencies, and foundation grants, the noncommercial stations have been forced to operate on modest budgets.

Another problem limiting the development of noncommercial television is that approximately two thirds of the channels originally reserved by the FCC for this purpose are in the ultra-high frequency (UHF) bands; and relatively few television sets are equipped to receive UHF telecasts. In order to overcome this limitation, federal legislation was enacted in 1962 requiring that all television receivers sold through interstate commerce be equipped to receive UHF as well as VHF beginning April, 1963. Although it will be some time before most families obtain all-channel receivers, the implications for the development of noncommercial television are enormous. Also in 1962, a federal bill was passed authorizing $32 million for expanding educational television facilities throughout the nation. While this is a very modest sum, it should have great impact in spurring the establishment of educational stations. It is estimated that at least 1,000 educational television stations are needed in the United States.[11]

INSTRUCTIONAL TELEVISION.   We have pointed out that while television has made its way into virtually every American home, it has not yet had a similar impact on our schools. Nevertheless, it is being used, at least to some extent, in a variety of ways at the school and college level.

During the 1950's and early 1960's, the Ford Foundation was a prime bulwark for instructional television. In supporting instructional television, the Ford Foundation was interested primarily in seeing the medium used for helping to solve the shortage of qualified teachers in the face of increasing school enrollments and rising educational costs. During 1955 the public schools of St. Louis and Pittsburgh experimented with open-circuit instructional TV under Ford Foundation support. In 1956 the Pittsburgh Schools enlisted Professor Harvey E. White of the University of California to develop and conduct a new high school physics course for televising to the schools. This entire course of 162 half-hour lessons was also recorded on film.

Beginning in 1956, also under Ford Foundation sponsorship, the public schools of Washington County (Hagerstown), Maryland inaugurated a closed-circuit system. Today, most of the county's schools are joined in the closed-circuit network. This system permits telecasting over several channels simultaneously. Hagerstown selects and trains its own television teachers, many of whom are from the regular teaching ranks of the school district. The project, no longer under Foundation support, has gained sufficient momentum to be financed through regular school funds. In 1957 the Ford Foundation announced its establishment of a coordinated series of projects called "The National Program in the Use of Television in the Public Schools." Participating in this program were the public school systems of Atlanta, Cincinnati, Dade County (Miami), Detroit, Milwaukee, Oklahoma City, Philadelphia, and elsewhere. This program was designed to use television for large classes in an effort to determine the feasibility of the medium for bringing about savings in teaching positions and classroom space, while improving the quality of education. The research results of this and other programs are discussed later in this chapter.

Similar closed-circuit television networks are in operation today on many state university campuses. Two of the pioneer universities that

---

[11] The *New York Times*, May 2, 1962, p. 63.

experimented with closed-circuit television are Pennsylvania State and Miami (Ohio). In 1956 the Chicago Board of Education, with Ford Foundation assistance, launched a city-wide, open-circuit program for course credit through the Chicago City Junior College. Except for registration and final examinations, it is possible for students to earn their Associate in Arts degree at home without attending classes. The at-home enrollment has roughly matched the total on-campus enrollments for the various branches. Most of the at-home students are adults who would otherwise be unable to attend college. Between the telecasts and their reading assignments they are able to gain sufficient verbal information to do well on the final examinations. Their attitudes toward television tend to be far more favorable than younger college students who prefer the stimulation of class discussion and interaction.

ITV AND N.D.E.A.   The National Defense Education Act of 1958 has replaced the Ford Foundation as the chief bulwark for instructional television. Under N.D.E.A., funds are available for research and experimentation in the effective use of television and other media for instruction. School districts are also eligible for funds on a matching basis for the purchase and installation of television systems and other equipment used for improving the instruction in science, mathematics, and modern foreign languages.

NATIONAL, STATE, AND REGIONAL ITV.   Under the support of the Ford Foundation and private business, a series in modern physics for high-school teachers was offered over the NBC network beginning in the fall of 1958. Known as Continental Classroom, this series was telecast five days per week beginning at 6:30 A.M. Courses in modern chemistry and modern mathematics were soon added. The CBS network also joined in with an early morning series called College of the Air, featuring a course in modern biology.

Although widely heralded, both Continental Classroom and College of the Air were terminated in 1963. Financial support was lacking and the networks were unwilling to assume the costs. The early morning hour of the telecasts was inconvenient for many teachers and the networks would not sacrifice prime revenue time by rescheduling the courses. Consequently, instructional television in the United States has been forced to develop outside the profit-motivated television networks.

Noncommercial state and regional networks have been making notable progress during the past several years. A noncommercial state TV network has been operating in Alabama since 1956. Through this state network, educational TV is available to schools and homes throughout most of the state. California, Florida, Oklahoma, Oregon, South Carolina, and other states have interconnected some or all of their noncommercial TV stations to form a network that facilitates the exchange of programs.

One of the most promising developments in the history of communications is the video-tape process, which permits the recording and exchange of programs. The video-tape process produces recordings of the highest quality. Schools operating their own closed-circuit systems can now make use of professional calibre programming. Through the repeated usage of these tapes it is economically feasible to increase the investment in better program content.

Perhaps the most spectacular ITV project is the Midwest Program on Airborne Television Instruction (MPATI). Established through grants from the Ford Foundation, MPATI was organized at Purdue University in 1959. During the spring of 1961 demonstration lessons were beamed to schools and colleges from a DC-6B aircraft hovering over Montpelier, Indiana at 23,000 feet and covering a region over 127,000 square miles in area. The first full year of airborne television transmission began in September of 1961. The purposes of MPATI are as follows:

The development of the video tape recorder has stimulated
the production of higher quality television lessons and
the wider use of television as a medium of instruction.

Courtesy the Midwest Program on Airborne Television Instruction

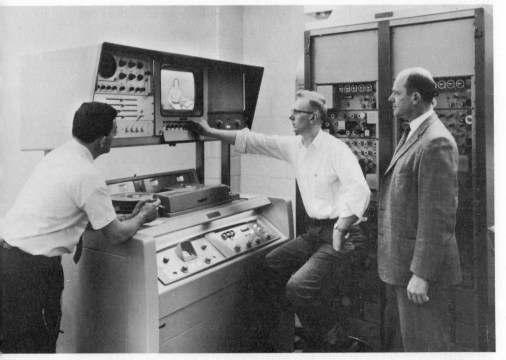

1. To broaden the range of educational offerings available to many schools.
2. To increase the quality of offerings in schools and colleges where resources are unavailable or inadequate.
3. To do these at a cost that is less than that for a comparable increase in quality achieved by other means.
4. To conduct the initial program in a manner that will assist the development of a permanent facility for the long range management and financing . . . by local and state educational authorities.[12]

MPATI transmits simultaneously over two UHF channels to schools and colleges throughout Indiana, most of Ohio, northern Kentucky, southern Michigan, eastern Illinois, and southeastern Wisconsin. During the 1963–64 academic year, 23 different courses were telecast four days per week to more than 1,000 participating schools in the six-state region. MPATI has produced the equivalent of over 1,000 full-length motion pictures, all recorded on video tape. The DC–6B aircraft contains two transmitters, and therefore functions as two television stations. A second aircraft is on hand for standby operations. Reliability has been remarkably high, since the aircraft operates above the weather. Twenty universities throughout the six-state region serve as resource centers to assist schools and colleges in utilizing MPATI courses. MPATI estimated a membership of some 1,500 schools during the 1964–65 academic year. Member schools help pay for this service.

THE NATIONAL EDUCATIONAL TELEVISION CENTER. There is no national network to serve educational television. However, the National Educational Television Center is a nonprofit agency that aims at producing high-quality informational and cultural programming for its affiliated noncommercial stations. Supported by foundation grants and fees from member stations, NET is giving major emphasis to producing the calibre of programming that is usually beyond the capacity of local noncommercial stations. Through its centralized resources, it will be possible for NET to make available to all affiliated stations a higher quality of programming.

ETV AND ITV IN BRITAIN. While television is employed as an educational medium in virtually all modern nations, a brief examination of the system in Britain reveals some interesting and valuable contrasts with the status of television in the United States. Britain is served by two networks: the British Broadcasting Corporation (BBC) and the Independent Television Authority (ITA). The BBC is a noncommercial public corporation supported by license fees on television receivers. ITA is a commercial company supported by advertising revenues. However, in

---

[12] Midwest Council on Airborne Television Instruction, *Midwest Program on Airborne Television Instruction* (Lafayette, Indiana: Purdue University, 1961), p. 1.

contrast to the minimum of 18 minutes per hour of advertising on American television, ITA is limited to an average of six minutes per hour.

The BBC has gained international recognition for its outstanding work in informational and cultural broadcasting. It has also provided high-quality programs for schools. But rather than use television for conveying conventional teaching, they use the medium primarily for the extension and enrichment of learning experiences. Most of the programs are designed to provide audio-visual experiences not otherwise possible in the classroom. Television is used as a "window to the world" rather than as a "talking face." Because of the shortage of highly competent teachers of mathematics, however, the BBC has been providing a two-year series of systematic instruction in pure mathematics for secondary students. Nevertheless, the principal use of school television in Britain is to break through the limitations of the four walls of the classroom, thereby linking school instruction with the fullest range of human experience. In the words of the Committee on Broadcasting,

> As a major purpose of broadcasting, education must be defined in its most liberal sense: as the development of the imagination, of the spirit of enquiry, of the critical attitude; as promoting breadth of interest and understanding; as making for the greatest awareness of the possibilities of mind and feeling open to human experience; in summary, as an essential part of a full life.[13]

The BBC relies on the School Broadcasting Council for determining the nature and extent of its school programming. The Council is composed of representatives from the Ministry of Education, local educational authorities, and the professional organizations of educators. During 1963–64 the BBC provided 25 television program series for schools and colleges. Pamphlets to accompany each program series are prepared by the BBC for teachers and students. These pamphlets contain information for preparatory and follow-up activities in connection with the telecasts. BBC telecasts for schools are noted for their high quality through the employment of the network's best resources. The School Television Service of the BBC draws upon the various BBC departments for design, film production, dramatization, and other resources.

Although the BBC is the leading producer of school television programming, some school television is also carried by the Independent Television Authority. However, ITA came under severe criticism in a 1962 report to the government by a committee of leading citizens.[14] The report criticized ITA for placing commercial considerations above the public interest, and recommended that the BBC expand to a second channel. It went on to recommend the continuation of school television

---

13 The Committee on Broadcasting, *The Future of Radio and Television* (London: H.M.S.O., 1962), p. 45.
14 *Ibid.*

through the auspices of the BBC and a reconstituted ITA. The system in the United States, which allows the networks to ignore school television, thereby leaving it to separate agencies and stations, was cited as an example of what not to do. When one realizes that the average youngster in the United States devotes one sixth of his waking hours to watching television, it is indeed a pity that our national networks have absolved themselves of any binding responsibility for educational and instructional broadcasting.

ITV RESEARCH. Hundreds of studies have been conducted to compare the effectiveness of televised instruction with classes receiving instruction under conventional conditions. Almost 90 per cent of the studies reveal no significant differences between the classes receiving television and the control classes, as measured by various achievement tests.

One of the important features claimed for television, according to the Ford Foundation, is that it extends the influence of our very best teachers. Yet the research does not reveal a vast superiority for television over conventional conditions. How can we account for this? There are several possible explanations. First of all, the Ford Foundation has been interested in promoting television primarily as a means of educational automation: to teach more students with fewer teachers and fewer classrooms. Under these circumstances television is used chiefly as an instrument to convey the talking face. The unique qualities of the medium for being a window to the world are almost completely ignored. Research by the author reveals that a considerable amount of instructional television closely resembles a conventional teacher who spends his time telling, explaining, showing, and even writing on the chalkboard.[15] Under these circumstances, the information is conveyed to the learner in much the same way as under traditional conditions. Attitudes of high-school and college students tend to be rather negative toward this type of television.

On the other hand, if we were to use television in the school as a window to the world or for expanded human vision, it is rather doubtful that such extended and enriched visualized learning could be measured adequately through conventional verbalized achievement tests. Yet the learning value of such lessons would be tremendous.

Our medical and dental schools have been using television as a means of expanded human vision. Through closed-circuit television, medical and dental students are able to see close-ups of surgical techniques. Microscopic views can be enlarged and projected through television, thereby giving the eyes of students new powers. Some law schools are employing closed-circuit television to link the law classroom with an

---

[15] Daniel Tanner, "Television and Learning," *Teachers College Record,* 65, December, 1963, 3:243–249.

actual courtroom. In this way law students and their professors can observe and discuss actual legal cases. Similar use is being made of television in teacher education where future teachers and their professors on the college campus can observe teaching methods and procedures in elementary and secondary schools. Video-tape recording permits the preservation and reuse of valuable sequences.

We have hardly capitalized on the unique powers of television for expanded human vision. Television not only can provide learning experiences not possible under conventional classroom conditions, but it can be used for stimulating student inquiry into important problems. Effective programs can present visual experiences to stimulate follow-up discussion, readings, and projects by the students and the classroom teacher.

The School Library

Too many teachers regard the textbook as the course of instruction. Not only do they fail to make systematic and effective use of audio-visual resources, but they neglect the vast potential of other reading materials. In the traditional school the textbook is such a dominant source of learning that students are expected to spend at least one period per day in a study hall. Except for the textbooks carried into the study hall, this room usually is barren of any learning resources. Is it any wonder that many students find the study hall a monotonous and stultifying environment?

CENTER FOR LEARNING RESOURCES. The modern concept of the school library is that it should serve as a learning resources center. Here students may be engaged not only in inquiring into a variety of reference works and other reading, but they may use specialized rooms for working with microfilm, audio-tape recordings, film strips, and various auto-instructional devices. Such an environment would stimulate student self-direction and self-impelled learning. In contrast to the policed environment of the study hall, the school library can be a center offering students a rich spectrum of learning experiences.

Teachers need to develop library assignments that stimulate inquiry and interpretation rather than fact-finding only. The power of the school library as a learning center has not been fully recognized. Studies reveal, for example, that students can make significantly greater achievement in English language skills through systematic library work than through conventional textbook work.[16]

School library experiences are more likely to carry over into adult

---

[16] Dorothy M. H. Hastings and Daniel Tanner, "The Influence of Library Work in Improving English Language Skills at the High School Level," *The Journal of Experimental Education*, 31, Summer, 1963, 4:401–405.

life than textbook assignments and class notes. If the joy of reading and self-impelled learning are cultivated in the school, such experiences are apt to exert positive influences on learning attitudes and behavior.

Instead of being a mere adjunct of the school facility, the library should be a key center in the learning process. And rather than be limited to reading materials, the school library should be a comprehensive center for learning resources.

SCHOOL LIBRARY STANDARDS. The American Library Association has formulated the following minimum quantitative standards for library programs in secondary schools:

A. Space and Location
1. Seating capacity for 10 per cent of the student enrollment.
2. Provision for classroom collections.
3. Audio-visual center as part of the school library suite or convenient to the library.

B. Annual Expenditures
1. Minimum of $4.00 to $6.00 per student for regular books.
2. Additional funds for reference works, newspapers, magazines, pamphlets, supplies and equipment.
3. Minimum of one per cent of the total instructional cost per pupil allocated for acquisition of audio-visual materials.

C. Size of Collections
1. Minimum of 10 books per student in schools with enrollment of 1,000 or more students; for smaller schools a collection of 6,000 to 10,000 volumes.
2. Collection of 70 magazine titles for junior high schools, and 120 titles for senior high schools.
3. Minimum of 3–6 newspapers.
4. Extensive pamphlet collection.
5. Professional books for faculty numbering 200–1,000 titles; and at least 25–50 professional magazines and journals.
6. Motion picture films used six or more times per year should be purchased.
7. Filmstrips and recordings used more than once a year should be purchased.

D. Personnel
1. Full-time librarian for first 900 students and additional full-time librarians for each 300–400 students or major fraction thereof.
2. One clerk for each 600 students or major fraction thereof.[17]

Programmed Learning

Throughout the history of education man has sought ways and means of improving the devices and systems of instruction. However, relatively

---

[17] Adapted from *Standards for School Library Programs* (Chicago: American Library Association, 1960), pp. 24–25.

What role can machines play in the learning process?

little progress was made in instructional technology before the twentieth century.

During the early 1920's, Professor S. L. Pressey at Ohio State developed a mechanical device that presented the student with a multiple-choice item, scored the response, and then automatically presented another item to be solved. The military employed various automated teaching devices during World War II for training in such tasks as aircraft identification. However, little interest was generated in this field among educators until the passage of the National Defense Education Act of 1958. With funds now available for research and for the acquisition of equipment by schools, a great deal of attention suddenly was being given to this field. In addition to support from N.D.E.A., the Carnegie Corporation and the Ford Foundation have financed a number of research and development projects in programmed learning.

Many private companies are marketing a variety of devices for home and school use. While much of the advertising for these instruments seems somewhat lavish and irresponsible, some reputable researchers regard programmed learning as a forerunner of a genuine revolution in educational method.

WHAT IS PROGRAMMED LEARNING? This rapidly developing field is labeled with such terminology as automated instruction, teaching machine, autoinstructional technology, and so on. However, regardless of the mechanical or electronic gadgetry, the essence of the system is the program—the series of questions, problems, processes, and solutions with which the learner is engaged. Such sequences are usually programmed in an order of increasing complexity. As the student responds to a question or problem, he receives immediate feedback as to whether his response is correct or incorrect. Some programs branch off into a review sequence whenever the student makes an error, while other programs simply follow a linear pattern that continues on to the next item without remedial sequences in case of student error. Branching is often called intrinsic programming because it anticipates errors on the part of the learner and provides for review or remedial work as an integral part of the sequence. In other words, branching or intrinsic programming provides a variable sequence that allows for differences in learner response. In contrast, the linear system provides a fixed sequence of items.

Some programs consist of multiple-choice items for selection, while others require the student to compose or construct each response. In either case the student receives immediate reinforcement as to whether his response is correct or incorrect. Branching attempts to help the student discover why he made an error in a given response.

Programmed learning systems may consist of nothing more elaborate than a scrambled book in which the subject matter is organized into units or items so arranged that each student may proceed through the text in a different pattern according to his error rate. For example, if a student makes an error on a given item he is directed to a special review exercise on another page. But the student making the correct response will continue on to the next item. The items are organized in careful sequence with prompts or cues built in to encourage the learner.

At the other extreme are electronic devices that use microfilm or 35 mm motion picture film. One device automatically selects and projects any one of 10,000 stored images, either still pictures or motion pictures, through a self-contained unit. Employing the branching principle, this device will alter its repertoire according to the response of the individual learner. Error rates are automatically recorded.

Yet another approach is the systems concept that links two or more devices in tandem. For example, a push-button (multiple choice) device is electronically linked to television. As the student is exposed to a problem on television, he selects his answer on an electronic keyboard. His response is automatically recorded on an IBM card and the student receives immediate feedback, through the flashing of a green light when he is correct, and a red light when he is incorrect. Meanwhile, the television teacher and the teacher in the classroom can get a total reading of the rate of correct or incorrect responses for all students.

An elaborate and expensive system employs a computer programmed to alter its strategy of providing questions and review lessons according to the responses of the individual learner. While for most teaching-learning exercises the instrumentation need not be so elaborate, it should be emphasized that expense is not always a limiting factor. For example, each of the major airlines has found it practical to use one or more mock-ups of jet aircraft for the training of flight crews. Each mock-up costs around a million dollars and provides simulated conditions of jet flight that are highly realistic. Responses to problem situations are automatically recorded for analysis. Such training eliminates the dangers of actual in-flight training while protecting the investment in jet aircraft.

WHAT ADVANTAGES ARE CLAIMED FOR PROGRAMMED LEARNING? In the conventional classroom the student is often treated as a passive recipient of information. It is the teacher who does most of the telling, explaining, and showing. Textbooks are designed as though all students are identical in aptitude, achievement, and rate of learning. Students are subjected to long delays before receiving their corrected papers after tests are administered. Tests are used as grading devices rather than as learning experiences. The entire class follows the same general lockstep of learning, even though some learners cannot keep pace, while others are bored by the slowness of activity.

It is argued by proponents of programmed learning that these limitations can be overcome. Some of the advantages offered for programmed learning are

1. The student is actively engaged in learning.
2. The material to be learned is organized and presented in a series of small steps, proceeding from relatively simple to complex processes, concepts, or skills.
3. Each step includes cues or prompts which help the student find the correct solutions.
4. The student receives immediate feedback as to whether his response is correct or incorrect, and thereby derives immediate reinforcement of correct responses.
5. The student progresses at his own rate of speed.
6. The student's level of performance and rate of progress are recorded.[18]

It is also claimed that programmed instruction can eliminate scholastic failure by providing nearly automatic achievement.[19] The brightest students are able to cover more ground, but all learners are reasonably assured of mastery at every stage.[20]

THEORY OF PROGRAMMED LEARNING. Professor B. F. Skinner of Harvard University maintains that learning occurs through a process of "operant conditioning" in which organisms develop a repertoire of operational responses through reinforcing stimuli or rewards. By using rewards in the form of food Skinner has been able to elicit complex responses on the part of rats and pigeons. In other words the organism is conditioned to respond operatively in order to gain its reward. Skinner and other proponents of operant conditioning maintain that human organisms and lower animals learn in much the same manner.

> Oddly enough, when one compares the behavior of verbalizing human organisms with the behavior of organisms such as pigeons and rats under otherwise identical conditions of instruction, one finds that the behavior of these differing species are essentially alike.[21]

Skinner believes that programmed learning should be governed by operant conditioning. In the case of the human learner, the reinforcing stimulus is the immediate feedback providing the learner with knowl-

---

[18] Daniel Tanner, "Automation in the Teaching-Learning Process," Ch. V, *The Outlook in Student Teaching*, Forty-first Yearbook, The Association for Student Teaching, 1962, p. 107.
[19] John W. Blyth, "Teaching Machines and Human Beings," *Educational Record*, 41, April, 1960, p. 119.
[20] B. F. Skinner, "Teaching Machines," *Science*, 128, October 24, 1958, p. 976.
[21] Edward J. Green, *The Learning Process and Programmed Instruction* (New York: Holt, Rinehart and Winston, Inc.), 1962, p. 10.

edge of the correct response. Whether such feedback is an adequate form of reward for higher forms of human learning is a moot question. Such reinforcement or reward ignores the intrinsic motivational aspects of learning. It gives no attention as to whether the learner is genuinely interested in the material itself.

For operant conditioning to be most effective, the reinforcing stimuli, according to Skinner, should be optimized. This means that the teaching machine or program should minimize error. If error rate is minimized, branching becomes unnecessary.

Some proponents of programmed learning differ sharply with Skinner on this and other points. They argue that effective learning can occur through errors provided that the learner is given the opportunity to discover the why of his errors. They reject Skinner's operant conditioning and would like to see programmed learning as a higher form of intellectual process.[22]

While space does not permit a thorough analysis of these issues, let us turn to a discussion of some of the chief criticisms of operant conditioning and programmed learning.

LIMITATIONS AND CRITICISMS. While it can be demonstrated that human behavior can be conditioned without the awareness or volition of the individual, such conditioned responses tend to be limited to rather rudimentary behaviors. Man also has the capacity for dissent. He has developed powers of imagination, creativeness, and value judgment that lead him to nonconforming behavior. In the words of H. L. Mencken, "human reason is a weak and paltry thing as long as it is not wholly free reason."

Skinner's operant conditioning runs counter to independent thinking. Under such conditioning, the learner is not allowed to seek novel and creative solutions. Skinner's thesis poses some ominous questions for a society that holds to democratic values and gives each man a voice in his own destiny.

The reduction of learning sequences into small parts and the standardization of these elements for programmed instruction would seem to lead to rigid habits of thinking. There is evidence to show that some forms of learning occur most effectively when one first deals with the total perspective and then proceeds to analyze the components in relation to the whole. Skinner's operant conditioning also conflicts with the cognitive process in which learning is geared to developing understandings rather than to evoking conditioned responses automatically.

In the years to come it seems likely that programmed learning and

---

22 See Noman A. Crowder, "On the Differences Between Linear and Intrinsic Programming," *Phi Delta Kappan,* XLIV, March, 1963, pp. 250–254.

autoinstructional technology will have to give greater emphasis to cognitive learning and reflective thinking (see Chapter 5). Teaching machines should not be used to make man more like a machine. After all, man can never compete with a machine in terms of endurance, precision, and persistence. Our world needs men who have the desire and capacity to inquire and discover, rather than to be mere instruments for information retention and retrieval.

The use of new educational media requires that the human teacher reassess his role in the school. The human teacher will need to concern himself more with human factors in the teaching-learning process. The human teacher can serve as a worthy model toward which learners might aspire. (What human would want to be like a machine?) The human teacher can seek to inspire motivation. He can develop the values of enlightened dissent through stimulating discussion. He can seek to know students as individual human beings. The human teacher can diagnose learning difficulties and provide individual guidance for solving unexpected problems. Research reveals that many important changes in human behavior are developed through human interaction rather than through verbalization.

It would be unwise to resist blindly the new media for learning. Through research we can determine what unique functions, if any, are offered by these media and how we can employ them to best advantage. In the case of programmed learning the research thus far fails to support the many unique advantages claimed for this approach.[23] Moreover, the research shows no marked superiority for one system of programming or type of instrumentation over another. Although it is obvious that, for the most part, the subject-matter specialists and curriculum workers have left programming to the amateurs, it also seems apparent that the claims have been vastly exaggerated in the interests of commercialism. Furthermore, most of the programming, including the kind that makes use of elaborate hardware, has been limited to verbal instruction. Perhaps it should not surprise us, then, if no significant learning increments are to be derived from such approaches over verbalized learning from other media.

And finally, while some observers regard programmed learning and autoinstructional technology as a system for individualized instruction, the content and process of this system is, in actuality, a mass production approach to learning. Ultimately it is the human teacher who holds the key position for developing a teaching-learning strategy that gives utmost importance to consideration for the individual learner.

---

[23] John F. Feldhusen, "Taps for Teaching Machines," *Phi Delta Kappan*, XLIV, March, 1963, pp. 265–267.

PROPOSALS FOR CHANGE IN THE DESIGN AND OPERATION OF THE SECONDARY SCHOOL

The effective utilization of new educational media requires changes in our traditional approaches to school design and operation. Recognizing the growing need for flexibility in school architecture and school management practices, the National Association of Secondary School Principals, with assistance of the Ford Foundation, established in 1956 a commission to study new approaches to school design and staff assignments. In this section we shall review some of the principal proposals of the commission and discuss their implications for the modern secondary school.[24]

The Traditional Secondary School

The architecture of the traditional secondary school resembles an egg crate. Each floor or tier is made up of an identical number of cells or classrooms and each classroom is designed to hold approximately 30 students and one teacher. Each class period is identical in length (approximately 50 minutes) with bells signaling the beginning and end of each period. The typical teacher is responsible for five or six classes daily, with one period for preparation, student conferences, and other responsibilities. Except for a possible study hall period each day, the student is given little responsibility and stimulation for individualized learning. The study hall is a place where there is no access to learning resources other than the textbooks brought there by the students themselves. And the study hall is regarded by students and teachers alike as a place where the teacher performs a custodial function.

A class of 30 pupils may be too small to justify the lecture method and too large for effective group discussion and student projects. Classrooms are ill-equipped for the new educational media, and consequently teachers find it inconvenient to make use of motion pictures, television, and other resources. The result is a classroom methodology of teacher talk, chalk, and textbook exercises. The school library is regarded as an adjunct to the instructional program, and not as an integral part of the learning environment.

The curriculum is cabined into the equal-time blocks of 50 minutes. The tendency is to fit the curriculum into the school schedule rather than to arrange the schedule to fit the curriculum.

Teachers tend to be isolated from one another as they work in their

---

[24] See J. Lloyd Trump and Dorsey Baynham, *Guide to Better Schools: Focus on Change* (Chicago: Rand McNally & Company, 1961).

separate classrooms. As a result, there is insufficient curriculum correlation and integration.

PROPOSALS FOR CHANGE: FLEXIBLE CLASS SIZE. Certain teaching-learning activities can be carried out effectively and efficiently in large groups. Classes may be combined for large group instruction during certain days of the week when motion pictures, television, or special lectures are provided. Large-group instruction makes it economically feasible not only to use motion pictures and television, but also to provide for small-group instruction. Small seminar groups could meet following each large-group session for purposes of student-centered discussion, projects, and other small-group learning activities.

For greatest effectiveness, the seminar groups should meet immediately following the large-group sessions. Seminar teachers should attend the large classes so that the follow-up discussion and activity in the seminar is carefully related to the combined class meetings. Teachers will need to learn how to conduct seminars effectively. There is little point in teaching a seminar group of 15 students in the same manner as a conventional class of 30.

Where no particular advantages are to be gained from combined classes or seminars, part of the school day will continue to be devoted to classes of conventional size.

Flexible class size does not guarantee improved learning. The key factor is the capability of the faculty and administration to develop effective teaching-learning strategies. Flexible class size should provide greater opportunities for the development of such strategies. But if faculties do not alter their methods and materials of instruction according to the nature and size of the learning group, no advantages will be gained through provisions for flexible class size.

PROPOSALS FOR CHANGE: FUNCTIONAL ARCHITECTURE. Buildings and facilities will be highly functional. While the rooms will be sound-proof, many areas will contain flexible wall partitions to accommodate various class sizes and learning activities. In this way, classes may be combined on short notice to take advantage of special films, guest speakers, or team teaching.

Rooms will be provided for small seminars, large instructional groups, and individualized study. The entire building will be wired for closed- and open-circuit television. The constant movement of audio-visual resources will be unnecessary since each learning center of the school will have the necessary installations.

PROPOSALS FOR CHANGE: INDEPENDENT STUDY AND INDIVIDUALIZED LEARNING. The traditional study hall will be eliminated. The school library will be part of the learning resources center, which will include private cubicles where learners will be able to dial films, recorded television lessons, and audiotapes for individual viewing and listening. Or the students may choose to work with programmed learning materials and teaching machines. Specialized work centers will also be available for each of the major disciplines, thereby enabling students to work on individual and small group projects under competent guidance and supervision.

PROPOSALS FOR CHANGE: MATERIALS PREPARATION CENTER. Technicians and artists will be available to assist teachers with the preparation of materials for instruction. These centers will be part of the larger learning resources center. A central television studio will broadcast both live and recorded programs to any area of the school. Viewing rooms will be available so that teachers may preview films and recorded television lessons. Clerk-typists and teacher assistants will also help professional teachers in preparing instructional materials.

PROPOSALS FOR CHANGE: TEAM TEACHING. When learning activities require close teacher collaboration in planning and conducting lessons, teachers will operate as instructional teams. This should facilitate faculty communication and also bring together the specialized talents of various teachers. Through team teaching, greater curriculum correlation and integration will be possible. Teacher assistants will function as part of the team to help relieve the professional teachers of certain routine tasks.

However, merely taking turns at teaching, while releasing other team members from the classroom, may effect no real improvement in the teaching-learning process. Teaching teams should function so as to bring about a significant improvement in instruction. Team members should be compatible and should be fully aware of their goals.

PROPOSALS FOR CHANGE: FLEXIBLE SCHEDULING. Flexible class size and varied learning activities will necessitate flexibility in class scheduling. A student's schedule will not be identical each day of the week. Certain classes and laboratory work may be scheduled two days per week for larger blocks of time. Students might also devote larger blocks of time (that is, 100 minutes) each day for individualized learning. Similarly, faculty schedules will feature greater flexibility to fit curriculum needs.

PROPOSALS FOR CHANGE: THE NONGRADED HIGH SCHOOL. In recent years, considerable interest has been generated in the nongraded high school. Having been developed successfully at the elementary level, a number of secondary school educators have attempted to pattern the high school along nongraded lines. Instead of grouping students by grade level, from 9 through 12, they are placed in various subject levels according to indices of aptitude and achievement. Each student, then,

Functional classroom design facilitates learning.

is allowed to progress at his own pace. While the traditional practice is to hold students to given grade levels according to chronological age, the nongraded approach represents an attempt at eliminating the grade-by-grade lockstep.

Under the nongraded approach, grade designations for subjects are also eliminated. For example, at Melbourne High School, in Melbourne, Florida, the curriculum is organized into five phases—ranging from those phases where students are provided with considerable remedial work, to those where the emphasis is on developing greater breadth and depth of learning.[25] In other words, while one fourteen-year-old might be placed in a remedial phase of English or mathematics, another would be designated for work at a highly advanced level. Placement is flexible to permit a given student to pursue studies, subject by subject, at a level appropriate to his aptitude and achievement. Thus, a student could be in an advanced phase of mathematics and in an intermediate phase of English. In the most advanced phase, the program is designed to provide the student with opportunity for self-direction under competent guidance.

[25] See B. Frank Brown, *The Nongraded High School* (Englewood Cliffs, N.J.: Prentice-Hall, Inc., 1963).

At Melbóurne High School it is claimed that the nongraded approach has improved student attitudes toward learning and has reduced the dropout rate significantly. It should be acknowledged that the traditional practice of grouping students and subjects by grade levels has been developed for administrative convenience, rather than for the improvement of learning. The nongraded high school is refreshingly irreverent of the tradition-bound Carnegie Unit. The nongraded approach also appears to be compatible with certain other innovations in secondary education such as flexible scheduling of classes, independent study, and team teaching.

But the most crucial factor in any school is the quality and dedication of its instructional staff. Organizational change, in and of itself, does not guarantee improvement in curriculum content and instruction. It can only facilitate such improvement. Administrators and faculty who are contemplating the nongraded approach must also be careful not to place excessive reliance on standardized aptitude testing for student placement. Multiple criteria, including previous academic records, motivation, maturity, teacher recommendations, and special problems and interests of the student must be taken into account in matching the youngster appropriately to the teaching-learning strategy.

SUMMARY

The provision for flexibility in educational design and the utilization of the most modern learning resources do not necessarily guarantee improved learning outcomes. The quality of the curriculum and the competency of the faculty and administration will determine how wisely, or how foolishly, modern facilities and media are used.

School facilities and learning resources do not, by themselves, determine the quality of learning experiences. A fancy package does not change the nature of its contents. Wisely used, however, functional educational design and modern learning resources will facilitate improvements in the quality of education. The underlying rationale for innovation in education should be the improvement of learning (behavior).

Television and the motion picture can provide the classroom with a window to the world. But we have hardly begun to use these media in education with any real degree of effectiveness. In the case of television, there has been the temptation to use it as an instrument of educational efficiency and economy, rather than a means of improving the learning process. Because traditional education is largely limited to verbal symbols, whether printed in the textbook or spoken by the teacher, there has been too great a tendency to use television as a means of verbalized instruction. Yet its greatest potential is in its power to extend man's time-life space.

In recent years, there have been some promising uses of television and the motion picture for the improvement of course content and methodology in science and modern foreign language instruction. Visual experiences are provided in situations that are beyond the capacity of any conventional classroom. It has been demonstrated that television and the motion picture do not have to be one-way forms of communication. These media can stimulate inquiry and discovery by exposing the student to new vistas and perspectives.

The newer learning resources and innovations should not be regarded as ends in themselves. These resources and innovations are the means of bringing new dimensions to classroom learning. The real test of these devices lies not in whether they are being used, but in how well they serve us.

As we gradually learn to exploit technology in education, we must not lose sight of the importance of the human model, the teacher and the peer, in learning. We need to keep in mind that, in education, we are dealing with human beings and not assembly-line components.

PROBLEMS FOR STUDY AND DISCUSSION

1. Some critics of audio-visual media hold the notion that because these devices deal with sensory experience, they are of poorer intellectual fiber than the printed word. In carrying this idea to its logical conclusion, how does one evaluate a painting by Rembrandt or a symphony by Beethoven?

2. Whitehead challenged the commonly accepted principle that easier subjects should precede the harder.

> It is not true that the easier subjects should precede the harder. On the contrary, some of the hardest must come first because nature so dictates, and because they are essential to life. The first intellectual task which confronts an infant is the acquirement of spoken language. What an appalling task, the correlation of meaning with sounds! It requires an analysis of ideas and an analysis of sounds. We all know that the infant does it, and that the miracle of his achievement is explicable.[26]

If educators were to make the schools more essential to life it would seem that our traditional ideas about learning sequences and the difficulty of subjects would have to be cast aside. How could audio-visual resources be used to make education more essential to life?

---

[26] Alfred North Whitehead, *The Aims of Education* (New York: The Macmillan Company, 1929), p. 25.

3. It is sometimes argued that television offers no advantages as a medium of instruction over the motion picture. What differences do you see between these two important media of instruction?

4. Do you favor a fourth national TV network that would operate in the United States on a noncommerical basis and in a manner similar to the British Broadcasting Corporation? Why or why not?

5. As a classroom teacher, under what circumstances, if any, would you favor the use of television as a medium for direct and systematic instruction? For expanded human vision?

6. What kinds of library assignments would you, as a teacher, give your students?

7. How does your own high-school library measure up to the minimum school library standards formulated by the American Library Association?

8. In the school of the future, what relationship do you see between the new educational media and the human teacher?

9. What are the alleged advantages of team teaching in the secondary school? Disadvantages?

10. Observe several classes at the secondary level and tabulate the approximate amount of time spent on the following:

    (a) Verbalization by the teacher.
    (b) Use of audio-visual media.
    (c) Use of chalkboard.
    (d) Use of textbook.
    (e) Other activities.

11. What architectural features would you incorporate in your ideal school of the future?

SELECTED REFERENCES

American Association of School Librarians. *Standards for School Library Programs.* Chicago: American Library Association, 1960.

Anderson, Charnel. *Technology in American Education 1650–1900.* Washington, D.C.: Office of Education, U.S. Department of Health, Education, and Welfare, 1962.

Brown, B. Frank. *The Nongraded High School.* Englewood Cliffs, N.J.: Prentice-Hall, Inc., 1963.

Brown, James W., Richard B. Lewis and Fred F. Harcleroad. *A-V Instruction: Materials and Methods.* New York: McGraw-Hill Company, Inc., 1959.

Bush, Robert N. and Dwight W. Allen. *A New Design for High School Education.* New York: McGraw-Hill Company, Inc., 1964.

Cassirer, Henry H. *Television Teaching Today*. Paris, France: UNESCO, 1960.

Chapman, Dave, Inc. *Design for ETV*. New York: Educational Facilities Laboratories, 1960.

Costello, Lawrence F. and George N. Gordon. *Teach With Television*. New York: Hastings House, 1961.

Coulson, John E. (ed.) *Programmed Learning and Computer Based Instruction*. New York: John Wiley and Sons, Inc., 1962.

Dale, Edgar. *Audio-Visual Methods in Teaching* (Revised). New York: Holt, Rinehart and Winston, Inc., 1954.

Fund for the Advancement of Education. *Teaching by Television* (2nd Ed.) New York: The Ford Foundation, January, 1961.

Green, Edward J. *The Learning Process and Programmed Instruction*. New York: Holt, Rinehart and Winston, Inc., 1962.

Hilgard, Ernest R. *Theories of Learning*. New York: Appleton-Century-Crofts, Inc., 1956, Ch. 4.

Himmelweit, Hilde T., A. N. Oppenheim and Pamela Vince. *Television and the Child*. London: Oxford University Press, 1958.

Lewis, Philip. *Educational Television Guidebook*. New York: McGraw-Hill Company, Inc., 1961.

Lumsdaine, A. A. "Instruments and Media of Instruction," Ch. 12 in *Handbook of Research on Teaching*, N. L. Gage (ed.) Chicago: Rand McNally & Company, 1963.

―――― and Robert Glaser (eds.) *Teaching Machines and Programmed Learning*. Washington, D.C.: National Education Association, 1960.

Margulies, Stuart and Lewis D. Eigen. *Applied Programmed Instruction*. New York: John Wiley and Sons, Inc., 1962.

Midwest Program on Airborne Television Instruction. *Using Television in the Classroom*. McGraw-Hill Company, Inc., 1961.

Office of Education. *New Teaching Aids for the American Classroom*. Washington, D.C.: U.S. Department of Health, Education, and Welfare, 1962.

――――. *The School Library as a Materials Center*. Washington, D.C.: U.S. Department of Health, Education, and Welfare, 1962.

Schramm, Wilbur (ed.) *Mass Communications*. Urbana, Illinois: University of Illinois Press, 1960.

――――. *The Impact of Educational Television*. Urbana, Illinois: University of Illinois Press, 1960.

Shaplin, Judson T. and Henry F. Olds, Jr. (eds.) *Team Teaching*. New York: Harper & Row, Publishers, Inc., 1964.

Stoddard, Alexander J. *Schools for Tomorrow: An Educator's Blueprint*. New York: The Fund for the Advancement of Education, 1957.

Stolurow, Lawrence M. *Teaching by Machine*. Washington, D.C.: Office of Education, U.S. Department of Health, Education, and Welfare, 1961.

Tanner, Daniel. "Automation in the eTaching-Learning Process," Ch. V in *The Outlook in Student Teaching*, Forty-first Yearbook of The Association for Student Teaching, 1962, pp. 102–117.

Trump, J. Lloyd and Dorsey Baynham. *Guide to Better Schools: Focus on Change*. Chicago: Rand McNally & Company, 1961.

――――. *Images of the Future*. Washington, D.C.: National Educational Association, 1959.

Wittich, Walter A. and Charles F. Schuller. *Audio-Visual Materials* (3rd Ed.). New York: Harper & Row, Publishers, Inc., 1962.

CHAPTER *11*

Administration,
Extra-Class Programs,
and Special Services

W HILE THE EDUCATIONAL FUNCTION of most nations resides with the national government, a different pattern of school organization and control has developed in the United States. In Chapter 1 we discussed the evolution of our system of education. The Tenth Amendment to the Constitution, ratified in 1791, stated that "the powers not delegated to the United States by the Constitution, nor prohibited by it to the States, are reserved to the States respectively, or to the people." Thus, education in the United States came to be recognized as a state function. The states, however, have delegated a great deal of operational responsibility to local school districts. If education is a state function with operational responsibility delegated to local levels, what then is the role of the Federal Government? The Preamble to the Constitution specifically includes the objective to "promote the general welfare." The words of our founding fathers and the Land Ordinances of 1785 and 1787 were testimony to the role of the Federal Government in supporting and promoting education. The Ordinance of 1787 declared that "schools and the means of education shall forever be encouraged."

While our founding fathers may have envisioned a more direct role of federal responsibility for education, the fact remains that a three-way, interrelated system has evolved. Nevertheless, federal activities in education have exerted great impact. The Land Ordinances of 1785 and 1787 provided lands from the public domain to be used for the support of education. The land-grant colleges and universities, vocational education programs, and G.I. Bill of Rights are but a few examples of the wide variety of federal activities in education over the years. In recent times, the role of the Federal Government in promoting and supporting certain

434

phases of our educational enterprise has been intensified and extended under the aegis of national defense.

This three-tiered structure of local-state-federal interrelatednesss confounds the European observer, who regards education as properly under the authority of the national government. After visiting many schools in several of our states a European educator commented to the author: "What you have in the United States is not a *system* of education, but rather many different, uncoordinated educational authorities and programs." Nevertheless, since World War II, and particularly during the past decade, the federal role in supporting education has grown significantly. Nationalizing influences have been felt not only in the area of school finance, but also in the domain of the curriculum.

In this chapter we shall examine the structure and function of educational administration at national, state, and local levels. And we shall give special attention to some administrative operations, responsibilities, and problems in the local secondary school.

THE FEDERAL LEVEL

While, historically, federal participation in education has been justified as promoting the general welfare, in more recent years the federal role has been stepped up for purposes of national defense. Nevertheless, in a message to Congress, the late President Kennedy observed that federal support for education does not need the threat to our nation's defense for its justification.

> We do not undertake to meet our growing educational problems merely to compare our achievements with those of our adversaries. These measures are justified on their own merits—in times of peace as well as peril—to educate better citizens as well as better scientists and soldiers. The Federal Government's responsibility in this area has been established since the earliest days of the Republic—it is time now to act decisively to fulfill that responsibility for the sixties.[1]

Federal support for education over the years has been provided through special programs passed by Congress as the need arose. While most modern countries provide for education through a national ministry at the cabinet level of government, our own Office of Education is only one of the agencies under the United States Department of Health, Education, and Welfare. Moreover, many different departments and agencies of our Federal Government have become engaged in education.

---

[1] Message to Congress on February 20, 1961, as quoted by Clayton D. Hutchins, Albert R. Munse, and Edna D. Booker in *Federal Funds for Education* (Washington, D.C.: U.S. Department of Health, Education, and Welfare, Office of Education, 1961), p. 5.

Table 11–1
State Rankings in High-School Graduates, Teachers' Salaries, and Per-Pupil Expenditures

State	Public high-school graduates in 1963 as per cent of ninth-graders in 1959–60		Average salary of public-school teachers, 1963–64		Expenditure per pupil in public elementary and secondary schools, 1963–64	
	Percent	Rank of state	Amount	Rank of state	Amount	Rank of state
50 states	72.7%	...	$5,963	...	$455	...
Alabama	61.5	42	4,615	44	280	48
Alaska	64.1	38	8,150	1	634	2
Arizona	77.2	16	6,500	8	455	22
Arkansas	65.0	37	4,031	49	302	44
California	87.5	1	7,375	2	530	7
Colorado	75.2	21	5,800	24	460	20
Connecticut	76.6	18	6,775	4	552	4
Delaware	74.5	23	6,500	9	498	11
Florida	65.7	36	5,940	21	388	34
Georgia	56.8	50	4,740	41	306	43
Hawaii	82.1	9	6,000	19	402	31
Idaho	74.8	22	4,940	39	316	42
Illinois	82.4	7	6,645	5	479	16
Indiana	69.9	31	6,280	12	467	18
Iowa	78.5	11	5,352	30	456	21
Kansas	84.5	4	5,312	31	448	24
Kentucky	58.2	48	4,400	46	300	45
Louisiana	60.9	43	5,090	36	399	32
Maine	68.6	34	4,950	38	378	38
Maryland	71.8	30	6,415	10	489	14
Massachusetts	78.4	12	6,275	13	475	17
Michigan	76.1	19	6,503	7	452	23
Minnesota	85.5	2	6,100	17	509	9
Mississippi	58.8	47	3,830	50	241	50
Missouri	72.4	28	5,488	27	419	29
Montana	73.8	25	5,420	28	493	13
Nebraska	84.8	3	4,800	40	385	37
Nevada	67.6	35	6,140	16	464	19
New Hampshire	69.7	32	5,185	32	427	27
New Jersey	75.9	20	6,511	6	568	3
New Mexico	57.4	49	6,040	18	440	26
New York	72.9	27	7,200	3	705	1
North Carolina	60.0	46	5,050	37	320	41
North Dakota	82.2	8	4,400	47	420	28
Ohio	73.9	24	5,850	23	446	25

Oklahoma	69.3	33	5,160	33	351	39
Oregon	78.2	14	6,240	14	549	5
Pennsylvania	77.6	15	5,908	22	485	15
Rhode Island	77.1	17	6,150	15	500	10
South Carolina	60.6	45	4,350	48	265	49
South Dakota	82.4	6	4,425	45	403	30
Tennessee	60.7	44	4,700	43	291	47
Texas	63.7	39	5,390	29	387	35
Utah	78.3	13	5,505	26	394	33
Vermont	73.6	26	5,150	34	387	36
Virginia	62.4	40	5,150	35	350	40
Washington	84.5	5	6,390	11	515	8
West Virginia	61.8	41	4,725	42	300	46
Wisconsin	81.8	10	5,985	20	498	12
Wyoming	72.0	29	5,725	25	540	6

SOURCE: *NEA Research Bulletin*, Vol. 41 (Washington, D.C.: National Education Association, 1964), p. 17.

For example, the Office of Education administers such programs as vocational education, school assistance in federally affected areas, and the several phases of the National Defense Education Act; the various branches of the armed services administer their own schools for the education of dependents of military personnel; the National Science Foundation provides scholarships and fellowships in the sciences, mathematics, and engineering; the Public Health Service gives training grants and fellowships in agriculture, education, the social sciences, and the various health fields; the Department of the Interior operates public schools for Indians; the Department of State operates the educational exchange program with other nations; the Atomic Energy Commission sponsors the public schools of Los Alamos, Oak Ridge, and other areas; the Veterans Administration provides funds for education and vocational rehabilitation; and the District of Columbia operates its own public schools through direct federal grants. Because federal programs in education have evolved on a piecemeal basis, we have a vast number of dissociated and uncoordinated programs administered by many different federal agencies.

The Need for Federal Support of Education

We have already cited the federal role in education as designed to promote the general welfare and to provide for the common defense— as stipulated in the Preamble to the Constitution. The tremendous rate of population mobility and the great inequities of educational support and opportunity from state to state serve to make education a national concern. In Table 11–1 we see the differences among the states in the proportion of high-school graduates, the salaries of public school teachers, and the expenditure per pupil in the public schools. The differences are glaring. For example, while New York State expended $705 per pupil during 1963–1964, Mississippi provided only $241. In California the high-school graduates of 1963 represented 87.5 per cent of the ninth-graders of 1959–1960, while the percentage in Georgia was only 56.8 over the same time period. The average salary of public-school teachers during 1963–1964 (Alaska excluded) ranged from $7,375 in California to $3,830 in Mississippi.

The per capita personal income of Mississippi is only 43 per cent of that for New York State. The percentage of Selective Service registrants failing the mental test varies sharply state by state and is closely related to educational expenditure. In 1961 fewer than one out of every ten registrants in 16 states failed the Selective Service mental test. Yet, that same year, more than three out of every 10 registrants in 11 states failed this test. In Mississippi and South Carolina the rate of failure exceeded 50 per cent.[2]

These great disparities in educational expenditure and achievement are good reason for federal support of education on a comprehensive rather than piecemeal basis. Obviously comprehensive federal support will need to be based on an equalization formula to provide optimum opportunities for youngsters in the schools of the poorer states.

The Office of Education has cited the following reasons for federal support of education through existing programs:

1. To encourage and support programs of education or services in the schools that are essential or beneficial to the national welfare and security.
2. To contribute to or provide for public education where there is a Federal responsibility or obligation.
3. To provide education and training services which are essential to the national defense but which are not the separate responsibilities of any local community, State, or segment of the population.
4. To assist students, selected on the basis of tests and recommendations, through scholarships for advanced training that will serve the national welfare.
5. To assist the economically developing areas of the world and to improve international relationships through the exchange of information and of students, teachers, professors, technicians, and leaders with other countries.
6. To maintain efficient governmental services and to increase the effectiveness of the Federal service.
7. To promote the general welfare of the Nation through research in the physical, biological, and social sciences that will develop new areas of learning and prepare more specialists with competencies in these fields.[3]

---

[2] National Committee for Support of the Public Schools, *Know Your Schools Fact Sheet No. 1*, Washington, D.C.: 1963.

[3] Hutchins, Munse, & Booker, *op. cit.*, pp. 3–4.

While the need to provide educational assistance to the economically developing areas of the world is recognized by our Federal Government, as indicated in number 5 of the above list, we have failed to provide for comprehensive equalization aid for improving educational opportunity in our poorer states. The principle of providing larger federal allotments to areas of lower financial ability has been established through such special federal programs as the National School Lunch Act, Vocational Rehabilitation, and Public Library Services for Rural Areas.

Despite the wide variety of federal programs for public education, we see in Table 11–2 that federal funds constitute less than five per cent of all school revenue receipts. The greatest burden falls on the local districts, which contribute 54 per cent, while the individual states provide 38.7 per cent. Back around the turn of the century, the Federal Government collected less than 20 per cent of our nation's total tax revenues. The major unit of tax revenues at that time was the local government. Today, the situation is completely reversed. The Federal Government now collects approximately 75 per cent of all tax revenues, while the states gather 15 per cent and the local communities receive only 10 per cent. Yet, although the Federal Government collects 75 per cent of the taxes, it contributes less than five per cent of the costs of public elementary and secondary education.

It should be noted, however, that there has been a gradual shift toward increased support for education on the part of the federal and state governments over the years. During 1919–20 the Federal Government contributed only 0.3 per cent of the funds for elementary and secondary schools; by 1961–62 the federal contribution rose to 4.5 per cent. Over this same period the state allocations to local districts increased from 16.5 per cent to 38.7 per cent.

The role of the Federal Government in supporting public elementary and secondary education, nevertheless, continues to fall far short of the great problem of unequal educational opportunity that faces our nation. While our nation's public elementary and secondary schools derive less than five per cent of their revenues from federal sources, our colleges and universities, both public and private, receive approximately 20 per cent of their income from the Federal Government. It is unfortunate that the universities, which have often been quick to criticize the work of the public schools, have lobbied vigorously for federal funds for higher education while avoiding any commitment to the public schools as far as federal support is concerned. In 1963 the eighty-eighth Congress passed a $1.2 billion dollar bill, known as the Higher Education Facilities Act, for the construction of classroom buildings and laboratory facilities in public and private institutions of higher education. This broad assistance program is probably the most significant piece of federal legisla-

Table 11-2

Public Elementary and Secondary School Revenue
Receipts from Federal, State, Intermediate, and Local Sources:
United States, 1919-20 to 1961-62

School year	Total	Federal	State	Intermediate	Local*
	AMOUNT IN THOUSANDS OF DOLLARS				
1919-20	$ 970,120	$ 2,475	$ 160,085	$110,814	$ 696,747
1929-30	2,088,557	7,334	353,670	216,747	1,510,806
1939-40	2,260,527	39,810	684,354	151,097	1,385,266
1941-42	2,416,580	34,305	759,993	150,223	1,472,058
1943-44	2,604,322	35,886	859,183	146,243	1,563,010
1945-46	3,059,845	41,378	1,062,057	185,097	1,771,312
1947-48	4,311,534	120,270	1,676,362	229,761	2,285,141
1949-50	5,437,044	155,848	2,165,689	328,849	2,786,658
1951-52	6,423,816	227,711	2,478,596	386,812	3,330,695
1953-54	7,866,852	355,237	2,944,103	240,733†	4,326,779†
1955-56	9,686,677	441,442	3,828,886	209,377†	5,206,973†
1957-58	12,181,513	486,484	4,800,368†	275,463†	6,619,198†
1959-60	14,746,618	651,639	5,768,047	382,870†	7,944,062†
1961-62**	17,483,120	781,495	6,760,723	507,010†	9,433,892†
	PERCENTAGE DISTRIBUTION				
1919-20	100.0	0.3	16.5	11.4	71.8
1929-30	100.0	.4	16.9	10.4	72.3
1939-40	100.0	1.8	30.3	6.7	61.3
1941-42	100.0	1.4	31.5	6.2	60.9
1943-44	100.0	1.4	33.0	5.6	60.0
1945-46	100.0	1.4	34.7	6.0	57.8
1947-48	100.0	2.8	38.9	5.3	53.0

1949–50	100.0	2.9	39.8	6.0	51.3
1951–52	100.0	3.5	38.6	6.0	51.8
1953–54	100.0	4.5	37.4	3.1†	55.0†
1955–56	100.0	4.6	39.5	2.2†	53.7†
1957–58	100.0	4.0	39.4†	2.3†‡	54.3†
1959–60	100.0	4.4	39.1	2.6†	53.9†
1961–62**	100.0	4.5	38.7	2.9†	54.0†

* Includes a relatively minor amount from other sources (transportation fees and tuition from patrons, and gifts) which accounted for 0.5 per cent of total revenue receipts in 1959–60.

† Data not comparable with those before 1953–54 because of reclassification of items comprising "intermediate," and "local."

‡ Revised since originally published.

** Estimated.

NOTE: Beginning in 1959–60, includes Alaska and Hawaii. Because of rounding, detail may not add to totals.

SOURCE: U.S. Department of Health, Education, and Welfare, Office of Education, *Statistics of State School Systems: 1959–60*, and unpublished data.

tion supporting higher education since the Morrill Act, which established the land-grant colleges and universities more than a century ago. While praising this bill, President Johnson pointed to the unfinished task of improving educational opportunity by providing omnibus support of public elementary and secondary education through the National Education Improvement Act.

> But these measures will still not do the whole job of extending educational opportunities to all who want and can benefit by them, nor in meeting our growing national needs. I therefore strongly urge the Congress to take early, positive action on the unfinished portion of the National Education Improvement Act, particularly those programs which will assist elementary and secondary schools.[4]

Opposition to Federal Support

One of the chief arguments against federal support for education is that it will lead to federal control. But federal participation in education is not a new development. It can be traced back to our very early history. In Chapter 1 we discussed the concern of our founding fathers on the national importance of education. The many special federal programs for aiding public education today do, of course, entail requirements and safeguards to ensure that the funds are legally administered. However, in virtually all of these programs, the Federal Government has consistently followed a policy of participation in order to aid and support education and not to control our schools. The individual states have always participated in these programs on a voluntary basis. Federal programs for elementary and secondary education typically have been administered through the various state departments of education. To assume that federal support for education brings dictatorial control over state and local systems implies powers that are alien to our Constitution.

Federal support for education is likely to increase over the long pull. However, if such support continues to be provided through a multiplicity of piecemeal and dissociated programs, the qualifications for participation in federally assisted programs will, of necessity, be administered on a piecemeal and dissociated basis. Certain pieces of emergency federal legislation, particularly the measures of the depression period, were administered independently of the state education authorities. The principle of education as a state function carried the expectation that federal educational programs would be administered through the appropriate state education agencies. As the federal role in supporting education is intensified and expanded, it becomes increasingly important that the federal programs are appropriately coordinated and channeled. A general

---

[4] The *New York Times*, January 16, 1964, p. 1.

rather than piecemeal program of educational support by the Federal Government would place the individual states in a better position to exercise their discretion in using these funds for school improvement.

The Higher Education Facilities Act of 1963 is an example of rather broad legislation to finance the construction of buildings for classroom and laboratory facilities on the college campuses of our nation. Leaders in higher education lobbied successfully for this measure. Very few, if any, colleges and universities will refuse these funds. It is unfortunate that our college and university leaders have lobbied for federal support for higher education only, while ignoring the critical needs of our public schools.

Although the National Education Association and other groups have been working for a comprehensive program of federal support of public education, there is no real grass roots awareness of the need for such assistance. The school board members who govern the 32,000 local school districts of our nation represent the conservative sectors of the community and have tended to oppose comprehensive federal support. They seem to fear big government even though lessons in political science tend to show no less wastage of public funds when derived and administered at state and local levels.

Opposition to federal support also stems from the church-state issue. Ironically, Catholic church leaders do not fear federal support as a means to federal control; such church leaders have been actively seeking federal funds for parochial schools. And they have vigorously opposed proposals for federal educational support that exclude church-related schools.

The school desegregation issue is another factor that has clouded the problem of federal support. Southern congressmen automatically oppose any federal bills that contain anti-segregation clauses. In view of the recent Supreme Court rulings, such clauses are obviously unnecessary.

Recent decisions by the United States Supreme Court on the church-state and school segregation issues have pointed to certain limitations on the states. The Supreme Court has upheld the principle of church-state separation by citing the First Amendment, in declaring that neither a state or any other agency of Government can support religious activities or institutions.[5] The Fourteenth Amendment, which established the principle of equal protection of the laws, was cited by the Supreme Court in its historic 1954 decision holding segregation in the public schools unconstitutional.[6] While the impact of various Supreme Court decisions is discussed in some detail in Chapter 4, we cite this now as

[5] McCollum vs. Board of Education, 333 (U.S.) 203 (1948); Everson vs. Board of Education, 330 (U.S.) 1 (1947).
[6] Brown vs. Board of Education, 347 (U.S.) 483 (1954).

evidence that, although education is recognized as a state function, the states or their agencies must not violate the Constitution of our Federal Government.

Role of the United States Office of Education

This federal agency was created by an act of Congress signed by President Andrew Johnson on March 2, 1867. The purposes of this agency were specified as follows:

> That there shall be established at the city of Washington, a Department of Education, for the purpose of collecting such statistics and facts as shall show the condition and progress of education in the several States and Territories, and of diffusing such information respecting the organization and management of schools and school systems and methods of teaching as shall aid the people of the United States in the establishment and maintenance of efficient school systems, and otherwise promote the cause of education throughout the country.[7]

However, there was considerable confusion as to just where this new agency should fit in the administrative framework of the Federal Government. Where most nations provided for a national educational agency coordinate with other departments of the national government, the United States kept its national educational agency at a subservient and ineffectual level. In 1869 the Department of Education was renamed the Office of Education. The following year it became the Bureau of Education. It remained a bureau in the Department of the Interior until 1929, when it was again renamed the Office of Education. In 1939 it was shifted to the Federal Security Agency. The Federal Security Agency became the Department of Health, Education, and Welfare in 1953. The Office of Education has continued as a unit of the Department of Health, Education, and Welfare to this day.

In Figure 11–1 we see an organization chart for the United States Office of Education. The head of the Office is the Commissioner of Education. He is appointed by the President with the advice and approval of the Senate. The operations of the Office are organized according to three bureaus: the Bureau of Research collects, analyzes and disseminates educational data; the Bureau of Educational Assistance Programs administers grants-in-aid such as vocational education and school assistance in federally affected areas; and the Bureau of International Education is concerned with gathering information on educational programs of other nations and assisting American and foreign teachers and students in certain programs of educational exchange.

The Office of Education not only collects and interprets educational

---

[7] Arthur B. Moehlman, *School Administration*, 2nd Ed. (Boston: Houghton Mifflin Company, 1951), p. 474.

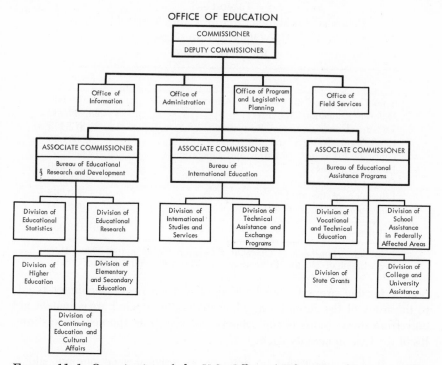

FIGURE 11–1. Organization of the U.S. Office of Education. [SOURCE: Office of Education, *Digest of Educational Statistics* (Washington, D.C.: U.S. Department of Health, Education, and Welfare, 1963), p. 134.]

data, but handles grants and contracts connected with more than 20 pieces of federal legislation—including such programs as vocational education, school assistance in federally affected areas, cooperative research, rural library services, and the various phases of the National Defense Education Act.

Table 11–3 shows the major programs and funds administered through the Office of Education during the 1963 fiscal year. It can be seen that the two largest programs by far are for school assistance in federally affected areas and defense education activities. These two programs accounted for more than 86 per cent of all the funds administered through the Office of Education during 1963. Since 1950 the Federal Government has been allocating funds to school districts in areas that are affected by federal activities. Under this program federal funds are granted to school districts having enrollment increases because of federal activities, and also to districts having tax losses as a result of the acquisi-

Table 11–3
Financial Assistance Programs Administered by the
U.S. Office of Education
Fiscal Year 1963

Program	Funds
School Assistance in Federally Affected Areas	$346,008,000
Defense Education Activities	229,450,000
Vocational and Technical Education	41,877,455
Land-Grant Colleges and Universities	14,500,000
Office of Education (Salaries and Operations)	12,300,000
Library Services	7,500,000
Cooperative Research	6,985,000
Education of the deaf	1,500,000
Education of the mentally retarded	1,000,000
TOTAL	$661,120,455

SOURCE: *Handbook of Office of Education* (Washington, D.C.: U.S. Department of Health, Education, and Welfare, 1963), p. 6.

tion of taxable property by the Federal Government. Hechinger points to the irony of the situation in which federally affected areas benefit not only from these grants to the schools, but also from the economic stimulus of the federal activity itself.

> It is no secret that, in spite of the original good purpose, aid to "Federally impacted" areas has in many places become no more than pork-barrel expenditure. Although Federal installations may take land off the tax rolls, the violent protests whenever an air base or a defense establishment is to be closed down offer some indication that their presence is hardly a drain on the local economy. While boom towns get aid, the truly distressed regions, both in rural sections and in city slums, go without support.[8]

The National Defense Education Act constitutes the next largest program administered through the Office of Education. As we have discussed in an earlier chapter, this legislation clearly favors the fields of science, mathematics, and modern foreign languages over other curricular areas.

As we have pointed out earlier, many different departments and agencies of the Federal Government continue to administer sizable programs for education. The need for a coherent policy and coordinated program becomes more urgent as the Federal Government increases and broadens its role in supporting education. The Office of Education appears to be the appropriate agency for coordinating federal educational programs and policies. But a Department of Education with cabinet

---

[8] Fred M. Hechinger, "Everybody Says He's for Education, But——," *The New York Times Magazine*, July 22, 1962, p. 63.

status may be necessary in the future if education is to receive adequate leadership and support.

THE STATE LEVEL

Although public education is a function of the state, the organization and operation of the schools have been delegated to the local school districts. Nevertheless, each state maintains an education agency that discharges important functions. The constitutions and amendments thereto in virtually all of the states make some provision for public education. Through subsequent legislation and court decisions in each of the states, the principle of maintaining schools at public expense has been firmly established. Most of the states have organized their education laws into a code that defines the functions and responsibilities of the state educational agency, the intermediate unit (that is, county), and the local school district. While public education is a function of the state, the constitutional provisions and laws of each state must not be in violation of the Federal Constitution and its amendments. For example, a state law requiring or resulting in the maintenance of racially segregated schools would be held illegal.

The State Board of Education

The Council of Chief State School Officers recommends that the duties of state boards of education be defined by statutes and that these boards perform such duties as (1) formulating policies and regulations for carrying out its responsibilities as indicated in the constitution and statutes of the state; (2) appointing the professional staff of the state education department upon recommendation of the chief state school officer; (3) establishing standards for teacher certification; (4) establishing standards for the classification, approval, and accreditation of public and private schools; (5) prescribing a uniform system of educational data on such matters as enrollment, finance, and evaluation of educational progress; (6) providing an annual report to the governor and legislature on educational progress and needs; (7) publishing the laws on education with notes for the guidance of those responsible for education; (8) providing for supervisory and consultative services through the state department of education; (9) distributing funds and commodities from the state and federal governments to the various school districts; and (10) defining its supervisory responsibilities over education, public and private, in accord with the law.[9]

In most of the states, the members of the state board of education are

---

[9] See National Council of Chief State School Officers, *The State Department of Education* (Washington, D.C.: The Council, 1952), pp. 14–16.

appointed by the governor. However, an increasing number of states are providing for the nonpartisan election of state board of education members. The number of members of the state board generally runs from seven to 10, with a term of office from two to four or more years. The typical state board of education is made up of lay people. Only a few states require that membership include professional educators. Many states actually exclude professional educators from membership on state boards of education. On the other hand, in most occupations that require state licensure (that is, medicine, law, dentistry, chiropody, pharmacy, optometry, nursing, accounting, and so on), the majority of the members of the licensing board are practitioners rather than lay people. This is also true for the barbers and beauticians. Lieberman argues that in education, as in the other professions, the composition of the state board should be made up of professional practitioners rather than laymen.[10] However, in view of the long tradition of holding to the principle of lay control of education, both at the state and local levels, it is highly unlikely that any significant measures will be taken in the foreseeable future toward shifting from lay control to professional control.

The Chief State School Officer

The chief state school officer typically carries the title of state superintendent of public instruction or state commissioner of education. The state superintendent or commissioner usually serves as the executive officer of the state board of education. He is responsible for administering the state department of education, advising the board on educational policies, operations, and standards, interpreting the school laws and rulings of the state board of education, preparing the budget for the education program of the state, and reporting to the state board, the governor, the legislature and the public on the status, progress, and the needs of the schools.

Although the chief state school officer should represent the most important educational position in the state, his salary is usually well below that of school superintendents of the larger urban districts. In about half the states the chief state school officer is elected by popular vote. This means that he must campaign for office and that his tenure is dependent upon his political ability. The other states provide for the appointment of the chief state school officer. The trend has been toward having this officer appointed by the state board of education. The appointment method is preferred over the method of popular election by most professional educators. In many states, there are no professional requirements or qualifications for this important office. However, the

---

[10] Myron Lieberman, *Education as a Profession* (Englewood Cliffs, N.J.: Prentice-Hall, Inc., 1956), p. 92.

trend appears to be toward improving the salary, status, and responsibilities of this office, and raising the professional qualifications so as to attract persons of higher competence.

The State Department of Education

This agency, headed by the chief state school officer, serves regulatory, operational, and leadership functions. It regulates teacher certification, school accreditation, attendance, finance, and certain curriculum requirements. The state education department frequently operates certain special schools for the handicapped, and in some states has jurisdiction over the operations of the state colleges. This agency also serves in a leadership capacity through planning, research, and consultation for educational improvement. Thus, while the state board of education determines educational policy within the legal framework of the state, the state department of education, under the chief state school officer, carries out the necessary regulatory, operational, and leadership functions. In some states the leadership of the education department has been outstanding, while in others it has been little more than a statistical and regulatory agency.

The State and School Finance

Almost 40 per cent of the revenues for operating the public schools are derived from the states. Local sources contribute 54 per cent, chiefly through property taxation. We have already pointed to the great disparaties from state to state in supporting education. But even within the same state or county there are tremendous differences in community wealth and expenditures for public education. For example, in Cook County, Illinois during 1961-62, the annual expenditure per pupil ranged from $283 to $1,090 for elementary-school districts, and from $522 to $1,535 for high-school districts.

It is a common practice for states to provide flat grants to local school districts based on average daily attendance, per census child, or a similarly related unit. Such flat grants ignore the financial status of the districts. In other words, these flat grants serve to aid the wealthy districts on the same basis as they aid the poorer districts.

Most of the states are now operating some type of foundation program intended to provide a minimum level of educational support for every child, regardless of the district in which he attends school. However, in only a few states is the foundation program effectively geared to the development of equalization of educational opportunity. In an effective foundation program, equitable measures for determining local ability to support schools are necessary. Through uniform assessment of property values, or an objective study of ratios between assessed and actual property value, the states could determine the ability of each locality to support the school foundation program. The poorer districts, then, would be allocated a proportionately greater amount of state aid per pupil than the wealthier districts. Of course, the wealthier districts would be free to provide any additional funds of their own for supporting their schools over and beyond the level provided through the foundation program. An effective foundation program not only includes equalization aid, but encourages more efficient and economical administration of the schools through effective district reorganization and school consolidation.

Relatively few states are providing a reasonable amount of assistance to local districts for school construction. In the years to come, the states, and particularly the Federal Government, with their infinitely greater tax resources than the local communities, will have to develop a program for supporting school construction.

THE LOCAL LEVEL

The School District

The responsibility for operating and maintaining the schools has been delegated by the state to the local school district. But, as we have seen, this does not mean that the states have absolved themselves from the legally established principle of education as a state function. Local responsibility for the operation and maintenance of schools has historic precedence in that locally administered schools existed in the colonies and early states long before state educational systems came into being. While such local administration of education is often likened to grass roots democracy and is considered by many educators to be the best means of making education responsive to the people, the large number of small districts is linked with problems of inadequate school finance, limited curricular offerings, and inequality of educational opportunity.

The local school district operates in most cases as autonomous and separate from other units of local government. School districts are of several types: (1) the common school district found most frequently in rural areas of certain states, having a single school or attendance area and confined to a small enrollment and geographic area; (2) the county unit district in which cities may or may not operate independent school districts of their own; (3) city school districts that derive their boundaries from those of the cities they serve; (4) special independent districts that operate separate systems of elementary schools, high schools, and junior colleges within the same geographic area; and (5) town or township districts. In some areas there are school districts that do not operate schools but choose to pay tuition and provide transportation so that their youngsters may attend the schools of neighboring districts. Such non-operating school districts, organized for tax advantages, are being eliminated gradually through state legislation. But as recently as 1963 there were over 4,000 nonoperating school districts out of a total of 32,000 districts in the United States.

More than half of our states have intermediate districts, usually at the county level, which were created by state action as a downward extension or adjunct of the state educational agency. Today, most of these intermediate units serve the smaller, rural school districts. Many of the city school districts are of sufficient size to operate independently of the intermediate unit. In some states the intermediate unit serves an important function in providing services that small rural districts would otherwise not be able to afford. In other states the intermediate unit is primarily a holdover from the days of inadequate transportation and communication.

SCHOOL DISTRICT REORGANIZATION. Despite the advantage of grass roots democracy claimed for the local school district, such localism has entailed a number of serious problems. The great number of small school districts in many states came about in eras when travel was mainly by foot or by horse and buggy. These numerous and tiny districts soon represented wide disparities in economic resources even within the same state. And these small administrative units, with their limited enrollments, were unable to keep pace with the societal demands for a comprehensive curriculum along with the need for specialized instructional staffs and facilities. The organization of elementary and secondary education into separate school districts within the same geographic area also revealed many serious disadvantages, such as hampering curriculum articulation and raising difficulties in passing bond issues.

Many districts attempted to solve the problem of school size by consolidating or combining two or more school units within the same district. But it soon became apparent that merely consolidating some of the schools within a district failed to improve the economic resources of the district and often failed to create schools of efficient size. The major impetus for school district reorganization, or the combining of two or more entire school districts, came about in the years following World War II. Studies at that time revealed that, for most areas, an enrollment of at least 100,000 was needed in the district if an effective and economical program of education through the high school was to be developed.[11] It was estimated as recently as 1959 that at least 85 per cent of the school districts of our nation were of insufficient size to provide an effective and

---

[11] Dawson, Howard A. *et al.*, *Your School District* (Washington, D.C.: Department of Rural Education, National Education Association, 1948), Ch. VI.

economical program of education.[12] In his report on the American high school, Conant recommended that in order to provide a comprehensive curriculum at reasonable cost the high school should have a graduating class of at least 100.[13] Investigations on pupil achievement show a significant advantage for those attending larger high schools over those in small high schools.[14]

Although many communities have resisted reorganization, notable progress has been made in recent years. Some states, such as California and New York, have been highly successful in reducing the number of small districts through legislation that has offered financial incentives for reorganization. In Table 11–4 we see that in 1947–48 the number of public school districts in the United States was over 101,000. By 1963–64 the number had declined to less than 32,000.

The Local Board of Education

The governing body of the local school district is commonly called the board of education. This body is legally a state agency, and is empowered to set local school policy consistent with the laws of the state. However, this local board of education represents the community in educational matters and tends to function very much like a local agency. Its members are chosen from the residents of the school district, usually by means of popular vote, but also through appointment by a local governmental body or local public official. In addition to setting local educational policy, the board selects the chief administrator or superintendent of schools, receives and allocates funds from local taxes and state aid for local school finance, secures land and develops educational facilities, and, through the superintendent, appoints the school staff and provides for all educational services.

While some 85 per cent of the nation's school board members are elected by popular vote, the appointment method is used in 26.6 per cent of the larger districts (enrolling 25,000 or more students), and in 38.3 per cent of the districts in the South.[15] Elections are usually nonpartisan in order to separate education from certain political pressures.

The usual number of members on a school board ranges from five to nine. The length of term ranges from three to six years. Overlapping

12 Edgar L. Morphet, Roe L. Johns, and Theodore L. Reller, *Educational Administration* (Englewood Cliffs, N.J.: Prentice-Hall, Inc., 1959), p. 226.

13 James Bryant Conant, *The American High School Today* (New York: McGraw-Hill Company, Inc., 1959), p. 81.

14 Stephen J. Knezevich, *Administration of Public Education* (New York: Harper & Row, Publishers, Inc., 1962), pp. 140-41.

15 Alpheus L. White, *Local School Boards: Organization and Practices* (Washington, D.C.: Office of Education, U.S. Department of Health, Education, and Welfare, 1962), p. 8.

Table 11–4
Number of Local School Districts
and Number of Public and Nonpublic Schools:
United States, 1929–30 to 1963–64

School year	School districts†	Public school systems		Secondary schools	Nonpublic schools°	
		Elementary schools			Elemen-	
		Total	One-teacher		tary	Secondary
1929–30 ...	‡	238,306	149,282	23,930	9,992	3,258
1931–32 ...	127,531	232,750	143,391	26,409	9,992	3,327
1933–34 ...	‡	236,236	139,166	24,714	9,992	3,289
1935–36 ...	‡	232,174	131,101	25,652	9,275	3,327
1937–38 ...	119,001	221,660	121,178	25,467	9,734	3,327
1939–40 ...	117,108	‡	113,600	‡	11,306	3,568
1941–42 ...	115,493	183,112	107,692	25,123	10,285	3,011
1943–44 ...	111,383	169,905	96,302	28,973	10,285	3,011
1945–46 ...	101,382	160,227	86,563	24,314	9,863	3,294
1947–48 ...	94,926	146,760	75,096	25,484	10,071	3,292
1949–50 ...	83,718	128,225	59,652	24,542	10,375	3,331
1951–52 ...	71,094	123,763	50,742	23,746	10,666	3,322
1953–54 ...	63,057	110,875	42,865	25,637	11,739	3,913
1955–56 ...	54,859	104,427	34,964	26,046	12,372	3,887
1957–58 ...	47,594	95,466	25,341	25,507	13,065	3,994
1959–60 ...	40,520	91,853	20,213	25,784	13,574	4,061
1961–62 ...	35,500	82,000	13,600	26,100	14,623	4,180
1962–63 ...	33,086					
1963–64 ...	31,705					

° Data for most years are partly estimated.
† Includes operating and nonoperating districts.
‡ Data not available.
NOTE.–Beginning in 1959–60, includes Alaska and Hawaii.
SOURCES. Office of Education, U.S. Department of Health, Education, and Welfare, *Digest of Educational Statistics*, 1963, p. 30; and *Fall 1963 Statistics on Enrollment, Teachers, and Schoolhousing*, Circular 735, 1964.

terms are the general rule, as this arrangement ensures continuity of policy. Most authorities in school administration are agreed that board members should serve without salary. About half of the boards are allowed travel expenses only, while half provide compensation in addition to travel.[16]

---

[16] *Ibid.*, p. 73.

A recent study reveals that 48.3 per cent of the nation's school board members are college graduates while 44 per cent are graduates of high school.[17] The level of educational attainment of school board members tends to be somewhat higher in the larger school districts and in the North. However, for the nation as a whole, college graduates and high-school graduates are several times more prevalent among school board members than among the general adult population. Approximately 10 per cent of our nation's board members are women.[18] The occupations of school board members fall into these categories: 34.5 per cent are owners, officials, or managers of businesses; 27.4 per cent are engaged in professional or technical services; 12.4 per cent are farmers; and 7.2 per cent are housewives.[19] Thus we see that most school board members are engaged in business or the professions. Skilled and unskilled workers obviously are not adequately represented.

Except for special executive sessions, all school board meetings should be open to the public. However, a recent survey revealed that while 89.1 per cent of the nation's school boards follow this practice of open public meetings, only 79.5 per cent of those in the South do so.[20] Unfortunately, citizen attendance at school board meetings is very low, except where highly controversial issues are being discussed.

A national survey of school board problems shows that those relating to policy were most frequently reported.[21] Next highest on the list were problems concerned with the selection of board members (that is, securing and retaining qualified people, changing from appointive to elective methods, and improving community representation). Third on the list were difficulties in board-superintendent relationships. This problem area concerning board-superintendent relationships is often connected with the failure of school boards to distinguish clearly between the policy-making role of the board and the administrative function of the superintendent.

The national survey also reported the following general problems, in order of rank according to frequency of mention, as seen by board members: school finance, buildings and facilities, district reorganization and consolidation, selection and retention of qualified teachers, school-community relations, improvement of instruction, pupil transportation, and rising enrollments.[22]

THE LOCAL SUPERINTENDENT OF SCHOOLS. We have emphasized that the chief function of the local school board is policy-making. The superintendent of schools, hired by the board, serves as its chief executive officer and is responsible for administering the educational program. In

[17] *Ibid.*, p. 18.   [18] *Ibid.*, p. 19.
[19] *Ibid.*, p. 24.   [20] *Ibid.*, p. 52.
[21] *Ibid.*, p. 81.   [22] *Ibid.*, p. 85.

other words, where the board formulates and adopts educational policy, the superintendent organizes the ways and means of carrying out that policy. However, the line of demarcation between policy-making and implementation need not be perfectly sharp. In attempting to develop sound educational policies, the board very often needs to seek the advice and guidance of its chief executive officer. And, in turn, the superintendent will involve the school staff in analyzing and implementing sound policy. Thus, policy-making and implementation involve a considerable amount of cooperative effort on the part of the board, the superintendent, and the entire educational staff. Conflicts tend to arise when the board attempts to administer the schools—a function that should be charged to the professional administrator. While the board is composed of lay representatives of the district, the superintendent is a professional educator. Obviously, one of the most vital tasks of the board is the selection of its chief executive officer—the superintendent of schools.

As the board's professional adviser, the superintendent makes recommendations concerning the appointment of school personnel and the adoption of personnel policies, the improvement and expansion of facilities and services, and the finance of educational operations. The superintendent prepares and submits the educational budget to the board, provides for the supervision of school personnel, provides leadership in curriculum development and evaluation, and serves as the educational leader for the district.

The function of the board and the administrative tasks of the superintendent and his staff should be designed for one central purpose: to provide the best possible program of education for the children and youth of the community.

THE PRINCIPAL. While the superintendent is the executive officer of the district's board of education, the principal is the chief executive officer of the school unit. The principal is responsible to the superintendent or to the superintendent's designated representative for implementing the educational policy of the school district. In essence the principal provides the instructional leadership for his school and the area it serves. The principal should have a voice in the selection of his teachers and other school personnel. He works with the faculty on curriculum development, evaluation, and other educational matters within the policy framework of the district. While the central office or intermediate unit may provide supervisory services to the schools and teachers, the supervisors are advisers rather than administrators. A common plan of high-school organization is the departmental system, each department head being responsible to the school principal. But regardless of the particular system of organizing the high school, lines of communication should be open to facilitate optimum working relationships with the faculty, students, parents, and the general school community. In democratic administration the principal will counsel with the faculty on many important phases of the educational program.

Although functioning at different levels, the superintendent and principal are involved in administrative tasks within the following operational areas: (1) school-community relationships, (2) curriculum development and appraisal, (3) pupil personnel (including enrollment, attendance, counseling, health, and remedial programs), (4) staff personnel (selection, supervision, evaluation, in-service education, retention, and so on), (5) physical facilities, (6) finance and business management, (7) organization and structure (centralized or decentralized systems, line and staff, and so on), and (8) communication and participation (to facilitate all administrative tasks).[23]

Some Strengths and Weaknesses of the Local System

The local school district is a unique mechanism of American education. Local responsibility for operating and maintaining schools tends to evoke greater interest and participation of citizens in educational affairs. In many communities in the United States, a home-school partnership has evolved that has no counterpart in the communities of any other modern nation. The local board of education has, for the most part, kept free of partisan politics.

On the other hand, it is generally agreed that the local district has too often tended to be of inadequate size for optimum economy of operation, diversification of curriculum, and provision of special services. The consolidation and reorganization trend since World War II has improved this situation, but much remains to be accomplished. The level of support for education varies unbelievably from community to community even within the same state. Although state equalization aid has helped the poorer districts somewhat, great disparities continue to exist because of the financial structure of American public education. Today, over 50 per cent of the revenues for the support of public education is derived from local sources through property taxes. Obviously, poor communities tend to have poorly financed schools. Since most people tend to leave the community in which they received their education, the matter of school finance becomes a state and national problem.

In many instances local boards of education have usurped the responsibilities of the superintendent in administering the schools. Pressures

---

[23] See Roald F. Campbell, John E. Corbally, Jr., and John A. Ramseyer, *Introduction to Educational Administration*, 2nd Ed. (Boston: Allyn and Bacon, Inc., 1962), Ch. 4.

by school boards and lay citizens have resulted in censorship and the avoidance of controversial material in the curriculum.

> Local control of the functions of education is largely responsible for the dull and uninspiring character of much school instruction. It enables local communities to protect dominant local points of view from analysis and criticism in the schools, while at the same time it deprives the teachers of any moral justification for refusing to be a party to indoctrination when it is sanctioned by a community. Teachers cannot criticize local points of view, no matter how much they may be questioned elsewhere in the state or in the country. The result is that the schools do not provide genuine intellectual stimulation.[24]

The actions of school boards and lay citizens on matters that are rightfully within the realm of the professional educator tend to subvert the principles upon which our educational system is based. There is a critical need in many districts to clarify the roles and responsibilities of the school board, administrator, and teacher. However, greater centralization of educational control through the state or federal level would not necessarily provide increased educational freedom and professional autonomy. Lieberman observes that the national systems of education in other modern nations are characterized by greater professional autonomy and less political interference than is present in our own decentralized system.[25] He contends that "local control of education has clearly outlived its usefulness on the American scene."[26] Others hold that "schools will flourish, in the final analysis, only as they are kept close to the people and to the communities they serve."[27]

In recent years we have seen a trend emerging toward nationalizing influences on education in our country through curriculum redesign by national bodies, nationwide testing programs, and federal legislation for the support of education in certain curricular areas. Notwithstanding these developments, no significant changes have been made in removing the actual operation of the schools from the local level. In the future we are likely to see the trend continued toward these nationalizing influences on curriculum and toward greater participation in financing the schools through state and federal funds. Population mobility, inequities of educational opportunities from community to community and from state to state, and national needs in science, technology, and the world of work are problems that cannot be dealt with effectively on the local

---

24 Myron Lieberman, *Education as a Profession* (Englewood Cliffs, N.J.: Prentice-Hall, Inc., 1956), p. 81.

25 Myron Lieberman, *The Future of Public Education* (Chicago: The University of Chicago Press, 1960), p. 52.

26 *Ibid.,* p. 34.

27 Gordon C. Lee, *Education in Modern America,* Revised (New York: Holt, Rinehart and Winston, Inc., 1957), p. 245.

level alone. The local-state-federal partnership in education can be strengthened without losing the close relationship that has developed between the people and the schools. This is one of the most important problems of the 1960's.

THE ECONOMIC FORCE OF EDUCATION

Renewed attention is being given to education as an economic force. It has been shown that the amount of lifetime earnings correlates highly with the amount of education completed. While such data do not provide proof of a cause and effect relationship, it can be concluded that higher incomes go with more education. It has been shown that nations high in educational development, although low in natural resources, can attain high standards of living. On the other hand, nations low in educational development, while high in natural resources, tend to have relatively low living standards.[28]

While some people fear that continued increases in the number of college graduates will result in an oversupply of such persons, the fact remains that our economy has continued to demand more education; at the same time, groups with low educational attainment tend to have a high rate of unemployment. Our nation is faced with the pressing problem of developing programs in high school that will be of recognized value for potential dropouts, while also providing training and employment for those who have already dropped out of school.

EDUCATIONAL LEADERSHIP

Many people tend to think of educational leadership in terms of status or position as represented by such titles as superintendent, principal, supervisor, coordinator, department head, or teacher. However, leadership is a product of process rather than of status or position. Leadership occurs when a person influences the behavior of others in working toward a given set of goals. Although there are many studies of leadership traits, the most fruitful are concerned with leadership behavior.

Leadership Behavior

The criteria for effective leadership behavior may differ sharply between autocratic and democratic societies. Research on leadership behavior in our own society tends to point to two important dimensions: (1) initiating structure, or organizing the ways and means of getting the

---

[28] John K. Norton, *Changing Demands on Education and Their Fiscal Implications* (Washington, D.C.: National Committee for Support of the Public Schools, 1963), pp. 38–42.

job done, and (2) consideration for the needs, feelings, and ideas of others.[29] Whether we are dealing with the leadership role of the school superintendent, the principal, or the teacher, we find these dimensions applicable. The leader not only needs to be an effective planner and organizer, but he needs to communicate effectively with others so that the processes of the group are contiguous with the goals. Since people often tend to resist change, the educational leader must have a good understanding of human behavior if educational improvements are to be attained.

Considerable study has been given to leadership functions in business, public administration, and the military. It is clear that there remains a great deal of research yet to be done on educational leadership in both sociological and psychological dimensions. We need to learn more about the relationship of the individual personality to the wider role and function of the school in a democratic society.

Existing research fails to identify leadership as any composite of given traits or personality factors. Increasing attention is being given to the role of the individual in relation to other individuals and to the total organizational setting.[30] Traditionally, we have been overly concerned with task-achievement or "getting the job done" without giving sufficient attention to human needs. This deficiency applies to relationships between school superintendents and principals, principals and teachers, and teachers and students. The traditional approach in task determination and process for these roles has tended to rely too heavily on hierarchical position. Insufficient attention has been given to the normal and positive human needs of recognition, self-actualization, and personal satisfaction in a job well done. The teacher who assumes that students are lazy and must be forced to work may well be creating a self-fulfilling prophecy. A substantial body of psychological evidence reveals that normal human beings shun boredom and seek positive activity (self-actualization). The effective leader can initiate structure and define the channels of operation within a setting that is compatible with human needs.

The dimension of consideration in the leadership process is manifested when the leader involves the group in decision making and when the feelings of the individuals within the group are taken into account. Under circumstances where a given decision must rest clearly and solely with the leader, it is desirable for the leader to communicate not only

---

29 John K. Hemphill *et al.*, "Relation Between Task Relevant Information and Attempts to Lead," *Psychological Monographs*, LXX, No. 7, 1956.

30 See National Society for the Study of Education, *Behavioral Science and Educational Administration*, Sixty-third Yearbook, Chapters VI and VII (Chicago: The University of Chicago Press, 1964).

the "what," "when," "where," and "how" of the decision, but also the "why" of the decision.

The challenge to the educational leader in a democratic society is to develop the milieu through which the needs and talents of each individual gain maximum fruition in contributing toward the common goal and the common good.

THE STRUCTURE OF EDUCATION

Every modern society has developed a framework or structure for organizing and administering public education. The obvious purpose of the organizational plan is to facilitate the process of education in the best interests of the individual and society. In the United States we have a unitary system of school organization extending from kindergarten through the graduate and professional schools of the university. The unitary system maintains open channels for continuous education. In contrast to the American unitary system, most European nations operate a dual system in which youngsters are differentiated, generally toward the end of their elementary schooling, for either an academic program leading to college entrance or a terminal program in a separate, general, or vocational type of secondary school.

As as result of the open educational channels characteristic of the American unitary system, no other nation can match ours in the proportion of the age groups enrolled in secondary and higher education. Although there is much to be done to improve educational opportunity in the United States, we have developed an educational structure unique for its openness for the continued pursuit of learning.

Vertical Organization

In Figure 11–2 we see the general structure of American education. The traditional pattern was an eight-year elementary school followed by a four-year high school. Although this pattern, known as the 8–4 plan, was dominant until the end of World War II, it actually began to decline significantly with the growth of the junior high school during the 1930's. While the 8–4 plan remains quite popular in rural areas, the most widespread plan is the 6–3–3, which includes a six-year elementary school, followed by a three-year junior high school and a three-year senior high school. The chief advantages of the junior high school are that it is designed for the early adolescent, provides for more specialized studies, facilitates the transition to the senior high school, and for many communities, offers an economical means of school plant expansion to accommodate increasing enrollments. In some areas, a 6–2–4 system is followed. The 6–3–3–2 plan provides for a junior college unit within

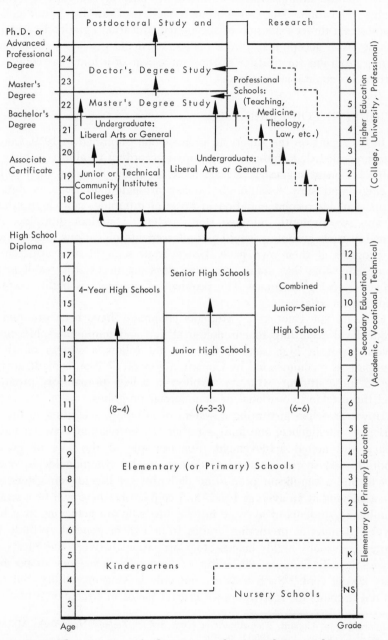

FIGURE 11–2. The structure of education in the United States. [SOURCE: U.S. Office of Education.]

the school district; although in many areas the junior college is operated as a separate administrative entity or as part of the state system of higher education. The 6–4–4 plan, which provides for junior college studies as a direct extension of secondary education (grades 13 and 14), has not won acceptance. Junior college curricula provide standard academic programs for transfer to the junior year of a four-year college, or terminal-occupational programs.

GROUPING FOR LEARNING

In his report on the American high school, published in 1959, Conant recommended that students be grouped according to ability, subject by subject. Conant suggested at least three grouping divisions: high ability, average, and slow.[31] Although Conant presented no research data in support of his recommendation in favor of grouping, most high schools of any size promptly adopted some system of student grouping. Presumably such grouping would permit students of various ability levels to progress at their own pace. However, it soon became apparent to many educators that ability grouping does not necessarily result in improved learning outcomes. The problem of grouping is highly complex and controversial.

CRITERIA FOR GROUPING. Students commonly have been grouped by grade level according to chronological age and minimum achievement levels. Even in high schools that do not follow a system of ability grouping as recommended by Conant, a general division is made according to those students who are enrolled in college-preparatory programs and those taking vocational or commercial programs.

However, when instituting a system of grouping according to the criterion of intelligence, one finds a rather low correlation between intelligence and actual achievement. For example, if the I.Q. or general aptitude test scores are used to determine the grouping levels, one is apt to find a significant proportion of highly intelligent youngsters who are achieving at an average level. And conversely, there will be a sizable number of students of average intelligence who are achieving at a high level. Attempts at predicting grades from I.Q. or general aptitude test scores are usually highly inaccurate. Correlations between these tests and grades usually come to .60 or less—a forecasting efficiency of no more than 20 per cent.[32] Such tests are not only lacking in validity, but they do not account for motivation—a crucial factor in educational perform-

---

[31] James Bryant Conant, *The American High School Today* (New York: McGraw-Hill Company, Inc., 1959), p. 49.

[32] Percival W. Hutson, *The Guidance Function in Education* (New York: Appleton-Century-Crofts, Inc., 1958), p. 402.

ance. This is not to say that aptitude tests are of little value; but they should not be used as the sole or even major determinant of pupil grouping or selection for college entrance.

Many high schools are now using multiple criteria for determining student-grouping. Such multiple criteria include aptitude, achievement, teacher recommendations, prior academic record (that is, in junior high school), social maturity, and pupil preferences or interests. The most accurate single criterion is the student's prior academic record, inasmuch as this most closely approximates the type of behavior one is attempting to predict. Nevertheless, because adolescence is a period of great psychosocial and physiological change, significant shifts in academic performance are not uncommon during this period. Moreover, academic performance may vary sharply from subject to subject according to aptitudes and interests. This means that if grouping is practiced in the school, it would be advisable to do so subject by subject and to have sufficient flexibility to allow for significant changes in student performance.

OTHER PROBLEMS IN GROUPING.   Many administrators and teachers assume that the grouping of students by ability levels will produce homogeneity. They often refer to this as homogeneous grouping. The research, however, reveals that even when students are grouped by I.Q.'s according to three levels, the range in achievement is reduced only by some 17 per cent.[33] Regardless of the schema for grouping, the motivation, interest, aptitude, personality, maturity, and socioeconomic variables are so complex that it would be folly to assume that homogeneity can be established.

As we have mentioned, grouping is most successful when it is flexible and when it is determined individually, subject by subject. But in too many instances, the practice of grouping fails to produce significant improvement in achievement on the part of high, average, and slow students. Perhaps one of the key reasons for this failure is that teachers do not use appropriate strategies for working with learning groups. Rather than attempt to stimulate and challenge brighter students so that they will want to inquire and discover, teachers often merely insist that these brighter students be pressured to do more work. As a result, even the brighter students develop negative attitudes toward learning. In the case of the slower students, instead of diagnosing learning difficulties and developing remedial procedures of a stimulating nature, teachers simply give these youngsters a watered-down version of the subject matter and proceed to cover this material at a slower pace. Many teachers are not only unenthusiastic about working with slower groups, but reveal strongly negative attitudes with these youngsters. Another

---

[33] National Education Association, *Schools for the Sixties* (New York: McGraw-Hill Company, Inc., 1963), p. 90.

factor that discourages the student who is placed in a slow group is the tendency for his aspiration level to fit the norm of the group.[34] The self-concept of students with latent abilities may deteriorate badly under such conditions. The creation of undesirable social consequences is also cited as a factor that should not be overlooked when decisions are made regarding the adoption of ability grouping.[35]

SIZE OF INSTRUCTIONAL GROUPS AND TEACHER LOAD. Most teachers would agree that smaller classes would enable them to improve the quality of their instruction. School administrators have tended to resist the reduction of class size on two accounts: first, and most obviously, such reduction would require a corresponding increase in per pupil expenditure, and second, it is alleged that the research regarding class size is inconclusive.

The typical secondary school teacher has five classes each day with 30 pupils in each class. This means that the teacher is working every day with 150 different adolescents. If, for example, a teacher of English or social studies were to require students to write a weekly theme, this would mean a total of 150 themes to read and evaluate each week. The result is that teachers resort largely to a mechanical type of exercises and tests that can be graded easily. While a reduction in class size would reduce the load of the teacher, it will not result in an improvement in the quality of instruction unless the teacher alters his strategy to fit the size of the class group. In other words, if the teacher works with a class of 20 students in much the same way as he would with a class of 35, the amount and quality of learning taking place may not be of any significant difference.

A summary of the research on the effects of class size reveals that in 22 carefully designed experiments, 16 favored small classes, three favored the large groups, and the remaining three were inconclusive.[36]

School administrators attempting to improve student achievement have been attracted by the practice of ability grouping rather than the reduction of class size. Ability grouping can be instituted without any great increase in per pupil expenditure, whereas reducing class size results in significant cost increases. One alternative is to increase the size of classes for certain learning activities while reducing them for other types of work. The most notable proposal for providing such flexibility has been advanced by Trump and Baynham.[37] This is discussed in

---

[34] Frederick J. McDonald, *Educational Psychology* (San Francisco: Wadsworth Publishing Company, Inc., 1959), p. 116.

[35] Hilda Taba, *Curriculum Development* (New York: Harcourt, Brace & World, Inc., 1962), p. 168.

[36] Donald H. Ross and Bernard McKenna, *Class Size: The Multi-Million Dollar Question* (New York: Columbia University Press, 1955), p. 2.

[37] J. Lloyd Trump and Dorsey Baynham, *Guide to Better Schools: Focus on Change* (Chicago: Rand McNally & Company, 1961).

greater detail in Chapter 10. However, in attempting to institute a program providing for such flexibility in class size, it is vitally important for administrators to work with their faculties in developing teaching-learning strategies that are best suited to the size of the learning group.

THE GUIDANCE PROGRAM

Relatively little attention was given to educational guidance prior to the twentieth century. The rise of technology, the disruptions of two world wars, and the unemployment of the Great Depression pointed to the need for vocational guidance and rehabilitation. The universalization of education and the diversification of the curriculum resulted in the first systematic attempts to provide programs of educational guidance in our secondary schools. Increases in crime, mental illness, and social maladjustment gave rise to the concept of adjustive guidance. And, most recently, we find national interest and support of guidance as a means of improving the productivity of our human resources.

Some Functions of Guidance

In recent years, the schools have been expected to assume a wide range of guidance functions. With the help of teachers and counselors, the student should develop an increasing awareness of his potentialities and interests, along with an understanding of educational and vocational opportunities. Teachers and counselors encounter situations, both formal and informal, where they work with youngsters on matters of (1) academic progress, (2) selection of subjects and school activities, (3) vocational choice, (4) discipline, (5) remedial instruction, (6) personal problems, (7) employment, and (8) maladjustment. While the school is clearly limited in its capacity for providing remedial treatment for severe cases of maladjustment, the teacher, the counselor, and the principal need to be able to spot certain symptoms or danger signals so that proper diagnosis and treatment are made available.

ROLE OF THE ADMINISTRATOR. The administrator is called upon to determine the needs for guidance resources and facilities in the school, and to facilitate the work of teachers, counselors, and other guidance specialists in providing for an effective program. He is responsible for selecting guidance personnel, dealing with budgetary requirements, and interpreting the program to parents and the community. The principal can perform an important leadership role in stimulating and supporting follow-up studies of graduates, transfers, and dropouts. He must see to it that the relationship between the guidance program and the curriculum is harmonious.

ROLE OF THE TEACHER. The effective teacher performs many important guidance functions. The teacher is in an ideal position to observe youngsters and to develop an understanding of their backgrounds, aptitudes, interests, and problems. Students frequently will go to certain teachers for counsel and advice. And the effective teacher will be aware of the early signs of learning difficulties and personal problems so that adequate assistance may be provided in the classroom and, when necessary, through the specialized guidance resources of the school. Fewer problems are likely to arise in a classroom where good teaching is taking place.

Because of the strong departmental organization in most junior and senior high schools, each teacher may be working with 150 or more individual students each day. In order to counteract the depersonalization of this system, homerooms are frequently provided so that a given teacher is identified more closely with a group of some 30 students. The homeroom teacher will have some general guidance functions relating to student progress, school activities, and individual problems.

Effective guidance, like effective education, enables the individual to make wise decisions on his own. In too many classrooms however, the teacher functions simply as a taskmaster who directs and tells students exactly what to do, how to do it, and when to do it. Students under such circumstances do not learn how to deal with situations of challenge and responsibility. And they do not develop the attitudes and skills for self-directed or self-impelled learning. A democratic society provides for responsible individual choice, but too frequently our schools function as autocratic institutions. Under such circumstances, students learn to regard the school as a threat or an obstacle, rather than as a means of developing responsible self-direction through challenging learning experiences. The successful students in such schools are the ones who are able to compete adequately for the higher grades, even though they may have no genuine thirst or love of learning. The unsuccessful ones become the discipline problems, the quiet ones, the truants, and the dropouts.

ROLE OF THE COUNSELOR. The school counselor is often a part-time teacher or former teacher who has developed some specialized training in guidance and educational psychology. An increasing number of states are establishing special certification requirements for school counselors. Many administrators prefer counselors who have had some successful teaching experience.

The counselor is engaged in assisting students to plan their school program, providing for individual and group psychological testing, maintaining and interpreting student personnel records, helping youngsters to understand their capabilities in relation to career opportunities, assisting students to progress toward educational and career goals, and working with students, teachers, and parents on educational problems.

However, in too many schools the student may see the counselor only when planning his academic program or when he is referred to the counselor by a teacher. In the event of disciplinary referrals, the counselor should work toward diagnosis and rehabilitation, and never in a threatening or punitive context. If constructive self-perception is to be developed, the counselor must be regarded as a friend and helper. In schools where mutual confidence is developed between student and counselor, the student often will come to the counselor voluntarily for guidance and assistance.

ROLE OF THE PSYCHOLOGIST. In the event of severe personal and emotional problems, the counselor may recommend to the principal that the student be referred to a psychologist. The psychologist is rarely involved in teaching. In some school districts, psychologists work as clinicians who treat youngsters with psychological problems, while in other systems the psychologist also may be engaged in consulting with teachers, counselors, and administrators. The work of the counselor is more broadly defined than that of the psychologist. The counselor will perform guidance functions with the perfectly normal youngster, as well as with youngsters having certain educational and personal difficulties.

The practice in the past has been to provide the services of school psychologists at the elementary level, while limiting the secondary school to the services of counselors. While the functions of the counselor and the psychologist may seem to overlap somewhat, the competent counselor will recognize when more highly specialized psychological services are required. And the school district should make such services available. Many of the larger school systems also employ a consulting psychiatrist who will be responsible for diagnosing and treating severely disturbed youngsters.

ROLE OF THE SCHOOL SOCIAL WORKER. The guidance program of a school should include the services of a social worker or visiting teacher. The school social worker will work closely with parents and various community agencies in improving the relationships of the youngster in the home, the school, and the community. The school social worker may deal with problems involving welfare agencies, the juvenile court, and the psychiatric clinic. The school social worker should consult with teachers, counselors, and principals on these problems. The usual practice is for the school social worker or visiting teacher to work out of the central office of the school district.

The Challenge of Educational Guidance

The guidance program and the school curriculum should be attuned to the goal of enabling the individual to make wise choices in fulfilling his personal needs and contributing to the needs of society. In a free society these needs are not mutually exclusive or incompatible. The individual who enjoys good mental health has a realistic understanding of his capacities and interests, seeks to improve himself through continued learning, recognizes his obligations to his fellowmen, and is better equipped for good citizenship than the person who is without these attributes.

Although we have made great strides in improving educational opportunity, socioeconomic inequities and problems have prevented many youths from developing their potentials. Studies reveal that of the high-school students in the top third in intellectual ability, some 40 per cent do not enter college; and of those who do begin college, 60 per cent drop out.[38] Studies by Havighurst and others reveal that socio-economic factors can have a greater bearing than aptitude or achievement on whether or not a youngster will go on to college.[39]

Research on juvenile delinquency points to the lack of successful experiences in school and society, and the feeling of inadequacy or low self-esteem as important factors in antisocial behavior.[40] A high proportion of our youth fail to see a realistic connection between high school and the world of work. Moreover, the poor mental health of large segments of our adult society has produced a high incidence of emotional problems among children and youth. The challenge to the guidance program and, indeed, to the total school in meeting these needs has never been more crucial.

THE NEW EMPHASIS ON NATIONAL NEEDS. In recent years, an unparalleled emphasis has been given to school guidance as a means of meeting national needs. It is generally agreed that there should be a full-time counselor or guidance officer for every 250 or 300 high-school students.[41] Nevertheless, as recently as 1959, the ratio was only one counselor for every 860 pupils in the secondary school. The National Defense Education Act, with its provisions under Title V for guidance, counseling, and testing, has improved this situation remarkably. In Figure 11–3 we see that, between 1959 and 1962, the ratio has been reduced from one counselor for every 860 pupils to one counselor for every 550 pupils at the secondary level. N.D.E.A. sponsored training institutes for school guidance workers and counselors have helped provide more and better qualified personnel for the secondary schools. Between 1959 and 1962 the

---

38 Dael L. Wolfle, "Diversity of Talent," The American Psychologist, 15:536, 1960.
39 See Leonard M. Miller (ed.), Guidance for the Underachiever with Superior Ability (Washington, D.C.: Office of Education, U.S. Department of Health, Education, and Welfare, 1961), p. 9.
40 Helen L. Witmer, Delinquency and the Adolescent Crisis (Washington, D.C.: Office of Education, U.S. Department of Health, Education, and Welfare, 1960), p. 3.
41 James Bryant Conant, The American High School Today (New York: McGraw-Hill Company, Inc., 1959), p. 44.

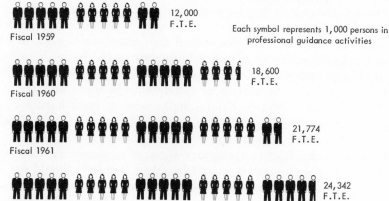

FIGURE 11–3. Number of full-time equivalent guidance personnel serving public secondary schools, 1959–1962. [SOURCE: Office of Education, *Report on the National Defense Education Act* (Washington, D.C.: U.S. Department of Health, Education, and Welfare, 1963), p. 25.]

number of qualified full-time equivalent guidance personnel in public secondary schools throughout the United States more than doubled.[42]

Notwithstanding these notable achievements through N.D.E.A., in our zeal for meeting national defense needs we must not lose sight of the individual and personal needs of our youth. Is it wise to put undue pressure on our intellectually superior youth merely to increase our national supply of mathematicians, scientists, and engineers? What about the creative arts, social service, and other important occupations? Will such undue pressure result in a striving for achievement without a corollary love of learning? What about the mental health needs of our society? In a free society, education and guidance must serve more than national defense. Otherwise, we shall be in danger of serving ends not very different from those of our adversaries.

Improving the Guidance Function of the Total School

Guidance is a total-school function. Each high school should investigate the factors causing students to drop out or to be forced out of school. Efforts should be made to reduce the dropout rate as much as possible. Follow-up studies should be conducted on a continuous basis to ascertain what adjustments graduates are making in college and in the world of work. Similar studies should be made of dropouts in the world

---

[42] Office of Education, *Report on the National Defense Education Act* (Washington, D.C.: U.S. Department of Health, Education, and Welfare, 1963), p. 25.

of work. Unemployed dropouts should be encouraged to return to school. Part-time enrollment in late afternoon and evening classes would enable employed youths to gain a high-school diploma. In too many high schools, the mid-year dropout faces the loss of the entire year's work, if and when he should return to school. Adjustments should be made, insofar as possible, to help the returnee to pick up his studies where he left off.

High schools need to work more closely with business, industry, and labor in assisting youths to obtain employment to meet financial and vocational needs. The high-school curriculum should be reassessed periodically to determine how it can better serve the needs of youth.

As soon as the teacher recognizes signs of academic or emotional problems, constructive action should be taken. Teachers should not ignore students with learning difficulties or emotional problems. The quiet, withdrawn student requires at least as much attention as the extrovert youngster. Special remedial work, tutoring, and counseling should be provided by the school at the earliest signs of academic trouble. The secondary school should not be a place where students are merely tried and tested. It should be a place where adolescents can come to realize the fullest measure of their potentials.

Close cooperation with parents is essential if the school is to serve youth properly. Information on home and family background, academic record in previous schools, health, educational interests and aspirations, work experience, personality, emotional adjustment, aptitudes and special interests—all are important for effective guidance. But such information should not be placed in cold storage. Properly used, these records can help the teacher and counselor to better understand the adolescent. And, in turn, the adolescent can be assisted in developing a more mature and satisfying level of self-realization.

HEALTH SERVICES

In addition to the provision of formal instruction in health and safety through the programs of studies in physical education, biology, and homemaking, certain health services are provided by the school. Such services differ widely from district to district and state to state. The school cannot afford to neglect health problems, since such problems not only interfere with learning, but also affect the well-being of all students and even the entire community. Schools should have the scheduled services of a registered nurse and the availability of a physician on call. Periodic physical examinations should be provided for all students. Parents should not only be informed as to needed corrective measures (eyesight, hearing, surgery, and so on), but follow-up should be provided to ensure proper action. In many areas, schools are cooperating with city, county, and state health departments in administering immunization programs. The use of the schools as centers for polio immunization is a case in point.

Common Deficiencies in School Health

The provisions for physical examinations are frequently sporadic and superficial. School authorities do not always see to it that youngsters and their parents are provided adequate guidance and follow-up on health matters. When parents are unwilling to take proper action, the school is not always in a position to see to it that these needs are provided. There is a serious need in many areas to coordinate health services with health education and welfare aid.

Although more than 15 million children and youths participate in federally subsidized school lunch programs each year, many schools in certain areas are not participating in the National School Lunch Program and are making no provision for hot lunches on school premises.

More work needs to be done on fostering mental and physical health through the school. Not only do we need to provide effective educational programs for the physically and emotionally handicapped, but we need to develop a healthful school environment for all children and youth.

EXTRACLASS ACTIVITIES

Most educators today regard student activity programs as integral to the school curriculum. They choose to identify such activities as extraclass rather than extracurricular. While such activities may carry no academic credit, they are, nevertheless, officially sponsored and scheduled by the school. Allied activities are designed to develop a wider range of student interests, provide a variety of flexible situations in which youngsters learn how to use their initiative and work effectively in group situations, enable students to discover and develop special abilities and talents, and motivate the student toward effective behavior in the total school program. Even in institutions of higher education, extraclass activities are under official sponsorship and have an important place in the lives of many students.

School Clubs

Often closely related to the academic program, school clubs enable youngsters to pursue projects that are not possible in their regular courses. These clubs may be organized around such special-interest areas of the curriculum as science, art, music, mathematics, dramatics, debating, French, Spanish, and homemaking. Other clubs may center on such hobby areas as photography, fencing, modern dance, electronics, and so forth. Another type of club may deal with vocational interests, such as the Future Teachers, Future Homemakers, and Future Farmers.

In some high schools, students have sought to imitate the fraternity or sorority type of organization common to our colleges and universities. It is generally agreed that such organizations and secret societies do not belong in the high school because they are arbitrarily restrictive and because their secretive tendencies make it impossible for the school to maintain proper supervision. Some state laws actually prohibit such organizations at the high-school level.

Student Government

In an effort to foster democratic values and processes, most secondary schools have a student council that serves as an advisory body to the administration and faculty and is often responsible for regulating the self-discipline of the student body outside of class. The student council is a representative body elected by homerooms or grade levels. The council functions according to a constitution and operates under faculty supervision. If student government is to develop democratic self-direction, students must have some decision-making responsibilities. This, of course, does not mean that they are to run the school. But the council can contribute to the morale and welfare of the school by maintaining close communication with the administration, faculty, and total student body on matters of common concern. The administration and faculty may want to seek out the opinions of the council on a variety of questions relating to student deportment, activities, and community-related programs. In addition, the student council may sponsor tutoring projects, assembly programs, and school elections. The student council can make an important contribution to the morale and welfare of the school.

Interscholastic Athletics

Varsity sports are credited with providing opportunities for athletically talented youth to be adequately challenged, building school and community spirit, and developing good sportsmanship. On the other hand, such activities have been badly abused in the name of education. The colleges and universities have created an impressive football and basketball industry that draws its recruits from our high schools through special grants-in-aid, job opportunities, alumni gifts, and other inducements. Ohio State University, for example, grosses over $2,000,000 annually from the game of football. The National Broadcasting Company paid more than $13 million to the National Collegiate Athletic Association for the rights to telecast the college football games during the 1964–65 season.

"Extracurricular activities must be thought of,
not as something apart from the classroom,
but as an extension of it."
—REPORT OF THE HARVARD COMMITTEE

The Notre Dame football coach, in a New York Times interview, properly referred to his players as personnel.[43]

The high schools, like our institutions of higher learning, have come to recognize the public relations value of successful teams. Many high schools invest far more in their athletic plants and operations than in their school libraries. High schools have installed expensive lighting systems for night football. Where varsity sports were once held during the daytime, the shift to evening events has attracted much greater community attendance. When the American Broadcasting Company attempted to negotiate with the National Football League in televising professional football on Friday nights, the National Federation of State

---

[43] Arthur Daley, "New Boy at Notre Dame," The *New York Times,* January 8, 1964, p. 29.

Are varsity sports overemphasized in high school and college? What pressures do colleges exert on the high school in recruiting star athletes?

Courtesy Northwestern University

High School Athletic Associations raised such a loud protest in Washington that the network backed down. The executive secretary of the Federation reported that 86 per cent of all high-school football is played on Friday nights and that the telecasting of professional games would detract from attendance.[44]

Varsity athletic coaches in the high schools, like their collegiate counterparts, are evaluated according to the won-lost column. Adult Boosters' Clubs, marching bands, and jumping cheerleaders are all part of the football scene. Yet, unless the colleges deemphasize athletics, it will be exceedingly difficult for the high schools to put interscholastic sports in their proper perspective. While such activities can be valuable for athletically talented students, and while interscholastic sports can contribute to school spirit, their overemphasis does more harm than good.

Intramural Athletics

While interscholastic athletics tend to develop spectatoritis, intramural sports foster active participation. In addition to the customary team sports, intramural athletics can include activities such as golf, tennis, and swimming—sports that are more likely to carry over into adult recreation. Intramural programs should be well planned and under competent supervision. Certain activities, such as golf, tennis, and volleyball could be organized on a coeducational basis.

Assemblies

In recent years students have been given increasing responsibility in planning and conducting school assemblies. The all-school assembly is the one activity in which the entire student body is gathered together. Assembly programs may feature concerts, plays, outside speakers, award ceremonies, and commencements. Assembly programs should have educational and cultural value. They should also contribute to the total school morale. Inasmuch as possible, students should be involved in planning and participating in these programs. If assemblies are to be truly an all-school activity, no admission fees should be charged.

Music, Dramatics, and Speech

In addition to student concerts and dramatic performances during school assemblies, special programs are provided during after-school hours for students, parents, and the general community. Although the marching band has become an important adjunct to the football spectacle, the student symphony orchestra can accomplish far more in im-

---

[44] The *New York Times*, February 15, 1964, p. 17.

Photo by Herb Comess

"They are not luxuries of education,
  but emphatic expressions of that which
makes any education worth while."
                        —JOHN DEWEY

proving the musical taste of adolescents. Student jazz and swing bands may perform at school dances and other social events. Good drama is educationally valuable not only for the student performers, but also for the student spectators. Students should have a voice in the selection of plays. In the area of the speech arts, students may be given opportunities for public speaking, debate, and panel discussions. Schools often tend to overemphasize debate contests; other forms of public speaking have great value for participants and audiences.

Student Publications

Student yearbooks, magazines, handbooks, and newspapers have come to play an important role in providing opportunities for interpreting school life, fostering literary expression, and building school morale. Arbitrary censorship of student publications should be avoided. Student publications should provide opportunities for responsible journalism, literary expression, and chronicling of school events. The solicitation of advertising and donations for financing student publications should be carefully assessed and controlled by cooperative agreement between the administration and students.

Camping and Outdoor Education

Camping activities sponsored by the school can provide unique opportunities for fostering democratic values, healthful living, and appreciation of nature. Regularly credentialed teachers may serve as camp instructors. However, camp activities should be focused on the interests and needs of the youngsters rather than on formal teaching. Certain school districts in California and Michigan have developed outstanding camping programs. But the potentials of school camping have hardly been tapped.

School Social Activities

School dances, parties, banquets, and other social activities can contribute to wholesome interpersonal and intergroup relationships. By virtue of its cross-sectional representation of society, the school is in a unique position to promote social acceptance among adolescents from all walks of life. Social activities sponsored by the school can contribute to developing responsible social behavior, building wholesome relations with peers of both sexes, and achieving effective masculine and feminine roles.[45]

---

[45] Robert J. Havighurst, *Developmental Tasks and Education* (New York: Longmans, Green and Co., 1950), p. 6.

EVALUATION, RESEARCH, AND IMPROVEMENT

Evaluation is the key to improvement. However, great public confusion has resulted from self-appointed judges of our schools who offer criticisms and recommendations based on opinion rather than objective research. Since we have dealt with a number of these critics in earlier chapters, our major purpose here is to review some of the procedures that have been developed in evaluating and accrediting our secondary schools.

Institutional Evaluation and Research

In many of our larger school districts, a type of action research is attempted by trying out various practices and applying to local school situations the results of research developed elsewhere. However, effective programs of self-evaluation and research require highly competent researchers. Furthermore, many school administrators are more interested in developing good public relations than in supporting research that may reveal serious weaknesses in the educational program.

Some school districts and newspapers have quoted data from standardized achievement tests, the number of students from the district who are finalists in the National Merit Scholarship Program, and other similar indices as evidence of educational quality. However, such measures often reflect the socioeconomic background of the students and the community, while having relatively little bearing on the actual quality of the school curriculum. Comparative studies between and among school districts must take into account the socioeconomic variables and other discrepancies that can produce significant distortions in research results.

Relatively few practices in our schools are developed through locally initiated research. In recent years, the trend has been toward utilizing and refining the materials developed by national agencies, publishers, and authorities in our universities.

Most school districts engage in useful attempts to analyze trends in community population and school enrollment with a view toward determining future needs for buildings, facilities, and teachers.

Follow-up studies of dropouts and graduates can be very useful. Important follow-up studies, conducted during the 1930's, helped identify the problems and needs of youth in relation to the secondary-school curriculum.[46] The more recent work of the Illinois Secondary School Curriculum Program, under the direction of the Illinois Department of Public Instruction and the University of Illinois, gathered much useful

---

[46] See Howard M. Bell, *Youth Tell Their Story* (Washington, D.C.: American Council on Education, 1939).

data in following up the students from 61 schools. Individual school districts and secondary schools can also gain valuable information in conducting their own follow-up studies.

School Surveys

Many school districts enlist the services of consultants from universities and other school systems to make periodic surveys of the educational program. Colleges of Education at most universities maintain an educational research bureau or field service that may be called upon to assist in conducting specific research or engaging in a comprehensive school survey. By going ,outside the school district, the local board and administration can gain the services of specialists not available locally.

It is important that such surveys be based on objective evaluation procedures and research, rather than on authoritative opinion only. A case in point is the *Report of the San Francisco Curriculum Survey Committee*, which represented the opinions of eight university scholars from the fields of English, economics, history, biology, chemistry, and mathematics.[47] While the report contained many important opinions and recommendations, none of the material was based on research findings or the results of research conducted elsewhere.

Universities, State Departments of Education, and National Agencies

Through the cooperation of university scholars, the National Science Foundation has supported course-content improvement programs in school science and mathematics. These programs have exerted great influence on curriculum revision at the local level. The United States Office of Education has been supporting projects at various universities designed to improve the curriculum in English and social studies in our elementary and secondary schools. The traditional gap between the findings of university research and school practices is being reduced as a result of comprehensive and coordinated planning.

An increasing number of state departments of education are employing research staffs that make educational data available to local districts. The National Education Association has not only been engaged in gathering and disseminating valuable research data, but has periodically supported projects for guiding local school districts in evaluating and improving their programs. The United States Office of Education prepares a wide variety of reports on educational progress that are of great benefit to school districts engaged in evaluation and research.

---

[47] *Report of the San Francisco Curriculum Survey Committee* (San Francisco: San Francisco Unified School District, April 1, 1960).

The Foundations

The Ford Foundation has supported a wide variety of research, demonstration, and promotional projects for improving the efficiency of the secondary school. These projects, discussed in some detail in Chapter 10, have been concerned with the architectural design of the school, the use of new educational media, and the application of various management procedures for instruction.

The Carnegie Corporation has supported the work of James B. Conant during the late 1950's in evaluating the secondary schools. Conant's opinions and recommendations, while seldom derived from actual research, have been enormously influential throughout the nation. His *Academic Inventory*, along with much of his other work, tends to focus on quantitative and bookkeeping criteria for evaluating and improving the secondary school. Although his works represent one man's opinions, they have carried great weight by virtue of his position as a prominent university educator and his avoidance of extremism.

ACCREDITATION OF THE SECONDARY SCHOOL

The accreditation of high schools is performed by state departments of education, special state agencies, voluntary regional associations, and in some cases by the state university. Accreditation of high schools by the state university is practiced in California and Michigan, although high schools in these states are also accredited by the voluntary regional association.

The Regional Accrediting Agencies

Most of these associations were established during the 1890's. Their major purposes are to improve educational standards and to develop cooperative relationships between secondary schools and colleges. Unlike the European practice of providing for accreditation functions through official national ministries, our decentralized educational system has produced regional associations that operate on a voluntary basis. These regional associations are New England, North Central, Northwest, Southern, and Western. As of 1964 the North Central Association included 19 states, with a membership of 3,671 high schools and 461 colleges and universities. The North Central Association is, by far, the largest of the five regional accrediting associations.

Accreditation procedures include a comprehensive self-evaluation of the school, conducted by the administration and faculty according to approved criteria and procedures established by the Association. This report is reviewed by the state committee, and a visiting team of school and college educators is provided to survey the school operations first-hand. Periodic reports are required of all member schools providing data on such phases of the school program as (1) philosophy and objectives, (2) the educational program, (3) organization, support, and control, (4) staff, (5) library and instructional materials, (6) administrative and supervisory services, (7) plant, (8) school year, day, and week, and (9) graduation requirements.[48]

Most regional accrediting associations use a guidebook, *Evaluative Criteria for Secondary Schools,* developed by the Associations of Secondary Schools and Colleges.[49] Schools are accredited as total institutions and, although certain basic standards are followed, flexibility is provided for reasonable variations and experimentation.

The Western Association, which consists of only one state, California, has developed its secondary school accreditation program through the California Association of School Administrators. This organization has developed its own set of evaluative instruments and puts heavy emphasis on self-appraisal followed by consultation and review through a visiting committee. Members of the visiting committee include a school administrator, a representative from the state department of education, a representative from the county education office, and a college professor. The State Accreditation Commission, which reviews the reports from the school and the visiting committee, includes representatives from the state university, state colleges, state department of education, junior college association, school board association, state teachers association, and state association of school administrators.

Educational Improvement

Schools should engage in a continuous program of evaluation and research. Changes in the school program should be based on the careful evaluation of existing procedures. Experimentation should be conducted as scientifically as possible for the purpose of improving the educational program. Innovations for the sake of following the fashion of other schools, or for publicity purposes, should be avoided. If schools are concerned primarily with public relations, their capacity for realistic self-appraisal and continued improvement will be impaired. Evaluation and research can help us to identify areas of strength and weakness, point to corrective measures, and give direction for fruitful innovation experimentation.

---

[48] The North Central Association of Colleges and Secondary Schools, *Policies and Criteria for the Approval of Secondary Schools* (Chicago: The Association, 1964).

[49] Cooperative Study of Secondary School Standards, *Evaluative Criteria* (Washington, D.C.: Association of Secondary Schools and Colleges, 1960).

SUMMARY

Although education in the United States is a state function, school systems are administered locally, and financial support is provided through local, state, and federal sources. In most nations of the world, education is a function of the national government.

In our own nation there is a trend toward greater federal participation in the support of education. The ever-increasing mobility of our nation's population has made education a national concern. Our Federal Government has come to recognize education as vital to national defense and well being. For·example, through the National Science Foundation, an agency of the Federal Government, a national curriculum in high school science is being created. Youth unemployment has become a national problem and, as a result, the Federal Government has broadened and intensified its program in supporting vocational education.

Nevertheless, federal participation in education has been provided through piecemeal legislation which tends to favor certain areas of the curriculum. In recent years, proposed federal legislation for the comprehensive support of education has failed by small margins. The efforts of some religious leaders to seek public funds for the support of church schools seems to have created an impasse.

Great inequities of educational opportunity continue to exist from community to community and from state to state. Our states need to work out better methods of improving educational opportunity in their poorer communities. But the great disparities in educational opportunity from state to state are not likely to be solved without federal participation.

At the local level, one of the most serious problems in recent years has been the tendency for some boards of education to confuse their role with that of the school administrator. The lay board should be responsible for educational policy while their chief executive officer, the superintendent of schools, should be responsible to the board for administering the educational program.

The three-tiered structure of local-state-federal interrelatedness is confusing, inefficient, and unwieldy. But it seems to work. While this structure poses many administrative problems, these problems are not insurmountable.

PROBLEMS FOR STUDY AND DISCUSSION

1. Earlier in our history, federal participation in education was intended "to promote the general welfare." In more recent times, federal educational

programs have been justified as necessary for national defense. What weaknesses do you see in federal programs in education that are geared to national defense only?

2. Do you favor comprehensive federal support for public elementary and secondary education? Why or why not?

3. How do you account for the lack of a grass roots movement in favor of comprehensive federal support of public education?

4. What financial provisions are made in your state for the equalization of educational opportunity?

5. How do you account for the slow progress in school district reorganization in many states? What relationship do you see between the size of school districts (and school units) and the quality of the educational program?

6. What differences do you see in the role of the local board of education and the superintendent of schools? How do you account for the great confusion in interpreting these roles in many school districts?

7. How do you explain the lack of clear-cut research showing improvements in learning as a result of ability grouping in the high school?

8. Why is it that one's socioeconomic status may be a more valid predictor of college attendance than one's I.Q.? What implications does this have for the guidance program of the high school?

9. How far should the school go in providing health services for students?

10. Do you feel that varsity athletics were overemphasized in your high school? Are they overemphasized at your college? Why or why not?

11. Under what circumstances, if any, would you justify administrative or faculty censorship of student publications?

12. What are the procedures for the accreditation of secondary schools in your state? What information is required of the school in the accreditation process?

SELECTED REFERENCES

Anderson, Vernon E. and William T. Gruhn. *Principles and Practices of Secondary Education* (2nd Ed.) New York: The Ronald Press Company, 1962. Chs. 15, 16, 17.

Austin, David B., Will French, and J. Dan Hull. *American High School Administration*. New York: Holt, Rinehart and Winston, Inc., 1962.

Boy, Angelo V. and Gerald J. Pine. *Client-Centered Counseling in the Secondary School*. Boston: Houghton Mifflin Company, 1963.

Campbell, Roald F., John E. Corbally, Jr., and John A. Ramseyer. *Introduction to Educational Administration* (2nd Ed.) Boston: Allyn and Bacon, Inc., 1962.

Conant, James Bryant. *The American High School Today*. New York: McGraw-Hill Company, Inc., 1959.

Cooperative Study of Secondary School Standards. *Evaluative Criteria*. Washington, D.C.: Associations of Secondary Schools and Colleges, 1960.

Corbally, John E., Jr., T. J. Jensen, and W. F. Staub. *Educational Administration: The Secondary School*. Boston: Allyn and Bacon, Inc., 1961.

Hutson, Percival W. *The Guidance Function in Education*. New York: Appleton-Century-Crofts, Inc., 1958.

Johnson, Mauritz, Jr., William E. Busacker and Fred Q. Bowman, Jr. *Junior High School Guidance*. New York: Harper and Row, Publishers, Inc., 1961.

Kilzer, Louis R., Harold H. Stephenson and H. O. Nordberg. *Allied Activities in the Secondary School*. New York: Harper & Row, Publishers, Inc., 1956.

Knezevich, Stephen J. *Administration of Public Education*. New York: Harper & Row, Publishers, Inc., 1962.

Lee, Gordon C. *Education in Modern America* (Revised) New York: Holt, Rinehart and Winston, Inc., 1957. Chs. 11, 12, 13, 14.

Lieberman, Myron. *Education as a Profession*. Englewood Cliffs, N.J.: Prentice-Hall, Inc., 1956.

———. *The Future of Public Education*. Chicago: The University of Chicago Press, 1960.

Miller, Carroll H. *Foundations of Guidance*. New York: Harper & Row, Publishers, Inc., 1961.

Miller, Frank W. *Guidance Principles and Services*. Columbus, Ohio: Charles E. Merrill Books, Inc., 1961.

Moehlman, Arthur B. *School Administration* (2nd Ed.) Boston: Houghton Mifflin Company, 1951.

Morphet, Edgar L., R. L. Johns and Theodore L. Reller. *Educational Administration*. Englewood Cliffs, N.J.: Prentice-Hall, Inc., 1959.

National Education Association. *Schools for the Sixties*. New York: McGraw-Hill Company, Inc., 1963.

National Society for the Study of Education. *Behavioral Science and Educational Administration*. Sixty-third Yearbook, Part II. Chicago: The University of Chicago Press, 1964.

Norton, John K. *Changing Demands on Education and Their Fiscal Implications*. Washington, D.C.: National Committee for Support of the Public Schools, 1963.

Office of Education. *Handbook of Office of Education* (Revised) Washington, D.C.: U.S. Department of Health, Education, and Welfare, 1963.

White, Alpheus L. *Local School Boards: Organization and Practices*. Washington, D.C.: Office of Education, U.S. Department of Health, Education, and Welfare, 1962.

V

The Profession

In brief, human reason is a weak and paltry thing
as long as it is not wholly free reason.
—*H. L. Mencken*

CHAPTER *12*

The Profession
of Teaching

THE TERM TEACHING PROFESSION is often used without a real understanding of its meaning. Is the occupation of teaching a true
profession? In considering this question, we must be concerned
with the role of the educational institution and the teacher in society,
the requirements for teacher certification and institutional accreditation,
ethics, teacher organizations, tenure, and other factors.

What distinguishes the professions from other occupations in our
society? There are several generally recognized criteria that fit the professional occupations.[1]

1. A unique and vital service in the public interest, with emphasis
   primarily on service, rather than personal gain or economic
   reward.
2. An advanced program of specialized education.
3. The application of skills and concepts at a high intellectual
   level.
4. A high level of responsibility, and latitude in decision-making
   within a context of reasonable operational autonomy.
5. A self-regulating membership with a code of ethics operationally
   supported by concrete cases.
6. Commitment on the part of individual members to the occupation as a lifetime career.

Although most teachers would regard themselves as professionals,
are the preceding criteria valid for the occupation of teaching? Let us
examine each criterion to determine the role and status of teaching as a
profession.

---

[1] See Myron Lieberman, *Education as a Profession* (Englewood Cliffs, N.J.: Prentice-
Hall, Inc., 1956), pp. 2–6.

"This is the most difficult profession in the world,
and the most important."
—H. G. WELLS

A UNIQUE AND VITAL SERVICE IN
THE PUBLIC INTEREST

Since education is a state function, and since every state enforces
compulsory education laws for children and youth, the teacher unques-
tionably performs a unique and vital social service. Moreover, each state
carefully regulates the licensing of teachers. The teacher, like members
of various professional groups in society, must meet the certification
requirements of the state in which he is to practice. Such requirements
are established and enforced by the state for every professional group,
since such groups are responsible for performing vital social services.

Although the professional worker should be motivated toward social
service rather than economic reward, the financial remuneration should
be sufficient to enable him to devote his full energies to professional

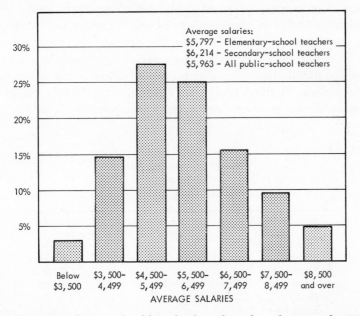

Average salaries:
$5,797 – Elementary-school teachers
$6,214 – Secondary-school teachers
$5,963 – All public-school teachers

AVERAGE SALARIES

FIGURE 12–1. Distribution of public-school teachers, by salaries paid, 1963–64. [SOURCE: Research Division, National Education Association, *NEA Research Bulletin*, Vol. 42 (Washington, D.C.: The Association, 1964), p. 5.]

endeavor. Unfortunately, the low level of teachers' salaries has compelled many to seek supplemental income through unrelated employment. But the situation is improving rapidly. The average salary of teachers for the 1959 calendar year was $5,013. The year 1959 marked the first time that the average salary of teachers in public elementary and secondary schools in the United States exceeded $5,000.[2] During 1963–64 the average salary had risen to almost $6,000.[3] Nevertheless, teachers' salaries continue to lag far behind the earnings of persons in other professions. And the actual income position of the teacher is even less favorable than other professional groups because our income tax structure is more advantageous to the independent fee taker than for the salaried employee.

Teachers' Salaries Vary

There is great disparity in the level of teachers' salaries according to the size and wealth of the school district, and according to geographic

---

[2] Research Division, National Education Association, *NEA Research Bulletin*, Vol. 38 (Washington, D.C.: The Association, May, 1960), p. 49.

[3] *Ibid.*, Vol. 42, February, 1964, p. 15.

location. The average salary of public school teachers during 1963–64 ranged from $3,975 in Mississippi to $7,800 in California.[4] While salary levels continue to rise year by year, the disparity by geographic location and wealth of the school district remains significant. In Figure 12–1 we see the distribution of salaries for public school teachers, elementary and secondary, in the United States during the 1963–64 school year. Regional differences in teachers' salaries are shown in Table 12–1.

Table 12–1
Average Teachers' Salaries
by Regions
1963–64

Region	Salary
New England	$6,340
Mideast	6,861
Southeast	5,000
Great Lakes	6,456
Plains	5,547
Southwest	5,667
Rocky Mountain	5,707
Far West	7,456
United States	$5,963

SOURCE: Research Division, National Education Association, *NEA Research Bulletin*, Vol. 42, 1964, p. 6.

The wide disparity of teachers' salaries in the various regions of our nation and from district to district means that many areas and districts cannot compete for the services of highly qualified teachers. This inequity has been so serious that proposals for federal support for education frequently include monies for improving teachers' salaries.

During 1963–64, minimum salary requirements for teachers were in effect by state law in 32 states. The minimum salary for teachers with the bachelor's degree ranged from $1,485 in South Carolina to $4,500 in California, Massachusetts, and New York. At the master's degree level the minimum salary requirement ranged from $2,570 in Idaho to $4,800 in New York.[5] Such minimum salary laws can be beneficial to teachers if the state legislatures continually adjust these minimums in line with inflationary trends and salary increases for college graduates in non-teaching occupations.

[4] *Ibid.*, p. 6.
[5] *Ibid.*, p. 13.

AN ADVANCED PROGRAM OF SPECIALIZED TRAINING

The requirements for teacher education and certification vary widely from state to state. In recent years, there has been a marked increase in the certification requirements. As recently as 1921, only four states required more than a high school education for the lowest standard teaching certificate. Even as late as 1940, the bachelor's degree was required for initial teacher certification in only nine states. Today, most of the states require it. During the 1963–64 school year, 45 states required the bachelor's degree for the lowest regular certificate for beginning elementary teachers, while at the high-school level 47 states required the bachelor's degree and the remaining three states required the master's degree or five years of college work.[6]

A very desirable trend in recent years is the reciprocity of certification between and among states. Such reciprocity is indicative of the growing recognition of certain uniform requirements and standards for the licensure of teachers, and the recognition that there is a core of professional knowledge and skills teachers should possess in common. Reciprocity in certification also facilitates the flow of teachers from state to state.

Teachers with Substandard Credentials

Although the requirements for teacher certification have become more stringent while salaries have been increasing, more than 83,000 teachers, or 5.3 per cent of the entire teaching force, held substandard certificates during 1963–64.[7] Some two thirds of these emergency teachers were employed at the elementary level where teacher turnover is highest. Moreover, the annual number of college graduates prepared for high-school teaching continues to outnumber those who are prepared for teaching at the elementary level.

At the secondary-school level, the shortage of qualified teachers exists only in certain fields such as women's physical education, home economics, mathematics, some modern foreign languages, industrial education, and certain areas of business education.

Most emergency teachers are employed by school districts that cannot compete in salaries with the larger and wealthier systems. Because teachers tend to move to the higher-paying positions in the more attractive communities, many substandard teachers must be contracted to fill these vacancies. The wide disparity in teachers' salaries is great not only between districts but also between states.

---

[6] Office of Education, *School Life*, Vol. 46, January–February, 1964, p. 18.
[7] *Ibid.*

Teachers Lack Interest in Professional Standards

While the practitioners of many other professions take a vital interest in establishing and maintaining stringent licensure requirements, rarely do classroom teachers exhibit an interest in this area.[8] Those professional groups engaged predominately in fee-taking (physicians, dentists, attorneys, and so on) look upon licensure as a vehicle for upholding standards and maintaining limits on the number entering the profession. Since teachers are employed mostly by public agencies, their bargaining power is extremely limited. And with a sizable portion of the teaching force comprised of women who are temporarily engaged in the occupation, one can understand why teachers as a group do not take an active interest in upholding and raising the licensure requirements.[9]

How Well Prepared are Teachers?

In recent years there has been much criticism of teacher education and certification requirements. The Bestors and Rickovers contend that teachers are incompetent because their programs of preparation are laden with methods courses and lack concentration in subject-matter specialization. A study by the Institute of Higher Education at Teachers College, Columbia University, involving a sample of 35 institutions of teacher education, revealed that prospective secondary teachers devoted only 17 per cent of their preservice curriculum to courses in professional teacher education.[10] Furthermore, a significant portion of this 17 per cent is concerned with the highly practical and essential experiences in observation of teaching and student teaching. This study revealed that the preservice program at the elementary level devotes an average of 36 per cent of the total curriculum to professional education course work. Because most elementary teachers are assigned to self-contained classrooms where they are responsible for instruction in virtually every area of the curriculum, their preservice education includes a broader and more intensive program in the so-called methods courses. Nevertheless, the evidence fails to support any contention that the education of teachers consists primarily of methods courses. Lieberman observes, however, that the demands of teaching require a program of preparation that goes far beyond that given in most contemporary teacher education curricula.

---

[8] Myron Lieberman, *Education as a Profession* (Englewood Cliffs, N.J.: Prentice-Hall, Inc., 1956), pp. 124–25.

[9] See Daniel Tanner, "The Case for Certification," *The Atlantic*, Vol. 202, July 1958, p. 35.

[10] The *New York Times*, Sunday, June 11, 1961, Section 1, p. 15.

Photo by Herb Comess

"We are only just realising that the
art and science of education require
a genius and a study of their own."
—ALFRED NORTH WHITEHEAD

Regardless of the actual status of teachers, teaching in the public
schools justifiably requires both general and specialized training far
beyond that given in contemporary teacher education programs. We
should not forget that there is no question as to the professional status
of the teacher in many countries. Hence if education is not a profession
in the United States, it is not because of anything inherent in education. The fact that in some countries the healing arts are in the hands
of medicine men instead of doctors does not mean that the intellectual
basis for a medical profession does not exist. It means only that other
factors are responsible for the absence of a medical profession in such
countries.[11]

If teachers, themselves, do not have a high regard for their calling
and if they do not strive for higher standards of selection and training,
then the occupation will not have a very high esteem in the eyes of the
general public.

---

[11] Lieberman, *op. cit.*, p. 196.

It seems contradictory that the critics of teacher education disparage the so-called methods courses, while many teachers desire greater emphasis on practical experience in their preparation. No professional group can exist without a theoretical framework on which to base its practice. For without a developing theory, practice becomes routine and repetitive. And conversely, theory without practice can be meaningless and dangerous.

> Teacher educators are the first to recognize that it would be a naive and serious mistake to conceive of teaching methods as being opposed to teaching content (and theory). Yet, many persons who attack our programs in professional teacher education tend to view content and method as antithetical. Does the nuclear physicist ignore the scientific method in his research work? Of course not. Teaching is a science and an art. It must be far more than drillwork in facts and skills. The teacher must be concerned with both content and process.
>
> It would be dangerous for society to license a medical doctor as a brain surgeon simply because he gave evidence of knowing the theory of brain surgery, without any preparation and demonstrated proficiency in actual surgery practice. Yet some people advocate that any person who manages to secure a bachelor's degree be given the privilege of walking into the classrooms of our nation and taking control of the minds of our children.
>
> . . . Teachers must see to it that only the highest calibre young men and women be permitted to join their ranks. If we are satisfied with less, then our society will have to be satisfied with a lower calibre of performance in the education of its future generations.[12]

Critics of teacher education ignore the fact that today's teachers are better qualified than ever before. Not only are teacher certification requirements becoming more stringent, but the type of institution for teacher education has undergone a significant transformation during the twentieth century. In 1900 the Normal School prepared teachers for the elementary levels. Prior to 1900, prospective teachers were admitted to the Normal School directly from elementary school. The curriculum of the Normal School ranged from a few weeks to one or two years' duration. After the turn of the century, the Normal Schools began to require high-school graduation for admission. With the offering of instruction at the college level and the granting of the bachelor's degree, the Normal Schools became publicly-supported teachers colleges during the 1920's. During the 1940's and 1950's, the teachers colleges were transformed into general state colleges or universities (See Figure 12–2.) These changes mean that the prospective teacher today can receive a better general education and can associate with college students in a wide variety of curricular specialties.

The most influential critique of teacher education and certification

---

12 Tanner, *op. cit.*, pp. 35–36.

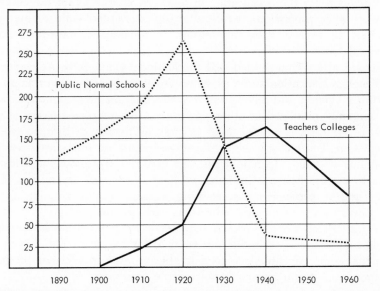

FIGURE 12–2. The rise and fall of the teachers college. [SOURCE: Paul Wood-ring, "The Short Happy Life of the Teachers College," *Saturday Review*, June 17, 1961, p. 61.]

standards came as the result of a study by James B. Conant, financed by the Carnegie Corporation.[13] Conant and his staff visited 77 colleges and universities in 22 states. They also studied the certification procedures in the 16 most populous states. Conant developed his recommendations from interviews, observations, and the perusal of catalogs and textbooks. While his study exerted considerable influence, it also generated much controversy. Most of Conant's recommendations were formulated on the basis of impressions. He appeared to be concerned more with the book-keeping arrangements of credit hours in teacher education than with the question of how to improve the quality of our teachers.

Among Conant's recommendations for the education of secondary-school teachers was that such teachers be prepared in a major field only. He also recommended that certification be provided by recommendation of the college or university upon completion of the bachelor's degree with a major in a teaching field and successful performance in student teaching. According to Conant, specific certification requirements, other than student teaching, should be left to the individual colleges and universities. Under present conditions, the states specify the minimum

[13] James Bryant Conant, *The Education of American Teachers* (New York: McGraw-Hill Company, Inc.), 1963.

requirements for the certification of teachers, as well as for the certification of other professions, while allowing accredited colleges and universities to exceed these minimums or to depart from them upon approval.

Conant also recommended that the National Council for Accreditation of Teacher Education serve as an advisory body rather than as an accrediting agency. But again, this recommendation runs counter to what is commonly practiced in other professions, where accreditation of preservice programs is administered through an agency of the professional association. Too many teacher-education institutions today are operating programs without adequate staffs and facilities. To allow these institutions to certify their own product, without the overall supervision of the state and a professional accrediting agency, would be akin to the proprietary days of medical education early in the century.

In his report, Conant argued that adequate preparation for teaching could be provided within the four years of the baccalaureate, despite the fact that some educators see considerable promise in five-year programs accompanied by an internship during the final year.

In recent years a few states have raised the requirements for certification of beginning high-school teachers from four to five years of college work. And in various sections of the nation, certain colleges and universities have developed fifth-year programs of teacher education at the graduate level and leading to the master's degree. These fifth-year programs were originally designed for those college graduates who had not been prepared for teaching. Since 1951 the Ford Foundation's Fund for the Advancement of Education has provided financial support for a number of these fifth-year programs.

But there is considerable disagreement about the curricular organization and content in programs of preservice teacher education. Such programs vary widely from institution to institution. Apparently, there is a lack of common recognition as to the body of educational theory to which prospective teachers should be exposed. This lack of coherence apparently is a result of the failure on the part of the behavioral sciences (psychology, sociology, and so on) to grapple adequately with problems related to the teaching-learning process. This does not imply that programs in teacher education should be everywhere the same. It does mean, however, that there is need for a sharper focus on teaching and learning through the behavioral sciences, and that the findings thereof should be directed toward the development of a coherent field of professional knowledge. Moreover, relatively few practicing teachers formulate their judgments and methods on the principles developed from educational research. In other words, relatively few teachers are effective consumers of educational research. Yet, practitioners in other professional fields (law, medicine, psychology, engineering, and so on) rely heavily upon research for their decisions.

Elements in Preservice Teacher Education

In summation, the total preservice education of the teacher includes the following four elements:

1. *General education:* This may be defined as "that part of a student's whole education which looks first of all to his life as a responsible human being and a citizen."[14] Historically, the term liberal education was the education designed for a ruling or leisure class, but a democracy requires that education for the good life is the privilege of all citizens.[15] Consequently, the term general education has gained common usage at both the secondary and collegiate levels. Approximately 40 to 50 per cent of the preservice curriculum for the prospective secondary-school teacher is devoted to general education. The National Commission on Teacher Education and Professional Standards identifies the following areas in the general or liberal education of teachers:

> Communication
> Humanities
> Social Sciences
> Natural Sciences
> Health and Personal Development[16]

2. *Specialization in teaching fields:* The preparation of the secondary-school teacher usually includes at least a major and a minor field of subject specialization. While in recent years it has been fashionable for some critics of public education to allege that teachers are ill prepared in subject specialties, the typical candidate's program devotes from 35 to 45 per cent to specialization in two or more teaching fields. However, many teachers fail to continue their academic pursuits in their teaching fields after they have attained full certification. And academic departments in our colleges and universities, until recently, have failed to meet the needs of in-service teachers.[17]

3. *Special-interest education:* This refers to the free electives, which permit the college student to select a limited amount of course work in

---

[14] Harvard University Committee on the Objectives of a General Education in a Free Society, *General Education in a Free Society* (Cambridge, Mass.: Harvard University Press, 1945), p. 51.

[15] *Ibid.,* pp. 52–53.

[16] National Commission on Teacher Education and Professional Standards, *Teacher Education: The Decade Ahead* (Washington, D.C.: National Education Association, 1955), pp. 70–71.

[17] In recent years, the National Science Foundation, for example, has granted fellowships at colleges and universities to secondary teachers for the purpose of improving their preparation and teaching proficiency.

areas beyond his specialty fields. This work may be largely of an avocational or general education character. Approximately 10 per cent of the candidate's program may be devoted to such electives.

4. *Professional education:* This refers to the so-called art and science of teaching, and is required of all college students who are preparing to teach at the elementary or secondary level. Professional teacher education usually includes introductory course work in the psychology of learning (including child and adolescent growth and development), history of education, philosophy of education, educational sociology, educational administration, principles and methods of education, and an internship of observational and practice teaching experience. While professional teacher education has been under severe criticism in recent years, with the allegation that prospective teachers learn only how to teach rather that what to teach, the evidence does not support this. Only 12 to 17 per cent of the preservice curriculum is devoted to the area of professional education. Alfred North Whitehead paid tribute to the need for developing professional education as a field for formal study.

> We are only just realising that the art and science of education require a study and genius of their own; and that this genius and this science are more than a bare knowledge of some branch of science or of literature.[18]

Principles for the Selection and Education of Teachers

A Statement by the Educational Policies Commission of the N.E.A. identifies seven broad principles that should govern the selection and education of teachers:

1. Every teacher should comprehend the purposes of public education in a democratic society and the contribution he makes through his teaching to the achievement of these purposes.
2. Every teacher should have both a liberal education and a knowledge in depth of the field in which he teaches. Specialization is essential, but alone is not enough. In the school of today the competent teacher must recognize and teach the relationships of his field to the whole of education and the whole of life.
3. Every teacher has the obligation to keep abreast of knowledge in his field and of developments in teaching materials and techniques which will help improve his performance.
4. Because of the prime importance of citizenship education in a democracy, every teacher should be well prepared to assume his own obligations as a citizen and should understand how the school may serve as an agency for developing civic responsibility.
5. Every teacher should have sympathetic understanding of boys and

---

[18] Alfred North Whitehead, *The Aims of Education* (New York: The Macmillan Company, 1929), p. 6

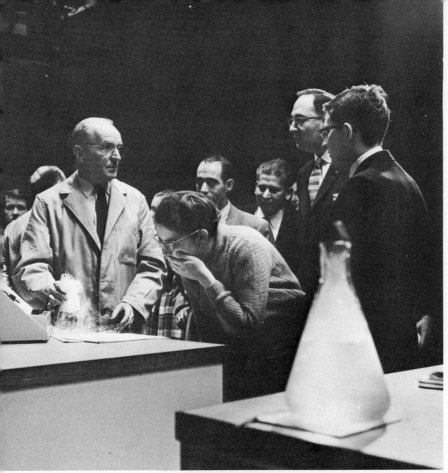

Photo by Martha Roberts; courtesy Learning Resources Institute

Subject matter is not static. Teachers need
to keep abreast of new developments.

girls and should be familiar with scientific knowledge regarding child
development and the psychology of learning.

6. Every teacher should understand the nature and purposes of guidance and should have had experience in individual and group
guidance as part of his training.

7. Teacher education should include supervised experience in dealing
with actual classroom problems.[19]

PERFORMANCE AT A HIGH INTELLECTUAL LEVEL

John Dewey emphasized that the function of education should be the
development of critical thinking.

---

[19] Educational Policies Commission, *The Contemporary Challenge to American Education* (Washington, D.C.: National Education Association, 1958), pp. 14–15.

The sole direct path to enduring improvement in the methods of instruction and learning consists in centering upon the conditions which exact, promote and test thinking.[20]

Although Hutchins, Bestor, Rickover, and other contemporary critics of American education have been extremely critical of Dewey's position on educational means, these critics, nevertheless, have argued that the main function of education is intellectual training. The Report of the Harvard Committee states that "the fruit of education is intelligence in action."[21] Thus we see that even among individuals embracing widely divergent educational philosophies, there is general agreement that one of the most important functions of the school is the development of critical thinking and intellectual facility. Although the teacher at the elementary and even high-school level is concerned with concepts and skills in relatively basic dimensions, even scholars are quick to agree that the task of the teacher is exceedingly difficult, for he must be able to make abstract concepts sufficiently clear and meaningful.

Intelligence and Teaching

Some studies reveal that students preparing for teaching have lower intelligence test scores as a group than students preparing for many other professional occupations.[22] This should not be interpreted to mean that a high level of intelligence is not generally necessary for successful teaching. Yet a number of educators have embraced the notion that superior intelligence is not an important requisite for successful teaching.[23] While it is true that emotional and attitudinal factors are vital to the success of the teacher, just as they are vital to the success of the physician and the attorney, the intellectual factor should not be minimized. While many studies fail to show a high positive correlation between intelligence and successful teaching, we must bear in mind that there is wide disagreement and confusion over what successful teaching really is. Furthermore, if one of the major functions of education is the development of critical thinking and the method of intelligence, then it is only reasonable to assume that teachers should have a high degree of intelligence. Lieberman asserts that a high degree of intelligence is a requirement common to all professions.

A high degree of intelligence is clearly one requirement common to all professions. The long period of formal training involving mastery of

---

[20] John Dewey, *Democracy and Education* (New York: The Macmillan Company, 1916), pp. 179–80.

[21] Harvard University Committee on The Objectives of a General Education in a Free Society, *op. cit.*, p. 75.

[22] Dael L. Wolfle, *America's Resources of Specialized Talent* (New York: Harper & Row, Publishers, Inc., 1954), pp. 199–200.

[23] Robert W. Richey, *Planning for Teaching* (New York: McGraw-Hill Company, Inc., 1952), pp. 218–19.

a body of theory would be useless unless the prospective practitioners possess enough intelligence to master theoretical problems. The work of the professions is not routine. It is varied and complex. Rule of thumb methods are inapplicable to professional work, because a profession requires thinking. Other characteristics will also be important, but they can never be *substituted* for intelligence.[24]

Recent studies reveal that an increasing proportion of our most able high-school seniors are giving teaching as their career choice. Among the 1963 National Merit Scholarship semifinalists, teaching ranked first among the girls and third among the boys in frequency of career choice. Moreover, during the past several years, there has been a significant increase in the proportion of semifinalists choosing the profession of teaching.[25]

A serious problem in professional education lies in the failure of in-service teachers to draw upon pertinent research concerning the teaching-learning process. In comparison to members of other professional groups, relatively few teachers utilize the findings of research to determine the content and methods for their professional practices. This failure on the part of practicing teachers to draw upon research in the behavioral sciences is a serious obstacle to the professionalization of teaching. And because many teachers use the textbook as the course of instruction and follow the textbook in dull routine, they automatically abrogate their professional responsibility for determining curricular content and process. Under such circumstances it can be argued that the teacher is not operating at a high level of professional and intellectual jurisdiction.

A HIGH LEVEL OF RESPONSIBILITY, AND LATITUDE IN DECISION-MAKING WITHIN A CONTEXT OF REASONABLE OPERATIONAL AUTONOMY

The standards for the licensing of professionals is governed by state legislation. Standards and rulings for entry and expulsion are delegated to state boards, which, for most professions, are composed of professional practitioners. In other words, the memberships of these boards are in most cases comprised of practitioners from the profession itself. This arrangement has evolved in recognition that the professionals themselves are the most competent to render judgment concerning standards of qualification and practice. Even in the case of registered nurses, barbers, and beauticians, the prevailing practice is the delegation of

---

24 Myron Lieberman, *Education as a Profession* (Englewood Cliffs, N.J.: Prentice-Hall, Inc., 1956), pp. 225–26.
25 Robert C. Nichols, "Career Decisions of Very Able Students," *Science*, Vol. 144, June 12, 1964, pp. 1315–1319.

licensing powers to boards composed of members who are from the profession concerned. A notable exception is in the case of teachers, where the state licensing board in most states is composed largely of persons *not* engaged in teaching.[26] In some states, professional educators are excluded by law from membership on the state board of education.[27] Presumably, this serves to ensure that the board of education is composed entirely of lay citizens. The rationale for such exclusion appears to be based on the fact that teaching is primarily a public profession, whereas many other professional groups are self-employed or privately employed. But one of the essential criteria distinguishing a profession from other occupations is that the professional group is dedicated to serving the public interest. Physicians and attorneys, for example, serve the public interest and may regard themselves as members of a public profession. Witness this statement from a study of the American legal profession:

> The legal profession is a public profession. Lawyers are public servants. They are stewards of all the legal rights and obligations of all the citizens.[28]

Should Boards of Education be Under Lay Control?

It is also significant that licensure for the professions is under the jurisdiction of public authorities. Nevertheless, teachers are a notable exception among the professions in that they are governed by state boards composed of lay persons or noneducators. The probable reason for this arrangement in the case of teachers is that they are employed predominantly by public agencies, namely the public schools. On the other hand, the majority of physicians, attorneys, engineers, and members of other professional groups are either self-employed or privately employed. This does not mean that the physician, attorney, or engineer who is employed by a public agency is less professional in his task than the one who is self-employed or privately employed. Historically, teachers as a group have not taken the position that state and local boards of education should be composed of professional educators rather than laymen. On the contrary the principle of lay control of state boards of education has had the approval of the N.E.A. since 1921, with the passage of the following resolution:

> We recognize the distinction between the lay control of education and the professional administration of our schools. We believe that the highest type of professional service in the offices of state superintendents or state commissioners of education, of county superintendents of schools,

---

[26] Lieberman, *op. cit.*, p. 95.
[27] *Ibid.*, p. 97.
[28] Albert P. Blaustein and Charles O. Porter, *The American Lawyer* (Chicago: The University of Chicago Press, 1954), p. VI.

and of city superintendents of schools can be secured by the selection of all such administrative officers by lay boards of education elected by the people.[29]

One of the most serious problems confronting school administrators at the district level is the tendency for lay boards of education to render decisions that should come under the jurisdiction of the professional administrator and teacher. Cases are on record in which the curriculum, grading system, and even the methods of instruction have been determined by lay boards of education and citizens' committees.[30] The structure of American education provides for the election of local school boards that are responsible for setting policy. Serious trouble arises when boards insist on telling the administrator how to carry out such educational policy.

Professional Standards

Unlike many other professional and even nonprofessional groups, teachers have shown relatively little interest in setting and upholding the standards for licensure and practice. This apathy may be attributed in part to the high rate of teacher turnover characteristic of an occupation with a high proportion of women members. Nevertheless, recent years have witnessed some significant developments relating to professional standards in teaching. In 1946, the National Education Association established the National Commission on Teacher Education and Professional Standards. The purposes of this commission are to develop "a continuing program for the profession in matters of recruitment, selection, preparation, certification, and advancement of professional standards, including standards for institutions which prepare teachers."[31] In 1952 a specialized agency for the accreditation of institutions of teacher education was established by the N.E.A. Known as the National Council for Accreditation of Teacher Education, this agency, by 1963, had accredited approximately 70 per cent of the colleges and universities. NCATE has been instrumental in bringing about reciprocity among the states in the certification of teachers.

Role of the Professional Teacher

The function of the teacher as a professional includes his degree of latitude in determining curriculum content, methods and materials of instruction, procedures and materials for testing and evaluation, ap-

[29] National Education Association, *Addresses and Proceedings,* Vol. 59 (Washington, D.C.: The Association, 1921), p. 27.

[30] Lieberman, *op. cit.,* pp. 115–16.

[31] National Education Association, *NEA Handbook 1963–64* (Washington, D.C.: The Association, 1963), p. 103.

proaches to the diagnosis of individual learning problems, and decision-making in various areas of classroom management. If, for economic reasons, it is not possible for a school district to permit textbook adoptions by individual teachers, it would not be an infringement on the professional role of the teacher to have such adoptions made by representative committees of fellow professionals. In cases where the adoption of textbooks is performed at the state level, such decisions should be made by educators.

Boards of education, at the local or state level, composed of lay citizens, are not professionally competent to exercise judgment concerning the selection or censorship of textbooks or curriculum materials. Yet it is not uncommon for such boards to perform censorship functions. Only a few years ago in San Francisco, for example, the Board of Education refused a gift subscription of the Christian Science Monitor to one of the city's junior high schools on the ground that "acceptance of the Monitor would oblige the Board to accept others, including magazines advocating the agnostic point of view."[32]

In most of the states, laws have been enacted requiring that specific subjects be taught in the public elementary and secondary schools. For example, a state statute may require the teaching of such subjects as state and United States history, physical education, and so on. Lieberman maintains that such laws are serious invasions of professional autonomy, since the implication is that educators either lack the competency for determining the curriculum or intend to ignore these curricular needs.[33]

Although we have raised several issues questioning the level of autonomy exercised by professional educators in comparison with that exercised by other professionals, we are not advocating that professional groups should be concerned primarily with the furtherance of their own interests and only secondarily with the public interest. We have stressed that one of the fundamental earmarks of a professional group is its dedication to the public interest. If the public lacks confidence in the expertness of the group concerned, then the professional status of the group is in doubt. The teaching profession has long been characterized by a high rate of turnover, a substantial portion of emergency and substandard personnel, and a general apathy with regard to the establishment and enforcement of standards for licensure and practice of its own membership. Recent developments in improving the financial status of the teacher, the establishment of the National Commission on Teacher Education and Professional Standards by the N.E.A., and the recognized importance of academic freedom are indicative of the developing status

---

[32] Quoted from The *San Francisco Chronicle,* January 27, 1960, p. 2.
[33] Lieberman, *op. cit.,* pp. 100–102.

of teaching as a profession. No other occupation can boast a higher level of public responsibility.

A SELF-REGULATING MEMBERSHIP WITH A CODE OF ETHICS OPERATIONALLY SUPPORTED BY CONCRETE CASES

We have observed that the teaching profession lacks the operational autonomy exercised by many other professional groups. Where control over licensure for teaching is relegated to state boards composed of lay persons, the boards governing many of the other professions are made up of representative practitioners from the profession itself. The professional status of the teacher is undermined by the 83,000 persons who presently hold emergency or substandard teaching licenses because of the shortage of qualified teachers. Moreover, teachers as a group have never exhibited a vital concern for establishing and upholding high standards for professional entry and expulsion.

An enforceable code of ethics derived and applied by the group itself is an important element for professional status. Codes of ethics were adopted by the American Bar Association in 1908 and the American Medical Association in 1912. In 1929 the National Education Association adopted a code of ethics, later revised in 1941 and 1952.

Most of the state education associations have either adopted the N.E.A. Code or have patterned their own code after the N.E.A. version. Despite the similarities among the various state codes of ethics, however, there is need for a singular code that will be accepted and adhered to by all state and local associations.

Problems in Professional Ethics

While the N.E.A. Code outlines the general principles governing the professional role and conduct of the teacher, it is exceedingly difficult to apply the Code to cases involving unprofessional conduct.[34] In many states, unprofessional conduct is grounds for dismissal of a teacher and, if judged sufficiently serious, may lead to the revocation of the teacher's license. In such cases, the state education association's Ethics Committee, the N.E.A.'s Committee on Professional Ethics, or the courts may be asked to make the determination. The following cases illustrate a variety of problems concerning professional ethics. How do you think they should be decided?

> Miss A refused to accept an assignment to teach a class of slow learners, even though she was legally qualified for this work. She main-

---

[34] See *NEA Handbook 1963–64* (Washington, D.C.: National Education Association, 1963), pp. 67–69.

tained that she was informed of this assignment only two weeks prior to the opening of school. And she pointed out that in six years of prior experience with the district, she had been assigned groups of "average" and "above-average" pupils.

Mr. B advocated, in his high school class in social studies, the election of a specific candidate for political office. In doing so, he distributed campaign literature to his students favoring the election of this candidate. No attempt was made to analyze the campaign literature of other candidates.

Mr. C did not maintain a complete and accurate record of student grades. When asked by his principal to show cause for failing several students, Mr. C argued that he knew each student individually and that each student's record of achievement was so well known to the teacher that he saw no reason for keeping a detailed grade book.

Mr. D, a teacher of social studies in an all-white Mississippi high school, advocated the "separate but equal" educational doctrine to his students. When a parent complained that this was in clear violation of the U.S. Supreme Court decision, Mr. D replied that "the maintenance of segregated schools is clearly the policy of the community and the state. To favor school desegregation would result in the loss of my job."

Mrs. E reported that she was "ill" and took a week of "sick leave" to accompany her husband on a business trip to Puerto Rico. Shortly after her return, the principal heard from another teacher that Mrs. E had been away on a trip. When asked for an explanation Mrs. E told the principal, "I was afraid that any request for a week's leave of absence to take a trip would have been denied."

Mr. F is author of a workbook in English grammar. Although the workbook has not been adopted by the school, Mr. F offers it for sale to his students at cost.

Mr. G, twenty-five years of age and unmarried, is dating a high school senior. The girl is not enrolled in any of Mr. G's classes. When asked by the principal to stop dating the girl, Mr. G refuses by arguing that he has the consent of the girl's parents.

Mrs. H had been negotiating with two school districts for a position during the coming year. A few weeks after signing a contract with the first district, she was offered a contract from the second district at a much higher salary. The second offer came one month prior to the opening of school. Mrs. H requested a release from her signed contract with the explanation that she had been offered a much higher paying position at a school much closer to her home. The superintendent of the first district told Mrs. H that he felt she was unethical in continuing negotiations with another district after having signed a contract with his district.

One week before the opening of school, the principal notified Miss I of some changes in her teaching assignment, explaining that he had to make these changes because of the sudden and unexpected resignation of a teacher. Miss I objected to these changes, explaining that the preparation and adjustment required for the new assignment meant a heavier load. The principal apologized, but stated that he had no choice in the matter. Miss I complained about these changes to her next door neighbor who was a member of the school board. When the superintendent learned of this case through the board member, he called Miss I and the principal to his office. After hearing the views of both parties, the superintendent expressed his belief that Miss I was unethical in going to the board member, rather than first arranging to see the superintendent through the principal.

The preceeding cases are illustrative of the variety of problem situations relating to the professional conduct of the teacher. The Committee on Professional Ethics of the National Education Association has compiled opinions on 32 cases, some of which are similar to the cases just described.[35]

A variety of cases are on record concerning the unprofessional conduct of the school administrator. The Defense Commission of the N.E.A. was established in 1941 to investigate criticisms of education, and to improve public understanding and support of public education.[36] At the request of professional organizations and citizens' groups in Chicago, this commission began an investigation in 1944 of the administration of the Chicago public schools. The investigation revealed evidence of unethical practices on the part of the administration, including questionable connections between the school administration and the city's political administration. Other findings indicated intimidation of capable teachers and attempted domination of teachers' organizations. The investigation eventually led to the expulsion of the superintendent from the N.E.A.[37] Whenever such cases cannot be resolved between or among the parties concerned, they may be referred to the state education association or the National Education Association, which claim to maintain machinery for the protection and discipline of its members. For example, most of the state associations, along with the N.E.A., maintain committees on professional ethics and tenure. But disciplinary actions by the N.E.A. and the state education associations are taken only under extreme circumstances. Although decisions by these committees on professional conduct cannot be enforced if any of the parties are unwilling, the major weapon is the publicity given to the findings and decisions of the committee. If necessary, such cases may be taken to court by the individual, the district, or the state association.

---

[35] National Education Association, Committee on Professional Ethics, *Opinions of the Committee on Professional Ethics* (Washington, D.C.: The Association, 1955).

[36] National Education Association, *Addresses and Proceedings* (79th Annual Meeting, Boston, 1941) (Washington, D.C.: The Association, 1941), pp. 778–79.

[37] "Ethics Committee Expels Chicago Superintendent from NEA Membership," *NEA Journal*, March, 1946, p. 161.

In certain instances concerning the legal rights of teachers, the state association has provided the legal services and assumed the court costs while giving financial aid to a suspended or dismissed teacher. One of the most notorious of such cases involved a teacher of social studies in a small community near San Francisco who was accused by a San Francisco radio commentator, in a series of broadcasts during 1951 and 1952, of being a Communist. The accusations were based on the fact that in a previous teaching position a housewife had demanded that the school board fire the teacher for serving as advisor to a student organization of United World Federalists. The board refused to discharge the teacher, but subsequently the teacher took a position in another school district. It was then that the housewife wrote to the radio commentator who in turn made a series of public accusations on his program. The Tenure and Ethics Committee of the California Teachers Association investigated the charges and cleared the teacher. But with the continued radio attacks directed against both the teacher and the C.T.A. Committee, the C.T.A., in behalf of the teacher, filed a libel suit against the commentator and the radio station. The court ordered the radio station and the commentator each to pay $25,000 in damages to the teacher, and the manager of the station was ordered to pay the teacher an additional $5,000.[38] The San Francisco Chronicle applauded the action of the California Teachers Association in this case.

Professional Self-Regulation

A significant milestone in the recognition of the need for professional responsibility and self-regulation in teaching occurred with the passage of a bill by the 1955 California State Legislature. This bill stipulates that a judge in a case involving teacher tenure may call upon the California Teachers Association or a similarly qualified teacher's group to nominate a panel of teachers to investigate and render a professional opinion to the court. This panel could be established at the request of the school board or the teacher involved. The California Teachers Association, largest of the state education associations, lobbied strenuously for the enactment of this piece of legislation. The significance of this bill was described in a national magazine.

> This is a legal prerogative that doctors and lawyers have had for a long time. Now the law gives teachers the same professional recognition and responsibility. The net effect is an official recognition that teaching is a profession in California. In this respect the state is unique.[39]

---

[38] Joseph Stocker, "Teachers in California: He Who Can, Must," *The Reporter*, February 21, 1957, p. 22.
[39] *Ibid.*, pp. 23–24.

This legislation is a move away from lay control of teacher practice, and a decisive step toward professional responsibility and self-regulation.

COMMITMENT ON THE PART OF INDIVIDUAL MEMBERS TO THE OCCUPATION AS A LIFETIME CAREER

The high rate of teacher turnover militates against the professionalization of teaching. In September of 1962, 125,000 teachers were needed to replace those who left the profession at the end of the preceding academic year.[40] Teacher turnover is high primarily because of the discontinuity of female employment. Approximately 70 to 75 per cent of the total teaching force is female. Lieberman considers the predominance of women in teaching one of the most important professional problems.

> The predominance of women in teaching is one of the most important and most neglected facts about American education. Under present conditions, it must be regarded as one of the two or three most important obstacles to the professionalization of education.
>
> This may sound like a criticism of women teachers, but it is not. Prejudiced attitudes toward women workers are facts, in education as well as in other occupations. Like other types of prejudice, it is costly to those who have it as well as to those who are the immediate objects of it. But the harsh unpleasant truth is this: Education will not become a leading profession unless either the proportion of men to women is drastically increased or there occurs a cultural revolution concerning the women in American society.[41]

Career Teachers Needed

The discontinuity of female employment is caused not only by marriage and maternity, but also by the fact that the husband's employment determines domicile. Consequently, when the husband's job requires him to move to another location, the wife may find that she must sacrifice her own teaching position and professional status. This intermittent character of female employment seriously hinders the organizability of teaching as a profession, since almost three fourths of the occupation is female. Caplow emphasizes that discontinuity of employment is fatal to occupational solidarity.

> Given the intermittent character of female employment, a woman's occupation must be one in which employment is typically by short term,

---

40 Research Division, National Education Association, "Interesting Facts and Figures on American Education," *NEA Research Bulletin*, Vol. 41 (Washington, D.C.: The Association, February, 1963), p. 3.

41 Myron Lieberman, *Education as a Profession* (Englewood Cliffs, N.J.: Prentice-Hall, Inc., 1956), pp. 241–42.

in which the gain in skill achieved by continuous experience is slight, in which interchangeability is very high, and in which the loss of skill during long periods of inactivity is relatively small. Note how closely the occupations of elementary teacher, nurse, librarian . . . conform to these criteria.

. . . Teaching, nursing, and other auxiliary professions do require substantial training, but it is notable that in the absence of fully qualified personnel, untrained teachers, nurses, librarians, or social workers are readily substituted. . . .

Occupation by occupation, unorganizability appears both as the cause and the effect of a preponderance of women. Well-organized occupations have usually been able to prevent the entry of women and have done so, for reasons previously outlined. . . . Above all, discontinuity of employment is fatal to the development of occupational solidarity.[42]

The aspirations for a career in teaching on the part of young women tend to be secondary to marriage and homemaking. A study was made of single women teachers, married women teachers, and married men teachers who were asked the following question: "What would you most like to be doing ten years from now?" Approximately three fourths of the men teachers indicated that they would like to continue teaching as a life work. On the other hand, three fourths of the single and married women teachers under 30 years of age expressed their desire to be housewives ten years hence.[43] Lieberman observes that because most young women teachers are not committed to education as a life work, these women drift in and out of teaching and are frequently opposed to the raising of professional standards.

It should be obvious that the fact that so many women teachers drift in and out of teaching means that it is very difficult for teachers to achieve occupational solidarity. The woman teacher interested chiefly in marriage and a home is not likely to take a strong interest in raising professional standards and in improving the conditions of teaching. Indeed, such women are frequently opposed to raising professional standards; such action runs contrary to *their* personal long term interests.[44]

This should not be construed as a criticism of women in the occupation of teaching. But it does mean that teaching will not become a leading profession until the overwhelming majority of teachers are committed to their work as a lifetime career. As long as teaching remains feminized, the development of professional solidarity will be exceedingly difficult.

---

[42] Theodore Caplow, *The Sociology of Work* (Minneapolis: University of Minnesota Press, 1954, pp. 245–46.

[43] R. G. Kuhlen and G. H. Johnson, "Changes in Goals with Increasing Adult Age," *Journal of Consulting Psychology,* Vol. 16, February, 1952, pp. 1–4.

[44] Lieberman, *op. cit.,* p. 253.

College Graduates and Teaching

Another serious professional problem is that despite the enormous number of new college graduates each year who are eligible to enter teaching, in recent years only about 68 per cent of the newly qualified high-school teachers actually enter classroom service. The class of 1960 included 77,573 qualified for high-school teaching, of which approximately 53,000 (68.1 per cent) actually accepted teaching positions. The approximate number of new teachers actually employed at the high-school level was 69,000. This means that almost one out of every four new high-school teachers employed in 1960 came from the general population. At the elementary level, the college graduates of 1960 contributed fewer than one half of the new recruits. In other words, a significant portion of the positions each year are filled by former teachers, homemakers, persons from other occupations, liberal arts college graduates with little or no professional preparation, and others who, if unqualified, are allowed to teach with an emergency license.[45]

Since 1950, the percentage of the total class of college baccalaureates prepared for teaching has ranged between 26 and 31.[46] With such a high proportion of undergraduates preparing for teaching, the shortage of teachers is obviously not caused by a lack of qualified candidates. The shortage is a result of the failure of these qualified graduates to enter teaching and to develop a commitment to the occupation as a lifetime career. From these data it seems reasonable to assume that a considerable portion of the college students pursuing programs in teacher education are doing so without a sound philosophical commitment to teaching as a career.

TEACHER TENURE

At the beginning of the 1960–61 school year, teacher tenure laws were in effect in 38 states and the District of Columbia. In six of these states, certain areas are exempted from tenure requirements. A probationary period of service prior to the granting of tenure status is required in 36 states. Iowa and Washington have no probationary period, while Minnesota exempts experienced teachers outside first-class cities. The usual probationary period is three years. If a tenured teacher resigns and later

---

[45] Research Division, National Education Association, "Colleges Producing 139,000 Teachers in 1961," *NEA Research Bulletin*, Vol. 39 (Washington, D.C.: The Association, May, 1961), pp. 37–40.

[46] Research Division, National Education Association, "Teacher Shortage Continues," *NEA Research Bulletin*, Vol. 41 (Washington, D.C.: The Association, October, 1963), p. 69.

takes a position in another school district, the teacher is again on probationary status. Pennsylvania is the only exception, in that a teacher
with tenure status does not lose it when moving to a new district. Connecticut, Ohio, and Kentucky have a reduced probationary period for
tenured teachers who affiliate with a new district. Table 12–2 lists the
states according to type of tenure or contract in effect.

Tenure and Dismissal

Tenure laws protect supervisors and principals, as well as teachers.
The purpose of tenure legislation is to protect teachers who have passed

Table 12–2
Type of State Tenure or Contract Provisions in Effect

States with Tenure Laws		States Without Tenure Laws
State-Wide		*State-Wide Continuing Contract of Spring Notification Type*
Alabama	Maine	Arkansas
Alaska	Maryland	Nevada
Arizona	Massachusetts	North Dakota
California°	Michigan°	Oklahoma
Colorado°	Minnesota	South Dakota
Connecticut†	Montana	Virginia (subject to local adoption)
Delaware	New Hampshire	*Annual or Long-Term Contracts*
District of Columbia	New Jersey	
Florida†	New York‡	Mississippi
Hawaii	New Mexico	North Carolina
Idaho	Ohio	South Carolina
Illinois‡	Pennsylvania	Texas
Indiana‡	Rhode Island	Utah
Iowa	Tennessee	Vermont
Kentucky	Washington	Wyoming
Louisiana	West Virginia	
In Certain Places Only°°		
Georgia	Nebraska	
Kansas	Oregon	
Missouri	Wisconsin	

° Subject to local adoption in small districts in California and Colorado; in Michigan, subject to local adoption throughout the state.
† Separate local tenure laws govern certain cities or counties.
‡ Illinois and New York exclude small districts; Indiana excludes township schools.
In the nontenure areas in Illinois and Indiana, continuing contract provisions of the
spring notification type apply.
°° In nontenure areas in Georgia and Kansas, annual contracts are the usual practice; nontenure areas in Missouri, Nebraska, Oregon, and Wisconsin are controlled by
continuing contract laws of the spring notification type.
SOURCE: Research Division, National Education Association, *NEA Research Bulletin,* Vol. 38 (Washington, D.C.: The Association, October, 1960), p. 83.

the probationary period from unfair dismissal. Tenure laws, however, do not protect the teacher who is guilty of incompetency, unethical conduct, insubordination, violation of board rules, or illegal activity. The competent tenured teacher, under most laws, can be dismissed as a result of abolition of position (for example, when a school drops a certain subject or department), reduced enrollment, and economic emergencies. But the laws do require districts to follow certain legal procedures before dismissal action can be taken. In some states, the board must file a statement showing cause of dismissal, while in other states the teacher is entitled to such a statement upon request. Ordinarily, the teacher also is entitled to request a hearing, but some states require that such a hearing be held. A 30-day advance notice of a hearing or dismissal is usually required.

The N.E.A. Committee on Tenure and Academic Freedom has identified eight essential conditions for a fair school-board hearing:

1. Adequate notice and statement of charges.
2. Presence of counsel.
3. Testimony of witnesses under oath or affirmation.
4. Right to subpoena witnesses.
5. Restriction of evidence to charges.
6. Right to argument on evidence and law.
7. Consideration of evidence and argument by the entire school board.
8. Vote of at least a majority of the entire school board.[47]

Although most of the states, through tenure laws, provide teachers with reasonable assurance of permanent employment status following a successful probationary period, 13 states have no tenure legislation and several other states have incomplete protection.

TEACHERS' ASSOCIATIONS

We have already discussed in some detail the role of professional organizations in representing the common interests of the group. Such organizations, by virtue of their professional status, are also responsible for protecting the general public. The interests of the professional group and those of society should not be antithetical. The professional group that exercises high standards to ensure that only competent persons are admitted to practice is acting in the interests of the public welfare as well as for the prestige of the group. On the other hand, an organization that functions merely as a closed shop to keep down competition and to heighten the economic position of its members is performing a dis-

---

[47] Research Division, National Education Association, "Teacher Tenure Laws," *NEA Research Bulletin*, Vol. 38 (Washington, D.C.: The Association, October, 1960), pp. 84–85.

service to society. Professional organizations are important to society, as well as to the membership concerned, because lay people are unable to distinguish the competent from the incompetent practitioner. Thus, society grants such organizations a reasonable degree of autonomy in maintaining standards of qualification and rules of ethical conduct. Such organizations not only rule on membership qualifications, but also help establish and enforce standards for the education of candidates for the profession, and exercise legal control over its practicing members.

In most professional fields, membership in the professional organization is a virtual necessity if the practitioner is to function effectively. The physician who is not a member of the American Medical Association or the attorney who does not hold membership in the American Bar Association is severely handicapped. There are, of course, many specialized associations within each profession, but every profession has a general organization that claims to represent all members regardless of specialty.

The National Education Association of the United States

This organization, founded in 1857 and chartered in 1906 by an Act of Congress, is the largest organization of educators in the United States. Originally established as the National Teachers Association, a merger was effected in 1870 with the National Association of School Superintendents and the American Normal School Association. The membership growth of the N.E.A. from 1870 to 1963 is shown in Table 12–3. While the growth in membership of the N.E.A. has been spectacular, only 52 per cent of the nation's public school teachers held membership during

Table 12–3
NEA Membership, 1870–1963

Year	Membership
1870	170
1880	354
1890	5,474
1900	2,332
1910	6,909
1920	52,850
1930	172,354
1940	203,429
1950	453,797
1960	713,994
1963	903,384

SOURCE: National Education Association, *NEA Handbook 1963–64* (Washington, D.C.: The Association, 1963), p. 344.

1963–64. The number of N.E.A. members in proportion of the total teaching force varies markedly state by state. While 95 per cent of the public school teachers in Kansas hold N.E.A. membership, only 8 per cent of the teachers in Rhode Island belong to the N.E.A.

ORGANIZATIONAL STRUCTURE OF THE N.E.A. The N.E.A.'s governing body is the Representative Assembly, composed of some 7,000 delegates who meet annually to establish broad policies. The delegates come from the state associations according to a ratio of five delegates for the first 500 members, plus a delegate for every 500 additional members. Local education associations also send one delegate for every 100 members. The Board of Directors interprets and acts upon the legislation approved by the Representative Assembly. The Board, elected by the Representative Assembly, is made up of one director from each state having less than 20,000 N.E.A. members, and two directors from states with higher membership.

The N.E.A.'s organizational structure, outlined in Figure 12–3, shows 33 departments, 26 commissions and committees, and 14 headquarters divisions. Many significant services are performed by these departments, divisions, commissions, and committees. For example, the Research Division is not only engaged in conducting educational research, but also reports research results in a variety of publications and provides consultative services. The Commission on Teacher Education and Professional Standards is charged with the development of a program for teacher selection, preparation, certification, and advancement of professional standards. This commission was established in 1946 and has been responsible for the professional standards movement in education—a movement that is crucial to the professionalization of teaching.

Each state maintains an association affiliated with the N.E.A. The state education associations provide field services, conduct research, and carry on legislative activities in the interests of their members. The largest state association is the California Teachers Association with 125,900 members reported in 1963. In addition to the state associations, there are many local associations affiliated with both the state organization and the N.E.A. The local association's membership usually includes the teachers of a school district or county, and the local association's activities are concerned with professional problems at the local level.

The N.E.A. also sponsors student N.E.A. chapters at colleges and universities with programs of teacher education. Also sponsored by the N.E.A. are the Future Teachers of America, with chapters in high schools throughout the United States.

CRITICISMS OF THE N.E.A. Despite the important functions and many accomplishments of the N.E.A., some serious criticisms can be directed at the organization. We have already stated that only 52 per cent of the

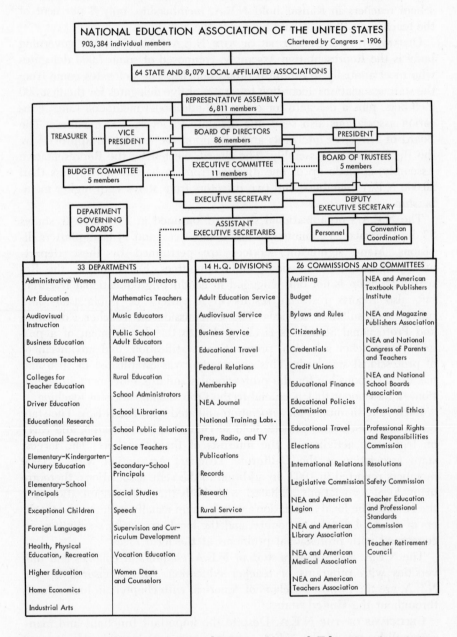

NATIONAL EDUCATION ASSOCIATION OF THE UNITED STATES
903,384 individual members   Chartered by Congress – 1906

64 STATE AND 8,079 LOCAL AFFILIATED ASSOCIATIONS

REPRESENTATIVE ASSEMBLY
6,811 members

TREASURER | VICE PRESIDENT | BOARD OF DIRECTORS 86 members | PRESIDENT

BUDGET COMMITTEE 5 members | EXECUTIVE COMMITTEE 11 members | BOARD OF TRUSTEES 5 members

EXECUTIVE SECRETARY

DEPARTMENT GOVERNING BOARDS

DEPUTY EXECUTIVE SECRETARY

ASSISTANT EXECUTIVE SECRETARIES

Personnel | Convention Coordination

33 DEPARTMENTS		14 H.Q. DIVISIONS	26 COMMISSIONS AND COMMITTEES	
Administrative Women	Journalism Directors	Accounts	Auditing	NEA and American Textbook Publishers Institute
Art Education	Mathematics Teachers	Adult Education Service	Budget	
Audiovisual Instruction	Music Educators	Audiovisual Service	Bylaws and Rules	NEA and Magazine Publishers Association
Business Education	Public School Adult Educators	Business Service	Citizenship	NEA and National Congress of Parents and Teachers
Classroom Teachers	Retired Teachers	Educational Travel	Credentials	
Colleges for Teacher Education	Rural Education	Federal Relations	Credit Unions	NEA and National School Boards Association
Driver Education	School Administrators	Membership	Educational Finance	
Educational Research	School Librarians	NEA Journal	Educational Policies Commission	Professional Ethics
Educational Secretaries	School Public Relations	National Training Labs.	Educational Travel	Professional Rights and Responsibilities Commission
Elementary–Kindergarten–Nursery Education	Science Teachers	Press, Radio, and TV	Elections	
Elementary–School Principals	Secondary–School Principals	Publications	International Relations	Resolutions
Exceptional Children	Social Studies	Records	Legislative Commission	Safety Commission
Foreign Languages	Speech	Research	NEA and American Legion	Teacher Education and Professional Standards Commission
Health, Physical Education, Recreation	Supervision and Curriculum Development	Rural Service	NEA and American Library Association	
Higher Education	Vocation Education		NEA and American Medical Association	Teacher Retirement Council
Home Economics	Women Deans and Counselors		NEA and American Teachers Association	
Industrial Arts				

FIGURE 12–3. NEA Organization. [SOURCE: National Education Association, NEA Handbook 1963–64 (Washington, D.C.: The Association, 1963).]

nation's public school teachers hold membership in the association. While this may be considered a weakness rather than a criticism, the association claims to represent the entire profession of teaching.

It is also argued that the organizational structure of the N.E.A. can be improved by paring down the size of the Representative Assembly. A delegate body with 7,000 members is too cumbersome to function effectively, although, admittedly, the present system permits considerable representation from each state and from the local associations.

But perhaps the most serious and controversial criticism levelled at the N.E.A. is the charge that the association is administrator-dominated. The teachers' unions have been most critical of the N.E.A. on this point, stressing that there is a conflict of interest between teachers and administrators, and teachers should therefore have their own organization. The N.E.A., on the other hand, maintains that there is no conflict of interest, and that teachers and administrators are working toward the same goals. As the executive officer of the school board, the superintendent is responsible to this body and is expected to represent it, as well as to see to it that the rights of the teaching staff are recognized. The teachers' unions point out that, as a go-between, the superintendent often finds himself in an awkward position. Furthermore, it is contended that teachers at the local level cannot freely criticize their administration, since they are members of the same organization. It is interesting to note that the American Association of University Professors has always excluded administrative personnel from membership.[48]

On the other hand, the Representative Assembly of the N.E.A. has a preponderance of teacher delegates (usually two thirds of the delegates are teachers). Also, most state education associations are so organized as to ensure adequate teacher representation. N.E.A. leaders stress the need for common interests and goals between administrators and teachers, rather than divisive interests and goals.

Teachers' Unions

The American Federation of Teachers, an affiliate of the AFL–CIO, is the largest teachers' union in the United States. The A.F.T. was organized in 1916 and affiliated with the American Federation of Labor that same year. In 1964, membership in the A.F.T. exceeded 81,000.[49] While this total is dwarfed by the N.E.A.'s membership of over 900,000, the A.F.T. functions as the dominant teachers' organization in some of our largest cities. A.F.T. membership exceeds N.E.A. membership in such

---

[48] See the Membership section of any recent issue of the *AAUP Bulletin*.

[49] *1964 Report of the President,* (Chicago, Illinois: American Federation of Teachers, 1964).

cities as New York, Atlanta, Boston, Chicago, Cleveland, Detroit, and Minneapolis. Only 3 per cent of the teachers in New York City held membership in the N.E.A. in 1963. The membership growth of the A.F.T. is shown in Table 12–4.

Table 12–4
AFT Membership, 1917–1960

Year	Membership
1917	2,433
1920	9,808
1925	3,497
1930	6,872
1935	13,705
1940	29,907
1945	31,089
1950	41,415
1955	46,583
1960	59,181
1964	81,798

SOURCES: Myron Lieberman, *Education as a Profession* (Englewood Cliffs, N.J.: Prentice-Hall, Inc., 1956).
Annual Reports of the President (Chicago, Illinois: American Federation of Teachers, 1960 and 1964).

Although principals, supervisors, and department heads are admitted to membership in the A.F.T., superintendents are not eligible, on the grounds that such administrators represent the interests of the employer. It has been pointed out that the N.E.A. has no such restriction in membership eligibility. Lieberman observes that while the A.F.T. constitution prohibits the granting of a charter to any local or state groups that practice racial distinctions, the N.E.A., on the other hand, has not yet acted to revoke charters where such discrimination exists.[50]

TEACHERS' UNIONS AND PROFESSIONAL STATUS. Although the professions, as a rule, do not affiliate with labor unions,[51] we find that a significant number of teachers in the larger metropolitan areas hold union membership. Obviously, the rank and file of labor union members are not college graduates and are not required to meet prescribed curricula in higher education. Consequently, the desirability of teacher affiliation

---

[50] Lieberman, *op. cit.*, p. 305.
[51] A notable exception is the American Federation of Musicians, an affiliate of the AFL–CIO, which includes among its members leading concert artists and symphony conductors. Some observers maintain that the American Medical Association is, in a sense, one of the most highly organized and effective unions.

with labor unions is a controversial issue. Teacher members of the A.F.T. maintain that the N.E.A., by virtue of its dual commitment to school superintendents as well as teachers, cannot properly represent the interests of the latter group. This assumes, of course, that there is a basic conflict of interest between the school administrator as the employer and the teacher as the employee.

Some members of teachers' unions maintain that since teachers are salaried employees, they cannot be true professionals. But one could hardly argue that the physician or attorney who is a salaried employee has lost his professional status.

The objectives of the A.F.T., as stated in the organization's constitution, refer to the occupation of teaching as a profession. A comparison between the stated objectives of the A.F.T. with those of the N.E.A. indicates no areas of conflict. Yet the two organizations have obvious differences, not only in competing for teacher membership, but also in several other operational respects. As mentioned previously, the A.F.T. sees a conflict of interest between the school superintendent and the teacher, and therefore prohibits the former from membership. The A.F.T. also seems to be more militant in protecting teachers from charges of incompetency and in improving the welfare of its members.

TEACHERS' UNIONS AND OCCUPATIONAL ENTRY. While most professional groups and unions continually strive to raise the requirements for occupational entry, the A.F.T. has occasionally lobbied for the reduction of such requirements—specifically, the required course work in preservice teacher education. When a bill was introduced in the California legislature in 1961 to limit the course requirements in teacher education, the California Federation of Teachers lobbied for the passage of this legislation, while the California Teachers Association opposed the bill.

Such legislation must be regarded as damaging to any professional group because it implies that the professional group should not establish and regulate its own standards for entry. Moreover, it indicates that the colleges that educate the teachers cannot be entrusted to set the requirements for professional teacher education.

While it is difficult to imagine a union or professional group advocating a reduction in requirements for occupational entry, the strategy of the California affiliate of the A.F.T. may be explained by its hostility toward the California Teachers Association and the N.E.A. Such agencies of the N.E.A. as the National Commission on Teacher Education and Professional Standards and the National Council for Accreditation of Teacher Education have been working to improve the standards for teacher education and certification. In this connection, NCTEPS and NCATE have been closely associated with the departments of education in various colleges and universities. On the other hand, the A.F.T. has never been

A.F.T. Objectives[52]	*N.E.A. Objectives*[53]
1. To bring associations of teachers into relations of mutual assistance and cooperation.	1. Educational opportunity for every individual to develop his full potential for responsible and useful citizenship and for intellectual and spiritual growth.
2. To obtain for them all the rights to which they are entitled.	2. Balanced educational programs to provide for the varied needs and talents of individual students and for the strength and progress of the nation.
3. To raise the standard of the teaching profession by securing the conditions essential to the best professional service.	3. The services of a professionally prepared and competent educator in every professional position.
4. To promote such a democratization of the schools as will enable them better to equip their pupils to take their places in the industrial, social and political life of the community.	4. School plant, equipment, and instructional materials appropriate to the educational needs of all learners.
5. To promote the welfare of the childhood of the nation by providing progressively better educational opportunities for all.	5. Effective organization, controls, administration, and financial support of public education in every state.
	6. A local-state-federal partnership in the financial support of public education with control of education residing in the states.
	7. Public understanding and appreciation of the vital role of education in our American democracy.
	8. Understanding and support of the teacher's right to participate fully in public affairs.
	9. Fair standards of professional welfare for teachers.
	10. Professional associations that evoke the active participation of all educators in working toward the highest goals for education.

---

52 *Constitution of the American Federation of Teachers,* Article II.
53 National Education Association, *NEA Handbook,* "The Platform of the National Education Association" (Washington, D.C.: The Association, 1961), pp. 50–53.

involved in any joint or cooperative efforts with these institutions of teacher education. Furthermore, the N.E.A. has developed student chapters of Future Teachers of America in hundreds of teacher education institutions throughout the nation. The A.F.T. has not been able to develop similar groups in the colleges and universities. And while some professors of education hold membership in the A.F.T., a much greater number have chosen to join the N.E.A. and its state affiliates. It would appear that these factors influence the negative attitude of the A.F.T. toward the college and university departments of education.

TEACHERS' UNIONS AND STRIKES.   Although labor unions commonly use the strike to secure improved salaries and working conditions, the A.F.T. has followed a nostrike policy since 1952. In the years following World War II, low salaries and poor working conditions catalyzed several strikes by local teachers' groups affiliated with the N.E.A. as well as the A.F.T. But both organizations have maintained a nostrike policy for several years. In many states, the right to strike is denied to public employees, including teachers.

TEACHERS' UNIONS AND THE WELFARE OF TEACHERS.   The concern of teachers' unions with matters of teachers' salaries, working conditions, academic freedom, retirement income, and other benefits, has probably spurred the N.E.A. to take a stronger interest in the welfare of teachers. This concern for teacher welfare should not imply that the unions are not interested in developing a high quality of public service. Indeed, these two factors are often interdependent. In recent years, the A.F.T. has indicated increasing concern with the quality of services rendered by teachers, as well as showing a continued concern for teacher welfare.

MERIT RATING

Merit rating of teachers is a highly controversial professional issue. It is based on the assumption that teachers should be paid according to their individual competence. In recent years, most school systems have adopted a single salary schedule in which each teacher, regardless of his subject specialization or merit, is paid according to his preparation and seniority of service. But we know that even with equal levels of preparation and experience, teachers differ greatly in their effectiveness. The idea of merit rating is to provide salary bonuses or rewards to outstanding teachers.

But there are many practical problems in merit-rating plans. Who is to do the rating of teachers? Do we have valid and reliable criteria for rating teaching effectiveness? Can such rating be done objectively? Will merit rating have an adverse affect on teacher morale? Will it lead to conformity of classroom teaching practices?

While many school districts use rating plans to assess the effectiveness of their teachers, only a few districts use such plans for purposes of merit pay. Teachers tend to be opposed to any system of merit rating for salaries.

THE TRUMP REPORT. In a study sponsored jointly by the National Association of Secondary School Principals and the Ford Foundation, a proposal was developed for a new approach to the secondary school. Included in this proposal was a merit plan in which so-called teacher specialists were to receive an average salary of $8,000, while the general teachers were to receive an average of $5,500. Trump's distinction between these two types of teachers is that the teacher specialists are those who "demonstrate career interests and abilities . . . possess a master's degree as a minimum . . . will be responsible for overseeing all the instruction in a given subject . . . will be even more competent than now . . . will have general charge of evaluating student achievement."[54] The general teachers, on the other hand, are those individuals found on many teaching staffs today who, according to Trump, "do not plan to continue in the profession on a long-term basis."[55] These general teachers will work under the teacher specialists, according to Trump's proposal. While this plan does not provide merit pay on the basis of man-to-man comparisons of effectiveness, it does provide for a dual level of salary according to qualifications and service to be performed.

> Certainly in the secondary school of the future there will be heavy emphasis on superior teaching. The fact that better teaching means better education will be fully appreciated. . . . Professional teachers will assume roles quite different from those they have today. The fetish of uniformity that seems to be dooming the teaching profession to mediocrity will be discarded. Moves to raise professional standards today are mainly concerned with higher certification requirements and uniform salary schedules. The teachers' new role in education will go far beyond that.[56]

Obviously, such a proposal has many controversial aspects. If salary levels can be raised sufficiently, teaching would become a more desirable occupation, and a much higher proportion of teachers would regard their work as a lifelong career. The Trump proposal, on the other hand, would distinguish two types of teachers, recognizing two distinct levels of qualitative performance, and would provide compensation accordingly. Some people would regard this as a type of caste system in teaching.

---

[54] J. Lloyd Trump, *Images of the Future* (Urbana, Illinois: Commission on the Experimental Study of the Utilization of the Staff in the Secondary School, National Association of Secondary School Principals, 1959), p. 15.
[55] *Ibid.*, p. 15.   [56] *Ibid.*, p. 27.

But, unfortunately, current practices provide only a very limited degree of upward mobility for the teacher who is outstanding.

ACADEMIC FREEDOM

One of the chief goals of education in a free society is to develop in students the capacity for critical thinking. But in order to think critically, one must be exposed to controversial issues and one must be free to reach his own conclusions. But there are those who consider such freedom of inquiry too risky even for a society such as ours. They would prefer to see the schools avoid controversial issues in teaching. Some would like to see the schools indoctrinate for Americanism.

Advocates of academic freedom point out that students should be taught how to think and not what to think. Since World War II we have witnessed a surging interest in academic freedom, with many attempts being made to censor textbooks and to avoid such controversial areas as the study of communism, race relations, separation of church and state, UNESCO, sex, and criticism of capitalism.

Most of the states now require loyalty oaths of teachers, despite the opposition to such oaths by the National Education Association, the American Federation of Teachers, and the American Association of University Professors. These organizations have expressed concern that such oaths have singled out teachers and have served to intimidate them by implying that they are suspect of abusing the civil rights of freedom of inquiry and speech accorded to other citizens.

Our society in time of peril finds itself in a schizoid position. On the one hand, it must be secure in knowing that its youth is developing the qualities of loyalty and patriotism essential to the preservation of society. But on the other hand, it must tolerate and stimulate the freedom of inquiry that produces the creative activity so necessary for societal improvement. In the words of Einstein,

> We are concerned not merely with the technical problem of securing and maintaining peace, but also with the important task of education and enlightenment. If we want to resist the powers which threaten to suppress intellectual and individual freedom we must keep clearly before us what is at stake, and what we owe to that freedom which our ancestors have won for us after hard struggles.
>
> Without such freedom there would have been no Shakespeare, no Goethe, no Newton, no Faraday, no Pasteur and no Lister. . . . It is only men who are free, who create the inventions and intellectual works which to us moderns make life worth while.[57]

---

[57] Albert Einstein, *Out of My Later Years* (New York: Philosophical Library, Inc., 1950), p. 149.

Robert M. Hutchins, a strong advocate of academic freedom, has this
to say:

> Academic freedom is simply a way of saying that we get the best
> results in education and research *if we leave their management to people
> who know something about them.* Attempts on the part of the public to
> regulate the methods and content of education and to determine the
> objects of research are encroachments on academic freedom. . . . The
> democratic view that the state may determine the amount of money
> to be spent on education and may regulate education and educators by
> law has nothing to do with the wholly undemocratic notion that citizens
> may tell educators how to conduct education and still less with the
> fantastic position that they may tell them how to live, vote, think, and
> speak.[58]

Many educators would agree that our society should not place any
restrictions on our freedom to teach and learn, except where license is
taken to advocate the destruction of such freedom and the destruction
of our free society. But perhaps fewer educators would agree with Jefferson's words in his first inaugural address:

> If there be any among us who wish to dissolve this union, or to change
> its republican form, let them stand undisturbed, as monuments of the
> safety with which error of opinion may be tolerated where reason is
> left free to combat it.[59]

THE TEACHER AND THE LAW

In 1954 the United States Supreme Court stated, "Today, education is
perhaps the most important function of state and local governments."
Laws have been established to cover such areas as school finance, compulsory school attendance, teacher certification requirements, courses of
instruction, teacher tenure, pupil transportation, and so on. Since many
of these areas are discussed in other sections of this book, we will attempt to examine briefly an area of great concern to the beginning
teacher: *liability for pupil injury.*

Immunity of the School District

Unless a state or local statute exists to the contrary, school districts
and municipalities are not liable for pupil injury. This immunity from
tort (injury) liability derives from the ancient doctrine that the king
(as an agent of God) can do no wrong. Such dogma was inherited by

---

[58] Robert Maynard Hutchins, *The Higher Learning in America* (New Haven, Conn.:
Yale University Press, 1936), p. 56.
[59] Thomas Jefferson, *First Inaugural Address.* As quoted in Gordon C. Lee, *Education in Modern America*, Revised (New York: Holt, Rinehart and Winston,
1957), p. 588.

the American courts, despite the fact that we have never had a king. But the theory of sovereignty, as represented in the rule of the king, was transposed to the state and its agencies. Since education is a function of government, school boards have been held immune from tort liability except where such immunity is waived by statute.

Obviously, such immunity may lead to great injustices and hardships where individuals, through no fault of their own, are injured or killed through the negligence of the school district and its agents. The courts of New York State have not held rigidly to this common-law doctrine and, until recently, have been the only courts to hold a school board liable for the negligent performance of duties, despite the absence of a statute waiving such immunity. The Illinois Supreme Court in 1959 ruled against the doctrine of governmental immunity, thereby concurring with the New York courts in this respect.

Recently, New York State passed the Court of Claims Act, which waives its governmental immunity from liability for negligent acts by its agents. Other states that have statutes specifically waiving this immunity are California and Washington.

Connecticut and New Jersey have laws that hold the district liable for injuries that occur as a result of the negligence of the district's employees during the time they are on duty. While such laws do not waive completely the district's immunity, they offer protection to the teacher and are commonly referred to as "save harmless" laws because they save the teacher from financial harm.

ARE TEACHERS IMMUNE FROM TORT LIABILITY? Since the laws in most states hold the school district immune from tort liability, the question arises whether the teacher enjoys similar immunity. After all, isn't the teacher, as an agent of the district, entitled to such immunity? The answer is emphatically no, because it is held that the teacher is not a public officer. Consequently, the teacher is personally liable for acts of negligence. Members of a school board, as officers, are not liable when acting in good faith and within the range of their corporate powers.

According to the courts, the teacher's relationship to his pupils is *in loco parentis*—that is, in the place of the parent. Consequently, a teacher must act in a manner of reasonable care and prudence, as any parent must. In other words, the teacher can be held liable for pupil injury if it can be established that such injury arose out of the negligence of the teacher. Such negligence includes nonfeasance (failure to perform a duty) as well as malfeasance (failure to perform a duty properly). While this would appear to put the teacher in a delicate and vulnerable position, the courts have repeatedly emphasized that unless a reasonable person could have foreseen the consequences of the act, the teacher cannot be held liable. Consequently, teachers do not have to be especially cautious or timid in the discharge of their duties. Teachers must act in a manner befitting that of a reasonable and prudent person. The following review of a recent court case will help illustrate this:

> In New Jersey a seventh-grade boy was punched by a taller boy while walking in the corridor in the direction of a room outside of which a teacher stood. The boy retaliated by tapping the other boy. He then started into the room, when, without warning, the taller boy pushed him from behind and shoved him into some desks, injuring him to such an extent that his leg was later amputated. As a result, an action for damages was brought against the teacher. In its decision, favoring the teacher, the court ruled that, in the absence of any evidence that the taller boy was known to be aggressive or known as a bully, the teacher's conduct in entering the classroom after the first encounter was not evidence of negligence. It was what an ordinarily prudent person might well have done and hence the teacher was not liable for damages.[60]

The above illustration is consistent with the stand taken by most courts with regard to teacher liability for pupil injury. Since this case occurred in a state that has no statute waiving the common-law immunity of governmental agencies, the plaintiff would find it useless to bring suit against the school district.

The following case also illustrates that it is difficult to prove negligence on the part of the teacher, since it must be shown that a reasonably prudent person would have been able to foresee the danger of injury.

> In New York, when a second-grade pupil was injured by a baseball bat swung by another girl, action for damages was brought against the child's teacher and the district. It was contended that the injury resulted from the lack of adequate supervision. The pupil was on the playground with her class under the supervision of her teacher when the accident occurred. The teacher testified that she did not notice that four older girls on the playground at the time were playing ball. The court held that no liability attached to the teacher as it was not shown that she was negligent. It did, however, hold the evidence was sufficient to justify a verdict for damages against the district.[61]

This case illustrates that in states, such as New York, that have enacted statutes to waive governmental immunity from tort liability, successful litigation can be brought against a school district even when the teacher is absolved of negligence. But in the other states where it is virtually futile to bring successful litigation against the school district, the plaintiff's only recourse is to sue the teacher for negligence. Nevertheless, the courts have not held the teacher liable unless it could be clearly shown

---

[60] Lee O. Garber, *The Yearbook of School Law 1961* (Danville, Illinois: Interstate Printers & Publishers, Inc., 1961), pp. 72–73. From Doktor vs. Greenberg, 115 A. (2d) 793 (N.J.).

[61] *Ibid.*, p. 72. Germond vs. Board of Education, 197 N.Y.S. (2d) 548.

that the teacher was negligent in contributing to the injury and that such injury could have been foreseen by a reasonably prudent person.

Examples of cases in which teacher negligence can be shown include the shop teacher who knowingly allows pupils to operate equipment without the required protective devices and clothing,[62] or the high-school football coach who, knowing that a player is injured, continues to use the youngster, resulting in a more serious injury.[63]

Teachers need not be Caspar Milquetoasts. The courts have consistently protected them from capricious actions. And many teachers' associations make available to individual members insurance protection against tort liability. Such policies carry very low premiums, since very few court cases against teachers have been successful.

SUMMARY

While teaching is widely recognized as a professional calling, teachers as a group differ from other professional groups in several ways. Many teachers lack interest in professional standards. There is a high rate of turnover, particularly among female teachers. A sizable proportion of the college graduates prepared for teaching choose to enter other occupations. In comparison to members of other professional groups, relatively few teachers draw upon research in their work. While most professional groups are licensed by state boards composed of professionals, teachers are licensed through state boards composed primarily of lay people. More than 5 per cent of the nation's full-time teachers have substandard certificates.

But despite these discouraging conditions, there is reason for much optimism. During the past decade, teachers' salaries and conditions of employment have improved markedly. State-wide tenure laws are in effect in most states. Academic freedom has been gaining greater protection. And a higher proportion of our more able high school seniors are declaring teaching as their career choice.

A recent study of the career choices of male National Merit Scholarship semifinalists revealed a remarkable increase in the proportion selecting teaching. Whereas in 1957 less than 8 per cent selected teaching, in 1963 over 15 per cent declared teaching as their career choice. Surprisingly, the field of engineering declined from 33.6 per cent to 20.8 per cent over this same period. Among female semifinalists, teaching was by far the number one choice. In 1963 more than 40 per cent of the girls chose teaching, while the next highest field (scientific research) was

---

[62] Edkins vs. Board of Education of New York City, 41 N.E. (2nd) 75.
[63] Robert R. Hamilton and Paul R. Mort, *The Law and Public Education* (Chicago: The Foundation Press, Inc., 1941), p. 274.

chosen by less than 19 per cent.[64] These data are all the more remarkable when one considers that, during recent years, there has been a great national campaign to encourage our most able students to select careers in science and engineering.

Teaching is the mother of all professions. Perhaps one day it will come to be regarded as one of our most honored professions.

PROBLEMS FOR STUDY AND DISCUSSION

1. What distinguishes the professions from other occupations in society? Is teaching a profession? Why?

2. What do you consider to be the most serious professional problems of teachers? Why?

3. Compared with physicians and attorneys, do teachers as a group lack interest in professional standards? Why?

4. How would you answer the following allegation?

> Teachers in our secondary schools are incompetent because they are trained mainly in *how to teach* rather than *what to teach*.

5. Should boards of education at local and state levels be made up of lay citizens or professional educators? Why?

6. What is meant by professional ethics?

7. What are the causes of teacher turnover? Is turnover a problem in most of the other professions? Why?

8. Under what conditions can a tenured teacher be fired?

9. What are the advantages of holding membership in the state teachers' association? The N.E.A? The teachers' union?

10. What are the advantages and disadvantages of merit rating? Are you in favor of merit rating for salary purposes? Why?

SELECTED REFERENCES

Chase, Francis S. and Harold A. Anderson (eds.) *The High School in a New Era.* Chicago: The University of Chicago Press, 1958.

Conant, James B. *The Education of American Teachers.* New York: McGraw-Hill Company, Inc., 1963.

---

[64] Robert C. Nichols, "Career Decisions of Very Able Students," *Science,* Vol. 144, June 12, 1964, p. 1316.

Ford Foundation. *Time, Talent, and Teachers.* New York: The Foundation, 1960.

Garber, Lee O. *The Yearbook of School Law, 1961.* Danville, Illinois: Interstate Printers & Publishers, Inc., 1961.

Kearney, Nolan C. *A Teacher's Professional Guide.* Englewood Cliffs, N.J.: Prentice-Hall, Inc., 1958.

Kinney, Lucien B. *Certification in Education.* Englewood Cliffs, N.J.: Prentice-Hall, Inc., 1964.

Lieberman, Myron. *Education as a Profession.* Englewood Cliffs, N.J.: Prentice-Hall, Inc., 1956.

————. *The Future of Public Education. Chicago:* The University of Chicago Press, 1960.

National Commission on Teacher Education and Professional Standards. *New Horizons for the Teaching Profession.* Washington, D.C.: National Education Association, 1961.

National Education Association. *NEA Handbook 1963–64.* Washington, D.C.: The Association, 1963.

Redefer, F. L. and Dorothy Reeves. *Planning a Teaching Career.* New York: Harper & Row, Publishers, Inc. 1960.

Ryans, David G. *Characteristics of Teachers.* Washington, D.C.: American Council on Education, 1960.

Smith, Elmer R. (ed.) *Teacher Education: A Reappraisal.* New York: Harper & Row, Publishers, Inc., 1962.

Stiles, Lindley J. *et. al. Teacher Education in the United States.* New York: Ronald Press Company, 1960.

Stinnett, T. M. and Albert J. Huggett. *Professional Problems of Teachers* (2nd. Ed.) New York: The Macmillan Company, 1963.

Trump, J. Lloyd. *Guide to Better Schools.* New York: Rand McNally & Company, 1961.

Woodring, Paul. *A Fourth of a Nation.* New York: McGraw-Hill Company, Inc., 1957.

————. *New Directions in Teaching Education.* New York: The Ford Foundation and the Fund for the Advancement of Education, 1957.

Wynn, Richard. *Careers in Education.* New York: McGraw-Hill Company, Inc., 1960.

Index